OXFORDSHIRE
COUNTY COUNCIL
Cultural Services

FOR USE
IN
THE LIBRARY
ONLY

THE ARCHAEOLOGY OF THE OXFORD REGION

edited by:
Grace Briggs,
Jean Cook
& Trevor Rowley

Oxford University Department
for External Studies

OXFORD   1986

© Oxford University Department for External Studies and individual authors 1986
Rewley House
3–7, Wellington Square
OXFORD OX1 2JA

ISBN 0 903736 20 9

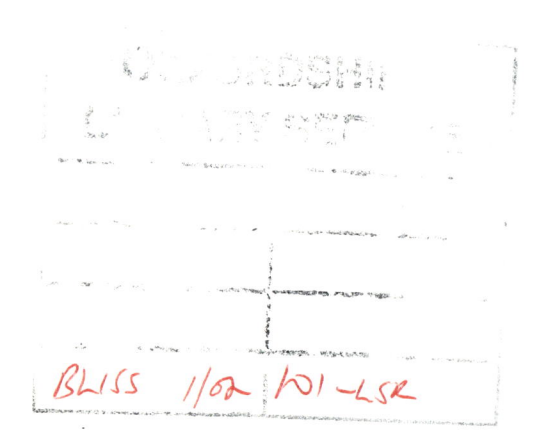

Typeset by Oxford Publishing Services, Oxford

Printed by Information Printing, Eynsham, Oxford

CONTENTS

List of figures

List of plates

List of maps

1	The Palaeolithic period in the Oxford Region Derek Roe	1
2	The Mesolithic and Neolithic in the Oxford Region Humphrey Case	18
3	The Bronze Age in the Oxford area – its local and regional significance Richard Bradley	38
4	The Iron Age David Miles	49
5	The Upper Thames Valley in the Roman period Christopher Young	58
6	The Early Saxon period Sonia Chadwick Hawkes	64
7	The Oxford Region from the Conversion to the Conquest Tom Hassall	109
8	Archaeology of Oxford City Tom Hassall	115
9	The Oxford Region in the Middle Ages James Bond	135
10	Commentary to accompany distribution maps of the archaeology of Oxfordshire John Steane	160

LIST OF FIGURES

1 Flint artefacts from the Highlands Farm Pit at Rotherfield Peppard: MacRae Collection	6–7
2 Handaxes from Iffley and the Wallingford Fan Gravels	8–9
3 Artefacts from Berinsfield: MacRae collection	10–11
4 Two typical Late Acheulian (Micoquian) handaxes from the Wolvercote Channel site	12–13
5 Map of Anglo-Saxon settlement of Britain by *c.* AD 475	97
6 Map of Saxon settlement of Wessex to *c.* AD 700	98
7 Map of Dorchester-on-Thames and immediate area, showing Saxon finds	100
8 Plan of the Abingdon cemetery (after Leeds & Harden 1936, fig. 3, with modifications and additions)	101
9 Map of early Anglo-Saxon sites around Cassington and Eynsham (after Berisford 1973, fig. 2)	102
10 Plan of Anglo-Saxon settlement at New Wintles, Eynsham (after Hawkes & Gray 1969, fig. 1, and Gray 1974, fig. 6)	103
11 Detail plan of the North Site, New Wintles, Eynsham	104
12 Cropmarks, University Parks	117
13 Reconstructed views of the North Gate, Oxford	119
14 North-south section through Castle Street, Oxford	121
15 Axonometric reconstruction of Grandpont *c.* 13th century	123
16 The Hamel, Oxford : conjectural reconstruction of medieval tenements	125
17 Oxford's north-western defences	126
18 All Saints Church : conjectural reconstructions	129
19 Greyfriars Church, *c.* 1350	131

LIST OF PLATES

1 Causewayed enclosures — 20

2 Ascott-under-Wychwood Long Barrow — 21

3 Cropmarks at Dorchester, Overy and Warborough — 28

4 The Devil's Quoits, Stanton Harcourt and Middle Beaker grave groups — 29

5 a Dorchester, Dyke Hills, reconstructed belt — 105
  b Dorchester, Minchin Rec., pair of applied brooches
  c Abingdon 1, grave 106, tutulus and applied brooch

6 a Frilford 1, grave 143, 6-spiral saucer brooches — 106
  b Fairford, grave 7, saucer brooches with star and Style I border
  c Oxford region, large saucer brooches modelled on Kentish discs

7 a–b Cuddesdon glass bowls — 107
    c Cuddesdon bronze Coptic bucket

8 a Dorchester, Bishop's Court, bronze Janus-head lock for book or casket — 108
  b Milton, North Field, one of two composite disc brooches
  c Air photograph, Saxon 'palace' complex, SE of Drayton

LIST OF MAPS

Map 1	Palaeolithic finds	172
Map 2	Mesolithic finds	173
Map 3	Neolithic sites	174
Map 4	Neolithic finds	175
Map 5	Bronze Age sites	176
Map 6	Bronze Age finds	177
Map 7	Iron Age sites	178
Map 8	Iron Age finds	179
Map 9	Romano-British sites	180
Map 10	Roman finds	181
Map 11	Early Anglo-Saxon sites and finds	182
Map 12	Later Saxon sites and finds	183
Map 13	Medieval boroughs and market centres	184
Map 14	Medieval rural settlement	185
Map 15	Deserted and shrunken villages	186
Map 16	Medieval monastic sites	187
Map 17	Medieval castles and moated sites	188
Map 18	Medieval forests and parks	189

PREFACE

The papers in this volume were first presented as part of a series of University Extension Lectures in 1980. Since that date there have been further significant archaeological finds in the Oxford Region and a number of the contributions have been revised accordingly. In order to provide a more complete picture of the archaeology of the Oxford Region an important additional paper on Oxford itself has been included. The distribution maps at the back were commissioned from the Field Department of Oxfordshire County Museum and are based on the information contained within the county Sites and Monuments Record. This record of archaeological information was initiated in the late 1960s as a pioneer county archive and has subsequently been the model for similar ventures in many other areas of Britain.

The authors have produced their papers quite independently and the editors have, quite rightly, made no attempt to reconcile conflicting individual view-points in the few cases where they exist; they have, however, endeavoured to standardize the presentation of the papers for ease of reading.

As several of the early papers explain, the Oxford Region is a relatively meaningless concept until the later Anglo-Saxon period when Oxford first emerges as a major urban centre with an identifiable hinterland. Nonetheless we have adopted the traditional regional approach as a convenient and understandable method by which to examine the surviving remains of man's past activities. The formula followed in this book is similar to that used in *The Oxford Region: a Scientific and Historic Survey* (edited by A.F. Martin and R.W. Steel in 1954) which was produced for the British Association for the Advancement of Science's visit to the city. This volume contains a series of archaeological papers along with contributions on other economic and social studies. In 1980 the Oxford University Department for External Studies published another book with the title of *The Oxford Region* to mark the centenary of the provision of institutional adult education in Oxford. That book deliberately omitted the archaeology of the region in anticipation of this present publication.

The survey of the archaeology of Oxfordshire published in the Victoria County History of Oxfordshire Volume I (1939) was the only other published attempt at a comprehensive survey of the region's archaeology. In this respect Oxford, for once, lagged behind Cambridge, which had an extremely important and influential regional archaeological survey published as early as 1928. *The Archaeology of the Cambridge Region* by Cyril Fox proved to be of immense importance and in particular helped to change attitudes to archaeological research and demonstrated the importance of the spatial approach to archaeological material at a local level. One of the reasons for publishing this book is that the maps produced for the 1954 *Oxford Region* still remain the only archaeological period maps in general circulation, and, whatever the limitations of such distribution maps, it is important that if they are to be used they should contain up-to-date information. We believe that the use of colour also significantly enhances their value.

The other major reason for the publication of these papers is that since 1954, and in particular over the past 20 years, an immense amount of new archaeological material has been uncovered in Oxford and in the Oxford Region, largely as a result of rescue archaeology ahead of redevelopment. In all periods there has been a tremendous increase in the amount of available information, added to which perceptions of what is important have radically altered. For instance, in 1954 environmental archaeology was virtually unheard of, whereas today the sampling and reconstruction of micro-environments are standard procedure, and are applied to the investigation of sites of all periods. Excavations of rural sites have been on a much larger scale over the past two decades, allowing a more thorough investigation of settlements and their associated agrarian systems, while in Oxford and the market towns of the Region every opportunity has been taken to excavate, enabling much more accurate chronologies and ancient topographies to be charted.

It has taken nearly 60 years for Oxford to produce a companion volume to that on Cambridgeshire. We believe that the time has been well spent and that the Oxford University Department for External Studies is proud to be associated with a volume of scholarship which we hope will survive well into the 21st century.

Trevor Rowley
Rewley House,
Wellington Square,
Oxford

October 1985

THE PALAEOLITHIC PERIOD IN THE OXFORD REGION

DEREK ROE

Introduction

To refer to 'the Oxford Region' in a Palaeolithic or Pleistocene context is meaningless: in considering the remoter end of the prehistoric period, one has to envisage a topography, environment and ecological situation quite different from those of today. Worse, one must envisage a whole succession of changing environments, corresponding to climatic changes on a vast scale, without being able to examine more than occasional fragments of some of them. So destructive are some of the geological processes involved (glaciation and deglaciation, for example), that often a whole landscape will be destroyed by the natural agencies that establish its successor; it is not a case of gentle superimposition of complete landscapes conformably one upon another to preserve for the archaeologist an unbroken record of the fluctuations of climate and temperature over half a million years or more. In the Oxford region, eloquent testimony of the magnitude of the environmental changes may, for example, be found in the deposits of the Summertown-Radley river terrace on which parts of Oxford itself are built. This terrace is a composite feature, incorporating 'warm' deposits overlying 'cold' ones (Sandford 1924, 1965; Briggs and Gilbertson 1980). The warm section represents interglacial conditions, in which hippopotamus and red deer were present, along with warmth-loving fresh-water mollusca including *Corbicula fluminalis* and *Unio littoralis*; on the other hand, the cold gravels contain abundant bones and teeth of woolly mammoth (*Mammuthus primigenius* Blumenbach) and they also incorporate many ice-wedge casts and cryoturbation features of periglacial origin. Consider on the one hand the modern environments in which hippopotamus thrives, and reflect on the other that the mammoth was highly specialized for existence in sub-arctic tundra (cf. Kurtén 1968: 136–8).

We are dealing, then, with a region which, over a long period of Middle and Upper Pleistocene time, saw many physical changes. It has also to be recalled that what is now Britain was for much of the Pleistocene a peninsula of the European land-mass, whose shape can only be vaguely guessed from a study of modern marine contours, though during certain interglacials the land-bridge may well have been drowned to leave Britain as a group of islands. The full history of this Pleistocene land-bridge, crucial to any understanding of access to Britain by successive human and animal populations, is simply not known. We are also dealing with a time-scale vastly greater than that of any other section included in this volume. Even the shortest chronology would place the beginning of the Palaeolithic period in Britain between 300,000 and 350,000 years ago, and some would prefer very much higher readings. Even the end of the period has to be set at about 10,000 years ago. It is not surprising that the nature of the archaeological evidence, the degree of its completeness, and the state of its preservation are all very different from what we encounter in more recent periods: the passing of time and the force of geological processes have deprived us of almost all trace of fragile and perishable objects in the British Lower and Middle Palaeolithic; dwelling structures and clear evidence concerning settlement patterns are unknown, and it is very rare to recover artefacts from an undisturbed primary context. It is true that cave sites offer rather better archaeological opportunities, but they are rare in Britain as a whole and entirely absent in the Oxford region.

From all of this it will be clear that the writing of palaeolithic prehistory in any part of Britain is fraught with grave difficulties. There is little alternative but to use modern geography, and we can at least be sure that there was a predecessor of the Thames in the Middle and Upper Pleistocene, which in our region flowed not so far away from its present course, though further downstream there were important differences at first (Gibbard 1979; Green *et al.* 1982). The courses and number of the tributaries are less certain. There would have been chalk and limestone hills, though the vertical intervals between hill-tops and valley bottoms will not have been exactly as we see them today. Rivers meander in their flood plains and, according to climatic circumstances, fill in or deepen their valleys, a process reflected in the occurrence of river terrace gravels at various heights and buried channels beneath modern flood plains. There is therefore no single demonstrable Upper Thames Valley that lasts for all our long period.

If we stand aside from local considerations and view the Oxford region in the full context of the Old World Lower and Middle Palaeolithic distributions, we find that it lies close to the north-western limit of human penetration in these periods. A scatter of find-spots lies to the north and west of Oxfordshire (Roe 1981: figs. 5.1–5.4) as far as Yorkshire and North Wales, but their sparseness contrasts notably with the richness of finds in East Anglia, south-east and central southern England. It might be argued that there has been greater destruction of evidence by geological processes in the north, but even allowing for this one may feel that palaeogeographical factors were more important: fewer resources of food and of raw material, and harsher climatic conditions, as the edges of the highland zone were approached. There was no population pressure to drive man into the remoter areas if they offered no obvious attraction. Even within the Oxford region, we pass beyond the limits of ready availability of flint, the principal lithic raw material of Palaeolithic Man in north-western Europe.

Palaeolithic settlement and Pleistocene deposits in the Oxford Region

All over western Europe, Early Man can be seen to have favoured settlement near water sources – lakes, and major and minor rivers. This makes sound economic sense for hunter-gatherer communities operating at a relatively simple technological level, and is reflected in the fact that in the Oxford region the river terrace gravels are the principal sources of Lower Palaeolithic artefacts. Middle and Upper Palaeolithic material is extremely rare, but the little that exists probably comes from sediments of Last Glacial age related to the Thames: the Late Pleistocene floodplain terraces, buried channels or alluvial deposits, for example. The fact that the Lower Palaeolithic material is mainly from gravel deposits is unfortunate, because almost all the finds are derived, swept into the gravel at the time of its formation by fluviatile or periglacial processes from an unknown number of original sites, whose actual relationships to each other in time and space we can never establish. Far more informative would be lake-margin sites in primary context, like Hoxne in Suffolk (Wymer 1974), or so many of the famous East African Lower Palaeolithic sites, but the Oxford region has none. The Wolvercote Channel site, discussed below, is perhaps the best of our local Lower Palaeolithic occurrences in river gravels, since the implements appear to have been closely associated with one particular stream channel and its beaches, at the base of the deposits, and were little disturbed. However, in this case the finds were made a long while ago by occasional collection, and although there were some distinguished geologists amongst those who observed the pit where the finds were made, there was never an archaeological excavation. The general nature of the Oxford region finds necessarily determines the strategy of our approach to them: in the absence of undisturbed datable sites locally, we can only look to the British Palaeolithic sequence as a whole and try to see which definable stages or industries are certainly represented in our own confused collections.

There are some hints of settlement on the higher ground in our region, away from immediate proximity to the main Thames. This would accord with the known existence of high-level sites on the chalk further to the east, in Bedfordshire and Hertfordshire particularly (W.G. Smith 1894, 1916), or to the south in Hampshire (Willis 1947), but as yet there are again no substantial undisturbed occurrences (cf. for example Peake 1918). Map 1 gives the general distribution of Oxford region Palaeolithic find-spots as recorded by the present writer in his *Lower and Middle Palaeolithic Gazetteer* (1968), with the addition of a few finds made since that work was published and older discoveries that have since come to his attention. The work of many local amateur archaeologists and collectors, past and present, has contributed to this map, with R.J. MacRae by far the most prolific single source of information.

As for the Pleistocene deposits of the region, the terrace sequences are crucial, though other forms of sedimentation exist. In the Upper Thames Valley (i.e. above the Goring Gap), the work of K.S. Sandford was the dominant influence from the middle of the 1920s to the end of the 1960s, and remains of basic importance; mainly on the basis of his research, though taking account of other contributions such as that of W.W. Bishop (1958), the following sequence of terraces and other gravels, in descending order of age, was suggested by Mitchell *et al.* (1973):

Gravels	*Suggested correlation*
Plateau Drift, also called Northern Drift (glacial origin)	Anglian glacial
Hanborough Terrace	Hoxnian interglacial
Wolvercote Terrace	Wolstonian glacial
Summertown-Radley Terrace:	
Lower part (cold)	Wolstonian glacial
Upper part (warm)	Ipswichian interglacial
Wolvercote Channel	Ipswichian interglacial
Floodplain Terraces:	
Upper	Middle Devensian
Lower (incorporating a buried channel)	Late Devensian

Sandford was of course envisaging a scheme with four principal Pleistocene glaciations, separated by interglacials. Recent researchers of many different kinds all over the world have shown this to be a grave oversimplification of the actual record of Pleistocene temperature fluctuations; the deep sea core oxygen isotope record perhaps offers the most striking evidence (cf. for example Shackleton and Opdyke 1976). In the last few years some interesting new evidence tending in the same direction has been obtained locally by those working on the Upper Thames gravels. Briggs and Gilbertson (1980) have suggested that the main accumulations of gravel on the various terraces represent aggradation in cold conditions by fluvio-periglacial processes; the Hanborough Terrace, for example, may be early Wolstonian rather than Hoxnian. The interglacials are most likely to be represented by local channel features containing organic deposits. The same authors give a preliminary report of the discovery at Linch Hill near Stanton Harcourt of just such a channel, filled with interglacial deposits, at the *base* of the Summertown-Radley Terrace. On stratigraphic grounds, this cannot belong to the same warm episode represented by the upper component of this terrace, since a substantial thickness of periglacial gravel intervenes. Exposures of the 'warm' upper part of the Summertown-Radley terrace, incidentally, have been lacking in recent years.

Meanwhile, Shotton *et al.* (1980) have reported on important Pleistocene sediments exposed at Sugworth, to the south-west of Oxford, during the construction of the A34 Abingdon by-pass. These included interglacial channels, whose age, on several lines of evidence, was Late Cromerian (Cromerian IIIb, in terms of the East Anglian sequence, for which see West 1980) – in other words, the channels belong to the interglacial preceding the Anglian. However, the fill of these channels was found to incorporate material derived from the Plateau Drift, showing that some parts at least of the Plateau Drift must belong not to the Anglian as previously believed, but to a glaciation older than the 'Cromerian' of the East Anglian sequence. This would doubtless correlate with one of the major cold phases well established within the 'Cromerian Complex' of north-west Continental Europe (cf. Zagwijn *et al.* 1971). The Sugworth channels are sealed in by a deposit of pebbly clay which itself closely resembles Plateau Drift, but this might have been redeposited during the Anglian glaciation.

We cannot here go deeply into the problems of Quaternary geology in our region, but it can at least be seen that recent work here has begun to attack the old oversimplified system of stages, in a manner wholly in keeping with the results of research elsewhere in the world. It may, however, be some while before a generally agreed correlation of the Upper Thames gravels with named Pleistocene climatic episodes, or numbered oxygen isotope stages, emerges.

It would in many ways be appropriate to draw the southern limit of our area at the downstream end of the Goring Gap, so far as the Thames Valley is concerned, but that is not quite possible in the present publication. The narrow route by which the Thames passes through the chalk barrier separates two different worlds of terrace nomenclature and of problems of correlation, and takes us from the Upper Thames to the Middle Thames Valley. It must suffice here simply to mention the principal Middle and Upper Pleistocene terrace names of the Middle Thames that are relevant, and we must leave aside the fascinating problems of the early high-level gravel deposits in that region and on the Chilterns, since they are of pre-Palaeolithic age. The main Middle Thames terraces, therefore, in descending order of height, are:

Winter Hill
Black Park
Boyn Hill
Lynch Hill
Taplow
Floodplain

Both Winter Hill and Taplow have sometimes been divided into Upper and Lower units; the Floodplain Terrace is probably not divisible until one has passed downstream beyond the limits of our area. The Boyn Hill Terrace was formerly regarded as having Upper and Lower divisions, but the name Lynch Hill has replaced 'Lower Boyn Hill'. Some authors have distinguished a separate 'Iver Terrace' at much the same height as the Lynch Hill feature; others regard them as identical. The Winter Hill Terrace is generally attributed to the Anglian and the Floodplain Terrace is evidently of Devensian age, but grave doubts must at present attend the attribution of the various gravels at intervening heights to specific named climatic stages, given that the deep sea cores and other evidence make it clear that there are more cold-warm cycles to be accommodated than we have previously allowed for in the British Quaternary succession, as we have just seen. Some of the Middle Thames gravels seem likely to be of fluvio-periglacial character; in particular, it is hard to point to any undisturbed deposit amongst them that is certainly of Hoxnian age. Various of the gravels also have important and sometimes subdivisible cappings of brickearth (e.g. at Iver), whose age is likely to be Ipswichian and Devensian in present terminology.

Correlations with the Upper Thames terraces mentioned above cannot at present be reliably established, one reason being major changes in the lithology of the gravels themselves after the Thames has passed through the chalk. There is also a terrace sequence in the Kennet Valley (Thomas 1961), with at least five terraces, for some of which correlations with Middle Thames features have been suggested.

For further information on the Middle Thames gravels, and for the development of research on them over the past half century, the reader should consult the work of W.B.R. King and K.P. Oakley (1936), A.D. Lacaille (1939, 1940, 1961), F.K. Hare (1947), K.R. and C.E. Sealy (1956), S.W. Wooldridge (1957), J.J. Wymer (1968), C.P. Green and D.W.F. McGregor (1980), and S. Cranshaw (1983). Two small guidebooks also contain useful information on the gravels of the Middle and Upper Thames and the Kennet: The Quaternary Research Association's *Field Guide to the Oxford Region* (April 1976), edited by the present writer, and the INQUA *Guidebook for Excursion A5: South-East England and the Thames Valley* (1977), compiled by E.R. Shepard-Thorn and J.J. Wymer.

After the terrace gravels, the most prolific source of Palaeolithic implements is certainly the Wallingford Fan Gravels – massive solifluction accumulations spreading out at the base of the Chiltern escarpment, known over a distance of at least 10 km. between Watlington and Ipsden (Arkell 1945; Wymer 1968: 99–107; Horton *et al.* 1981). A major factor in the formation of these gravels has been the sludging downhill of material under periglacial permafrost conditions, and the artefacts in them are mixed and derived, many no doubt having come from the upper slopes of the chalk hills. The geological evidence, including studies of the lithology of the gravels, suggests that they are younger than the Plateau Drift, but that is not particularly helpful from the archaeological point of view, and several separate phases of periglacial conditions may well have contributed to their deposition and to various post-depositional effects which they have suffered; it is certainly not possible to assign to them any single well-established date. In the most recent study, Horton *et al.* described (1981) a recently observed soil horizon with organic remains (the Gould's

Grove Member) within the Fan Gravel deposits and argued that the bulk of the Fan Gravel may be of Upper Winter Hill Terrace age. One would certainly expect the implements to be substantially later than that in date according to our present knowledge of the British Lower Palaeolithic (Roe 1981), but until new specimens are found *in situ* we are unlikely to reach firm conclusions regarding their actual relationship to the deposits.

The British Palaeolithic sequence

It is necessary to summarize the main features of the British Palaeolithic period in order to understand the Oxford Region finds because, as already indicated, in the absence of undisturbed, stratified, dated sites, no purely local sequence can be established. Instead, we must try to assess the local Palaeolithic assemblages by comparing them with industries recognized in better archaeological circumstances elsewhere in Britain, to see what parts of the full sequence are represented in our own area, and whether any of our occurrences have special interest or importance.

The present writer has recently published (1981) a full account of the British Lower and Middle Palaeolithic, with comprehensive references for the sites mentioned and detailed arguments in support of the conclusions drawn. For the British Upper Palaeolithic, there is the two-volume account by J. B. Campbell (1977), with extensive documentation. Shorter general accounts are those of A. Morrison (1980) and P. Mellars (1974), and, for the Upper Palaeolithic, R. Jacobi (1980). J.J. Wymer's account of the British Lower Palaeolithic (1968), based heavily on the Thames Valley material, remains very useful but naturally does not include all the ground covered by the more recent books. In view of the availability of all this literature, which should be consulted for technical detail, the writer feels justified in stating quite baldly here the stages of the British sequence as he understands it. The order of events in the Lower Palaeolithic is deduced mainly from stratified occurrences in North Kent, especially in the Swanscombe area, with occasional independent geochronological evidence from individual sites elsewhere. The crucial sites for the Upper Palaeolithic are caves in western Britain (notably Devonshire, the Mendips, North and South Wales) and in the Midlands (notably the Creswell Crags sites), though some finds from open sites are known, notably in East Anglia and East Dorset.

Industry	Probable age
LOWER PALAEOLITHIC	(terminology as in Mitchell *et al.* 1973)
Clactonian, with simple cores, choppers and flakes; no handaxes present at all	From Late Anglian to some time in the Hoxnian
Acheulian:	
(a) Early Acheulian, with crude, thick handaxes	Present during the Anglian, presumably in a mild phase; duration uncertain
(b) Middle Acheulian, well made handaxe industries with several variants, classifiable within general 'Pointed' and 'Ovate' traditions	Begins in the Hoxnian; present also in the Wolstonian complex and probably also in the Ipswichian
(c) Final Acheulian, belonging to the *Micoquian* tradition seen in various parts of Continental Europe	Present in the Ipswichian
LOWER/MIDDLE PALAEOLITHIC	
Levalloisian. Although this is properly the name of a specialized knapping technique, a few British industries specialize in its use to the extent of being able to be designated as 'Levalloisian Industries'. They stand somewhat on the threshold between the Lower and Middle Palaeolithic industries of classic type, but ought not to be thought of as 'transitional' in the sense of implying some 'evolutionary' process in Britain itself.	

(a) Earlier style, with large flakes from prepared cores, often showing a radial pattern of preparatory scars

(b) Later style, with flake-blades showing mainly longitudinal preparatory scars

Present by an early stage of the Wolstonian; probably a brief episode, reflecting a technique used only when raw material of high quality was particularly abundant.

Present in the Ipswichian and also the Devensian; similar technology may be a part of the British Mousterian

MIDDLE PALAEOLITHIC
Mousterian. Industries characterized by the use of prepared core flaking techniques and the manufacture of fine, regular flake tools and of characteristic handaxes, notably the so-called *'bout coupé'* type. There may be a few signs of precocious Middle Palaeolithic industries in Britain, but the main body of the British Middle Palaeolithic comprises isolated finds or occasional industries, mostly small-scale, specifically attributable to one variant of the West European Middle Palaeolithic, the Mousterian of Acheulian Tradition, which is well known in France (cf. for example Bordes 1961)

The precocious industries apparently belong to some part of the Wolstonian complex. There is just a hint that the Mousterian of Acheulian Tradition may be present before the end of the Ipswichian, but the majority of datable occurrences apparently belong to one or more milder periods in the first half of the Devensian

UPPER PALAEOLITHIC
Earlier Upper Palaeolithic. Sporadic episodes of probably brief occupation by makers of blade-tool industries took place (Campbell 1977; Jacobi 1980). Certain characteristic tool types, notably projectile points and gravers (burins), suggest direct connections with various Upper Palaeolithic traditions better seen in Continental Europe, notably the Central European leaf-point industries, though there are lesser amounts of material attributable to the Aurignacian and perhaps to one particular facies of the Gravettian (Upper Perigordian). A long gap in the occupation record follows, coinciding with the coldest phase of the Devensian

Wholly within the second half of the Devensian; on the basis of radiocarbon dating, the older limit could be as early as $c.38,000$ years ago (Campbell 1977) and the younger one $c.25,000$.

Later Upper Palaeolithic. There is a scatter of industries, whose small backed blade tools and other artefacts are wholly in keeping with various Late Glacial traditions of north-west Continental Europe, notably the *'Federmesser'* series of northwest Germany and the Low Countries, though there may also be some Late Magdalenian influences; some sites have produced a little bonework, including barbed spearheads and occasional decorated objects.

Campbell (1977) published various radiocarbon dates, the earliest being 14,275 BP ± 120, from Kent's Cavern, Torquay, 12,375 BP ± 150, from Sun Hole, Cheddar and 12,180 BP ± 100, from Kent's Cavern. Jacobi (1980) argued that the association of these particular dates with the artefacts was doubtful and that the Late Upper Palaeolithic occupation of Britain probably began after 10,000 BP. However, a site at Hengistbury Head in Dorset has since yielded good dates of $c.12,500$ BP (Barton 1983). The Later Upper Palaeolithic is succeeded by the Early Mesolithic early in the Flandrian, possibly with a period of overlap.

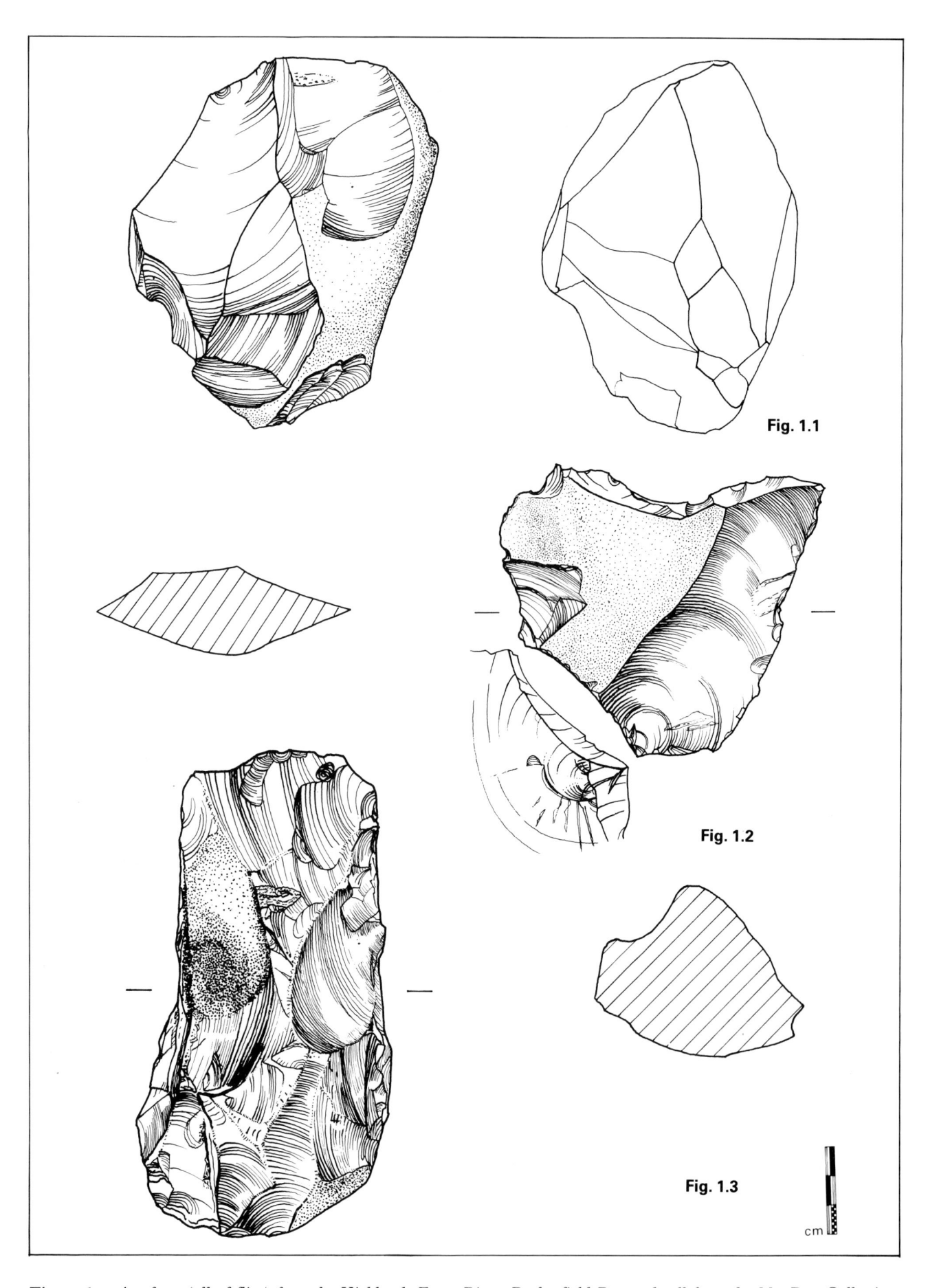

Figure 1. *Artefacts (all of flint) from the Highlands Farm Pit at Rotherfield Peppard, all from the MacRae Collection, now at the Pitt Rivers Museum. 1, Clactonian core; 2, Clactonian flake; 3 and 4, crude, thick, abraded handaxes attributed to the Early Acheulian; 5, Middle Acheulian ovate handaxe. Drawings by M.H.R. Cook.*

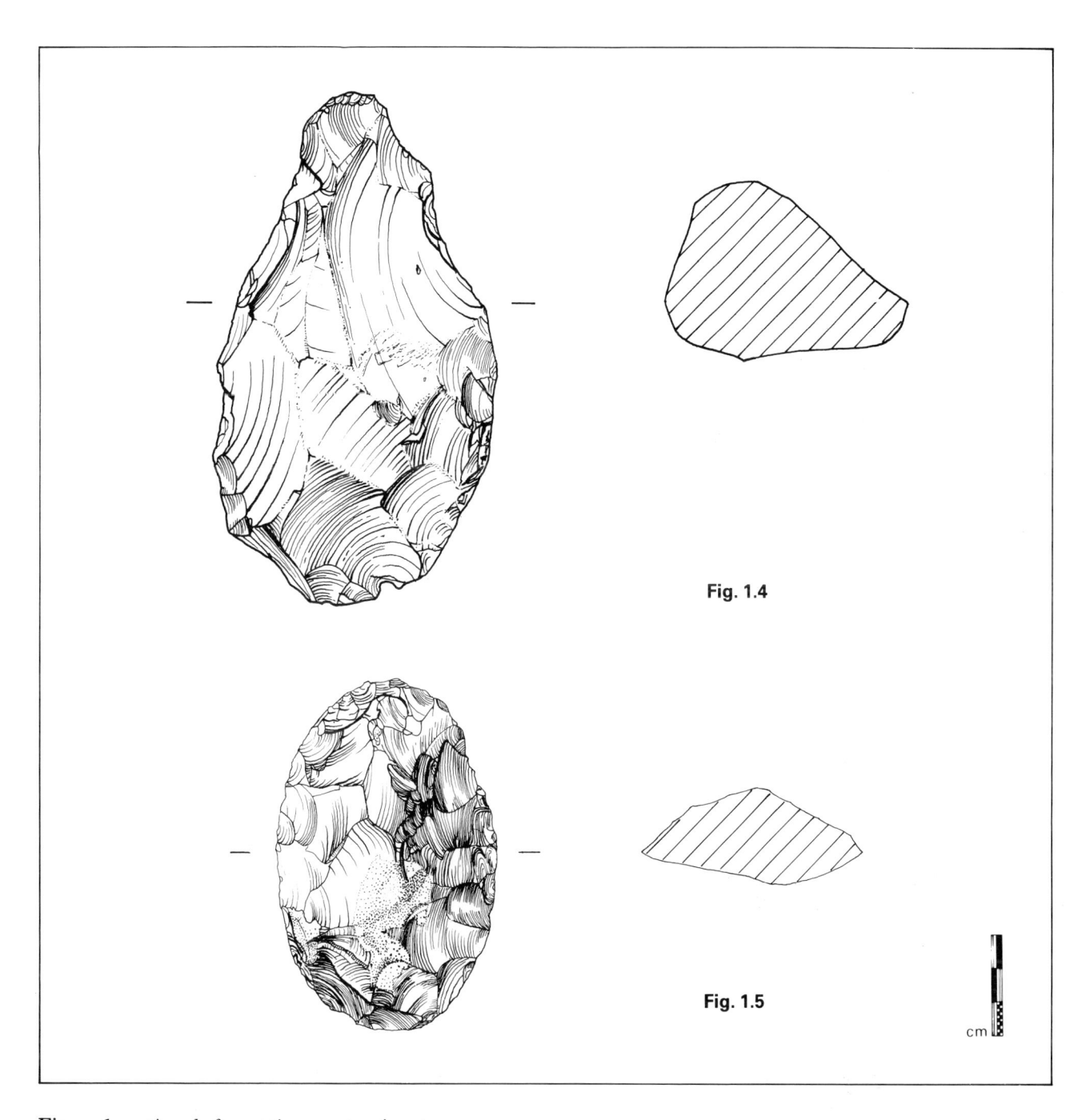

Figure 1 *continued: for captions see previous page*

The Palaeolithic of the Oxford Region

If we now check over the list given in the preceding section, and follow a mainly technological and typological argument, it is possible to conclude that a surprising number of the stages are represented in the Oxford area, albeit in some cases very sparsely.

Clactonian. At Highlands Farm Pit, Rotherfield Peppard, immense quantities of artefacts (several thousand) have been recovered from gravels of the so-called 'Ancient Channel of the Thames' that cuts across a loop of the modern river at an altitude some 150 feet higher, between Caversham and Henley. Numerous collectors obtained material from the pit during its working life, and excavations were also carried out by J. J. Wymer, who has published the results (1956, 1961, 1968: 191–209). Wymer's work casts doubt on the original 'Ancient Channel' interpretation of the gravels into which the Highlands Farm pit is cut (Treacher *et al.* 1948) and on the date of their formation; they may have been extensively reworked. In assessing the artefacts, he concluded that the strongest element represented in the collections was Clactonian, with plenty of the characteristic cores as well as flakes, flake tools and choppers, and the present writer sees no reason to disagree (Fig. 1, nos. 1, 2). The gravels are much disturbed and the artefacts in them jumbled together, so this is not a pure Clactonian industry in a primary context. There are a

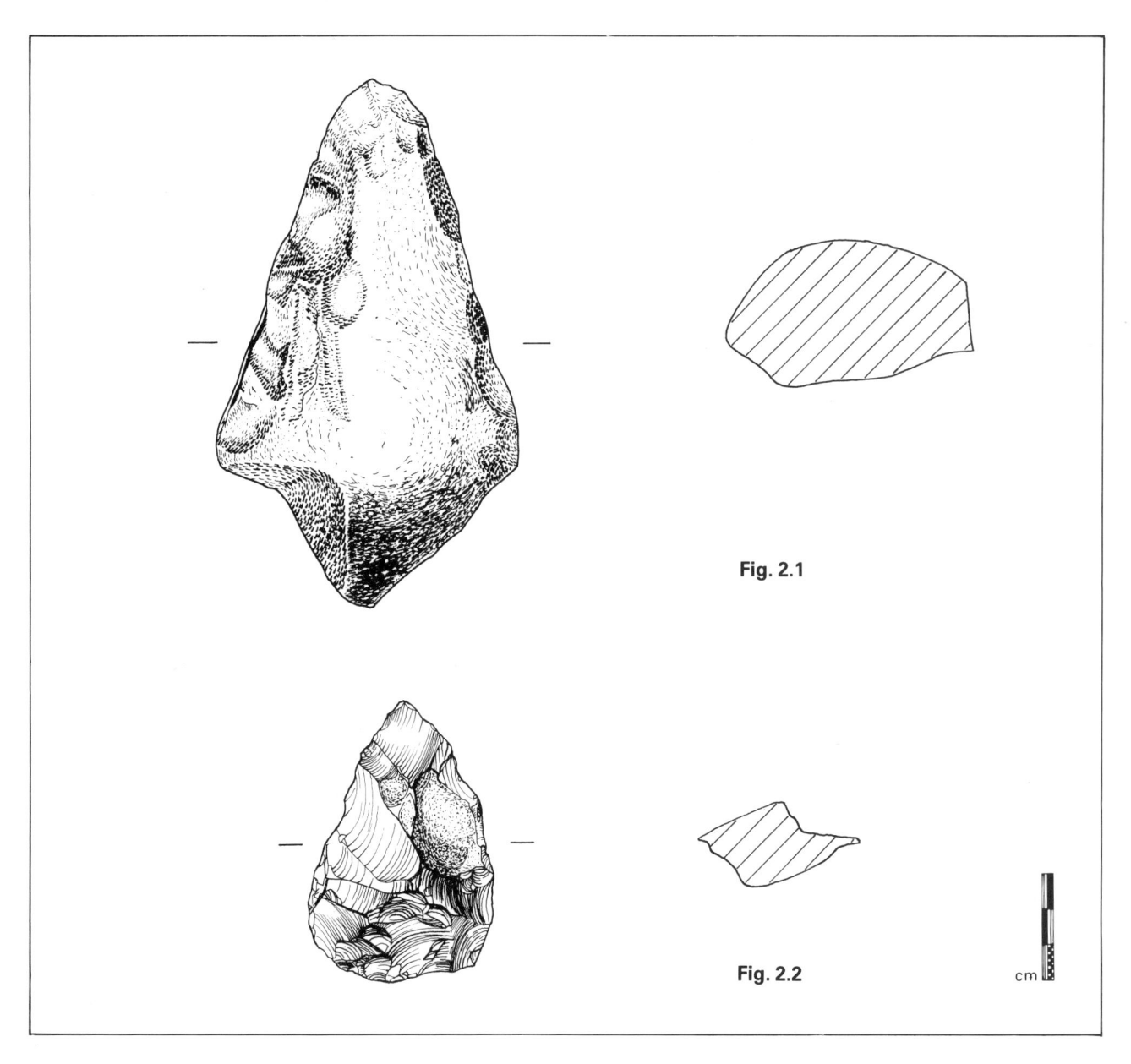

Figure 2. *Handaxes from Iffley and the Wallingford Fan Gravels, all now in the Pitt Rivers Museum collections. 1, pointed handaxe of quartzite from Iffley; 2, pointed handaxe of flint from Iffley; 3, pointed handaxe of flint from Rumbolds Pit, Ewelme (Fan Gravels); 4, ovate handaxe of flint, same source as no. 3. Drawings by M.H.R. Cook.*

few other possible Clactonian occurrences in the Middle Thames Valley, and a few more pieces from some of the other pits in the Ancient Channel gravels, but no certain finds of Clactonian have been made in the Upper Thames area.

Early Acheulian. Wymer also argues for the presence of a small amount of Early Acheulian in the mixed assemblage at Highlands Farm: crude handaxes, made by 'hard hammer' technique only (Fig. 1, nos 3, 4) certainly occur, and they are often much more worn and stained than the numerous fine ovate handaxes which are also common at this prolific pit. Though 'rough-outs' or unfinished handaxes, superficially of crude appearance, may occur in any Acheulian industry of whatever date, one would expect them to be in the same condition as the finished pieces; in any case, these handaxes do not appear to be unfinished, so much as completed at a low level of technological competence. Some of the other Ancient Channel pits also yielded similar material. Wymer's diagnosis is perhaps unprovable, and dating evidence for the manufacture of the crude handaxes would still be lacking even if the date of the formation of the gravel deposit were clear, but the present writer finds the hypothesis perfectly acceptable pending further information and has noted with interest the occurrence of similar material here and there in the Kennet Valley (1981: 151–2).

Middle Acheulian. There are a number of local occurrences atrributable to this rather vague stage, which covers a long period of time and a considerable

Fig. 2.3

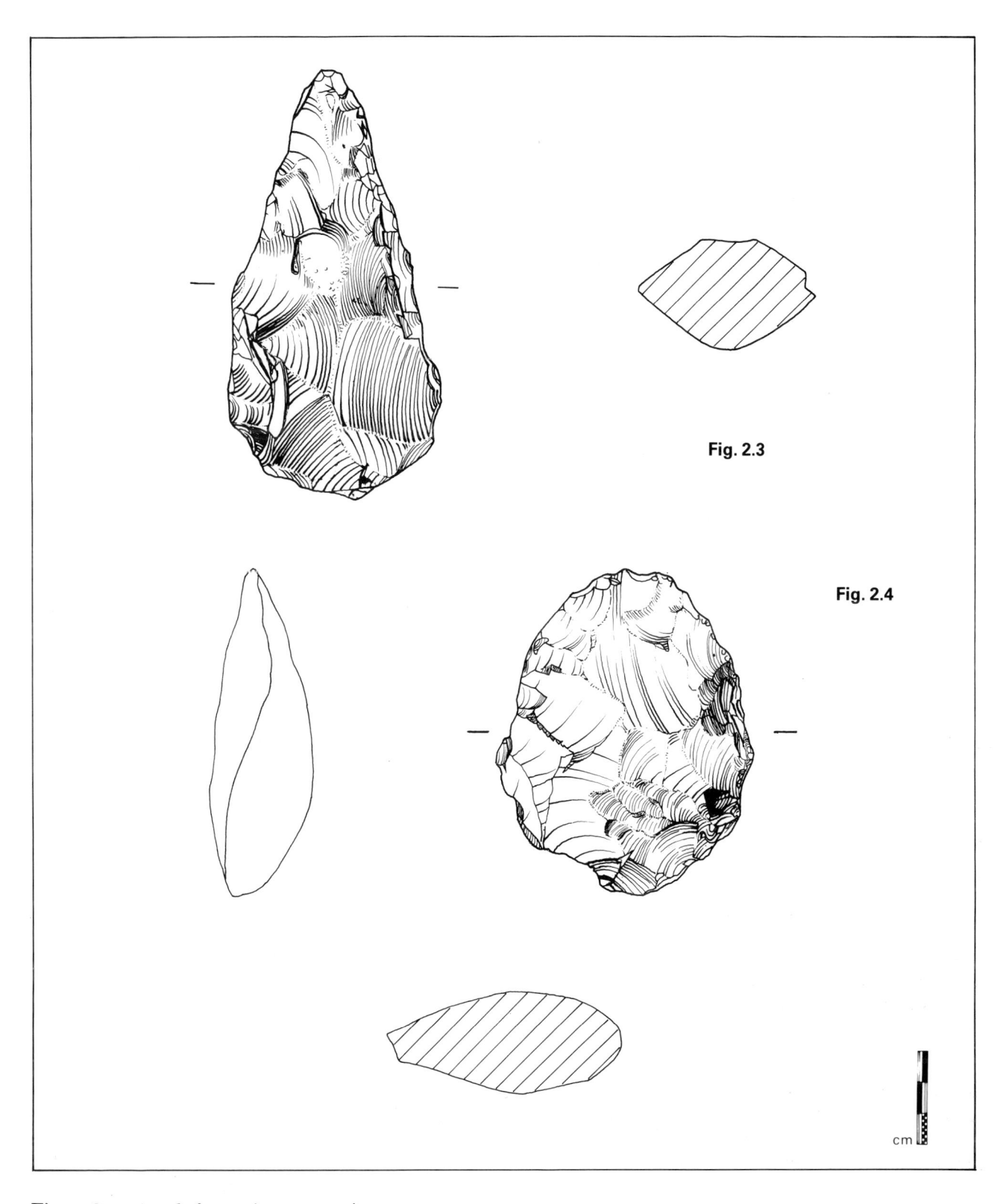

Fig. 2.4

Figure 2 *continued: for captions see previous page*

typological range. Highlands Farm Pit is again a contributing site; so are virtually all of the Ancient Channel pits, but at Highlands Wymer's excavation seems to have coincided with a concentration of two or three hundred fine handaxes, with a strong preference for ovate shapes (in the sense of plan forms), made by very skilful 'soft-hammer' flaking, giving flat cross-sections and straight cutting edges round all or most of their circumferences (Fig. 1, no. 5). They resemble each other strikingly in condition (pretty fresh) and raw material, though they occurred at greatly varying depths in the gravel, and we may guess that there was a substantial Acheulian site close by from which these pieces came at the time when the gravels were deposited or reworked into the state in which we see them now. Middle Acheulian 'ovate' industries of this kind are

Fig. 3.1

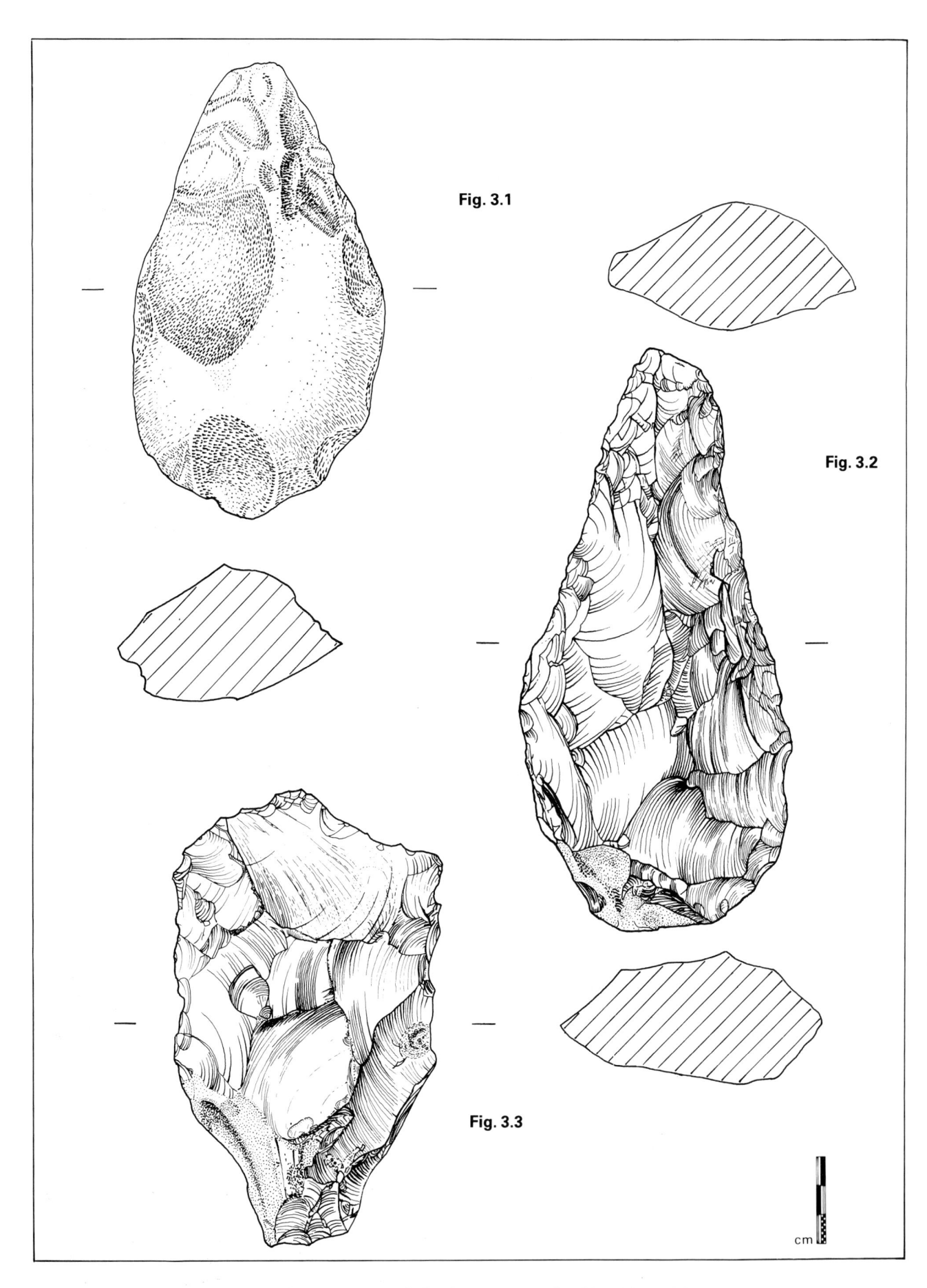

Fig. 3.2

Fig. 3.3

Figure 3. *Artefacts from Berinsfield: MacRae Collection, now at the Pitt Rivers Museum. 1, quartzite handaxe; 2, pointed handaxe of flint, approaching the* ficron *form; 3, cleaver, made of flint; 4, ovate handaxe of flint, with an oblique 'tranchet' scar at the tip on one face; 5, flint Levalloisian flake, with faceted striking platform. Drawings by M.H.R. Cook.*

Fig. 3.4

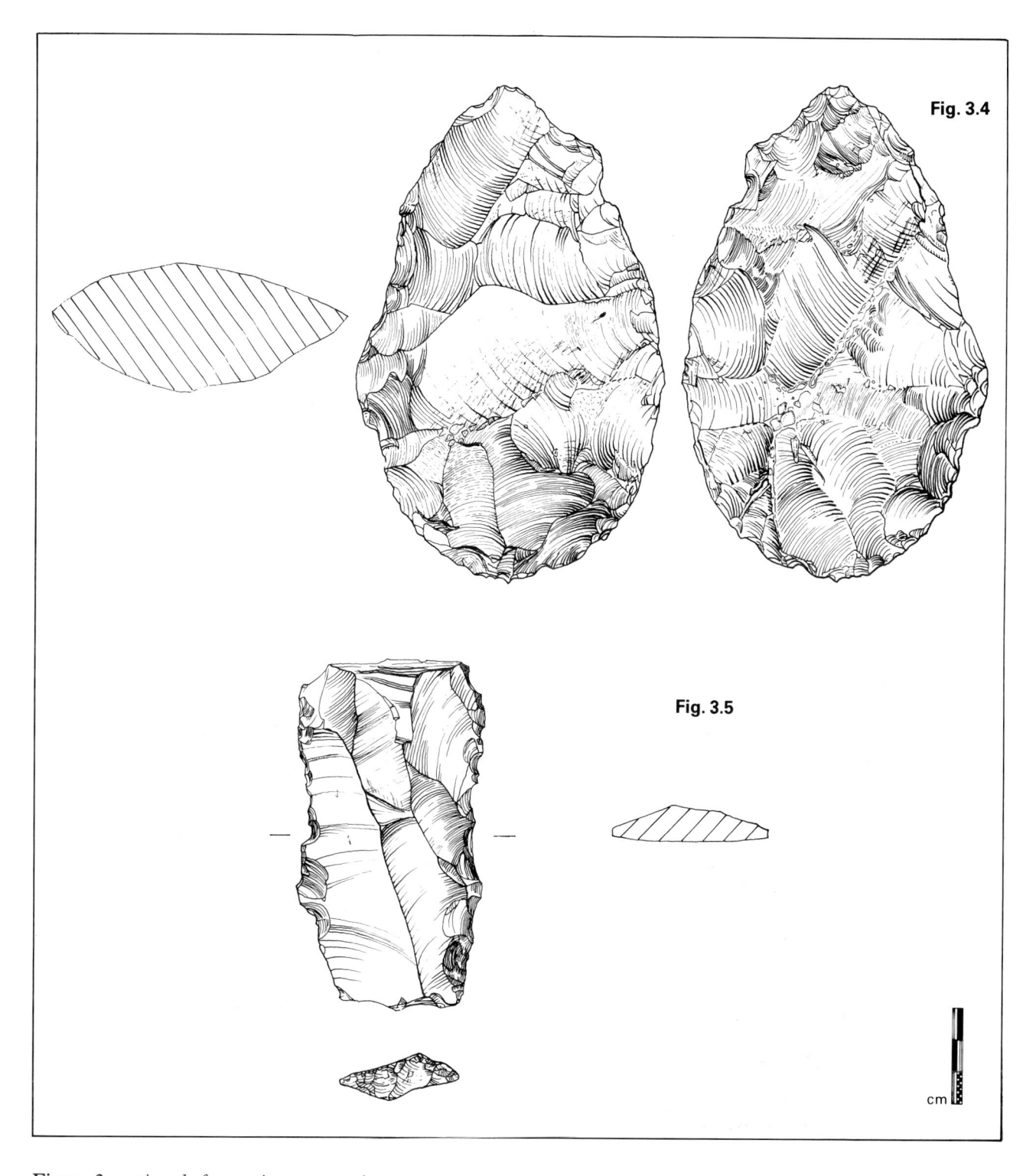

Fig. 3.5

Figure 3 *continued: for captions see previous page*

known from many places in England (Roe 1981: 152–211): for example, in the loam overlying the main gravels of the so-called 90′ terrace in North Kent in the Swanscombe-Dartford area, or in East Anglia at Warren Hill, Mildenhall (the fresh series) or at nearby High Lodge (in gravel overlying the lake sediments), or in Dorset at Cogdean Pit, Corfe Mullen. Nearer to home, as it were, there was a fine series of ovates from the Roebuck Pit, Tilehurst, near Reading, found in a gravel probably formed under periglacial conditions (Smith 1915; Wymer 1968: 148–50, 165).

On the southern edge of Oxford, old finds at Cornish's Pit, Iffley, are also classifiable as Middle Acheulian (Wymer 1968: 91–2). This time, pointed handaxe shapes are in the majority (Fig. 2, nos. 1, 2) and the industry is of interest because of the raw materials: flint was evidently scarce and the implement sizes are all small, while quartzite is frequently used and one or two other exotic rocks, presumably in the form of pebbles collected from Plateau Drift deposits. Wymer lists 28 handaxes from this site, now at the Pitt Rivers Museum, Oxford, and there are also various flakes and

Fig. 4.1

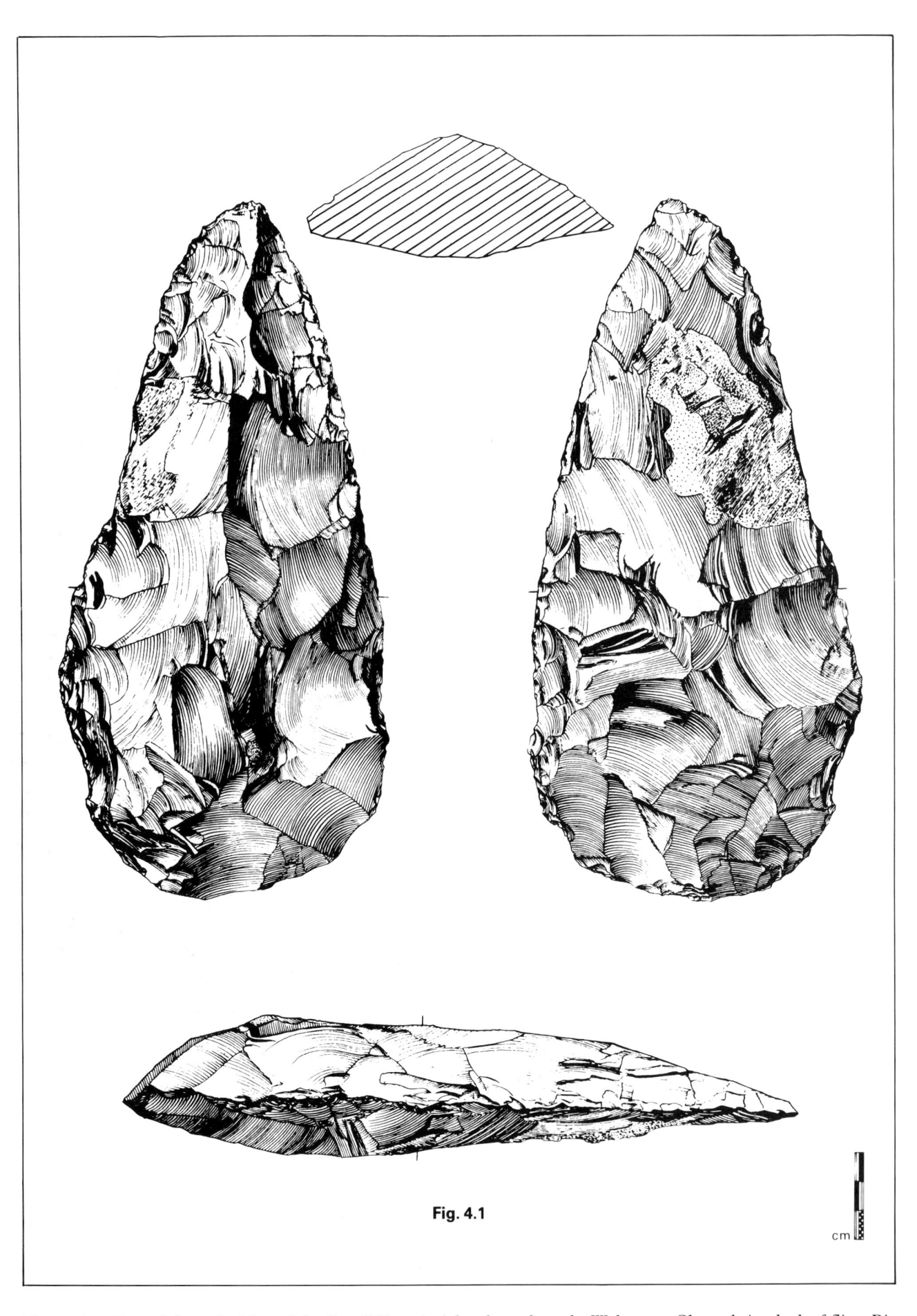

Figure 4. *Two of the typical Late Acheulian (Micoquian) handaxes from the Wolvercote Channel site, both of flint. Pitt Rivers Museum collections; drawn by the late C.O. Waterhouse.*

Fig. 4.2

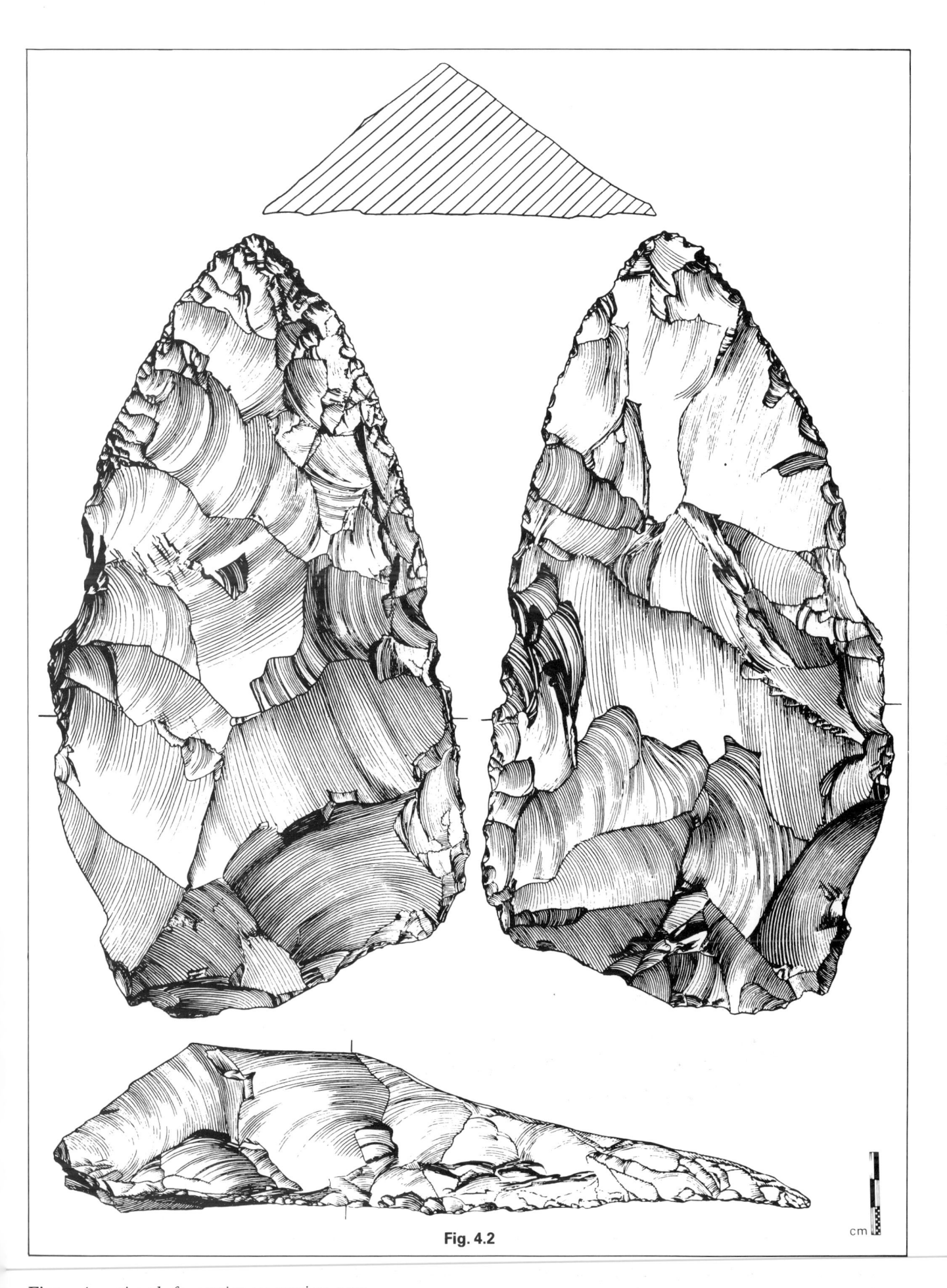

Figure 4 *continued: for caption see previous page*

fragments. They appear to have come from the extreme base of the Summertown-Radley gravels (see above), but could of course be older than the gravels themselves. Faunal remains were found at the same level, including both mammoth and hippopotamus, but one cannot regard any of them as necessarily being properly associated with the industry. Middle Acheulian industries specializing in pointed handaxes are well known in Britain (Roe 1980: 152–213): the most famous example is that from the Middle gravels at Barnfield Pit, Swanscombe, Kent, the deposit that also yielded the fragments of the Swanscombe hominid skull. It is a pity that the Iffley finds were all made long ago, most of them in the early years of the present century: the site would probably have rewarded a close study using modern archaeological methods.

The handaxes from the Wallingford Fan Gravels (see above) are also Middle Acheulian, in a broad typological and technological sense, but their actual age is uncertain and the collections are a mixture from pits at several places in this deposit of solifluctued material on the slope of the Chilterns (Arkell 1945; Wymer 1968: 99–107). Pits near Benson and Crowmarsh were the most productive, notably Turner's Court, Gould's Grove and Rumbold's Pit. The handaxes (Fig. 2, nos. 3, 4) show much damage and include examples of various classic Middle Acheulian types – *ficrons*, twisted ovates, and so forth. Over a hundred survive.

Lastly under this heading should be mentioned some interesting finds, recently published by R. J. MacRae (1982) from a group of gravel pits near Berinsfield: examples of the implements are illustrated here (Fig. 3). Some 250 artefacts were collected, mostly at the gravel screening plant, though pits at Queensford Farm and Mount Farm were clearly the principal sources. It was possible to trace the origin of some of the artefacts at least to the extreme base of the gravel, where they probably lay right on the surface of the Oxford Clay over which the gravel (tentatively attributed to the Summertown-Radley terrace) was deposited – a situation reminiscent of the old descriptions of the finds at Cornish's Pit, Iffley. No contemporary fauna was recovered at Berinsfield. There are various handaxe types (Fig. 3), including some large, bold, pointed handaxes of flint and other rocks, mainly quartzite: flint was evidently more readily available, in larger pieces, than at Iffley and the site is certainly much nearer to the chalk. It is interesting to note the presence of at least one typical cleaver (Fig. 3, no. 3), a *ficron*, and some broad, flat, round-ended handaxes. The combination of such types is reminiscent of a Middle Acheulian variant seen at various places in southern England, including the Middle Thames sites of Baker's Farm, Farnham Royal, Bucks, and Furze Platt, Maidenhead, Berks (Lacaille 1940, 1961; Wymer 1968: 217–227, 239–243; Roe 1981: 164–8; for a recent detailed account, see Cranshaw 1983). It would perhaps be unwise to attribute MacRae's finds specifically to this facies of the British Middle Acheulian, especially since we cannot be sure that only a single industry is represented at the find-spots, but the possibility is worth noting. Cleavers are a distinctive element at the British sites of this kind; it is interesting to recall that P. J. Tester recovered a quartzite cleaver at Dorchester, not far away, in the early 1950s, from a pit near the site of the Neolithic henge, apparently dug into the same gravel (Roe 1968: 248).

Final Acheulian (Micoquian). In the present writer's view (cf. 1981: 117–30), the finds from the Wolvercote Channel site at the old brick pit in Upper Wolvercote are of major significance in the British Lower Palaeolithic. Some two hundred artefacts survive in museum collections in Oxford, including 75 handaxes, various flake tools and other flakes and fragments, amongst which is some typical *débitage* of handaxe manufacture. Certainly some and possibly all of this material was associated with the beaches of a stream channel, and with the artefacts were found faunal remains of 'interglacial' character, including *Elephas (Palaeoloxodon) antiquus*, *Dicerorhinus hemitoechus*, *Bos primigenius*, *Cervus elaphus* and *Equus caballus*. Many of the artefacts are in fresh condition, and the site was probably a good one which had been little disturbed, but it was discovered too early for proper archaeological examination. Sandford argued (1924, 1926, 1939) that the stream channel was cut through, and therefore younger than, a fragment of the (Wolstonian) Wolvercote Terrace, making its age Last Interglacial (Ipswichian). W. W. Bishop (1958) argued differently and concluded that the age was more likely to be Hoxnian. The present writer has laid stress on the rather striking technology of the Wolvercote handaxes: their planoconvexity, especially towards the tip, and the strong preference for pointed, narrow, pyriform shapes; the consistent order and disposition of the flake removals; the frequent occurrence of a line of minute flake scars down one long edge, and so forth (Fig. 4). These features, so frequent at Wolvercote, do not regularly occur in the British Middle Acheulian, but can readily be found in the Central and West European Micoquian (Bosinski 1967; Gábori 1976), where the industries, when dated, appear to belong to the Last Interglacial or even, on occasion, to the earliest part of the final glaciation. It therefore seems likely that the Wolvercote occurrence is the best Micoquian site in Britain, and offers the leading evidence at present for the representation in the 'British peninsula' of this particular late handaxe tradition, whose source lies rather to the east of Britain than to the south, one would think. If this view is correct, Sandford's view of the chronology would be more likely to be right than that of Bishop, and we might envisage the Wolvercote Channel as belonging to the period when interglacial channels were incised into the top of the periglacial gravels that make up the bulk of the Summertown-Radley terrace (see above). However, with the increasing doubt over the number of Middle and Upper Pleistocene interglacials in Britain and Europe, it would be wiser not to insist on that correlation at present. A few other examples of classic 'Wolvercote type' handaxes are known in our region, none of the find-spots being far from the main site: North Rise (Banbury Road), Summertown, and a gravel pit near Eynsham Station.

Levalloisian. There are no finds of major 'Levalloisian' industries in our area, but a few individual artefacts made by the Levalloisian technique are known. The most interesting come from the Berinsfield pits already mentioned as a source of Middle Acheulian material (MacRae 1982). We have already noted that no stratigraphic observation of the artefacts *in situ* was possible, but it is worth noting that the Levalloisian flakes, of which one is shown in Fig. 3, no. 5, seem fresher and less patinated than most of the handaxes: they might have come from a separate level, some pocket of loam overlying the gravel, for example, though we cannot be sure. Traces of a fine-grained deposit certainly adhere to the specimen illustrated, but lenses of fine sand are common enough within gravel deposits. As noted earlier, Levalloisian technique is merely a knapping method: it occurs within many different Palaeolithic industries and indeed even in industries of Holocene age, so no clear attribution of the isolated examples known from Oxfordshire can be made.

Mousterian. It has already been observed that major concentrations of Mousterian artefacts are rare anywhere within Britain, though single finds are scattered over much of the south. The Oxford region conforms precisely to this general pattern: there are no major sites, but there are two fine and typical *bout coupé* handaxes (Tyldesley, in press b). The first comes from Abingdon (see also Roe 1981: 264 and Plate 35), found in 1972 in an alluvial deposit perhaps of Devensian age; the implement is fresh and unpatinated. The second comes from Tuckwell's Pit, Radley, where it was found in 1983 lying on the Tertiary Clay surface at the base of gravel of the Floodplain Terrace, which is certainly of Devensian age. The implement bears only slight abrasion and patination. From Chaundy's Pit at Radley comes a stray find of a disc core, a type that is more common in the Mousterian than at any other stage of the Palaeolithic (unpublished: teaching collections of the Department of Ethnology & Prehistory, Oxford University). This pit was also dug into Floodplain Terrace gravel, though the artefact was a loose find and not *in situ* in the gravel; a tentative Middle Palaeolithic attribution seems not unreasonable. One more artefact that is probably Mousterian is a small cordiform handaxe, picked up as a stray surface find at Mount Skippitt near Finstock (Tyldesley, in press a). These four items make up the total list of Middle Palaeolithic artefacts from Oxfordshire known to the writer at the present time, though other finds can be expected. It is worth noting that the adjacent counties to the east, south and west have each produced one or more *bout coupé* handaxes (list in Roe 1981: 254–267).

Upper Palaeolithic. Only a single fragmentary artefact from the Oxford region seems certainly to represent the whole Upper Palaeolithic: a water-worn piece of a flat, bifacial leaf-point, which came from 'river-ballast' at Osney Lock, in or before 1911, in which year it was given to the Pitt Rivers Museum. The present writer noted it in the collections and tentatively identified it as of Earlier Upper Palaeolithic age on grounds of typology and technology; this opinion was later confirmed by R. M. Jacobi, who has studied the British Upper Palaeolithic leaf-points in much more detail, and he duly mapped the find-spot in his recent account of the British Upper Palaeolithic (1980: fig. 2.2). One might guess that the artefact was dredged up from some buried channel of Devensian age below the modern river, like comparable finds in the Gipping Valley at Ipswich, Suffolk, but that is a purely speculative suggestion for which no supporting evidence exists, worth making only for the sake of urging that a watch be kept locally on dredged material for other artefacts of Upper Palaeolithic age. No Later Upper Palaeolithic material is yet known from Oxfordshire, though a look at the distribution maps prepared by Campbell and Jacobi in the works cited earlier suggests the strong likelihood that Upper Palaeolithic people did at least pass across what is now the Oxford region, even if they did not settle there. Jacobi's map (1980: fig. 2.8) of finds of *Federmesser*-type artefacts in the British Isles is a case in point; the nearest actual find-spot to our area is at Crown Acres, Newbury (see also Campbell 1977: 177–8).

Conclusion

The review of the Oxford region palaeolithic finds in the preceding section was deliberately selective rather than comprehensive, concentrating on the prolific sites and those of particular importance. Map 1 shows the distribution of the rest of the material and space does not permit a commentary on what each minor find-spot yielded; the majority of this information can be obtained from the present writer's *British Lower and Middle Palaeolithic Gazetteer*, from the pages devoted to Oxfordshire – and Berkshire, since different county boundaries were then in force. Wymer (1968) is also an admirable source. It is of course difficult to classify single finds with confidence, except when they are such striking objects as *bout coupé* handaxes, Middle Acheulian cleavers, Levalloisian flakes or disc cores.

From what has been said in the present account, it should be clear that the greater part of the British Palaeolithic sequence is actually represented in the Oxford region, even if mainly by minor occurrences. The sites are all to some extent disturbed or mixed, often considerably, though when the artefacts are numerous the general nature of the assemblage is usually clear. The finds have the geographical interest of proximity to the very edge of the Lower and Middle Palaeolithic settlement of Europe, and the regular use of rocks other than flint is also an unusual feature so far as

Britain is concerned. Though these are not primary context sites, they are far from unimportant: the Wolvercote Channel site in particular has genuine significance and much more than local interest.

There is in fact no reason why primary context sites should not await discovery in the Oxford region, perhaps associated with interglacial channels or possibly with patches of high level brickearth on the chalk uplands, if any can be found like those away to the east and south, mentioned in the section on Palaeolithic settlement and Pleistocene deposits. There should still be more Acheulian material to come from the Upper Thames gravels, and there should eventually be more too in the way of Mousterian and Upper Palaeolithic artefacts. Finally the important evidence recently obtained from the quite unsuspected Quaternary deposits at Sugworth and Linch Hill shows that the Oxford region has already made and should continue to make major contributions to the current debate on the British Pleistocene succession, the outcome of which is absolutely crucial to Palaeolithic archaeology and all branches of Quaternary research in Britain and indeed beyond.

Note: This article was written in 1982 and revised early in 1984. It does not therefore take account of two relevant works which have appeared very recently (Briggs *et al.*, 1985 and Gibbard, 1985)

References

Arkell, W.J. (1945) 'Palaeoliths from the Wallingford Fan-Gravels', *Oxoniensia* 8/9: 1–17

Barton, R.N.E. (1983) 'New dates for Hengistbury Head, Dorset', *Antiquity* 47:220: 133–135

Bishop, W.W. (1958) 'The Pleistocene geology and geomorphology of three gaps in the Midland Jurassic escarpment', *Phil. Trans. Roy. Soc.*(Series B) 241: 255–306

Bordes, F. (1961) 'Mousterian cultures in France', *Science* 134: 803–810

Bosinski, G. (1967) *Die mittelpaläolithischen Funde im westlichen Mitteleuropa. Fundamenta* Reihe A, Band 4, ed. H. Schwabedissen

Briggs, D.J. and Gilbertson, D.D. (1980) 'Quaternary processes and environments in the upper Thames Valley', *Trans. Inst. British Geographers* N.S. 5: 1: 53–65

Briggs, D.J., Coope, G.R. and Gilbertson, D.D. (1985) *The Chronology and Environmental Framework of Early Man in the Upper Thames Valley: a new model.* BAR British Series 137

Campbell, J.B., Jr. (1977) *The Upper Palaeolithic of Britain: a study of man and nature in the late Ice Age.* 2 vols.

Cranshaw, S. (1983) *Handaxes and Cleavers: Selected English Acheulian Industries.* BAR British Series 113

Gábori, M. (1976) *Les civilisations du Paléolithique moyen entre les Alpes et l'Oural*

Gibbard, P.L. (1979) 'Middle Pleistocene drainage in the Thames Valley', *Geol. Mag.* 116: 35–44

Gibbard, P.L. (1985) *Pleistocene History of the Middle Thames Valley*

Green, C.P. and McGregor, D.F.M. (1980) 'Quaternary evolution of the River Thames', in *The Shaping of Southern England*, ed. D.K.C. Jones, pp. 177–202. Institute of British Geographers Special Publication, no. 11

Green, C.P., McGregor, D.F.M. and Evans, A.H. (1982) 'Development of the Thames drainage system in Early and Middle Pleistocene times', *Geol. Mag.* 119: 281–290

Hare, F.K. (1947) 'The geomorphology of a part of the Middle Thames', *Proc. Geol. Assoc. Lond.* 58: 294–339

Horton, A., Worssam, B.C. and Whittow, J.B. (1981) 'The Wallingford Fan Gravel', *Phil. Trans. Roy. Soc.* (Series B) 293: 215–255

Jacobi, R.M. (1980) 'The Upper Palaeolithic of Britain with special reference to Wales', in *Culture and Environment in Prehistoric Wales: selected essays*, ed. J.A. Taylor, pp. 15–100. BAR British Series 76

King, W.B.R. and Oakley, K.P. (1936) 'The Pleistocene succession in the lower part of the Thames Valley', *Proc. Prehist. Soc.* 2: 52–76

Kurtén, B. (1968) *Pleistocene mammals of Europe*

Lacaille, A.D. (1939) 'The Palaeolithic contents of the gravels at East Burnham, Bucks', *Antiq. Journ.* 19: 166–181

Lacaille, A.D. (1940) 'The palaeoliths from the gravels of the Lower Boyn Hill Terrace around Maidenhead', *Antiq. Journ.* 20: 245–271

Lacaille, A.D. (1961) 'The palaeoliths of Boyn Hill, Maidenhead', *Antiq. Journ.* 41: 154–185

MacRae, R.J. (with a contribution by P.R. Jones) (1982) 'Palaeolithic artefacts from Berinsfield, Oxfordshire', *Oxoniensia* 47: 1–11

Mellars, P.A. (1974) 'The Palaeolithic and Mesolithic', in *British Prehistory: a new outline*, ed. A.C. Renfrew, pp. 41–99, 268–79

Mitchell, G.F., Penny, L.F., Shotton, F.W. and West, R.G. (1973) *A correlation of Quaternary Deposits in the British Isles.* Geol. Soc. Lond. Special Report no. 4

Morrison, A. (1980) *Early Man in Britain and Ireland: an introduction to Palaeolithic and Mesolithic cultures*

Peake, A.E. (1918) 'Surface Palaeolithic implements from the Chilterns', *Proc. Prehist. Soc. East Anglia* 2: 4: 578–587

Roe, D.A. (1968) *A Gazetteer of British Lower and Middle Palaeolithic sites.* CBA Research Report no. 8

Roe, D.A. (1981) *The Lower and Middle Palaeolithic Periods in Britain*

Sandford, K.S. (1924) 'The river gravels of the Oxford district', *Quart. Journ. Geol. Soc. Lond.* 80: 113–179

Sandford, K.S. (1926) 'Pleistocene deposits', in *The Geology of the country around Oxford* (2nd ed.), eds. T.I. Pocock and J. Pringle, pp. 104–172. Memoirs of the Geological Survey, England: explanation of special Oxford sheet

Sandford, K.S. (1939) 'The Quaternary Geology of Oxfordshire, with reference to Palaeolithic Man', in *VCH Oxfordshire*, vol. I: 223–238

Sandford, K.S. (1965) 'Notes on the gravels of the Upper Thames floodplain between Lechlade and Dorchester', *Proc. Geol. Assoc. Lond.* 76: 61–75

Sealy, K.R. and Sealy, C.E. (1956) 'The terraces of the Middle Thames', *Proc. Geol. Assoc. Lond.* 67: 369–392

Shackleton, N.J. and Opdyke, N.D. (1976) 'Oxygen-isotopes and palaeomagnetic stratigraphy of Pacific core V28-239: Late Pliocene to Latest Pleistocene', *Geol. Soc. Amer. Mem.* 145: 449–464

Shotton, F.W., Goudie, A.S., Briggs, D.J. and Osmaston, H.A. (1980) 'Cromerian interglacial deposits at Sugworth, near Oxford, England, and their relation to the Plateau Drift of the Cotswolds and the terrace sequence of the Upper and Middle Thames', *Phil. Trans. Roy. Soc.* (Series B) 289: 55–86

Smith, R.A. (1915) 'High level finds in the Upper Thames Valley', *Proc. Prehist. Soc. East Anglia* 2: 99–107

Smith, W.G. (1894) *Man the Primeval Savage: his haunts and relics from the hill-tops of Bedfordshire to Blackwall*

Thomas, M.F. (1961) 'River terraces and drainage development in the Reading area', *Proc. Geol. Assoc. Lond.* 72: 415–436

Treacher, M.S., Arkell, W.J. and Oakley, K.P. (1948) 'On the ancient channel between Caversham and Henley, Oxfordshire, and its contained flint implements', *Proc. Prehist. Soc.* 14: 126–154

Tyldesley, J. (1984*a*) 'A Palaeolithic biface from Finstock, Oxfordshire', *Oxoniensia* 48: 143–4

Tyldesley, J. (1984*b*) 'Two *bout coupé* handaxes from Oxfordshire', *Oxoniensia* 48: 149–152

West, R.G. (1980) *The pre-glacial Pleistocene of the Norfolk and Suffolk coasts*

Willis, G.W. (1947) 'Hampshire palaeoliths and the clay-with-flints', *Proc. Hants Field Club.* 16: 3: 253–256

Wooldridge, S.W. (1957) 'Some aspects of the physiography of the Thames Valley in relation to the Ice Age and Early Man', *Proc. Prehist. Soc.* 23: 1–19

Wymer, J.J. (1956) 'Palaeoliths from the gravel of the Ancient Channel between Caversham and Henley at Highlands, near Henley', *Proc. Prehist. Soc.* 22: 29–36

Wymer, J.J. (1968) *Lower Palaeolithic archaeology in Britain as represented by the Thames Valley*

Wymer, J.J. (1974) 'Clactonian and Acheulian industries in Britain: their chronology and significance', *Proc. Geol. Assoc. Lond.* 85: 3: 391–421

Zagwijn, W.H., Montfrans, H.M. van and Zandstra, J.G. (1971) 'Subdivision of the 'Cromerian' in the Netherlands: pollen analysis, paleomagnetism, sedimentary petrology', *Geologie en Mijnbouw* 50: 41–58

THE MESOLITHIC AND NEOLITHIC IN THE OXFORD REGION

HUMPHREY CASE

The Mesolithic

As in the Palaeolithic, most of the data relating to the Mesolithic consists of surface or derived finds, but there have been modern excavations of settlement sites in the Kennet valley on the southern fringes of the region, and at Ascott-under-Wychwood in the Cotswolds. Settlement in the Kennet valley can be traced from the Early Mesolithic in the 9th millennium at Thatcham, Berks (Wymer 1962, radiocarbon dates summarized in Mellars 1974), into the Later Mesolithic, approaching the end of the 5th millennium at the Wawcott sites (Froom 1971/2a 2/2b, 1976). There seems reason to doubt the 4th millennium date obtained at Wawcott I (3310± 130 bc, BM–449; Froom 1971/2b, Jacobi 1982). (Uncalibrated radiocarbon chronology is used throughout this contribution; definitions of Early and Later Mesolithic may be found in Jacobi 1973, 1976; Mellars 1974, 1976a.)

The Kennet valley sites, on the drier parts of the floodplain alongside lakes or streams, can be interpreted as base-camps for communities which will have exploited a variety of local environments for hunting and gathering, including the Berkshire Downs (Jacobi 1973; also Mellars 1976a for activities at various types of British site, and cp. Newell 1973 for Dutch sites). A wide range of habitats will have been exploited, as seen for example in the animal bones recovered at Thatcham (King in Wymer 1962). Northwards, an appreciable number of characteristic flint axes, or so-called picks, extending to Oxford (and not certainly beyond), seem likely to represent the activities of *Early Mesolithic* communities centred on the Thames, similar to that at Thatcham on the Kennet dating from the 9th millennium. Surface finds at Goring may indicate more than one base-camp. An Early Mesolithic upland site at Nettlebed on Eocene Sand in the Chilterns can possibly be connected with flint collecting. Similar sites on the Berkshire Downs and relating to the Kennet valley may be represented by finds of axes at Lambourn, East Garston and Fawley. Other possible upland sites were at Cumnor, Wootton and Shotover, all on Lower Greensand of the Corallian ridge near Oxford. (Local references throughout this section in Case 1952/3; if not there or of later date, in records of Oxfordshire Museum Services or Ashmolean Museum.)

Later Mesolithic assemblages (from the 7th millennium onwards in a national context) are characterized by so-called geometric microliths. Well-known sites in the Kennet valley are Wawcott III (4170± 134 bc, BM–767; Froom 1976) and XXIII (4129± 113 bc, BM–826; Froom 1971/2a, 15–17 for preliminary report). As in the Early Mesolithic, other base-camps may have been by or near the floodplain of the Thames. Cores or microliths from Warborough, Abingdon (Corporation Farm) and Brighthampton and some of the finds of axes following the course of the Thames probably belonged to this period; and activities will have extended over the higher-terrace gravels, for example at Iffley and Cholsey (Case 1952/3), and places where Neolithic farmers later settled as at Abingdon, both at the causewayed enclosure and Corporation Farm (p. 23). Microliths and other flints near the confluence of the Cherwell and Ray south of Islip may have been associated with a riverside settlement, and there have been a few finds northwards up the Cherwell valley. Activity along the Thame is shown by a microlith from Waterperry.

The landscape may now have become more densely settled with base-camps spreading onto higher ground, although generally following the river-courses. Sites at somewhat higher elevation associated with the Thames or Ock may be represented by microliths (and sometimes microlithic cores) at Coleshill, Great Coxwell, Hatford, Buckland and Longworth on the Corallian ridge (where no doubt more remains to be found, as finds at Kingston Bagpuize suggest: CBA Gp. 9 *Newsletter* 10 (1980), 145) and at Fawler and Kiddington on the Great Oolite towards the southern edge of the Cotswolds.

Most of the Cotswold finds appear to be associated with the course of the Evenlode, and this is true of the base-camp on the Great Oolite at Ascott-under-Wychwood, sealed under a Neolithic long barrow (Benson 1971 and information from Mr. D. Benson and from study of the finds). The site thus shows a similar sequence of settlement to that on the river gravels at Abingdon. A Later Mesolithic flint assemblage with scalene triangles and crescents and also non-geometric microliths occurred with Neolithic settlement finds in the soil-profile under the barrow and possibly in pits. The Mesolithic flints can be taken to represent a settlement which may date from early in the 5th millennium – since similarly mixed geometric and non-geometric industries date nationally from the 6th, and at Wawcott III geometric forms had replaced non-geometric by the late 5th. The activity extended over some 750 sq. metres, a very large area in both English and Dutch contexts, comparable with that at Thatcham. The assemblage, with neither microliths nor scrapers dominant, can be taken to represent normal domestic as well as hunting activities, and suggests a base-camp at the boundary of contrasting upland and lowland environments, within reach of varied resources and possibly attracting concentrations of game. A low density of finds may represent a relatively short occupation or perhaps an agglomeration of small ones.

Mesolithic inhabitants will have made their mark on the region. If boats were widely used river-courses will have needed freeing of fallen trunks and branches, although modifications to lakes or streams may have been only of a minor nature, as at Thatcham III (Wymer 1962, 336). More permanent features of the landscape will have been tracks to fords and watering-places, to seasonal hunting and collecting grounds, and to sources of raw material such as flint, and along which finished products may have been transported in a network of exchanges (Care 1979); fragments of chert and slate of West Country origin at Wawcott I, III and XXIII suggest far-reaching connections in the Later Mesolithic (Froom 1971/2a, 1976). More extensive alterations of the regional landscape may have been clearances of woodland to provide not only optimum conditions for favoured game and wild fruits and nuts (Jacobi 1978) but killing-grounds where the quarry could be driven and trapped or shot. Fire may have been deliberately used for this purpose (Mellars 1975, 1976b; Simmons 1976) as by the pre-European Australians (Hallam 1975). Clearances are unlikely however to have produced the enduring changes in the regional lowland forest which are seen for example in upland forest in north Britain at the edge of the tree-line. At Thatcham, Early Mesolithic occupation had little effect on the vegetation (Churchill 1962, 369, based on pollen samples), but Bradley has drawn attention to possible disturbance of the forest at Cothill Fen, near Abingdon (Bradley & Ellison 1975, 177), and at Ascott-under-Wychwood a connection between a phase of open woodland and the Later Mesolithic settlement cannot be overlooked, although Evans considered it unlikely that Mesolithic man was directly responsible for opening the canopy (1972, 256, cp. 1971, 39, based on molluscan samples). Nonetheless, in a region which was plainly well-settled, repeated clearances along the fringes of forest both in the lower parts of the river valleys, and perhaps towards the escarpment of the Berkshire Downs, may have produced in parts a parkland landscape with tracks very suitable for pioneering farming and thus similar to the landscape which early 19th-century European settlers found in south-western Australia (Hallam 1975).

The Neolithic

The Neolithic can be defined as the period which saw the introduction and prevalence of mixed-farming among stone-using people. Three phases can be recognized in Britain and Ireland: *Early*, representing the first traces of farming (early 4th millennium bc); *Middle*, the stable adjustment (from the mid 4th millennium bc) of communities which had adopted farming; and *Late*, representing developments from the Middle phase (late 3rd millennium bc). Regionally a fair number of modern excavations amplify the record of monuments and of surface or derived finds.

Early Neolithic. Vestiges of pioneering mixed-farming however are likely to be sparse and elusive here and elsewhere, and arguments for an Early Neolithic will generally have to depend largely on palynological evidence (for forest clearing or selective felling, or for cultivated crops). Possibilities for sampling continuously evolving polliniferous deposits may exist only on the region's fringes in the Kennet Valley, where Mesolithic occupation lasted into the late 5th millennium (p. 18); deposits at Cothill Fen near Abingdon (Bradley & Ellison 1975) were too early to be relevant. Elsewhere however abandoned river channels may provide opportunities (as in the Upper Thames at Buscot, near Lechlade: information from Mr. M. Robinson). Moreover, if one accepts that the Holocene climax vegetation on the southern English Cretaceous uplands was indeed forest (but cp. Barker & Webley 1978, 166–8 and comments by Evans, *loc. cit.*, 185–6), then molluscan evidence for open grass-land in the buried soil beneath the Lambourn long barrow and in the primary silting of its ditch (information from Mr. R. Bradley) goes some way to suggest Early Neolithic activity on the dip-slope of the Berkshire Downs in the first half of the 4th millennium.

Middle Neolithic. In the Oxford region and its surroundings, as almost invariably elsewhere, the unambiguous record begins in the Middle Neolithic, especially with monuments which survive conspicuously in the archaeological record (causewayed enclosures, long barrows, cursuses, and others) indicating communities possessing capacity for monumental works, past the pioneering stage, with their subsistence in stable adjustment to their environment. Most of these monuments may be dated to the 3rd millennium, the Lambourn long barrow appearing exceptionally early (3415± 180 bc, GX–1178).

Causewayed enclosures. Five causewayed enclosures (so-called 'camps') are known from the region, at: Eastleach, Langford (Pl. 1, A, B; Palmer 1976, Pls. 17, 18 respectively), Broadwell (Pl. 1, C; Wilson 1975, Pl. XXI), Aston, Bampton and Shifford (Pl. 1, D; Palmer 1976, Pl. 18) and Abingdon. (Segmented ditches on Port Meadow, Oxford are generally interpreted as a former water course: Atkinson 1942, pl. II.) The 5 enclosures are part of a group of 9 so far recognized as associated with the Thames, extending to Orsett, Essex, on the estuary, and were probably all sited alongside streams draining into the main river. On varying bedrocks (Eastleach, on Forest Marble; Langford, Broadwell and Abingdon at the edge of second terrace gravel; Aston on alluvium and first terrace gravel), all overlook the floodplain and are within easy reach of other soils of varying characteristics. A sixth possible causewayed enclosure, single-ditched and transversed by a possible cursus, has recently been identified at Burford, Upton and Signet (Forest Marble) some 800 metres north-north-east of the Westwell henge monument (p. 32 Information kindly given by Mr. John Steane).

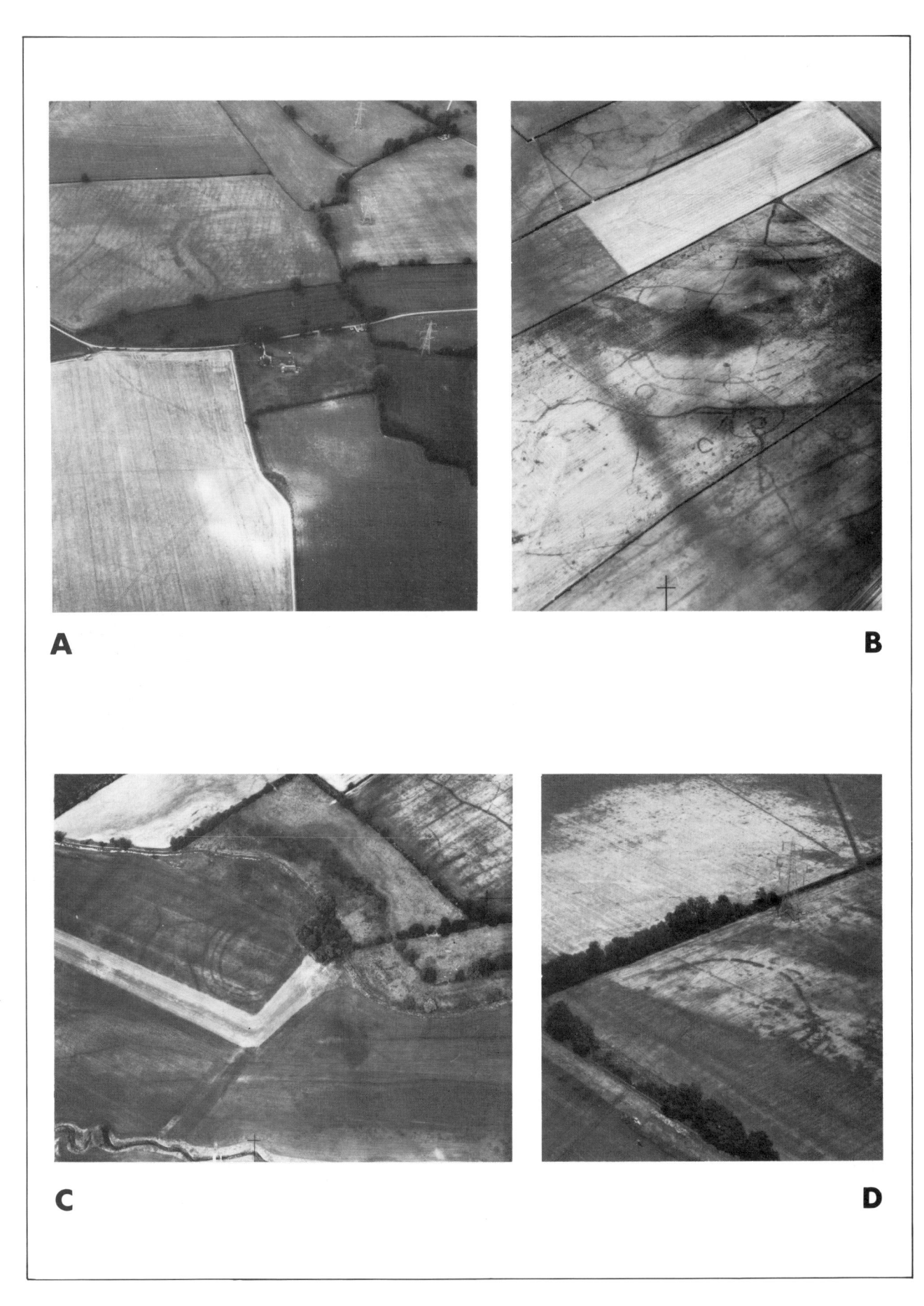

PL. 1. *Causewayed enclosures*. A, *Eastleach*; B, *Langford*; C, *Broadwell*; D, *Aston, Bampton, Shifford*. *(A, D, National Monuments Record Air photographs: A, Crown Copyright reserved; D, Copyright W.A. Baker. B, C, Cambridge University Collection: Copyright reserved)*

PL. 2. *Ascott-under-Wychwood long barrow.* A, *General view of east end.* B, *longitudinal section towards west end; left-right, bays 8 and 9.* C, *vertical view of southern pair of cists: top-bottom, burial deposits C, B, A.* D, *Burial deposit B, during excavation.* (A, B, D, photographs D. Benson: C, B.V. Arthur. Copyright Oxfordshire County Council)

Langford and Broadwell are little over 2 kms. apart and thus seem unlikely to have been in use at the same time or even perhaps used for the same purpose. Indeed one can reasonably assume that this class of enclosure, while demonstrating the common constructional technique of earthworks derived from segmented ditches, served a variety of functions. This seems emphasized for example by excavations recently concluded on two enclosures at Hambledon Hill, nr. Shroton, Dorset, where the Main Causewayed Enclosure is best interpreted as having a ritual purpose for the exposure of the dead and the Stepleton Enclosure, some 800 metres south-west on an adjoining spur, is best seen as a settlement enclosure (Mercer 1980).

Abingdon is the only regional enclosure to have been excavated (Leeds 1927, 1928; Case 1956a; Avery 1982). Unusual in being a promontory enclosure, it cut off a slight spur of second terrace gravel at the confluence of two streams, and may have stood by a trackway running along the edge of the terrace. It was a settlement enclosure at which Avery recognised 3 periods. *Period 1* was represented by the inner ditch, which enclosed about one and a quarter hectares. The upcast was used to make a low bank on the inner edge of the ditch and was possibly surmounted by a palisade. The works would have served as a barrier for animals rather than any defensive purpose, and occupation continued while the ditch silted considerably. In *Period 2* the ditch was recut and then filled in immediately with the settlement refuse of the occupation so far, in more than one layer intercalated between layers of soil and gravel. Structures surviving in the interior may have been burnt. The inner ditch and possibly the whole enclosure having been thus levelled, the outer ditch was dug to make a larger enclosure, about 3½ hectares. The upcast on the inner edge of the ditch, probably revetted with turf, will now have formed a bank of more defensive proportions, some 3 m. high and more than 3 m. broad. In *Period 3* occupation continued, while the ditch silted normally without any traces of recutting or the burying of settlement refuse; it was however partly levelled, near the conclusion of its silting.

The layers of settlement refuse buried in the inner ditch were prolific in finds and consisted of continuous linear deposits along the longitudinal axis of the ditch, heaped apparently from individual basketfuls. How can they be explained? Tidiness of mind in clearing up the site for new occupation? Taboos concerning the possessions and detritus of previous occupants? Some explanation of the latter kind is perhaps partly involved since a closely similar process has been noted both at the ritual Main Causewayed Enclosure, Hambledon Hill and in the ditches of the adjoining long barrow (Mercer 1980); something like it may be recognized too at Windmill Hill (Smith 1966).

7 radiocarbon determinations were made on the settlement refuse buried in the inner ditch, the mean dates ranging from the late 5th millennium to the mid 3rd. The most reliable ones for Periods 1 or 2 are second quarter to mid third millennium (2760 ± 135 bc, BM–352; 2510 ± 140 bc, BM–355; 2500 ± 145 bc, BM–354). The isolated 5th millennium date (4070 ± 110 bc, BM–349), taken in context with a sub-geometric microlith recorded unstratified by Leeds, should relate to material derived from previous occupation of the area in the Later Mesolithic.

The occupants' farming followed normal Middle Neolithic practice. Emmer wheat and barley (including a 6-row variety) were cultivated, and crab apples were collected. Cattle were grazed mainly, then pig, and least of all sheep or goat, on stable grassland with woodland not far distant, and in a warmer climate than today. Hunting was not an important activity.

The builders and occupiers of the enclosures used pottery in the so-called Decorated style, current in most of southern England and East Anglia, but the clays employed were obtainable from the more or less immediate region. Surface flint was almost invariably used for implements and was probably collected from the Berkshire Downs, being nearer than the Chilterns. Flint for axes appears to have come from another source; the nearest potential centres of axe production were at Rotherfield Peppard in the Chilterns (Peake 1913, 1914) and another possibly in north-east Wiltshire near Aldbourne (Passmore Collection, Department of Antiquities, Ashmolean); the nearest known more or less contemporary flint mine is at Easton Down, Winterslow on Salisbury Plain. Axes of igneous rock deriving from Cumberland (Group VI) were also probably similarly obtained through exchanges or gifts (axe identifications throughout this contribution from Evens *et al.* 1962, 1972, with additions from records of Oxfordshire Museum Services, Woodstock).

Information relating to the duration and nature of the occupation at Abingdon can be obtained by calculating the manpower involved in building the enclosures and comparing the figures with the volume of settlement refuse produced in Period 1. Startin (in Avery 1982) has calculated that digging the inner enclosure involved some 1,400 man-hours, and the outer one about 9,600, about 7 times greater. In view of the size of its segments, a convenient labour force for digging the inner enclosure within a single season would have been 12 able-bodied adults. Bearing in mind subsistence needs, it should have been possible to spare this number from a community as small as 30 persons (excluding infants), who on analogy with primitive societies generally would have been of one kin.

How would such a community have used the Period 1 enclosure? There would have been adequate room for them all within it and for storage and herding. However, calculations based both on observation from the animal bones that the enclosure was occupied throughout the year and on the assumption that a major part of the refuse of the Period 1 occupation was buried in the ditch, and inferring thence the number of pots broken on the site, the weight of flint knapped and used and the weight of meat represented, although covering wide ranges and involving many uncertainties, at least converge on the conclusion that a continuous settlement of 30 persons would only have lasted for a few decades. This is rather unlikely bearing in mind the very long time span of the Middle Neolithic. Thus, since not fewer than 30 persons are likely to have been involved with the enclosure (since its construction would otherwise have been too great a task, unless it was spread over several seasons), the conclusion must be that not all the kinship group resided there all the time. This would be consistent with settlement evidence throughout Great Britain and Ireland and over much of northern Europe that Middle Neolithic settlement was dispersed not nucleated. Thus one or two families may have resided permanently at the enclosure as caretakers and the remainder of the group have been dispersed about the more or less immediate neighbourhood in isolated farmsteads only resorting to the enclosure periodically for tasks which involved the cooperation of the whole group. These tasks may have been economic or social as much as ritual: say, for rendering fat, working antler, arranging exchanges and marriages. Movement to assemblies of this kind may have been a part of seasonal movements of many kinds, including some to temporary settlements for special purposes: say, for gathering or hunting, or grazing cattle in the spring and summer on the Thames floodplain or first terrace which all the regional causewayed enclosures overlook.

It would be a mistake to assume that such a small group (or even a much larger one) was self-sufficient within its own territory. On analogy with the general behaviour of primitive societies, a complex pattern of exchanges will have been required to maintain the necessities of life (Case 1982a). A group thus situated overlooking extensive grazing grounds could have offered partial rights in the grazing to communities based on the chalk, in exchange for supplies of flint or the right to collect them. Similarly axes of fine-grained rock (having already passed through many hands) may have been offered by other descent groups for similar rights to grazing: exceptionally large arrowheads (represented in the region although not at Abingdon) may have similarly been tokens of exchange. Excursions may also have had to be made outside the territory to temporarily unsettled waste for forest grazing, for example, or for hunting (p. 18) or gathering antler, and here again descent groups who claimed control may have required gifts. Exchanges throughout would have included nubile men or women (depending on whether residence was matrilocal or otherwise), since such a small descent group would not have been reproductively self-sufficient for long, even with only the most rudimentary mating prohibitions.

Such contacts with other groups will have led eventually to large, more or less self-sufficient lineages, widespread, powerful and competitive in the possession of resources. Such groups would have been capable of constructing long barrows, cursuses and the larger causewayed enclosures. Such a development may explain at Abingdon the suppression of the Period 1 enclosure and the building of a much larger one in Period 2. The labour involved was about 7 times greater, indeed more than 14 times (about 20,000 man-hours) if the rampart was revetted with turf as seems probable (Startin in Avery 1982). The rampart would have been of defensible proportions. Warfare may have been inherent in the clan system which had now developed. The Stepleton Enclosure, Dorset, referred to above (p. 22; Mercer 1980) was fortified by a palisade which had been fired in an attack. Another defended enclosure nearer the Oxford region is Crickley Hill, Glos. (Dixon & Borne 1977).

Small settlement enclosures. Two small enclosures, recently excavated, both by the floodplain and near the Abingdon causewayed enclosures can perhaps be connected with summer grazing and other special activities. At Corporation Farm, Abingdon, an oval ditched enclosure with 2 opposed entrances, some 15 metres by 14, excavated by the Abingdon Archaeological Society, was associated with pottery and flints which can be matched in a general way at the causewayed enclosure (information from Mr. and Mrs. R.P. Henderson). The absence of a large repertoire of implements and also of large charcoal concentrations suggests temporary occupation, and its specialized nature seems emphasized by the high proportion of red deer bones in the food refuse (17%) with a suggestion of fishing (pike). Bones of wild animals were rarely brought to the causewayed enclosures, and hunting may therefore have been practised away from them. Hunting may explain large concentrations of arrow-heads, for example in the North Stoke-Crowmarsh area or at Stonesfield, Kiddington or Sarsden in the Cotswolds in or around the medieval Wychwood Forest (but the preference of collectors for these intrinsically attractive specimens should not be overlooked; Bradley & Ellison 1975, 175). Microliths show the area of Corporation Farm to have been frequented in the Mesolithic like that of the causewayed enclosure, and Grooved Ware and Peterborough pottery in the Mortlake style in the upper filling of the enclosure ditch indicate Late Neolithic activity.

At Thrupp Farm, Abingdon, a penannular ditched enclosure of similar size (about 16 metres in diameter), on a sandy rise slightly above the floodplain, was excavated by the Oxfordshire Archaeological Unit (information from Mr. D. Miles). The small sample of bones included aurochs. Pottery generally comparable to that from the causewayed enclosure occurred here too, also Peterborough ware.

Long barrows. Three long barrows have recently been excavated in the region or on its fringes: Lambourn on the dip-slope of the Berkshire Downs (Wymer 1965/6), Wayland's Smithy, Ashbury on the escarpment (Atkinson 1965; Evans 1972, 265) and Ascott-under-Wychwood towards the southern edge of the Cotswolds (Benson 1971; my account of this long barrow is also based on personal information and detailed examination of the finds). All these barrows had been built on open grassland.

Whatever the pre-Neolithic climax vegetation of the Berkshire Downs may have been (p. 19), forest had thickened at *Ascott* since the Mesolithic occupation (p. 18) and been cleared during Neolithic settlement of the area which preceded the building of the barrow. The Neolithic occupation covered a smaller area than the Mesolithic one. Possibly connected with building the barrow, this occupation may however have been older and if so, judging from its extent and the quantity of finds, have represented a single outlying farmstead of the kind surmised at Abingdon (p. 22). The pottery of this occupation and most of that in the burial cists of the overlying barrow was of the so-called South Western style as found mainly in Dorset, Somerset, Devon and Cornwall; but one bowl from deposit C was in the Decorated style as at Abingdon and in other Cotswold-Severn long barrows.

The best conclusion from 7 radiocarbon dates (BM–491b, –492, –832–7) is that the barrow was built at the turn of the 4th and 3rd millennia bc, somewhat earlier therefore than the Period 1 enclosure at Abingdon. Aligned east-west and trapezoidal, some 7–16 metres wide, about 50 long and 1.5 high, it contained towards its western (narrower) end 2 pairs of opposed burial cists of limestone slabs (e.g. Pl. 2, C). There was an inturned false entrance at the east end (Pl. 2, A). The trapezoidal barrow and its irregular quarry pits, from which the rubble and earth mound was derived, together show a striking resemblance in plan to the long houses and their associated quarry pits of the central and north-west European Middle Neolithic.

The barrow was constructed in 21 bays, defined by hurdling or stone partitions (Pl. 2, B). Similar bays have been noted at the Beckhampton road long barrow, Bishop's Cannings, Wilts. and at the nearby South Street long barrow, Avebury (Ashbee *et al.* 1979) and may be taken to have defined the constructional tasks of individual teams; the strikingly different filling of some of the bays confirms this suggestion. The work of construction may be estimated at some 7,000 man-hours at most. It was thus a much bigger task than the Period 1 enclosure at Abingdon, but not as big as the Period 2.

Perhaps some indication of the labour force can be obtained by considering the nature of the chambers and burial deposits. One of the 4 cists at Ascott was empty, the other 3 contained human bones (*e.g.* Pl. 2, D). Additionally there were 3 secondary deposits of bones in the area of the cists (*e.g.* deposit C, Pl. 2, C). One deposit contained cremated bones, the remainder were unburnt. No recognizable individual's bones occurred in more than one deposit or cist, and each deposit or cist was different in arrangement and to some extent in composition of bones. All shared in common the fact that the bones when buried had either lost their flesh or represented only portions of corpses in very partial articulation (Pl. 2, C, D). The bodies had thus either been previously exposed for an appreciable period, say, in an enclosure similar to the Main Enclosure at Hambledon Hill (p. 22) or of some other kind (p. 31), or had been exhumed from graves. The evidence is also not inconsistent with some bones having been removed from the chambers and replaced.

47 individuals were represented, with ages from one to 45 years but mostly between 20 and 30. The bones can thus have represented only a very incomplete selection from the community which will have built the barrow or from those which may have used it – all the more so since one must allow for the possibility that some of the bones may have been of ancestors long since dead when the barrow was built. The burials were thus as it were token deposits in a co-operative shrine.

Each of the 6 burial deposits (3 in cists, and 3 in structurally secondary positions) was different in a number of ways. May not the 4 primary cists represent the 4 descent groups in the clan which together provided the labour force for its construction? If each group was about twice the size of the minimum envisaged at Abingdon 1, the manpower available should have been able to complete the work in a season. Interestingly a group about twice the minimum envisaged at Abingdon 1, say 12–13 nuclear families, is the minimum size Startin assumes would have been necessary to co-operate in building one of the major long houses of the central and north-west European Middle Neolithic (Startin 1978). Such a group may have been a fairly basic unit – about the minimum which could have supported the necessary technology for constructing and maintaining boats for maritime explorations or to carry livestock and stores on colonizing expeditions.

Finally, pursuing the interpretation of the Ascott burial deposits, may not the 3 secondary deposits represent other groups who joined or superseded the original builders? If so, the barrow would show a similar sequence to that at Abingdon; and in view of the possibility that this was a period of warfare (p. 23), it is interesting to note that an individual represented in one of the cists at Ascott had an arrow wound, and the same may have been true of another in another cist.

The *Wayland's Smithy* long barrow was certainly two-period. The first monument was a long barrow aligned south-north with maximum length and breadth 54 ft. and 27 ft. respectively, standing at least 6 ft. high, and flanked by quarry-ditches. Preliminary report (Atkinson 1965) suggests that the unburnt bones of at least 14 individuals (a significant proportion being young adults), whose corpses had disintegrated to varying degrees through exposure before burial, had been buried in a wooden chamber of ridge-pole structure within the barrow. A platform on which their bodies may originally have been exposed may have stood immediately to the chamber's south. Three leaf-shaped flint arrowheads were with the burials. Two split-trunk posts some 4 ft. in diameter stood one immediately north and the other south of the chamber; they may have reached the surface of the barrow and extended upwards as markers.

Not more than a few decades are held to have separated the building of this monument and its incorporation into a trapezoidal long barrow of earth and rubble on the same alignment, 180 ft. long and 48 – 20 ft. wide, derived from flanking quarry ditches. This mound had a sarsen kerb and at its south end a straight façade of orthostatic sarsen slabs and dry-walling up to 10 ft. high. From the façade a passage led into the barrow; it was up to 6 ft. high of sarsen slabs and dry-walling with 2 opposed transepts up to 4½ ft. high of similar construction. This chamber-complex contained the bones of at least 8 individuals. It appears to have been eventually filled with chalk rubble as at the somewhat similar West Kennet long barrow, Wilts. (Piggott 1962).

Pottery from the surface under the second barrow at Wayland's Smithy was in the Decorated style as at Abingdon, and its construction was broadly contemporary with the Period 1 enclosure there (2820±130 bc, I–1468). The minimum labour force required for excavating and building the first barrow would have been about the same as that needed for the Period 1 enclosure at Abingdon, and that required for the second barrow would have been of the same order as that at the Ascott long barrow. Exceptional effort would have been needed to erect the wooden posts at the first barrow, and the façade stones at the second. The lengths of the posts are unknown. However, if they were 7½ ft. long the minimum excavating team, assuming it to have been 12 able-bodied men, could probably have brought them to the site unaided and put them up. Erecting the façade stones of the secondary barrow may have required a labour force of 35 to 50 able-bodied people, which could have been supplied comfortably by a community of the size envisaged at Ascott-under-Wychwood.

There may thus have been growth in the social unit involved at Wayland's Smithy, similar to that seen in the two periods at Abingdon. In a prominent position, both stages of the barrow may have been conspicuous over a considerable region, including both upland and lowland. The territory settled or controlled by their builders will have included chalk downland, since the monuments are likely to have been built on land already taken into cultivation (Evans 1972, 265; although possibly for only a short period, Bradley & Ellison 1975, 177), and also have included the Corallian ridge in the valley below, in view of the use of coral ragstone in the dry-walling of the second barrow. Surface finds of flints on the Corallian, including leaf-shaped arrowheads at Great Coxwell, Fernham, Hatford, Charney Bassett, Hinton Waldrist, Pusey and Longworth, show Middle Neolithic activity there (see also Bradley & Ellison 1975, 175–6). The barrows too may have overlooked an important route across the ridge to the Thames valley and the eastern Cotswolds (Case et al. 1964/5, 50–3).

Three miles south-west, the *Lambourn* long barrow (Wymer 1965/6), aligned northeast-southwest, trapezoidal and some 215 ft. long judging by its quarry ditches, stood near the source of a stream draining to the Lambourn and Kennet and may have been a focus for a number of territories as at Ascott and Wayland's Smithy – in this case territories both on the chalk dip-slope and in the valleys. It was built in open grassland (p. 23) and its core of sarsen boulders suggests as at Wayland's Smithy that this land too may have been already cultivated. Very little evidence could be obtained by excavation as to structures, since the mound had largely been destroyed through modern ploughing; but at the north-east end there may have been a burial platform as at Wayland's Smithy. The ditch showed traces of gang-work as inferred at Ascott; but the earthwork may have been a slightly bigger task than there or at the second stage at Wayland's Smithy. Pottery in the Decorated style was represented as at Wayland's Smithy and Abingdon. The radiocarbon determination (3415+180 bc, GX–1178) is significantly older than the 3rd millennium mean dates obtained for the previously quoted sites, although consistent with that from Fussell's Lodge long barrow, Hants. (3230±150 bc, BM–314: Ashbee 1966), similarly with Decorated style pottery.

The Ascott barrow is on the fringe of the numerous Cotswold-Severn group of long barrows, which mainly extends south-westwards along the Cotswolds into Wales; Wayland's Smithy belongs to the same group and with Lambourn is towards the extremity of a great mass of long barrows on the chalk uplands from the Berkshire Downs to Cranborne Chase. Very few have been recorded from the valley system between Cotswolds and Downs. This largely upland distribution of long barrows is a national feature. It is unlikely to reflect primarily the use of marginal land, since we have seen that ground on which local examples stood is likely to have been settled as at Ascott and cultivated as at Wayland's Smithy and Lambourn. A more likely explanation is that a more or less commanding position over a number of territories was felt appropriate for shrines which involved co-operative effort.

Exceptionally, however, cropmarks on second terrace Thames gravel at Drayton appear to show ditches of a ploughed-out long barrow (Benson & Miles 1974, 62) and the North Stoke linear ditches at first terrace level, some 740 ft. long aligned north-south, represent a variant form of *bank barrow* (Case 1982b) not recognized until recently north of Cranborne Chase. Similar ditches to those at North Stoke but straighter also appear to run tangentially from the north-east corner of the Warborough cursus (p. 26: National Monuments Record photograph SU 5993/14/61: Benson & Miles 1974, map 36) towards the Thame (Pl. 3, B). If they represent a bank barrow, its relationship would be somewhat similar to that of Pentridge barrow 21/22 to the Dorset cursus (RCHM 1975, fp 25). Linear ditches at Clanfield are possibly similar (Benson & Miles 1974, 36, map 7), but others at Little Faringdon seem too close together (*ibid.*, 27).

It seems likely that the North Stoke monument was at least partly revetted. If unrevetted, the labour involved (5,300 man-hours) would have been rather less than that required at the Ascott long barrow; but if fully revetted, about twice as much (some 11,700 man-hours). A radiocarbon-date (2722±49, BM–1405) from antler sealed by the primary silt of the east linear ditch of the bank barrow is equivalent to that of the Period 1 enclosure, Abingdon. Cropmarks suggest it had a forecourt at its north end similar to that at the Maiden Castle bank barrow (RCHM 1970), and overlay an oval ditched enclosure, the dimensions of which would have been appropriate to a settlement enclosure as at Corporation Farm, Abingdon (p. 23) or a cremation-cemetery of New Wintles kind.

Long mortuary enclosures. At its excavated southern end the North Stoke bank barrow was later than a long mortuary enclosure, the ditch of which had been twice recut and which yielded pottery which can be matched at the causewayed enclosure, Abingdon. A characteristic long mortuary enclosure was Dorchester site VIII, subrectangular, 210 ft by 70 ft, with an internal bank to its ditch. The enclosure was earlier than the adjoining cursus (p. 27) and aligned along its western ditch. Ebbsfleet style Peterborough ware occurred in later silting of the enclosure ditch (Atkinson 1951; Atkinson *et al.* 1951). Another similar enclosure appears represented by cropmarks across the Thame at Overy, west of the Warborough Cursus (Pl. 3, B). Cropmarks at North Stoke may show other examples besides the one excavated at the south end of the bank barrow. Another may be represented by cropmarks east of the south end of the Benson cursus (Allen photograph 151, Ashmolean Museum). An excavated enclosure at Sonning (Slade 1963/4) rather squarer than the others, associated with Peterborough ware, is a possible example. These enclosures could have been dug comfortably by an extended family within a season. Similar enclosures have been recorded in southern and northern England as representing early stages at long barrows, and a generally held opinion is that all these enclosures were for exposing corpses for stripping of their flesh by carrion feeders as surmised at the Main Causewayed Enclosure, Hambledon Hill (p. 22), before their bones were selectively incorporated in barrow deposits as at Ascott.

Single graves. Single graves represent quite different treatment of the dead. An example excavated on first terrace level gravel at Newnham Murren, near Wallingford, contained a contracted inhumed adult woman, with a sherd and flint flake characteristic of the Abingdon causewayed enclosures (Moorey 1982). It was within a ring-ditch, showing this characteristic Thames Valley monument to have originated in the Middle Neolithic. The ring-ditch was double, both concentric ditches having been dug with outer banks. The outer ditch, diameter about 75 ft., had been recut and the spoil then heaped on its inner edge, showing that even small monuments had continuity of use or veneration. The inner ditch had an apparent interruption suggesting that it may possibly have been a settlement enclosure as at Corporation Farm and Thrupp Farm, Abingdon (p. 23), later used for burial. The burial itself is comparable to that at Pangbourne, Berks., downstream some 8 miles, likewise of an inhumed woman, with a Decorated style bowl, antler and animal bone (Piggott 1929). The labour involved in the Wallingford monument would have been trivial, and like the long mortuary enclosures it could have been constructed by an extended family in a season.

Cremation cemeteries. Another burial-site, in this case showing the rite of cremation as already seen in one of the secondary deposits at Ascott, was represented by a ditched enclosure at New Wintles Farm, Eynsham, on second terrace gravel by the Evenlode (Kenward 1982). The oval outer ditch, 10–12 metres in diameter, had 5 segments, and the inner ditch 2. Pits were at either end of the inner ditch and 3 other pits were in the ditch filling or between the ditches. The ditches had been filled with soil as soon as dug. This material had presumably been derived from clearing the area, and the gravel obtained from the ditches had been spread over the site as a low platform or mound, or perhaps even used to build an enclosing bank as at Wallingford. Four pits contained cremated bone and charcoal; the only identifiable bones were of children. The associated pottery was in the Decorated style and one sherd could be compared in fabric with Peterborough ware. As at Wallingford, the labour-input involved was trivial and well within the capacity of a single or extended family in a season.

New Wintles is plainly a Middle Neolithic precursor of the well-known Dorchester cremation cemeteries or so-called sanctuaries (Atkinson *et al.* 1951; Atkinson 1951). These however seem very largely Late Neolithic, only Site XI (Pl. 3, A) with Peterborough pottery in the Ebbsfleet style being possibly Middle Neolithic (p. 30).

Cursuses. This third major group of monuments may also largely be Late Neolithic, although with Middle Neolithic origins. It is represented by crop or soil marks of more or less parallel linear ditches sometimes with terminals forming complete enclosures. Well-authenticated or likely examples are at Dorchester (Pl. 3, A), Drayton and Benson, and others with varying degrees of likelihood are at Lechlade, Warborough (Pl. 3, C), Sonning; and Burford-Upton-Signet, Buscot, Oxford, Abingdon, Shillingford, North Stoke and Goring (Sonning & Goring in Gates 1975; North Stoke, south of the bank barrow, Case 1982b; others, Benson & Miles 1974). The enclosure at Warborough (Pl. 3, C; Benson & Miles 1974, map 36) seems plainly analogous to cursuses, although unusually broad and short. Nearby, the south-west terminal of the Benson cursus appears formed by a cross-ditch which has been claimed as another cursus (RCHM 1960, 27), and ditches at Shillingford (Warborough) cannot be dismissed for appearing sinuous (Allen photograph 1067, Ashmolean Museum). Linear marks similar to those of a cursus appeared in the University Parks, Oxford in the summer 1976.

Cuttings have been dug at Dorchester and at two

cursuses at Drayton: 1, north and west of Brook Farm; 2, south-east of Oday Hill (Benson & Miles 1974, map 33). Dorchester, more than 4,000 ft. long and some 200 ft. wide, is among the largest nationally (Atkinson 1951; Atkinson et al. 1951; CBA Gp. 9 Newsletter, 12 (1982), 143–6; information from Mr. R. Chambers). Its north-west terminal is uncertain. The alignment of the south-east one suggests that it may possibly be of a different period from the main body of the monument, and the ditches here (excavated by Chambers) were shallower than those to the north-west (excavated by Atkinson). To the north-west, ditch-silting indicated that the banks were at the inner edges of the ditches (as for example at the immense Dorset cursus: RCHM 1975); this position of the banks at Dorchester would be consistent with the positions of monuments between the ditches (including a cremation cemetery probably of well-known Dorchester type, a post-circle monument and an Early Bronze Age ring-ditch). The bank of the east ditch at Drayton 2 was also internal (information Mr. J. Wallis).

A date for Dorchester rather late in the Middle Neolithic seems the most likely possibility both from its finds and from its stratigraphical and inferred relationships with adjoining sites. To the north-west, a leaf-shaped arrowhead and edge-polished flint axe came from primary silting and Ebbsfleet style Peterborough pottery from upper filling. The cursus here was stratigraphically earlier than a ditch complex (site IX, later stage) associated with unusual flat-based pottery in the Middle Neolithic tradition, but later than 3 adjoining sites: a long mortuary enclosure (site VIII, p. 26); the earliest stage at site IX, represented by an enclosure possibly similar to that at Warborough (p.26); and the outer ditch at site XI (Pl. 3, A), a cremation cemetery and 'sanctuary', which had Ebbsfleet pottery in primary silting. A Late Neolithic transverse arrowhead of oblique type came from upper silting at the south-east. At Drayton 1 (Leeds 1943b, 415) a hearth with presumably Late Neolithic flints including a chisel-shaped transverse arrowhead was similarly stratified. However, at Drayton 2 Peterborough pottery came from primary silting (information Mr. J. Wallis) which suggests a Late Neolithic constructional date, and this appears confirmed by similarly stratified Peterborough pottery in the Mortlake style at the Springfield cursus, Chelmsford, Essex (information from Mr. J. Hedges).

Unlike the long barrows, the regional cursuses are valley monuments, on second or first terrace gravel of the Thames. They appear somewhat clustered throughout the valley, and with a conspicuous gap between Buscot and Oxford. Clearly the landscape was open in at least their immediate vicinity and they may conceivably have been connected with large seasonal gatherings for spring and summer grazing along the river. The Dorchester and Warborough cursuses, for example, appear to demarcate suitable areas of grazing on either bank of the Thame at its confluence with the Thames. The North Stoke bank barrow appears to limit another similar area. The scale of the monuments suggests that large numbers of people were involved at times. If the ditches at Dorchester were overall as deep as at the north-west, a labour-input approaching 30,000 man-hours would have been required, more than 4 times that required for excavating and building one of the local long barrows and half as much again as the maximum assumed at the Period 2 enclosure, Abingdon; but the shallower ditches at the south-east suggest that this figure is somewhat too high.

Social groups. Regional Middle Neolithic monuments may thus be arranged into those requiring *small effort* (Corporation and Thrupp Farm enclosures; Wallingford ring ditch; New Wintles and Dorchester XI cremation cemeteries or sanctuaries; the long mortuary enclosures), which could have been dug without too much difficulty by a single nuclear or extended family; those requiring *medium* effort (Abingdon Period 1 and Wayland's Smithy 1; Ascott, Lambourn and Wayland's Smithy 2), which could each probably have been constructed in a season by descent groups ranging from 30 to 250 persons, excluding infants; and those requiring *large* effort (North Stoke bank barrow; Abingdon 2; Dorchester cursus), presupposing greater numbers or more prolonged work.

The monuments thus arranged according to the effort involved in their construction tend to confirm the organization of Middle Neolithic society suggested by the Abingdon excavation: dispersed settlement in individual farmsteads of extended family size, which were nonetheless closely linked in social groups by kinship ties and clan obligations. The distribution of monuments and finds appears to suggest provisionally the existence of 6 such groups:–

(1) The causewayed enclosures between Eastleach and Shifford can probably be linked with the long barrows in the southern Cotswolds; and with Group VI axes from Alvescot, Minster Lovell, Bampton and a possible example from Enstone.

(2) A more northerly group may be represented by long barrows in the northern Cotswolds and Group VI axes from Tadmarton, Swalcliffe and Broughton.

(3) The nearest source of flint for both these groups would have been the Berkshire Downs across the Thames and the Corallian ridge. Very numerous finds of arrowheads and other struck flints on the Corallian ridge suggest that a causewayed enclosure may be found there, possibly near Cherbury Camp; with it could be associated the Wayland's Smithy long barrows and Group VI axes from Faringdon, Buckland, West Hanney and possible examples from Ram's Hill and Hinton Waldrist.

(4) This group in turn would be associated with another on the dip-slope of the Downs as suggested by the Lambourn long barrow.

(5) In the Thames valley downstream from Oxford, the Abingdon-Drayton monuments constitute another group, with Group VI axes from both localities and from Appleford and Sutton Courtenay. Contacts with the chalk may have been in the Blewbury area.

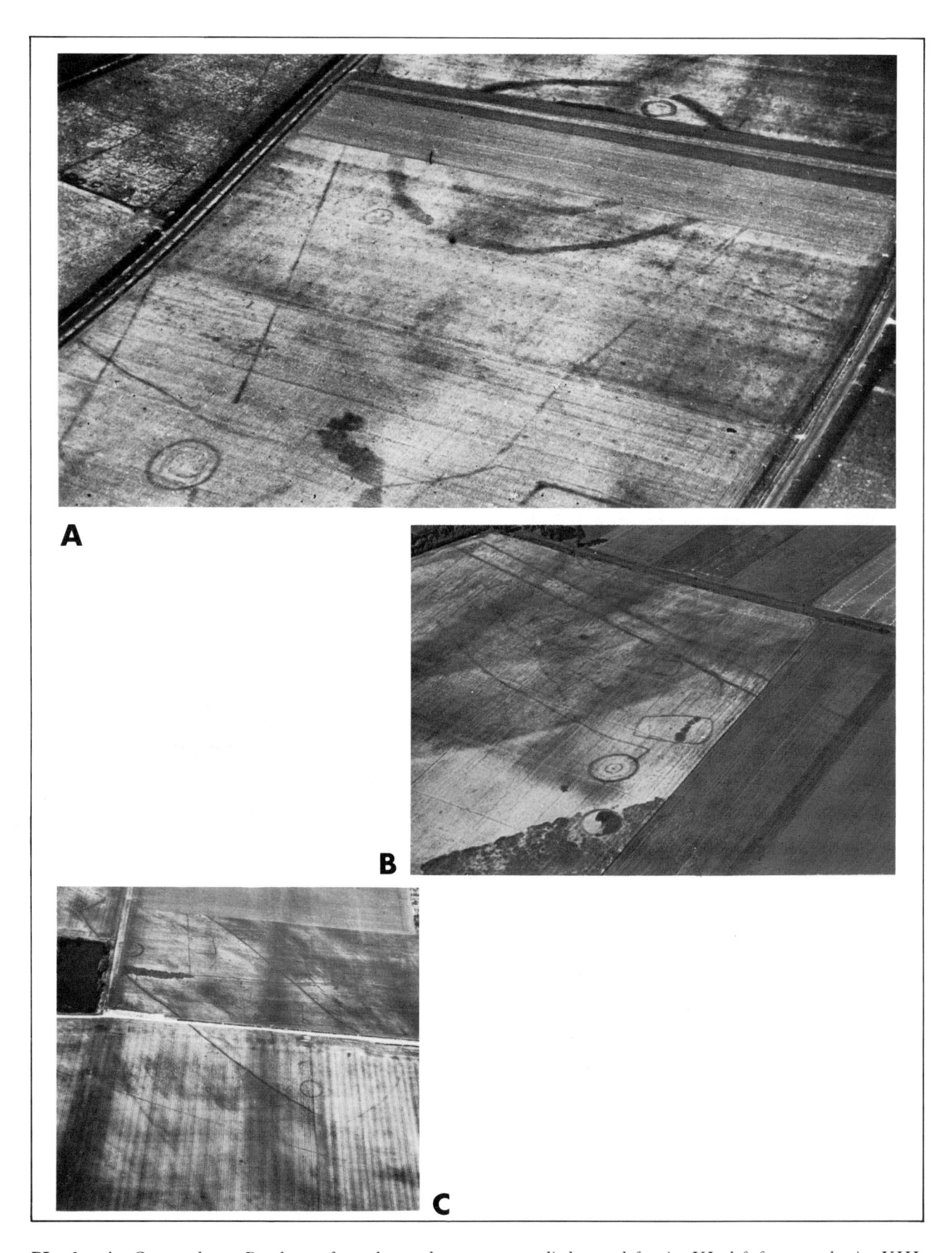

PL. 3. A, *Cropmarks at Dorchester from the north-west; cursus ditches to left; site XI, left-foreground; site XIII, background; site XII between north entrance of site XIII and west cursus ditch; site XIV inside south entrance of site XIII.*

B, *Cropmarks at Overy from the south, including linear ditches running towards river Thame; long mortuary enclosure, central.*

C, *Warborough cursus from south-west, and other cropmarks.* (A, B, Allen air photographs: Copyright Ashmolean Museum; C, Cambridge University Collection: Copyright reserved)

PL. 4. A, *The Devil's Quoits, Stanton Harcourt, from the north-west; excavations 1972/3 by M. Gray showing west and east entrances and setting of stoneholes around inner edge of ditch. (Photograph M. Aston: Copyright Oxfordshire County Council)*

B, *Middle Beaker grave groups.* Left: *Beaker, barbed-and-tanged flint arrowheads and gold ear-rings from Radley 4a.* Centre: *Beaker (height 22 cms.), copper and bronze knives, stone wristguard from Dorchester XII.* Right: *Beaker, flint flake, bone tool from Stanton Harcourt grave 1 near XV, 1–5. (Photograph and Copyright Ashmolean Museum)*

(6) Downstream, Dorchester may not have been settled until late in the Middle Neolithic but the Warborough-Benson-Wallingford-North Stoke monuments can be associated with Group VI axes from Chalgrove and Benson and from across the Thames at Cholsey. Flint will have been available both in the Chilterns and over the river in the Sinodun Hill-Brightwell outcrop; flint axes in the Chilterns and on its fringes can be associated with this group. A causewayed enclosure may remain to be discovered here too.

The end of the Middle Neolithic, and the Late Neolithic. Viewed nationally, the construction of causewayed enclosures and long barrows tended to cease around the mid 3rd millennium. Some changes in material culture came at about the same time. The emergence of *Peterborough ware* was somewhat before the mid 3rd millennium. Its typologically early Ebbsfleet style can be seen as a development from preceding Neolithic pottery, including the Decorated style; its developed Mortlake style should span the second half of the millennium and survive later; and its final Fengate style should characterize the end of the 3rd millennium and the early 2nd. These styles are likely to have overlapped somewhat. The later 3rd millennium saw the emergence too of another group of Neolithic pottery, *Grooved ware*, which as far as southern England was concerned was prevalent towards the end of the millennium and in the early 2nd. Its characteristic flat-based jars are different in form and decoration from preceding native Neolithic pottery but show a somewhat similar fashion in shape to that current on the continent of Europe. It is consistently associated too with a flint industry different from that of the Middle Neolithic, somewhat heavier and less blade-like, in which flakes with polished edges and arrowheads of transverse type were conspicuous.

Associations with Peterborough ware. The national tendency for the construction of causewayed enclosures and long barrows to cease around the mid 3rd millennium can be seen to have coincided to some extent with the regeneration of former clearings to woodland, and it has been suggested that this may show a fall in population (Bradley 1978a, b; Whittle 1978), brought on by farming failure as a result, say, of overcropping. Farming practice may indeed have changed to some extent; and there may have been fluctuations in population, although they are not everywhere apparent. For example, if old clearings reverted to woodland, some new ones continued to be made (Bradley 1978b, fig. 2). The later 3rd millennium saw the construction of some massive works in Britain and Ireland, as at Meldon Bridge, Peebles, associated there with a variety of Peterborough ware (Burgess 1976); and some of the local cursuses may date from now.

We must remember too that we are entering a period when the Middle Neolithic practice of burying large masses of settlement rubbish (as at the onset of Period 2 at Abingdon) ceased, not to be resumed until the Iron Age; and this may give a misleading impression of impoverishment. Viewed in this way, the Oxford region may show shifts in settlement rather than a decline. Peterborough pottery in the Mortlake and Fengate styles, in surface scatters and sometimes associated with burials or other evidence of occupation, indicates the first definite Neolithic settlement (apart from New Wintles and possibly a burial from Cassington 6, pp. 26, 33) of the great expanses of second terrace Thames gravels at Stanton Harcourt–Eynsham–Cassington, and also at Wytham on the floodplain across the river; conversely there were only 3 sherds of Peterborough pottery at the Abingdon causewayed enclosure. Three Mortlake style bowls from the Thames at Cholsey indicate a settlement in the North Stoke-Wallingford area, with which a Group VIII stone axe (deriving from Graig Lwyd, Caernarvons.) may also possibly have been associated. No Peterborough pottery occurred at Wayland's Smithy or at Ascott, but sherds at the Lambourn long barrow and at Farncombe Down, at Blewbury (Wymer 1965/6; Rahtz 1962; Peake 1936), and East Hendred, and at Asthall (Leeds 1922, 235–6) and Astrop, Northants., about a mile east of the Cherwell (Leeds 1913), show that both the dip-slope of the Downs and the eastern Cotswolds continued to be occupied.

The Asthall sherds appear to be a variant of the Ebbsfleet style and interestingly this style is the earliest pottery from the Dorchester cremation cemeteries and so-called 'sanctuaries'; it occurred also at Mount Farm, Dorchester (information Mr. G. Lambrick). Middle Neolithic Decorated style pottery was totally absent from the Dorchester cremation cemeteries. Atkinson (1951; *et al.* 1951) was rightly cautious about dating these sites (especially writing at a time when the existence of Neolithic cremation cemeteries was not generally accepted), but it is noteworthy that Peterborough ware or sherds which it seems reasonable to identify with it represented the pottery which was consistently associated with them, occurring at Sites I, II, V, VI, and XI and at Site VIII, the long mortuary enclosure, and Site III, the cursus. Other finds at the Dorchester sites (bone skewer pins, chisel arrowheads, a stone macehead) can also be linked nationally with Peterborough ware, although they are more consistently associated with Grooved ware. The relationship between Grooved ware and Peterborough ware was however exclusive at Dorchester, as in settlement assemblages in pits throughout the region. Grooved ware occurred only at Site I where it was contemporary in phase 1 with rather indeterminate primary Neolithic pottery in the Middle Neolithic tradition, although not associated with it; phase 2 (the recutting of the oval ditch) was exclusively associated with the Mortlake style of Peterborough ware. Pottery in the Middle Neolithic tradition, also indeterminate, occurred unambiguously elsewhere at Dorchester only at Sites IX and XI. This indeterminate pottery from Sites I and XI could conceivably be regarded as a variant of the Ebbsfleet style, but this would be less likely in the case of that from Site IX. It seems therefore that there were three groups using the region more or less contemporaneously in the Late Neolithic, with exclusive styles of pottery but otherwise similar material culture; and that the Peterborough ware element was dominant at Dorchester.

It may also have been closely associated with the cursus. Clearly defined Ebbsfleet style sherds occurred in its later silting and in that of the long mortuary enclosure; but were also primary in the outer ditch of Site XI, which may have been earlier than the adjacent cursus ditch (Pl. 3, A). Drayton 2 was plainly associated with Peterborough ware (p. 30) but this may not be an invariable association, in view of the absence of a cursus from the Stanton Harcourt–Eynsham–Cassington area (p. 26). In any event, if some at least of the cursuses belong towards the end of the Middle and to the Late Neolithic, any local fall in population would represent quite a minor fluctuation; and if one can judge by numbers of individuals recorded at the Dorchester cemeteries (55 at Site VI, 25 at IV and 22 at II and V), the populations involved do not appear to have been less than those concerned with Middle Neolithic long barrows.

Another burial tradition is represented by the *single grave* inhumation burial of a woman in Stanton Harcourt XXI, 1, (Grimes 1943/4). Like the similar Middle Neolithic burial at Wallingford (p. 26), it was central to a double ring-ditch, the inner penannular ditch of which may conceivably also have been first used for settlement; the burial was furnished with a flint knife with polished edge and a jet belt-fastener, types which are characteristic associations with Peterborough ware. Other ring-ditches nearby may also have been associated with Peterborough ware and first dug for settlement (Hamlin & Case 1963). Some at least of the Dorchester sites may similarly originally have been settlement enclosures along the edge of the floodplain and only later used for burial (in a manner analogous to Bronze Age barrows, as suggested at City Farm 3, Case *et al.* 1964/5); and it is conceivable that the Thrupp and Corporation Farm enclosures date from this period and not earlier (p. 23). A burial platform and pits with multiple dismembered skeletons associated with a Peterborough ware sherd at Cassington (grave 7 at the edge of the Late Beaker culture cemetery: Leeds 1934a, 272) also appears to continue Middle Neolithic burial traditions. In this context it is noteworthy too that at the Nympsfield long barrow, Glos., in the eastern Cotswolds, construction and use are dated by the Ebbsfleet and Mortlake styles respectively (Smith in Saville 1979, 77 and references); here as in the Thames Valley population may not have fallen greatly.

Environmental evidence associated with Peterborough ware is slight both regionally and nationally. At Mount Farm, Dorchester, less than 2 kms from the cursus and other sites, Burial 602 (p. 32) gave evidence of cereal cultivation (cp. emmer wheat: information kindly given by Messrs. G. Lambrick and M. Jones).

Bones or teeth of pig have occurred consistently with Peterborough ware locally: unassociated with other bones at Asthall and Cassington (Leeds 1922; 1940, 5: Ebbsfleet and Fengate styles respectively), with ox at Eynsham (Bradford & Morris, 1941; information from Mr. R. Wilson: Mortlake style), but in a minority to ox and sheep or goat at Stanton Harcourt (Hamlin & Case 1963, 2) and at Dorchester Site II (Zeuner *et al.* in Atkinson *et al.* 1951). It remains to be seen whether, taken in conjunction with evidence for regeneration of woodland (p. 30), this may not indicate farming practice somewhat more dependent on an animal adaptable to woodland, scrub and pasture alike. Hunting too may have become important (cp. Bradley 1978a, 108) and the Thrupp and Corporation Farm enclosures (p. 23) if dated now could illustrate this trend.

A pit at Stanton Harcourt probably to be associated with a nearby settlement (with the Fengate style) contained flint-workers' material including apparently mined flint (Hamlin & Case 1963, 19), which may have come from the Downs east of Swindon across the Corallian ridge along a route which may have been important in the Middle Neolithic (p. 27) and continued to be important in the Bronze and Iron Ages (Case *et al.* 1964/5, 50–3).

Associations with Grooved ware. Most of the regional Grooved ware is likely to date towards the end of the 3rd millennium or to the early 2nd, although 2 unstratified sherds of Grooved ware affinity from the Abingdon causewayed enclosure suggest some overlap with the Decorated style. The distribution of Grooved ware suggests further extensions of the settled area; it occurs on Thames alluvial deposits (second terrace to floodplain) at Lechlade (Jones 1976), Stanton Harcourt (Thomas 1955; Case 1982c), Cassington (Leeds 1940; Case 1982d), Radley (CBA Gp 9 *Newsletter* 11 (1981), 136), Abingdon (Corporation and Barton Court Farms, information from Mr. & Mrs. R.P. Henderson and Mr. D. Miles; Bypass, Parrington 1978, 31), Drayton (Leeds 1934a and references) and Dorchester (Atkinson 1951, *et al.* 1951), and on the dip-slope of the chalk at Farncombe Down, Lambourn and Blewbury (Rahtz 1962, Peake 1936). Group I axes from Spelsbury in the eastern Cotswolds, Tackley and Kirtlington athwart the Cherwell, from Oxford, from Charney Bassett (Cherbury Camp), Frilford and Sunningwell on the Corallian ridge, from Abingdon and Dorchester, and from Ewelme in the Chilterns, and a Group Ia axe from Wallingford are likely to amplify this pattern; and similarly some of the transverse arrowheads found in the eastern Cotswolds, towards the foothills of the Chilterns in the North Stoke-Crowmarsh area, and on the Corallian ridge (see also Bradley & Ellison 1975, 175–6).

Settlement traces are confined to pits. At Drayton they extended over some 100 metres and even further at Cassington, although the distribution was discontinuous (Case 1982d); there were smaller clusters at Stanton Harcourt (Case 1982c) and at Barton Court

Farm, Abingdon (information from Mr. D. Miles). Some of these may have stood alongside ditched enclosures or field boundaries similar to those discovered at Peterborough (Pryor 1978); ditches at Dorchester (Site IX, second phase: Atkinson 1951) may have been of this kind.

Emmer and hexaploid wheat and barley occurred in pits at Barton Court Farm, Abingdon (Jones 1980); hazel nuts and crab apple were also found, indicating a diet supplemented by gathering. Pig bones were more frequent than those of cattle at Barton Court (information from Mr. R. Wilson) and at Cassington where sheep were also reported (Jackson in Case 1982d); pig has been recorded consistently with Grooved ware regionally as generally in southern England, and may confirm a somewhat changed farming practice.

Grooved ware has also repeatedly been associated in southern England with constructional phases of the largest henge monuments. Two monuments of this kind (map in Lambrick 1983, fig. 10) have been excavated in the region: The Devil's Quoits, Stanton Harcourt (Pl. 4, A: Grimes 1943/4, Gray 1974) and Dorchester XIII (Pl. 3, A: Atkinson 1951), to which may be added the smaller Dorchester XIV (Pl. 3, A: excavations by Atkinson and Thomas, noted in Case & Kirk 1952/3). The ditch of the Devil's Quoits, perhaps some 150 metres in greatest diameter, had opposed entrances, outer bank and inner stone-circle. Apparently no identifiable pottery was found but a radiocarbon determination from the primary silts (2060± 120 bc, Har–1887, information from Mrs. M. Gray) agrees well with those dating similar constructional phases elsewhere with Grooved ware. Inhabitants of the Grooved ware settlement nearby at Vicarage field may thus have been involved with the monument, although Peterborough ware finds at Linch Hill Corner and further north were closer (references in Case 1982c). The labour involved in the ditch and earthwork may have been some 26,000 man-hours, a figure which suggests the existence of populations at the end of the 3rd millennium bc at least as large as those of the Middle Neolithic. The ditches showed evidence of 'frequent clearing out' (Gray 1974) and the monument may have been periodically resorted to both now and into the Bronze Age by groups grazing in spring and summer the extensive floodplains and lowest terraces of the Evenlode and Thames between Newbridge and Standlake (Case 1982c). It may thus have played a role as a seasonal gathering point similar to that of the cursuses elsewhere; and this may explain the absence of a cursus at Stanton Harcourt. A possible major henge-monument at Eynsham (Case 1955, cp. Benson & Miles 1974, 44) could be similarly explained.

Dorchester XIV, a smaller monument 70 ft. in diameter (Pl. 3, A), was unusual in having an internal bank; finds of a Group I stone axe and of marine shells (cp. Wainwright & Longworth 1971, 265) would be consistent with a Grooved ware date. It had been abandoned before the very much larger Site XIII (Pl. 3, A) was constructed over it; judging by its Late Beaker pottery (personal examination thanks to Mr. N. Thomas) the major period of use of Site XIII and perhaps its construction should date to the Early Bronze Age. It could be taken as superseding the cursus there as a seasonal gathering point.

The major henge-monument recorded at Westwell, near Burford (Atkinson 1949), on the Great Oolite, however, is not close to a major river or its floodplain, being some 2 miles south of the Windrush on higher ground; and the site at Condicote, Glos., is at the head of the Windrush valley system (Lambrick 1983, 51).

The Beaker culture. The Beaker culture as generally elsewhere in southern England represents the fourth component of the Late Neolithic. For the purposes of this contribution, account is taken only of the culture's Middle phase; the few Early style beakers or sherds (Stanton Harcourt II, grave 2; Stanton Harcourt XV, 1–5, grave 3; Cassington 1; and Clifton Hampden) are assumed regionally to belong to that phase, and the Late phase is taken as best considered with the Early Bronze Age (Beaker culture phases are according to Case 1977a; regional beaker pottery and associations based on Case 1956b and references, amplified by Hamlin & Case 1963, Case 1982c and information from Messrs. G. Lambrick and J. Wallis). The Middle Beaker phase may be dated from within the 20th century to within the 17th century bc. In calibrated chronology it is likely thus to have endured for some 400 calendar years or more, during at least a part of which time it will have overlapped with the use of Peterborough and Grooved wares. However, at Stanton Harcourt XXII, 1, there was apparently an appreciable interval: the ring-ditch around the Beaker culture burial was dug only after tertiary silting had begun in that around the Peterborough culture one (above, p. 31; Grimes 1943/4, 40). A similar interval may have occurred at Mount Farm, Berinsfield, where an oval ring-ditch (feature 528, about 13 metres in widest dimension) enclosed two pit-graves (information given by Mr. G. Lambrick). One pit (Burial 602; 2500 ± 100 bc: HAR–4673, provisional date) contained a primary man's burial with sherds of fabric comparable to Peterborough ware and struck flints including an unpolished knife comparable to the finely flaked and polished one with the central burial of Stanton Harcourt XXI, 1 (Grimes 1943/4, fig 15,a). An adjoining pit was cut by a secondary woman's grave (Burial 618: 1760 ± 110 bc: HAR–4792) with a Middle style beaker, somewhat comparable to that from the secondary grave at Stanton Harcourt XXI, 1 (Grimes 1943/4, fig 18; Clarke 1970, fig 772), and two boar's-tusk pendants, a split-bone pin and a flint end-scraper. Partial recutting of the ditch may also have been associated with the Beaker culture activity.

Regional evidence in the Middle Beaker phase is confined to graves and surface scatters; more or less closed settlement assemblages in pits such as found elsewhere, have unfortunately not been located here. Regionally pits with Peterborough and Grooved wares do not contain Beaker ware. This is the general rule elsewhere, where conversely pits with Beaker ware do not as a general rule contain either of these two wares. One may assume therefore with reasonable confidence that users of beakers were a fourth group with more or less divergent material culture using the region during the Late Neolithic.

Middle style beakers, sherds or their associations have been recorded on the left bank of the Thames, from Standlake (possibly), Stanton Harcourt, Eynsham, Cassington, Yarnton, Culham (probably), Drayton St. Leonard and Dorchester; and on the right bank at Radley, Abingdon, Sutton Courtenay, Clifton Hampden, Long Wittenham, Wallingford and Cholsey. These were all probably from second terrace gravel, but a recent find from Radley was from the first terrace (CBA Gp 9 *Newsletter* 11 (1981), 137) and more may appear eventually. Finds at Little Rollright and at Lambourn (Case 1956/7: barrow 31) show continuing occupation of the eastern Cotswolds and the Berkshire Downs; sherds have been claimed as Middle Beaker at Farncombe Down, Lambourn (Smith in Rahtz 1962), but others at the Lambourn long barrow and at Blewbury are not entirely distinctive (Wymer 1965/6, Peake 1936). There are no finds from the Oxfordshire Chilterns or the Corallian ridge, but some of the flint barbed-and-tanged arrowheads in these areas should supplement the pattern; barbed-and-tanged arrowheads have also occurred frequently in the eastern Cotswolds.

The Beaker Culture Middle phase thus shows continued infilling of the landscape, especially in the Thames Valley itself where it appears to indicate the earliest Neolithic settlement in several parishes. This may be partly an accident of recording, in that graves are more conspicuous than pits; but the density of settlement may be real enough in that graves are likely to have been near occupation sites, and it is note-worthy that small groups of finds or scattered graves occur in several parishes, suggesting clustered or protracted settlement. For example there are 4 groups at *Stanton Harcourt* (Vicarage field, 2 graves; around XV, 1–5, some 6 graves; Linch Hill corner, one grave; Linch Hill, numerous finds); 3 groups at *Radley* (around Barrow Hills, summarized in Riley 1982); possibly more than 2 groups at *Cassington* (Tolley's pit; Smith's 2 pit, ring-ditch 1 and possibly ring-ditch 6, summarized in Case 1982d); 2 groups at *Dorchester* (Mount Farm, one grave, above, p. 33, and Site XII, a grave near the Big Rings henge monument); and 2 groups at *Oxford* (Summertown, 2 graves; Polstead road). Finally there may have been more than one grave at Yarnton.

The characteristic form of burial as generally elsewhere was contracted inhumation with a beaker and sometimes other grave goods in an individual grave pit. The graves may have been covered by small mounds (as at Graves 1 and 2, Vicarage field: Case 1982c) and were sometimes within small ring-ditches of around 10 metres diameter or less as at Stanton Harcourt XXII, 1, or at Mount Farm or Lambourn 31; the ring-ditch of larger size at Cassington 1 (Bradford 1951) may be Late Beaker like Radley 15 (Riley 1981). Two burials may be unstratified in a single grave as at Summertown, Oxford, or superimposed as at Lambourn 31; and more than one burial may occur within a ring-ditch as at Lambourn 31. Standlake 20, a small ring-ditch with post-circle, may belong to this phase (Catling 1982).

The infilling of the landscape which the graves suggest is consistent with palynological evidence nationally for a surge of clearings which coincides with the maturity of the Beaker culture (Case 1977a). The economy associated with the Beaker culture (more so than that of any other Late Neolithic group) shows a strong emphasis on cattle grazing, which was combined with cereal cultivation and grazing other livestock. (Regional evidence on the farming economy is however slight, confined to impressions of emmer wheat on beakers from Little Rollright, and from Stanton Harcourt XXII, 1 where sheep also occurred; Murphy 1982, Grimes 1943/4. Wheat and barley grains have recently been identified associated with burial 618, Mount Farm, Dorchester; information Mr. G. Lambrick.) The continued attractiveness of the region as a centre for spring and summer grazing may explain the exotic products which were brought into it, and its participation in advanced technology. Examples include not only shale or jet (Cassington, Clarke 1970, fig. 240, and nearby at Purwell Farm, Case & Sturdy 1959, 58), but pottery possibly made by specialists (the beaker at Dorchester, Site XII, Pl. 4, B); slate wristguards from a source as yet unknown (Stanton Harcourt XV, 1–5, grave 3, Purwell Farm, Cassington, Dorchester site XII, Pl. 4, B); gold ear-rings possibly from Ireland (Pl. 4, B, Radley 4a, Williams 1948; context discussed in Case 1977b); knives of copper from Ireland (Sutton Courtenay, Britton 1963, 298, Table 2, no. 1) and from another source in Central Europe or Great Britain (Pl. 4, B, Dorchester site XII, Case 1965), one of the Dorchester knives being of tin-bronze (*loc. cit.*). The Yarnton torc (VCH 1939, 258, fig. 16), another exotic object of non-Irish copper, is also likely to belong to this phase.

The cluster of finds in Stanton Harcourt (p. 32) around the Devil's Quoits suggests that the monument continued to be frequented, and a radiocarbon determination from the secondary silting of its ditch (1640±70 bc, Har–1888; information from Mrs. M. Gray) is appropriate to the climax of the Middle Beaker phase and transition to the Late. This date matches those for rebuilding in stone both at Stonehenge and at the Mount Pleasant henge-monument, near Dorchester, Dorset, both of which events may be associated with the Middle Beaker phase (Case 1977, 80). It is thus possible that the stone-circle within the Devil's Quoits (Pl. 4, A) dates from this stage too, and likewise the undated Rollright Stones (Lambrick 1983) near which a Middle phase beaker was also found (Case 1956b).

Beaker culture graves, although unlikely to represent more than a small proportion of the population, enable some inferences to be made about divisions of society towards the end of the Late Neolithic. Generally, children's graves tend to be the most poorly furnished, then women's, then men's. There was perhaps already a tendency in the Middle phase for women and children to be buried apart from men (as noted in the Late phase in Case 1977a, 80) but it was not invariable: 2 women's graves were grouped at Vicarage field, Stanton Harcourt (Case 1982c), but a man, adolescent boy and child at Lambourn barrow 31 (Case 1956/7).

The furniture of some burials suggests recognizable activities and their status; such burials may be classified as Artisans, Arrowhead and Exceptionally Rich (Case 1977a, 81–2). An Artisan's burial is represented by one of the women's graves at Vicarage field, Stanton Harcourt, where finds suggest flint-knapping (Case 1982c). Arrowhead graves are represented by Radley, 4a (Pl. 4, B; also with gold ear-rings; Williams 1948) and Stanton Harcourt XXII, 1 (also with a bone so-called pendant or belt-fastener, possibly better interpreted as a bow-stringer). Such graves are never of women and children and suggest the practice of occasional feuding; hunting was not an important Beaker Culture activity, nor was warfare judging by the almost complete absence of evidence for defended settlements.

Exceptionally Rich burials in the Middle phase are generally also of men; the young man's burial at Dorchester XII (Pl. 4, B, with stone wristguard, bronze and copper knives and exceptional beaker: Atkinson 1951; Inventaria, GB 1) qualifies as one. Adjoining the Late Neolithic sites near the confluence of the Thames and Thame (p. 30), this burial may conceivably have been of the kin of those responsible for the seasonal allotment of the grazing rights and their overseeing (cp. Kehoe 1974) – practices which survived regionally until very recently at Yarnton (references in Case 1982c). A similar but largely robbed burial may have been represented in grave 1 near Stanton Harcourt XV, 1–5 (Pl. 4, B, Hamlin & Case 1963), and have been a predecessor to the even richer Early Bronze burial in the nearby Stanton Harcourt Barrow (Harden & Treweeks 1945).

Late Neolithic social structure. Whatever the fluctuations in the later Neolithic population, the beliefs and eventually somewhat warlike social system connected with long barrows and causewayed enclosures plainly lapsed. The large, rich and powerful lineages which had produced it may have disintegrated. Regional evidence suggests a shift in settlement towards the Stanton Harcourt-Cassington-Eynsham and the Dorchester areas, and there is a little evidence that grazing swine became relatively more important in a less rigid mixed-farming economy. Cattle may perhaps have declined in importance as a status symbol and as a major token of exchange (as bridewealth for example) although with the Beaker period they became once more the major livestock.

Exchanges will have been needed in the later Neolithic as before to obtain the necessities of life, but their focal points may have become the ritual monuments. The Dorchester evidence may suggest a pattern of dispersed settlements, with their cremation cemeteries by the floodplain – settlements exchanging as in the Middle Neolithic grazing rights on the floodplain for flint from the chalk and for exotic rocks from various sources (Case 1982a).

By the end of the 3rd millennium there seems no evidence for population decline: the manpower needed for digging the Devil's Quoits henge monument, Stanton Harcourt, seems somewhat greater than that for digging and revetting the Period 2 enclosure at Abingdon (pp. 22–3); and then and in the early 2nd millennium, the distribution of Peterborough and Grooved wares and of Beaker pottery and its associations suggests a landscape more filled in than before. Henge monuments may have replaced cursuses as focuses for exchange: the Devil's Quoits, for example, dominating an extensive area of alluvium, providing the place of spring and summer resort for a group of communities at least as big as those of the hypothetical Middle Neolithic clans, and commanding as wide a variety of environments both upland and lowland; around the monument, the individual farmsteads of members of the leading families, their burials in individual graves, ring-ditches and barrows spread along the margins of their plots (p. 27). These leading families may have been responsible both for the monument's upkeep (and presumably for the ceremonial associated with it) and for allocating rights to the nearby grazing to those coming from far and near, receiving in return exchanges of necessary substances such as flint and prestigious objects of copper, bronze or exotic rocks. Grave groups of the Beaker period and the Early Bronze Age suggest that exotic substances came generally into the hands of men, rather than women, which may suggest that residence was generally patrilocal.

This *barrow-henge* system in some ways implies a more loosely-knit, less fragmented and basically simpler social system than that of the Middle Neolithic; all who used the area, despite considerable differences in material culture, may have been bound in some loose tribal unity, dependent perhaps on religious belief; inter-clan rivalries were plainly not such as to necessitate defensive works. Conversely, religious belief as seen in the Beaker Culture may have sanctioned social stratification in somewhat rigid castes.

Finally, a henge monument itself is not an essential part of this system: a barrow-group alone might suffice, as at Radley (p. 33). Such a group without a henge monument may indicate a development which began after the late 3rd-millennium fashion for building these monuments *ab initio* had largely declined.

Acknowledgements. Thanks are expressed in the text to numerous excavators and researchers who have generously given me access to unpublished material on which I have based my account. The use of imperial or metric measurements follows individual excavators' practice. Mr. D.W.A. Startin most kindly made the calculations of manpower quoted throughout; but the wider inferences drawn from them have been largely my responsibility. References are made to excavation reports in *Settlement patterns in the Oxford Region* edited by myself and Dr. A.W.R. Whittle, with whom I have discussed the sites concerned in detail: and I am thus grateful too for his help. We also collaborated in studying the finds from the Ascott-under-Wychwood long barrow.

I am most grateful to Mr. J. Steane, Keeper of Field Section, Department of Museum Services, Oxfordshire County Council, Woodstock, for much helpful topographical information, and to Mr. J. Rhodes, Keeper of Antiquities, for lending me negatives of the Ascott excavations (with Mr. D. Benson's consent). Mrs. F.E.S. Roe kindly gave me information on unpublished Group I axes. The plates were prepared by Mr. N.A. Griffiths of the Department of Antiquities, Ashmolean Museum.

Postscript. This contribution was submitted in May 1981. As publication of the volume did not then proceed, opportunity for revision was taken in December 1982. This postscript notes some developments since December 1982, kindly made known to me by those responsible.

In the summer of 1983, Mr. R.J. Bradley excavated the double-ditched subrectangular cropmark enclosure about 25 metres long and within 100 metres east of the Abingdon causewayed enclosure (Benson & Miles 1974, 57; Map 31, SU 51289824). A small fenced enclosure was found to have been covered by a low oval mound, which had covered a grave with 2 crouched male inhumation burials, one with a polished flint knife and the other with a jet or shale belt slider. The earthwork was finally enclosed by a causewayed ditch. The monument has affinities with long mortuary enclosures (p. 26) and in its later state it was in effect a very small long barrow (p. 23). The burial has affinities with that of Stanton Harcourt XXI, 1 and is one more variation on later Neolithic burial practice (p. 31). About 200 metres east-south-east, 2 Beaker culture burials (Middle and Late phase) were excavated by Ms. C. Halpin and Mr. J. Wallis, adding to the Radley concentration (p. 33).

Ms. Halpin and Ms. Wallis excavated pits with Grooved ware and struck flints at Blewbury (p. 31) in December 1983.

Intensive and systematic field-walking has been undertaken by Messrs S. Ford and R. Holgate. Mr. Ford is surveying a transect of soils from the Thames Valley floor at North Stoke eastwards to the Chilterns. Struck flints are more or less continuously distributed throughout the landscape, but some concentrations occur and a notable blank at the North Stoke cropmark sites (p. 26). The bulk of the earlier material (Mesolithic and earlier Neolithic) has been found on lower ground towards the river (p. 25) but later material (Late Neolithic and Bronze Age) is more widespread.

Mr. Holgate's survey is part of a project to map settlement patterns in the whole Thames basin. His provisional conclusions are that Later Mesolithic settlement on the Upper Thames gravels was restricted to areas immediately adjacent to the river, at the forest margin (p. 18). In the Middle Neolithic, increased numbers of sites exploited the same general areas (p. 27), principally on the edge of the gravel terraces alongside the river. The Late Neolithic shows settlements increased in numbers expanding into previously unoccupied areas (p. 30). The Cotswolds may show a contrasting pattern similar to that in the Avebury region, Wilts., with settlement tending to move down the slopes.

Finally I am grateful for discussions with Mr. G. Lambrick on general aspects of settlement, and specifically on the apparently generally complementary distributions of long barrows in the Cotswolds, neighbouring the upper tributary reaches of the Thames; and of causewayed enclosures alongside the Thames or its floodplain on the low-lying broad valley, with the long barrows on the Berkshire Downs mirroring those in the Cotswolds (Lambrick 1983, fig. 9). It might be possible from this to infer some specialization in function in the settled areas thus:

(1) Intensive mixed-farming settlement in the Cotswolds exploiting varying soils in conveniently narrow valley cross-sections, associated with long barrows.

(2) Specialization towards grazing in the broad valley, associated with causewayed enclosures.

(3) Specialization towards flint-collecting on the Berkshire Downs, associated with long barrows.

Thus the causewayed enclosures may be assumed to have served as markets, where the Cotswold settlers obtained flint and where they and the inhabitants of the Berkshire Downs obtained valley grazing rights in spring and summer. Kinship ties may be assumed to have spread across this pattern, so that those living in the valley had rights in the upland long barrows. Eventually this Middle Neolithic cross-valley pattern may have been replaced by a Late Neolithic communications pattern more emphatically up and down the valley systems.

Recent trace-element analysis of more than 400 polished flint axes from southern England (Craddock *et al.* 1983) concludes that individual axes cannot be provenanced with any great certainty. Despite this reservation, it is suggested that the majority of the axes in the sample were of South Downs flint. The 'best mines' for 4 out of the 5 samples from the Abingdon causewayed enclosure were there – Easton Down, Wilts., being the 'best mine' for the remaining sample (p. 22). Peppard, Oxon., was the 'best mine' for 26 axes: 13 from East Anglia, 9 from Wiltshire and 4 from Sussex.

Bibliography

Ashbee, P. (1966) 'The Fussell's Lodge long barrow excavations 1957', *Archaeologia*, 100, 1–80

Ashbee, P., Smith, I.F. & Evans, J.G. (1979) 'Excavation of three long barrows near Avebury, Wiltshire', *Proc. Prehist. Soc.* 45, 207–30

Atkinson, R.J.C. (1949) 'A henge monument at Westwell, near Burford, Oxon.', *Oxoniensia* 14, 84–7
Atkinson, R.J.C. (1951) 'The excavations at Dorchester, Oxfordshire, 1946–1951', *Archaeol. Newsletter* 4, 56–9
Atkinson, R.J.C. (1942) 'Archaeological sites on Port Meadow, Oxford', *Oxoniensia* 7, 24–35
Atkinson, R.J.C. (1965) 'Wayland's Smithy', *Antiquity* 39, 126–33
Atkinson, R.J.C., Piggott, C.M. & Sandars, N.K. (1951) *Excavations at Dorchester*
Avery, M. (1982) 'The Neolithic causewayed enclosure, Abingdon', in *Settlement patterns in the Oxford Region*, eds. H. Case & A.W.R. Whittle, 10–52
Barker, G. & Webley, D. (1978) 'Causewayed camps and Early Neolithic economies in central southern England, *Proc. Prehist. Soc.* 44, 161–86
Benson, D. (1971) 'Ascott-under-Wychwood', *Current Archaeology* 3, 7–10
Benson, D. & Miles, D. (1974) *The Upper Thames Valley: An Archaeological Survey of the River Gravels*
Bradford, J.S.P. (1951) 'Excavations at Cassington, Oxon, 1947', *Oxoniensia* 16, 1–4
Bradford, J.S.P. & Morris, J.M. (1941) Archaeological notes, *Oxoniensia* 6, 84–9
Bradley, R. (1978a) *The Prehistoric Settlement of Britain*
Bradley, R. (1978b) 'Colonisation and land use in the Late Neolithic and Early Bronze Age', in *The effect of man on the landscape: the Lowland Zone*, eds. S. Limbrey & J.G. Evans, 95–103
Bradley, R. & Ellison, A. (1975) *Rams Hill*. BAR 19
Britton, D. (1963) 'Traditions of metal-working in the Later Neolithic and Early Bronze Age of Britain: Part 1', *Proc. Prehist. Soc.* 29, 258–325
Burgess, C. (1976) 'Meldon Bridge: a Neolithic defended promontory complex near Peebles', in *Settlement and Economy in the Third and Second Millennia B.C.*, eds. C. Burgess & R. Miket, 151–79
Care, V. (1979) 'The production and distribution of Mesolithic axes in southern England', *Proc. Prehist. Soc.* 45, 93–102
Case, H. (1952/3) 'Mesolithic finds in the Oxford area', *Oxoniensia* 17/18, 1–13
Case, H. (1955) 'Deadman's burial, Eynsham, Oxon.', *Antiquity* 29, 233–6
Case, H. (1956a) 'The Neolithic causewayed camp at Abingdon, Berks', *Antiq. J.* 36, 11–30
Case, H. (1956b) 'Beaker pottery from the Oxford Region: 1939–1955', *Oxoniensia* 21, 1–21
Case, H. (1956–7) 'The Lambourn seven barrows', *Berks. Archaeol. J.* 55, 15–31
Case, H. (1965) 'A tin-bronze in Bell-Beaker association', *Antiquity* 39, 219–22
Case, H. (1977a) 'The Beaker Culture in Britain and Ireland', in *Beakers in Britain and Europe: Four Studies*, ed. R. Mercer, BAR SS 26, 71–101
Case, H. (1977b) 'An early accession to the Ashmolean Museum', in *Ancient Europe and the Mediterranean*, ed. V. Markotic, 18–34
Case, H. (1982a) Introduction, *Settlement patterns in the Oxford Region*, eds. H.J. Case & A.W.R. Whittle
Case, H. (1982b) 'The linear ditches and southern enclosure North Stoke', in *op. cit.* above
Case, H. (1982c) 'The Vicarage field, Stanton Harcourt', in *op. cit.* above
Case, H. (1982d) 'Cassington, 1950–2: Late Neolithic pits and the big enclosure', in *op. cit.* above
Case, H. & Kirk, J.R. (1952/53) Archaeological notes, 1952, *Oxoniensia* 17/18, 216–8
Case, H. & Sturdy, D. (1959) Notes and News, *Oxoniensia* 24, 98–102
Case, H., Bayne, N., Steele, S., Avery, G. & Sutermeister, H. (1964/5) 'Excavations at City Farm, Hanborough, Oxon.', *Oxoniensia* 29/30, 1–98
Catling, H. (1982) 'Six ring-ditches at Standlake', in *Settlement patterns in the Oxford Region*, eds. H. Case & A.W.R. Whittle
Churchill, D.M. (1962) 'The stratigraphy of the Mesolithic sites III and V at Thatcham', *Proc. Prehist. Soc.* 28, 362–70

Clarke, D.L. (1970) *Beaker Pottery of Great Britain and Ireland*, 1, 2
Craddock, P.T., Cowell, M.R., Leese, M.N. & Hughes, M.J. (1983) 'The trace element composition of polished flint axes as an indicator of source', *Archaeometry* 25, 135–63
Dixon, P. & Borne, P. (1977) *Crickley Hill and Gloucestershire Prehistory*. Crickley Hill Trust
Evans, J.G. (1971) 'Habitat change on the calcareous soils of Britain: the impact of Neolithic man', in *Economy and settlement in Neolithic and Early Bronze Age Britain and Europe*, ed. D.D.A. Simpson, 27–73
Evans, J.G. (1972) *Land Snails in Archaeology*
Evens, E.D., Grinsell, L.V., Piggott, S. & Wallis, F.S. (1962) 'Fourth Report of the Sub-Committee of the South-western group of Museums and Art Galleries (England) on the petrological identification of stone axes', *Proc. Prehist. Soc.* 28, 209–66
Evens, E.D., Grinsell, L.V. & Wallis, F.S. (1972) 'The petrological identification of stone implements from south-western England', *Proc. Prehist. Soc.* 38, 235–75
Froom, F.R. (1971/2a) 'Some Mesolithic sites in south-west Berkshire', *Berks. Archaeol. J.* 66, 11–22
Froom, F.R. (1971/2b) 'A Mesolithic site at Wawcott, Kintbury', *Berks. Archaeol. J.* 66, 23–44
Froom, F.R. (1976) *Wawcott III. A Stratified Mesolithic Succession*. BAR 27
Gates, T. (1975) *The Middle Thames Valley: An Archaeological Survey of the River Gravels*
Gray, M. (1974) 'The Devil's Quoits, Stanton Harcourt, Oxon.', *Oxoniensia* 39, 96–7
Grimes, W.F. (1943–4) 'Excavation at Stanton Harcourt, 1940', *Oxoniensia* 8/9, 16–43
Hallam, S.J. (1975) *Fire and Hearth: a study of aboriginal usage and European usurpation in south-western Australia*
Hamlin, A. & Case, H. (1963) 'Excavations of ring-ditches and other sites at Stanton Harcourt', *Oxoniensia* 28, 1–19; 'Notes on the finds and on ring-ditches in the Oxford region', 19–52
Harden, D.B. & Treweeks, R.C. (1945) 'Excavations at Stanton Harcourt, Oxon., 1940, II', *Oxoniensia* 10, 16–41
Inventaria *Inventaria Archaeologica:* Great Britain, 1st set, GB. 1–8, ed. C.F.C. Hawkes
Jacobi, R.M. (1973) 'Aspects of the 'Mesolithic Age' in Great Britain', in *The Mesolithic in Europe*, ed. S.K. Kozowski, 237–65
Jacobi, R.M. (1976) 'Britain inside and outside Mesolithic Europe', *Proc. Prehist. Soc.* 42, 67–84
Jacobi, R.M. (1978) 'Population and landscape in Mesolithic lowland Britain', in *The effect of man on the landscape: the Lowland Zone*, eds. S. Limbrey & J.G. Evans, 75–85
Jacobi, R.M. (1982) 'Later Hunters in Kent', in *Archaeology in Kent to AD 1500*, ed. P. Leach,
Jones, M. (1980) 'Carbonised cereals from Grooved Ware Contexts', *Proc. Prehist. Soc.* 46, 61–3
Jones, M.U. (1976) 'Neolithic pottery found at Lechlade, Glos.', *Oxoniensia* 41, 1–5
Kehoe, A.B. (1974) 'Saints of Wessex?', *Antiquity* 48, 232–3
Kenward, R. (1982) 'A Neolithic burial enclosure at New Wintles Farm, Eynsham', in *Settlement patterns in the Oxford Region*, eds. H. Case & A.W.R. Whittle
Lambrick, G. (1983) *The Rollright Stones*
Leeds, E.T. (1913) 'On 'Neolithic' pottery from Boston Farm, Astrop', *Oxfords. Archaeol. Soc. Report* for the year 1912, 114–8
Leeds, E.T. (1922) 'Further discoveries of the Neolithic and Bronze Ages at Peterborough', *Antiq. J.* 2, 210–37
Leeds, E.T. (1927) 'A Neolithic site at Abingdon, Berks', *Antiq. J.* 7, 438–64
Leeds, E.T. (1928) 'A Neolithic site at Abingdon, Berks, (Second Report)', *Antiq. J.* 8, 461–77
Leeds, E.T. (1934a) 'Recent Bronze Age discoveries in Berkshire and Oxfordshire', *Antiq. J.* 14, 264–76
Leeds, E.T. (1934b) 'Rectangular enclosures of the Bronze Age in the Upper Thames Valley', *Antiq. J.* 14, 414–6
Leeds, E.T. (1940) 'New discoveries of Neolithic pottery in Oxford-

shire', *Oxoniensia* 5, 1–22
Mellars, P. (1974) 'The palaeolithic and mesolithic in Britain', in *British Prehistory: A New Outline*, ed. C. Renfrew, 41–99
Mellars, P. (1975) 'Ungulate populations, economic patterns and the Mesolithic population', in *The effect of man on the landscape: the Highland zone*, eds. J.G. Evans, S. Limbrey & H. Cleere, CBA Research Report 11, 49–56
Mellars, P. (1976a) 'Settlement patterns and industrial variability in the British Mesolithic', in *Problems in Economic and Social Archaeology*, eds. G. de G. Sieveking, I.H. Longworth & K.E. Wilson, 375–99
Mellars, P. (1976b) 'Fire ecology, animal populations and man; a study of some ecological relationships in prehistory', *Proc. Prehist. Soc.* 42, 15–45
Mercer, R. (1980) *Hambledon Hill: A Neolithic Landscape*
Moorey, P.R.S. (1982) 'A Neolithic ring-ditch and Iron Age enclosure at Newnham Murren, near Wallingford', in *Settlement patterns in the Oxford Region*, eds. H. Case & A.W.R. Whittle
Murphy, P. (1982) 'Plant impressions on local Neolithic and Bronze Age pottery and daub in the Department of Antiquities, Ashmolean Museum', in *Settlement patterns in the Oxford Region*, eds. H. Case & A.W.R. Whittle
Newell, R.R. (1973) 'The post-glacial adaptations of the indigenous population of the north-west European plain', in *The Mesolithic in Europe*, ed. S.K. Kozowski, 339–440
Palmer, R. (1976) 'Interrupted ditch enclosures in Britain: the use of aerial photography for comparative studies', *Proc. Prehist. Soc.* 42, 161–86
Parrington, M. (1978) *The excavation of an Iron Age Settlement, Bronze Age ring-ditches and Roman features at Ashville Trading Estate, Abingdon (Oxfordshire) 1974–6*. Oxfordshire Archaeological Unit Report 1
Peake, A.E. (1913) 'An account of a flint factory, with some new types of flints excavated at Peppard Common, Oxon.', *Archaeol. J.* 70, 33–68
Peake, A.E. (1914) 'Notes on the implements from the factory site at Peppard, Oxon.', *Proc. Prehist. Soc. East Anglia* 1, pt. 4, 404–20
Peake, H.J.E. (1936) 'Excavations on Churn Plain, Blewbury, Berks', *Trans. Newbury Dist. Field Club* 7, 160–174
Piggott, S. (1929) 'Neolithic pottery and other remains from Pangbourne, Berks. and Caversham, Oxon.', *Proc. Prehist. Soc. East Anglia* 6, 30–9
Piggott, S. (1962) *The West Kennet Long Barrow*
Pryor, F. (1978) *Excavation at Fengate, Peterborough, England: The Second Report*. Royal Ontario Museum, Archaeology Monograph 5
Rahtz, P.A. (1962) 'Farncombe Down Barrow, Berkshire', *Berks. Archaeol. J.* 60, 1–24
Riley, D. (1982) 'Radley 15, a Late Beaker ring-ditch', in *Settlement patterns in the Oxford Region*, eds. H. Case & A.W.R. Whittle
RCHM (Eng.) (1960) *A Matter of Time*. Royal Commission on Historical Monuments (England)
RCHM (Eng.) (1970) *An Inventory of the Historical Monuments in the County of Dorset, 2: South-East (Part 3)*. Roy. Comm. on Hist. Monuments (England)
RCHM (Eng.) (1975) *An Inventory of the Historical Monuments in Dorset, 5: East Dorset*. Roy. Comm. on Hist. Monuments (England)
Savile, A. (1979) 'Further excavations at Nympsfield chambered tomb, Gloucestershire', *Proc. Prehist. Soc.* 45, 53–91
Simmons, I.G. (1976) 'The ecological setting of Mesolithic man in the Highland Zone', in *The effect of man on the landscape: the Highland zone*, eds. J.G. Evans, S. Limbrey & H. Cleeve, CBA Research Report 11, 57–63
Slade, C.F. (1963/4) 'A Late Neolithic site of Sonning, Berkshire', *Berks. Archaeol. J.* 61, 4–19
Smith, I.F. (1966) 'Windmill Hill and its implications', *Palaeohistoria* 12, 469–81
Startin, W. (1978) 'Linear pottery culture houses: reconstruction and manpower', *Proc. Prehist. Soc.* 44, 143–59
VCH (1939) *A History of Oxfordshire*, 1
Wainwright, G.J. & Longworth, I.H. (1971) *Durrington Walls: Excavations 1966–1968*
Whittle, A.W.R. (1978) 'Resources and population in the British Neolithic', *Antiquity* 52, 34–42
Williams, A. (1948) 'Excavations in Barrow Hills Field, Radley, Berkshire, 1944', *Oxoniensia* 13, 1–17
Wilson, D.R. (1975) '"Causewayed camps" and "interrupted ditch systems"', *Antiquity* 49, 178–86
Wymer, J.J. (1962) 'Excavations at the Maglemosian sites at Thatcham, Berkshire, England', *Proc. Prehist. Soc.* 28, 329–61
Wymer, J.J (1965/6) 'Excavations of the Lambourn long barrow', *Berks. Archaeol. J.* 62, 1–16

THE BRONZE AGE IN THE OXFORD AREA – ITS LOCAL AND REGIONAL SIGNIFICANCE

RICHARD BRADLEY

'The old river . . . rested unruffled at the decline of day, after ages of good service done to the race that peopled its banks, spread out in the tranquil dignity of a waterway leading to the uttermost ends of the earth . . . And indeed nothing is easier . . . than to evoke the great spirit of the past on the . . . reaches of the Thames.'

Joseph Conrad, *Heart of Darkness*

Introduction

Both parts of my title are artificial. The term 'Bronze Age' is virtually obsolete, and the traditional period framework is only followed in order to achieve a division of labour among the contributors to this volume. At one extreme this period fuses so closely into the Beaker phenomenon that different writers have been able to describe the same finds as 'Neolithic', 'Copper Age', or 'Early Bronze Age', whilst some of the material published a few years ago in a book on the 'Iron Age' of this area (Harding 1972) now appears to have been made at an earlier date, with the result that the importance of the Bronze/Iron Age transition needs fresh research. Within the arbitrary limits of my survey, this account will be largely thematic. As the quotation from Conrad suggests, we must consider the local inhabitants of the Thames Valley as well as their long-distance contacts.

There are similar problems in talking about an Oxford region, and still more if we attempt to follow modern county boundaries. It is essential to think in terms of wider geographical zones. The most important of these are the Thames corridor itself, constricted by the Goring Gap but broadening out to either side of this barrier, the limestone of the Cotswolds and the Corallian ridge, and the chalk of the Berkshire Downs. In cultural terms, we have to widen the frame still further to take into account the regional contrasts which emerge between the gravel terraces and the Wessex chalk, and between the upper Thames Valley and the middle and lower reaches of the same river. The Kennet Valley must also be considered, since it forms an essential link between the Thames and the downland. At different stages in this paper I shall be comparing the evidence from all of these regions, and it is worth making the point at this stage that developments within the modern county of Oxfordshire will never be explained unless it is understood that throughout the Bronze Age this area was only part of a much larger whole.

If this approach seems over-ambitious, at least the broader geographical framework will help to compensate for more local biases in the available evidence. The modern county of Oxfordshire is composed of several distinct zones of survival and destruction, so that the ring-ditches of the low-lying ground are merely the equivalent of the barrows in upland areas (Map 5). This evidence is often considered on such a small scale that these groups of sites are treated in isolation (Grinsell 1935; Case 1963). One way in which we can cope with such distortions is to look for wider tendencies in the evidence.

The Earlier Bronze Age burial record

The first point to consider is the relationship between the Thames gravels and the Wessex chalkland during the period between 1600 and 1100 bc, the time of the so-called Wessex Culture. It is well known that the upper Thames basin contains some of the unusual types of artefact found in the barrows of Wiltshire and Dorset, and that the siting of elaborate burials in both areas was apparently influenced by the presence of earlier monuments. The major ceremonial centres in Wessex were Mount Pleasant, Knowlton, Stonehenge, Avebury, and Marden, and at least the first four of these were accompanied by barrow cemeteries, often in the immediate vicinity (Renfrew 1973). This pattern continues into the area studied here, with quite large clusters of ring-ditches close to the Devil's Quoits and Big Rings, Dorchester. Even more important was the Barrow Hills, Radley, cemetery, aligned on the Earlier Neolithic enclosure at Abingdon.

Apart from these superficial similarities, there are more exact relationships. It is possible that a stone circle was added to the monument at Devil's Quoits several centuries after the original earthwork on the site had been constructed (Case, this volume, p. 33). This may represent an attempt to reassert the power of traditional centres at a time when contemporary society was undergoing rapid change. The same development is seen at Mount Pleasant and the Sanctuary on the Wessex chalk (Wainwright 1979). There is also a conspicuous contrast between the artefacts from different henge monuments. Mount Pleasant, Durrington Walls and Marden are extremely prolific sites and are dominated by finds of Grooved ware, but the various monuments at Avebury contain far fewer artefacts and a lower proportion of this particular style of pottery. The henges of the upper Thames show the same pattern and seem to have produced little or no material. The distribution of major sites can perhaps be divided into two zones. The southern area was based on rivers discharging into the English Channel, and contains sites with a large number of finds, whilst those henge monuments along the Thames, or its tributary the Kennet, could belong to a different system with its emphasis to the east. The henges at Westwell and Condicote may also conform to this scheme.

It is uncertain to what extent henge monuments remained in active use at the same time as rich burials. At one level the two features suggest different and perhaps contradictory emphases on the group and the individual (cf. Bradley 1984, chapter 4): the conscious renewal of ancestral monuments may have been used to legitimize the position of local leaders. The cemeteries themselves show regional variations. Case's (1963) study of ring-ditches in the Thames Valley defined a number of embanked enclosures which have no obvious counterparts on the chalk, and it is possible that larger burial mounds were the exception rather than the rule. Only at Radley was there a linear cemetery of the type characteristic of the downland, and here the mounds had other features in common with sites in Wessex, including the size and construction of the barrows, and the complexity of the burials underneath them. Because of the damage caused by ploughing, it is rarely possible to tell how far burial mounds in the Oxford region adopted the specialized forms found close to the ceremonial centres of Wessex. The presence of bell barrows at Radley (Williams 1948; Atkinson 1953) and Stanton Harcourt (Harden and Treweeks 1945) stands out from a generally undifferentiated pattern, although some of the embanked ring-ditches could have been disc barrows. There were also flat burials and a pond barrow at Radley, but we should not exaggerate these links, for even on the Wessex chalk there are regional differences in the character of the main barrow groups (Fleming 1971).

In spite of these qualifications, the links between the Thames gravels and the Wessex chalk are fairly clear. First, burials in Oxfordshire contain some of the specialized types which define the 'Wessex Culture', including bronze daggers and knife daggers, incense cups, goldwork and faience beads. Among these burials are a growing number of examples at Radley (Williams 1948, Atkinson 1953; C. Halpin pers. comm.), one at Abingdon (Parrington 1978, 25–30), and another at Stanton Harcourt (Harden and Treweeks 1945). There are faience beads from City Farm, Hanborough (Case et al. 1965), two bronze daggers from the river at Sandford-on-Thames (Gerloff 1975) and another found in the Thames between Abingdon and Sutton Courtenay (Thomas 1978). Some of these special items come from the main concentration of burials, and this certainly applies to the Barrow Hills cemetery, which has such clear parallels in Wessex. Case's study of the ring-ditches also reveals a relationship between graves with special contents and some of the larger mounds (1963, 41–2).

If we are to take this comparison any further, we have to move the emphasis from the centre of this region to its edge. The Berkshire Downs are a rather neglected area, but for present purposes they are important precisely because they form a bridge between the main areas of Wessex Culture barrows and the gravels of the Thames Valley. The burial mounds on the Berkshire Downs were listed by Grinsell in 1935 and 1936, and his work has now been supplemented by two further surveys (Bradley and Ellison 1975, chapter 5; Richards 1978), as well as a reassessment of the Lambourn cemetery (Case 1956). Like the site at Radley already mentioned, the latter group stands out from the other evidence, since it contains an unusually large number of barrows with a high proportion of special types of mound. The name 'Seven Barrows' is inappropriate, since over forty are now known. The layout of this site again recalls the classic cemeteries of Salisbury Plain. The Lambourn group has a long history and may show a horizontal sequence from a Beaker nucleus at its centre in barrows 17 and 31. Although this site is rather different from the other cemeteries on the downland, there are isolated barrows which also contain specialized types of artefact. Wessex daggers or knife daggers are known from seven sites on the Berkshire Downs (Gerloff 1975), and an axe hammer, an incense cup and a razor were found in a barrow at Stancombe Down (Greenwell 1890). The most recently excavated barrow is at Hodcott and has produced a Wessex dagger, retaining traces of its sheath, and radiocarbon dates of 1390 ± 70 bc and 1420 ± 70 bc (Har 3599 and 3608; J. Richards pers. comm.). Like barrows at Beedon and Farncombe Down, this mound included a stake circle. These features are well known in Dorset and Wiltshire but have not been recognized on the Thames gravels.

The remaining evidence for barrow burials is very limited. Little is known about the burial mounds of the Oxfordshire Cotswolds, although one ceremonial focus might have been provided by the Rollright Stones, an enigmatic monument whose original character has been slow to emerge (Burl 1976, 292; Lambrick 1983). Air photography also suggests the existence of round barrows on the Corallian limestone, and perhaps in the Vale of the White Horse (Bradley and Ellison 1975, 239–40). These areas cannot be discussed for lack of evidence, although it should be noted that even in Wessex the areas of rich burials were flanked by regions with less elaborate mounds.

The problems of Earlier Bronze Age settlement

All too often this period is treated as if it had no settlements and the burial of the dead consumed the whole energies of the living. This view probably arises because field archaeologists have underestimated the degree of mobility in the settlement pattern. They have made repeated appeals to chemical solution and other agencies as ways of explaining the rarity of pits and post-holes, when it might have been easier to adopt a different conception of contemporary land use. Although Deverel-Rimbury settlements do overlap the period of the late Wessex Culture, it looks as if earlier domestic activities rarely left subsoil features. It follows that much of the relevant data ought to be in the ploughsoil, if it survives at all. It is just this layer that is machined away on so many excavations of prehistoric sites. The importance of surface fieldwork cannot be overemphasized.

Until field survey is further advanced, we cannot do more than summarize some of the approaches already taken to earlier second-millennium settlement and the main possibilities that have arisen so far. Two components of the archaeological record have been considered, usually in isolation: the distributions of monuments and those of lithic scatters. Not until about 1400 bc are these problems alleviated.

a) Barrows, flint scatters and earlier second-millennium settlement. For some time Bronze Age specialists have been trying to reconstruct settlement patterns from the distribution of burial monuments. In our study area Case (1963) has suggested that the main groups of ring-ditches on the gravels were located close to tracts of seasonal grazing. Fleming (1971) has taken a rather similar approach to the positioning of barrow groups on the chalk. In both areas different cemeteries have been connected with the activities of single communities and seem to show a long history, from the Late Neolithic or Beaker phases to the late second millennium bc (cf. Case and Whittle 1982, III ff.). At Stanton Harcourt and Radley the scale of these different cemeteries has been extended through the discovery of flat burials, both inhumations and cremations, beyond the mounds themselves (Case and Whittle, 1982, 103ff.; C. Halpin and R. Chambers pers. comm.). Such evidence does suggest continuity in the *use* of these locations, but this is not enough to show that the cemeteries were set in an agricultural landscape. Case has also suggested a link between the river gravels and the chalk, arguing that the detailed distribution of ring-ditches around Hanborough follows a route between the two zones, perhaps used in seasonal grazing (in Case *et al.* 1965, 50). This reconstruction is not easy to assess and raises the problem that different authorities have suggested that summer grazing took place in both of these areas, making movement between them unnecessary. We know all too little about the pattern of land use on the Downs, and recent work on the Thames gravels has suggested that the present floodplain did not develop until a later period (Bowler and Robinson 1980), meaning that the apparent association between ring-ditches and seasonal grazing land may in fact be misleading. For example, a recently excavated barrow on the modern floodplain of the Thames was originally built on dry land (ibid.); work elsewhere on the lower ground indicates that this area might even have been ploughed (Palmer 1980, 128). Possible ard marks at the Hamel, Oxford, may have been associated with scattered artefacts of earlier second-millennium date. Even the lower ground could have been used all year.

In any event there is too little information concerning the siting of barrows in the landscape. It is important to make more use of lithic scatters as a source of information. Promising work is now in progress in this area (S. Ford pers. comm.; M. Tingle pers. comm.; R. Holgate pers. comm.), but it is too soon to decide the relationship between these finds and the burial monuments. On a broader scale, however, we can already see patterns in the use of different parts of the region.

It has always been hard to decide whether the distribution of complex burials on the chalk necessarily reflects the areas of major settlement. Green's recent study of flint arrowheads (1980) sheds some light on this question, since this is one of the few artefact types with a secure chronology. He provides summary figures for four contrasting regions, to which we can add the results of more limited work on finds from the Corallian ridge and the Vale of the White Horse (Green 1980, table VII. 8; Bradley and Ellison 1975, fig 5.1).

	Earlier Neolithic Leaf-shaped arrowheads	Later Neolithic Transverse
Upper Thames	24%	10%
Lower Thames	25%	10%
Corallian & Vale	10%	15%
Wessex	23%	49%
Bournemouth area	17%	37%

	Earlier 2nd mill. bc Barbed and Tanged	Misc.
Upper Thames	62%	4% *
Lower Thames	63%	2% *
Corallian & Vale	70%	5%
Wessex	25%	3%
Bournemouth area	43%	3%

* percentage recalculated because of errors in Green's tables

These figures suggest two contrasting sequences. In three regions, the Thames Valley, the Corallian limestone, and the Vale of the White Horse, the major activity appears to have been during the second millennium bc, with a massive increase in the number of arrowheads deposited during this period. Further south in Wessex, the main period of activity was in the Later Neolithic. The same phase saw considerable activity in the Bournemouth area, but this continued on a slightly increased scale during the earlier second millennium whilst the number of arrowheads in Wessex diminished rapidly. This trend is seen even more clearly in the results of recent fieldwork (Barrett *et al.* 1981, 215–7). Taken at face value, these figures suggest that after a period of intensive use during the late third millennium bc, activity on the chalkland may have slackened as the surrounding lowlands were exploited more intensively. One exception may be the west

Berkshire Downs where field survey reveals a high proportion of barbed and tanged arrowheads (M. Tingle pers. comm.).

This does not preclude the use of some of these areas, particularly the downland, for summer grazing, but such a specific reconstruction need not be justified by the available evidence, although in Wessex it offers one explanation for the sparse distribution of earlier second-millennium flintwork. The higher proportion of barbed and tanged arrowheads on the Berkshire Downs seems to be exceptional, and may be a local phenomenon which follows the general trend for the Thames Valley and adjacent areas. Year-round settlement would be feasible throughout this part of the region, although it need not presuppose a sedentary pattern of residence. Much depends on a more detailed study of the lithic evidence, but already enough is known to make it very doubtful whether we will find a consistent relationship between the siting of cemeteries and broader patterns of land use. Moreover, it is always possible that large parts of the landscape were set aside for non-subsistence activities. To suggest otherwise may be to impose our own priorities on the past.

b) Ceramic variation and later second-millennium settlement. The specialized nature of some areas of the landscape is also highlighted by the character of second-millennium pottery, and in particular by the later stages of the ceramic sequence. Until radiocarbon dates became widely available, it seemed as if there might be a break in the sequence of domestic pottery throughout large parts of southern England. This view was based on the expectation that the same styles of pottery would be found in living sites and in graves, and that this material could eventually be organized into a clearcut sequence in which one style would follow another in an orderly progression. Recent work has started to undermine these assumptions. Whittle (1981) has suggested that Beaker pottery remained the principal domestic ware after its main use in complex burials was over (cf. Bradley 1984, chapter 4), and Barrett (1980a) has shown that Deverel Rimbury ceramics could have played the same role later in the second millennium. The Beaker material from this area is considered by Case (this volume, p. 32). In subsequent phases the burials were associated mainly with Collared Urns, whilst Deverel Rimbury types were perhaps limited to the poorer graves.

However, this can be only part of the answer, for it soon appears that, like the 'Wessex' burials, Deverel Rimbury pottery has a rather restricted distribution. It seems as if the weight of the Deverel Rimbury material is found in the middle and lower Thames Valley, where it complements the pattern of rich burials above the Goring Gap (Barrett and Bradley 1980a). The same may be true in Wessex, where most Deverel Rimbury activity is known from the coastal area, south of the main barrow groups (Barrett and Bradley 1980b). In each case, the concentrations of Deverel Rimbury material occurred in just the areas which had shown the highest proportion of barbed and tanged arrowheads. There are two ways of interpreting these patterns. Either we are seeing signs of a general separation between the areas with burials and those with more lasting settlements, or the separation between Beaker coarseware, Collared Urns and Deverel Rimbury types may be a reflection of relative status. Since the lithic evidence indicates quite intensive activity on the upper Thames gravels, at any rate during the earlier second millennium bc, there seems little alternative to suggesting that in this area contrasting styles of pottery were being used to express differences of status. The subordinate position of Deverel Rimbury and related vessels may be illustrated by the organization of two cemeteries in this region: Lambourn, where Deverel Rimbury cremations were confined to the outer edge of the barrow group (Smith 1921); and Barrow Hills, Radley, where biconical urns were used in secondary burials, again towards either limit of the cemetery (Leeds 1938; C. Halpin pers. comm.).

The Earlier Bronze Age sites on either side of the Goring Gap contain different types of archaeological material, but may have been linked by complex reciprocal relations, for the lower Thames was the area through which exotic items must first have entered the region. These originated in other parts of Britain, and even in Europe (Barrett and Bradley 1980a). The same observation applies to the coastal basin of Wessex, where Deverel Rimbury material is equally common (Barrett and Bradley 1980b). This duality may go back to the period around 2000 bc when ceremonial centres were constructed in the landlocked areas, rather than the 'supply zone'. Although the lower Thames Valley was as suitable for settlement as the Oxford region, it seems as though little imported material was retained in this area. Perhaps the upper Thames kept its importance after henge monuments had gone out of use and possessed a higher degree of political organization than neighbouring communities. Their ability to secure exotic objects allies these groups to those in Wessex, and however we explain the links between the two areas it is clear that the Oxford region should be thought of as one part of a larger unit. The development of a major enclosure at Rams Hill may be relevant at this point, since the site recalls some of the features of earlier henge monuments, but is located for easy access from the Thames gravels and the Wessex chalk (Bradley and Ellison 1975).

Ten years after Rams Hill was excavated, the site remains enigmatic. The first enclosure had a massive ditch and an internal rampart, probably faced by a rubble wall. It is rather poorly dated, with a well preserved Collared Urn in the lower filling of the ditch but no material suitable for radiocarbon analysis. It is not clear how long such Collared Urns remained in use, but the rebuilding of this earthwork after what seems to have been a fairly short interval may have taken place as early as the 11th century bc. No Deverel Rimbury pottery was found on the site, despite its occurrence in the Lambourn cemetery only 4 km. away. It is difficult to envisage a 'missing' phase at Rams Hill, and it seems more likely that this distinctive material was excluded from sites of special status. The same could have happened at Mount Pleasant (Wainwright 1979).

Unfortunately, excavation inside this enclosure was uninformative and only one small group of post-holes could be assigned to this phase. On the other hand this area did contain residual pottery in Earlier Bronze Age fabrics. Other features were interpreted as 'root holes', on the assumption that chalk solution must have destroyed all unprotected stakeholes (Atkinson 1957). Since then, this orthodoxy has been questioned (Groube and Bowden 1982, 17), and there may be grounds for reconsidering the interpretation of these features, particularly since the published plan seems to show some regularities in their layout (Bradley and Ellison 1975, fig 2.18).

Given the links between Wessex and the upper Thames, Rams Hill could have played a strategic role in a variety of social and economic transactions, but since so many of the links between these two areas concern the burial record, it is difficult to pursue this point in detail. The particular importance of this site seems to lie in its pivotal position at the junction of two regions that might have been engaged in long distance exchange. The construction of such a massive monument may appear to form the culmination of a long period of interchange, but in fact it marks only a transitory stage in a much longer process.

c) Agricultural intensification in the later second millennium bc. The continuous consumption of wealth must have demanded the production of an agricultural surplus in order to maintain the supply of exotic objects (Bradley 1980). For this reason it can be argued that the Earlier Bronze Age, far from representing a settlement vacuum, should be marked by a vigorous attempt to increase economic flows through greater food production. The first stage of this process is probably represented by the colonization of new areas, but after some of these had proved unproductive land use seems to have intensified in regions of long-standing settlement. Both stages can perhaps be recognized in the Thames Valley and its hinterland. The first is probably marked by the settlement of the Vale of the White Horse (Bradley and Ellison 1975), and further downstream by the clearance of parts of Berkshire, north Hampshire and Surrey which are now covered by heathland. A heathland barrow at Ascot preserved a buried soil with traces of cultivation, and provided a date of 1480 ± 70 bc (Har 478; Bradley and Keith-Lucas 1975). The second stage was retrenchment within the river corridor and may account for some of the first traces of Deverel Rimbury settlement. Unfortunately there are few radiocarbon dates for this episode from the Thames Valley.

The Deverel Rimbury presence takes three forms: settlements, cemeteries and clearance horizons. Few details of the settlements are available, although a series of conjoined enclosures with a possible round house have been found at Corporation Farm, Abingdon (E. and R. Henderson pers. comm.; Barrett and Bradley 1980a, fig. 4). There are traces of similar enclosures at Thorpe in Surrey (Johnson 1975, 19–23). The Abingdon site was associated with pottery, animal burials and loom-weights, and its rather rectilinear layout might mean that originally it had been integrated with fields which no longer survive. Field systems of this date are known from the Thames corridor at Thorpe and at Mucking (Johnson 1975; Jones and Bond 1980). As well as the terrace gravels, the Abingdon site commands an area of low-lying ground, and in this respect it recalls Deverel Rimbury find-spots in the Kennet Valley. These include Brimpton, where pottery and a side-looped spearhead were found in a flood deposit (S. Lobb pers. comm.); Burghfield, where a group of pits and cylindrical loom-weights has given a radiocarbon date of 1245 ± 95 bc (BM 1594; Bradley, Lobb, Richards and Robinson 1980, 256ff.); and Pingewood, where another spread of post-holes and pits has been excavated (J. Johnson pers. comm.). The latter site was located on land with a high water table and included pottery, animal bones and loom-weights. It seems likely that these sites participated in a mixed economy which included seasonal grazing of the wetlands, and that much of the available land in the river valley was now being put to use (Bradley, Lobb, Richards and Robinson 1980). There are numerous finds of cylindrical loom-weights on the middle and lower Thames gravels, and these provide a useful clue to settlement location. By contrast, there is less sign of occupation in the Oxford area or on the Berkshire Downs.

The same distinction applies to the burial evidence, although Deverel Rimbury cemeteries do occur at Long Wittenham and Standlake in the upper Thames Valley (Leeds 1929; Riley 1947; Case and Whittle 1982, 101–2). The site at Long Wittenham also produced sherds of Collared Urn. Recent work in parts of Wessex and Sussex has suggested that such cemeteries are often located within a few hundred metres of contemporary settlements (Bradley 1981), but in the Thames Valley there has been little opportunity of exploring this relationship. The most recently discovered example of this pattern is at Basingstoke in Hampshire (T. Schadla-Hall, pers. comm.), but there are hints that this also occurred at Burghfield in the Kennet Valley (Bradley, Lobb, Richards and Robinson 1980, 286) and perhaps at Lambourn, where the cremation urns in Barrow 1 may be contemporary with some of the Bronze Age domestic debris in the ditch of the nearby long barrow (Smith 1921; Wymer 1965, 9–13).

Lastly, there are signs that the ground around earlier monuments was being cleared of vegetation at this time, perhaps in preparation for farming. Clearance layers in the Great Ouse valley date from the later second millennium (Green 1974), and the same seems to be true of a limited number of sites in the middle Thames and Kennet valleys, all of which are found within the main distribution of Deverel Rimbury ceramics (Bradley and Richards 1980). The only absolute dating evidence is a radiocarbon determination of 1090 ± 90 bc from Heron's House, Burghfield, where secondary scrub was being cleared from an earlier ring-ditch (Har 2749; Bradley and Richards 1980). There is similar evidence for clearance at Rams Hill, probably in the eleventh century bc (Bradley and Ellison 1975, 35). In addition, a ring ditch at Mount Farm, Berinsfield, may show evidence of a longer sequence of activity (G. Lambrick pers. comm.).

The importance of settlement and agriculture in the middle Thames seems to have increased as other changes happened in neighbouring regions. By the late second millennium, the power of communities on the Wessex chalk may have been in decline. Fewer rich burials were being deposited, and it seems as if the supply of fresh items was failing (Bradley 1980). Once large barrow cemeteries went out of use, areas of the downland were taken into cultivation and regular field systems seem to have developed. As the flow of materials and artefacts from outside diminished, greater reliance was placed on reorganizing food production.

The upper Thames shows similarities but also differences. Again a region which had played a major part in the settlement pattern of the early second millennium lost its dominant position as the middle and lower Thames became more important. This process seems to have started at an earlier date than it did in Wessex. The first sign of change is probably the growth of the Arreton bronze industry in the middle and lower Thames (Barrett and Bradley 1980a). Thereafter the latter areas seem to have eclipsed the upper Thames basin fairly rapidly, and by the end of the Wessex Culture fewer imported objects travelled upstream. The material which had originally found its way into the Oxford region was now confined to the lower reaches of the river. The essential difference between Wessex and the Thames Valley, however, is that the movement of wealth into central southern England seems to have diminished altogether, whilst it entered the lower Thames on a greater scale. Such a change is not easy to explain, but one important factor may have been the greater fertility of the latter area, especially compared with Wessex (Bradley 1980). This meant that economic growth could continue here, whereas the constant wasting of the heathlands of south Wessex may have proved disastrous.

Later Bronze Age developments

We have reached the transition between the Earlier and Later Bronze Ages. In the second millennium bc, the upper Thames Valley had seen ceremonial centres, burial mounds and rich graves. Most of the wealth items were deposited with the dead, and this area may have dominated its hinterland partly through its links with Wessex and that area's tradition of complex burials. In the early first millennium the pattern changed decisively. None of these monuments remained in use, and some were soon ploughed out. Pottery styles changed completely; there were no burials with grave goods, and by this time the rich metalwork was deposited in rivers.

The evidence of metalwork

At first sight these changes seem to confirm popular ideas of the Bronze Age sequence. After the disuse of Deverel Rimbury pottery, a period seems to ensue in which settlements and ceramics are extremely uncommon, and metal finds dominate the available evidence (cf. Burgess 1969). More recent work on the chronology of first-millennium pottery has shown that this view is unjustified (Barrett 1980a), but even so it is understandable how the metalwork did appear to assume a more central role in this period.

Even at the most superficial level, the distribution of evidence appears to document major shifts in the settlement pattern (Map 6). Many of the Earlier Bronze Age barrows were in the uplands (Map 5), whilst the majority of Later Bronze Age metalwork comes from lower ground, with a great concentration around the rivers. It has already been shown that the earlier distribution is deceptive and that subsequent disturbance has created the distinction between round barrows and ring-ditches (Map 5). It is harder to appreciate that the metal distribution may be just as misleading.

The metalwork of this period is usually divided into four categories: single finds, settlement finds, hoards, and river finds. This evidence is very ill-balanced. The only settlement finds from the Oxford region are three items from Rams Hill (Bradley and Ellison 1975, 88–9), and one from Weathercock Hill (Bowden, Ford and Gaffney 1983), although other possible examples are known from Wayland's Smithy (Atkinson 1965) and from Wallingford, where a Late Bronze Age occupation site is eroding into the Thames (Collins 1949; Wymer 1960). The character of settlement finds is understood fairly well and for the most part these consist of small objects, dominated by personal equipment like pins (Needham and Burgess 1980). The other deposits are quite different and need not be regarded as evidence of domestic activity, the main exceptions being the so-called scrap hoards, some of which may represent the remains of foundries. The single finds from the Oxford area are uninformative, whilst the high proportion of complete weapons discovered in the rivers distinguishes this material from other types of deposit (cf. Ehrenberg 1977 and 1980). The reasons for these differences will be considered shortly, but the important point is that many of these finds must have entered the archaeological record as deliberate deposits. For this reason the distribution of metalwork need not represent the full extent of the settled landscape. To take one example from the edge of this region, there is clear evidence from excavations and chance finds that settlement on the Kennet gravels was increasing in intensity throughout the earlier first millennium, but there is very little metalwork from the same area. If anything, the rate of deposition was inversely related to the scale of settlement (Bradley, Lobb, Richards and Robinson 1980,

292). Map 6 therefore maps the distribution of rather specialized, if easily dated deposits.

Apart from the domestic finds already mentioned, two types of deposit are important. Very little is known about the hoards of the Oxford region, not all of which are adequately provenanced. Tool hoards in particular may be connected with the operation of foundries, perhaps in the vicinity of settlements. There are five possible hoards from Oxfordshire, two of which, those from Burgesses Meadow and Leopold Street, Oxford, include pieces made in the same mould. Here at least we find evidence of a smith at work (Rowlands 1976, 252–3).

The other main group consists of river finds. Here two observations can be made. It is clear that these deposits first entered the archaeological record in any number as the Wessex grave series came to an end. The rapiers found in the Thames were the direct successors of the daggers of the previous phase, which had been deposited with burials. Indeed, the Snowshill daggers found in the river at Sandford-on-Thames represent a transitional find (Gerloff 1975, 246), as does an Acton Park dagger from the river between Abingdon and Sutton Courtenay (Thomas 1978). After 1200 bc about the only skeletal material demonstrably of Bronze Age date comes from Dorchester-on-Thames and includes a human pelvis pierced by a metal spearhead (Ehrenberg 1977, 37). This can hardly be considered as a normal burial. We might suggest that the deposition of these weapons in the rivers was partly the result of a new type of funerary ritual (Bradley 1982). There are numerous examples of fine metalwork from Oxfordshire rivers, but two particular discoveries are worth mentioning here. One is a recently discovered shield from Long Wittenham which had again been pierced by a spear before it was placed in the river (Needham 1979). The second find came from Shipton-upon-Cherwell and consisted of a complete cauldron (Leeds 1930). Such cauldrons may have been used in feasting and it is likely that this was another 'high status' find. Elaborate river deposits seem to be grouped around confluences (Map 6), and it will be worth checking whether this is a result of dredging.

In another sense, the evidence from the Oxford region *does* give some clue to the character of settlement. Despite the high proportion of 'water finds' in Map 6, their absolute number is fairly limited, compared with finds from further downstream (Barrett and Bradley 1980a). Also, the number of river finds falls between the Middle and Late Bronze Ages (Ehrenberg 1980), and by the latter period most of the metalwork comes from Greater London. This effect may be enhanced by dredging, but it is by no means created by this process. In fact the changing number of river finds roughly matches the density of settlement sites within the river corridor, although the character of these deposits makes it most unlikely that they were accidental losses (cf. Barrett and Bradley 1980a; Needham and Burgess 1980).

At this larger scale the Oxford region occupied an increasingly peripheral position in relation to the middle and lower Thames. Although there are some signs of domestic activity, mainly in the form of pottery, the most extensive settlement evidence comes from the lower reaches of the river, the Berkshire Downs, and the Kennet gravels. To some extent the rarity of metal finds in this area may be because this region was dependent on an outside source of supply, but here it is necessary to draw a sharp distinction between high status occupation sites, which might well have been involved in the consumption and deposition of fine metalwork, and those lower ranking communities which were less radically affected by change. Having moved the emphasis away from the more elaborate metalwork, let us turn to the settlement evidence.

Settlement evidence

The clearest signs of continuity come from the Berkshire Downs, where Later Bronze Age occupation sites have been excavated at Beedon Manor Farm, Rams Hill, Weathercock Hill, and Wittenham Clumps (J. Richards pers. comm.; Bradley and Ellison 1975; Bowden, Ford and Gaffney 1983; Hingley 1980). On parts of the Wessex chalk it appears that remarkably regular field systems were now developing in the areas around the main barrow groups. In Berkshire the best dating evidence comes from Stancombe Down where part of a very large field system apparently respected a round barrow containing a late Early Bronze Age razor, whilst the field groups closer to Lambourn completely avoided the main burial sites, although they may not necessarily be of prehistoric date (Bradley and Ellison, chapters 5 and 6). The direct evidence for the extension of cultivation comes from only three sites: a field system at Streatley Warren (J. Richards pers. comm.); the chambered tomb at Wayland's Smithy, which was disturbed by later agricultural activity (Atkinson 1965); and the hill-top enclosure at Rams Hill (Bradley and Ellison 1975, 65). In each case the fields date from the latter part of the Bronze Age. Otherwise their chronology depends on their relationship with boundary ditches, which occasionally seem to cut the field earthworks. Most of these boundaries have now been investigated and current work suggests that the system as a whole was established by the end of this period (S. Ford in prep.; Bradley and Ellison 1975, 185).

There is less evidence for land division on the Thames gravels, although there are signs of some kind of boundary system at Mount Farm, Berinsfield (G. Lambrick pers. comm.). Its full extent is uncertain but parts of a similar system overlie the Dorchester-on-Thames cursus. It is possible that a fragmentary field system at Northfield Farm, Long Wittenham, also belongs to this period (Thomas 1980). It is known to predate Roman activity on the same site and is loosely associated with 'Bronze Age' pottery (Gray 1977, 4ff. and 20). Paired ditches like those at Mount Farm are known at Burghfield on the Kennet gravels, where they probably date from the ninth century bc (Bradley,

Lobb, Richards and Robinson 1980, 263).

The settlements contemporary with these fields are not known in much detail. On the chalk a small part of an unenclosed settlement at Beedon Manor Farm contained a round house, and a working area from which flint nodules were being quarried, but there is no information on the economic character of the site (J. Richards pers. comm.). Pits have been found on the upper Thames gravels, notably at Appleford (Hinchliffe and Thomas 1980), but at present more is known about contemporary settlements on the Kennet gravels (Bradley, Lobb, Richards and Robinson 1980). Here there are further round houses, one example at Burghfield having a radiocarbon date of 870 ± 110 bc (BM 1596). The sites in this area are also characterized by pits and waterholes. The pits at Aldermaston Wharf have been analysed in detail. They are dated between 1100 and 800 bc and seem to have been used mainly for storing grain. Large amounts of carbonized wheat and barley were recovered in excavation, and some of the pits seem to have possessed a special lining of fired clay (Bradley, Lobb, Richards and Robinson 1980, 221). The density of pits on sites in the river valley far exceeds that on downland sites of the same period. The waterholes are mainly a feature of a nearby site at Knights Farm, Burghfield, which was occupied between about 1250 and 550 bc. The site was located in an area of seasonally waterlogged ground, and analysis of the environmental evidence from two of these features confirms their identification as ponds, but also suggests that they were located in an area predominantly of pasture. The sites in the Kennet Valley occupy a series of contrasting locations and were probably able to make use of all the land in this area, ranging from the floodplain to the best arable soils on the higher ground (Bradley, Lobb, Richards and Robinson 1980). Further downstream, possible wells have been identified in a Late Bronze Age occupation site at Furze Platt, which also provided evidence of pits and round houses (Lobb 1980).

The one completely excavated settlement was at Aldermaston Wharf (Bradley, Lobb, Richards and Robinson 1980, 219ff.), and this gives some indication of the arrangements which might also have existed on the Thames gravels. Indeed, there is some similarity between the Aldermaston site and a settlement, possibly of this period, at Standlake (Riley 1947). There was a pair of post-built houses at Aldermaston, each accompanied by two clusters of storage pits of contrasting character. Each 'household cluster' was associated with the same range of artefacts, but one contained a higher proportion of fine pottery than the other. It also had a greater volume of pits. The settlement seems to have made use of the freely draining terraces of the Kennet, and also of the river floodplain, which may have assumed its present form during this period. Textile production was very important in the Kennet Valley, whilst bronze objects of uncertain character were also being made at Aldermaston. Both activities seem to be largely confined to the river gravels.

It is precisely because settlement on the gravels differs from that on the chalk that the relationship between the two areas becomes so important. Apart from these hints of regional specialization, sites on the gravels could have produced or stored more grain. It was also in the latter area that fine metalwork was freely discarded. By contrast, linear ditches are a feature of the chalk. At the upper level of the settlement hierarchy these contrasts become more evident.

In the uplands it is possible to suggest two types of evidence for change: the development of major defended enclosures and the imposition of boundary ditches on the less differentiated pattern of Celtic fields. The first point needs particularly careful analysis, since the discussion involves complicated matters of chronology. Although it is possible to invoke a Bronze Age origin for a number of hill-top sites around the edge of the Wessex chalkland, their defences may have developed only later (Barrett and Bradley 1980b, 201). The same seems to have happened on the Chilterns (Needham and Burgess 1980, fig. 4). The recognition of 'early' hill-forts is not particularly helpful in itself, since such earthworks may have been built in two phases, between about 1050 and 800 bc and between 600 and 450 bc, the latter group overlapping the start of the Iron Age (Burgess 1980, 273). At present only two Oxfordshire sites can be placed in the first group, the inner enclosure at Rams Hill and Chastleton Camp on the Cotswolds, whilst the other earthwork at Rams Hill, together with other hill-top settlements on the Wessex downland, seems to belong to the later period (Leeds 1931; Bradley and Ellison 1975). It does not follow that the functions of both groups were the same, and at Rams Hill nearly all the excavated buildings have been assigned to a period of occupation in between these two defensive phases, albeit on tenuous evidence.

Virtually nothing is known about the interior of Chastleton Camp, and the Rams Hill enclosure itself is unusual, if not unique, in being an adaptation of a still earlier earthwork, apparently constructed during the late Wessex Culture. There are no radiocarbon dates for the first enclosure, but it was probably in the eleventh century bc that its rampart was rebuilt with a timber front face. This seems to be the earliest box rampart in Britain, although the very early dates could result from the use of heartwood and now need independent confirmation. There is little evidence for the function of Rams Hill at this time, but after the rampart had started to decay it was probably supplemented by two palisades constructed over the partly filled ditch. At this stage the enclosure became a settlement of some pretension, with round houses, internal fences and an array of four-post buildings. There are eleventh-century dates for this phase too, but the narrow spread of all but one of the dates from the site may result from the reuse of timbers taken from the box rampart. The metalwork from Rams Hill does not compare with the rich finds from the Thames Valley, but there is some reason to suppose that this site was of special character. It contains a series of buildings suitable for storing grain (cf. Gent 1983), yet the absence of querns suggests that cereals were not being consumed here. Close connections with other sites are also suggested by the presence of a number of stones occurring naturally in the Vale of the White Horse or on the Corallian limestone. The reasons for their introduction are unknown.

The linear ditches are equally important, and recent work has favoured a date for those on the Berkshire Downs as late as the 8th century BC (S. Ford in prep.). We know very little about their function. All that is certain is that their construction must have involved a considerable dislocation to existing patterns of settlement. Indeed, it is likely that this rearrangement influenced the siting of certain of the Late Bronze Age/Early Iron Age hill-forts. Although the Rams Hill report did not reach any conclusion on the function of these ditches, some new evidence can be considered. The fact that they were built towards the end of the Bronze Age sequence means that they are little, if at all, earlier than the first hill-forts on the chalk – their construction may be part of the same processes of political change as these defended centres. The linear ditches also appear to define a series of distinct valley-based land units (Ford 1983). It is apparent that the line of the Berkshire Grim's Ditch corresponds with a major change in the styles of latest Bronze Age pottery (Barrett 1980b, fig. 3), and may have formed the boundary between two different groups (Ford 1982). The hill-forts possibly followed the same division. At the same time there may be evidence of a connection between the building of linear boundaries and environmental changes on the downland. This cannot be proved, but the dates now available for the Berkshire ditches fall within the period when open grassland was first established on the ridge top, as reflected by the molluscan sequences at Wayland's Smithy and Rams Hill, and also by land snails from the Grim's Ditch itself (Bradley and Ellison 1975, 217–8; Bowden in Ford 1982). This need not imply a general emphasis on pastoral farming, but it could indicate some measure of economic specialization to balance the changes already suggested for the gravels.

In the latter area it is even harder to locate the upper levels of the settlement hierarchy, although one clue is provided by the riverine distribution of fine metalwork, much of it of exotic origin. For other indications of the likely character of such sites it is necessary to turn our attention to areas further downstream. Two classes of higher ranking site have been suggested in the middle and lower Thames, the part of the river valley where imported material was being consumed in greatest quantity. First, there is the discovery of a rich settlement at Egham which seems to have controlled the movement of prestige goods along the river (Needham and Longley 1980). Excavation of this site has revealed the remains of the Bronze Age river frontage and has brought to light a remarkable concentration of fine pottery and continental metalwork. The excavators have drawn attention to finds from the middle Thames which might indicate the presence of similar sites. In the Oxford area it is possible that another high status settlement is eroding into the Thames at Wallingford. Very limited investigations have found several bronzes and even a tiny piece of gold (Collins 1949; Wymer 1960), whilst the river itself has produced a substantial series of artefacts. The dating of this site still presents some difficulties, but it is worth noting that it is well placed to control riverine traffic close to the territorial boundary marked by the Berkshire Grim's Ditch.

The second class of monument has recently been described by Champion (1980) and consists of a series of small circular enclosures, sometimes containing one major round house. The most extensively excavated of these sites are at Mucking (Jones and Bond 1980), Thwing (Manby 1980, 321) and West Harling (Clark and Fell 1953). Although these were once thought to be Iron Age sites, a substantially earlier date is now established. Several of these earthworks are associated with evidence of metalworking. For example, weapons were being made at Mucking. There also seems to be evidence of feasting at Thwing.

Until recently, it seemed that no sites of this type were known further up the Thames than Surrey, but it seems possible that another example once existed near the confluence of the Thames and the Kennet. This site, at Marshall's Hill, Reading, was first published as a disc barrow (L.A.G. 1927) and was later dated to the Iron Age (Seaby 1932). The associated pottery could well be Late Bronze Age, and a bronze socketed knife and a spearhead have both been found nearby. Not long ago, the writer drew attention to the apparent contradiction between the signs of intensive agriculture and craft production in the Kennet Valley and the deposition of weaponry in the Thames at Reading (Bradley, Lobb, Richards and Robinson 1980, 292–3). Marshall's Hill overlooks both of these areas and it is particularly tempting to suggest that this site was of some importance. It is possible that another important settlement may have existed close to the Thames at Moulsford. A ditch containing Late Bronze Age occupation debris has been investigated at the site, which is also the find-spot of a Middle Bronze Age torc (Wymer 1961).

Epilogue

To sum up. In the Later Bronze Age the richest communities seem to have been those along the river corridor. They were well placed to control the movement of fine metalwork and may even have been involved in its deposition in the river. Most of the settlements known so far are less remarkable and seem to have been engaged in agricultural production and the making of textiles. It is tempting to see a reciprocal relationship developing between these two patterns, in which an elite who were able to control riverine traffic in prestige goods might have been receiving tribute from a wider hinterland. The settlement of the chalk may belong within the same framework. Here there is less evidence for the consumption of wealth, although the distinctive character of the latest Bronze Age settlement pattern perhaps carries hints of regional specialization. As in the Earlier Bronze Age, a site like Rams Hill must have been perfectly located for long distance exchange with the communities controlling the Thames waterway. Indeed, this enclosure could have channelled exchange at one outlet, just as the site at Wallingford could have done at another point. Both sites were possibly located on the same territorial boundary. This reconstruction is very speculative, but once again it implies that communities in the Oxford area did not exist in isolation.

Taking a still broader perspective, we can observe that the Later Bronze Age pattern is almost the mirror image of the Earlier Bronze Age scheme. This time the lower Thames dominates the upper Thames and the Wessex chalkland is reduced to a rather peripheral area whose inhabitants may have engaged in exchange with more powerful groups who dominated the river corridor. A key to this system could have been control over the distribution of fine metalwork. As long as bronze technology retained its high status, exchange between lowland and highland Britain, and between the Thames Valley and the continent, would remain very basic patterns. The Oxford area had only a limited role to play in this arrangement.

This paper could well end with that statement, for it is an open invitation to carry the story on into the Early Iron Age. That temptation will be resisted, but one final contrast must be considered if we are to look at this region in a wider context; for in the Early Iron Age the upper Thames Valley does see a massive increase in the evidence of human activity. To some extent this may have come about with the final collapse of the bronze trade, but it was not iron technology itself that was to be so important: rather, it was the reshaping of exchange relations that allowed such rapid growth in this area and finally freed local communities from a dependence on outside groups which had become increasingly rigid (cf. Thomas in prep.). With the rise of Wessex and the Upper Thames during the Early Iron Age, history came close to repeating itself, and more than a millennium after the flowering of the Wessex Culture we are practically back where we started.

Acknowledgements

It will be evident from the bibliography that much of this material was originally published jointly with a number of colleagues, in particular John Barrett and Julian Richards. The distribution maps (Maps 5 and 6) were compiled by Mike Heaton from the county Sites and Monuments Record at Woodstock and were drawn initially by Mark Bowden. They have been prepared for publication by Mélanie Steiner.

Bibliography

Atkinson, R.J.C. (1953) 'Excavations in Barrow Hills Field, Radley, Berks. in 1944', *Oxoniensia* 13, 1–14

Atkinson, R.J.C. (1957) 'Worms and weathering', *Antiquity* 31, 219–33

Atkinson, R.J.C. (1965) 'Wayland's Smithy', *Antiquity* 39, 126–33

Barrett, J. (1980a) 'The pottery of the Later Bronze Age in lowland England', *Proc. Prehist. Soc.* 46, 297–319

Barrett, J. (1980b) 'The evolution of Later Bronze Age settlement', in *Settlement and Society in the British Later Bronze Age*, eds. J. Barrett & R. Bradley, 77–100

Barrett, J. and Bradley, R. (1980a) 'The Later Bronze Age in the Thames Valley', in *Settlement and Society in the British Later Bronze Age*, eds. J. Barrett & R. Bradley, 247–69

Barrett, J. and Bradley, R. (1980b) 'The Later Bronze Age in South Wessex and Cranborne Chase', in *Settlement and Society in the British Later Bronze Age*, eds. J. Barrett & R. Bradley, 181–208

Barrett, J., Bradley, R., Green, M. and Lewis, B. (1981) 'The earlier prehistoric settlement of Cranborne Chase: the first results of current fieldwork', *Antiq. J.* 61, 203–37

Bowden, M., Ford, S. and Gaffney, V. (1983) 'A Late Bronze Age site on Weathercock Hill, Lambourn, Berkshire', *Recent Archaeology in Berkshire*, 32–4

Bowler, D. and Robinson, M. (1980) 'Two round barrows at King's Weir, Wytham, Oxon.', *Oxoniensia* 45, 1–8

Bradley, R. (1980) 'Subsistence, exchange and technology – a social framework for the Bronze Age in Southern England c. 1400–700 bc', in *Settlement and Society in the British Later Bronze Age*, eds. J. Barrett & R. Bradley, 57–75

Bradley, R. (1981) 'Various styles of urn-cemeteries and settlement in Southern England c. 1400–1000 bc', in *The Archaeology of Death*, eds. R. Chapman, I. Kinnes & K. Randsborg, 93–104

Bradley, R. (1982) 'The destruction of wealth in later prehistory', *Man* 18, 108–22

Bradley, R. (1984) *The Social Foundations of Prehistoric Britain*

Bradley, R. and Ellison, A. (1975) *Rams Hill – A Bronze Age Defended Enclosure and its Landscape*

Bradley, R. and Keith-Lucas, M. (1975) 'Excavation and pollen analysis on a bell barrow at Ascot, Berkshire', *J. Archaeol. Science* 2, 95–108

Bradley, R., Lobb, S., Richards, J. and Robinson, M. (1980) 'Two Late Bronze Age settlements on the Kennet gravels – excavations at Aldermaston Wharf and Knight's Farm, Burghfield, Berkshire', *Proc. Prehist. Soc.* 46, 217–95

Bradley, R. and Richards, J. (1980) 'The excavation of two ring-ditches at Heron's House, Burghfield', *Berks. Archaeol. J.* 70, 1–7

Burgess, C. (1969) 'Chronology and terminology in the British Bronze Age', *Antiq. J.* 49, 22–29

Burgess, C. (1980) 'The Bronze Age in Wales', in *Culture and Environment in Prehistoric Wales*, ed. J.A. Taylor, 243–86

Burl, A. (1976) *The Stone Circles of the British Isles*

Case, H. (1956) 'The Lambourn Seven Barrows', *Berks. Archaeol. J.* 55, 15–31

Case, H. (1963) 'Notes . . . on ring-ditches in the Oxford region', *Oxoniensia* 28, 19–53

Case, H., Steele, S., Avery, G. and Sutermeister, H. (1965) 'Excavations at City Farm, Hanborough, Oxon.', *Oxoniensia* 29/30, 1–98

Case, H. and Whittle, A., eds. (1982) *Settlement Patterns in the Oxford Region: Excavations at the Abingdon Causewayed Enclosure and Other Sites*

Champion, T. (1980) 'Settlement and environment in Later Bronze Age Kent', in *Settlement and Society in the British Later Bronze Age*, eds. J. Barrett & R. Bradley, 223–43

Clark, J.D.G. and Fell, C. (1953) 'The Early Iron Age site at Micklemoor Hill, West Harling, Norfolk and its pottery', *Proc. Prehist. Soc.* 19, 1–40

Collins, A.E.P. (1949) 'Bronzes and pottery from Wallingford', *Berks. Archaeol. J.* 51, 65.

Ehrenberg, M. (1977) *Bronze Age Spearheads from Berkshire, Buckinghamshire and Oxfordshire*

Ehrenberg, M. (1980) 'The occurrence of Bronze Age metalwork in the Thames: an investigation', *Trans. London and Middlesex Archaeol. Soc.* 31, 1–15

Fleming, A. (1971) 'Territorial patterns in Bronze Age Wessex', *Proc. Prehist. Soc.* 37(1), 138–66

Ford, S. (1982) 'Excavation and fieldwork on the Berkshire Grim's Ditch', *Oxoniensia* 47, 13–36

Ford, S. (1983) 'Berkshire Downs linear earthwork project', in *Recent Archaeology in Berkshire*, 27

G.L.A. (1927) 'Discovery of a disc barrow', *Berks., Bucks. and Oxon. Archaeol. J.* 31, 72

Gent, H. (1983) 'Centralised storage in later prehistoric Britain', *Proc. Prehist. Soc.* 49, 243–67

Gerloff, S. (1975) *The Early Bronze Age Daggers in Great Britain*

Gray, M. (1977) 'Northfield Farm, Long Wittenham', *Oxoniensia* 42, 1–29

Green, H.S. (1974) 'Early Bronze Age burial, territory and population in Milton Keynes, Buckinghamshire and the Great Ouse Valley', *Archaeol. J.* 131, 75–139

Green, H.S. (1980) *The Flint Arrowheads of the British Isles*

Greenwell, W. (1890) 'Recent researches on barrows in Yorkshire, Wiltshire, Berkshire etc.', *Archaeologia* 52, 1–72

Grinsell, L.V. (1935) 'An analysis and list of Berkshire barrows: part 1', *Berks. Archaeol. J.* 39, 171–91

Grinsell, L.V. (1936) 'An analysis and list of Berkshire barrows: part 2', *Berks. Archaeol. J.* 40, 20–58

Groube, L. and Bowden, M. (1982) *The Archaeology of Rural Dorset*

Harden, D. and Treweeks, R.C. (1945) 'Excavations at Stanton Harcourt, Oxon., 1940', *Oxoniensia* 10, 16–41

Harding, D. (1972) *The Iron Age in the Upper Thames Basin*

Hinchliffe, J. and Thomas, R. (1980) 'Archaeological investigations at Appleford', *Oxoniensia* 45, 9–111

Hingley, R. (1980) 'Excavations by R.A. Rutland on an Iron Age site at Wittenham Clumps', *Berks. Archaeol. J.* 70, 21–55

Johnson, B. (1975) *Archaeology and the M25*

Jones, M.U. and Bond, D. (1980) 'Later Bronze Age settlement at Mucking, Essex', in *Settlement and Society in the British Later Bronze Age*, eds. J. Barrett & R. Bradley, 471–82

Lambrick, G. (1983) *The Rollright Stones*

Leeds, E.T. (1929) 'Bronze Age urns from Long Wittenham', *Antiq. J.* 9, 153–4

Leeds, E.T. (1930) 'A bronze cauldron from the River Cherwell, Oxfordshire, with notes on cauldrons and other vessels of allied type', *Archaeologia* 80, 1–36

Leeds, E.T. (1931) 'Chastleton Camp, Oxfordshire: a hill fort of the Early Iron Age', *Antiq. J.* 11, 399–404

Leeds, E.T. (1938) 'Further excavations in Barrow Hills Field, Radley, Berks.', *Oxoniensia* 3, 31–40

Lobb, S. (1980) 'Notes from the Wessex Archaeological Committee', *Berks. Archaeol. J.* 70, 9–20

Manby, T.G. (1980) 'Bronze Age settlement in Eastern Yorkshire', in *Settlement and Society in the British Later Bronze Age*, eds. J. Barrett & R. Bradley, 307–70

Needham, S. (1979) 'Two recent British shield finds and their continental parallels', *Proc. Prehist. Soc.* 45, 111–34

Needham, S. and Burgess, C. (1980) 'The Later Bronze Age in the Lower Thames Valley: the metalwork evidence', in *Settlement and Society in the British Later Bronze Age*, eds. J. Barrett & R. Bradley, 437–69

Needham, S. and Longley, D. (1980) 'Runnymede Bridge, Egham: a Late Bronze Age riverside settlement', in *Settlement and Society in the British Later Bronze Age*, eds. J. Barrett & R. Bradley, 397–436

Palmer, N. (1980) 'A Beaker burial and medieval tenements in The Hamel, Oxford', *Oxoniensia* 45, 124–225

Parrington, M. (1978) *The Excavation of an Iron Age Settlement, Bronze Age Ring Ditches and Roman Features at Ashville Trading Estate, Abingdon (Oxfordshire), 1974–6*

Renfrew, C. (1973) 'Monuments, mobilisation and social organisation in Neolithic Wessex', in *The Explanation of Culture Change*, ed. C. Renfrew, 539–58

Richards, J.C. (1978) *The Archaeology of the Berkshire Downs – an Introductory Survey*

Riley, D.N. (1947) 'A Late Bronze Age and Iron Age site at Standlake Downs, Oxon.', *Oxoniensia* 11/12, 26–43

Rowlands, M.J. (1976) *The Production and Distribution of Metalwork in the Middle Bronze Age in Southern Britain*

Seaby, W.A. (1932) 'Some pre-Roman remains from south Reading', *Berks. Archaeol. J.* 36, 121–5

Smith, R.A. (1921) 'The Seven Barrows at Lambourn', *Archaeol. J.* 78, 47–54

Thomas, R. (1978) 'Three Bronze Age implements from the Thames', *Oxoniensia* 43, 246–8

Thomas, R. (1980) 'A Bronze Age field system at Northfield Farm?', *Oxoniensia* 45, 310–11

Thomas, R. (in prep.) 'The bronze-iron transition in southern England'

Wainwright, G.J. (1979) *Mount Pleasant, Dorset. Excavations 1970–71*

Whittle, A. (1981) 'Later Neolithic society in Britain: a realignment', in *Astronomy and Society 4000–1500 BC*, eds. C. Ruggles & A. Whittle, 297–342

Williams, A. (1948) 'Excavations in Barrow Hills Field, Radley, Berks., 1944–5', *Oxoniensia* 13, 14–35

Wymer, J. (1960) 'Archaeological notes from Reading Museum', *Berks. Archaeol. J.* 58, 52–64

Wymer, J. (1961) 'The discovery of a gold torc at Moulsford', *Berks. Archaeol. J.* 59, 36–7

Wymer, J. (1965) 'Excavations of the Lambourn long barrow, 1964', *Berks. Archaeol. J.* 62, 1–16

THE IRON AGE

DAVID MILES

Introduction

The Oxford Region has been in the forefront of British Iron Age studies since the pioneering work of Stephen Stone at Standlake in the 1850s. The area is not noted, with a few exceptions, for its spectacular sites but as Stone emphasized, 'if the acquisition of knowledge be more his (the antiquary's) object than the acquisition of wealth, he may perchance reap a rich harvest here.' (Stone 1957, 99). The region presents considerable potential for the student of pre- and protohistory. It has contrasting landscapes within a limited area: limestone dip-slopes and ridges, broad clay vales, gravel terraces, tributary valleys and chalk downlands offer varying environmental niches and resources. Alkaline soils provide good conditions for the preservation of animal bones and mollusca; waterlogged deposits in the valleys and in the perched water tables below the gravel terraces allow the recovery of organic artefacts and biological evidence. The Thames Valley is prolific in late prehistoric cropmarks and is, from the air, one of the most thoroughly surveyed parts of the British Isles (Benson & Miles 1974; Hingley 1981a). Centuries of ploughing have flattened most of the upstanding remains of prehistoric settlement in the Thames Valley and more recently on the uplands. Ironically this arable farming allows many buried sites to be located by fieldwalking (but for the problems see Miles 1983). The region is also an interesting one culturally and politically, forming as it does a traditional frontier or boundary zone between Central and Southern England.

Because of the favourable conditions for the recovery of archaeological evidence and the central location of Britain's oldest university, large quantities of Iron Age data are available. Unfortunately much of this has been recovered piecemeal, in difficult circumstances, and is often of limited value. Aerial photography, fieldwalking, excavation and environmental sampling have all been biased towards the gravel terraces of the Thames and its major tributaries. In contrast the Cotswolds, north Oxfordshire and the Chilterns have seen little archaeological investigation.

In the predecessor of this volume Humphrey Case wrote, 'The Iron Age saw a colonization of the region by new-comers probably late in the fourth century BC as abrupt as that of the Beaker people, but farther reaching; for their culture, as reflected in pottery, carried all before it. . . . The culture of these newcomers, and perhaps of others still to be recognized, became that of the existing population, and in time the later Iron Age A culture of the region settled down to a fair and rustic uniformity, and is traceable until the Roman Conquest' (Case 1954, 81).

Since 1954 attitudes and fashions have developed in archaeology. The invasion hypothesis, promoted by pseudo-historical models, can no longer be maintained as the exclusive or even major explanation of change; the chronology of the Iron Age has been extended thanks to radiocarbon dating; interpretations of ceramic assemblages and other artefacts are more circumspect. The Iron Age can now be seen not as a static and uniform period but one which witnessed periodic if not constant social change within a complex agricultural landscape (Jones 1981, 116–9).

The Oxford Region is unusual and fortunate in having two major studies of the Iron Age devoted to it. It is neither necessary nor desirable, therefore, for this paper to repeat the detailed evidence which can conveniently be consulted in them. Dr. D.W. Harding's *The Iron Age in the Upper Thames Basin* (1972) describes the regional background and synthesizes the evidence that was available in the early 1970s. The invasion hypothesis looms large in Dr. Harding's book, supported for the most part by his study of the pottery accumulated over several decades in salvage excavations, but mostly lacking detailed stratified contexts. In 1972 the evidence of settlements, structures and subsistence was meagre. In the following decade knowledge of the Iron Age was transformed in several respects. However, with regard to hillforts or defended enclosures little advance has been made in the region since the small-scale research campaigns of the 1930s, 50s and 60s (Harding 1972, 45–60; Harding 1976).

Following the publication of *The Upper Thames Valley: an archaeological survey of the river gravels* (Benson & Miles 1974) and the formation of the Oxford Archaeological Unit, more systematic attempts have been made to pursue specific research designs and problems within the context of rescue excavation. The dependence upon Department of Environment rescue funding has generated an even greater bias towards the gravel terraces as far as excavation is concerned (10 out of 12, or 84%, in the 1970s), but this has in some small part been counteracted by survey projects and sample excavations on the Thames floodplain, the Corallian ridge south-west of Oxford and the Cotswold slopes (Hingley & Miles 1984; Lambrick 1981a; Hingley 1980b). The most recent summary of current work can be found in the collection of papers entitled *Aspects of the Iron Age in Central Southern Britain* (Cunliffe & Miles 1984) which contrasts research in the Upper Thames with that in Wessex.

In the Thames Valley the emphasis has been placed on the large-scale excavation of well-preserved settlements of differing forms and functions in as wide a variety of environmental niches as possible. There has been a move away from the concept of the type-site towards the reconstruction of socio-economic systems. Much emphasis has been placed on the systematic recovery of biological evidence in order to investigate the nature of Iron Age subsistence and the environmental background. Increasingly 'the site' becomes difficult to define both spatially and as a concept. In the Iron Age the landscape as a whole was utilized; settlements and activity areas become increasingly inter-dependent.

In a brief review such as this it would be desirable to operate within a clear-cut chronological framework. Unfortunately there are at present relatively few radiocarbon dates available and some of these are not consistent with other forms of evidence (e.g. Parrington 1978, 39). Instead a deliberately loose tripartite scheme of Early, Middle and Late Iron Age is generally adopted. The introduction of iron is logically the beginning of this period; in practice this is an event or more properly a process which cannot, on specific sites, usually be recognized. Increasingly at hillforts and other settlements the distinction between the Late Bronze Age and Early Iron Age is blurred. In general terms however, the Early Iron Age is dated *c.* 800/700 BC to *c.* 400 BC. The Middle Iron Age, for which in Oxfordshire the evidence is at present most prolific, runs up to *c.* 100 BC. The Late Iron Age, the first century BC until the Roman Conquest, sees the bow wave of Continental and Roman influence affecting Southern Britain and is still sometimes, though unsatisfactorily, referred to as the Belgic period.

The Environment

There is patchy but increasing evidence for the character of the Iron Age landscape and the impact of human communities upon it. Previous papers (see Bradley in this volume) have emphasized the importance of ceremonial centres and the conspicuous consumption of prestige metalwork in the Neolithic and Bronze Age. About the 8th century BC, around the period traditionally regarded as the late Bronze Age or Early Iron Age, the emphasis of society appears to have taken on a different direction. Farming settlements become more numerous, and increasingly more specialized. A wider variety of soil types was utilized for agriculture, particularly less tractable soils, and in the Thames Valley woodland occupied only limited areas. The increasing importance of agricultural land and control over it must be seen against a background of population growth and slightly deteriorating climate.

Climatologists (Turner 1981; Lamb 1981) have postulated a sequence of climatic deterioration in the first millennium BC, with conditions generally becoming colder by about 2°C and wetter. This would have shortened the growing season by about five weeks. Opinions differ as to the impact of these worsening climatic conditions from the catastrophic school (summarized by Mercer 1981, xviii-xix) to those who would see the impact as slight (Robinson 1984, 7-8). It should be remembered that the climatic conditions in the Iron Age would not have been very different from those of today. In the Upper Thames region the response to this adversity seems to be increasing agricultural intensification. The slightly increased wetness may have actually proved to be an advantage on gravel terraces and a floodplain whose main summer problems may have been draughtiness.

In the Thames Valley forest clearance seems to have been extensive during the Neolithic and Bronze Age. On the floodplain and first terrace, at Port Meadow, Oxford and Mingie's Ditch, Hardwick (alongside the River Windrush), the lack of preserved organic material or gleyed soils in early first millennium contexts suggests that this low-lying land was dry. During the course of the Iron Age there is, however, increasing evidence for seasonal flooding and by the late Iron Age for the deposition of alluvium (Robinson 1984; Lambrick & Robinson 1979). Robinson has emphasized that alluviation in the Thames Valley, like colluviation on the chalk downland (Bell 1981, 1982), should be regarded not simply as the result of climatic deterioration but, more importantly, as stimulated by the impact of man. The clearance of forest on the higher ground combined with the increasing trend towards winter-sown arable land would result in greater run-off from the hills and increased sediment load in the drainage system (Goudie 1981, 128). The deposition of alluvium has important connotations for land use in the Upper Thames region as a whole. The sequences of deposition are complex; they almost certainly continue in the Roman and again in the late Saxon periods (Lambrick & Robinson 1984). A more precise chronology is required for these sequences. The uplands, in particular the Cotswolds, also require closer investigation in order to develop fully a regional model of land use in later prehistory.

In the valley bottom evidence of land use has been accumulating in recent years. At Farmoor Iron Age compounds on the floodplain and first terrace, radiocarbon dated *c.* 250–100 BC, occupied an open grassland environment. Only about 3% of the pollen found there belonged to tree/shrub species. Grass pollen predominated, as did dung beetles among the Coleoptera. Just west of the county boundary at Claydon Pike, Lechlade (Gloucestershire), round houses of about the same date as Farmoor occupied islands of first-terrace gravel. Drainage ditches controlled flooding and bounded paddocks of wet grassland. At Mingies Ditch, Hardwick, a pioneer settlement (*c.* 220 ± 90 BC) in the valley of the Windrush also exploited a pastoral area.

On the higher terraces there is evidence for grassland and patches of arable cultivation in the late Neolithic and Bronze Age, but during the first millennium arable becomes predominant (for example at Mount Farm, north of Dorchester, and Ashville, Abingdon). Evidence of woodland is rare; the region at present lacks useful pollen sequences. The Thames Valley was essentially cleared but timber and wood were nevertheless vital for building material, fencing, tools and fuel –

particularly for the smelting and smithing of iron (Salter & Ehrenreich 1984). In the Stanton Harcourt area recent excavations at Northmoor, Gravelly Guy and on the Black Ditch by-pass indicate land usage similar to that in familiar medieval strip parishes: meadowland by the River Windrush, arable on the second terrace, and localized hazel woodland, probably cropped as coppice, on the edge of the higher third terrace (Robinson 1984, 6). A similar sequence has been observed in a Roman context at Barton Court Farm, Abingdon (author's excavation). An oak/hazel coppice probably occupied the present Bagley Wood area, overlooking Oxford, in the fourth century AD but was an ancient wood at that time.

On the Cotswold slopes numerous settlements recently located by aerial photography in addition to the well-known hillforts suggest that the population was not inconsiderable. Unfortunately there are few data available to clarify the nature of the landscape. At Eynsham Hall Camp, on acidic glacial drift in Wychwood Forest, pollen from beneath the rampart, identified by Professor G. Dimbleby, indicated the presence of oak woodland prior to the construction of the hillfort. Woodland may have been retained on the intractable clay-with-flint soils of the Chilterns. There is however some evidence for clearance in that area: a ploughsoil was found sealed beneath the Iron Age linear earthwork known as the South Oxfordshire Grim's Ditch (Hinchliffe 1975, 129–32). Some of the most spectacular Iron Age sites in the county are to be found in the south on the scarp edge of the chalk downland. Hillforts, 'celtic' fields, linear boundaries and colluvial deposits leave no doubt about the extent of late prehistoric activity here. But there has been little excavation within Oxfordshire, and the interpretation of these features is dependent largely upon analogy with more thoroughly investigated areas of Wessex (Cunliffe 1984; but for Rams Hill see Bradley & Ellison 1975).

Settlement

Evidence of Iron Age settlement in the region is plentiful and complex. There is a wide variety of settlement types and notable variation in their patterning within the different regional zones (Map 9). With the exception of the Thames Valley, however, we can do no more than speculate about the chronological range, subsistence basis, social organization and interrelationships of these settlements. The most prominent of them are the hillforts or, more properly, the defended enclosures. Whereas these have attracted much of the excavation activity in Wessex (Cunliffe 1984) or the West Country and Welsh borders (see papers in Harding 1976), no Oxfordshire hillfort has been excavated on any scale. Results of the sampling exercises of the 1930s to 1960s at sites such as Chastleton, Lyneham Camp and Cherbury Camp were summarized by Harding (1972, 45–60). In the past decade further information has become available about earlier work at Blewburton Hill (Harding 1976), the external areas of Castle Hill, Wittenham Clumps (Hingley 1983a) and the Big Enclosure, Cassington Mill (Case and Whittle 1982, 118–51). Limited excavations have also taken place at Rams Hill (Bradley & Ellison 1975) and the interesting and, at present, well-preserved valley fortification of Burroway, Clanfield (Benson & Miles 1974, map 11; Lambrick 1984). Nine excavations have taken place in Gloucestershire hillforts, notably at Crickley Hill and Salmonsbury, the results of which have been recently summarized by Saville (1984).

On the Oxfordshire Cotswold slopes small univallate hillforts such as Lyneham and Chastleton have phases of occupation as early as the late Bronze Age/early Iron Age (Bayne 1957; Leeds 1931; for wider discussion Marshall 1978). In the south on a prominent outlying hill of the Downs, Blewburton Hill had a stockaded enclosure of about 2ha in the 7th to 6th centuries BC, replaced by a timber-laced rampart a century later, a dump rampart about 100 BC, and abandoned soon afterwards.

Not all defended enclosures are found on prominent positions. The multivallate site of Cherbury Camp occupies a low promontory of limestone and sand on the northern edge of the Vale of the White Horse. Its position was probably more secure than it now appears as the land to the east is likely to have been marsh in the Iron Age. Although its excavator (Bradford 1940) proposed a short chronology for Cherbury Camp it seems probable that the site's history is long and complex. Its size (c. 5ha) may also be misleading as an extensive open settlement lies to the west which may in part be contemporary (Hingley 1983b). At Castle Hill, Long Wittenham an external settlement area has been partially excavated, well preserved beneath colluvial deposits (Hingley 1983a).

The limited evidence available suggests that local hillforts were no longer occupied in the late Iron Age. However, certain low-lying defended sites may, like Salmonsbury in Gloucestershire, belong to this period. Dyke Hills, Dorchester encloses a large area (c. 47 ha) at the confluence of the River Thames and the Thame which cropmarks indicate was densely occupied (Benson & Miles 1974, 91–4; Hingley & Miles 1984, fig. 4.9). Except for a trial trench by Lane-Fox in the 19th century Dyke Hills has not been excavated; it is nevertheless usually regarded as a late Iron Age enclosed *oppidum* (e.g. Cunliffe 1976, fig. 5), the location of which influenced the siting of the Roman fort at Dorchester.

A late Iron Age date has been confirmed for the c. 5.5 ha enclosure at Cassington Mill, though in view of its six causeways Startin (in Case & Whittle 1982) has suggested that the earthwork construction was never completed.

The defended enclosures of the region are of varying form, size and location; little is known of their detailed chronology or of their function. For Wessex Cunliffe (1984) has been able to postulate a model of hillfort development in which some sites like Danebury in the middle Iron Age emerge as densely occupied centres, with large-scale storage facilities for foodstuffs and craft specialization. In Oxfordshire the defended enclosures lack investigation so it is impossible to assess their role in Iron Age society with any degree of confidence. This role need not follow the Wessex model and at present we cannot be certain that the Oxfordshire hillforts are central to the organization of the communities in the Upper Thames region.

In contrast to the hillforts the Iron Age settlements of the Thames Valley are relatively well-known thanks to recent rescue excavations and to aerial photography (Hingley & Miles 1984, 54–63). The cropmark evidence indicates that different zones of the valley can be associated with different types of site and this has been confirmed by excavation. At Farmoor, for example, scattered compounds of middle Iron Age date have been associated with the short-term, seasonal grazing of the Thames floodplain (Lambrick & Robinson 1979). The floodplain, with its waterlogged deposits preserved beneath alluvium, has great potential for archaeological investigation, although sites are often difficult to locate by conventional means. On the first terrace settlements are more easily discovered by aerial photography, yet their margins and deeper features are often waterlogged. (Unfortunately the recent lowering of the water-table is having a drastic effect on the preservation of organic deposits.)

The first gravel terrace has pastoral sites which were probably occupied on a longer term basis, such as the double-ditched enclosure of Mingie's Ditch, Hardwick (Allen & Robinson 1979; Benson & Miles 1974, Map 21, SP 3905). At Claydon Pike, Lechlade (Gloucs.), middle Iron Age round houses were integrated into a system of ditched fields, which provided year-round pasture for cattle and sheep (Miles & Palmer 1982; Miles 1984, fig. 2). A similar, and possibly contemporary, layout is visible on aerial photographs of Port Meadow, Oxford, though not confirmed by excavation.

Fields are rare in the Thames Valley (Miles 1978). On the Downs the outlines of Celtic fields are visible because of surface stone clearance and the movement of soil downhill, which cause lynchets to form. In the wetter valley bottoms drainage ditches are necessary. In contrast on the flat, dry, second terrace – which was probably the most prolific arable area – little trace remains of Iron Age fields.

Settlements are most prolific on the second gravel terrace. They can often be recognized from the air by the dense clusters of pits, used for food – notably grain – storage, and scatters of round houses. The site at Ashville, Abingdon (Parrington 1978), is the most thoroughly published of these, though at present a larger scale and more coherent investigation is under way at the site of Gravelly Guy, Stanton Harcourt (Benson & Miles 1974, frontispiece; Lambrick 1984).

Round house/pit complexes have also been recognized from the air on the Corallian ridge, south-west of Oxford, and excavated during the construction of the M40 on the plateau gravels at Milton Common to the east (Rowley 1973).

In the late Iron Age rectilinear blocks of enclosure and isolated rectangular enclosures appear on the gravel terraces, sometimes overlying the pit clusters. Some of these belong to the Roman period but pre-Conquest origins have been confirmed at Ashville, Barton Court Farm, Abingdon, and possibly at Claydon Pike. Some of these rectilinear blocks are very extensive and associated with trackways as at Northfield Farm, Long Wittenham (Gray 1977).

Until recently relatively few Iron Age settlements were known on the Cotswold slopes other than the hillforts; now as a result of the analysis of aerial photographs (mostly vertical photographs not taken for archaeological purposes) a considerable number of so-called banjo enclosures have been located (Hingley & Miles 1984, fig 4.3). These tend to lie on hill slopes, at the junction of different soil types, with well-watered valleys in front and dry plateaux behind. Banjo enclosures in Wessex have in the past been interpreted as animal pens; however excavations indicate that they also acted as settlement areas, dating to the mid/late Iron Age. The location of the Cotswold examples suggests that they were involved in mixed farming, though excavated evidence is lacking (for the only trial excavation, at Tomlins Gate, Kiddington see Hingley 1982). A small number of banjo enclosures on the gravel terraces occur within settlement complexes and may be specialized stock-holding compounds.

As a result of several large-scale and carefully conducted excavations there is considerable evidence for the layout and organization of Thames Valley settlements. It is essential, however, not to take site plans or cropmark plots at face value. Where stratigraphical relationships are available clusters of round houses, for example, can be seen to have a complex history. Large-scale excavations have also shown the danger of interpreting settlements on the basis of even relatively large, key-hole trenches.

Most of the middle Iron Age open settlements were laid out in an apparently unstructured way. There is, however, evidence of zoning: storage pits in clusters, areas of round houses, sometimes in lines or forming opposing pairs, and trackways. Four-post structures – usually interpreted as above ground storage units (Gent 1983) – are rare on the higher valley sites where pits are frequent though recently several have been found at Gravelly Guy, Stanton Harcourt (Lambrick pers. comm.). They occur in small numbers on low-lying sites such as Mingie's Ditch and Claydon Pike, perhaps because dampness inhibited pit-digging and because seed grain (which is thought to have been kept in the underground pits) was not an important requirement at these pastoral sites. The systematic sampling of biological material indicates that activities such as crop processing took place around the houses at Ashville and work on animal bones is beginning to show patterning in the distribution of debris (Wilson 1978).

One of the greatest advances in recent years has been in the study of Iron Age houses. Large numbers of house plans have now been recovered (Allen, Miles &

Palmer 1984). Early Iron Age houses are still rare, though they probably were of a post-ring type – that is, circular structures of about 10m in diameter. The outer wall was of wattle and daub and the inner ring of posts, which penetrated the subsoil, bore the weight of the thatch roof. In a few cases a closely set post-ring may have represented the line of the outer wall (e.g. at Frilford: Allen, Miles & Palmer 1984, fig 6.2).

A characteristic of Upper Thames Iron Age houses is that they were bounded by shallow gulleys. These penannular gullies are sometimes interpreted as the foundations for walls, but the evidence is conclusive in local examples that these gullies acted as drains, to protect the foundations of the house from damp. Sometimes the houses set inside these penannular gullies leave little trace. Well-preserved examples such as House 5 at Mingie's Ditch and House XV at Claydon Pike suggest that most of them probably had stake-built walls 7–8m in diameter which did not penetrate the subsoil. Sometimes only the pair of post-holes formed by the strongly built doorposts survives in the archaeological record.

The vast majority of the doorways faced east or south-east and thus allowed the optimum amount of light into the house while avoiding the prevailing westerly winds. Traces of internal activities are disappointingly few: the occasional hearth, clay-lined rectangular pits, stake holes and cobbled areas but little *in situ* debris to indicate the activities which took place within the houses. Most artefacts, mainly pottery, are found in the terminals of the drainage gullies where they were discarded.

Subsistence

Evidence of Iron Age subsistence has become more plentiful in the past decade as a result of the concerted campaigns of excavations in the 1970s and 80s. Only a few of these projects have, however, been fully published and work is still in progress on much of the recently recovered material. Carbonized plant and animal remains are virtually ubiquitous at local Iron Age settlements: the same domesticated species occur on most of them. However with modern sampling and flotation techniques it is possible to draw comparisons between sites, to investigate the differences between biological assemblages, and to propose inter-relationships between different types of settlement.

In the Oxford region a number of sites have been excavated on a large scale with the specific aim of recovering a wide variety of quantifiable subsistence information. We are not therefore dependent simply upon a few isolated plant remains or on animal bones lacking a detailed context (Jones 1984, 120–1). In Oxfordshire the most productive sites at which integrated analyses have taken place are the Ashville Trading Estate and Barton Court Farm, both on the second gravel terrace near Abingdon (Parrington 1978; Miles in press); Mount Farm on the third terrace near Dorchester (Lambrick 1979, 1981b); Farmoor on the floodplain (Lambrick & Robinson 1979); Mingie's Ditch, Hardwick (Allen & Robinson 1979) and Watkins Farm, Northmoor (Allen 1984), both on the first terrace by the Windrush, and Gravelly Guy, Stanton Harcourt on the second terrace. A further large-scale excavation at Claydon Pike, Lechlade, on the first terrace is 4 km west of the Oxfordshire county boundary. It will be obvious that all these sites are on the gravel terraces or the floodplain of the river valleys. No upland site in the region has received the same kind of systematic investigation.

The Iron Age is notable for the increase of crop species observable in the archaeological record (Helbaek 1952; Jones 1981). There is an expansion of arable land and a tendency to crop diversification at the expense of pasture, also involving the colonization of new relatively difficult soils.

For the Iron Age the dominant crops in the archaeological record are spelt (*Triticum spelta*), 6-row barley (*Hordeum spp*), breadwheat (*T. aestivum/compactum*) and beans (*Vicia faba*). In the Oxford region the earlier staples – emmer wheat and naked barley – go into decline. The first millennium appears to be a period of major innovation in farming in Southern Britain. Jones (1981; 1984) has emphasized that all of these species are suited to adverse conditions of various kinds and are adaptable to a farming regime faced with worsening climate, declining fertility and the need to expand on to more difficult soils. This process can best be observed locally at the Ashville site near Abingdon (Parrington 1978). Although this settlement sits on the second gravel terrace it has a wide variety of soil types in close proximity: damp alluvial floodplain to the south, clay to the west and limestone to the north. The carbonized weed seeds recovered at Ashville indicate that all of these soils were to some extent exploited as arable land. Significant proportions of the spike rush *Eleocharis palustris* in the seed assemblages indicate that even parts of the low-lying damp ground had been brought into cultivation by the middle Iron Age.

The colonization of heavier soils may have in part been a reaction to the declining fertility of the long exploited second terrace soils. At Ashville the increase of leguminous weeds such as vetches and tares has been interpreted by Jones (1978, 109) as an indication of nitrogen depletion in these traditional arable soils.

The apparent development of large-scale arable production during the course of the first millennium BC is consistent with the needs of a growing population. There is a substantial loss of energy at each trophic level in the food chain. As a result, observations in a modern British context record food output (in calories) from cereal farming as about six times that of milk and up to twenty-two times that of meat production (Duckham and Lloyd 1966, recorded in Grigg 1982, 71).

The intensification of cereal farming was probably also promoted by the gradual expansion of the practice of autumn sowing. At Ashville cleavers (*Galium aparine*) and other autumn germinating plants are a major component of the weed flora and are more likely to occur in autumn rather than spring sown crops (Jones 1978, 106). The practice of autumn sowing, which spreads the labour load and increases productivity, may also account for the predominance of spelt. This cereal is frost-hardy, slow-growing and well adapted to autumn sowing; it is also tolerant of heavy, damp soils.

In spite of the statistics of the food chain animals remained an essential part of the Iron Age economy. Ruminants like cattle and sheep can convert parts of plants inedible to man into meat and milk and, particularly in the case of sheep, exploit soils too poor for arable. Erosion on parts of the chalk downland as a result of ploughing in the second and early first millennia BC may even have led to the restoration of pasture there and the introduction of sheep flocks. Animal dung was also an important by-product, particularly for the arable fields, whose straw stubble could be grazed after harvest. Sheep and cattle were not only useful for milk and meat; wool, hides and tallow were essentials. Oxen were also used for traction, particularly for pulling the plough.

Our information on Iron Age livestock comes mainly from a small number of extensively excavated sites with good bone preservation. A number of trends can tentatively be identified. Sheep tend to be found in greater proportions on higher and drier settlements, not surprisingly in view of their lower nutritional requirements and limited need for water. Cattle on the other hand are more frequent on the lower valley sites such as Farmoor and Appleford, where water supplies are more plentiful and the grass is lush and available, at least on the first terrace, all year round. Sheep are present at low-lying sites in spite of the presence at Appleford of the snail which acts as the secondary host for liver fluke (Robinson 1980, 84).

The presence of weights from warp-weighted looms at low-lying sites such as Farmoor and Claydon Pike, as well as Ashville and Gravelly Guy on the second terrace, suggests that woollen textile production was an important element in the local economy. In view of the small number of adequate samples it would be unwise to underestimate the importance of sheep in the lowlands of the Thames Valley.

The importance of wool is also reflected in the age at which sheep were killed: the majority were beyond the optimum age for meat production (Grant 1978, 107). The predominance of female sheep at Appleford, Ashville and Barton Court Farm (Wilson 1978, 115) also suggests that flocks were kept predominantly for milk and wool.

The animal bones indicate that Iron Age communities were exploiting relatively wide territories. At Farmoor, for example, the floodplain pasture was grazed on a seasonal basis, possibly communally. The flocks and herds were probably driven down in spring/early summer from their higher winter grazing grounds. The presence of pigs (Grant 1984, fig. 7.7) on most Iron Age sites also suggests that woodland pannage was available, though not necessarily adjacent to the settlement.

Horses were a high-status animal in the Iron Age, kept principally for riding and pulling light carts or chariots, whose main advantage was speed (Piggott 1983, 89). Considerable skill was lavished upon the accessories of horsemanship such as bridles and terrets. The finest material of this kind from the region was found in 1803 on Hagbourne Hill (Harding 1972, 91, pl. 77).

Horse bone assemblages are notable for their lack of the remains of young animals, particularly on downland sites (Grant 1984, 113–41) suggesting that relatively free-roaming herds were periodically rounded up and selected animals caught for training. As a prestige animal the horse was not kept predominantly as a source of meat; however, butchery marks on bones from Ashville (Wilson 1978) indicate that horses were occasionally eaten.

In contrast with earlier periods wild plants and animals do not seem to have been an important element in Iron Age diet. Red deer and to a lesser extent roe deer are indicated, usually by the presence of antlers. Pine marten and badger have also been found at Mount Farm (Wilson pers. comm.) Fish bones are rare, though chub and pike were present at Ashville. Conditions for preservation are generally good in the Thames Valley and fish bones survive well on sites of other periods (for example, Saxon Barton Court Farm). The lack of fish bones may therefore reflect a real decline in fishing as a subsistence activity at a time when intensification of farming was taking place. Birds also do not occur very frequently in the Iron Age record. Bones of water birds, mallard, larger duck, heron and red shank have been found in all the Iron Age phases at Ashville (Bramwell 1978), suggesting that fowling took place in the marshland south of the settlement. There is also at Ashville a rare occurrence of house sparrow. Domestic fowl bones have only been found in a late Iron Age context (Bramwell 1978). Although Caesar (*Gallic War* V.13) specifically mentions the keeping of fowl, in south-east Britain at least, (and a taboo on eating them), they may in his time have been a recent introduction.

An interesting sidelight on the Iron Age economy was the discovery of the head of a worker honey bee (*Apis mellifera L.*) preserved in peat in an Iron Age sump at Mingie's Ditch, Hardwick (Robinson 1984b) radiocarbon dated to 220 ± 90 BC. This is the earliest find of the honey bee in Britain to date. Presumably therefore honey and beeswax were available to Iron Age communities. Northover (1984) notes that there is only evidence for the use of the lost wax process in casting bronze in Britain from about 300 BC.

The availability of iron tools must have played a major role in the expansion of settlement and arable areas. Iron tools however are relatively rare from excavated sites in comparison with the Roman period (for knives, iron ploughshares and a reaping hook see Harding 1972, 176; Parrington 1978, 78–9). In contrast with copper and tin used in bronze manufacture, iron ores were widely available, notably in the Jurassic belt of the South Midlands (Salter & Ehrenreich 1984,

147–9). Iron smelting, which requires charcoal, must have had considerable impact on local woodland management, the production of one kilogram of finished iron requiring the consumption of about 630 kg of timber. For this purpose, woodland would best be cropped rather than cleared.

The Process of Change

Iron Age (usually equated with Celtic) society is traditionally regarded by historians as tribal. In anthropological terms the Celts were not organized into egalitarian 'tribes' but into chiefdoms with a pyramid-shaped social structure based on inheritance (Collis 1984, 18–9): that is, 'hierarchic, aristocratic and familiar'.

According to Service (1971 edition, 133–4) 'a chiefdom occupies a level of social integration which transcends tribal society in two important respects. First a chiefdom is usually a denser society than a tribe, a gain made possible by greater productivity. But second and more indicative of the evolutionary stage, the society is more complex and organised, being particularly distinguished from tribes by the presence of centres which co-ordinate economic, social and religious activities'.

Service suggests that increased productivity and population are a characteristic of chiefdoms, not necessarily based upon technological innovation but on the structuring of the whole environment towards specialization, central control and redistribution so that 'the increased efficiency in production and distribution made possible a denser society'.

It is apparent from the archaeological evidence in the Upper Thames region that Iron Age society was in the process of transformation in the course of the first millennium BC. In Wessex Cunliffe (1978; 1984) has proposed a model of development in which certain hillforts such as Danebury functioned as the principal sites in a hierarchy of settlement. There is as yet no evidence in the Oxford region to support this hypothesis. On the Cotswold slopes hillforts may represent peripheral and insecure border settlements in the less densely occupied landscape (Hingley 1984). The valley settlements may not have been dependent upon these fortified sites for their defence, redistribution of foodstuff or any other centralized activity. Similarly to the south Barrett (in Bradley & Ellison 1975, 111–2) has noted that the Rams Hill pottery suggests that this hillfort was functioning in a different economic sphere from Blewburton Hill and the Upper Thames Valley settlements. It is at Blewburton Hill, Cherbury Camp and Castle Hill, Long Wittenham, that we have the potential to investigate this key question: 'How were Celtic society and its settlements integrated in the early and middle Iron Age?'

In other respects the Upper Thames region conforms to the chiefdom model. There was certainly a growing emphasis on agricultural productivity and there is some evidence for agricultural specialization and interdependence between settlements. A site like Claydon Pike with its emphasis on animal products may have imported cereals from its neighbours. It certainly imported salt and fine pottery from the Malverns 70 km to the north-west as did Mingie's Ditch. Such new settlements also indicate an ability and a desire to exploit what had previously been marginal land exploited on a seasonal basis (and was to become so again in the post-Roman period). This required a greater investment of labour in order to create efficient drainage systems in spite of the worsening climate.

New colonization is probably also reflected in the appearance of banjo enclosures on the Cotswolds. The sheer number of middle Iron Age sites known in the Upper Thames is convincing evidence of an expanding population and a far higher one than used to be thought. At present it is possible to estimate population in only the most vague and relative terms. Perhaps it is naive to assume that it could be otherwise, when even Domesday historians chose to work in relative rather than absolute terms (for discussion of the Iron Age population problems in Hampshire equally relevant in the Oxford region see Champion & Champion 1981, 38–9; Cunliffe 1978). In order to introduce rigour into any discussion of relative populations it is necessary to conduct systematic field surveys. In recent years fieldwork has not kept pace with excavation. The distribution of intensively surveyed areas in the region is relatively arbitrary and these have been conducted with minimal funding. Population is one of the most important but at present least understood variables in any study of the Iron Age.

In some periods (e.g. the Bronze Age and the Anglo-Saxon period) archaeologists can investigate social hierarchy through mortuary data. Unfortunately burials are relatively rare in the Oxford region though a high-status sword burial was found at Sutton Courtenay (Whimster 1981, 135, 216–7). Other swords and daggers have been found in riverine or marshy deposits, reflecting the Celtic elite's tendency to dispose of prestige goods, particularly weapons, as votive offerings and as a public display of wealth (Fitzpatrick 1984, fig. 12.1). In contrast such objects are rarely found in excavations of settlement sites, nor is there any convincing evidence (e.g. in the size and form of buildings) for social stratification within the excavated settlements.

In the late Iron Age social stratification may have become more pronounced. New types of enclosed sites appear, such as Barton Court Farm, Abingdon (Miles 1978a), at the same time as the landscape is more systematically divided and delineated by trackways and rectangular enclosures. Many of these settlements continue into the Roman period; Barton Court Farm, for example, develops into a small villa. It may be significant that the middle Iron Age site of Ashville, Abingdon, shows signs of nitrogen depletion in the soil and the continued use of old-fashioned tools in the Roman period (a wooden ard) while the new site of Barton Court Farm seems to prosper and develop.

In the late Iron Age the Upper Thames region was a

frontier zone between the Dobunni to the west, the Atrebates to the south and the Catuvellauni to the east. The influences of these groups are reflected in the spread of the coinage (Sellwood 1984). The most dramatic changes in late Iron Age society took place in the south-east. Large territorial *oppida* with urban characteristics, such as Verulamium and Camulodunum, developed at nodal points from *c*. 100 BC. Dyke Hills, Dorchester, may have risen to prominence as a gateway settlement, promoting contact between separate social and economic groupings; hence the impressive number of Iron Age coins from the area around Dorchester. With the Roman Conquest and the absorption of the region into the province of Britannia such a gateway community would no longer have a major role to play: as a result Dorchester became no more than a minor Romano-British town.

The role of the possible territorial *oppidum* of Grim's Ditch around the river Evenlode is even more enigmatic. No major occupation focus of the Iron Age has been found within its considerable bounds (the enclosed area is about 9 km across). However a cluster of Romano-British villas emerged within and just outside its earthworks. Hingley (1984) has suggested that the development of these Cotswold villas may reflect the character of the Iron Age communities from which they sprang – individual pioneering family groups in a less densely inhabited landscape, in contrast to the more traditional, communally organized and highly populated settlements of the valley, whose way of life, as reflected in the archaeological record, scarcely changed after the Roman Conquest.

Acknowledgements

I would like to thank all those archaeologists upon whose work I have drawn, particularly my colleagues: Tim Allen, Richard Hingley, Martin Jones, George Lambrick, Simon Palmer, Mark Robinson, Bob Wilson. Any misuse of their hard-earned data remains, of course, my responsibility.

References

Allen, T. (1984) 'Northmoor; Watkins Farm', *South Midlands Archaeology (CBA Group 9 Newsletter)* 14, 106–109
Allen, T., Miles, D. & Palmer, S. (1984) 'Iron Age Buildings in the Upper Thames Valley' in Cunliffe & Miles 1984, 89–101
Allen, T. & Robinson, M. (1979) 'Mingies Ditch, Hardwick', *CBA Group 9 Newsletter* 9, 115–7
Bayne, N. (1957) 'Excavations at Lyneham Camp, Lyneham, Oxon.', *Oxoniensia* 22, 1–10
Bell, M. (1981) 'Valley sediments and environmental change' in *The Environment of Man: the Iron Age to the Anglo-Saxon period*, eds. M. Jones and G. W. Dimbleby, (BAR 87), 75–91
Bell, M. (1982) 'The effects of land-use and climate on valley sedimentation' in *Climatic change in later prehistory*, 127–42
Bradford, J.S.P. (1942) 'The excavation at Cherbury Camp 1939', *Oxoniensia* 5, 13–20.
Bradley, R. & Ellison, A. (1975) *Rams Hill*. BAR 19
Bramwell, D. (1978) 'The bird bones' in Parrington 1978, 133
Case, H.J. (1954) 'The Prehistoric Period' in *The Oxford Region*, eds. A.F. Martin & R.W. Steel, 76–84
Case, H.J. & Whittle, A.W.R. (1982) *Settlement patterns in the Oxford Region: excavations at the Abingdon causewayed enclosure and other sites*. CBA Res. Rept. 44

Champion, T. and S. (1981) 'The Iron Age in Hampshire' in *The Archaeology of Hampshire*, eds. S.J. Shennan and R.T. Schadla Hall, (Hants. Field Club and Archaeol. Soc. Monograph 1), 37–45
Collis, J. (1984) *The European Iron Age*
Cunliffe, B.W. (1976) *Iron Age Communities in Britain*
Cunliffe, B.W. (1978) 'Settlement and population in the British Iron Age: some facts, figures and fantasies' in *Lowland Iron Age Communities in Europe*, eds. B. Cunliffe and T. Rowley, (BAR Internat. Ser. 48), 3–24
Cunliffe, B.W. & Miles, D. (1984) *Aspects of the Iron Age in Central Southern Britain*. OUCA 2
Duckham, A.N. & Lloyd, D.H. (1966) 'Production of dietary energy and protein on University of Reading farm', *Farm Economist* 11, 95–97
Gent, H. (1983) 'Centralised storage in later prehistoric Britain', *Proc. Prehist. Soc.* 49, 243–67
Goudie, A.S. (1981) *The Human Impact: Man's role in environmental change*
Grant, A. (1984) 'Animal husbandry in Wessex and the Thames Valley' in Cunliffe & Miles 1984, 102–19
Gray, M. (1977) 'Northfield Farm, Long Wittenham', *Oxoniensia* 42, 1–29
Grigg, D. (1982) *The Dynamics of Agricultural Change*
Harding, D.W. (1972) *The Iron Age in the Upper Thames Basin*
Harding, D.W. (ed.) (1976) *Hillforts: Later Prehistoric Earthworks in Britain and Ireland*
Helbaek, H. (1952) 'Early crops in Southern Britain', *Proc. Prehist. Soc.* 18, 194–233
Hinchliffe, J. (1975) 'Excavations at Grim's Ditch, Mongewell, 1974', *Oxoniensia* 40, 122–35
Hinchliffe, J. & Thomas, R. (1980) 'Archaeological investigations at Appleford', *Oxoniensia* 45, 9–111
Hingley, R. (1980a) 'The Upper Thames Valley survey', *CBA Group 9 Newsletter* 10, 141–3
Hingley, R. (1980b) 'The Frilford/Marcham/Garfords survey', *CBA Group 9 Newsletter* 11, 104–7
Hingley, R. (1981) 'The Upper Thames Valley survey', *CBA Group 9 Newsletter* 11, 104–7
Hingley, R. (1982) 'Kiddington: Tomlin's Gate', *CBA Group 9 Newsletter* 12, 154–5
Hingley, R. (1983a) 'Excavations by R. A. Rutland on an Iron Age site at Wittenham Clumps', *Berks. Archaeol. J.* 70, 21–55
Hingley, R. (1983b) 'Charney Bassett: Cherbury Camp', *CBA Group 9 Newsletter* 13, 123
Hingley, R. (1984) 'Towards social analysis in archaeology: Celtic society in the Iron Age of the Upper Thames Valley' in Cunliffe & Miles 1984, 72–88
Hingley, R. & Miles, D. (1984) 'Aspects of Iron Age settlement in the Upper Thames Valley' in Cunliffe & Miles 1984, 52–71
Jones, M. (1978) 'The plant remains' in Parrington 1978, 83–8
Jones, M. (1981) 'The development of crop husbandry' in *The Environment of Man: the Iron Age to the Anglo-Saxon Period*, eds. G. Dimbleby & M. Jones, 95–127
Jones, M. (1984) 'Regional patterns in crop production' in Cunliffe & Miles 1984, 120–5
Jones, M. & Miles, D. (1979) 'Celt and Roman in the Upper Thames Valley: approaches to culture change' in *Invasion and Response*, eds. B. Burnham & H.B. Johnson, 315–25
Lamb, H.H. (1981) 'Climate from 1000 BC to AD 100' in *The Environment of Man: the Iron Age to the Anglo-Saxon Period*, eds. G. Dimbleby & M. Jones, 53–65
Miles, D. (1978) 'The Upper Thames Valley' in *Early Land Allotment in the British Isles*, eds. P.J. Fowler & H.C. Bowen, 81–8
Miles, D. (1979) 'Claydon Pike, Fairford/Lechlade', *CBA Group 9 Newsletter* 10, 160–4
Miles, D. (1983) 'An integrated approach to the study of ancient landscapes: the Claydon Pike project' in *The Impact of Aerial Reconnaissance on Archaeology*, ed. G.S. Maxwell, 74–84
Miles, D. (1984) 'Romano-British settlement in the Gloucestershire Thames Valley' in *Archaeology in Gloucestershire*, ed. A. Saville, 191–211

Miles, D. (forthcoming) *Archaeology at Barton Court Farm, Abingdon*

Miles, D. & Palmer, S. (1983) *Figures in a Landscape: archaeological investigations at Claydon Pike, an interim report*

Northover, P. (1984) 'Iron Age bronze metallurgy in Central Southern England' in Cunliffe & Miles 1984, 126–145

Parrington, M. (1978) *The excavation at Ashville, Abingdon (Oxfordshire) 1974-76.* CBA Res. Rept. 28

Piggott, S. (1983) *The Earliest Wheeled Transport*

Robinson, M.A. (1980) 'Roman waterlogged plant and invertebrate evidence from Appleford', *Oxoniensia* 45, 90–106

Robinson, M.A. & Lambrick, G. (1984) 'Holocene alluviation and hydrology in the Upper Thames Basin', *Nature* 308, 809–14

Robinson, M.A. (1984a) 'Landscape and environment of Central Southern Britain in the Iron Age' in Cunliffe & Miles 1984, 1–11

Robinson, M.'. (1984b) 'An apicultural postscript: the honey bee in the Iron Age' in Cunliffe & Miles 1984, 119.

Rowley, T. (1973) 'An Iron Age settlement site at Heath Farm, Milton Common', *Oxoniensia* 38, 23–40

Salter, C. & Ehrenreich, R. (1984) 'Iron Age metallurgy in Central Southern Britain' in Cunliffe & Miles 1984, 146–162

Saville, A. (1984) 'The Iron Age in Gloucestershire: a review of the evidence' in *Archaeology in Gloucestershire*, ed. A. Saville, 140–178

Sellwood, L. (1984) 'Tribal boundaries viewed from the perspectives of numismatic evidence' in Cunliffe & Miles 1984, 191–204

Service, E.R. (1971) *Primitive Social Organisation: an evolutionary perspective*. 2nd ed.

Sherratt, A. (1983) 'An Iron Age sword from Little Wittenham', *Oxford J. Archaeol.* 2, 115–8

Stone, S. (1857) 'Account of certain (supposed) British and Saxon remains', *Proc. Soc. Antiq. Lond.* 1st ser. 4 (1856–9), 92–100

Turner, J. (1981) 'The Iron Age' in *The environment in British prehistory*, eds. I.G. Simmons & M.J. Tooley, 250–81

Whimster, R.P. (1981) *Burial practices in Iron Age Britain: a discussion and gazetteer of the evidence c. 700BC – AD43.*

Wilson, B. (1978) 'The animal bones' in Parrington 1978, 110–37.

THE UPPER THAMES VALLEY IN THE ROMAN PERIOD
CHRISTOPHER YOUNG

Roman Oxfordshire is to a certain extent an anachronistic misnomer since the modern county does not apparently conform to any administrative unit of the Roman period. As boundaries have run since 1974, the county does form the nucleus of a convenient geographical unit, comprising the Upper Thames Valley and the adjoining high ground of the chalk downs to the east and south, and of the limestone and ironstone plateaux to north and west.

On this basic geology is superimposed the drainage pattern of the Thames and its tributaries, with which are associated extensive gravel and alluvial deposits. Away from these, the alternating bands of hard and soft rocks give rise in succession from the north-west to the limestone and cornbrash of the Cotswolds, the Oxford clay vale, the sandstone and Coral Rag of the Oxfordshire Heights, the Gault clay vale south of Oxford, and, finally, the rising steps of the chalk escarpment, capped by clay-with-flints in many areas (Emery 1974, fig. 1).

In the past there have been two major attempts to survey the Roman occupation of the Upper Thames Valley as a whole, in the *Victoria County History* before the last War, and in *The Oxford Region* thirty years ago. These two papers (Taylor, Harden, Sutherland 1939, Taylor 1954) present a coherent picture of Roman Oxfordshire as a backwater, ignored by the Romans at the conquest and dependent on political centres many miles away. Only Dorchester and Alchester were recognised as small towns with any claim to Romanization. Major areas of settlement were thought to be the river gravels, the limestone west of the Cherwell, and the north of the county. The land to the east of the Cherwell was regarded as being lightly settled only. Settlement along the gravels was thought of as being primarily peasant in character and little different from what had gone before in the Iron Age. This was sharply contrasted to the prosperous villas on the foothills of the Cotswolds. Elsewhere in the county less prosperous villas were recognized along with peasant settlements and farmsteads. A pottery industry of mainly local importance lay between Alchester and Dorchester.

Over the intervening decades there has been an enormous explosion of evidence which has in some respects radically altered this picture. This has several causes. On the gravels, and more recently on the Corallian ridge, air photography has greatly increased our knowledge, while increased amateur and professional archaeological effort has located many more sites by fieldwork and general observation. The vastly speeded-up pace of destruction has paradoxically revealed many new sites. This has been of particular use in areas hitherto thought to be largely devoid of occupation. The construction of the M40 motorway revealed Roman settlement of the plateau gravels and on the greensand step at the foot of the Chilterns (Hinton, Rowley 1974). West and north of Oxford linear threats such as roads and pipeline have uncovered peasant settlements and major population centres on the cornbrash (Chambers 1977, 1979).

Increased resources have also made it possible to carry out excavations on a much greater scale. For almost the first time it has been possible to dig sites virtually in their entirety and this has greatly increased knowledge and understanding of certain aspects of settlement. The development of new techniques, particularly in the field of environmental archaeology, has opened up entire new aspects of the evidence.

Taken on its own, this vast explosion of information might have done little more than confuse us by its complexity and profusion. Hence the efforts of the Oxford Archaeological Unit and of others to improve the quality of this information by codification and analysis of existing evidence on the one hand, and by problem-oriented excavation on the other, have been of particular importance. Surveys of the Thames gravels (Benson, Miles 1974, Leach 1977) and of the Oxfordshire towns (Rodwell 1975) have been particularly useful in the former field, while the present writer has discussed the Roman pottery industry of the region (1977).

Among excavations, the Unit's work on the Thames gravels has been particularly significant. This series of research-based projects within a rescue framework has been designed to explore the nature of, and relationships between, the different categories of settlement visible on the gravels, with particular reference to the environmental aspects. Also important has been the total excavation of the villa at Shakenoak on the Cotswold foothills (Brodribb *et al.* 1968, 1971, 1972, 1973, 1978). There have also been important excavations in Dorchester (Bradley 1979, Frere 1964, Rowley, Brown 1982).

This vast increase in the quality and quantity of the evidence for the Upper Thames Valley in the Roman period makes possible a new assessment of the area. It is of course not possible to look at the Roman period without reference to what had gone before or came after. The region appears to have been reasonably heavily settled in the immediate pre-Roman period. On the gravels, where the evidence is best, the range of Iron Age settlement was wide, including rectangular enclosures, possible villages and single huts (Miles 1978b, 84). For most of the Iron Age evidence of field boundaries is lacking.

There is some evidence for change in the settlement pattern in the century prior to the Roman conquest. In that time three major defended centres appeared at Dyke Hills, Dorchester, the major enclosed site at Cassington Mill and the North Oxfordshire Grim's Ditch. Of these Dyke Hills is the most impressive with aerial photographic evidence of settlement within the defences (Benson, Miles 1974, map 36). The Cassington enclosure is enigmatic, but was clearly defensive (Case, Whittle 1982). There is also some evidence on the gravels for the development of ditched trackways and enclosed rectangular paddocks which may herald a major re-organization of the landscape (Jones, Miles 1979). The development of new defended centres and, possibly, of major changes in the landscape may indicate that changes in society and economy were taking place before the Roman conquest itself, presumably reflecting increasing Belgic influences on the area. The effects of the Roman conquest are difficult to measure. In the long term a complex hierarchy of settlement types and distribution emerged (see below p. 62). This pattern clearly reflects a complex and socially-differentiated society, though archaeological evidence alone will never give us a detailed picture of how it worked as opposed to its material remains. It is far from clear, though, how the transition from the pattern of the immediate pre-Roman period to that of the second century A.D. was effected. It is also far from clear how far the changes were the result solely of the Roman conquest or how far they reflect trends within late Iron Age society.

The immediately recognizable physical effects of the conquest were the establishment of military occupation and a communications system. A fort almost certainly existed at Dorchester (Rowley 1975, 117–8). Alchester too probably has military origins: although no fort has yet been located, military equipment has been found near the town (Webster 1978), and it is situated at the junction of the north-south road from Towcester on Watling Street to Silchester, with Akeman Street running from Verulamium to Cirencester (Margary 1973, 155–166). Both these roads must have been established at or shortly after the conquest, though the bridge across the River Ray on the Alchester-Dorchester Road was not built until the end of the first century (Grew 1981, 343). Presumably it was preceded by a ford.

The third major road in the region ran south-west from the Oxford area via Frilford and towards Wantage and probably thence to the Roman town of Cunetio (Lambrick 1970, 86–90). Fieldwork and aerial photography have shown already that a dense network of minor roads and track existed alongside these major routes. Many of the minor roads must have been Iron Age in origin and can never have been more than rough lanes. As well as these directly recognizable physical effects, the conquest must have had equally tangible, but less archaeologically discoverable, effects on the economy. The imposition of tribute and taxation sufficient to supply the needs of the Roman army and administration in Britain must have had substantial effects and should either have diverted existing agricultural surplus towards new users or stimulated agricultural production to produce sufficient to meet the demands of the conqueror. In the first instance, there would have been little profit in this since the levies would have been in the form of tribute. Later, army supplies must have had a stimulating effect on the economy (cf. Rivet 1969, 189–198).

More immediately the effect of garrisons within the area would have been to create a market for various goods around the forts themselves. Thus *vici* must have developed at Alchester and Dorchester though no evidence of them has been found. Other developments within the second half of the first century have been recognized. At both Appleford and Claydon Pike, near Lechlade, new patterns of trackways and field-systems were laid out, presumably reflecting changes in the use of the land. At North Leigh, Barton Court and Shakenoak the first Romanized rectangular buildings were built before the end of the first century. This presumably implies that within a generation or two of the conquest sufficient wealth was available locally to pay for such things.

Fieldwork, aerial photography and chance finds have revealed a dense settlement pattern throughout most of the region. Dating of individual sites is difficult since so few have been excavated, but those that have been, by and large, in existence in the second century. Probably, therefore, the pattern can be taken as indicative of that reached within a century of the Roman conquest. It must have continued to develop and change during the remaining centuries of the Roman occupation of Britain, and traces of this can be detected in the archaeological record. A large number of different types of site are known and these must be indicative of the varied economic and social activities of the components of the society that they supported.

The most obvious settlements in the landscape of the Upper Thames Valley must have been the towns. No major Roman cities existed in the area, the nearest being Silchester, Cirencester and Verulamium, but a network of small market centres through the region has been suggested (Rodwell 1975, 13–15). Because of their defences, the most apparent towns are Alchester and Dorchester. Both lay on the main north-south road through the area. The defences presumably indicate an official and administrative status for these two towns, since their building in the late second century must have been at official instigation. Alchester at least shows some signs of a formal grid layout, apparently extending well beyond the area later enclosed by defences (Wilson 1975, pl. VI; Rowley 1975, fig. 4). It was by far the largest town in the region, extending over a total area of *c.* 43 hectares, although the defences enclosed only 10.5 hectares. It also contained the most substantial structures of any town in the Upper Thames Valley, including a large courtyard building in the centre of the town, and a number of other stone buildings (Rowley 1975). Dorchester was much smaller. Its defences enclosed about 5 hectares although the total settled area was larger. It succeeded the late Iron Age settlement of

Dyke Hills just to the south of it, and its buildings seem predominantly to be of timber, although some stone houses have been found. Administrative significance is again suggested by the now lost altar set up by a *beneficarius consularis*, a minor official of the provincial government (Rowley 1975).

The other large settlements in the area were all undefended, though this does not mean that they were necessarily less significant economically and commercially than the two which did receive walls. All were sited on or close by good road or river routes. Large settlements were situated on the Thames at Abingdon (Thomas 1979) and Wallingford (Rodwell 1975, 154), as well as that at Dorchester already discussed. Off the Thames, other possible sites are either at road junctions or at road-crossings over rivers.

In the south of the county a large settlement underlies Wantage in the area where the Cunetio road would have crossed the ancient route along the Downs (Rodwell 1975, 163). Where the same road crosses the Ock recent fieldwork has established that the well-known temple at Frilford lies in a dense settlement which also contains an apparent amphitheatre (Hingley 1982).

North of the Thames there is a chain of settlements along Akeman Street to the west of Alchester at the crossings of the Glyme, the Evenlode and the Windrush (Sansom's Platt, Wilcote, Asthall respectively). Fieldwork has shown that the Wilcote settlement stretches along the road for nearly a mile (Brodribb *et al.* 1978, 183). There are also very large settlements in the north of the county at Swalcliffe Lea (Webster 1975) and just over the modern county boundary at King's Sutton (Rodwell 1975, 13–15), and in the north-west there seems to have been an extensive site at Chipping Norton (Rodwell 1975).

The extent to which these sites discharged functions which we regard as being urban or, indeed, whether a Roman would have recognized any of them as towns is debatable. Of the dozen sites mentioned Alchester and Dorchester are the most likely to have had administrative functions. Of the others, several must have acted as *mutationes* or posting-stations along the main roads, and some must have contained *mansiones* or rest-houses (Rivet 1975). Frilford may have drawn much of its livelihood from the temple it surrounded.

Even these settlements must have depended principally on agriculture as the basis of their existence. Some can have been hardly more than villages. Others probably served also as local markets. If, as has often been suggested, the proximity of villas is indicative of economic activity, apart from Alchester and Dorchester, Abingdon and Frilford in particular stand out as potential market centres. On this argument one or more of the three Akeman Street sites may also have been important commercially.

There were also many smaller nucleated settlements which cannot by any stretch of the imagination be construed as potentially urban, for example, at Ducklington (Chambers 1976) and Appleford (Hinchliffe, Thomas 1981). At the latter site settlement focused on a triangular space, perhaps a village green. On this part of the Thames gravels, to the west of Dorchester, settlements are spaced at intervals of one to one-and-a-half kilometres. Such settlements could contain substantial buildings, as for example at Ducklington (Chambers 1976, 199), which if found on their own might well be interpreted as villas.

Villas tend, in the public eye, to be the most prominent surviving element of the Roman countryside and the Oxford region has a large number of examples. The term is now used to cover almost any isolated but rural building showing pretensions on the part of its owner towards a Romanized manner of life. Buildings included within the definition thus range from simple 'cottages' of four or five rooms, such as the first phase of Shakenoak Building B or of Ditchley, to the elaborate country houses of the late Roman period such as North Leigh. Apart from reflecting widely differing wealth on the part of their occupiers, they must also signify wide ranges of status and of power. It is also possible that similar buildings which are not isolated but in nucleated settlements of one sort or another, occupied similar niches within society and economy but are not classified as villas.

Nonetheless, the distribution of villas and also their size and degree of refinement do provide some evidence on where wealth was concentrated. Within the Oxford region there are clear patterns both in the distribution of villas in general and also in the apparent aspirations of these villas. They are concentrated in four main areas (see Miles 1982, fig. 1 and Appendix 1). In the north of the county there are a number of villas such as Thenford (just over the modern county boundary), and it is also possible that there are villa-type houses within the major settlement at Swalcliffe Lea.

Further south and to the east of the Cherwell there is a scatter of villas, running from Middleton Stoney north-east of Alchester (Rowley 1973) down towards Dorchester. With the exception of the villa at Islip, these lie mainly to the east of the Alchester-Dorchester road, perhaps because the area to the west of it was so intensively exploited by the pottery industry. Apart from Middleton Stoney none have been excavated since the nineteenth century, but records of work done at sites such as Headington Wick (Jewitt 1851) and of aerial photography (e.g. Miles 1982, fig. 3 b, h) suggest that these sites were modest in plan and in aspiration, being mainly of corridor or winged-corridor type.

The gravel terraces of the Thames and its tributaries, despite their dense occupation, are markedly lacking in villas, except for the area between Dorchester and Abingdon and to the west of Abingdon up the Ock Valley. This may partly reflect a tendency to build in timber, as in the early phases at Barton Court, making it difficult to distinguish important buildings from other settlement evidence by aerial photography, our major source of evidence in this area. It may also reflect a real gap in the distribution of this type of site, reflecting in its turn an absence of wealth.

Certainly the only villa to be investigated on the

gravels in recent years, at Barton Court Farm, near Abingdon, appears to have developed on a modest rather than a grand scale. Set in an enclosure in the middle of a field-system of small paddocks, the house was until the late third century of timber construction. Only in the late Roman period was a stone building erected. Even this was on a modest scale (Miles 1978a).

The densest concentration of villas in the region was in the foothills of the Cotswolds running north from the valley of the Windrush. At its northern end this concentration fades into the general scatter of villas in the north of the county. We are fortunate that several villas in this area have been intensively investigated in this century. Most recently the total excavation of the Shakenoak villa, between North Leigh and Akeman Street, has enabled its excavators to re-interpret the development of this area (Brodribb *el al.* 1968, 1971, 1972, 1973, 1978). The three villas investigated in this century (Shakenoak, Ditchley, North Leigh) all seem to have begun their development as simple rectangular 'cottage'-type buildings in the late first century on the site of an earlier native farmstead, perhaps representing the Romanization of their owners. Ditchley and Shakenoak both seem to have reached their greatest extent in the second century and the excavation of the latter has suggested that the status of both sites declined *c*.200 A.D. (Brodribb *et al.* 1972, 140–2; 1978, 202–5). This was not true of North Leigh, however (Wilson, Sherlock 1980). This site shows a continuous pattern of development and expansion and by the fourth century North Leigh was a massive courtyard villa with elaborate bath-suites, mosaic floors and wall-plaster. Clearly this must represent a great increase in wealth on the part of the site's owners, and perhaps at the expense of the estates supporting Ditchley and Shakenoak (Brodribb *et al.* 1978, 202–5). The general wealth of this part of the region in the late Roman period is indicated by the development of at least two other villas, at Stonesfield and Great Tew, on a similar scale to North Leigh.

Traditionally, the typical non-villa rural settlement type in Roman Britain is the isolated farmhouse sitting within its field-system. Peasant settlements appear to occur most commonly on the river gravels and many of the enclosures identified by aerial photography (Benson, Miles 1974, *passim*) may have been used for this sort of farm. Such farmsteads clearly existed off the river gravels in the early Roman period, since they have been found to precede the villas at North Leigh and Shakenoak. It is less clear that they are common later in the Roman period. The admittedly limited excavation evidence suggests that by the second century isolated enclosures were tending to develop as villas. Presumably other elements of society in these areas were tending to live in nucleated settlements such as Ducklington (Chambers 1975). The economic basis to this society was varied but must, as in all pre-industrial societies, have relied primarily on agriculture. In recent years the work of the Oxfordshire Archaeological Unit has greatly increased our understanding of this agricultural basis, particularly on the river gravels (e.g. Lambrick, Robinson 1979; Miles 1982), though much still remains to be done.

A recurrent pattern on the river gravels is one of settlements surrounded by clusters of paddocks and lying on long driveways. The paddocks often have wells in one corner and were possibly used for keeping stock. Field-systems as such are very rare (Miles 1982, 61) but it is likely that the apparently open areas between the settlements and their associated enclosures were used for arable. This pattern of land use is found around both villas (e.g. Barton Court Farm, Miles 1982, fig. 10) and native settlements.

Environmental evidence has added considerably to our knowledge of the use of the Thames gravels and floodplain (Robinson 1981). Lambrick and Robinson (1979) have suggested, for example, that the floodplain was used primarily for grazing and for hay meadows, while arable was restricted to the drier gravel terraces. Clearly the agriculture practised along the river valleys was mixed, with predominant products being spelt wheat among the crops, and cattle among livestock (Lambrick, Robinson 1979, 135–6), though sheep were obviously of considerable importance also. Another significant crop was flax (Robinson 1981, 273).

It is important not to make too rigid and artificial distinctions between agriculture on the gravels and what happened on other soil types, since it is likely that many settlements or estates may have exploited several different soil types (cf. Robinson 1981, 272–3). However, with the exception of Shakenoak, there is much less environmental evidence for agricultural practice off the gravels. Aerial photographic evidence suggests a similar pattern of small paddocks, often with a water supply, around villa enclosures with open, unditched areas beyond (cf. Miles 1982, figs. 8, 9, 10) perhaps used for arable. The predominant grain is spelt wheat, as on the gravels, and the predominant animal, at Shakenoak at least, cattle, followed by sheep. This suggest a broadly similar agricultural pattern to that on the gravels, apart from such exotica as the fish-farming practised at Shakenoak (Brodribb, Hands, Walker 1978, 15–19).

After agriculture the most important rural industries were probably extractive in type. The Oxford region, particularly the Cotswolds, contains good sources of building materials and they may well have been very significant economically. Stonesfield slate has been found as far away as Silchester and, possibly, Verulamium, while Taynton stone occurs at Colchester. Oolite was used extensively for architectural detail across the south-east, for example in London and at Richborough (Williams 1971) and Oxfordshire is a likely source, particularly given the potential use of the Thames as a route. It is, perhaps, tempting to see this industry as contributing to the obvious wealth of the owners of villas in the Cotswold foothills.

Manufacturing in the ancient world was, largely, organized on a small scale. Many crafts must have been carried on within the various urban and semi-urban centres in the area and thus added to their importance as market centres. The only form of production to leave any trace is, paradoxically, a rural one. This was the pottery industry of the Oxford region (Young 1977, *passim*).

As well as small and traditional potteries catering solely to local communities and slightly better established ones marketing over a wider area, there was to the east of the Cherwell and Thames and to the north of Dorchester, a much more substantial industry. This began in the early second century and from the start aspired to the production of wares such as mortaria. After achieving a modest distribution in the second and early third centuries, the Oxford potters c. 250 A.D. added to their range the production of fine table-wares and by the early to mid-fourth century were one of the major pottery producers of Roman Britain. Their success was probably due to a combination of factors such as availability of raw materials, good communications and the ability to produce wares which found a ready market (Young 1977, 231–241).

For any economic system of this type to produce a surplus it must have a market or markets. This the Oxford region clearly did. Part of this market must have been generated within the region itself through the various small towns, whose population would have absorbed part at least of the surplus production of the countryside in exchange for the services and goods they provided. It is unlikely though that such internal trade within the region would have generated wealth sufficient to support establishments such as North Leigh.

The two biggest potential consumers of agricultural surpluses were the army and the cities. It is doubtful that the army would have been a major source of profit since for long periods its needs for grain and, presumably, for livestock were levied as taxation. Large towns, however, must have been another matter. Unable to support themselves from their immediate hinterlands, they must have drawn supplies from further afield.

The region is however relatively close to four of the largest cities in Roman Britain – Verulamium, London, Silchester, and Cirencester. London, in particular, as the largest Roman city north of the Alps, must have had a voracious appetite for agricultural produce. The use of the Thames as a communication route would have made the city a particularly apposite market for the Oxford region.

There is the possibility also that in the fourth century British grain was exported to the continent though it is unclear whether this was an exceptional or a regular occurrence. Here again the Thames would have provided a cheap transport route for exporting agricultural produce. It is doubtful though that overseas trade was a major component of the Oxford region's market.

We have discussed the archaeological evidence for the Upper Thames Valley and have examined the various settlement types and the economic basis of the region. It is now necessary to conclude by discussing the type of society which lived in these settlements and derived its subsistence from this economy. Here archaeological evidence is at its least helpful. From it we have been able to deduce that certain types of site reflect certain activities or concentration of wealth. It will not reveal the mechanism by which activities were regulated or wealth concentrated.

For this type of analysis it is necessary to turn to documentary sources which are sadly lacking throughout this period of British history. The changing basis and organization of society within Roman Britain has to be gleaned from a few direct references and by analogy with what we know to have been happening in Gaul and further afield within the Empire.

Pre-Roman society in Britain was Celtic and thus tribally based, ruled by kings and composed of nobles and of peasants, although it must already have undergone considerable changes as the result of the impact of Roman influence and ideas (Todd 1981, 33–6). Power certainly lay in the hands of the nobility but it is unclear that land was personally owned by them. It may well have belonged to the tribe and the noble may merely have controlled the use of it (Todd 1981, 132).

The Roman system also vested power and wealth in the hands of relatively few people, with the essential difference that they had much less fettered control of their property and land and were much more able to exercise personal ownership. Society was also much more complex in that it had to cope with a degree of urbanization and with much larger trading and industrial elements.

It is far from clear how far, and over what period, the basically Celtic society of Britain was transformed into a Roman one. Certainly the nobility of the various tribes must have been relatively easily transformed into the decurions of the various self-governing *civitates* through which the Romans governed the province. The impact of the seizure of land for imperial estates, for the army and for the establishment of colonies must have altered the concept of property ownership. The development of taxation must have accelerated moves towards a cash economy.

It is likely that these pressures would have tended towards an assimilation of British customs to Roman ways. Certainly by the fourth century (and, presumably earlier), it was possible for members of the senatorial class, such as Saint Melania the Younger, to own estates in Britain. This would suggest that by the late Roman period British society, at least at the upper levels, was entirely within the Roman system. Certainly the taste of the wealthy, as evidenced by their mosaics and other artefacts, was entirely Romanized. It is less clear how far this Romanization had penetrated down to the peasantry who must still have formed the vast bulk of the population, and it may well be that they persisted relatively untouched.

Probably, therefore, it would be reasonable to see society in the Upper Thames Valley as one dominated by the landowners, themselves the successors of the pre-Roman Celtic tribal aristocracy, and increasingly Romanized over the generations. Their wealth would have derived principally from agriculture and, to a lesser extent, from the exploitation of raw materials for building and for pottery manufacture, though the exact mechanics by which this happened will never be clear. The vast bulk of the population would still have been working on the land and probably living in ways little different from those of their ancestors.

The two walled towns would have provided administrative centres and, with some of the large unwalled settlements such as Abingdon, local market centres servicing the predominantly rural population. Possibly, as suggested above, there were major movements of bulk commodities such as grain, pottery and stone to large towns well outside the region. This economic and social system would have taken many generations to develop and would have been in a state of continuous change and development. For example, it is possible that certain estates were growing at the expense of others in the third and fourth centuries, as suggested for North Leigh, presumably meaning that certain landowners were getting a great deal wealthier at the expense of others. Probably the system was at its most developed in the fourth century. Certainly this was the period at which the great villas like North Leigh reached their full size.

Yet within one or two generations of 400 A.D. the complex culture of the Roman Upper Thames Valley appears to have collapsed, as occurred over the whole of Roman Britain. The reasons for this are still very unclear, as is the timing. Clearly major problems included the increasing Saxon pressure indicated by the evidence for Germanic mercenaries at Dorchester, and the progressive withdrawal of troops either to protect the other, and in the last resort, more important parts of the Empire, or to support their generals in bids for the purple on the continent.

These reasons, of themselves, do not fully account for total collapse of Romano-British culture though undoubtedly they would have assisted. Possibly the increased insecurity led to the collapse of trade routes on which prosperity was based, thus removing much of the wealth of the landowners. Possibly also the replacement of a Romanized landowning aristocracy by incoming Saxon settlers in the fifth century would ultimately have removed those elements principally interested in appearing Romanized.

References

Benson, D. & Miles, D. (1974) *The Upper Thames Valley: an archaeological Survey of the River Gravels*
Bradley, R.J. (1979) 'Rescue excavations in Dorchester-on-Thames', Oxoniensia 43, 17–39
Brodribb, A.C.C., Hands, A.R., Walker, D.R. (1968) *Excavations at Shakenoak I*
Brodribb et al. (1971) *Excavations at Shakenoak II*
Brodribb et al. (1972) *Excavations at Shakenoak III*
Brodribb et al. (1973) *Excavations at Shakenoak IV*
Brodribb et al. (1978) *Excavations at Shakenoak V*
Case, H. & Whittle, A. (1982) *Settlement patterns in the Oxford Region: excavations at the Abingdon causewayed enclosure and other sites*. CBA Res. Rept. 44
Chambers, R.A. (1976) 'A Romano-British settlement site and seventh century burial, Ducklington, Oxon, 1974', Oxoniensia 40, 171–200
Chambers, R.A. (1977) 'Excavations in the Witney area', Oxoniensia 41, 17–55
Chambers, R.A. (1979) 'The Archaeology of the Charlbury to Arncott gas pipeline, 1972', Oxoniensia 43, 40–47
Emery, F. (1974) *The Oxfordshire Landscape*
Frere, S.S. (1964) 'Excavations at Dorchester-on-Thames, 1961', Archaeol. J. 119, 114–149
Grew, F.O. (1981) 'Roman Britain in 1980', Britannia 12, 313–68
Hinchliffe, J. & Thomas, R. (1981) 'Archaeological excavations at Appleford', Oxoniensia 45, 9–111
Hingley, R. (1982) 'Frilford: Noah's Ark', CBA Group 9 Newsletter 12, 150–152
Hinton D. & Rowley, T. (1974) 'Excavations on the route of the M40', Oxoniensia 38, 1–183
Jevitt, L. (1851) 'On Roman remains, recently discovered at Headington, near Oxford', J. Brit. Archaeol. Ass. 6, 52–67
Jones, M. & Miles, D. (1979) 'Celt and Roman in the Thames Valley: approaches to cultural change' in *Invasion and Response: the case of Roman Britain*, eds. B.C. Burnham, H.B. Johnson, BAR 73, 315–27
Lambrick, G. (1970) 'Some old roads of North Berkshire', Oxoniensia 34, 78–93
Lambrick, G. & Robinson, M. (1969) *Iron Age and Roman riverside settlements at Farmoor, Oxfordshire*. CBA Res. Rept. 32
Leech, R. (1977) *The Upper Thames Valley in Gloucestershire and Wiltshire*
Margary, I. (1973) *Roman Roads in Britain*. 3rd ed.
Miles, D. (1978a) 'Barton Court Farm, 1972-6', CBA Group 9 Newsletter 8, 106–108
Miles, D. (1978b) 'The Upper Thames Valley', in *Early Land Allotment*, eds. H.C. Bowen, P.J. Fowler, BAR 48, 81–8
Miles, D. (1982) 'Confusion in the countryside: some comments from the Upper Thames Valley' in *The Romano-British Countryside: Studies in Rural Settlement and Economy*, ed. D. Miles, BAR 103, 53–80
Miles, D. (forthcoming) *Archaeology at Barton Court Farm, Abingdon*
Rivet, A.L.F. (1969) 'Social and economic aspects' in *The Roman Villa in Britain*, ed. A.L.F. Rivet
Rivet, A.L.F. (1975) 'Summing up: the classification of minor towns and related settlements' in Rodwell & Rowley 1975, 111–114
Robinson, M. (1981) 'The Iron Age to Early Saxon environment of the Upper Thames terrace' in *The Environment of Man: the Iron Age to the Anglo-Saxon Period*, ed. M. Jones, G. Dimbleby, BAR 87, 251–286
Rodwell, K.A., ed. (1975) *Historic Towns in Oxfordshire: a survey of the new county*
Rodwell, W. & Rowley, T., eds. (1975) *The Small Towns of Roman Britain*. BAR 15
Rowley, T. (1973) 'First report on the excavations at Middleton Stoney Castle', Oxoniensia 37, 109–136
Rowley, T. (1975) 'The Roman towns of Oxfordshire' in Rodwell & Rowley 1975, 115–124
Rowley, T. & Brown, L. (1982) 'Excavations at Beech House Hotel, Dorchester-on-Thames, 1972', Oxoniensia 46, 1–55
Taylor, M.V., Harden, D.B., Sutherland, C.H.V. (1939) 'Romano-British remains', in *Victoria County History of Oxfordshire* 1, 267–345
Taylor, M.V. (1954) 'The Roman period' in *The Oxford Region*, eds. A.F. Martin and R.W. Steel, 85–95
Thomas, R.M. (1979) *Roman Abingdon: an assessment of the evidence*. Unpublished B.A. thesis, University of Southampton
Todd, M. (1981) *Roman Britain*
Webster, G. (1974) 'A Romano-British fragment of military equipment from Alchester', Oxoniensia 38, 385–6
Webster, G. (1975) 'Small towns without defences', in Rodwell & Rowley 1975, 53–66
Williams, J.H. (1971) 'Roman building-materials in south-east England', Britannia 2, 166–195
Wilson, D.R. (1975) 'The 'small towns' of Roman Britain from the air', in Rodwell & Rowley 1975, 9–50
Wilson, D.R. & Sherlock, D.A. (1980) *North Leigh Roman Villa*
Young, C.J. (1977) *The Roman Pottery Industry of the Oxford Region*. BAR 43

THE EARLY SAXON PERIOD

SONIA CHADWICK HAWKES

Introduction and Background

None of our early historical sources, nor any of the founder legends or genealogies relating to the kingdoms of the Germanic peoples who eventually came collectively to be known as the English, bear directly on the West Saxon settlement of the valley of the river Thames around Oxford in the fifth century.

And even had we such sources, it is doubtful indeed whether they would now be regarded as any more reliable in detail than the recorded traditions about the Germanic takeover of Kent or the Saxon incursions into Sussex and southern, or Chalk Wessex at this period. It is not so much that the battles and landtakings which form the chief part of what has come down to us, principally in the *Anglo-Saxon Chronicle* but also in the *Historia Brittonum*, both works compiled in the ninth century, are necessarily fictional, nor that some of the personalities involved did not actually exist as remembered heroes, warleaders and founders of dynasties. It is that one has to reckon with human fallibility in transmitting accurately what must have originated in purely oral traditions, and the errors and omissions which may have crept in; with later embroidery of events; and, by the ninth century, the strong probability of manipulation of sources, deliberate editing, to suit the bias of later times. What was finally committed to vellum in our surviving insular sources, Anglo-Saxon and Celtic alike, has been shown by recent work on Dark Age historiography all to be flawed to a greater or lesser extent in these respects. The texts require rigorous evaluation, of both their sources and the contexts in which they were written, and, though it has begun, such exact criticism of even such a fundamental work as the *Anglo-Saxon Chronicle* is still in its early stages (Sims-Williams 1983b, 26–410).

What is abundantly clear already, however, is that our insular texts must be discounted when it comes to dates. Recent research has already shown that, at least for the fifth century, probably also the sixth, dates of events were computed by later writers and should nowadays be regarded as quite artificial. This applies especially to the so-called *Adventus Saxonum*, the first arrival of the English in Britain, the exact pin-pointing of which, in terms of the new *Anno Domini* dating which he was introducing to historical writing in his *Historia Ecclesiastica* in AD 731 (Harrison 1976, 76 ff.), was to preoccupy and tax the resources of the Venerable Bede (Plummer 1896, II, 27 f.). On this subject his sources were slight indeed, essentially only the historical section of the *De Excidio et Conquestu Britanniae*, composed, probably towards the middle of the sixth century (Miller 1975a; Sims-Williams 1983a, 3–5), by the western British cleric Gildas. Primarily this was not a work of history at all, but a thundering homily denouncing the misdeeds of the clergy and laity of his own time. The historical essay, giving the saga of the Pictish wars, and the horrors of the later Saxon conquest which followed just such a period of inertia and corruption as Gildas saw in his own day, is a moralising tract carefully constructed to remind his readers that 'God doubtless had an equally crushing punishment in store for his own generation' (Winterbottom 1978, 5). His history, such as it is, was from the start subordinated to moral aims; and this, its errors of fact, its ignorance of or indifference to names and dates, its deliberate or inadvertent selectivity, its rhetorical style and formulaic construction – three wars, three appeals, the Saxons' three ships – almost rob it of all credibility. Indeed, Sims-Williams (1983a) argues that Gildas was almost wholly dependent on inaccurate oral tradition, and that his conscious use of these traditions to parallel the situation in his own time 'is also a warning against taking him at face value.' And yet, as we shall see, there are details which demand our attention. For Bede, the fatal fascination was the single datable reference, a quotation from a letter in which Britons appealed for help against unnamed barbarians, to *Agitius ter consul*, whom he interpreted, rightly in the view of most modern scholars, as the Roman *Magister Militum* in the West, Aetius, whose third consulship in 446 gave him the title 'thrice consul' till his death in AD 453 or 454.

This appeal prefaced a whole sequence of events – a famine, civil war, a victory over northern enemies, a time of prosperity, the rise and fall of tyrants, vice and corruption in church and state, a rumour of a new attack and, finally, a plague. Only after all this did a council of Britons, and the 'proud tyrant', whom Bede (and probably Gildas himself) named as Vortigern (Dumville 1977, 183 f.), decide to invite in Saxons to act as mercenaries, from Gildas's viewpoint the ultimate act of folly, with all the dire consequences that followed before the British began to fight back successfully under Ambrosius Aurelianus, and subsequently scored a famous victory at a place called *Mons Badonicus*. This secured them an interval of comparative peace which still endured at the time when Gildas himself was writing, in the forty-fourth year after. Bede, having no means of cross-checking his source, had perforce to accept the letter to Aetius as a *terminus a quo* for the *Adventus*; but that he was not happy with it, and was well aware how badly it constricted the timetable of subsequent events, has been shown by Morris (1965), and Miller (1975b), who reveal how he edited Gildas' text in taking the narrative over into his own *Historia*, to minimise the interval between the letter and the invitation to the Saxons. His own dates for their coming, variously 445, 446/7, 449, 450–55, seem all his own computations, without external authority of any kind at all. However, AD 449, the date at which the *Anglo-Saxon Chronicle* introduces Hengest and his federates into Kent, might have been obtained by Bede from a Kentish source (Alcock 1971, 108 f.), but if so it can scarcely have been anything but another computed date (Harrison 1976, 123 ff.) of dubious accuracy. Finally, the *Historia Brittonum* gives a quite different and, from the modern archaeological view, more attractive date for the invitation to Hengest by Vortigern, but AD 428 has likewise been shown to be a computation, and a manifestly false one (Dumville 1974).

Such revelations, however, are very recent. Bede in particular, because of his high reputation as a historian, was very influential from Anglo-Saxon times onwards, and his mid-fifth century dating for the *Adventus Saxonum* remained unchallenged for too long. An important paper by C.E. Stevens (1941), which shed new light on the whole subject, did not receive the attention it deserved, and the first major shake-up came only with Morris's 'Dark Age Dates' (1965). Though now overtaken by newer and more austere critical studies, this provocative essay was very attractive and influential at the time. Probably it and the book which followed (Morris 1973) were largely responsible for the great upsurge in source criticism for the history of Dark Age Britain which has followed in the last decade: certainly it caused archaeologists to re-evaluate their own evidence for the date of the Anglo-Saxon settlements. Hitherto they had mostly allowed Bede and the Chronicler to mislead them into dating their earliest artefacts at least a generation too late. Even such a sceptic about the value of the historical sources as Oxford's E.T. Leeds never really managed to expunge from his thinking the assumption of a mid-fifth century beginning for the material culture of the insular Anglo-Saxons whose study he dominated for forty years, from 1913 to 1954. And his successors still have to be alert to adjust to the implications of the changed situation and above all be careful not to over-react and rush to extremes. The new-model *Adventus*, based on independent work on the archaeology as well as stringent criticism of the history, is only just beginning to take shape. And the outline I give here, as an introduction to the Saxon settlement of the Upper Thames, may yet be subject to some shape-changing in response to future finds and future researchers. However, provisionally it is as follows.

Roman Britain had been under attack by sea-borne raiders, Picts and Scots as well as North-Sea coastal peoples known to the ancient world collectively as Saxons, since the later third century AD. Of the three the Saxons posed the greatest threat because for them piracy was no mere adventure but a response to a genuine and increasing hardship, rising to desperation, for their whole livelihood was under threat. War had destroyed their once prosperous trade with the western Roman provinces, and the sea was destroying the precarious economy which had supported it. All along the North Sea coast from what is now Dutch Friesland to western Holstein, the villages established on the fertile clay marsh had begun to be inundated by the rising sea-level of a major marine transgression which reached its peak in the fifth century. As fewer people could be supported by local resources, more of the menfolk had either to take service in the Roman army or resort to piracy, gaining a livelihood by plunder. Late Roman writers tell us that these Saxon pirates were formidable. The defensive measures taken against them, the maintenance of a fleet in the Channel and the construction on both sides of strong stone forts garrisoned to defend the key harbours of what became known as the 'Saxon Shore', in Britain extending from Norfolk to Hampshire, were only partially successful (Johnson 1976). Despite the continued maintenance of the northern frontier on Hadrian's Wall and the building of west-coast forts, Britain was overrun in 367 by a combined assault of all her foes.

Valentinian I's general Count Theodosius came to repair the situation and apparently added yet one more element to the defence, if this had not begun even earlier, the equipping of already walled towns with new arrangements for active defence in the form of *ballistae*, heavy artillery firing iron bolts, which almost certainly required professionals of a sort to man them (Johnson 1980, 95 ff.). Campbell (1982, 13 f.), from the viewpoint of a medieval historian, comments with amaze on 'the military effort of which Rome was capable' and which it expended on Britain. In addition to the various garrisons there was a Field Army of 6,000 men under the *Comes Britanniarum*, 'about the same size as William the Conqueror's army at Hastings'. The quality and character of these troops in the later fourth century is very obscure, but many of them, in all ranks, were certainly Germans (Salway 1981, 374 ff.). Archaeological evidence, in the form of their distinctive burials, shows officially-equipped Franks and Saxons as a major presence in military units attached to forts and towns, also county estates, in northern Gaul at this period (Böhme 1974). In Britain there has been less excavation of the cemeteries which alone can attest them beyond doubt, but it is safe to say that there were German officers in the latest garrison at Richborough (Hawkes and Dunning 1961, 17), headquarters fort of the Saxon Shore; in towns such as Winchester (Clarke 1979, 377 ff.), perhaps Colchester (Crummy 1981, 16) and, in the early fifth century, certainly Dorchester-on-Thames. The official employment of Saxons at the latter site and, apparently, also at the Roman villa at Shakenoak, both in Oxfordshire, will be discussed further below. Such barbarian soldiers, with their sometimes flashy equipment, often accompanied by their own women wearing their own national dress, must have become familiar to late Roman eyes in the western provinces, and, indeed, may have influenced provincial taste.

In 383, the Roman general Magnus Maximus, victor against Picts and Scots in the previous year, was elected Emperor by the army in Britain, and took part of it with him in his bid for Italy which was scotched by Theodosius the Great in 388. Despite this, the defences of Britain seem to have been maintained, and it was not until the closing years of the century that another expeditionary force had to be sent from Rome, this time commanded by Rome's most senior general, the *Magister Militum* Stilicho, himself a Vandal and the classic example of how high German officers could rise in the service. From the little information we have, he seems to have busied himself with frontier defence, but also to have withdrawn troops from Britain to help against the Goths in Italy in 401. How large an army remained behind is problematic, but it was enough to stage a major revolt against Stilicho in 406–7, electing three British emperors in rapid succession (Thompson 1977 *pace* Stevens 1957). The motivation is obscure but may have concerned lack of pay, since the last major shipment of Imperial coin had been in 402 (Salway 1981, 424 f.). An increasing sense of isolation there must have been and this must have intensified when, on the last day of the year 406, a great horde of Suebi, Vandals and Alans crossed the frozen Rhine at Mainz, defeated the Frankish federates who opposed them, and swept on into Gaul causing devastation wherever they went. By May 407 there seemed to be a real threat to the Channel ports and Britain itself, so the third British emperor Constantine III, elected for the purpose, crossed over to Gaul to deal with the situation, certainly taking part of the army of Britain with him. Like Maximus he never returned and was soon killed. In 409, however, he was in such a strong position in Gaul that the legitimate emperor Honorius had to recognize him as Augustus and joint consul. But before the year was out the major part of his forces, in Spain now under his general Gerontius, had revolted from him and Britain was again undefended. What happened next is recorded by the late fifth-century Byzantine historian Zosimus (vi.5.2 f.), in a difficult passage which has been subject to various interpretations. Thompson (1977, 306) translates as follows: In 409, when Constantine was powerless to prevent them, 'barbarians from beyond the Rhine overran everything at will and reduced the inhabitants of the British Island and some of the peoples in Gaul to the necessity of rebelling from the Roman Empire and living by themselves, no longer obeying the Romans' laws. The Britons, therefore, taking up arms and fighting on their own behalf, freed the cities from the barbarians who were pressing upon them.' Recently Bartholomew (1982, 263 f.) came up with a new translation of the last few words, 'freed the cities from the barbarians who were billeted there'. This seemed very attractive and convincing because it appeared to refer to the dismissal of the units of largely barbarian troops, whether of the field army or merely local garrisons, whom Constantine III, if not Stilicho before him, had left stationed in the fortified towns of lowland Britain. If left unpaid, they must have been becoming troublesome and a burden to the civic authorities. However, Thompson's dismissive rejoinder (1983) has great authority, and his version must be reinstated. Returning again to Zosimus, he tells how the Britons expelled the Roman officials and set up their own administration; presumably it was Constantine's officials who were dismissed. If Honorius's letters of 410 to the cities, instructing them to defend themselves (Zosimus vi. 10. 2), were really addressed to Britain (and there is debate on this point, viz. Thompson 1982 & 1983), it seems likely that they may have been in reply to loyalist appeals for help to Rome itself. But Rome never intervened in Britain again: according to Procopius (*De Bello Vandalico* i. 2. 38), after the defeat of Constantine in 411, 'The Romans were never able to recover Britain, but from that time it remained under the rule of tyrants' (local usurpers). The Byzantine sources here link us to the insular: at any time after AD 409 any rulers set up by the Britons would to Roman eyes be seen as usurpers; 'tyrants' as both Gildas and Procopius called them.

The 'barbarians from beyond the Rhine' who caused the Britons to take matters into their own hands in 409 are hardly likely to have been the horde which invaded Gaul in 406, for this had now moved down to Spain. The *Gallic Chronicle of 452* provides the predictable identification: at the time in question 'Britain was devastated by an incursion of Saxons'. Some years ago the authenticity of this Chronicle was called into question (Miller 1978) but, happily, a more recent and authoritative examination of it has proved both its independence and date of composition 'before Valentinian's murder in 455' beyond reasonable doubt (Wood 1984). There are problems in arriving at precise dates from it, thanks to the Chronicler's original errors and 'inability to correlate two dating systems', but there can be no reason to doubt his information that while Constantine III was having problems in Europe, Britain was invaded by Saxons. We can similarly believe his later reference to events in either 442–3 or 445–6, depending on whether one uses his dating by regnal years or olympiads, written quite independently of Bede, probably using the same source as the *Gallic Chronicle of 511*, which dates the same events to AD 440. The events are of course those enshrined in the long famous passage, 'The provinces of Britain, continually up to this time oppressed by various disastrous events, are subjected to the power of Saxons'. Now that the credibility of these two key entries in the *Gallic Chronicle of 452* has been restored to us, it is possible once again to place the insular traditions for the *Adventus Saxonum* and its aftermath within an independently-dated framework.

It has long been acknowledged that the Gallic Chronicler's second entry for fifth-century Britain must refer to something which from across the Channel appeared to be decisive: a takeover, no less, probably in south-east Britain, which radically changed the balance of power. This would fit well with the Kentish traditions, most fully preserved in the *Historia Brittonum*, but also outlined in the *Anglo-Saxon Chronicle*, which start with the story of Hengest, his employment as a federate by Vortigern, his treachery, and the revolt that resulted in the ceding of all Kent, Essex, Middlesex and Sussex, with some other places (*H.B.* 46), to the Germanic peoples concerned. The archaeological evidence fits well, too (Fig. 5). The years around and after the middle of the fifth century saw the beginnings of widespread settlement in East Kent, evidenced chiefly by the jewellery brought by women from the homeland (Hawkes and Pollard 1981, 320 ff.; Hawkes 1982, 70). In the present state of the evidence, mid-fifth century developments are not so clear in Essex and Middlesex, but an impressive case has been made for a new land allotment in East Sussex, to predominantly Saxon groups who settled between the rivers Ouse and Cuckmere (Welch 1983, 217 ff.). And there is evidence for Germanic penetration further west along the south coast during the second half of the fifth century, in southern Hampshire at Portchester, in Portsmouth Harbour (Cunliffe 1976), in the valleys of the rivers Meon (Aldsworth 1978) and Itchen (Biddle 1976), and also on the Isle of Wight (Arnold 1982). By the early sixth century there were Anglo-Saxon settlers in the region around Salisbury in Wiltshire, at such sites as Petersfinger (Leeds and Shortt 1953), Winterbourne Gunner (Musty 1964) and Collingbourne Ducis (Gingell 1978). Some of these, at least, must have reached their destination by boat up the river Avon from Christchurch Harbour (Fig. 6), which is by far the most plausible identification of the Chronicler's *Cerdicesora*. In fact, the sequence of events recorded in the *Anglo-Saxon Chronicle* seems nowadays to be remarkably well vindicated by the evidence of archeology, to an extent undreamed of until recently. Of course the precise dates and some of the personal names remain suspect, but the various cemeteries and settlement sites are evidence, if not of battles, at least of Anglo-Saxon landtaking at the approximate times and places indicated by the Chronicler.

The fact that the ninth-century Chronicler could use some apparently accurate sources about fifth-century events along the south coast implies the preservation of traditions of great antiquity relating to the founder legends of what became three separate Anglo-Saxon kingdoms. Bede apparently did not know all these stories but learned just enough from his informants in Kent to link Gildas's first federates in their three ships with Hengest. What may have influenced Bede is that his copy of the *De Excidio* named the 'proud tyrant' Vortigern (Miller 1975b, 252–3), and Vortigern was already an indispensable part of the Hengest story. Whether Gildas meant to refer to Kent when writing about the arrival of three boat-loads of German federates *in orientali parte insulae* we shall never now know. There are several details in his story at this point, his use of the Germanic word for ship, *cēol*, in referring to the three 'keels', *cyulis* (23, 3), and his correct use of late Roman technical terms for the billeting and supplying of federate troops – *hospites, annona, epimenia* (23, 5) –

which imply that he was not relying for this episode on mere oral tradition but had a contemporary written source at his elbow (Hawkes 1982, 66). If that source, presumably a British one, named the place to which the federates came, then Gildas was being deliberately vague: to his British readers in the west perhaps 'the eastern part of the island' would have had more impact than either the old Roman or the new Anglo-Saxon names for specific places. By the time Gildas was writing the whole east coast was lost territory and must have seemed very remote. However, if as most critics believe (*pace* Thompson 1979), Gildas wrote the *De Excidio* in the British south-west, in south Wales or the kingdom of Dumnonia, then it is very tempting to assume it was the federate revolt in the south-east and its consequences which concerned him. The Saxon expansion westwards in the fifth and earlier sixth centuries actually threatened Dumnonia itself. But, if present archaeological evidence is representative, it seems not to have been very successful: the cemetery at Kingsworthy near Winchester in Hampshire indicates a community in deep trouble; settlement in Wiltshire was sparse and limited to the east side of the modern county; and, except for a small group of Saxons buried on Hardown Hill in west Dorset, there seems to have been no Germanic expansion further west until the later seventh century. Twenty-five years ago Kenneth Jackson (1958) made a good case, on philological and historical grounds, for locating the British victory at *Mons Badonicus* at Badbury Rings in east Dorset (Fig. 6). Only excavation of the hillfort itself, and the discovery of a battle cemetery and perhaps Dark Age refortification, as at Cadbury Castle to the north-west, could positively prove it. But what archaeology now tells us about the setback to Saxon hopes in this area – Poole Harbour, which Badbury dominates, should logically have been their next objective – reinforces Jackson's identification and leaves Badbury Rings very much the front runner amongst all possible candidates. Much in its favour is that it guarded territory which Gildas knew and was concerned with. It stood at the very portals of Dumnonia.

Whether or not Gildas indeed meant to stage his *Adventus Saxonum* and the federate revolt which followed in southern Britain, most modern commentators agree that he must have misplaced the letter to Aetius in his narrative (Sims-Williams 1983b, 14), confusing it with a much earlier appeal (Stevens 1941). He quoted from it: 'To Aetius, thrice consul: the groans of the British . . . The barbarians push us back to the sea, the sea pushes us back to the barbarians; between these two kinds of death we are either drowned or slaughtered.' As always he seems to have been striving for dramatic effect, and for his purposes probably it did not matter whether he used the letter to climax the Pictish wars rather than the Saxon revolt. With the aid of the *Gallic Chronicle of 452*, however, and with benefit of modern archaeology, we, unlike Bede, can put the record straight. The British appeal to Aetius between 446 and 454 makes best sense in the context of the Saxon revolt, which caused so many of the Britons to take refuge overseas, in Gaul and Brittany, by the 460s (Salway 1981, 491 f.).

According to the *Historia Brittonum* (31), Vortigern, the man chiefly responsible for the recruitment of Saxon federates, 'ruled in Britain' (Gildas's term for him was *superbus tyrannus* (23), hence perhaps as a successor of Constantine III), 'and during his rule . . . he was under pressure, from fear of the Picts and Irish, and of a Roman invasion, and, not least, from dread of Ambrosius.' Ambrosius, probably the same British leader who fought successfully against the Saxons after the Saxon revolt, possibly led an opposition party to Vortigern (Myres 1960), which might have attempted to call in help from Rome. It has been suggested that the time when Vortigern would have had most to fear from intervention from across the Channel was between 425 and 429, when the ambitious Aetius was *Magister Militum* in Gaul with a large Hunnic army at his back (Salway 1981, 474 ff.). The stationing of Hengest and his federates on Thanet in east Kent could have been a move to block the approach route from Gaul (C.F.C. Hawkes 1956) at this date twenty years before the revolt. Depending on one's reading of Gildas, whether he meant to refer to the federates in Kent or took a wider view of affairs in the east, it is possible to agree with most modern writers on the subject that Hengest and his following were not necessarily the first Germanic federates in Britain. By Vortigern's time large-scale federate settlement was normal Imperial policy and the build-up in Britain could have begun earlier. The historical sources can take us no further and it is time now to put the archaeology to question.

The Saxon Settlement of the Upper Thames – the Federate Phase.

The earliest Saxons of whom we know in the Oxford region were living, during the first decades of the fifth century, in the Roman villa at Shakenoak, in the parish of North Leigh (Brodribb, Hands & Walker 1968, 1972 & 1978, 205 ff.). By this date the villa buildings were ruinous and only the long barn-like Room I in Building A, internally 13.5 × 4.5m, remained roofed. It was intensively occupied, however, by a group of people who dumped their refuse immediately outside in what had once been adjacent rooms. Excavation of their midden revealed that they had used unusually large quantities of local Oxford colour-coated pottery, disposed of worn Theodosian coinage, and threw away the outworn remnants of metal fittings from at least one late Roman 'military' belt which had originated on the Continent (Hawkes 1968). Amongst the latter, the most diagnostic item was part of a strap-slide (Brodribb *et al.* 1968, fig. 29, 15) which can be paralleled in German officers' graves at Krefeld Gellep in the Rhineland and at Vermand in France (Böhme 1974, Taf. 81, 10 & 136, 9) and amongst the finds from Richborough, Kent, headquarters fort of the British Saxon Shore defences (Hawkes 1968, fig. 33, 2–3). Originally it must have formed part of a chip-carved belt-set of Böhme's Type A (1974, 55 ff.). Such sets were produced in Imperial workshops, possibly at Trier, during the later fourth century, as standard issue to officials and high-ranking military personnel especially, and became distributed all along the frontiers of the Western Roman Empire, with a heavy concentration in northern Gaul and the Rhineland (Böhme 1974, Karte 11). Here the numbers are high because of the large numbers of German troops buried with their equipment. It seems likely that the original wearer of the Type A belt from Shakenoak was a foreign mercenary, a regular officer serving under Count Theodosius or in one of the later relieving armies down to that of Stilicho, who settled at Shakenoak after retirement from active service. It has been suggested that he was placed there, in what had become a primitive dwelling on a perhaps subordinate estate, to help protect the flourishing late Roman villa at nearby North Leigh. Whether more than one old soldier was involved cannot be known: the rosette-attachment found could have formed part of the same *cingulum* or official belt, while the third piece of late fourth-century belt equipment was a battered plate from a British-made Type I buckle (Brodribb *et al.* 1968, fig. 32, 58), meant for a very narrow belt (Hawkes & Dunning 1961; Hawkes 1973). It is becoming increasingly likely that such buckles were female gear (Hawkes 1974): certainly the Saxon womenfolk of the early fifth-century military personnel at Mucking (Evison 1981, fig. 4, d) and Dorchester-on-Thames (discussed below) chose to wear them. Perhaps they were a special issue, comparable to the brooches made by official workshops for the women of the German officer-class in northern Gaul in the later fourth century, or perhaps they had become the fashion in civilian circles too. Good primary contexts for them are still insufficient to tell us precisely who wore them before the fifth century.

Thus far there has been nothing very specific, except perhaps their style of living, to indicate that the Shakenoak people were in fact Saxons: their material goods were all Roman (as were those of the military Germans in Gaul). But when *c*. 420/30 their dwelling burnt down and they moved to an undiscovered place somewhere else in the vicinity, they began to use the enclosure ditch of the villa (Site F) as a rubbish tip (Brodribb *et al.* 1972); and here were found further pieces of belt-equipment similar to those from Building A (Hawkes 1972), no longer with coins or colour-coated pottery, but with freshly broken wheel-made calcite-gritted wares, hand-made Saxon pottery (Berisford 1972) and a North German small-long brooch of the first half of the fifth century (Vierck 1972). There seems to be a continuity (*pace* Brown 1972). Shakenoak is by no means central to the early fifth-century Saxon settlement of the Upper Thames, and the presence there, attested by brooch and handmade pottery, of at least one female immigrant of this period is most easily explained if the Romanized military veteran had been a Saxon, whose descendants would have been glad to make contact with new arrivals from the homeland, and perhaps arrange a marriage with a daughter of one of the Dorchester Saxons or their neighbours.

Amongst the earliest Saxon burials in the Oxford region, the famous trio found at Dorchester-on-Thames in the late nineteenth century have long been central to the debate about the beginnings of Anglo-Saxon settlement in Britain. Already in his first pioneering book, E.T. Leeds (1913, 55f., fig. 8) recognized them as unusually early, and J.N.L. Myres, seeking to accommodate them to Bede's dating for the first Germanic settlements, came up with the idea that they must have been 'some nest of Teutonic river-pirates established on the Thames even before the final collapse of Roman government' (Collingwood & Myres 1936, 394 f.; Myres 1954, 96). The first full publication of the finds clarified matters considerably (Kirk & Leeds 1952/3). There had been three graves of Saxons: two found 500m south of the Roman town in the eastern end of the Iron Age earthwork known as the Dyke Hills, where late Roman burials had been found some years previously (Dickinson 1976, II, 76 f.: Dorchester I); and a third, found in unknown circumstances in the Minchin recreation ground (Dorchester II) 400m north of the town, near to the Roman road where one would have expected a late Roman cemetery. Further excavation of both sites is sorely needed, to determine the numbers of this important Saxon community, and the relationship of their burials to those of any surviving British population. But their context seems definitely late- or sub-Roman (Fig. 7). Dyke Hills grave 1 (Kirk & Leeds 1952/3, fig. 27) contained a six-foot male buried with weapons: a knife, a Continental type B2 spearhead (Swanton 1974, 41) and, to judge from the bone sword-knot bead (Evison 1975, 309 f., pl. LXV, c), a sword which must have been included amongst the ironwork found in 1874 but thrown into the river. The bronze objects from this grave have received much attention, but it was not until twenty-five years ago that they were identified correctly as the fittings for a particularly broad and late form of the Roman official belt (Werner 1958, 381 ff.), and even then some time elapsed, while systematic work on such assemblages was done on the Continent, before it was possible to date and reconstruct them (Bullinger 1969; Ypey 1969; Böhme 1974). The photograph published here is the Ashmolean's reconstruction (Pl. 5a): a slightly different version has been figured by Evison (1968, fig. 1). In either case we see how the tubular-sided plate and its non-matching counterpart formed the end-plates for a stout leather belt about 9.3 cm broad, which was stiffened at back and sides by cast and riveted metal strips, and cinched in at centre waist by means of a separate, narrower strap, attached by shorter riveted strips, which passed through the buckle and terminated in a strap-tag. Close parallels from recent excavated graves in Holland, where the lay-out was preserved, indicate that the rosette attachments depended downwards and served to attach implements (Ypey 1969, Abb. 13, 15 etc.). The Dorchester belt-set is made of plain bronze, as are most of its parallels on the Continent, which are normally decorated, if at all, by simple punch-work. The contrast with the elaborate chip-carved belt-sets of the Valentinianic army is very marked, and Werner, Ypey and Böhme have all made a chronological distinction without arriving at any very precise date for the Dorchester type, which Ypey calls Type B and Böhme 'Simple'. It should be possible to be more precise.

The earliest form of the belt with slim tubular end-plates is Böhme's Type Vieuxville (1974, 61, Fundliste 13, Karte 13), in which zoomorphic buckle with hinged plate, strap-tag, end-plates and strap-slide are all still chip-carved, and the belt-width ranges from 45–100 mm. A couple have been found in Lower Saxony, suggesting some recruitment from that area, but the majority indicate the area of service; the Rhineland from Mainz northwards to Nymegen, and northern Gaul from the Meuse around Namur to the Aisne and Somme rivers, with single outliers in south Germany, Thuringia, the Alps and Italy (Böhme 1974, Karte 12). As one might expect from this restricted distribution, so different from the Valentinianic period, the date appears to be early fifth century. The rich grave from Vieuxville, the only one with associated coins, is dated by silver *siliquae* of Constantine III (407–11) and Jovinus (411–13), both in fresh condition, at earliest to the second decade of the fifth century (Breuer & Roosens 1957, 343 ff., figs. 31–4; Werner 1958, 373 ff., Taf. 72–5; Böhme 1974, 61 f., Taf. 110–11). That the dead man had obtained these coins suggests that he had served in the armies of both usurpers. Recent research has shown that his was not a single burial, but the founder grave in an early Frankish cemetery similar to several others in the Namur region of Belgium (J. Alenus-Lecerf 1981). This fits very well with what we know of the military strategy of Constantine III, who sought Frankish aid in securing the Rhine frontier and clearing Gaul of its invaders, had a German *Magister Militum* Edobich whom he sent to enlist Frankish and Alamannic help in raising the siege of Arles in 411, and struck his own gold and silver coin with which to pay them. Werner (1958, 400 ff.) stresses the great treasure Constantine must have taken from Britain to finance his undertaking – perhaps a major grievance in the British revolt against him in 409 – and considers his coins and those of Jovinus found between the Meuse and the Weser as evidence of payments to Frankish officers within the province (as at Vieuxville) and German allies beyond the Rhine (Werner 1958, Abb. 21). Their distribution across the Rhine is most numerous amongst the Franks, but takes in the Alamanni, the Thuringians, the Frisians but apparently not the Continental Saxons, though among them so little Roman coin of any period survives that the lacuna may be misleading.

If belt-sets of Type Vieuxville belong to the time and reflect the activities of Constantine III, what of the broader (80–160 mm) and plainer *cingula* of 'Simple' or B type? Their distribution indicates fairly massive recruitment from the Saxon homeland and also from the hinterland of Frisia, then deployment in strength along the Rhine frontier, the region of Namur and in northern Gaul generally; in other words, the Type Vieuxville distribution thickened up, but with no outliers south of the Alamans (Böhme 1974, Karte 13). Unfortunately not one of them has been found associated with a useful coin, but study of the components of the belts makes it clear that they underwent considerable typological and chronological development. The earliest form appears to be that of the belt from Furfooz grave 3, Belgium, with its chip-carved strap-tag, which must date from the very end of the fourth or earliest fifth century (Dasnoy 1969, 190, figs. 1–2; Böhme 1974, Taf. 88). The Dorchester type, with its lanceolate plain strap-end and zoomorphic buckle with hinged plate, appears to belong to the next phase, best paralleled in Frankish cemeteries, at Wijster and at Rhenen on the Lower Rhine (Böhme 1974, Taf. 62–5 & 71). Rhenen grave 829 has short plates with key-hole perforation similar to that from Dorchester. However, excepting the buckle itself, the closest parallels to the Dorchester belt as a whole, with its set of stiffeners, occur at Krefeld Gellep and Nymegen on the Lower Rhine frontier, and Tournai in Belgium (Böhme 1974, Taf. 79, 84 & 109), all belts with fixed-plate buckles, cast in one piece. This type of buckle constitutes a further development and simplification, which is likely to date from the second quarter of the fifth century (Werner in Breuer & Roosens 1957, 320 ff.; Böhme 1974, 79 ff.). By the middle of the century the official workshops, probably in the Meuse and Lower Rhine valleys, which had been supplying these variations of the military belt to troops now almost entirely composed of German federates, began to make a narrower form of belt on which the fixed-plate buckle might be worn alone, as in Haillot grave XI, Belgium (Breuer & Roosens 1957, fig. 12), or with different types of plates and strap-tag, as in the commander's grave 43 at Krefeld Gellep in the Lower Rhineland (Böhme 1974, Taf. 77). Fixed-plate buckles occur in Lower Saxony, but they represent the last form common to Franks and Saxons and probably the last 'official' uniform of late Roman derivation. After their time Saxony had nearly emptied of people and the Franks developed their own types of metalwork under different influences from central Europe.

I have devoted so much discussion to the development of the late Roman military belt in order to correct the currently received dating of the Saxon officer in the Dyke Hills at Dorchester. There is still a tendency for people to bury him *c.* 400 (e.g. Johnson 1980, 137), but this is patently too early: had he been a veteran of Count Theodosius or one of Stilicho's officers, his uniform would have been quite different, and his accompanying women would have been wearing brooches from the Gallic factories rather than Saxon brooches direct from the homeland. The latest date for his recruitment is the period *c.* 425, when Aetius became active as Roman *magister equitum* in Gaul: coins of the empress regent Galla Placidia and her young son the future Valentinian III show that Aetius was at this time recruiting beyond the frontiers (De Boone 1954, Kaart 13). He is not known to have intervened in Britain, however, though it has been suggested above that the British feared he might and took steps accordingly by introducing federates (p. 68). However, the Dorchester Saxon and his relationship to the late Roman town are better suited by an earlier date and context. It is just possible that Constantine III, in his successful two years in Gaul and on the Rhine between 407 and 409, found time to commission new-style military belt-fittings for his new officers from east of the Rhine and Lower Saxony, and that, responding to the Saxon invasion of 409, he sent some of these men to Britain to stiffen the defences. It is easy to imagine how an influx of such barbarian mercenaries, at this date barely Romanized at all, looking and sounding little different from their invading kinsfolk, might have alarmed the Romano-British authorities at home; and that orders to billet them in the towns and generally supply and feed them might have provoked the revolt recorded by Zosimus (p. 66).

However, the Dorchester officer and his female following, whether sent by Constantine or recruited by the British themselves in the years following, were not in fact dismissed from their post. Excavations within the town revealed the presence of what have been interpreted as late Roman barracks, the best preserved of which, a three-room structure *c.* 12 × 6m, had been built over a worn coin of Honorius 394–5 (Frere 1962, 121 ff.; 1966, 93 f.). These structures, the presence of early fifth-century Saxon pottery nearby (Frere 1962, fig. 21, nos. 16 & 17) and the relatively high percentage of worn Theodosian coinage found in the town, surely indicates that the German garrison was being properly housed and paid. Their length of service is suggested by the state of the officer's belt-fittings when he was buried: they show so much wear and evidence of repair that it is not inconceivable to think of him still at his post when the federate revolt broke out in the 440s. The female buried alongside him seems to have been similarly long-lived: her dress accessories had all seen long use before burial. They were a late Romano-British buckle of Type IB, broken and repaired in antiquity and terribly worn, and North German brooches currently dated late fourth/early fifth century (Böhme 1974, Stufe II, AD 380–420), a very worn protocruciform brooch and the backplate of an early applied brooch minus its decorated frontplate or any means of attachment (Kirk & Leeds 1952/3, fig. 27, 14–16; Hawkes & Dunning 1961, fig. 1, 14–16). The second woman, whose resting-place across the town was in another cemetery altogether, though apparently an exact contemporary of the Dyke Hills Saxons, had clearly died younger. Though she had one outworn piece of the later fourth century, a backplate from a tutulus brooch (Böhme 1974, 349, no. 31), her pair of applied brooches (Pl. 5b) seem to have been buried in working condition (Kirk & Leeds 1952/3, fig. 30, pl. V, 8). They are imported brooches whose repoussé plates, decorated with fivefold whirligig, are paralleled only on an undated silver brooch from the Frisian terp at

Jouswier (Kirk & Leeds 1952/3, pl. IV, C), but the form of the pin-catch is typologically early (Dickinson 1976, 101; Evison 1978, II, 264), and they can hardly have been buried later than the first decades of the fifth century. Supporting such a date is the collection the woman had made of Roman bronzes: late Roman bracelets, key and rings, two of which came from male belt-fittings (Kirk & Leeds 1952/3, fig. 29, 8 & 10), which link her definitively to the military. The presence of burials of such character on opposite sides of the town suggests that the Germanic military presence may have been larger than present evidence attests.

Dorchester, a small town strongly fortified and provided with *ballista* defence in the late fourth century (Frere 1962, 130), was of great strategic importance since it controlled the only major Roman road crossing the river Thames between Staines and Cricklade, and also river traffic on the Thames itself and its tributary the Thame (Map 11 and Figs. 5–7). A strong garrison here in the early fifth century could have contributed much, theoretically at any rate, to the security of Cirencester to the west, Silchester to the south, and the still prosperous Romano-British estates in the region and also in the British south-west. As things look at the moment the Saxon mercenaries at Dorchester seem to have been a key part of a whole chain of defensive emplacements along the Thames in the early fifth century (Fig. 5). The Dorchester belt-fittings are closely paralleled by a set found on the south bank of the Thames at Milton Regis in Kent (Hawkes & Dunning 1961, fig. 2), which suggest a military burial of similar date and type at a place, strategic to the policing of the Lower Thames estuary and Watling Street, which eventually became a royal vill of the Kentish kings. Further upstream at Croydon, opposite London, an ill-recorded Saxon cemetery has yielded an unworn lanceolate strap-tag and rosette-attachment (Hawkes and Dunning 1961, figs. 23, c & 24, e) which suggest there was an early fifth-century military presence there too.

Defence of London, which remained a British centre with some overseas trade in the fifth century (Biddle & Hudson 1973, 14), and the prevention of unwanted ingress up the Thames, probably explains the establishment of two groups of officer-class Saxons or Franks, revealed by founder burials in cemeteries I & II at Mucking, Essex (Jones 1979 for general refs.; Evison 1968 & 1981). The site, on an eminence which commands a view down the whole upper part of the Thames estuary, was obviously chosen to give its military command power to see and intercept any hostiles coming up-river. The most prestigious of its German officers had been provided with an insular version, in early Quoit Brooch Style, of a late fourth/early fifth-century five-piece chip-carved belt-set, which should date from the second or third decades of the fifth century (Evison 1968, pls. LIII & LIV). This is a very significant burial: the German officer was considered important enough to have very high-class insignia, in the form of *cingulum* fittings, made for him expensively in a sub-Roman or Anglo-Saxon workshop. In the other cemetery on the same hill, the founding male was evidently less high-ranking: his simpler bronze suite incorporated a fixed-plate buckle cast in one with the belt's tubular-sided end-plate, representing a later development by perhaps a generation than the Dorchester and Milton Regis fittings. It dates not earlier than the second quarter of the century (Evison 1981, 139, fig. 6). Evison thinks that this and the North German brooches of the accompanying women were also made in local workshops. The proposition is unprovable at present, but certainly the early Germans at Mucking, like those at Dorchester-on-Thames, had access to genuine examples of late Romano-British 'official' buckles (Evison 1981, fig. 4, d & 5, a), which they carried with them in worn condition into their graves. The map (Fig. 5) shows that such insular buckles in fifth-century German graves have a very similar distribution to the Continental-type military belt-fittings, notably from the Upper Thames down to its lower estuary. The groups concerned seem to have been well provided for by their sub-Roman employers, and they seem just the kind of people, similar to the partially romanized Saxons and Franks already employed on the Continent, and thus familiar and accessible, whom the British would have sought first when recruiting Germanic mercenaries or federates in the years after AD 409 (Hawkes 1978, 78 f.; Hawkes 1982, 67). They could well have been amongst the first comers referred to by Gildas as receiving official rewards in the form of *hospites, annona* and *epimenia* for their services.

The archaeological evidence suggests that Hengest's federates in Kent came later, after this initial stationing of troops along the Thames. A key factor here is in the distribution and chronology of buckles, brooches and other objects decorated in the so-called Quoit Brooch Style (Fig. 5). Since Leeds first discussed them in 1936 (3 ff.), they have been the subject of much research (Hawkes 1961; Evison 1965, 46 ff.; Evison 1968; Ager 1985), and, thanks to significant new finds such as the Mucking grave 117 chip-carved belt-set, we now know that the period of manufacture extended from early in the fifth century to perhaps *c.* 460/75. The finest examples may have been of Germanic workmanship, but probably the earliest were produced in British workshops and, as they have never been found elsewhere than in an Anglo-Saxon grave, Vera Evison (1981, 142) is probably right in thinking them to have been primarily a special issue for federates. The earliest examples, all belt-fittings, tend to come from the cemeteries along the Lower Thames, not just at Mucking, but on the Surrey side, at Orpington and Mitcham as well as Croydon, making the apparent federate build-up here look quite impressive. In East Kent, Hengest's territory, the Quoit Brooch Style objects are both grander – big disc-brooches inlaid with silver and glass settings, and the sumptuous quoit-brooches themselves, made of gilded silver – and arguably stylistically later. Already by around the middle of the fifth century, it seems, the Jutes of Kent had begun to emerge as a prestigious and wealthy élite amongst the first Germanic settlers, a status they were to retain and exploit for another two hundred years, thanks to their unique geographical situation. As to the Upper Thames Saxons, they received no Quoit Brooch Style objects – the nearest to approach them being the plate from Bishopstone in Buckinghamshire – unlike the other federates. Either the workshops making them were supplying only the Germanic settlers in the south-east, or their inland situation rapidly rendered their usefulness as federates secondary to that of the peoples lower down the Thames.

The reasons for recruiting all these federates may have varied with time. It has already been suggested (p. 68) that the enlistment of Hengest to hold Thanet and East Kent had to do with Vortigern's fear of a Roman attempt to recover Britain for the Empire, perhaps by Aetius between 425 and 429. The earlier establishments along the Thames may have been made to counter Pictish raiders, but a glance at the map (Fig. 5) will show that a possible threat to southern British interests existed nearer at hand. Some, possibly many, of the Anglo-Saxon cremation cemeteries of Norfolk and the East Midlands had come into use very early in the fifth century. Our leading expert on Anglo-Saxon cremation pottery has long maintained that some of the pots at such places as Caistor-by-Norwich (Myres & Green 1973) are old enough to suggest Germanic settlement outside this Roman town, and in other places too, as early as the fourth century (Myres 1977, 121 ff.). Not many people agree with him on the dating, nor with his idea that these people were recruited to serve in some official capacity, as *laeti* or as *foederati*. Indeed, he has been severely criticised (Hawkes 1974, 412 ff.; Morris 1974), the chief objection being that the very mixed groups of Angles, Saxons and other North Sea coastal peoples interred in these cremation cemeteries were totally unromanized in every way, both as to burial rite and to the lack of Roman objects amongst their grave goods. There is not a scrap of official 'military' gear to be found in their cemeteries in England, and this contrasts strikingly with the archaeological situation in the homeland, especially in Niedersachsen, which shows that many Saxon men took service in the Roman army (on the historical evidence for this see Bartholomew 1984). In England, however, it seems improbable that any of the purely cremating groups of North Germans should have inhabited any part of Roman Britain, in any capacity, let alone as part of the military establishment, before the demise of *Romanitas* there. Caistor, in fact, seems to have had its own officially equipped garrison, which was quite distinct from the barbarians buried outside its walls. Excavation in the town has been slight, of course, and further work is needed, but the town seems to have survived until early in the fifth century (Myres & Green 1973, 31 ff.; Wacher 1974, 238). Then apparently it met with a violent end. Perhaps Constantine III removed the garrison, and the barbarians now buried in the two cemeteries outside its walls put the surviving population to flame and sword. The present evidence is not good enough to testify with certainty. But we must not forget the Saxon invasion of 409.

Without historical detail, we can only surmise that news of Constantine's departure for Gaul in 407, and his withdrawal of troops from Britain, rapidly reached the now desperate peoples of the North Sea Coast of Holland and West Germany; that the phase of mere piracy was over and that they were now bent on taking new, dry, land for settlement. Norfolk, which they had raided for a century, had been well known to their warbands, and it was here that they made some of their first landfalls. The circumstances were very different now and it cannot have been easy to organize a full-scale migration in boats laden to the gunwales with women, children, animals and such other possessions as could be crammed in. Doubtless there were disasters both during the crossing and on first landing. There is growing realization now that the absolute numbers of Anglo-Saxons who actually settled eastern England in the fifth century were much fewer than used to be realized (Campbell 1982, 29). Probably they met with resistance from the British, but once the first comers had obtained a foothold it must have been very difficult to stop the influx of refugees, for there was nowhere else for them to go. In the event, it seems, many were accommodated peacefully alongside the British wherever land could be spared them, though elsewhere warbands may have concerted to take out major British centres of resistance. Caistor-by-Norwich is likely to have been such a case: once abandoned by the British, its rich townlands must have been a prime attraction for the Anglo-Saxons. As to the town itself, when one surveys the empty circuit of its walls today, occupied only by the church, and imagines it full of stinking ruins, it is easy to understand how irrelevant it must have seemed to barbarian settlers, accustomed to rural timber-built farms and villages, except perhaps as a quarry for useful pots and scrap metal. Archaeologists have been mesmerised by the proximity of the early Anglo-Saxon cemeteries, without considering that their placing close to the town may have been the fortuitous result of extra-mural land use.

The Caistor cemetery, on gently rising ground, would elsewhere be considered typically sited, with the added incentive that previous Roman occupation had rendered it unfit for other purposes than burial. The contrast with Dorchester-on-Thames, where Saxon mercenaries helped ensure its survival as the central place in the West Saxon scheme of things for the Oxford region, could not be more marked.

Possibly the Dorchester Saxons were brought in partly to deter peoples such as the Caistor Anglo-Saxons from invading the Thames Valley by the Icknield Way out of East Anglia. Despite the modern tendency to play down the threat posed by these peoples, to the Romano-British in the early fifth century their presence must have been very worrying. However much they may have tried to contain them, by *foedus* or other measures, they clearly did not succeed except in the very short term, for the archaeological evidence shows that more and more immigrants from the North German homelands poured into the whole area around the Wash until a date quite late in the fifth century (Böhme 1974; Evison 1977; Myres 1977). Shortly after their arrival the Dorchester Saxons were reinforced by further Saxon groups who settled at sites near the confluences of tributary rivers such as the Thame and Ock. Probably this represents official policy not unconnected with the placement of other early Saxon groups at strategic sites along the Icknield Way itself (Rutherford Davis 1982, 51–3), notably at Luton, Beds., but probably also at Bishopstone, Bucks. (Meaney 1964, 38 & 56), both in an area that remained British territory till the seventh century (Matthews & Hawkes, 1985). Some of the sites in the Cambridge region may have begun as federate establishments, the best attested of which is the recently excavated settlement at West Stow, in south-west Suffolk (West 1969 & 1978). The British may at first have attempted to bring all the Anglo-Saxon immigrants under control, but nearer the coast events must rapidly have got out of hand.

The course of Saxon settlement-history on the Upper Thames, as elsewhere, is best studied by means of the cemeteries with their copious and datable grave-goods. There has been no modern publication of the great mass of evidence, but it was handled for a doctoral thesis by my ex-pupil Tania Dickinson, and her invaluable three-volume work is on open access in the Bodleian Library. Much of what will follow here will inevitably derive in greater or lesser part from her unpublished research (Dickinson 1976). I acknowledge my debt to her from the outset, partly to avoid incessant referencing, but also because the detail on the regional map (Map 11) was checked and amended, and dated, according to her catalogue and maps. The maps, however, are published, though without their primary documentation (Dickinson 1980, figs. 1. 2–1. 4). For many of the data about settlement sites, though they are far less numerous and voluminous, I should like to acknowledge my debt to another ex-pupil, Freda Berisford, author of an unpublished B. Litt. thesis, also in the Bodleian Library (Berisford 1973). However, neither should be held responsible for the interpretations of the evidence expressed here.

Until the advent of aerial photography cemeteries were the most easily recognizable class of evidence. But even now not so very many have been found. For the whole great area she studied, from North Oxfordshire southwards to the river Kennet and extreme North Wiltshire, and from the Middle Thames and the Chiltern Hills westwards to the river's source and high Cotswold, deep in Gloucestershire, a region much larger than that under survey here, Tania Dickinson was able to record only 168 sites, definite or probable, of Saxon burial in the fifth, sixth and seventh centuries (Dickinson 1976, vol. II). Of these the great majority had been excavated before 1950, most in the last century, and ill recorded. Given the increased building activity and gravel extraction during the last decades, and the increased awareness and rescue activity, it is remarkable indeed how very few major Saxon cemeteries have come to light in recent years (Dickinson 1980, 13 f, fig. 1.1). Saxon settlement sites began to be recognised only in the 1920s (Leeds 1922–3, 1926–7 & 1947), so fewer have been excavated, though more are known now than have been explored (pp. 83–5; Pl. 8c; also Benson & Miles 1974, *passim*). Even so, one's impression is that the Saxon population was never exactly thick on the ground, and that in absolute numbers it never approached that of the British in the Roman period. Until we have more completely excavated cemeteries, the actual numbers will elude us: at present we can make estimates for very few sites. At Berinsfield (Dorchester VI), the only totally excavated site, as yet unpublished, just over 100 burials in approximately 200 years, at a time when human life-expectancy, including sub-adult deaths, averaged not more than 25 years, suggests a population of not more than 12 or 13 alive at any one time. Some sites, such as Abingdon I (Fig. 8; Leeds & Harden 1936), with some 128 inhumations and 99 cremations (Dickinson 1976), but evidently only half excavated, obviously accommodated larger communities of perhaps 40–50 people. On the other hand, there are many sites where population size was even smaller than at Berinsfield. At Purwell Farm, Cassington (Leeds & Riley 1942; Arthur & Jope 1962–3), and New Wintles Farm, Eynsham (Hawkes and Gray 1969; Gray 1974), funerary and settlement evidence combine to indicate farming-units of single-family size. Comparably small-scale groups from the Oxford region colonized marginal land in the Chilterns during the seventh century (Matthews and Hawkes 1985).

At no time is the smallness of family numbers more remarkable than in the early fifth century. It will not have escaped notice that the military establishments at Mucking, and of course at Dorchester-on-Thames itself, seem to have depended on just one or two officer-class males, not on a whole detachment of regular troops. Presumably they led and trained local recruits whom we cannot recognize archaeologically. Similarly, the next groups of Saxons to appear in the Oxford region early in the fifth century, at Berinsfield, Abingdon I and Frilford, all in the close vicinity of Dorchester (Dickinson 1980, fig. 1. 2), came in small numbers. At all three sites there were just two graves apiece which definitely date from the first half of the fifth century, though a few others, less diagnostic, might be as early (Dickinson 1980, Table 1.2). My own analysis of the Abingdon cemetery (Fig. 8) led me to conclude that perhaps four burials in the southern part of the cemetery might date from before c. 450: the female inhumation B106, with late fourth-century tutulus brooch in very worn state, another imported brooch, with applied 5-spiral ornament, and a Romano-British finger-ring (Pl. 5c), which is indistinguishable in date from the Dorchester graves themselves; and cremations 64, 67 and 74, in urns with early-looking standing-arc decoration (Myres 1968, fig. 7). I agree with Dickinson (1976, 344 f.) *pace* Myres that not all the urns in this style from Abingdon need be so early. Even if we double their numbers to allow for burials not excavated, the first-comers in this and other early cemeteries along the Upper Thames seem remarkably few. One's first reaction is of amazement that such small Saxon groups could have been effective either as protectors or invaders. But we should remember the words of the late John Morris (1973, 58): 'In a society that had relied for centuries upon professional soldiers, a few armed men might terrify thousands of civilians.' To the local Britons, the Saxon menfolk, physically taller and longer in the arm, and accustomed from childhood to carry and use weapons, must have seemed both impressive and intimidating. Certainly it seems that a very few of them went a very long way in establishing Germanic control of the Upper Thames in the fifth century.

It has long been assumed that the Saxons at such sites as Berinsfield, Abingdon, Frilford, and other relatively early sites from Reading up-river to Brighthampton (Map 11), must have been brought in initially by sub-Roman authority as federates. As an extension of the policy of defending the line of the Thames the idea makes sense, and the archaeological evidence tends to support it. Considering that cremation was the regular burial-rite in the Saxon homeland, and that the mixed North German peoples who settled in East Anglia, around the Wash and parts north, continued to cremate long after they had settled in Britain (Fig. 5), the high incidence of inhumation amongst the Germanic peoples on the Upper Thames (Kirk 1956), is strikingly different. It suggests a high level of Roman influence. Though no other cemetery has yielded full sets of imported military equipment comparable to that at Dorchester, the man in grave 6 at Berinsfield (a cemetery with very little cremation) had a single tubular-sided end-plate from just such a military belt, suggesting that he had had some contact with official forces. Other bits and pieces of late Roman belt-fittings occur as heirlooms or amulets in women's graves of the later fifth or earliest sixth centuries: at Long Wittenham, in grave 31, a suspension-ring from a military belt; in grave 111 a late Romano-British strap-tag; at Purwell Farm, Cassington, in grave 2, a Dorchester-type strap-tag (Leeds & Riley 1942, fig. 15); in Minster Lovell grave 3, a propeller-shaped fourth-century belt-stiffener. These need not have been casual gleanings – indeed such things are very rare in Anglo-Saxon cemeteries elsewhere – but could mean that the families concerned had once seen military service in official Roman forces. As we have noticed already (Fig. 5), a number of late or sub-Romano-British buckles, all probably of early fifth-century date and all, where ascertainable, actually being worn, have been found at Reading, in grave 13, and Blewburton, grave 2 (Hawkes & Dunning 1961, fig. 14), also at Frilford and Long Wittenham I, grave 165 (Evison 1968, fig. 2d & 4a). Again these are unusual, and deliberate supply by the British seems likelier than that the women concerned all acquired them by chance. There are also a few instances, at Abingdon I, B70, Long Wittenham I, 127 and Fairford, as well as Dorchester II, of burials, usually children, with late Roman bracelets, which Dickinson regards as a significant continuity of custom into the early Saxon period (1976, I, 200).

Though the Upper Thames Saxons were not supplied with major metalwork in the Quoit Brooch Style (p. 71), Dickinson was able to point to a number of side-fastening composite belts, including tubular end-pieces as well as a variety of buckles and other fittings – from Blewburton Hill grave 20, Abingdon I grave 30 and Minster Lovell grave 3 – which look like local attempts to produce a form of military belt (Dickinson 1976, I, 247 f., 419; III, pl. 63, a,b,). It seems probable that they were fifth-century products of British workshops, and thus 'official' gear of local workmanship, cheaper and less glamorous than the equipment supplied to the federates in the south-east. Finally, there is the strong possibility that, already before the middle of the fifth century, sub-Roman workshops on the Upper Thames had begun to cater for Saxon female national dress by producing a more durable brooch-type than the flimsy applied brooches brought by the first comers from North Germany. This was the cast disc brooch, worn in pairs on the shoulders like the applied and later cast saucer brooches, which was to become the most common brooch type in the Oxford region from the fifth until well on in the sixth century (Dickinson 1979). In conclusion, then, there is ample evidence from study of the contents of their cemeteries to suggest that the early fifth-century Saxons in the Oxford region were in the employ of the Britons. But it is still unclear whose taxes and workshops supported them, and whose federates they actually were.

Myres suggested that they were settled along the Thames to protect the *Civitas* of Silchester (1969, 89), by creating a 'political frontier' along the Berkshire bank of the river Thames. But this idea will not stand long scrutiny. The initial billeting of troops at Dorchester itself would have benefited Silchester, but not exclusively. Dorchester and its region must always have lain outside the territories of both the neighbouring *civitates*, of Silchester to the south and Cirencester to the west. As the seat of an Imperial official, a *Beneficiarius Consularis* (RIB 235), it had probably always been independent. As a strong-point at a critical road and river junction, a police post and administrative centre concerned with the control and movement of traffic and supplies along and across the river – pottery from the Oxford kilns, wool from the Cotswolds, corn from the fertile Thames Valley itself – it was of central importance. At the beginning of the fifth century, the now self-governing cities which had depended on it, not just Silchester to the south, nor Cirencester up-river, but also London itself, the major port down-river, may all have been concerned to ensure that an official remained, not with the same title, perhaps, after the late fourth century, but with the same function: to maintain the safety of the river and the free flow of trade and staple goods. The Dorchester Saxons could well have been under the command of this official, helping to enforce by their presence the payment of customs dues, perhaps, which would have provided their own pay and support, their *annona* and *epimenia*. By such means the costs of maintaining a defence force at Dorchester would have been spread amongst all users of the river and its crossing. But once one imagines such a situation, the likely consequences at once become apparent. With Constantine III dead and no expeditionary force from Rome likely to come again, with the various *civitates* becoming increasingly concerned for their own survival and increasingly cut off from each other, an ambitious sub-Roman official with armed soldiers at his back could easily have set himself up as a petty tyrant at Dorchester. Myres' idea of a 'nest of river pirates' would not have been so wide of the mark after all, though not in the sense he meant it. The presence of a sub-Roman tyrant based on Dorchester would explain much that is odd and puzzling about the Saxon settlement of the Upper Thames, and it is tempting to adopt the notion at least as a working hypothesis.

The Birth of a Kingdom.

The early and rapid build-up of fifth-century Germanic settlement in the Oxford region has always looked peculiar, requiring special explanation. Even Tania Dickinson, who is far more cautious than I am in jumping to conclusions, remarked the orderly progress of the settlement, the apparently deliberate placement of communities at strategic intervals, as opposed to the haphazard agglomeration of newcomers which must otherwise have happened as the Thames Valley filled up during the course of the century. In considering the nature of the controlling power which dictated settlement tactics, Dickinson thought in terms of federate settlement and revolt, followed by the emergence of Saxon 'chieftains' at Dorchester who orchestrated the further recruitment and settlement of Germans in the region (Dickinson 1976, I, 422 ff.). She implies but does not specify that the foundations of the West Saxon kingdom had been laid already by the end of the fifth century.

My own impression is that deliberate kingdom-building began very soon after the recruitment of the Dorchester Saxons, with the appearance of the Saxons at Berinsfield, Abingdon and Frilford, perhaps also Long Wittenham, at latest by *c.* 425/30. The usefulness of these people as federates has never been questioned, but when one looks closely at their positions, at or very near late Roman sites, notably the temple at Frilford, close around the town but so placed as to control movement along the nearer reaches of the Thames and its local tributaries the Thame and Ock rivers, they seem more relevant to the build-up of a power-base centred on Dorchester itself rather than any larger strategy. In the next phase, starting probably before the middle of the century, we seem to see the thoughtful construction of a defence in depth. Saxons were settled at Reading and Wallingford, where they could control the Thames below Dorchester and its tributary the Kennet, and others at Blewburton Hill, an old Iron Age hillfort, and East Shefford, whence they could command the Berkshire Downs. Others were placed upstream, at Oxford and Cassington, Minster Lovell, Brighthampton and as far west as Fairford, thus controlling the Thames below Cirencester and its various feeder streams from the Cherwell, Evenlode and Windrush to the Coln. At the same time other Saxons were settled at Bishopstone and Dinton, Bucks., seemingly to control access by the Icknield Way. As we have seen, none of these groups can have been large initially, and the economical placing of a few armed men and their families at places where they could do most good, seems the action of leaders with sound strategic sense. Perhaps the Saxons policed the local British and led them in action when necessary, but it is impossible to say anything with confidence about an indigenous population which virtually did an archaeological vanishing-act after the beginning of the fifth century and about which we know nothing historically.

It is unfashionable nowadays to believe the Gildasian account of the fate of the Britons in the mid-fifth century. It is dismissed as exaggerated for dramatic effect, or even as borrowed from other writers (Sims-Williams 1983a). Yet we know from external sources that a great many, presumably of the more mobile and affluent socio-economic classes, such as the villa owners, did in fact emigrate overseas to Brittany, and archaeology has long confirmed that many Roman towns did indeed remain 'deserted, in ruins, unkempt', with 'no burial to be had except in the ruins of houses' (Gildas, 24, 4 & 26, 2). As we have seen already, Caistor-by-Norwich was one such town, and as we shall see, Silchester and Cirencester were others. Archaeology has also begun to find traces of those who fled 'to the high hills, steep, menacing and fortified' (Gildas, 25, 1), in the form of crude sub-Roman dwellings in refortified hillforts such as Cadbury Congresbury in Somerset (Fowler *et al.* 1970) and, nearer the Oxford region, Crickley Hill, Gloucs. (P. Dixon pers. comm. 1982). A certain amount of slaughter must have taken place, as always in times of war or invasion, and, as the Anglo-Saxons dealt in slavery, no doubt many Britons were enslaved by them. But wholesale massacre and mass enslavement remain unproven, probably unprovable, definitely unpalatable, and, for the Oxford region at least, given the small numbers of Saxons involved and their apparent role, most unlikely. Nonetheless, the fact remains that one of the more bewildering results of modern archaeological research in the Upper Thames Valley is the tale of abandonment of late Roman rural sites before the middle of the fifth century. In no case so far, even where Saxons took over the farming of the land, as at Shakenoak and Barton Court Farm, Abingdon (Miles *et al.* forthcoming), can the incomers be shown to have been directly responsible for this sudden break with tradition. It happened equally where no Saxons are evident at all, as at Appleford (Hinchliffe & Thomas 1980) or not until at least two centuries later, as at Ducklington (Chambers 1975). So much evidence now building up for rural dislocation and abandonment in the early sub-Roman period must add up to an economic disaster of great magnitude, which is hard to explain except in terms of a human tragedy far exceeding anything which could have been caused by a few Saxons, however bloodthirsty. For this period Gildas is our only historian, and given that he may have been right about other happenings, might he not have been correct when he referred to the famine and the great plague – *famosa pestis* (Gildas 2) – which preceded the invitation to the Saxons? Todd (1977) makes no very convincing case for discrediting it. Others (Stevens 1941; Wacher 1974, 413 ff.) have tended to connect it with the only other plague recorded for this time, by Hydatius, which was scourging the western Mediterranean in the early 440s. Discussion of this plague has so far assumed that it spread from the Mediterranean to western Britain, but this is exactly the period when refugees from Britain began fleeing abroad in great numbers, and its spread could have been in the reverse direction, from Britain, which had been experiencing it earlier. In the fourteenth century in England, the Black Death did not just depopulate the towns but destroyed whole rural communities, killing a third of the total population and changing the course of economic history. Gildas's plague need not have been the same, but whether it was indeed the bubonic plague, or, more likely perhaps, typhoid or a major outbreak of influenza (and here one must remember that influenza killed more people at the end of the Great War than all the slaughter in the trenches), some such killer disease could explain the great population shift and decline which archaeology is now spelling out for us as marking the final end of Roman Britain.

But even the worst disasters leave survivors. Certainly it is impossible to imagine the large late-Roman population of the Oxford region being wiped out in its entirety even in such a great composite catastrophe as Gildas outlines for us. Some of the Britons must have survived somewhere, but our problem at present is not knowing where to search or what to look for in the way of evidence. Place-names are unlikely to help much, for names indicating the survival of Britons in Anglo-Saxon contexts are extremely rare in Berkshire, Oxfordshire and eastern parts of Gloucestershire (Smith 1956, I, map 2; Gelling 1978, 90). As for the suggestion that the Britons might have merged with the Saxons, adopting their dress-style and burial customs (Dickinson 1980, 23), it is quite unrealistic. Neither the cemeteries nor the settlements of the Saxons are large enough to have housed more than a tiny fraction of Britons, as well as allowing for natural expansion amongst the Germans themselves.

But of course we need good new excavations of many more cemeteries to establish maximum population size and, not least, to permit modern research on skeletal data which might detect ethnic differences within communities on the Upper Thames. At present I can only quote reliable evidence from one south Wessex cemetery, Worthy Park, Kingsworthy near Winchester, where archaeological and osteological research (Hawkes and Wells 1983) has combined to suggest that, amongst the inhuming population of just over 90 excavated individuals, 5 showed up definitely as the 'overworked drudges', ie. lowest class of slave, in the community, 3 of whom seem to have been British. In the Oxford region, likewise, we should expect to find a few British amongst the slaves and also amongst the women, with the effects of resultant interbreeding appearing by the sixth and seventh centuries. As noted above, some of the craftsmen working for the Saxon incomers in the fifth century will have been Britons, and may have been integrated into some of the larger communities such as those at Abingdon and Long Wittenham, unless they had workshops, as yet not found, in Dorchester itself. But the bulk of the surviving sub-Roman population must be elsewhere.

Recently attention has been drawn to the existence of major rural complexes, of large size and regularly spaced, which, it has been suggested (D. Miles, unpubl. lecture 1982), might have functioned as the Roman equivalents to the medieval market towns in the region. There is one at Abingdon, under the present town (Biddle *et al.* 1968; Miles *et al.* 1975), and others at Long Wittenham, Frilford, Fairford and elsewhere. The hope now must be that the elusive sub-Romans will show up in some way at such sites as these, having regrouped, or been regrouped, into nucleated settlements, as some Anglo-Saxons seem to have done, or been, in the later seventh and eighth centuries (p. 85). It is surely no coincidence that it is near these larger Roman rural centres that the fifth-century Saxon federates were settled, presumably to guard or police them.

As to the controlling intelligence, the more one considers the fifth-century situation in the Oxford region, the more impressive appears the case for a ruling power at Dorchester. The suggested 'tyrant' will probably have been British, but apparently one more successful in maintaining control over his federates than Vortigern in the south-east. Perhaps, to maintain his authority and that of his successors, he intermarried with the Saxons, or his sons and daughters did. Such an idea is not pure fantasy, for the genealogy of the Upper Thames West Saxons, though we can trace it certainly only from Ceawlin in the second half of the sixth century, contains quite a number of names with a British flavour. Ceawlin himself had a British name, and his descendant Caedwalla had another, while his great-grandson Cenwalh's name contains the Anglo-Saxon element -*walh*, meaning Briton. British names or names with the element -*walh* occur in other royal genealogies, where the Anglo-Saxons came first as a minority element in the population; thus Cerdic, the traditional ancestor of the Wiltshire branch of the West Saxon kings, with the British name *Caraticos*, and the various -*walh* names in the Mercian royal genealogy. Margaret Gelling (1978, 95) has suggested that 'probably the Saxon royal families in which the -*walh* theme occurs were acknowledging a Celtic strain in their ancestry', and this would fit well with what is being suggested here about the mixed origins of the West Saxon royal house.

The suggested build-up of strength around Dorchester seems to have alarmed the authorities at Silchester, for, from a date probably early in the fifth century, the existing earthworks around the townland were supplemented by the construction of a massive linear earthwork, known now as Grim's Bank (Boon 1974, 78 ff., fig. 5f; Johnson 1980, 156 f., fig. 17). This lies some 3 km from the town and runs from just short of the Roman road to Cirencester and Bath across country for 3.8 km, blocking the Dorchester road in such a fashion that travellers from the north would have had to make a detour around it and then negotiate a control-point to the rear created by a further arrangement of earthworks. The Cirencester/Bath road was left open, but Grim's Bank was brought near enough to enable this line of approach to be blockaded rapidly should the need arise. Apparently it never did, but then by the time the Saxons were settling around Cirencester, *c.* 500, sub-Roman life in Silchester, too, was probably at an end, and may have been defunct already half a century earlier (Boon 1974, 80 ff.). In the event, the road from Dorchester seems to have gone out of use, its line now being hard to trace. At Cirencester the sub-Roman authorities seem to have concentrated on fortifying the amphitheatre, possibly as a residence for the local tyrant there. Life in the town itself is thought to have ceased by the middle of the fifth century (Wacher 1976). Excavations at both Silchester and Cirencester have produced evidence, in the form of unburied bodies (Boon 1974, 81 f.; Wacher 1976, 16), which may have been the victims of plague, of forays by the Saxons, or, in Boon's words, 'of casual lawlessness at a time when duly-constituted authority had disappeared'. Such unburied bodies have not turned up in the various excavations within the walls of Dorchester, where conditions were obviously different (pp. 70, 88).

Before finally abandoning the topic of British reactions to developments based on Dorchester, a word or two must be said about East Wansdyke (Fig. 6). This great linear earthwork, which runs for some 20 km along the crests of the North Wiltshire Downs, with its formidable ditch facing northwards, was so engineered as to block completely the Roman road to Bath from Mildenhall, and eventually both Cirencester and Silchester, and to control access to the Vale of Pewsey and Salisbury Plain by way of the Ridgeway out of Berkshire (Fox & Fox 1960). There is no close evidence of dating, but clearly it is either a late or post-Roman work, constructed, according to recent evidence, as a military barrier (Green 1971) against aggression from the north. Two alternative contexts for its original appearance in the landscape have been proposed: that it was a sub-Roman defence against the growing threat posed by the Upper Thames Saxons in the fifth century; or that it was built to play a major role in events during the later sixth century, when the West Saxon king, and bruising warleader, Ceawlin, was actively extending his territory (Myres 1964). Most writers on the subject have tended to prefer the later date for East Wansdyke, but there is much to be said in favour of a sub-Roman origin, and that is the alternative I shall adopt here. The blocking of the Roman road suggests that the great dyke was not dug until Silchester and Cirencester had become irrelevant to the situation in Wiltshire; hence one may tentatively suggest that its construction dates from the middle rather than the beginning of the fifth century. The middle of the fifth century saw the beginning of the British military revival under Ambrosius, according to Gildas, and Ambrosius is traditionally associated with Amesbury and Wiltshire. Wiltshire was still British territory, as yet unthreatened by Saxons coming from the south, the nearest of whom at this time were probably no nearer than Sussex or, just possibly, at Portchester (p. 67). East Wansdyke has always seemed an excessive reaction to any possible threat posed by a bunch of dissident Saxons miles away on the Upper Thames. However, if one accepts the hypothesis that there was a British 'tyrant' at Dorchester, with his Saxons well in hand, gradually extending their deployment with the result that, around the middle of the century, they were already taking up land as close as the Berkshire Downs at East Shefford; and if that Dorchester 'tyrant' was actively recruiting yet more militarily effective Germans to his following during this same period, as we shall see in a moment; then one could imagine a major confrontation between the two leaders, inevitably involving the Ridgeway, in which the construction of East Wansdyke would have made immediate sense militarily and in the longer term provided a useful territorial boundary.

Ethnic Origins – Saxons and Franks

The German people on the Upper Thames came to be known as the West Saxons, and initially they all seem indeed to have come from Old Saxony, the part of North Germany between the rivers Elbe and Weser, which was materially very distinct from its neighbours. As we have seen, the best evidence for their ethnic and cultural origins are the women's brooches and the types of cremation pottery they brought from their homeland. Some of these, notably the typologically late equal-armed brooch of Böhme's Type Nesse from Abingdon C26 (Leeds & Harden 1936, fig. 4, pl. IV, B; Evison 1977, fig. 5, b), and the *Buckelurnen* from Abingdon CX, C48, C68, C82, and others from Wallingford, Harwell, Osney and Souldern (Myres 1969, 45 ff., 102 ff.; Myres 1977, 31 ff.), indicate that Saxon immigration into the Oxford region continued into the second half of the fifth century. At the same time other Saxons were continuing to arrive in the East Midlands and were also colonizing Sussex. The firstcomers were refugees from the west side of Continental Saxony, and the area west of the river Oste was depopulated by the middle of the century, while the second wave was composed of easterners from between Oste and Elbe who, though not leaving a desert behind them, left so few people in the homeland that they came quickly under the heel of the Thuringians (Böhme 1976). By at least *c.* 500 there were no more Saxons to come, and the dearth of new recruits from North Germany is nowhere more apparent than amongst the mongrel bands, second-generation settlers from Sussex and elsewhere, who made up the colonists in southern Wessex, in Hampshire and Wiltshire, in the late fifth and early sixth centuries.

Amongst the second wave of Germans who settled southern England in the second half of the fifth century, there were certainly some Franks from northern Gaul or the lower Rhine. When she first recognized these, Vera Evison (1965) definitely overstressed their role, attributing to them almost sole leadership of the Germanic population in southern England, including the Upper Thames. Her tendency to promote Franks at the expense of Saxons and Jutes is reasserted in her most recent publication on the subject (Evison 1981), and should be treated with caution. Whatever their role or number they were not remembered by the Anglo-Saxons themselves as founding any dynasties or kingdoms. Evison has tended to adduce Franks wherever there are imports of Frankish weapons, inlaid iron buckles or luxury goods from the late Gallo-Roman workshops of the Meuse and Lower Rhine valleys, which equipped and catered for Franks. However, some of these things could have been acquired by Saxons on the Continent and others introduced by trade; yet others, especially the inlaid iron buckles which appear most frequently in Sussex and Kent, are likely in large part to have been made in sub-Romano-British workshops such as those which may have produced the Quoit Brooch Style. One has to weigh all these possibilities in evaluating the evidence before allowing oneself to infer the presence of actual Franks in England in the fifth century. However, in his recent work on Sussex, a region rich in 'Frankish' goods, Martin Welch (1983) has probably erred on the side of caution in his handling of this material.

In the Oxford region, mid/late-fifth century 'Frankish' imports are rarities, appearing in just a few cemeteries – Abingdon I, Long Wittenham and East Shefford attracting most of them – and tend to be prestige goods rather than items of everyday use. The one inlaid buckle loop and the one bronze fixed-plate buckle from the Upper Thames both came from Long Wittenham; the former (Evison 1955, pl. III, e) from grave 111, together with objects that date the grave to the first half of the sixth century, including a pair of cast saucer brooches with scroll ornament (Dickinson 1982, pl. 7) which are not so early as Evison (1981, 137) would have them; the latter (Hawkes & Dunning 1961, fig. 20, g; Evison 1965, fig. 12, a–c) from grave 57, together with an insular long-boss pot which Myres (1977, 44) would date early in the sixth century. Both were old when buried, therefore, and by themselves not evidence of fifth-century Franks. However, grave 93 in the same cemetery is more conclusive. It contained the burial of a boy with a spearhead and two undeniably Gaulish objects of the fifth century: a cauldron with triangular lugs made in the workshops of the Meuse valley in Belgium, and the famous 'stoup' with repoussé ornament representing scenes from the New Testament (Evison 1965, fig. 13, b–c), which was probably made in the same north French workshop that produced the equally famous 'buire chrétienne' that ended its days in grave 319 at Lavoye, Meuse: the founder-grave, datable *c.* 500/520 in an important cemetery of Franks (Chenet 1935; Joffroy 1974, 95 ff.). It would be hard to quarrel with the conclusion that burial 93 was the child of a wealthy family of Franks at Long Wittenham. Dickinson (1976) regards the man in grave 26 in this cemetery, with late Roman bronze dish and bucket and cauldron of early Frankish type, as another member of this Continental élite. Imported fifth-century glasses occur singly at Cassington, Smith's Pit, and at Dinton, Bucks., but no less than four examples were found at East Shefford (Harden 1956; Evison 1972). The only one from a closed find, the 'Kempston'-type cone-beaker from grave XXIV, was buried with a woman wearing applied brooches of Böhme's Type Muids, a distinctively French variant which he places late in the type's development, around the middle of the century (Böhme 1974, 28, Karte 7: Evison 1965, 101, pl. 17b & 1978, II, 265, pl. LVIa). This combination suggests that there were Franks also at East Shefford.

At Abingdon the question of Franks revolves around the famous swords from graves 42 and 49. These were long ago recognized as products of the same Meuse-valley workshops which supplied swords to Frankish federate chieftains at Krefeld-Gellep on the Lower Rhine and Samson and Éprave near Namur in Belgium (Leeds & Harden 1936, 59 f., pl. IX & XIX; Werner 1953 & 1956; Hawkes & Dunning 1961, 39f.; Hawkes & Dunning 1962–3, 200, Abb. 11; Evison 1965, 40 f., fig. 22). The problem has always been how to decide whether they had been acquired as prestige goods by Saxons, or whether their owners really were Franks. My detailed analysis of the plan of the Abingdon cemetery (Fig. 8) was undertaken primarily with this question in mind, and, most gratifyingly, it seems to have resolved it. The early burials of people with Saxon artefacts, mostly cremations, lie mainly in the southern and eastern parts of the burial-ground, as excavated. Inhumations 42 and 49, however, are on its western side, and integral to a discrete group of NE-oriented graves which, in the fifth century, will have been apart from the majority of Saxons. Their occupants, overwhelmingly male, look like an intrusive warrior/military group, which remained distinct for at most two generations. Burial 42, with the bronze-mounted Frankish sword and the remains of a lyre, and 49 with a similar but iron-mounted sword and spearhead with ferrule, of Swanton (1973) Type K1, were probably the founder-leaders of the group; and 48 with bronze-bound bucket, K1 spearhead and Dickinson Group 1.1

shield boss, 55 with K2 spearhead and ferrule, and Group 1.2 boss, either their followers or perhaps their successors. Except for 52, with just an H1 spearhead, the remaining five males went into their graves unfurnished, suggesting that each armed male had an unarmed retainer. Female inhumations closely related spatially with this group consist only of 46 (between 48 & 49), an adult whose glass beads and trefoil-headed small-long brooches (Leeds & Harden 1936, pl. X) might be as early as the later fifth century (*pace* Leeds & Dickinson), and the young teenager in 51, whose two pots, pair of button-brooches and handsome string of glass beads (Leeds and Harden 1936, pl. XI) might also be as early as the late fifth century (Avent & Evison 1982, 99). From their jewellery these were local ladies, not Franks, but of sufficient social status to have been the consorts or offspring of this warrior élite. There are also a few cremations in what appears to be significant association with the male inhumers, not well preserved admittedly, but some, C31 and C36, were definitely female, and another, C35, adjacent to inhumation 52, was certainly fifth-century in date. These could be the remains of other Saxon girls who, though taken up by the inhuming male newcomers, were buried according to the practice of their own families. That the male group was indeed Frankish seems likely, not just because of the swords, but because of certain objects of Frankish origin buried in sixth-century graves on the fringes of the fifth-century founder-group; two angons in the male grave 69 (Leeds & Harden 1936, pl. XIX) and a cloisonné buckle-plate of *c*. 500 buried in the otherwise Saxon female grave 119 (Leeds & Harden 1936, pl. XVII). These look like heirlooms.

One other male burial on the Upper Thames has been described as that of a fifth-century Frank, namely grave 31 at Brighthampton (Evison 1965, 31–2, fig. 11). I agree with Dickinson (1976, 257 ff. *contra* Evison) that the now famous sword is likely to have been a composite piece, originally from South Scandinavia and retaining its original pommel and scabbard mouthpiece, but with a replacement chape, either Scandinavian- or British-made, and silvered scabbard edgings and cross-headed stud added either in Britain or northern Gaul. Like many heroic swords of the Migration Age it seems to have been much-travelled before it found its final resting-place in the grave. The bucket from this same burial seems definitely fifth-century Frankish, suggesting that its owner had served amongst Franks before coming to Britain. It would be interesting to know the relationship between him and the woman buried in grave 22 at Brighthampton, with earlier sixth-century local zoomorphic applied brooches, great numbers of glass beads and a knife with elaborate silver or tinned bronze sheath-binding and U-shaped chape, and a unique knife sling, obviously constructed by a bucket-maker, with ornament in minor Quoit Brooch Style (AM 1966. 61–2; Dickinson 1976, pl. 68). I am sure Dickinson is right in suggesting that this is local British work, but equally sure that the person who commissioned it had in mind Frankish prototypes, such as the gold-mounted knives worn by the Frankish princely class in the early sixth century, such as were buried in Krefeld-Gellep 1782 (Pirling 1964, 201, Taf. 54; Pirling 1974, 168 f., Taf. 46) and under Cologne Cathedral in both the woman's and the boy's grave (Doppelfeld 1960, 100, Taf. 18; Doppelfeld 1964, 164 ff., Taf. 40). If I am right, it means that minor Frankish aristocrats on the Upper Thames retained cross-Channel contacts during the first third of the sixth century, and that sub-Roman craftsmen survived, still working in fifth-century style, until this relatively late date.

One could speculate endlessly as to the circumstances that brought such high-ranking Franks to the Upper Thames, and that gave them the confidence or bravado to sacrifice valuable prestige goods and weapons in the graves of their first leaders. If we follow modern thinking in interpreting extravagant funerals of this sort as deliberate statements on the part of the families involved about their own views of their economic and political situation, then the statement the fifth-century Franks were making seems clear enough. They were telling the peoples of the Oxford region that they had arrived, were to be noticed and reckoned with, were the top people and expected to remain so. For themselves they were probably also establishing an ancestor-cult in their respective communities, by giving the founder-figures memorably lavish funerals. We can see the same thing happening at a slightly later date and on a much richer scale in Frankish cemeteries such as Lavoye (p. 78), where the burial of the founder of the new community on its new estate, grave 319, was infinitely better provided for than any of his successors. But while the status of the Frankish aristocrat at Lavoye is not in doubt (James 1982, 129 ff.), that of the fifth-century Franks in the Upper Thames cemeteries is obscure, and will remain so until there has been a great deal more excavation on a modern scale. However, we can make an informed guess or two, which may come somewhere near the truth. Let us take another look at the distinct group of male burials at Abingdon, with their two swordsmen-leaders, whose military look has already been remarked on. Their swords, 'official' issue it seems, dating from the time of the Frankish federate king Chlodio and the end of the career of the Roman *Magister Militum* Aetius, and the time of the federate revolt in south-east England, suggest that we may be dealing with something other than just an opportunist influx of self-motivated German peoples. If the Saxon revolt spread to the Upper Thames, and if Gildas was wrong in saying that the British got no help from their appeal to Aetius, the Abingdon Franks represent just the kind of troops he might have sent to bring the dissident Saxons to heel and subsequently police them. Alternatively, the Dorchester 'tyrant' himself could have sent to Gaul for further federates, this now being the only source of fresh recruits, to strengthen his position vis-à-vis his own Saxons and/or his British neighbours. Given the frustrating situation for Franks in Gaul at this time, with Aetius and later Aegidius hampering their prospects of territorial expansion, many young men – and the Abingdon grave 42 swordsman was still 'adolescent' when he died – would probably have welcomed the opportunity offered for adventure and reward overseas.

Once arrived in the Oxford region the new recruits were well catered for as regards equipment. Few weapons survive from the earlier fifth century, but the Saxon officer buried in the Dyke Hills at Dorchester is thought to have had a Continental mid-ribbed spear of Swanton's Type B2 (Swanton 1973, 47), and other such spears are known from Pangbourne, Berinsfield grave 20, Frilford and Fairford grave 2 (Swanton 1973, fig. 7, b). However, from about the middle of the century, production of weapons began locally. Initially, one supposes, this will have taken place under central control or at least under the aegis of officer-chiefs at such places as Abingdon, for at the outset there will have been the problems of organizing supplies of iron, presumably from surviving British bloomsmiths, and of training enough weapon-smiths, the latter no light undertaking because the craft could only be learned by an apprenticeship, which, in Germanic society, was presumably steeped in ancient mystique (Swanton 1973, 9). In the event, the earliest insular spear-type produced on the Upper Thames seems to have been Swanton's K1, with broad leaf-shaped blade, on which the expense of metal and technical problems involved in producing the Continental mid-rib were resolved by making the blade stepped or helicoidal in section, a trick that may have originated abroad (Dickinson 1976, 315, *pace* Swanton 1973). These spears seem to have been particularly prestigious, occurring not only with the Abingdon 49 swordsman and his companions in graves 48 and 55, but also with the bearer of another fifth-century Frankish sword in grave 86 at Riseley in Saxon West Kent (Swanton 1973, 128 ff., figs. 86–7). There are about a dozen examples from the Upper Thames – from Berinsfield, Frilford, Long Wittenham, Eynsham, Brighthampton, Fairford and Shipton-on-Cherwell – and some were found with ferrules, which are rare in the region, and with shields of the early Group 4 and 1.1 and 1.2 varieties. The dating of the type seems not to extend much beyond AD 500; that from Finglesham grave 204 in East Kent, a well-dated grave of *c*. 525 (Hawkes 1982b), being perhaps amongst the latest. However, even such a very early type as this is represented, not just along the Lower Thames, the communication route to the Continent, but also in significant numbers in Hampshire, suggesting that the newly arrived Germanic peoples in this region were already in touch with the longer established groups in the Oxford region. Another early type of short-lived spear, Swanton's I2, with slim leaf-shaped blade and lunate fullering, occurs on the Upper Thames as early as the middle of the fifth century, in Abingdon grave 111 with Saxon bowl with facetted carination (Swanton 1973, fig. 84, a–c). It may have been a local version of the Hampshire-based type I1, or vice versa. Type J with angular blade and lunate fullering occurs both in Hampshire and the Upper Thames, also downstream and in the East Midlands. It appears to have had a short life from sometime in the fifth to the earlier sixth century. More successful was type L, of which Tania Dickinson counted about 15 examples in the region she studied, an angular blade with the profile of the H-series spears but the stepped section of K1. Probably it began as early as the other spears with modified sections, but its broader distribution, taking in the Warwickshire Avon and more of Wiltshire suggests a longer life in the first half of the sixth century (Swanton 1973, 134 ff.). Finally, we come to the most common spear-types used in the Oxford region, the small to medium-sized blades, with angular profiles and lozenge-shaped sections, of series E1/E2 and especially H1/H2. They began to be made in the latter part of the fifth century, for there was a type E1 in Long Wittenham I, grave 93, with the famous stoup (p. 78) and a type H1 in Brighthampton grave 31, with the famous sword (p. 79), but manufacture continued well into the sixth century and perhaps even the seventh. With such spears the Saxons seem to have achieved types which were economical of iron and apparently able to be mass-produced in numerous local forges, for their distribution extends to all areas colonized by these people, including the Warwickshire Avon and the region around Cambridge. The cultural affinities between Saxon groups in different parts of England, the close contact they kept with each other, are really remarkable, and demonstrable also, of course, through the brooches of the women as well as the weapons of the men.

The shield-fittings of the Oxford region are not especially remarkable, though a good percentage of spear-bearing males in fact carried shields. Dickinson subjected the bosses to a computer-based analysis, which broke them down into groups. Of these Group 4 was perhaps the most interesting, being a fifth-century development from the tall, narrow boss with spike apex produced by late Roman workshops on the Continent for Saxon and Frankish troops and federates (Böhme 1974, 111 ff.), but there is nothing from the Upper Thames as early-looking as the boss from Mucking, Essex, grave 272 (Evison 1981, fig. 7). Most belong to the later derivative, and thoroughly local, Group 1, while a very few belong to Group 3, with low convex cones, which is an early sixth-century Frankish type perhaps introduced via Kent.

Few swords were buried after the fifth century, but the region is remarkable for a small group of late fifth- or early sixth-century swords, with unusual scabbard-fittings (Menghin 1975). From Burford comes a sword with long, broad chape, which seems, like another from Bredon's Norton, Worcs., to have been West-Saxon work, modelled on that from Brighthampton 31. The cast gilt-bronze scabbard-mouthpiece from the Burford sword, with its transverse ribbing, derives originally from the Continent, but probably reached the Upper Thames via Kent (Brown 1976, 23 f.). Other examples are known from Mitcham, Surrey and the region of Cambridge (Kennett 1971, 12–14), and from our region we also have the example on the sword from Long Wittenham I, grave 67, and a fine piece, detached from its sword, from Cirencester itself (Brown 1976, fig. 3.1).

By contrast with the men, most women in the fifth and earliest sixth century present a thoroughly, conservatively Saxon appearance, with few exotic features. The native dress, apparently a tubular peplos-type garment, required shoulder-fastening brooches, which, in the homeland, could be either circular or bowed (Böhme 1974, 158 ff., Abb. 53; Vierck 1978a), and a single brooch, usually an equal-armed brooch, for fastening cloak or shawl. The elaborate equal-armed brooches manufactured in Old Saxony, which the richer immigrants brought with them (p. 77), have usually been considered beyond the technical competence and resources of the Saxons in Britain, but it has recently been suggested that some of the simpler variants, including the rather stylishly simple brooch from Berinsfield grave 8, were made here (Evison 1977, 136, fig. 5 c). That may be so, but many women, like the one whose fine silver-gilt equal-arm brooch of Type Dösemoor was found broken and terribly worn in the infilling of hut X, 2 at Sutton Courtenay (Leeds 1922–3, 171, fig. 11), must have been long dead before their descendants were supplied with an alternative type of cloak-fastener, the square-headed brooch of Scandinavian origin, which finally reached the Upper Thames, via Kent, sometime early in the sixth century.

In the matter of the shoulder-brooches they fared better. As mentioned above, many Saxon women came over wearing Continental applied saucer brooches. In her recent survey of insular applied brooches, Vera Evison (1978) tends as usual to date them indiscriminately early and assume most were imports. However, in his study of applied brooches with floriate-cross motif, Martin Welch (1975) made a convincing case for their production in England before the middle of the fifth century, by a jeweller, domiciled and working in Surrey, perhaps, who could have supplied the brooches in Wallingford grave 15 (Leeds 1938, 98 f., pl. 7) and Long Wittenham 108 (Welch 1975, pl. 20, 9). Similar brooches with repoussé star-patterns seem definitely to have been made in this country (Welch 1976) and Dickinson has isolated a little group, die-linked by their ornament – from Blewburton Hill grave 2 and Fairford – which she thinks were made in the Oxford region during the fifth century (Dickinson 1976, I, 107 f., III, pl. 25, a–c). However, provided there was enough metal to hand, cast brooches were to prove more practical. The fifth-century production of cast disc-brooches with simple concentric grooved or stamped ornament, possibly by British workshops, has been noticed above (p. 74). The production of cast saucer brooches, which nearly rival them in numbers, may have begun a little later, during the second half of the fifth century. Both Dickinson (1976) and Welch (1983) have pointed out the rarity of fully developed cast saucer brooches on the Continent, and the implication that they represent a technical innovation which was only just achieving currency when the last Saxons left their northern homeland for England. Böhme (1976) clearly regards the one-piece cast form as a development of the second half of the fifth century in Old Saxony, and it is surely no coincidence that it is in Sussex, which recruited its Saxons at this relatively late date, that we find the brooches most closely modelled on Continental Saxon prototypes. Evison's statement that one of the commonest types, with five-spiral ornament 'was not made later than the middle of the fifth century' (Evison 1981, 137) is very misleading, and totally unfounded. Dickinson and Welch, our two saucer-brooch experts, are wholly in agreement that very few cast saucer brooches of any kind were made in England before the end of the fifth century, and that the spiral types were produced mainly in the sixth century. In the Oxford region Tania Dickinson regards the fine five-spiral brooches from Abingdon I, 60 (Leeds & Harden 1936, pl. 12) and the very crisp six-spiral pair from Frilford I, 143 (Pl. 6a) as possible imports from Sussex or Surrey, from which craftsmen on the Upper Thames derived the inspiration for their own large series of spiral-ornamented brooches in weaker relief (Dickinson 1976, 51 ff.). However, to one series, that with leg-whirligig motif in various combinations, she does accord primacy on the Upper Thames, with possible fifth-century beginnings in her type 2.1 from Long Wittenham I, 5. It is type 2.2, however, with leg-swastika inside an egg-and-tongue border, with three find-spots on the Upper Thames – Long Wittenham 1, East Shefford and Broughton Poggs grave 16 – and die-linked parallels as far away as Orpington and Risely in West Kent, as well as Broadway in Worcestershire (Cook 1958, fig. 4, 1–2), which appears to show the late fifth-century beginnings of the prolific saucer-brooch industry which was to develop in the region of Oxford. A study of the finer points of construction of these brooches from first to last, leads her to suggest that in early days, during the later fifth and earlier sixth centuries, production may have been in the hands of travelling craftsmen with a limited number of models to work from, but that later a mass-producing industry churned them out from a centralized workshop (Dickinson 1982).

Expansion and Consolidation.

By the end of the fifth century or the beginning of the sixth, the Germanic population of the Upper Thames had ceased to recruit itself from overseas and had settled down to work out its destiny amongst the surviving Romano-British. The cemeteries suggest that the population in existing communities had increased sufficiently to allow further geographical expansion to take place (Dickinson 1980). Perhaps the most dramatic example of this is to be found at Cirencester, where Saxons settled, close to the Gloucester gate, on the site of the Roman villa at Barton Mill (Brown 1976), burying their dead, as at the similarly-named Barton Court villa near Abingdon (Miles forthcoming), actually in the ruins of the Roman buildings, at Cirencester mutilating the Orpheus mosaic pavement. In both places, presumably, they were cultivating the lands of the villa estates, and interring their dead where they would make least waste of useful space. Another Saxon cemetery, similarly in use from *c.* 500, lies 4 miles south-west of Cirencester, along the Bath road, at Kemble. By the early sixth century, therefore, West Saxon settlement had by-passed Cirencester, and the scabbard mouthpiece found in the town itself (p. 81) may be a mute witness to the events, a minor skirmish perhaps, or even a major battle, in which the last Britons there relinquished any autonomy. The archaeological evidence is consistent in dating the end of sub-Roman Cirencester some three generations earlier than the Anglo-Saxon Chronicler, who accredited its capture to Ceawlin *sub anno* 577. There was no further sixth-century expansion towards Bath, but early in the century West Saxons crossed high Cotswold to settle the Severn/Avon valleys at such sites as Bishop's Cleeve, north of Gloucester; Broadway, Worcs.; Bidford-on-Avon and Stretton-on-Fosse, Warwicks. In the Oxford region itself Saxon settlement thickened up during the sixth century, both on the Thames itself and on its tributary rivers, and there was more occupation of the Berkshire Downs and the valley of the river Kennet (Dickinson 1980, fig. 1.4). Further south, whether or not the settlers themselves came from the north, strong cultural influence from the Oxford region can be seen south of East Wansdyke in such cemeteries as Black Patch, Pewsey, Collingbourne Ducis and Winterbourne Gunner, in east Wiltshire, and Andover in west Hampshire (Fig. 6). These communities in southern Wessex seem to have been dependent on the Upper Thames workshops especially for their supply of female brooches, whether brought by traders or on the persons of brides, and perhaps also for weapons.

Looking at all the evidence, the sixth century was a time of steady West Saxon expansion, both in territory and in influence. Anyone who is still tempted to stage the siege of *Mons Badonicus* at either of the Upper Thames Badbury sites, whether Badbury Hill itself or Liddington Castle next the village of Badbury (Fig. 6), must reckon with the fact that local Saxon archaeology offers nothing to support their candidature. Unlike the situation in west Wiltshire and east Dorset (p. 67), there is nothing in the Oxford region to reflect Gildas' tale of Saxon defeat and retrenchment in the first half of the sixth century. The West Saxons were very much on the make during these decades.

Perhaps the one serious setback for them was the phenomenal success of the kingdom of Kent at this time. Thanks to its unique geographical situation and to an enterprising and early-emerging royal dynasty, Kent seems to have been able to create for itself a monopoly of overseas trade from early in the sixth century. By some means, perhaps by keeping coastguard watch, or even some sort of fleet ready to move against them, Kent seems to have been able to prevent both the South Saxons and the West Saxons, and probably all the other Saxon peoples, too, from maintaining any direct contact with the Continent (Hawkes 1982a. 72). The Thames, which had been a highway for so many Saxon peoples and their Frankish reinforcements, now became a backwater, blocked at its mouth by the small but powerful Juto-Frankish kingdom in East Kent. All the trade of southern England seems now to have been channelled through Kent, travelling by way of its surviving Roman roads and its ports. The wealth of Kent shows up in the cemetery archaeology of the sixth and earliest seventh centuries as far exceeding that of any other region of Anglo-Saxon England. Even the wealthiest women on the Upper Thames had to make do with brooches of copper alloy with a surface dressing of gilding and silver plating to add glamour, but in Kent their counterparts regularly had their jewellery made of silver-gilt or, when gold made its appearance in quantity towards *c.* 600, of gold, with settings of garnets and exotic shell from the orient. Their menfolk had swords with silver-gilt hilts and ring-pommels and, because much more iron was available, their spears tended to be much larger than those carried elsewhere. Their tables were decked with imported bronze vessels and glassware, much of it made in Frankia but much also produced by imported glassblowers who had become domiciled in Kent. Towards the end of the sixth century and during the first quarter of the seventh, Kent was enjoying the fruits of a variety of trade connections: a cross-Channel trade with the Neustrian Franks, which brought in wine, wheel-made pottery and gold; a Frisian trade which probably brought in goods from the Baltic; and a long-distance international trade from the Far East via Alexandria, Aquileia, the Alps, the Rhine and thence cross-Channel to Kent, which brought in cast-bronze Byzantine vessels, amethyst beads, cowrie shells and, not least, almandine garnets for use on jewellery. These are just the tangibles which have survived; doubtless there were perishable goods, too, such as silks and spices. What Kent sent to pay for these luxuries certainly included slaves, by far the most frequently-mentioned commodity in the documentary sources (Verhulst 1970), but there must have been staple goods sufficient in importance and quantity to give Kent the international status it clearly enjoyed. The famous hunting dogs will probably have been more in the nature of diplomatic gifts to notables overseas than regular trade-goods, which are likely to have been commodities such as honey, wool and woven cloth (Hodges 1982, 105).

Kent by itself would not have had the surplus with which to trade on such a scale, so it seems likely that it trafficked in goods from neighbouring kingdoms. The distribution of Kentish jewellery, the pervasive influence of Kentish style generally, the occasional redistributed import such as a Frankish bronze bowl and the rather widespread distribution of glass claw-beakers of types 3 and 4 (Evison 1982), which could all have been made in Kent and exported thence, suggest that Kent was having dealings with most of the peoples of southern England during the sixth century. There is evidence that the Upper Thames may have been important to Kent in this internal trade. From Long Wittenham I and Fairford grave 57 (Leeds 1936, pl. XX, b; Dickinson 1976, I, 251 f., III, pl. 64) come fine examples of Kentish buckles with Style I ornamented plates, such as were worn by well-to-do males during the second quarter of the sixth century (Hawkes & Hogarth 1974, 78 f.) and which provoked local copying. Others are known from Sussex, southern Wessex and East Anglia, and are just the kind of object which local traders might have carried proudly back home after completing a successful deal in Kent. About seven West Saxon saucer brooches are known from East Kent (Dickinson 1976, III, 82). In view of Kent's own prolific and more elegant brooch production, these seem unlikely import-goods, but they could have reached their burial places, in cemeteries such as Lyminge (Warhurst 1955, pl. VIII, 1) and Faversham, on the persons of West Saxon women who had been married into East Kentish families to seal trade agreements. Archaeological evidence from coastal France and Kent, chiefly brooches, suggests that bridal exchanges cemented cross-Channel agreements. However, Kentish female jewellery occurs very rarely elsewhere in England, and such as there is on the Upper Thames, notably the small square-headed brooches from East Shefford, Brighthampton 40 and Abingdon I, B117, may well prove to be local copies of Kentish types, just as the great square-headed brooches from the Oxford region are all from local non-Kentish workshops. There is thus no evidence that Kent returned the compliment and married its own girls amongst the West Saxons.

However, Kentish influence on West Saxon female fashion was strong nonetheless. The Upper Thames workshops were quick to adopt Kentish Style I to ornament their own products, chiefly square-headed and saucer brooches (Pl. 6b), copying on the latter, too, some of the designs from Kentish jewelled disc brooches. The unprovenanced pair of large saucer brooches illustrated here (Pl. 6c), which must date from the very end of the sixth century at earliest, bear a close copy of the ornament of some Kentish Class 3 disc brooches (Avent 1975), though with a stylishness and difference of detail in the modelling of the heads flanking the mock-garnet wedges, which places them in a major class of their own. West Saxon women seem not to have abandoned their two-brooch dress until perhaps the second quarter of the seventh century (Matthews and Hawkes 1985), but their saucer brooches continued to ape developments taking place in Kent on the single circular cloak-brooches which had become the fashion there. I have suggested recently that some of the largest and latest saucer brooches from the Upper Thames workshops, such as those from Stone, Bucks., and Puddlehill, Dunstable, Beds., were modelled on Kent's plated disc-brooches of the latest sixth and earliest seventh centuries, while the vast brooch from Ashendon, Bucks. (Akerman 1855, pl. 38), was definitely conceived with one of the equally large Kentish composite brooches in mind (Matthews & Hawkes 1985). By this date in the second quarter of the seventh century, Kentish jewellery had begun to circulate more freely, at least in aristocratic circles, and composite brooches which could have served as models are known from Leighton Buzzard, Beds. (Hyslop 1963, fig. 10; Avent 1975, pl. 65), and, in the Oxford region itself, from Milton near Abingdon (Pl. 8a).

Before this date, when the progress of the conversion to Christianity had begun lowering the barriers between jealous and often hostile kingdoms and their royal houses, actual imports to the West Saxons in terms of staple goods seem to have been rather limited. The two glass claw-beakers, from Fairford and East Shefford (Evison 1982, nos. 34–5, pl. XI, c), too few to have been regular trade-goods, would make sense as gifts to individuals. Kent could have supplied iron from its copious Wealden resources, but once they had tapped the North Oxfordshire ironstone, which the Souldern settlers (Kennett 1975) may have been placed to do in the fifth century already, and once there were colonists in the Avon valley by the early sixth, the West Saxons should have been self-sufficient. The supply of copper alloy was another matter, however. Scavenge as they might, and undoubtedly did, to salvage scrap-bronze from Roman sites for recycling, the great production of often large brooches from the Upper Thames workshops must have depended on a more constant supply of metal. Kent could have provided this, as it must have supplied its own workshops with silver, by importing ingots or sacks of scrap metal from the Continent, and passing them on by way of internal trade. Another feature of wealthy sixth-century female dress in the West Saxon area was the necklace, suspended between the saucer brooches and comprising a great festoon of glass, crystal, and amber beads. Glass and crystal beads must have been trade-goods from the Continent, while amber could possibly have come from the East Anglian coast via West Saxon contacts in the Cambridge region. However, the amber beads are so numerous that an overseas source, in the Baltic, seems more realistic. Both the Anglian kingdoms and Kent in the sixth century disposed of large quantities of amber beads, and either could have supplied the West Saxons with that particular luxury from the sea, as well as the much more basic and necessary commodity, salt.

Had we more excavated sites of settlement, we might be better placed to determine which commodities the Saxons were exporting from the Oxford region. However, thus far the only site to be completely excavated under controlled modern conditions is that of a small farmstead at New Wintles, near Eynsham (Figs. 9–11). Only interim publications have appeared (Hawkes & Gray 1969; Gray 1974), but Freda Berisford produced a useful summary of results in her B. Litt. thesis (1973). It will be seen from the general plan (Fig. 10; Gray 1974, fig. 6) that the Saxon features excavated were broadcast over an amazingly large area of some 4.5 hectares (11 acres), and yet they add up to no more than a couple of farms or, more likely, several phases of a single farm. The South Site, probably not excavated totally, consisted of nine dug-out huts of normal two-post construction, which afforded very little dating evidence except pottery. Berisford's work on the region's pottery, which produced a rough but convenient chronological classification, showing increase of grass-tempering in the seventh century, enabled her to suggest that the South Site had been occupied first, in the sixth century, by people who buried their dead across the Torres Mear stream on what was to become the North Site. This appears to have been occupied from the end of the sixth until the late seventh or early eighth centuries, and it would be interesting to know whether these people were responsible for the seventh-century barrow-burial on the South Site or the strange mixture of late inhumations and cremations just across the present parish boundary at City Farm, Long Hanborough (Fig. 9). Even such a large excavation as this was not able to establish the relations between settlements and burials with enough certainty.

The excavation of the North Site produced the first post-built structures, without sunken floors, to be recognized in the Oxford region since Leeds (1947, 84, fig. 1) found parts of such buildings at Sutton Courtenay, and dismissed them as sheds. Actually, from Berisford's reworking of his plans (1973, fig. 20), at 7 × 3.5m the smaller of the post-built structures at Sutton Courtenay closely resembles building 255 at New Wintles, which may have been either farmhouse or barn. And the larger was bigger than the 8 × 4m structure at New Wintles, which is regarded as the main farmhouse. This is situated in the north-west corner of the site, with a dug-out hut on the same axis just outside its east end, and a well just to the north. Others among the eleven dug-out huts on the North Site have the same alignment as House 9 D and may be its contemporaries (Fig. 11), in which case they date it early in the seventh century. A successor-farmhouse contemporary with the later-dated huts is not immediately obvious, but the well-preserved paths leading to gaps in the palisade fences draw the eye to the eastern side of the site. Here there are the less regular post-built structures 255 and 122, the square 130 with its central post, which may have been a granary, and some less determinate features which were interpreted as sheep-folds. Berisford interpreted the whole south-eastern corner of the site as devised for the control of livestock. At New Wintles, as elsewhere, the dug-out huts probably served as ancillary buildings – store-rooms, workshops, and so forth – but evidence of function was disappointingly sparse. A pit with slag suggested that smithing took place on site, but where the smithy was located was not determinable. There was no pottery workshop, as in hut XXI at Sutton Courtenay (Leeds 1947) and no pottery kilns, as at Purwell Farm, Cassington, just across the Evenlode valley (Arthur & Jope 1962–3). There was no obvious cooking-hut or bakehouse, as found on the farmstead-site on Puddlehill, Dunstable (Matthews & Hawkes 1985), but there were several weaving-sheds (absent on Puddlehill) and much spinning and weaving gear was distributed about the site generally. The animal food-bones from New Wintles showed 16% pig and 38% each of cattle and sheep/goat. But at this period the sheep were too small to be kept mainly for eating, so it is interesting to find from B. Noddle's bone-report that they were slaughtered only when old, having been kept primarily for their wool. This was not everywhere the case. The Puddlehill community ate plenty of young animals, including lambs. At Purwell Farm, Cassington, the proportions of animal bones were quite different, with sheep accounting for only 15% of domestic animals eaten, as against 30% pigs and 50% cattle.

It is extremely interesting that these three farmstead sites, the only ones in the region so far to yield adequate information about their respective economies, should prove to have been so different. The Puddlehill Saxons, aristocrats to judge from the lady's opulent beads and brooches, obviously lived off the fat of the land and may have bought in, or been supplied through taxes with, most of the goods they needed. In contrast with them we have the people at Purwell Farm, Cassington, middle-class and prosperous to judge from their grave-goods, who seem to have concentrated on the production of meat and dairy produce. They also seem to have run a small potting industry to serve local needs and, on the testimony of a failed casting from one of their huts, either went in for a little saucer-brooch production themselves, or on occasion entertained a visiting jeweller. Across the Evenlode from them were the people at New Wintles Farm, who were obviously sheep-farmers primarily, concentrating on producing surplus wool and perhaps cloth. Finally, a few kilometres up-river, there was the seventh-century community which left so much refuse in the boundary Ditch F of the old Roman villa at Shakenoak (Brodribb *et al.* 1972, *passim*). The finds there show nearly 50% sheep and goats amongst the animals kept, an abundance of bone-working connected with weaving, and also of evidence for smithing and production of iron tools. These small settlements along the Evenlode valley show both a remarkable degree of self-sufficiency and also an unexpectedly developed amount of specialization at such a comparatively early date.

Other, apparently similar, farmstead sites have recently been excavated in the vicinity of Abingdon. The, as yet not fully-published, Saxon settlement adjacent to the Roman villa at Barton Court comprised at least two post-built houses measuring 6.7 × 9m and 5.2 × 10m respectively, seven dug-out huts, a well, and post-built fence enclosures (Miles 1977, fig. 15; Miles forthcoming). The economy here seems also to have been dominated by sheep and textile production, and there is some evidence for bead-making on the site. At the time of writing, considerable interest focusses on the excavations in the Barrow Hills nearby in Radley parish (Benson & Miles 1974a, 87 f., map 31, figs. 15, 16), where more post-built houses and dug-out huts may represent a continuation of the Barton Court settlement (which would make it huge) but are more likely to be another farmstead.

Thus far settlement evidence in the Oxford region supports the hypothesis proposed by Christopher Taylor (1983, 109 ff.), that the early Saxon landscape was largely filled with 'varied, small and mobile' settlements, and that the nucleated village at this period was pretty much a myth. However, the cemeteries tell us quite clearly that there must have been larger sites than the farmsteads we have been studying here. The settlement belonging to the Abingdon I cemetery, for example, could we but find it, must have been very substantial. Moreover, the only sites available for total excavation are precisely the minor sites, or the 'failed' sites, which were abandoned in the seventh or eighth centuries – whether because of Mercian agression or for less dramatic socio-economic reasons – and which have never been occupied since. If we return to the map of the New Wintles and Purwell Farm sites (Fig. 9), the eye is drawn at once to the medieval/modern villages of Cassington and Eynsham, both with Old English place-names and both with evidence of early Saxon occupation, though very scrappy because the overlying houses make systematic excavation virtually impossible. Eynsham, at least, must have been an important place in our period, because it is documented by the Anglo-Saxon Chronicler *sub anno* 571 as one of the four *tunas* captured by Ceawlin's brother Cuthwulf. The circumstances are obscure, and will remain so, but clearly the place was no mere farm. Perhaps it was a major seat of some rival family, perhaps even the early Saxon equivalent to the small market town which Eynsham became in the later Middle Ages (Rodwell 1975, 109 ff.). If the Oxford region was already producing wool and perhaps cloth in a big way, and to some extent also meat and hides, as the evidence from the farm-sites suggests, local markets will have been needed to organize their redistribution and export to Kent, and also to enable the king to extract his toll of the profit.

Kingship

Given the economic domination of Kent during the sixth century, it is not surprising that an early act in the reign of Ceawlin, the one West Saxon king whom Bede describes as some kind of overlord in southern England (*H.E.* ii, v), was a successful clash with his young contemporary Æthelbert of Kent (*A.S.C. sub anno* 568) at *Wibbandun*, probably Wimbledon in Surrey. From the Chronicle's numerous references to his military campaigns, he seems to have been a warleader of ability and aggression, with notably expansionist aims. It would have been natural for him to attempt West Saxon recovery of the Thames highway to the sea, but there is nothing to suggest that he was successful in that regard. Æthelbert's setback seems to have been temporary. But confrontation between the two kings may explain one of the most puzzling single burials of this period, that of the man buried with great wealth under the great mound at Taplow (Meaney 1964, 59) in Buckingham-shire. The burial still awaits proper publication, after excavation a century ago now, but the mound is still there, about 5m high by 24.5m in diameter, standing proud on its riverside terrace, which commands an immense view of the Thames upstream towards the territory of the West Saxons. *Taeppa*, if that indeed was his name, was given a burial of truly royal proportions, in a large grave-chamber and with lavish grave-goods second only in splendour to those of Raedwald of East Anglia at Sutton Hoo (Bruce-Mitford 1975 & 1978). It would have been a fitting monument to Ceawlin himself, but Taplow is well outside West Saxon territory and remote from any other major kingdom in the late sixth or early seventh century. One is forced to conclude, therefore, that *Taeppa* was a regional ruler of a small riverine territory, centred on the fertile Taplow terrace where, doubtless, he had his own estate. One of the most remarkable things about his burial is that nearly everything in it, his gold buckle and gilt clasps, his great silver-mounted drinking-horns, some of the decorated cups (Speake 1980, fig. 7, pls. I, a–b, 7, c, f, 14, k, 1), and probably his four glass claw-beakers (Evison 1982, pl. xii) are all high-class pieces from Kent. His unusual Coptic 'fruit-stand' is also likely to have reached him via Kent. Obviously he was of great importance to Kent; very much Æthelbert's 'man'; possibly even a Kentish prince himself; but, if not, certainly the recipient of lavish diplomatic gifts from Æthelbert. It is difficult not to conclude that he performed some vital function, and from his strategic situation and status, he could well have been acting as the Kentish king's ally against Ceawlin, helping to ensure that Kent maintained its control of trade down the Thames.

There used to be a great debate about whether Ceawlin ruled the West Saxons on the Upper Thames or originated in the south from the ruling house of Wiltshire settlers, whose royal line traced its ancestry back to Cerdic, 'son of Elesa, son of Esla, son of Gewis . . .' (*A.S.C. sub anno* 552). Ceawlin's attribution to this same dynasty has in modern times been based on a simplistic reading of the Anglo-Saxon Chronicle, which appears to narrate the advance of Cerdic and his son Cynric from the New Forest to the region of Salisbury, where (*sub anno* 552) Cynric vanquished Britons at Old Sarum, then couples the names of Cynric and Ceawlin in another victory over Britons at Barbury Castle in North Wiltshire (*sub anno* 556). Thereafter, Ceawlin and his kinsmen are recorded as conducting campaigns in and around the Upper Thames Valley, which people used to interpret as a southern takeover. However, Kirby (1965) pointed out that in none of these entries relating to Ceawlin is he described as the son of Cynric, that in fact he is given no pedigree at all until 'Ceadwalla began to contend for the kingdom' (*A.S.C. sub anno* 685), and suggests that Ceadwalla, a great-great-grandson of Ceawlin, now laying claim to the lordship of greater Wessex, found it expedient to add Cerdic and Cynric to his nothern pedigree to buttress his claim to rule Wiltshire as well as the Upper Thames. The practice was continued by King Ine, another and very distinguished descendant of Ceawlin. Thus, from the end of the seventh century, the two genealogies became mixed, and, as northerners and southerners used similar, often identical names, disentangling their true relationships is difficult, often impossible, given the limited amount of information at our disposal (Kirby 1965).

Dickinson (1976, 452 ff.) argued that the use of similar, sometimes identical C-alliterative names by the descendants of both Cerdic and Ceawlin, implies that the northern and southern kings belonged to branches of the same family, preferring to believe that Ceawlin was indeed the son of Cynric, as his succession date *sub anno* 560, which corresponds with that of the death of Cynric, would indeed imply. However, this could have been the result of editing by the Anglo-Saxon Chronicler, wishing to tidy up the record in the light of the pedigrees of Ceadwalla and Ine. Ceawlin's own lack of pedigree remains to perplex us, and it could even be that the Chronicler suppressed it deliberately because it named ancestors other than Cerdic and Cynric, earlier rulers on the Upper Thames, whose greater antiquity might have challenged the seniority of the line of Cerdic. A possible explanation for the similarity of royal names is that Cerdic and Cynric had been scions of the dynasty ruling the Oxford region, who went adventuring early in the sixth century and became the founding kings in the south. Upper Thames involvement in the settlement of Wiltshire could certainly explain the close archaeological connections between the regions from the outset of the landtakings in the south.

From his recorded doings, there can be little doubt that Ceawlin operated in the north. He was a great war-leader, whose deeds were sung in heroic tales, snippets of which are actually quoted in the Anglo-Saxon Chronicle, notably *sub annis* 584 & 592. The Chronicler's dates for events in the sixth century are as likely to be computations as those for the fifth, but there is not much obviously discrepant about them as regards Wessex. We anyway have no choice but to accept them with caution as pegs on which to hang the small amount of historical information afforded us. There is archaeological support for the arrival of Saxons in the Salisbury region at about the time, *sub anno* 519, of the foundation of the southern kingdom by Cerdic and Cynric. The latter is said to have succeeded *sub anno* 534 and to have ruled for 26/7 years, ie. until 560/1. Again this is quite plausible and permits the alliance between the old southern king (whose name Cynric, meaning 'Kingdom', sounds like a nickname, suggesting that perhaps he was the real force behind the creation of the southern kingdom) and the young West Saxon prince from the north, Ceawlin, with whom he fought against unnamed Britons at Barbury Castle, *sub anno* 556. By about that date, Saxon settlement seems to have spread to the west side of the Berkshire Downs and the headwaters of the river Kennet (Dickinson 1980, fig. 1.4), north of East Wansdyke, as it were closing the gap between West Saxons and the original settlers of chalk Wessex. It is not improbable that some Britons, in and around Bath for example, might have felt threatened and have sent a raiding party which based itself on Barbury Castle. This Iron Age hillfort bestrides the Ridgeway leading from the Oxford region into Wiltshire (Fig. 6) and would have made a formidable base from which to harry both north and south, thus producing just the kind of situation in which a joint operation by Cynric and Ceawlin would have made tactical good sense. Just over twenty years later, *sub anno* 577, Ceawlin and his son Cuthwine are said to have taken the war into the enemy's camp, killing three British kings at the battle of Dyrham (another Iron Age hillfort), which lies a few miles north of Bath (Fig. 6). Bath must have been the chief objective, and it is said to have been captured and its king killed. Perhaps this was a reprisal for further British attacks meanwhile on what they would have considered the increasing Saxon menace. Dumnonia certainly seems to have felt itself threatened, if the second Dark-Age refortification of South Cadbury Castle is anything to go by (Alcock 1971, 222). Saxon settlement did not reach as far west as Bath until at least a century later, so landtaking was not Ceawlin's aim. The other cities mentioned as captured in 577 were Gloucester, which at the time was just on the edge of Ceawlin's sphere of influence, and Cirencester which, as we have noticed above, must have been his already. The names of the British kings are apparently suspect (Sims-Williams 1983b), so we await new critical work on this annal before we can judge what to accept.

Problems also attach to the annal for 571, the only one for his reign not to mention Ceawlin in person. Cuthwulf or Cutha, said in two manuscripts of the Chronicle to have been Ceawlin's brother, fought against Britons at *Biedcanford* (on philological grounds apparently not identifiable with Bedford) 'and captured four towns, Limbury, Aylesbury, Benson and Eynsham'. Sims-Williams has suggested some later interpolation here, connected with a dispute between Wessex and Mercia over some of this territory in the late eighth century. However, leaving Eynsham aside, the other towns captured seem to mark West Saxon expansion into the Chiltern-foot zone, which, from the fifth century, had remained British apart from originally federate colonies of Saxons (p. 73). Archaeological evidence suggests that these, as at Bishopstone, by Aylesbury, and Luton, by Limbury, had kept in touch with the West Saxons but did not increase their numbers until late in the sixth and earlier seventh centuries. Then, presumably as a result of Cuthwulf's military coup, other Saxon groups arrived, chiefly small aristocratic groups, to help administer the new territory and back up its new West Saxon *sub-regulus* (Matthews & Hawkes 1985). The real problem is that the archaeological evidence, the imposing women's brooches from Stone, Ashendon and Puddlehill, Dunstable, would better fit a West Saxon takeover after Ceawlin's time, during the earlier seventh century. The Preface to MS A of the Anglo-Saxon Chronicle records a grandson of Ceawlin's called Cuthwulf, who was the brother of Cynegils, who succeeded in 611. Cuthwulf died immediately after his Chilterns campaign. Might scribal error have copied 611 as 571, thus wiping out all record of the West Saxon king who intervened between Ceawlin and Cynegils? Cuthwulf might well have reigned between 593 and 611, Cutha (either his uncle Cutha or his father Cuthwine – the pet-name forms are confusing) having been killed in 584 and Ceawlin himself in 593. His being credited with sole conduct of the Chilterns campaign certainly suggests that Cuthwulf was king at the time. The Chronicle's candidates for the succession to Ceawlin have never quite fitted chronologically: Ceol succeeded *s.a.* 591, two years before Ceawlin's death, and Ceolwulf in 597, four years after. When one looks at their pedigrees (*s.a.* 597 & 611), one realises that they were brothers and, as sons of Cutha, son of Cynric, kings of southern Wessex and not of the Upper Thames (Kirby 1965, 23). I shall return to them shortly.

Perhaps the least problematic of the annals relating to Ceawlin are the two where the deadpan jottings of the Chronicler give way to what appear to be quotations from a heroic tale about the 'Deeds of Ceawlin'. *Sub anno* 584 Ceawlin and Cutha fought against the Britons at *Fethanleag*, usually identified with a place in Stoke Lyne in north-east Oxfordshire, 8 km north of the old Roman town of Alchester, a region where Anglo-Saxon settlement in this period is quite absent, except for a few sites well to the west on the upper Cherwell (Map 11). Ceawlin is said to have captured many villages and taken countless spoils, presumably from the British, and one can only speculate that perhaps Ceawlin was bent on controlling some surviving British communities there, who were working the North Oxfordshire ironstone. Obtaining sufficient iron to arm his following must always have been an anxiety. However, Cutha was slain, and Ceawlin returned in anger to his own county. Even worse fated was his campaign in 592: 'Her micel waelfill waes at Woddesbeorge, Ceawlin waes ut adrifen.' The great slaughter at Woden's barrow was one of the inspirations behind the major study of Wansdyke by Aileen and Cyril Fox (1960). The annal has been interpreted variously, and their reading of it differs radically from mine. We have seen that Wansdyke – O.E. *Wodenesdic* – might originally have been a British work of the fifth century (p. 77), but it would still have been a major boundary and defensive work in the time of Ceawlin. If it turns out after all to have been constructed in his day, it would merely stress the gravity of the political rift between the northern and southern sides of the Wessex hegemony, which the battle of 592 already implies. *Wodnesbeorge* is the Neolithic long-barrow, known now as Adam's Grave, which stands on a commanding hill beside the Ridgeway about 1 km south of Wansdyke, dominating the two approach-routes from the north, across the plateau from the Red Gate and up Woden's Dene from Woden's Gate (Fox & Fox 1960, fig. 28). The concentration of Woden names in this small area suggested to the Foxes that the barrow was a site of heathen worship. It must certainly have been of great importance strategically against invaders from the north, for it was here that the Mercian king Ceolred fought Ine of Wessex *sub anno* 715, just as Ceawlin suffered a bloody defeat and 'was driven out' in 592. The circumstances are not difficult to imagine. Ceol had become king in Wiltshire in the previous year and had presumably challenged the overlordship of the veteran West Saxon king. The following year, 593, must have seen a further outbreak of hostilities, to the detriment of the West Saxons, for Ceawlin perished, along with Cwichelm and Crida, presumably two of his kinsmen.

As a kind of footnote here one may add that the otherwise unknown Crida provides a clue to the ancestry of Ceawlin. In some late Wessex genealogies a Creoda, an archaic form of the name Crida, appears as the son of Cerdic (Sisam 1953, 291), and Kirby has made the attractive suggestion that this 'Creoda was a prince of the Thames valley, as Ceawlin was, whose name was transmitted to Wessex in its archaic Anglian spelling, and it is not impossible that he was the father or grandfather or some other ancestor of Ceawlin whose name was dropped when the Ceawlin line adopted Cerdic and Cynric as its ancestors, later being added to the West Saxon genealogy when the dynasty of Egbert was seeking to clarify its historical background' (Kirby 1965, 24). The Crida of 593 will thus have been the bearer of a proud and ancient West Saxon family name.

To resume, however, the line of Ceawlin must have suffered a great blow in 593, and, with Ceol and Ceolwulf presumably claiming lordship of the hegemony, it is perhaps hardly surprising that the Anglo-Saxon Chronicle demoted Cuthwulf. If he was indeed king on the Upper Thames after the death of Ceawlin, he will have been well occupied dealing with possible rebellion at Eynsham and carving out new territory in the Chilterns to the north-east. The next king, Cynegils, though described by the Chronicler as a son of Ceol, of the Wiltshire line, must from his recorded deeds have been a West Saxon. The pedigree of Ine *sub anno* 688 describes him as the grandson of Ceolwold who was the brother of Cynegils, and they both were the sons of Cuthwine, son of Ceawlin. Cynegils would not have been mentioned in this pedigree had he not been a king, and a well remembered one, too, because it was in his reign that Christianity came to Wessex. For present purposes, however, it is sufficient to take the story forward just as far as the year 628, when the Chronicle records that Cynegils and his son Cwichelm 'fought against Penda at Cirencester, and afterwards came to terms'. This is the earliest intimation that the West Saxons had now to contend with a new enemy: the internecine wars were at an end: the new problem was Mercia under Penda, a warleader after the manner of Ceawlin. This dispute over Cirencester was the beginning of the end of West Saxon control over the whole of the Oxford region.

But before handing the region over to the Mercians, or even introducing St. Birinus and Christianity, it is time to look briefly at the evidence for the West Saxon kings' administration of their large territory. The maps (Map 11 & Fig. 6) make it abundantly clear that it could not have been governed from a single centre, but that there must from early times have been *villae regales*, royal estates strategically placed so as to enable the kings to reach, control, take council with and legislate over their widely dispersed subjects. And of course such estates will have had to provide the maintenance, the food and clothing, perhaps also the weapons and jewellery, etc., needed by the kings, their families and their following. Like medieval kings, early Anglo-Saxon kings will have been continually on the move from place to place, and in the Oxford region certainly they must have travelled by river as well as by such roads as existed. Therefore, amongst the specialist services required by them will have been both ship-building and horsebreeding. As we have seen already, settlement-site excavation is in its infancy and nothing approaching a royal vill has yet been explored in the Oxford region, though Yeavering in Northumberland (Hope-Taylor 1977) gives us some idea of what to look for.

Dorchester itself must be considered first, for it was in the king's gift in 635 when Cynegils established St. Birinus there. Tania Dickinson has pointed out that more gold finds of the late sixth and earlier seventh centuries have been found in or around Dorchester than anywhere else in the region and that one of them, a gold cloisonné pyramidal sword-knot, probably from the same workshop that made the regalia buried with Raedwald at East Anglia at Sutton Hoo c. 625, could have come from a royal burial in the close vicinity of Dorchester (Dickinson 1974, 25 ff., pl. iv, b). If there is any substance in the notion of a sub-Roman 'tyrant' at Dorchester who became the ancestor of the West Saxon royal house, one would expect to find evidence of a palace-site within the circuit of the Roman walls. Excavation has been possible on a limited scale in three areas of the town (Fig. 7) and the actual amount of Saxon material, chiefly pottery and building foundations, recovered is quite remarkable. Excavations in the north-west corner of the town produced a sequence of Saxon occupation from the fifth century through to the ninth, the last phase dated by a coin of Burgred of Mercia, 825–74. The buildings here were all small, flimsy and un-palacelike (Rowley & Brown, 1981). In the south-east corner the sequence of material found was of similar date but the features were less determinate (Bradley 1978). Much more impressive, though unhappily fragmented by inability to do any large area-excavation, were the traces of Saxon buildings found in the south-western sector of the town under the present-day allotments (Frere 1962 & forthcoming). I am most indebted to Professor Frere for letting me see the text of his report on the 1963 excavations, which provided evidence for the existence of large trench-built timber buildings cutting through the latest Roman levels and associated with well-fired hard sand-tempered pottery which Berisford would date any time between the fifth and seventh centuries (1973, 148 ff., see also Rowley & Brown 1981, 39 f.). Some pieces are definitely of the fifth century, others not closely datable on form or fabric, because grass-tempered pottery, which elsewhere is a useful indicator of seventh-century date, is hardly represented at all at Dorchester. I was allowed to look through the pottery from the 1963 season, only a fraction of which will be published of course, and the sheer quantity of Saxon sherds represented was very impressive. Altogether, it looks as if the allotments cover the site of a major building complex, in which the sixth-century hut found in 1962 will have been merely a bakehouse (Frere 1962, 123 ff., figs. 7–9). The whole complex might well represent a palatial establishment in the town before the arrival of Birinus, but obviously its identity, scale and date must remain speculative until large area-excavations become possible.

One of the most tragic occurrences in the whole history of gravel extraction in the Oxford region has been the near-total loss of information about a Saxon extra-mural settlement to the west of Dorchester (Fig. 7; Benson & Miles 1974a, 68, 91, Map 36, Figs. 17–18). Just to the north-east is Bishop's Court, traditionally associated with the ninth-century Mercian bishopric, but parts of a sixth- and of a seventh-century cemetery have been dug in the near vicinity, together with settlement evidence of similar date (May 1977). At present the chief clue to the importance of this site is provided by a single bronze artefact (Pl. 8b), an exquisite little ornamental lock for a book or casket (May 1977, fig. 11). It is unique but its human-head decoration looks like Anglo-Saxon work of the seventh century. It was found in a ditch near the seventh-century burials, and is not the kind of thing which would be at all commonplace. It suggests a community of status somewhere nearby. Might this have been a royal site, or actually the site of Birinus's seventh-century palace? It is also possible that the burials and clasp may have had to do with one of the shadowy Mercian bishops at Dorchester in the late seventh or early eighth centuries. One can only hope that enough remains for sense to be made of the situation at Bishop's Court sometime in the future.

There is no early written reference to the *villae regales* of the West Saxon kings, those mapped by Myres (1954, fig. 33) being late-attested sites, dating from after the Mercian takeover, not all of which may be relevant to the early situation I am writing about here. However, aerial photography is revealing some distinct possibilities. The one shown here (Pl. 8c) lies just over 1 km SE of Drayton village, and comprises an L-shaped alignment of rectangular structures in a palaeo-landscape dominated by prehistoric features (Benson & Miles 1974b). The largest structure in the complex, overlying a ploughed-down Bronze Age barrow, appears to be a great hall some 25 × 8m in size, as long but not as wide as Edwin of Northumbria's great hall at Yeavering. It lies E–W and aligned on it at its east end, just as at Yeavering, is a smaller 9 × 6m building, which is probably to be interpreted as the women's quarters or 'bower', O.E. *Bur*. Set a little distance apart from these buildings A and B, and at right angles to them, is a line of smaller buildings (not all of one period because there are overlaps and rebuilds) the largest of which, 16 × 6m, is likely to have been a guest-hall. Across the modern road is another major rectangular building, which has shown up since first publication of the site, the photograph used here being one taken by D.R. Wilson in 1975. Apart from the lack of a 'grandstand' for open-air meetings, this site at Drayton seems not much inferior in the scale of its accommodation to Yeavering itself. It can hardly be other than a royal residence. As to dating, the buildings appear to be of post-in-trench construction, which suggests seventh century at earliest, but the site is littered with dug-out structures whose contents would quickly resolve the problem were excavation ever to take place. It has even been suggested that Leeds' old site at Sutton Courtenay, not too far off on the same wedge of plateau, may be a domestic area of the 'palace' complex, and there the occupation extends from the fifth until late in the seventh century. Finally, just 650m south across the Mill Stream, is the richest seventh-century cemetery so far discovered in the whole of the Upper Thames. Though never systematically excavated, finds made in the last century included two female graves with imported Kentish composite jewelled disc brooches (Pl. 8b), datable to the second quarter or middle of the century, and other status-denoting objects such as a hanging bowl and a sugar-loaf shield-boss. This cemetery, known as Milton II, may well have been the burial ground of the 'palace' folk, and if so would suggest that the building complex I am assuming to have been a royal vill belonged to Cynegils and/or his son Cenwalh. Alternatively, the sites might have been early Mercian.

Just 6 km to the east, on the river Thames itself, immediately south of the centre of Long Wittenham village, aerial photography in 1975 discovered another site with major timber buildings. I am grateful to David Miles for mentioning this to me and David R. Wilson for providing photographs. The site would repay proper analysis and mapping, as was done for the Drayton complex. But meanwhile one can say that the Saxon date of the site is attested by the presence of unmistakable dug-out huts around the edges of an L-shaped arrangement of at least three hall-houses, the largest of which seems about 20 × 8m in size, the others perhaps 14m long. The Long Wittenham I cemetery, which dates from the fifth to the early seventh century, was situated not more than 200–300 metres to the west of this settlement, and the two must surely belong together. The cemetery was a large one and it may be that we have found one of the large village-sites I was speculating about earlier (p. 84). On the other hand, the scale of the buildings suggests a site of some status, and Dickinson picked out the cemetery as being the most 'military', with more burials of armed males than anywhere else in the Oxford region. Considering also the numbers of high-status objects from this cemetery, the likelihood remains that this was another royal vill, with a big ancillary population. It should prove to be earlier in date than the Drayton site, and thus part of the earlier organization of the region, perhaps in the time of Ceawlin, perhaps earlier still.

Both sites are very close to Dorchester, and now we know what we are looking for, it is certain that more will be identified as survey work in the region continues. One would expect to find others in major settlement centres such as the Eynsham and Brighthampton districts, and parts further west still. The very recent discovery of an important and rich cemetery close to Shrivenham (containing a man's grave with scales and weights for weighing precious metals) perhaps suggests that there was a royal vill here, at the foot of Ashdown, in early as well as late Saxon times (Scull forthcoming). The importance of rich cemeteries and burials as a means of identifying royal vills in this period should not be underestimated. The archaeological evidence for the appearance of West Saxon aristocrats in the wake of Cuthwulf's campaign in the Chiltern-foot zone (the rich women's burials at Stone and Ashendon near Aylesbury, for example, and Puddlehill near Dunstable) probably date the foundation of otherwise late-attested vills, Kingsbury by Quarrenden and Kingsbury in Houghton Regis, as early as the beginning of the seventh century (Matthews & Hawkes 1985).

Burial-sites of royalty are of course of prime importance. In the Oxford region we are tantalized by documentary references to burial-mounds with names suffixed by O.E. -*hlaew*, as in Taplow, and prefixed by personal names used in the West Saxon royal line. In south-east Oxfordshire a charter of 995 mentions a *Cudan hlaew*, Cuda or Cutha's tumulus, on the boundary of Cuxham with Easington, and Dickinson was surely right to suggest that this same individual's name survived as a field-name in the next parish of Watlington (Dickinson 1974, 32), where Cuddington goes back to *Cudesdon*, Cuda or Cutha's hill (EPNS XXIII, 97, 126). Cutha being the favourite pet-name in Ceawlin's dynasty, there seems a good chance that one of his kindred held an estate and was buried here. Perhaps the same man held Cuddington just over the boundary in Buckinghamshire, very close to the two early Saxon settlements there of Dinton and Bishopstone. Much more famous, of course, is the burial-mound of Cutha or Cuthwine, the *Cuthnes hlawe*, which gave rise to the place-name Cutteslowe, once a separate parish, now an almost-obliterated place under Oxford's northernmost suburbs (EPNS XXIV, 267). In 1935 Helen Cam made the priceless discovery in the public records that, in 1261, two strangers having been found murdered 'under' the 'how' of Cutteslowe, the place being a notorious haunt of evil-doers, the Sheriff of Oxford was ordered to have the place levelled. O.G.S. Crawford added his opinion, with which one must surely agree, that for a 'robber's den' a stone-chambered long-barrow of Neolithic date would best fit the book. So, there is still a chance that a Saxon royal burial survives, with its mound quite ploughed down, somewhere on the farm of St. Frideswide, known as Old Cutchlow on the

Ordance map of 1814 (Cam & Crawford 1935). The tendency of Anglo-Saxon barrows to be eroded to the point of invisibility is well illustrated by the fate of the boat-barrow at Snape in Suffolk (Bruce-Mitford 1974, 114 ff.), and the smaller barrows at Finglesham in Kent (Hawkes 1982b), while their normal lack of ditches could render them invisible to aerial photography. So at almost any time during rescue excavation, e.g. at Long Wittenham, a royal burial might just turn up.

An original barrow, long ploughed away, must certainly explain the extraordinary situation at Cuddesdon (O.E. name *Cuthenes dune*, 'Cuthwine's hill') in 1847 when Samuel Wilberforce, bishop of Oxford, decided to improve the carriageway to his palace. Workmen found a radial arrangement of skeletons and some very fine objects which must have come from a princely grave of latest sixth or earliest seventh century. The site was re-excavated and republished by Tania Dickinson (1974), and she came out in favour of sacrificial burials around a still-pagan West Saxon prince. There were two swords, two blue glass bowls, probably of Kentish make, a Coptic bronze miniature bucket, probably another diplomatic gift from Kent (Pl. 7a–c), and a fragment of something set with garnets. The date of acquisition of these things is likely to have been during the overlordship of Æthelbert, after Ceawlin's death in 593 and before Æthelbert's in 616. The dead man might well have been Cuthwine, the brother of Ceawlin, whose son Cuthwulf would have needed Kentish help and patronage, if, as I have suggested (p. 87), he ruled the West Saxons in the teeth of Gewissan opposition until the accession of Cynegils in 611. Cuthwine will have been Ceawlin's major *sub-regulus*, and giving him this estate at Cuddesdon, on the fringe of West Saxon territory vis-à-vis the Chilterns, would have made sound tactical sense.

The name Cwichelm appears twice in the region, at Ardley in North Oxfordshire, where a charter of 995 names a *Cwicelmes hlaew* (EPNS XXIII, 197), and on the boundary of the parishes of East and West Hendred, just south of the Ridgeway, where the originally vast mound now called Scutchamer Knob was named *Cwicelmes hlaew* both in a document of the late tenth century and in the Anglo-Saxon Chronicle *sub anno* 1006 (EPNS L, 481 f.). Ardley is the village immediately west of Stoke Lyne, where Ceawlin fought at *Fethanleag* in 584, and nothing is more likely than that he placed a member of his kindred in charge of this quarter of his kingdom. It could perfectly well have been the Cwichelm who later died with him in 593. The great mound by the Ridgeway was traditionally associated with another Cwichelm, the son of Cynegils, who died immediately after converting to Christianity, *A.S.C. sub anno* 636. He died within the lifetime of his father, who was succeeded by another son Cenwealh. Yet Bede (*H.E.* ii, 9) described him as king of the West Saxons, so clearly he was a major figure, and must have governed a large block of country. The Berkshire Downs, or Ashdown, the accepted name in Old English being *Aescesdune* (EPNS XLIX, 2 ff.), could well have been his territory. It may not be a coincidence that Cenwealh made a vast grant of land on Ashdown, 3,000 hides, to Cwichelm's son Cuthred (*A.S.C.*, s.a. 648), thus leaving him in charge of this huge buffer territory between the Upper Thames and southern Wessex, when Mercian aggression made the West Saxon king shift his centre of operations south to Winchester. This may just have been official confirmation of Cuthred's title to a sub-kingdom which his father had held before him. *Cwicelmes hlaew* on Ashdown was a well-known landmark in Saxon times, with its own special aura and folklore, which the Vikings went out of their way to discredit in AD 1006. It was so prominent a feature that by c. 990 it had become a meeting place of the Shire and later the site of a fair and regular local market. It was opened up in the nineteenth century by a local farmer and excavated more scientifically in 1934 (Peake *et al.* 1935) but the results were inconclusive: a primary burial could have been missed and the Iron Age pottery found could have derived from disturbance of a settlement site of that date thereabouts. So the alternatives remain: it could have been Cwichelm's mound or something of another date and purpose subsequently named after him.

The two best-attested Anglo-Saxon barrow-burials in the region are those of people unnamed, but they interestingly reflect the political situation as it developed in the reigns of Cynegils and Cenwealh. From 628, when the Anglo-Saxon Chronicle records Cynegils and Cwichelm fighting Penda over Cirencester and having to come to terms, it was a mere twenty years before Cenwealh had to give up Dorchester and move to Winchester, where he is recorded as building a Minster in 648 (A.S.C. MS E). The terms exacted by Penda, in 628, were apparently sealed by the marriage of his sister with Cenwealh (Bede, *H.E.* iii, 7). What the terms were we do not know, and can only guess that the West Saxons lost territory in and around Cirencester. In 645 Cenwealh repudiated his Mercian wife and Penda attacked and drove him from his kingdom. When he returned from exile in East Anglia, quite clearly he had made arrangements to try his fortunes elsewhere, Winchester being a prudent choice in view of the rival dynasty in Wiltshire. Thenceforth all his recorded activities seem to be directed at expansion in the south-west, and there is no clear evidence that he returned to Dorchester at all. This seems to have been left to bishop Birinus and perhaps his successor Agilbert, though Agilbert, too, could have been at Winchester. Meanwhile, Cenwealh's nephew Cuthred maintained a West Saxon military presence on Ashdown to prevent Mercian invasion of the south. This was not long coming, for in 661, according to the Chronicle, while Cenwealh himself was campaigning in Somerset, Wulfhere son of Penda 'harried on Ashdown', and, presumably as a result, Cuthred and the Wiltshire king Cenberht died. By this time the whole West Saxon territory north of the Thames, including Dorchester itself, must have passed to Mercia, being mostly absorbed into the territory of the

Hwicce. These people, originally of mixed West Saxon and Anglian stock, and centred on the Severn/Avon valleys, thrived under the Mercians as a powerful sub-kingdom with their own Anglian rulers (Finberg 1961, 167–80).

Representing the Mercians, in all probability, there is the Asthall barrow on the edge of Wychwood, which used to stand proud on the skyline, dominating the ridge where the Roman road to Cirencester crossed the river Windrush. It is an imposing monument, originally at least 18m in diameter and 4 high, which a local farmer could not resist exploring in 1923–4, though luckily he conveyed his findings to E.T Leeds, who subsequently wrote a summary report (Leeds 1924). The burial proved to be a total cremation, a purely Anglian rite in the seventh century, of a personage who had been lavishly equipped with at least six vessels, including at least one of silver, a Coptic bowl and perhaps a Celtic hanging bowl of bronze, one or more drinking-horns, a wheel-made pottery bottle and two hand-made pots; an ivory mounted casket; bone pieces and die from a board-game; and decorated belt-fittings of bronze, including a gilt Style II ornamented object with bird-heads. There were the remains of a pyre and the bones of a horse, a sheep and perhaps a woman (Dickinson 1976, II, 35 ff.). The chief burial is likely to have been a man, perhaps with human and animal sacrifices, after contemporary Scandinavian fashion; a pagan of course, and probably datable to the second quarter or middle of the seventh century. One must agree with the conclusion that Asthall may be the burial of 'either one of the early and still pagan princes of the Hwicce, or some Mercian Angle charged with the administration of this district' (Dickinson 1976, I, 442).

About four miles south-east of the Asthall barrow, across the valley of the Norton Ditch (now occupied by RAF Brize Norton), is the even larger mound at Lew, which stands on high ground overlooking the vale and is visible for miles around. The place, mentioned in a charter of 984 as *aet Hlaewe* (EPNS XXIV, 327), clearly takes its name from the mound which is the most prominent feature in the landscape. It seems astonishing, therefore, that the connection was not made in the place-name survey, and that the mound has not previously been mentioned in the archaeological literature. From its form there can be no doubt at all that it is an Anglo-Saxon barrow. And the great mound at Leafield, four miles north-east of Asthall, has every appearance of being another Anglo-Saxon barrow. Both barrows were first drawn to my attention by Dr. John Blair, the first person in modern times to recognize their true character, and I am deeply indebted to him. Neither Lew nor Leafield has been excavated, of course, but their position in relation to Asthall looks significant enough to suggest that these too may have been the burial-places of Mercian or Hwiccan notables.

Representing the embattled West Saxons on Ashdown, we have the nobleman buried outside the Roman temple-enclosure on Lowbury Hill, beside the Ridgeway, about 9 km ESE of *Cwicelmes hlaew* (Atkinson 1916, 15 ff., figs. 7–10, pls. IV–VI; Evison 1963, 46 ff., figs. 26–28). His barrow was about 17.5m in diameter and originally at least 3m high, made of scraped-up soil, without a ditch, covering a grave 2.7 × 1m – not a chamber-grave like Taplow, therefore, but a large coffin-size grave – in which the dead man was laid out with his personal goods. These included a sword, spear, more than usually elaborately-fitted shield with sugar-loaf boss, archer's bone bracer, iron fire-steel, ornamented humped-back comb, and a bronze hanging-bowl with enamelled escutcheons in trumpet-spiral patterns, like one from the seax-grave at Oliver's Battery near Winchester (Andrew & Smith 1931). A new, as yet unpublished find of a very tall sugar-loaf shield boss, found at Updown, Eastry, in Kent, with a buckle with triangular plate, suggests that Evison's very late seventh century dating for this type of boss may need some revision. The Updown grave can scarcely be much later than the middle of the century, and the Lowbury barrow-burial could therefore date from the third rather than the fourth quarter of the seventh century. In either case he could have been Cuthred's man. He is said to have been elderly when he died, 'stiff and bent with rheumatism', so presumably his fighting days were long over and he was not an active victim of Wulfhere's campaign in 661. His precise status is hard to determine. Comparing the large numbers of vessels in the Taplow and Asthall barrows – entertainment-gear being an important feature of royal burials – the Lowbury man could scarcely be mistaken for Cuthred himself, for example. But the sword, the sugar-loaf boss and certainly the hanging-bowl are all prestigious, and, together with the status of the barrow-rite of burial, suggest a man of considerable substance. It is tempting to equate him with one of the *Gesithcund* men who feature as major gentry in the Laws of Ine, and whom Loyn characterised as powerful military leaders, 'possibly of the royal kin, settled on an estate, possessing a hall, and surrounded by retainers' (Loyn 1962, 202). Archaeologically he has some counterparts in barrow-burials in Wiltshire. More interestingly in this context, the sugar-loaf shield-boss and hanging bowl from Milton II, the cemetery which produced the composite brooches (p. 89), suggest a family of comparable status – aristocratic but sub-royal – burying their dead near what we have interpreted as a seventh-century royal vill at Drayton. Here perhaps we have evidence of something known in literature, a *Gesithcund* man functioning as a royal reeve.

The funerary evidence of the late sixth and seventh centuries sheds much light on the social and economic polarization that was going on in Anglo-Saxon England once royal dynasties were established, and began to create the major kingdoms with their sub-divided and tiered administration. Not only have we the barrow-burials illustrating the upper ranks of society, the kings, their *sub-reguli* and the *Gesithcund* men on whom they depended to provide supporters and administrators, but we get a glimpse of what the maintenance of this super-structure cost the lesser folk, who were doubtless taxed to pay for it. A phenomenon of Anglo-Saxon cemeteries nearly everywhere is a sudden cessation of well-furnished burials shortly after the middle of the sixth century. Since it is most noticeable in the case of women, some people have put it down to a change of dress-fashion, such as certainly took place in Kent from about 560, a kingdom where sufficient rich burials continued to illustrate the change. In the Oxford region, however, though Saxon women abandoned the square-headed brooch, they clung to their saucer brooches, which were worn into the second quarter of the seventh century, when, as we have seen, they became ostentatiously large (Pl. 6c; p. 83), as did their festoons of beads. The chief difference between the middle sixth century and the early seventh is the disappearance of what looked like prosperous upper-middle-class rivalry in displays of funerary ostentation. In the pagan-period cemeteries which continued in use into the early seventh century, sites such as Abingdon I, Berinsfield, Long Wittenham and Wheatley, the majority of people buried in the latest graves are without jewellery and weapons, while just a 'few high-ranking families continued to display their wealth in burial' (Dickinson 1976, 439). And absolute numbers of these are quite small. At Abingdon, for example, only the woman in grave 5 was buried with large early seventh-century saucer brooches, compared with the numerous women buried with saucer brooches of earlier date. It is difficult not to conclude that the political situation, with its new economic and social pressures, was responsible for the change. Society as a whole seems to have been becoming more rigidly stratified.

Conversion and Conclusion

In about 635 St. Birinus arrived to preach Christianity to the West Saxons, and King Cynegils was baptized, with Oswald of Northumbria present to stand as his sponsor, either because he was there in his capacity as *Bretwalda*, or overlord, or because he was there to marry Cynegils' daughter Cyneburh (Bede *H.E.* iii, 7; Wormald 1983, 112), or both. The two kings gave Dorchester to Birinus for his episcopal see, and the bishop subsequently converted Cwichelm and Cuthred, and 'brought many to the Lord by his pious labours'. So far archaeology has failed to disclose the site of the churches he built, but it has given us a glimpse of some of his converts.

The introduction of Christianity into Kent at the very end of the sixth century, thence, always with royal mediation, into Essex, East Anglia, and Northumbria, whence into Wessex, Mercia and finally Sussex, brought about some profound changes (very useful for the archaeologist) not only in the burial customs but also in the dress and material culture of the Germanic peoples of England in the course of the seventh century. New fashions were introduced from the Mediterranean into Kent, and as the missionary work progressed from royal court to royal court, with one king sponsoring the baptism of another, usually as a precondition of a marriage alliance between kingdoms, as we have just seen between Wessex and Northumbria, so the cultural barriers between kingdoms were laid low. By the latter part of the century, a great lady in Wessex, such as the one buried on Roundway Down in Wiltshire, might be wearing gold jewellery almost identical with that worn by Mercian ladies buried at Desborough, Northants., or Cow Low and Brassington Moor, Derbyshire (Campbell 1982, colour figs. 31, 41, 36). Apparently they were all now wearing a sewn dress that required none of the old heavy brooches to pin it together, the only functional jewellery being a pair of delicate chain-linked pins to fasten the headdress, the remaining adornment an elegant necklet of jewelled pendants and beads. The overall effect is of 'a uniquely English adaptation of the classic style of Byzantium' (Hawkes 1982c, 49). The new style of dress and ornament filtered down through society very quickly, at least to the level of the *Gesithcund* and probably to that of the womenfolk of the more prosperous *Ceorl* families, and silver versions of the mode can be seen in cemeteries such as Winnall II, near Winchester (Meaney & Hawkes 1970), Leighton Buzzard II, Bedfordshire (Hyslop 1963), and Burwell and Shudy Camps, Cambridgeshire (Lethbridge 1931 & 1936). These are good examples of cemeteries of a date and type which Leeds characterized as belonging to his 'Final Phase': he did not know all of them, but he illustrated and discussed others in Northumbria, for example (Leeds 1936, 96 ff.). Common to them all is a marked tendency towards WE orientation, a high percentage of unfurnished burials, scarcity of weapons in male graves except for the occasional late type such as a seax or sugar-loaf shield-boss, the new types of female jewellery described above, and certain artefacts, such as wooden caskets and bronze amulet-capsules (in old parlance 'work-boxes'), which are totally unknown in normal pagan-period cemeteries. Just occasionally there is an object overtly Christian (Hawkes 1982c). Except in Kent it is very rare for true pagan cemeteries to continue into this phase, which seems elsewhere to start from some time just before or after the middle of the seventh century. Leeds hesitated to call these cemeteries Christian, but he was of course hampered by an inaccurate chronology, trying to cram them into the first half of the seventh century, whereas now, thanks to advances in numismatics, we know that many of these 'Final Phase' cemeteries continued in use into the first half of the eight century (Meaney & Hawkes 1970, 50 ff.; Hawkes 1973). Lethbridge and Hyslop were happy to call them 'Christian', but for me now the term proto-Christian seems best to define such cemeteries, which are transitional between those of the fully pagan period and the time when Christian burial was transferred to a formal churchyard or burial-enclosure sanctified by a cross, and grave-goods were finally abandoned.

Perhaps the most convincingly proto-Christian cemeteries are those where, at the known time of the Conversion, burial can be seen to have been transferred from the old pagan site to a new cemetery slightly at a distance. The classic examples of this are at Leighton

Buzzard and Winnall, but Leeds was shrewd to remark an earlier-excavated example of this at Long Wittenham in our region. The cemetery which had been in use from the fifth century was abandoned during the earlier seventh, and a new cemetery, some 400m to the west, apparently came into use during the 'Final Phase'. Only ten graves were found, but two of them contained females with silver chain-linked pins, characteristic of the phase under discussion, and another a copy of a Kentish triangular-plate buckle. Another case is even closer to Dorchester, at Bishop's Court (Fig. 7), where a pagan cemetery was apparently succeeded by the later seventh-century site which yielded eight graves, of which one contained a seax (May 1977, 52 f., figs. 4, 12). Finally, turning for the last time to the plan of the Abingdon I cemetery (Fig. 8), it will be noticed that some 40m west of the fifth-century Frankish graves, and separated from them by what Leeds regarded as a genuine gap, are five WE oriented burials without significant grave-goods. He did not explore further west, but these might well have proven to be part of another proto-Christian cemetery, a little less distanced from its pagan predecessors than the others.

Here then, in the immediate vicinity of Dorchester, we have three sites where there are signs that Birinus' preaching may have borne fruit, and at least the first steps towards Christian burial have taken place at sub-royal level. Just as at Winnall by Winchester, all three communities were so close to the episcopal centre that rapid conversion and, at least outward, conformation would have been inevitable. But in view of Cynegils' death in 641/2, Cenwealh's flight into East Anglia and subsequent retreat to Winchester, and the short life of the West Saxon see at Dorchester, it is hardly surprising that these West Saxon proto-Christian cemeteries seem to have been so small. After Birinus, whose death-date is unknown, if bishop Agilbert was at Dorchester at all, he remained only till 661, and the translation of Birinus' bones to Winchester, by bishop Haedde, perhaps as early as 676, clearly means that there was an active Christian leadership for a very short time indeed. Probably the king evacuated his people, for he would have needed every weapon-bearing male he could muster to help Cuthred defend his rear on Ashdown and further his own landtakings westwards into British Dumnonia – Dorset, Somerset and Devon.

In complete contrast with the dearth of late seventh-century cemeteries in the region of Dorchester and Abingdon, is the evidence for new settlements of this date to the north-west, in the country around the lower Windrush and upper Evenlode valleys (Map 11). The largest complex of burials, some 2 km NNW of Standlake village, may have begun around or just before the middle of the century, though most seem late (Brown 1973; Dickinson 1973). They have yielded some unusually rich finds, including a Style II-decorated disc (Speake 1980, pl. 16, c), an amulet capsule or 'work-box', and, from a single woman's grave, two garnet-set gold pendants of the kind worn in Kent and by the rich ladies of Wessex and Mercia mentioned above (p. 92; Brown & Schweizer 1973, AM 8–9), together with a chatelaine bearing an interlace-ornamented foil cross. Just across the Windrush, 1 km SW of Stanton Harcourt, was a similar but less rich cemetery of some twenty-three inhumations dating from the late seventh/early eight centuries (Harden & Treweeks 1945, 33 ff.). About the same distance from Standlake to the north-west, close to a destroyed settlement-site in Yelford parish, twenty-six inhumations of this date were found, only one with significant jewellery (Benson & Miles 1974a, 42). At Ducklington, 3 km NNW of the Yelford site, there are two separate sites of burial for this period, one belonging to a deserted site near Breech Farm, the other close to the church of the present village (Brown 1975). Though only few burials were found both sites boasted rich women, the one near the church having two fine pendants, one with cabochon garnet, the other with filigree cross and garnet (Brown & Schweizer 1973, AM 10). The late seventh-century colonization here is remarkably concentrated, and its leading women were buried with some display of wealth. One would suggest that these communities were socially strongly stratified with *Gesithcund* families at their heads. Further north the situation differs only in that contemporary settlement appears less dense. The small cemetery at North Leigh contained one rich female burial with an amulet-capsule decorated with an engraved Christian cross, its arms divided by panels of interlace; a girl with necklet composed of silver rings and beads; and a man with a seax (Leeds 1940, 21 ff., pls. VI–VII). Further north again at Chadlington, part of a cemetery of WE-oriented graves, of which sixteen excavated were all of the later seventh/early eighth centuries, yielded one or two important finds, including a composite bead made of gold with shell settings and a seax 42.5 cm long (Leeds 1940, 23 ff., pl. VII). Finally, close to the church in the next village 2 km to the east, Spelsbury, a disturbed burial ground produced another interlace-ornamented disc, not unlike the one from Standlake, and of similar middle or late seventh-century date (Speake 1980, pl. 15, i).

Leeds (1940, 29) followed by Dickinson (1973, 249), suggested that these late colonists represented an expansion of West Saxon settlement from 'a centre in the main valley of the Upper Thames'. But in view of what the evidence from the Dorchester area has told us about West Saxon contraction and emigration by this date such a theory will no longer hold. These new settlers in the second half of the seventh century were taking up land around the fringes of Wychwood, O.E. *Hwiccewudu* (EPNS XXIV 1954, 386), meaning 'the forest of the Hwicce', the people who have been introduced already as allies of Mercia who became the inheritors of the Oxford region in the seventh century (pp. 91–2). It is far more likely that the later seventh century colonization of north-west Oxfordshire, east of the Wood, which we have been reviewing here, was carried out by minor aristocracy of the Hwicce, and that the cemeteries give us a precious first glimpse of their initial landtakings. Everying fits. By this time the Hwiccan nobility was Christian, so the proto-Christian character of their cemeteries is explained. They were partially Anglian, so the un-Saxon appearance of their Style II-decorated jewellery is also explained. Finally, there is the Asthall barrow, generally agreed to be Mercian, standing between the Windrush and Evenlode valleys, and, equally strategically sited to south and north respectively, the great barrows at Lew and Leafield, which could well be contemporary and also Mercian. Even from Asthall alone, however, one could infer that pagan Hwiccan or Mercian royalty annexed West Oxfordshire, maybe not long after 628. The territory thus secured was further colonized by the now Christian Hwicce during the half-century following.

Thus the seventh-century archaeology of the Upper Thames valley does seem to be fulfilling a very rare function, that of helping to write a hitherto very obscure piece of political history.

Bibliography

Akerman, J.Y. (1855) *Remains of pagan Saxondom*
Alenus-Lecerf, J. (1981) 'Découverte d'un cimetière des Ve–VIe siècles à Vieuxville', *Archaeologia Belgica* 238, 59–63
Andrew, W.J. & Smith, R.A. (1931) 'The Winchester Anglo-Saxon bowl', *Antiq. J.* 11, 1–13
Atkinson, D. (1916) *The Romano-British site on Lowbury Hill in Berkshire*
Avent, R. (1975) *Anglo-Saxon disc and composite brooches*. Brit. Archaeol. Rept. 11
Alcock, L. (1971) *Arthur's Britain*
Aldsworth, F. (1979) 'Droxford Anglo-Saxon cemetery, Soberton, Hampshire', *Proc. Hants. Field Club* 35, 93–182
Arnold, C.J. (1982) *The Anglo-Saxon cemeteries of the Isle of Wight*
Arthur, B.V. & Jope, E.M. (1962–3) 'Early Saxon pottery kilns at Purwell Farm, Cassington, Oxfordshire', *Med. Archaeol.* 6–7, 1–14
Bartholomew, P. (1982) 'Fifth-century facts', *Britannia* 13, 261–70
Bartholomew, P. (1984) 'Fourth-century Saxons', *Britannia* 15, 169–185
Benson, D. & Miles, D. (1974a) *The Upper Thames valley: an archaeological survey of the river gravels*. Oxfordshire Archaeol. Unit, survey no. 2
Benson, D. & Miles, D. (1974b) 'Cropmarks near the Sutton Courtenay Saxon site', *Antiquity* 48, 223–6
Berisford, F. (1972) 'The Anglo-Saxon pottery', in Brodribb *et al.* 55–66
Berisford, F. (1973) *The early Anglo-Saxon settlement sites in the Upper Thames basin with special reference to the area around Cassington and Eynsham*, unpublished B. Litt. thesis, Oxford University
Biddle, M. (1976) 'Hampshire and the origins of Wessex', in *Problems in economic and social archaeology*, ed. G.de G. Sieveking *et al.*, 323–342
Biddle, M. *et al.* (1968) 'The early history of Abingdon, Berkshire, and its abbey', *Med. Archaeol.* 12, 26–69
Biddle, M. & Hudson, D. (1973) *The future of London's past*
Böhme, H.W. (1974) *Germanische Grabfunde des 4 bis 5 Jahrhunderts zwischen unterer Elbe und Loire*. Münchner Beiträge zur Vor- und Frühgeschichte 19
Böhme, H.W. (1976) 'Das Land zwischen Elbe und Wesermundung vom 4. bis 6. J H', *Führer zu vor- und frühgeschichtliche Denkmälern* 29, 205–226
Boon, G.C. (1974) *Silchester: the Roman town of Calleva*
Bradley, R. (1978) 'Rescue excavations at Dorchester-on-Thames 1972', *Oxoniensia* 43, 17–39
Breuer, J. & Roosens, H. (1957) *Le cimetière franc de Haillot*. Archaeologia Belgica, 34

Brodribb, A.C.C., Hands, A.R. & Walker, D.R. (1968) *Excavations at Shakenoak I*
Brodribb, A.C.C., Hands, A.R. & Walker, D.R. (1972) *Excavations at Shakenoak III*
Brodribb, A.C.C., Hands, A.R. & Walker, D.R. (1978) *Excavations at Shakenoak V*
Brown, D. (1972) Review of Brodribb *et al.* 1972, *Britannia* 3, 376–7
Brown, D. (1973) 'The site of Stephen Stone's Saxon cemetery at Standlake', *Oxoniensia* 38, 233–238
Brown, D. (1975) 'Objects from the grave', in Chambers 1975, 191–7
Brown, D. (1976) 'Archaeological evidence for the Anglo-Saxon period', in *Archaeology and history of Cirencester*, ed. A. McWhirr. Brit. Archaeol Rept. 30, 19–45
Brown, D. & Schweizer, F. (1973) 'X-Ray fluorescent analysis of Anglo-Saxon jewellery', *Archaeometry* 15, 179–192
Bruce-Mitford, R.L.S. (1974) *Aspects of Anglo-Saxon archaeology: Sutton Hoo and other studies*
Bruce-Mitford, R.L.S. (1975) *The Sutton Hoo Ship Burial I*
Bruce-Mitford, R.L.S. (1978) *The Sutton Hoo Ship Burial II*
Bullinger, H. (1969) *Spätantike Gürtelbeschläge*. Diss. Archaeol. Gandenses, 12
Cam, H. & Crawford, O.G.S. (1935) 'The *Hoga* of Cutteslowe', *Antiquity* 9, 96–98
Campbell, J. (1982) *The Anglo-Saxons*
Chambers, R.A. (1975) 'A Romano-British settlement site and seventh-century burial, Ducklington, Oxon. 1974', *Oxoniensia* 40, 171–200
Chenet, C. (1935) 'La tombe 319 et la buire chrétienne du cimetière mérovingienne de Lavoye (Meuse)', *Préhistoire* 4, 34–118
Clarke, G. (1979) *Pre-Roman and Roman Winchester, II: The Roman cemetery at Lankhills*. Winchester Studies 3
Collingwood, R.G. & Myres, J.N.L. (1937) *Roman Britain and the English settlements*
Cook, J. (1958) 'An Anglo-Saxon cemetery at Broadway Hill, Broadway, Worcestershire', *Antiq. J.* 38, 58–84
Crowfoot, E. & Hawkes, S. Chadwick (1967) 'Early Anglo-Saxon gold braids', *Med. Archaeol.* 11, 42–86
Cunliffe, B. (1976) *Excavations at Portchester Castle, II: Saxon*. Res. Rept. Soc. Antiq. London 33
Crummy, P. (1981) *Aspects of Anglo-Saxon and Norman Colchester*. CBA Res. Rept. 39
Dasnoy, A. (1969) 'La nécropole de Furfooz', *Annales de la Soc. Archéol. de Namur* 55, 121–94
Davies, W. & Vierck, H. (1974) 'The Contexts of *Tribal Hidage*: social aggregates and settlement patterns', *Frühmittelalterliche Studien* 8, 223–93
Dickinson, T.M. (1973) 'Excavations at Standlake Down in 1954: The Anglo-Saxon graves', *Oxoniensia* 38, 239–257
Dickinson, T.M. (1974) *Cuddesdon and Dorchester-on-Thames*. Brit. Archaeol. Rept. I
Dickinson, T.M. (1979) *The Anglo-Saxon burial sites of the Upper Thames region and their bearing upon the history of Wessex, circa AD 400–700*, unpublished D. Phil. thesis, Oxford University
Dickinson, T.M. (1976) 'On the origin and chronology of the early Anglo-Saxon disc brooch', in *Anglo-Saxon Studies*, I, Brit. Archaeol. Rept. 72, 39–80
Dickinson, T.M. (1980) 'The present state of Anglo-Saxon cemetery studies', in *Anglo-Saxon cemeteries 1979*, Brit. Archaeol. Rept. 82, 11–33
Dickinson, T.M. (1982) 'Ornament variation in pairs of cast saucer brooches: a case study from the Upper Thames region', in *Aspects of production and style in Dark Age metalwork: selected papers given to the British Museum seminar on Jewellery AD 500–600*, British Museum Occ. Paper 34, ed. L. Webster, 21–50
Doppelfeld, O. (1960) 'Das Frauengrab unter dem Chor des Kölner Domes', *Germania* 38, 41–119
Doppelfeld, O. (1964) 'Das Fränkische Knabengrab unter dem Chor des Kölner Domes', *Germania* 42, 3–45
Dumville, D.N. (1974) 'Some aspects of the chronology of the *Historia Brittonum*', *Bull. Board Celtic Stud.* 25, 439–45
Dumville, D.N. (1977) 'Sub-Roman Britain: history and legend', *History* 62, 173–92

Evison, V.I. (1955) 'Early Anglo-Saxon inlaid metalwork', *Antiq. J.* 35, 20–45

Evison, V.I. (1963) 'Sugar-loaf shield-bosses', *Antiq. J.* 43, 38–96

Evison, V.I. (1965) *The fifth-century invasions south of the Thames*

Evison, V.I. (1968) 'Quoit Brooch style buckles', *Antiq. J.* 48, 231–246

Evison, V.I. (1972) 'Glass cone beakers of the 'Kempston' type', *J. Glass Stud.* 14, 48–66

Evison, V.I. (1975) 'Sword rings and beads', *Archaeologia* 105, 303–315

Evison, V.I. (1977) 'Supporting-arm brooches and equal-arm brooches in England', *Studien zur Sachsenforschung*, ed. H.J. Hässler, 127–147

Evison, V.I. (1981) 'Distribution maps and England in the first two phases', in *Angles, Saxons and Jutes: essays presented to J.N.L. Myres*, ed. V.I. Evison, 126–67

Evison, V.I. (1982) 'Anglo-Saxon glass claw-beakers', *Archaeologia* 107, 43–76

Finberg, H.P.R. (1961) *The early charters of the West Midlands*

Fowler, P.J. *et al.* (1970) *Cadbury Congresbury, Somerset, 1968: an introductory report*

Fox, A. & Fox, C. (1980) 'Wansdyke reconsidered', *Archaeol. J.* 115, 1–48

Frere, S.S. (1962) 'Excavations at Dorchester-on-Thames, 1962', *Archaeol. J.* 119, 114–149

Frere, S.S. (1966) 'The end of towns in Roman Britain', in *The Civitas Capitals of Roman Britain*, ed. J. Wacher, 87–100

Frere, S.S. (forthcoming) 'Excavations at Dorchester-on-Thames, 1963', *Archaeol. J.* forthcoming

Gelling, M. (1978) *Signposts to the past: place-names and the history of England*

Gingell, C.J. (1978) 'The excavation of an early Anglo-Saxon cemetery at Collingbourne Ducis', *Wilts. Archaeol. Mag.* 70/71, 61–98

Gray, M. (1974) 'The Saxon settlement at New Wintles, Eynsham', in *Anglo-Saxon settlement and landscape*, ed. T. Rowley, Brit. Archaeol. Rept. 6, 51–5

Green, H.S. (1971) 'Wansdyke, excavations 1966–1970', *Wilts. Archaeol. Mag.* 66, 129–146

Harden, D.B. (1956) 'Glass vessels in Britain and Ireland, AD 400 – 1000', in *Dark-Age Britain: studies presented to E.T. Leeds*, ed. D.B. Harden, 132–167

Harden, D.B. & Treweeks, R.C. (1945) 'Excavations at Stanton Harcourt, Oxon, 1940, II', *Oxoniensia* 10, 16–41

Harrison, K. (1976) *The framework of Anglo-Saxon history to A.D. 900*

Hawkes, C.F.C. (1956) 'The Jutes of Kent', in *Dark-Age Britain: studies presented to E.T. Leeds*, ed. D.B. Harden, 91–111

Hawkes, S. Chadwick (1961) 'The Jutish Style A. A study of Germanic animal art in southern England in the fifth century A.D.', *Archaeologia* 98, 29–74

Hawkes, S. Chadwick (1968) 'The late Roman military belt-fittings', in Brodribb *et al.*, 96–101

Hawkes, S. Chadwick (1972) More late Roman military belt-fittings, in Brodribb *et al.*, 74–77

Hawkes, S. Chadwick (1973a) 'A late Roman buckle from Tripontium', *Tr. Birmingham & Warwickshire Archaeol. Soc.* 85, 145–59

Hawkes, S. Chadwick (1973b) 'The dating and social significance of the burials in the Polhill cemetery', in *Excavations in West Kent 1960–1970*, ed. B. Philp, 186–201

Hawkes, S. Chadwick (1974a) 'Some recent finds of late Roman buckles', *Britannia* 5, 386–93

Hawkes, S. Chadwick (1974b) 'British Antiquity 1973–4: post-Roman and pagan Anglo-Saxon', *Archaeol. J.* 131, 408–20

Hawkes, S. Chadwick (1978) 'Die anglo-sächsische Invasion Britanniens', in *Sachsen und Angelsachsen*, ed. C. Ahrens, 71–84

Hawkes, S. Chadwick (1982a) 'Anglo-Saxon Kent c. 425–725', in *Archaeology in Kent to AD 1500*, CBA Res. Rept. 48, 64–78

Hawkes, S. Chadwick (1982b) 'Finglesham. A cemetery in East Kent', in *The Anglo-Saxons*, ed. J. Campbell, 24–25

Hawkes, S. Chadwick (1982c) 'The archaeology of conversion: cemeteries', in *The Anglo-Saxons*, ed. J. Campbell, 48–9

Hawkes, S. Chadwick & Dunning, G.C. (1961) 'Soldiers and settlers in Britain, fourth to fifth century', *Med. Archaeol.* 5, 1–70

Hawkes, S. Chadwick & Dunning, G.C. (1962/3) 'Krieger und Siedler in Britannien während des 4. bis 5. Jahrhunderts', *43–44 Bericht der Römisch-Germanischen Kommission*, 156–231

Hawkes, S. Chadwick & Gray, M. (1969) 'Preliminary note on the early Anglo-Saxon settlement at New Wintles Farm, Eynsham', *Oxoniensia* 34, 1–4

Hawkes, S. Chadwick & Hogarth, A.C. (1974) 'The Anglo-Saxon cemetery at Monkton, Thanet', *Archaeol. Cantiana* 89, 49–89

Hawkes, S. Chadwick & Pollard, M. (1981) 'The gold bracteates from sixth-century Anglo-Saxon graves in Kent', *Frühmittelalterliche Studien* 15, 316–70

Hawkes, S. Chadwick & Wells, C. (1983) 'The inhumed skeletal material from an early Anglo-Saxon cemetery at Worthy Park, Kingsworthy, near Winchester, Hampshire, South England', *Paleobios* 1

Hinchliffe, J. & Thomas, R. (1980) 'Archaeological investigations at Appleford', *Oxoniensia* 45, 9–111

Hodges, R. (1982) *Dark Age Economics. The origins of towns and trade, AD 600–1000*

Hope-Taylor, B. (1977) *Yeavering. An Anglo-British centre of early Northumbria*

Hyslop, M. (1963) 'Two Anglo-Saxon cemeteries at Chamberlains Barn, Leighton Buzzard, Bedfordshire', *Archaeol. J.* 120, 161–200

Jackson, K. (1958) 'The site of Mount Badon', *J. Celtic Stud.* 2, 152–5

James, E. (1982) *The origins of France from Clovis to the Capetians, 500–1000*

Joffroy, R. (1974) *Le cimetière de Lavoye, nécropole mérovingienne*

Johnson, S. (1976) *The Roman forts of the Saxon Shore*

Johnson, S. (1980) *Later Roman Britain*

Jones, M.U. (1979) 'Saxon Mucking – a post-excavation note', in *Anglo-Saxon Studies* 1, Brit. Archaeol. Rept. 72, 21–37

Kennett, D.H. (1971) 'Graves with swords at Little Wilbraham and Linton Heath', *Proc. Cambr. Antiq. Soc.* 63, 9–26

Kennett, D.H. (1975) 'The Souldern burials', *Oxoniensia* 40, 201–210

Kirby, D.P. (1975) 'Problems of early West Saxon history', *Eng. Hist. Rev.* 80, 10–29

Kirk, J.R. (1956) 'Anglo-Saxon cremation and inhumation in the Upper Thames valley in pagan times', in *Dark-Age Britain: studies presented to E.T. Leeds*, ed. D.B. Harden, 123–131

Kirk, J.R. & Leeds, E.T. (1952/3) 'Three early Anglo-Saxon graves from Dorchester, Oxon', *Oxoniensia* 17/18, 63–76

Leeds, E.T. (1913) *The archaeology of the Anglo-Saxon settlements*

Leeds, E.T. (1922/3) 'A Saxon village near Sutton Courtenay, Berkshire', *Archaeologia* 73, 147–92

Leeds, E.T. (1924) 'An Anglo-Saxon cremation-burial of the seventh century in Asthall Barrow, Oxfordshire', *Antiq. J.* 4, 113–126

Leeds, E.T. (1926/7) 'A Saxon village at Sutton Courtenay, Berkshire: second report', *Archaeologia* 76, 59–80

Leeds, E.T. (1936) *Early Anglo-Saxon art and archaeology*

Leeds, E.T. (1938) 'An Anglo-Saxon cemetery at Wallingford, Berkshire,' *Berks. Archaeol. J.* 42, 93–101

Leeds, E.T. (1940) 'Two Saxon cemeteries in North Oxfordshire', *Oxoniensia* 5, 21–30

Leeds, E.T. (1947) 'A Saxon village at Sutton Courtenay, Berkshire: third report', *Archaeologia* 92, 79–94

Leeds, E.T. & Harden, D.B. (1936) *The Anglo-Saxon cemetery at Abingdon, Berkshire*

Leeds, E.T. & Riley, M. (1942) 'Two early Anglo-Saxon cemeteries at Cassington, Oxon', *Oxoniensia* 7, 61–70

Leeds, E.T. & Shortt, H. de S. (1953) *An Anglo-Saxon cemetery at Petersfinger, near Salisbury, Wilts.*

Lethbridge, T.C. (1931) *Recent excavations in Anglo-Saxon cemeteries in Cambridgeshire and Suffolk*, Cambr. Antiq. Soc. 4to Publ. 3

Lethbridge, T.C. (1936) *A cemetery at Shudy Camps, Cambridgeshire*, Cambr. Antiq. Soc. 4to Publ. 5

Loyn, H. R. (1962) *Anglo-Saxon England and the Norman Conquest*

Matthews, C.L. & Hawkes, S. Chadwick (1985) 'Saxon settlements and burials on Puddlehill, near Dunstable, Bedfordshire', *Anglo-Saxon Studies* 4, (in press)

May, J. (1977) 'Romano-British and Saxon sites near Dorchester, Oxon', *Oxoniensia* 42, 42–79

Meaney, A.L. (1964) *A Gazetteer of early Anglo-Saxon burial-sites*

Meaney, A.L. & Hawkes, S. Chadwick (1970) *Two Anglo-Saxon cemeteries at Winnall, Winchester, Hampshire*, Soc. Med. Archaeol. monograph 4

Menghin, W. (1975) 'Schwertortbänder der frühen Merowingerzeit', in *Studien zur Vor- und Frügeschichtlichen Archäologie: Festschrift für Joachim Werner, II*, ed. G. Kossack & G. Ulbert, 435–69

Miles, D. (1977) 'Abingdon/Radley, Barton Court Farm', *CBA Group 9 Newsletter* 6, 10–13

Miles, D. (forthcoming) *Archaeology at Barton Court Farm, Abingdon*

Miles, D. *et al.* (1975) 'Excavations at Abingdon, 1972–4', *Oxoniensia* 40, 1–121

Miller, M. (1975a) 'Relative and absolute publication dates of Gildas's *De Excidio* in medieval scholarship', *Bull. Board Celtic Stud.* 26, 169–74

Miller, M. (1975b) 'Bede's use of Gildas', *Eng. Hist. Rev.* 355, 241–61

Miller, M. (1978) 'The last British entry in the ''Gallic Chronicles''', *Britannia* 9, 315–318

Morris, J. (1965) 'Dark Age dates', in *Britain and Rome: essays presented to Eric Birley*, ed. M.G. Jarrett & B. Dobson, 145–185

Morris, J. (1973) *The Age of Arthur*

Morris, J. (1974) Review of Myres & Green 1973, *Med. Archaeol.* 18, 225–32

Musty, J. & Stratton, J.E.D. (1964) 'A Saxon cemetery at Winterbourne Gunner, near Salisbury', *Wilts. Archaeol. Mag.* 59, 86–109

Myres, J.N.L. (1954) 'The Anglo-Saxon period', in *The Oxford Region: a scientific and historical survey*, ed. A.F. Martin & R.W. Steel, 96–102

Myres, J.N.L. (1960) 'Pelagius and the end of Roman rule in Britain', *J. Roman Stud.* 50, 21–36

Myres, J.N.L. (1964) 'Wansdyke and the origin of Wessex', in *Essays in British History presented to Sir Keith Feiling*, ed. H.R. Trevor-Roper, 1–27

Myres, J.N.L. (1968) 'The Anglo-Saxon cemetery', in *Biddle et al. 1968*, 35–41

Myres, J.N.L. (1969) *Anglo-Saxon pottery and the settlement of England*

Myres, J.N.L. (1977) *A Corpus of Anglo-Saxon pottery of the pagan period*

Myres, J.N.L. & Green, B. (1973) *The Anglo-Saxon cemeteries of Caistor-by-Norwich and Markshall, Norfolk*. Res. Rept. Soc. Antiq. London 30

Peake, H.J.E. *et al.* (1935) 'Excavations on the Berkshire Downs: Cuckamsley', *Tr. Newbury Field Club* 7 ii, 93–102

Pirling, R. (1964) 'Ein fränkisches Fürstengrab aus Krefeld-Gellep', *Germania* 42, 188–216

Pirling, R. (1974) *Das Römisch-Fränkische Gräberfeld von Krefeld-Gellep, 1960–1963*, Germanische Denkmäler der Völkerwanderungszeit, Ser. B, Die Fränkischen Altertümer des Rheinlandes, 8

Plummer, C. (1896) *Venerabilis Bedae opera historica*

Rodwell, K. (1975) *Historic towns in Oxfordshire: a survey of the new county*. Oxfordshire Archaeol. Unit, survey no. 2

Rowley, T. & Brown, L. (1981) 'Excavations at Beech House hotel, Dorchester-on-Thames 1972', *Oxoniensia* 46, 1–55

Rutherford Davis, K. (1982) *Britons and Saxons: the Chiltern Region 400–700*

Salway, P. (1981) *Roman Britain*

Sims-Williams, P. (1983a) 'Gildas and the Anglo-Saxons', *Cambridge Medieval Celtic Studies* 6, 1–30

Sims-Williams, P. (1983b) 'The settlement of England in Bede and the Chronicle', *Anglo-Saxon England* 12, 1–41

Sisam, K. (1953) 'Anglo-Saxon royal genealogies', *Proc. Brit. Acad.* 39, 287–346

Smith, A.H. (1956) *English place-name elements, I & II*, English place-name soc. 25 & 26

Speake, G. (1980) *Anglo-Saxon animal art and its Germanic background*

Stevens, C.E. (1941) 'Gildas Sapiens', *Eng. Hist. Rev.* 223, 353–73

Stevens, C.E. (1957) 'Marcus, Gratian, Constantine', *Athenaeum (Pavia)* 35, 316–347

Swanton, M.J. (1974) *The spearheads of the Anglo-Saxon settlements*

Taylor, C. (1983) *Village and farmstead. A history of rural settlement in England*

Thompson, E.A. (1977) 'Britain, A.D. 406–410', *Britannia* 8, 303–18

Thompson, E.A. (1979) 'Gildas and the history of Britain', *Britannia* 10, 203–26

Thompson, E.A. (1982) 'Zosimus, 6.10.2, and the letter of Honorius', *Classical Quarterly* 32, 445–62

Thompson, E.A. (1983) 'Fifth century facts?', *Britannia* 14, 272–4

Verhulst, A. (1970) 'Der Handel im Merowingerreich: Gesamtdarstellung nach schriftlichen Quellen', *Early Med. Studies* 2, 2–52

Vierck, H. (1972) 'Date and origin of a small-long brooch', in *Brodribb et al.* 78–83

Vierck, H. (1978) 'Trachtenkunde und Trachtgeschichte in der Sachsen-Forschung, ihre Quellen, Ziele und Methoden', in *Sachsen und Angelsachsen*, ed. C. Ahrens, 231–243

Wacher, J. (1974) *The towns of Roman Britain*

Warhurst, A. (1955) 'The Jutish cemetery at Lyminge', *Archaeol. Cantiana* 69, 1–40

Welch, M. (1975) 'Mitcham grave 205 and the chronology of applied brooches with floriate cross decoration', *Antiq. J.* 55, 86–95

Welch, M.G. (1976) Contribution to B. Cunliffe, *Excavations at Portchester Castle, II: Saxon*, Res. Rept. Soc. Antiq. London 33, 206–211

Welch, M.G. (1983) *Early Anglo-Saxon Sussex*. Brit. Archaeol. Rept. 112

Werner, J. (1953) 'Zu fränkischen Schwertern des 5. Jahrhunderts', *Germania* 31, 38–44

Werner, J. (1956) 'Fränkische Schwerter des 5. Jahrhunderts aus Samson und Petersfinger', *Germania* 34, 156–8

Werner, J. (1958) 'Kriegergräber aus der ersten Hälfte des 5. Jahrhunderts zwischen Schelde und Weser', *Bonner Jahrbücher* 158, 372–413

West, S.E. (1969) 'The Anglo-Saxon village at West Stow: an interim report on the excavations, 1965–8', *Med. Archaeol.* 13, 1–20

West, S.E. (1978) 'Die Siedlung West Stow in Suffolk', *Sachsen und Angelsachsen*, ed. C. Ahrens, 395–412

Winterbottom, M. (1978) *Gildas: the ruin of Britain*

Wood, I. (1984) 'The end of Roman Britain: Continental evidence and parallels', in *Gildas: new approaches*, ed. D.M. Dumville & M. Lapidge, 1–25

Wormald, P. (1983) 'Bede, the *Bretwaldas* and the origins of the *Gens Anglorum*', in *Ideal and Reality in Frankish and Anglo-Saxon society: studies presented to J.M. Wallace-Hadrill*, ed. P. Wormald *et al.*, 99–129

Ypey, Y. (1969) 'Zur tragweise frühfränkische Gurtelgarnituren auf Grund niederländischer Befunde', *ROB* 19, 89–127

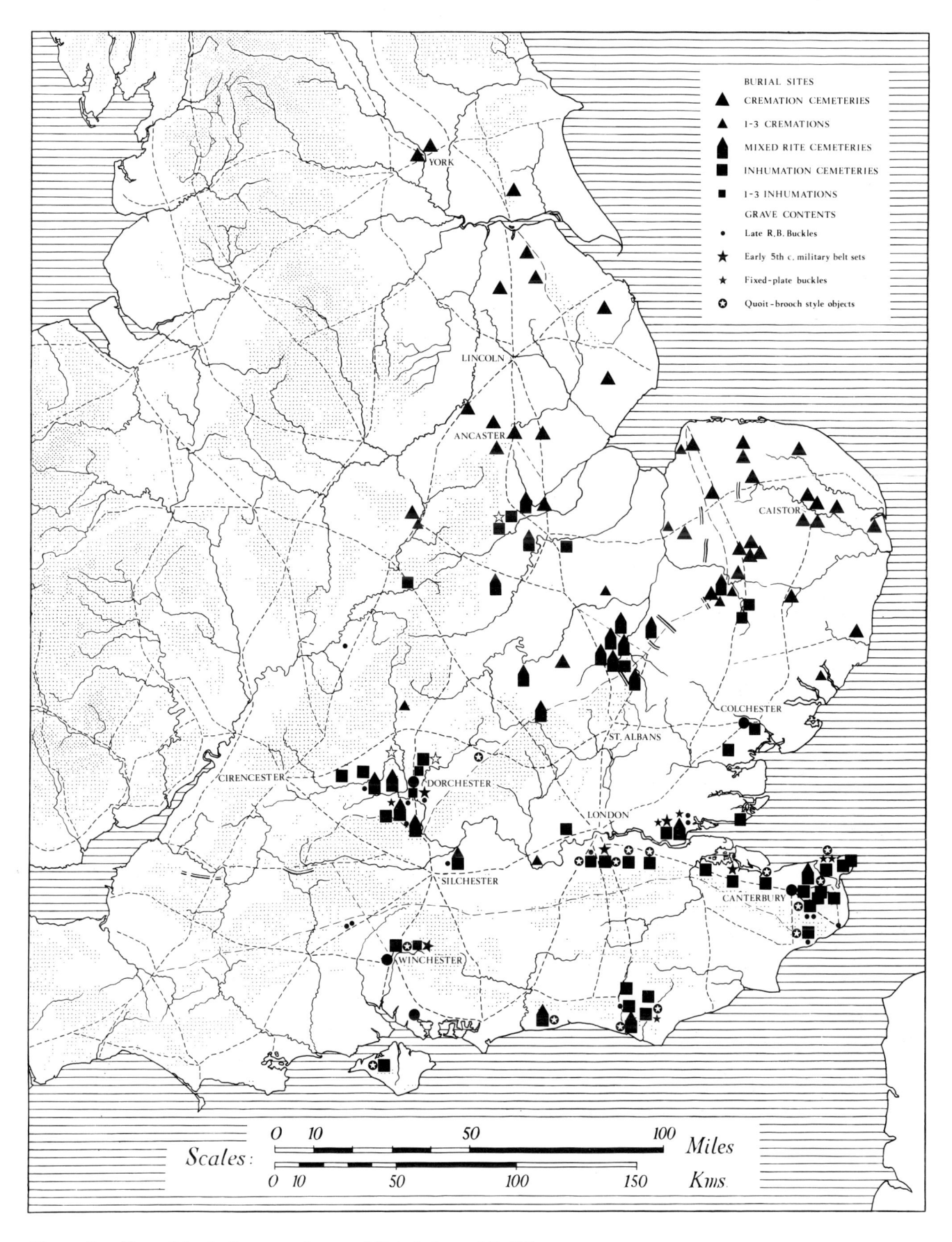

Figure 5. *Map of Anglo-Saxon settlement of Britain by c. AD 475*

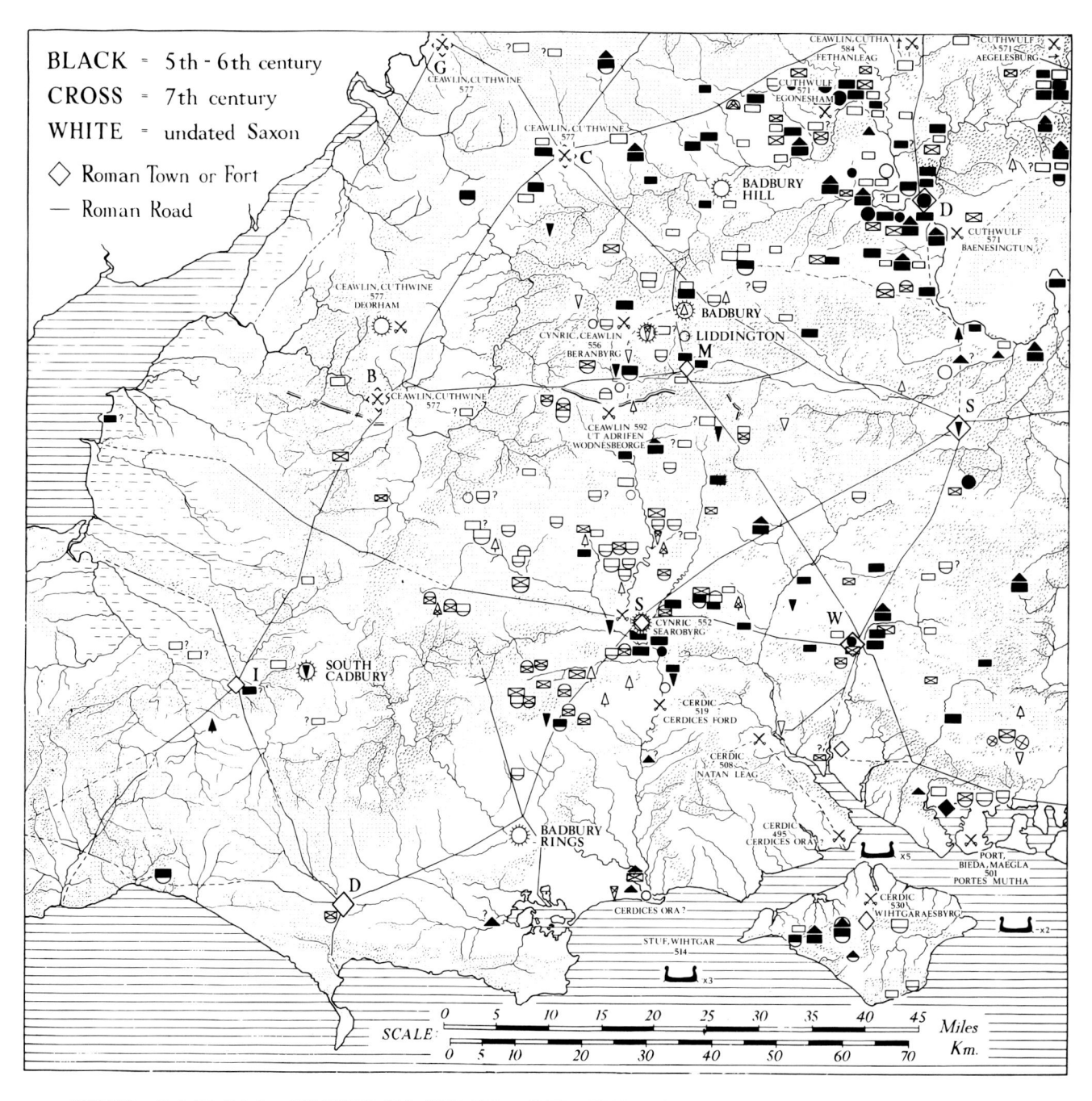

Figure 6. *Map of Saxon settlement of Wessex to c. AD 700*

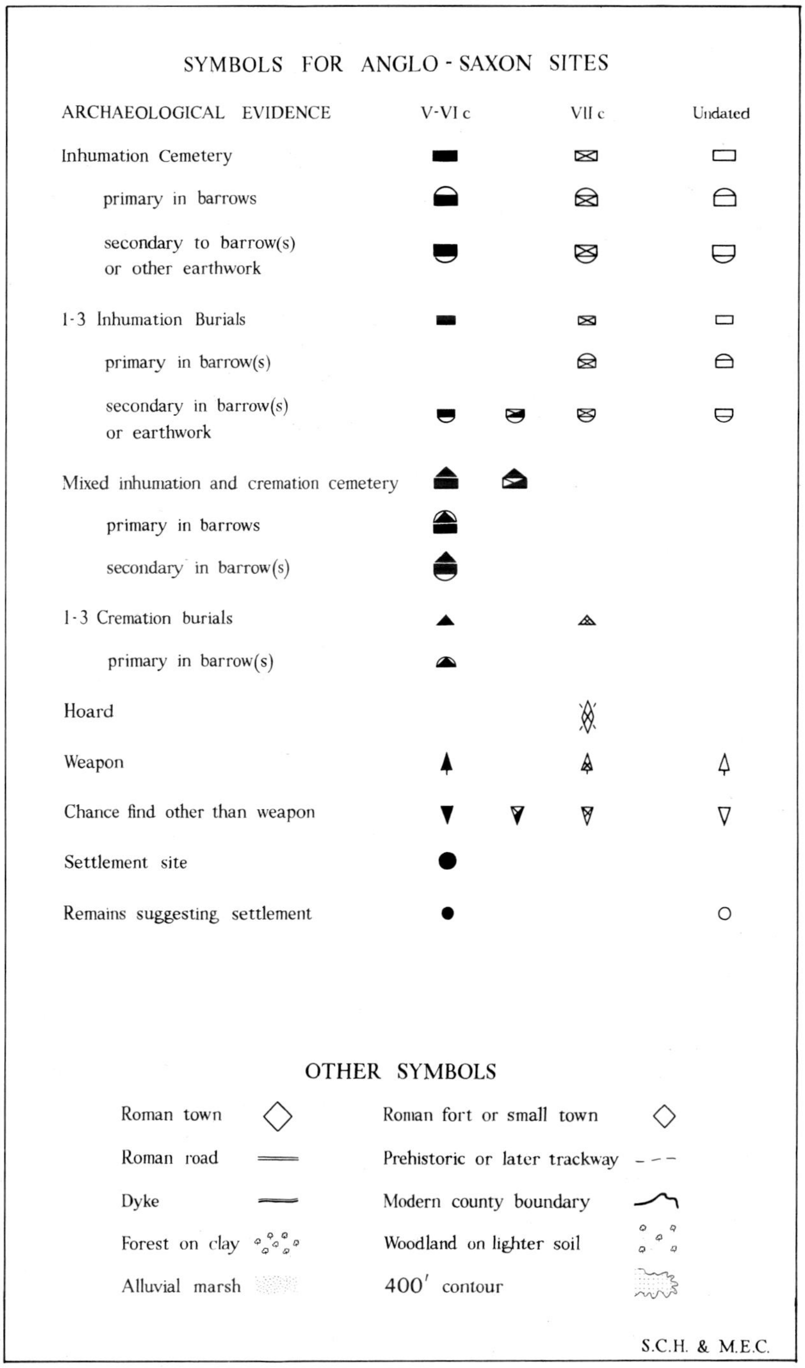

SYMBOLS FOR ANGLO-SAXON SITES

ARCHAEOLOGICAL EVIDENCE	V-VI c	VII c	Undated
Inhumation Cemetery	■	⊠	▭
primary in barrows	⬬	⊠	⌒
secondary to barrow(s) or other earthwork	⬯	⊠	⌣
1-3 Inhumation Burials	■	⊠	▭
primary in barrow(s)		⊠	⌒
secondary in barrow(s) or earthwork	⬯ ⬮	⊠	⌣
Mixed inhumation and cremation cemetery	⬥ ⬦		
primary in barrows	⬥		
secondary in barrow(s)	⬥		
1-3 Cremation burials	▲	△	
primary in barrow(s)	⬭		
Hoard		✦	
Weapon	▲	△	△
Chance find other than weapon	▼ ▽	▽	▽
Settlement site	●		
Remains suggesting settlement	●		○

OTHER SYMBOLS

Roman town	◇	Roman fort or small town	◇
Roman road	═	Prehistoric or later trackway	- - -
Dyke	━	Modern county boundary	⌒
Forest on clay	° ° °	Woodland on lighter soil	° °
Alluvial marsh		400' contour	

S.C.H. & M.E.C.

Figure 6b. *Key to Figure 6*

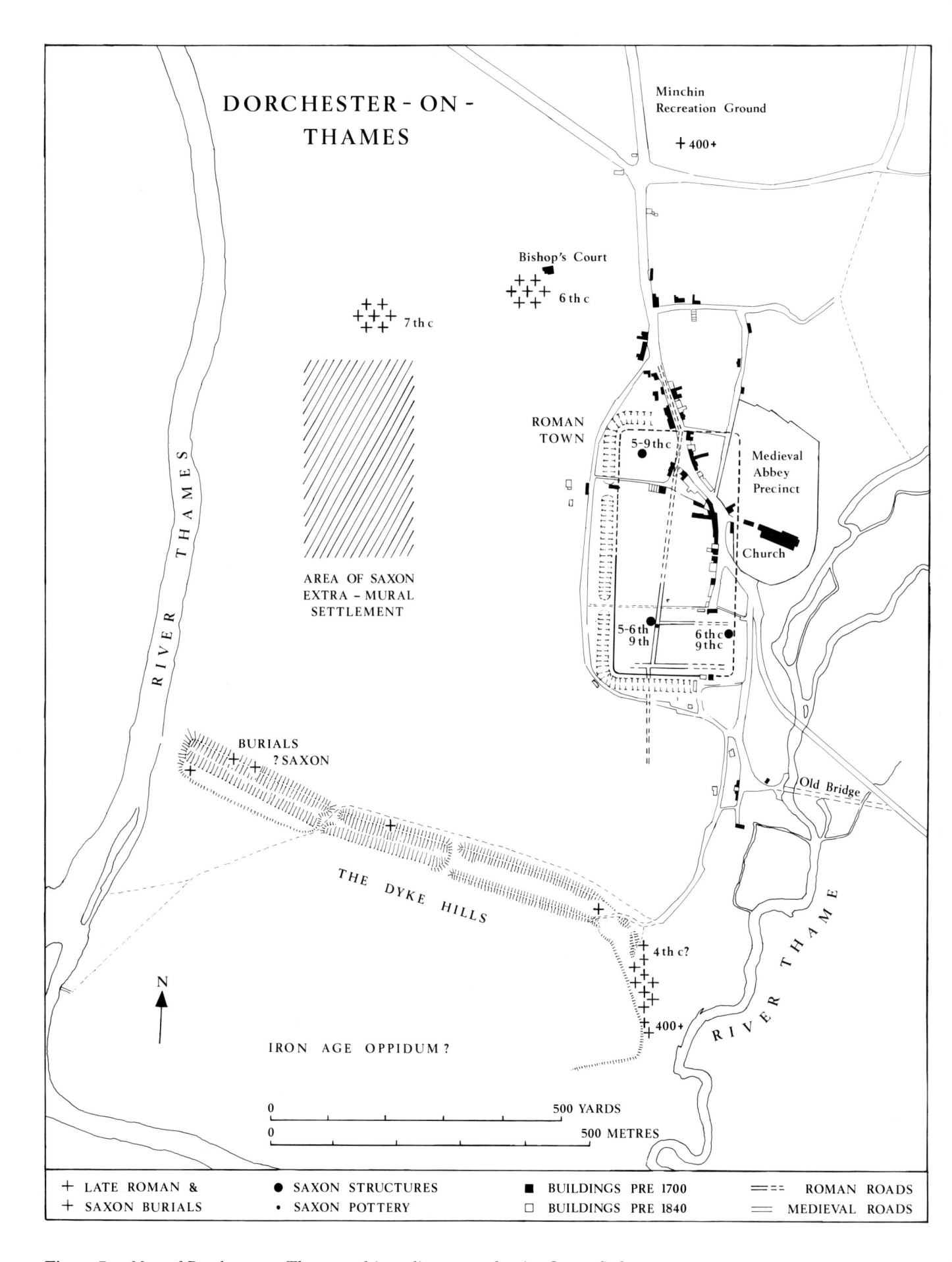

Figure 7. *Map of Dorchester-on-Thames and immediate area, showing Saxon finds*

ABINGDON, SAXTON ROAD

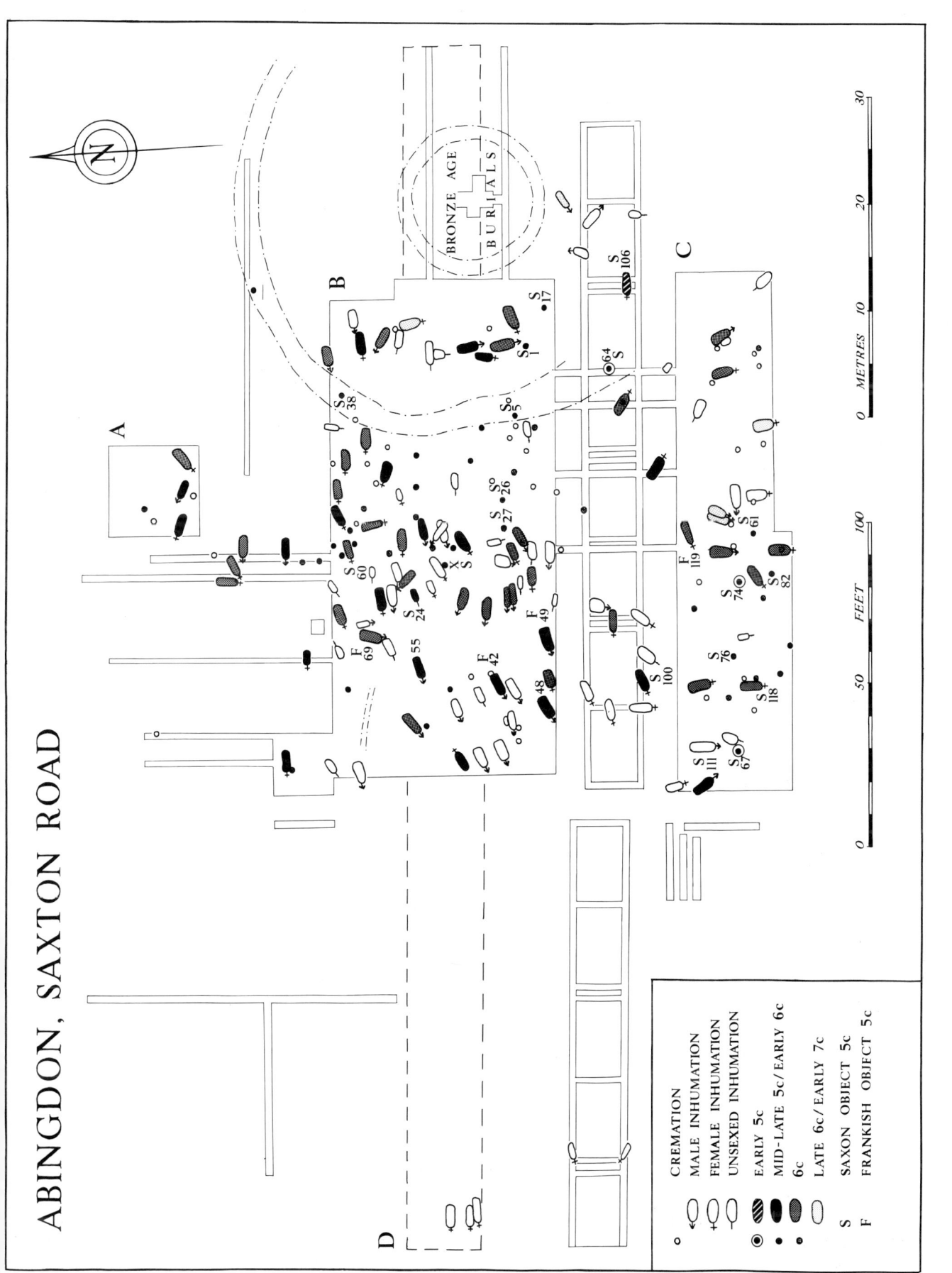

Figure 8. *Plan of the Abingdon cemetery (after Leeds & Harden 1936, fig. 3 with modifications and additions)*

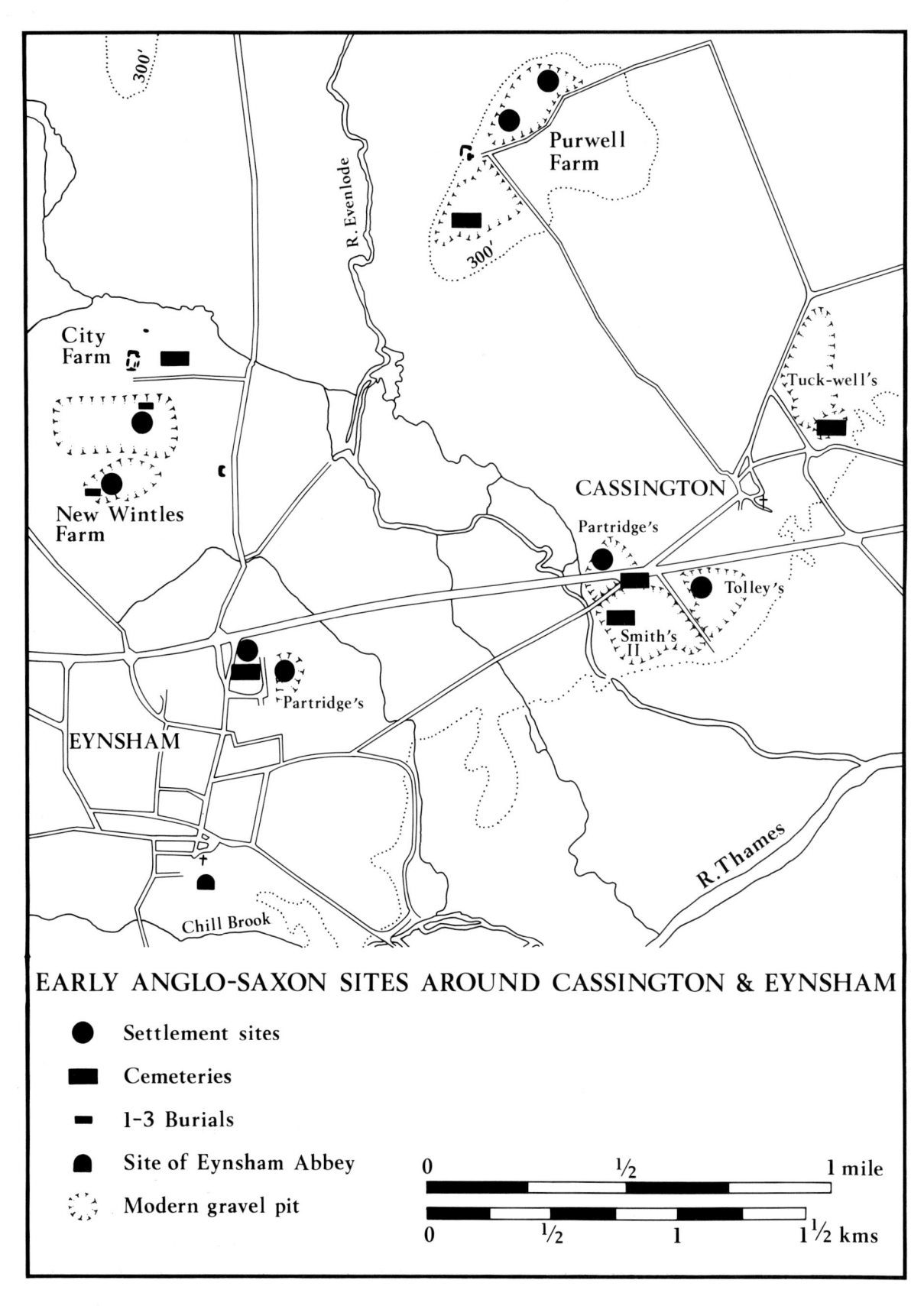

Figure 9. *Map of early Anglo-Saxon sites around Cassington and Eynsham (after Berisford 1973, fig. 2)*

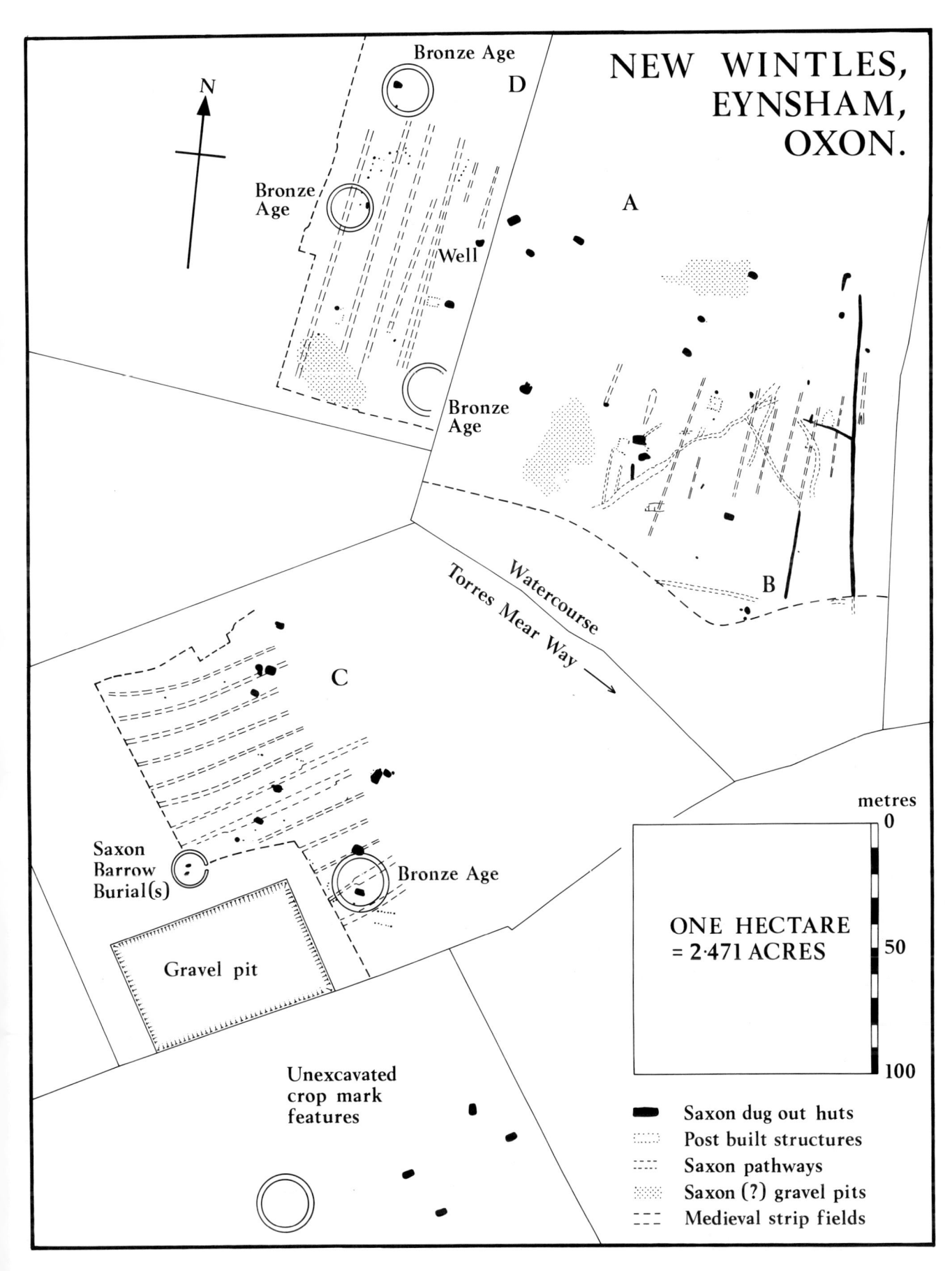

Figure 10. *Plan of Anglo-Saxon settlement at New Wintles, Eynsham (after Hawkes & Gray, 1969, fig. 1, & Gray 1974, fig. 6)*

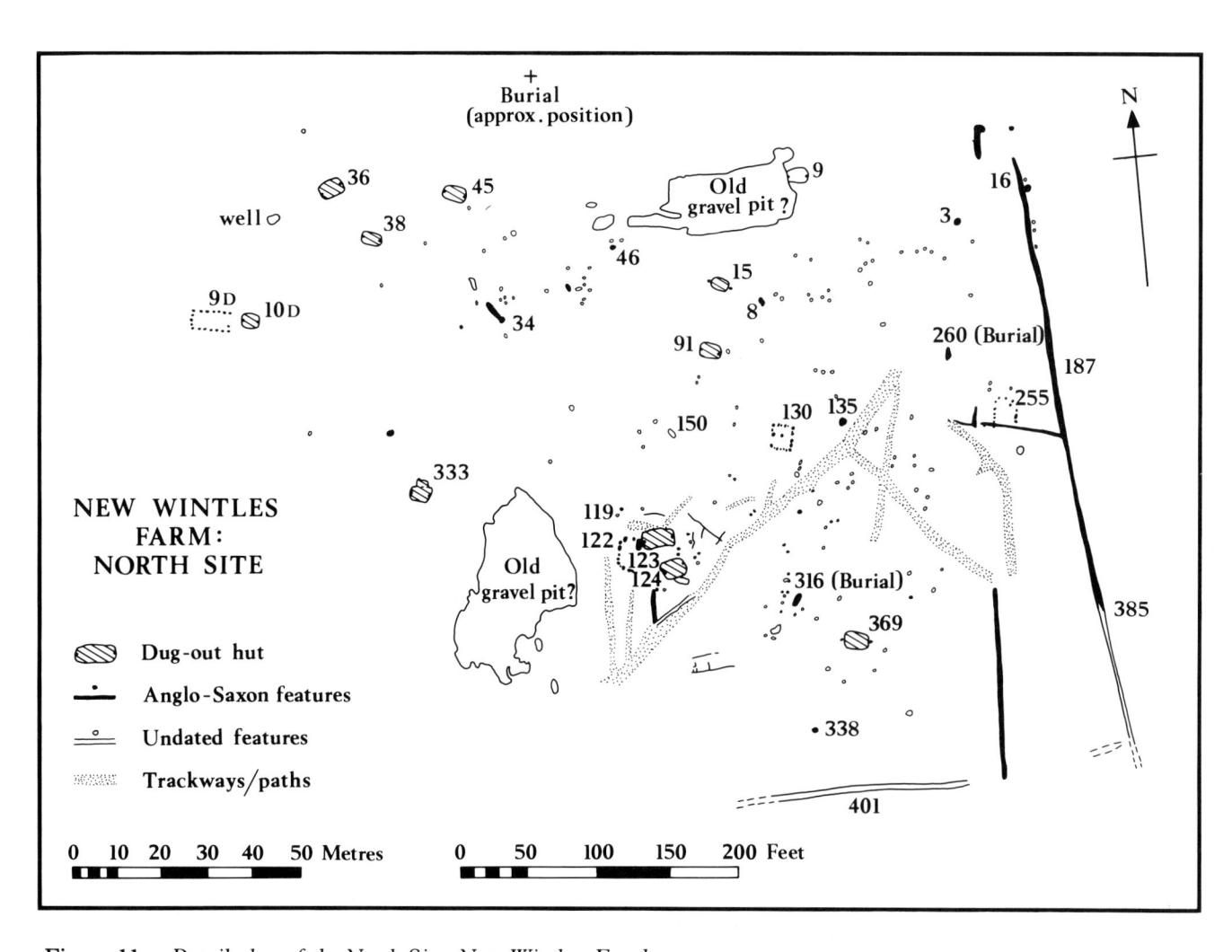

Figure 11. *Detail plan of the North Site, New Wintles, Eynsham*

Plate 5a. Dorchester, Dyke Hills, belt reconstructed, @ ¼ actual (Ash. Mus.)

Plate 5b. Dorchester, Minchin Rec., pair of applied brooches ¹/₁ (Ash. Mus.)

Plate 5c. Abingdon I, grave 106, tutulus and applied brooch etc. ¹/₁ (Ash. Mus.)

Plate 6a. *Frilford I, grave 143, 6-spiral saucer brooches c. ¹/₁ (Ash. Mus.)*

Plate 6b. *Frilford, grave 7, saucer brooches with star & Style I border c. ¹/₁ (Ash. Mus.)*

Plate 6c. *Oxford region, large saucer brooches modelled on Kentish discs c. ¹/₁ (Ash. Mus.)*

Plate 7a–b. *Cuddesdon glass bowls, @ ½ actual (after Akerman 1855, pl. vi)*

Plate 7c. *Cuddesdon bronze Coptic bucket @ ¼ actual (after Akerman 1855, pl. xiii)*

Plate 8a. *Milton, North Field, one of two composite disc brooches, 1/1 (V & A photo)*

Plate 8b. *Dorchester, Bishop's Court, bronze Janus-head lock for book or casket 2/1 (R L Wilkins photo)*

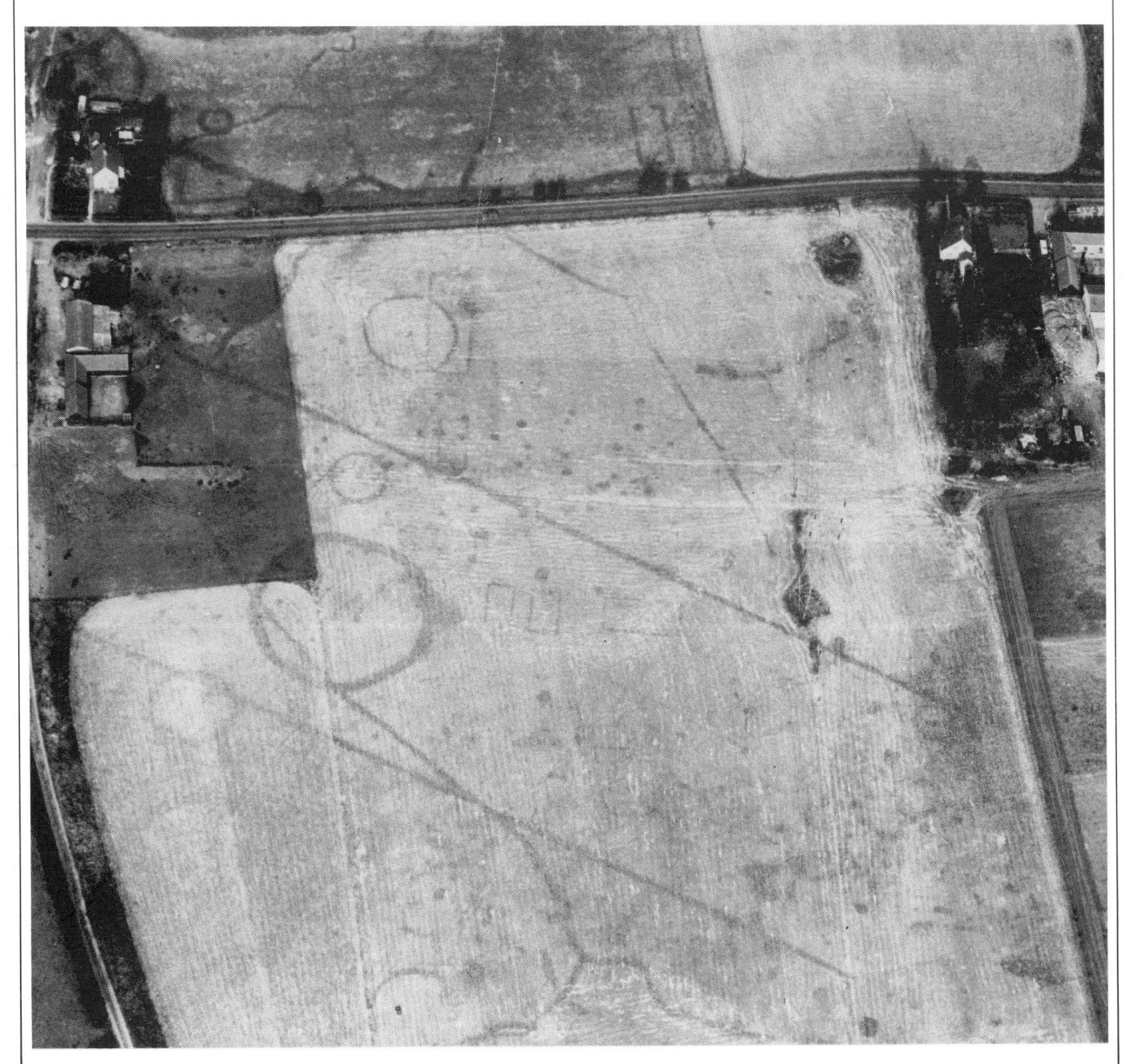

Plate 8c. *Air photograph, Saxon 'palace' complex, SE of Drayton. (Cambr. photo)*

THE OXFORD REGION FROM THE CONVERSION TO THE CONQUEST

TOM HASSALL

Bede's account (1969) of the conversion of the West Saxons to Christianity by Birinus is the natural starting point of a discussion of the region in the middle and late Saxon periods. The period began with Dorchester in its traditional role as the focus for activity in the Upper Thames, but by the end of the period Dorchester had sunk into decline and its role had been assumed by Wallingford and Oxford. By the Conquest one can for the first time truly speak of the Oxford region. This process can now be much more fully understood thanks to the discovery of new material remains and the re-interpretation of older finds, while for the first time in this survey of the archaeology of the region documentary sources, such as the Anglo-Saxon Chronicle and charters, complement and illuminate the physical remains. But it is only in recent years that archaeology has been able to make any significant contribution to the more familiar historical narrative (Rait 1939; Salter 1907).

According to Bede the West Saxons whose cemeteries dominate the archaeology of the Oxford region in the period before the coming of Birinus in 634 were a 'most pagan people'. The conversion was not a rapid process. The West Saxon king Cynegils had his centre of power based in Dorchester so that he must have had a palace in or near the site of the Roman town (Dickinson 1974). Cynegils' conversion by Birinus in 635 may have owed much to his desire to strengthen his ties with his overlord, Oswald, the Christian king of Northumbria. This overlordship certainly seems to have had a reality for Oswald stood sponsor for Cynegils at his baptism. Oswald was also associated with the grant of Dorchester as Birinus' episcopal seat. The site of Birinus' cathedral is uncertain. The suggestion that it might have lain to the east of the Roman town in one of the suburban cemeteries at Church Piece, Warborough, seems to have been disproved (Mary Harman *et al.* 1978). A second possibility is that it lay north-west of the town at Bishop's Court Farm (May 1978). It is more probable that the later Abbey church marks the site. The excavations at the Old Minster at Winchester (Biddle 1970) give an indication as to the type of building which might be expected.

Dorchester was a sensible choice for the bishopric so long as West Saxon patronage and power were based there, but for the immediate future, the kingdom of Wessex was to be largely restricted south of the Thames which was to form a debated natural frontier with Wessex's northern neighbour Mercia. Penda, the heathen king of Mercia, expelled Cynegils' successor, Cenwalh, from Wessex. Cenwalh himself was not a Christian but he was converted in exile and eventually regained power in Wessex. Once he was re-established Cenwalh gave Birinus' see at Dorchester to a Frank, Agilbert, but the king and the bishop disagreed and Cenwalh promoted a new bishopric at Winchester about 660. Agilbert abandoned Dorchester and the bones of Birinus were transferred to Winchester. The creation of the see at Winchester was a recognition of the realities of Saxon power. From 675 the Mercians were in control in Dorchester and they established their own bishopric.

Dorchester was no more relevant to 7th-century Mercia than it was to Wessex and the Mercian bishopric came to an end in 686 when Caedwalla, king of Wessex, temporarily regained control. The area was to come under the see of Leicester, while the church of Dorchester itself became a house of secular canons. South of the river the West Saxon control seems to have been more certain, so that contemporary with the brief Mercian bishopric at Dorchester a West Saxon under-king Cissa made a grant of land for the foundation of a monastery to a nobleman called Hean at Abingdon (Stenton 1913).

Abingdon's early history is similar to that of Dorchester. It too had been a focus of activity. Extensive Romano-British finds within the boundaries of the modern town suggest a substantial settlement with clear early Saxon occupation (Biddle *et al.* 1968). The later traditions of the monastery included the foundation by Hean's sister, Cilla, of a nunnery dedicated to the Holy Cross and St. Helen on the site of the medieval parish church. Certainly the topography of the medieval town suggests two foci, one in front of St. Helen's and another in front of the Abbey gates (Rodwell 1975, 33–40). In the 10th century the monks of Abingdon discovered an open-work disc-headed pin near St. Helen's church. The pin became known as the Black Cross of Abingdon and was revered as a relic. A 13th-century illustration shows a pin of late 7th- to early 8th-century date and certainly supports the theory of an early religious establishment near the site. As for Hean's monastery, the buildings are described in the Abingdon Chronicle as being 120 feet long with an apse at each end (Clapham 193, 36). It presumably had aisles. There was no cloister but instead there were 12 cells each with its own oratory. The whole complex was surrounded by a wall.

Although Abingdon was a West Saxon foundation many of the early charters later put forward by the Abbey as evidence for its land-holding south of the Thames were apparently issued by Mercian kings (Stenton 1913). These charters reflect the successive attempts by Mercia to gain control south of the river. Æthelbald, the Mercian king from 715 to 757, was to be particularly successful in this respect. The details are obscure but from 733 to 752 Wessex south of the Thames seems to have been under Mercian control. In the 730s Æthelbald gave the monastery of Cookham in Berkshire to Christchurch, Canterbury and he may also have given privileges to Abingdon.

Simple political control over the Oxford region may not have been Æthelbald's only motive for expansion. He seems to have begun a Mercian policy to achieve access to international trade for his landlocked kingdom (Metcalf 1972). By the early 730s London and, later, the rich trading centres of east Kent had fallen under Mercian domination. The route to the south through the Oxford region to the great international port of Hamwih, Saxon Southampton, offered an easy and accessible alternative route to the continent as it has continued to do until today. Metcalf's analysis (1977) of finds of sceattas from the region leads to the conclusion that a Mercian coinage existed at this time. Stylistic evidence suggests a hint of this trade between the Solent and the Oxford region (Metcalf 1972). The distribution of these coins points towards a frontier mint existing at the point of entry where goods from Wessex and in particular from Southampton came overland into Mercia. The obvious siting for such a mint would seem to be at Dorchester-on-Thames. Excavations by Rowley (1974; Rowley and Brown 1981) have demonstrated a series of stone-based structures existing in the town at this period. There is also some evidence for the internal organization of Dorchester (Bradley et al. 1978). However, it was not Dorchester which was to provide Mercia with its major crossing of the Thames into Wessex. Dorchester's historic role as the focus of the region was slowly but surely to be eroded by the rise of Oxford and Wallingford. It is precisely at the period of the sceatta finds that Oxford begins to emerge as an important centre. It was at this time that St. Frideswide was presumed to have established her minster at Oxford and the first archaeological evidence for Saxon occupation dates from the same time (Stenton 1936; Durham 1977).

However, in 752 Æthelbald was defeated by Cuthred of Wessex at a battle which has been identified with Burford. Robert Plot connected a faint memory of this battle with the Burford dragon ceremony (Plot 1705, 356). Mercian control south of the river was lost and five years later Æthelbald himself was murdered. The revival of West Saxon power in the Upper Thames was to be comparatively short-lived, for in 777 (s.a. 779) Offa captured Benson and the Oxford region both north and south of the Thames was brought back into Mercian hands. The role of Benson in relation to Dorchester is far from clear. It was certainly an important royal estate. Offa's role in the Oxford region may have been critical and it has been argued that it was he who established Oxford as the main crossing-point of the Thames for Mercia's southern commercial and political ambitions (Durham 1977). If this suggestion is correct then it was his action which was ultimately to lead to the rise of Oxford at the expense of Dorchester.

Until the Danish invasion of nearly a century later lands north of the Thames were to remain in Mercia. South of the river the Mercians retained control of what was to become Berkshire even after Egbert of Wessex defeated the Mercians at the battle of Ellandun in 825. Beorhtwulf, king of Mercia, certainly possessed Berkshire as late as 844 through a Mercian Ealdorman, named Æthulwulf. Even so the land south of the river came under the jurisdiction of the West Saxon bishops of Winchester and Alfred of Wessex himself was born at Wantage in 849. Æthulwulf is known to have transferred his allegiance to the West Saxons. He died in 871 fighting for the West Saxons against the Danes. It was the resistance to the Danes by the West Saxon kings which was finally to secure the region for them.

The Mercian territories north of the Thames first felt the force of the Danish raids, but in 870/871 the Danish army wintered at Reading. Reading was described as a royal vill and the Danes were said to have built a rampart from the Thames to the Kennet. The entrance was unsuccessfully attacked by king Ethelred of Wessex and his brother Alfred. However Ethelred and Alfred were to win the famous victory at Ashdown. The precise position of the battle on the Downs is uncertain, but it is not necessarily to be associated with the present Ashdown Park (Gelling 1973, 2–3). The early name for Uffington Castle is similar and folklore has also always associated the White Horse at Uffington with Alfred. Recent research on the Horse itself also now seems to support its origins as being of Saxon date rather than earlier (Woolner 1965), although the connection with Alfred cannot be sustained. The victory itself seems to have been only a temporary setback for the Danes.

Archaeology can provide some further evidence for Danish and later Saxon activity in the area. At Reading a burial of a man and his horse has been found together with a sword (Akerman 1867). At Sonning, immediately opposite the Danish site at Reading, two skeletons were discovered in 1966 associated with a sword, pin, knife and arrowheads (Evison 1969). Evison considers these to be connected with other Viking burials. The precise dating of these Viking burials is difficult and their existence so close to Reading may be only chance, but it is certainly tempting to see them dating from the years 870–1. At Shifford a Viking-type sword together with spears, knife and sword blades and a spur were all of similar date and dredged from the river in 1914 (Oakeshott 1962). These finds may mark the site of another skirmish in the late 9th or early 10th century which it is tempting to associate with a 13th-century name Knightsbridge (Gelling 1946–7) found in the same parish. A Saxon sword with the maker's name, Ulfberht, comes from the river above Tenfoot Bridge in the same parish, similar to the splendidly decorated sword from Wallingford bridge (Evison 1967). Also from the Saxon side comes the Abingdon sword with its elaborate ornament in the Trewhiddle style depicting biting beasts and the symbols of the four evangelists

(Hinton 1970). Hinton has suggested that these symbols may have fortified the Christian Saxon warrior as he went out to do battle with the invading pagan Vikings (Hinton 1977, 53).

In 874 the Danes set up a puppet king in Mercia and three years later the kingdom was divided. Eastern Mercia came firmly under Danish control. This annexation by the Danes led to the revival of a second Mercian bishopric at Dorchester to serve the unoccupied territories between the Thames and the Humber. This diocese was to survive until after the Norman conquest in spite of the military re-conquest of Mercia by the West Saxon kings.

The resurgence of West Saxon power was the work of Alfred and his son, Edward the Elder. By 878 Oxfordshire was brought back under West Saxon control: in that year Oxfordshire was given to Ethelred as Ealdorman of the Mercians. Ethelred was to marry Alfred's daughter, Ethelflaed, while her brother Edward the Elder was to take direct possession of Oxford in 911.

One of the key elements in the process of consolidating royal power in Wessex and annexing Mercia, was the establishment of fortified centres known as *burhs* (Radford 1970). The *burhs* themselves ranged in size from small forts to much larger fortresses capable of providing communal defence for a resident population as well as the neighbourhood. The defences themselves were either constructed from new or else made use of pre-existing fortifications. Control of the Thames and its crossing-places was vital to the re-conquest and a chain of forts guarded the fords and provided springboards for the advance into Mercia. Significantly Dorchester with its Roman defences and episcopal tradition was not chosen as a *burh* although a rectangular hall-like structure dated by sherds of 9th- or 10th-century ware has been suggested there (Frere 1962). The lack of defence at Dorchester must imply that by this time the Roman north to south road was no longer of any commercial or strategic significance. Instead of Dorchester three much larger *burhs* were built at Wallingford, Oxford and Cricklade. These three *burhs* display a great similarity. Wallingford and Cricklade were certainly rectangular in plan (Biddle and Hill 1971) and all the evidence suggests that Oxford was also (Hassall 1975). The defences consisted of an earth rampart which has been examined in all three *burhs* (Brooks 1965–66; Durham *et al.* 1972; Radford 1972). At all three *burhs* the rampart was strengthened by a stone wall which may have been a later addition. The street pattern in all three may also date from the same period. Each *burh* has a grid of streets and sections of intramural street. Doubt has recently been cast on Wallingford's intramural street (Durham 1983). Good quality stone cobbling was a feature of the streets at Oxford (Durham 1982; Hassall 1971) and possibly also at Cricklade. Excavations have uncovered much of the details of the topography and life of the *burh* at Oxford from this period (Hassall 1975). A substantial wooden building has been excavated in part at Wallingford (Durham 1981a).

Outside Oxford, the archaeological evidence is scant for the period from Alfred to the Norman Conquest. The outstanding single find is the Minster Lovell Jewel (Clarke and Hinton 1971). The context of the find is obscure; however, its manufacture must be associated with a royal workshop which was probably also responsible for the Alfred Jewel itself. Hinton, however, sees these jewels as one of the last manifestations of a barbaric tradition. They belong firmly to the Pagan and middle Saxon traditions rather than to the archaeology of late Saxon England.

The 10th century also reflected the national monastic revival. The buildings of Abingdon Abbey around 954 were described as ruined and neglected because of the aftermath of the earlier Danish raids (Biddle *et al.* 1968). King Edward (947–955) refounded the monastery under Ethelwold. It may be that the apsidal church excavated in 1922 and published by Biddle in 1968 was Ethelwold's church. Between 990 and 994 Ethelred founded a further monastery at Cholsey on an extensive royal estate. Gem (1978) has argued that the central tower which sits uneasily on the present 12th-century church may actually form part of the original monastic church. If this is indeed the case then it would make Cholsey the only monastic church of new foundation associated with 10th-century reform with any significant portion remaining. By the early 11th century other religious houses were founded at St. Frideswide's at Oxford and at Eynsham. There may have been a minster as early as 864 (Birch, 119–20) at Eynsham where Ælfric the Grammarian, the greatest scholar of the Benedictine Reformation, became Abbot in 1005. Pre-Conquest burials have come from the site (Gray and Clayton 1978).

The degree of Danish settlement in the 10th century in the region is obscure, but it was probably never very extensive. It was probably Oxford's central position which was to make it such a crucial centre during the establishment of the Anglo-Danish state which was finally achieved following the assembly at Oxford in 1018. There was certainly some settlement north of the Thames. The Danish personal name Clac is found in Shifford and Eynsham (Gelling 1946–7, 481). Other personal names occur in a number of parishes, in Pyrton, Crowsley Park, Stanton Harcourt, Great Tew, Goring, Wychwood, Barford St. Michael, Stanton St. John and Hanborough. South of the river the evidence is even less. A few Scandanavian personal names are recorded (Gelling 1976, 921), while at Stratton Burgh Castle Farm at Coleshill there is an enigmatic Danish sculpture (Pevsner 1966, 119). The sculpture is an 11th-century tympanum decorated with the Lamb of God in a circle in the middle with tendrils in Ringerike style. While the sculpture is certainly in Danish/Viking style its origin is obscure since it is set in a farm built as an eyecatcher in 1792.

The massacre at Oxford of the Danes on St. Brice's day in 1002 suggests an extensive Danish population in the town. Mellor has suggested (1980) that the presence of St. Neots type pottery may indicate likely areas of such settlement. However the massacre itself did not deter the Danes. The Danish army burnt Wallingford in 1006 and defeated the Wiltshire militia at Cuckhamsley Knob in East Hendred. In 1009 the army burnt Oxford itself. The stirrups of Anglo-Danish manufacture found at Magdalen Bridge may be associated with this raid (Seaby and Woodfield 1980). The radio-carbon date for a burnt fence from All Saints, Oxford is tantalizingly close in time to this traumatic event (Durham 1981b). Lyon (1966) has pointed out that the Oxford Mint ceased production for some time afterwards.

A sidelight on the way in which Danegeld could be paid at this time is given by a charter dated to 1005–12 in which Ethelred sold Beckley and Horton to a Dane named Toti for 1lb of gold in order to pay Geld (Gelling 1953, XXIV–XXV). Before the Conquest, Azor son of Toti appears as the holder of the estate (Wolffe 1957). He also held Iffley, Lillingstone Lovell, and lands in Marsh Baldon and Chastleton.

By the 11th century one can probably speak of the Oxford region which was beginning to take on clearly its familiar pre-feudal structure. The major administrative divisions, the shires, were established. The origins of Berkshire as a county are not totally clear (Gelling 1976, 838–847). As a name it first appears in 893. Unlike Oxfordshire it did not take its name from its county town. Oxfordshire is more clearly an artificial creation, probably by Edward the Elder. The smaller administrative divisions, the Hundreds, were also in existence (Stenton 1939, 374). For instance, probably in Edgar's reign the endowments of the see of Dorchester were grouped for administrative purposes in the three Hundreds of Banbury, Thame and Dorchester of 100 Hides each (Sawyer 1962). These three Hundreds were probably grouped together to help provide ships for the naval defence against the continued Viking threat. Such a system might seem rather bizarre; however the Thames was navigable from its mouth to Oxford at this time (Bond 1979, 69–71), so that Dorchester might not have seemed quite so remote from the sea.

The prolific evidence of charters, paramount amongst which is the great series of Abingdon charters, shows that many estate boundaries were firmly fixed (Gelling 1976, 615–794). For the series of Abingdon estates on the Downs it has been suggested that some of these estate boundaries were probably already ancient before the two administrative tiers of Hundreds and Shires were created (Gelling 1976, 822–835; cf. Bradley 1975). A number of boundary earthworks are recorded in the charter evidence. While the major tenurial pattern is emerging the details of the location of actual settlements and their fields have been more elusive. Research elsewhere has provided the cautionary note that the middle and late Saxon settlements of the region may not necessarily lie under the modern villages which bear names to be found in Domesday. The discovery of early Saxon settlement sites such as Radley (Avery and Brown 1972) and Eynsham (Hawkes and Gray 1969)

point in the same general direction. However, the Domesday evidence certainly suggests that the region was fully settled with the possible exception of parts of Wychwood and the Chilterns (Campbell 1962; Jope and Terrett 1962).

Settlement archaeology of the region is again dominated by Oxford whose late Saxon topography has been clear in broad outline since Jope's pioneering studies (Jope 1956). Jope's general picture has been confirmed and refined. Wallingford, the other *burh*, is also beginning to yield late Saxon material though perhaps not in the quantities one might have expected. The other two key centres, Dorchester and Abingdon, have not however produced much material. Other places too, which were to emerge in the medieval period as market towns, were probably already of some importance, if not truly urban. Royal vills, such as Bampton, Faringdon and Wantage, and episcopal estates such as Banbury, Thame and Witney were probably important local centres of administration and are likely to have possessed minster churches serving a large surrounding area. Little is known of their archaeology and it is an assumption that the sites of their parish churches, later often in the periphery of the medieval town, mark the original settlement nucleus (Rodwell 1975).

It is the same picture in the villages. There is virtually no evidence from which to argue either a static or a shifting settlement pattern (Jope and Terrett 1962, 193). No village plans can be dated with certainty to the period, although finds of Late Saxon pottery have come from a number of sites. However, some more clues to the future potential of village sites has been provided by Davison's excavation at Sulgrave (Davison 1977) in the extreme north of the region, where excavation of part of a small ringwork showed that the later Norman manorial centre had been established on the site of earlier buildings. These buildings belong presumably to a late 10th-century estate complex of sufficient status to warrant an abortive attempt to fortify the site in the early 11th century. Nearer to Oxford, at Middleton Stoney, Rowley's excavation showed that the 12th-century castle had buried a stone based building of possible late Saxon date presumably analogous to Sulgrave (Rahtz and Rowley 1984, 49–53).

The region contains the physical remains of a number of late Saxon churches and others can be inferred from Domesday (Campbell 1962, 271–2; Jope and Terrett 1962, 233). Langford with its imposing tower and sculpture is perhaps the best known (Taylor and Taylor 1965, 367–72), but traces survive at Bampton (Sherwood and Pevsner 1974, 429), Northleigh (Taylor and Taylor 1965, 464–5), St. Michael's, Oxford (Taylor and Taylor 1965, 481–2), and the lower stages of the tower at Caversfield (Sherwood and Pevsner 1974, 523–4). An 11th-century church may exist at Tackley (Sherwood and Pevsner 1974, 802), while at Swalcliffe three bays of a late Saxon nave survive (Taylor and Taylor 1965, 599–601). At Waterperry the discovery of the chancel was a dramatic example of archaeology above ground and the subsequent excavations have demonstrated that the nave walls belong to the same date and not as was previously thought to a later church (Hassall 1972). Excavations at All Saints (Hassall and Durham 1974) and St. Peter's-in-the-East (Sturdy 1972), both at Oxford, have confirmed that further late Saxon churches are likely to be discovered by excavation within existing buildings. A similar conclusion can be derived from excavations at Westcote Barton (Chambers 1979). The numerous burials from Dorchester may also be associated with the number of the churches said to have existed there (CBA 9 1976). At Wallingford, the site of the former church of St. Rumbold's, possibly a late Saxon foundation, has been recognized (Halpin 1983). In addition to surviving remains a number of other churches are known or suspected: for instance, a number of minster churches were probably associated with royal estates, while some are recorded in place names such as Minster Lovell. Charlbury was said to have been the resting-place of St. Diuma (Rollason 1978, 90; Stenton 1939, 378), while St. Fremund, martyred son of king Offa of Mercia, is said to have had a shrine at Cropredy (Mason 1972, 158). There are also casual references such as the priests mentioned at Bampton where there was probably a minster (Stenton 1939, 377–8) or a church mentioned in Ducklington in 958 (Grundy 1933, 29).

No remains of peasant houses have been excavated within existing villages. Admittedly excavations have been limited. However at Tetsworth, where the settlement has shifted, the earliest pottery found in the excavation showed that there was a settlement by the 10th or 11th century (Robinson 1973), while the excavation at Deddington Castle provided tantalizing clues suggesting that a large portion of the 11th-century village may lie under the enormous outer bailey of the post-Conquest castle (Ivens 1983).

The agricultural arrangements within villages are even more obscure than the villages themselves. The general picture has been described by Jope and Terrett (1962). There is little information on tenure although one can suspect that there may have been a variety of tenures. Jones (1981, 222) has, for instance, drawn attention to the Domesday reference to the 23 men who had gardens at Holywell, near Oxford, probably being analogous to the small nucleated parcels arranged in a radial fashion around a nucleus such as a church. Agricultural arrangements elsewhere may have had equally old origins and just as estate boundaries may have reflected much earlier divisons, so too Roman and pre-Roman field boundaries may have influenced their late Saxon counterparts. At Great Bourton, Taylor (1975, 58) has pointed out the tantalizing relationship between a cropmark field division and a later furlong boundary.

Apart from agriculture archaeology, coupled with documentary evidence, provides a few glimpses on other aspects of the region's economy. There must have been a flourishing local pottery industry. Although the Domesday kilns at Bladon have not been identified, Mellor (1980) has suggested that they were probably producing fabric tempered with calcareous gravel classified as AC, other local potteries were producing fabric tempered with fossil shell (fabric B), fossil shell and limestone (fabric R), and flint and quartz (fabric BF). These sources were complemented by imported wares from such well-known centres as Stamford but also from the continent. Such wares were certainly available in Oxford. They could have reached the town by way of either the Southampton route discussed above or from London either overland or via the Thames. Stone had already become a local industry and was exported from the region (Jope 1956, 251–44), whilst salt was imported from Droitwich (Jope and Terrett 1962, 232) and hone stones from the continent.

It is clear that the potential for archaeological discoveries is very great. With the exception of excavations in Oxford and, to a lesser extent, Wallingford, no recent fieldwork has been aimed specifically at examining Middle and Late Saxon sites, so that comparatively little can be added to earlier surveys of the region (Leeds 1939; Myres 1954). An obvious priority where rescue archaeological situations are likely to arise would be to examine the original nuclei of royal and episcopal estates at those places which became market centres in the Middle Ages. Church archaeology both above and below ground is a second area where future discoveries can be expected. The problems of rural settlement by contrast seem to be more intractable, but if any well-preserved sites are identified they should either be preserved or fully excavated.

Bibliography

Akerman, J.Y. (1867) *Antiq. J.*, 2nd ser. J, 321–2

Avery, M. & Brown, D. (1972) 'Saxon features at Abingdon', *Oxoniensia* 37, 66–81

Bede (1969) *Bede's Ecclesiastical history of the English people*, ed. B. Colgrove & R.A.B. Mynors

Biddle, M., Lambrick, Mrs. & Myres, J.N.L. (1968) 'The early history of Abingdon, Berkshire and its abbey', *Med. Archaeol.* 12, 26–68

Biddle, M. (1970) 'Excavations at Winchester: eighth interim report', *Antiq. J.* 50, 311–321

Biddle, M. & Hill, D.H. (1971) 'Late Saxon planned towns', *Antiq. J.* 51, 70–85

Birch, W. de G., ed. (1887) *Cartularium Saxonicum: a collection of charters relating to Anglo-Saxon history*

Bond, C.J. (1979) 'The reconstruction of the medieval landscape: the estates of Abingdon Abbey', *Landscape History* 1, 59–75

Bradley, R. (1975) 'The landscape in its wider context', in R. Bradley and A. Ellison, *Rams Hill: a Bronze Age Defended Enclosure and its Landscape*, BAR 19, 190–203

Bradley, R. (1978) 'Rescue excavation in Dorchester-on-Thames, 1972', *Oxoniensia* 43, 17–39

Brooks, N.P. (1965–66) 'Excavations at Wallingford Castle, 1965: an interim report', *Berks. Archaeol. J.* 62, 17–21

CBA 9 (1976) 'Dorchester 7 Rotten Row', *CBA 9 Newsletter* 6, 73

Campbell, E.M.J. (1962) 'Berkshire' in H.C. Darby and E.M.J. Campbell eds., *The Domesday Geography of south-east England*, 239–86

Chambers, R.A. (1979) 'Excavations in Westcote Barton parish church, Oxon., 1977', *Oxoniensia* 44, 99–101

Clapham, A.W. (1930) *English Romanesque Architecture before the Conquest*

Clarke, J.R. & Hinton, D.A. (1971) *The Alfred and Minster Lovell Jewels*
Davison, B.K. (1977) 'Excavations at Sulgrave, Northamptonshire, 1960–76, *Archaeol. J.* 134, 105–114
Dickinson, T.M. (1974) *Cuddesdon and Dorchester-on-Thames, Oxfordshire: two early Saxon 'princely' sites in Wessex*, BAR 1
Durham, B., Hassall, T., Rowley, T. & Simpson, C. (1972) 'A cutting across the Saxon defences at Wallingford, Berkshire 1971', *Oxoniensia* 37, 82–85
Durham, B. (1977) 'Archaeological Investigations in St. Aldates, Oxford', *Oxoniensia* 43, 83–203
Durham, B. (1981a) 'Wallingford: 9–11 St. Martin's Street', *CBA 9 Newsletter* 11, 44–47
Durham, B. (1981b) 'Oxford: All Saints', *CBA 9 Newsletter* 11, 155–6
Durham, B. (1982) 'Oxford: High Street', *CBA 9 Newsletter* 12, 158–60
Durham, B. (1983) 'Wallingford: The Mill, St. Mary's Street', *CBA 9 Newsletter* 13, 150
Evison, V. (1967) 'A sword from the Thames at Wallingford Bridge', *Archaeol. J.* 124, 160–189
Evison, V. (1969) 'A Viking Grave at Sonning, Berks.', *Antiq. J.* 49, 330–345
Frere, S. (1962) 'Excavations at Dorchester-on-Thames, 1962', *Archaeol. J.* 119, 114–149
Gelling, M. (1953) *The Place-Names of Oxfordshire*. Pt. i. English Place-Name Society vol. 23
Gelling, M. (1954) *The Place-Names of Oxfordshire*. Pt. ii. English Place-Name Society vol. 24
Gelling, M. (1973) *The Place-Names of Berkshire*. Pt. i. English Place-Name Society vol. 49
Gelling, M. (1976) *The Place-Names of Berkshire*. Pt. iii. English Place-Name Society vol. 51
Gem, R. (1978) 'Church architecture in the reign of King Aethelred', in D.H. Hill ed., *Ethelred the Unready: Papers from the Millenary Conference*, BAR 59, 105–114
Gray, M. & Clayton, N. (1978) 'Excavations on the site of Eynsham Abbey, 1971', *Oxoniensia* 43, 100–122
Grundy, G.B. (1933) *Saxon Oxfordshire*. Oxfordshire Record Soc. 15
Halpin, C. (1983) 'Wallingford: John Wilder's, Goldsmith's Lane', *CBA 9 Newsletter* 13, 148–149
Harman, M., Lambrick, G., Miles, D. & Rowley, T. (1978) 'Roman burials around Dorchester-on-Thames', *Oxoniensia* 43, 1–16
Hassall, T.G. (1971) 'Excavations at Oxford, 1970. Third interim report', *Oxoniensia* 36, 1–14
Hassall, T.G. (1972) 'Excavations at the Saxon church at Waterperry, Oxon', *Oxoniensia* 37, 245
Hassall, T.G. & Durham, B.G. (1974) 'Excavations at Oxford, 1973–74', *Oxoniensia* 39, 54–57
Hassall, T.G. (1975) 'Topography of pre-University Oxford', in C.G. Smith & D.I. Scargill eds., *Oxford and its Region*
Hawkes, S. & Gray, M. (1969) 'Preliminary note on the early Anglo-Saxon settlement at New Wintles Farm, Eynsham', *Oxoniensia* 34, 1–4
Hinton, D.A. (1970) 'Two late Saxon swords', *Oxoniensia* 35, 1–4
Hinton, D.A. (1977) *Alfred's Kingdom: Wessex and the South, 800–1500*
Hoskins, W.G. & Jope, E.M. (1954) 'The Medieval period', in A.F. Martin & R.W. Steel eds., *The Oxford Region*, 103–121
Jones, G.R.J. (1981) 'Early customary tenures in Wales and open-field agriculture', in T. Rowley ed., *The Origins of Open-Field Agriculture*, 202–225
Ivens, R.J. (1983) 'Deddington Castle, Oxfordshire. A summary of excavations 1977–79', *South Midlands Archaeology (CBA 9 Newsletter 13)*, 34–41
Jope, E.M. (1956) 'Saxon Oxford and its region', in D.B. Harden ed., *Dark-Age Britain*, 234–58
Jope, E.M. & Terrett, I.B. (1962) 'Oxfordshire', in H.C. Darby and E.M.J. Campbell eds., *The Domesday Geography of south-east England*, 184–238
Leeds, E.T. (1939) 'Anglo-Saxon remains', in L.F. Salzman, *Victoria County History, Oxfordshire* 1, 346–72
Lyon, C.S.S. (1966) 'Chronology of the coinage of Ethelred II', *Brit. Numis. J.* 35, 34–7
Mason, J.F.A. (1972) 'Cropredy', in A. Crossley ed., *Victoria County History, Oxfordshire*, 10, 157–175
May, J. (1978) 'Romano-British and Saxon sites near Dorchester-on-Thames, Oxfordshire', *Oxoniensia* 42, 42–81
Mellor, M. (1980) 'Late Saxon pottery from Oxfordshire: evidence and speculation', *Medieval Ceramics* 4, 17–27
Metcalf, D.M. (1972) 'The "Bird and Branch" Sceattas in the light of a find from Abingdon', *Oxoniensia* 37, 51–65
Metcalf, D.M. (1977) 'Monetary affairs in Mercia in the time of Aethelbald', in A. Dornier ed., *Mercian Studies*, 87–106
Myres, J.N.L. (1954) 'The Anglo-Saxon period', in A.F. Martin & R.W. Steel, *The Oxford Region*, 96–102
Oakeshott, R.E. (1962) 'The Shifford sword', in H.R.E. Davidson, *The Sword in Anglo-Saxon England: its archaeology and literature*, 225
Pevsner, N. (1966) *Buildings of England: Berkshire*
Plot, R. (1705) *The Natural History of Oxfordshire*
Radford, C.A.R. (1970) 'The later pre-Conquest boroughs and their defences', *Med. Archaeol.* 14, 83–103
Radford, C.A.R. (1972) 'Excavations at Cricklade, 1948–63', *Wilts. Archaeol. Nat. Hist. Mag.* 67, 61–111
Rahtz, S. & Rowley, T. (1984) *Middleton Stoney, Excavation and Survey in a North Oxfordshire Parish*
Rait, J.M. (1939) 'Political history', in L.F. Salzman ed., *Victoria County History, Oxfordshire* 1, 429–435
Robinson, M. (1973) 'Excavations at Copt Hay, Tetsworth', in D.A. Hinton & T. Rowley eds., 'Excavations on the route of the M40', *Oxoniensia* 38, 41–115
Rodwell, K. ed. (1975) *Historic Towns in Oxfordshire*. Oxfordshire Archaeol. Unit Survey No. 3
Rollason, D. (1978) 'List of saints' resting places in Anglo-Saxon England', *Anglo-Saxon England* 7, 61–94
Rowley, T. (1974) 'Early Saxon settlement in Dorchester', in T. Rowley ed., *Anglo-Saxon Settlement and Landscape*. BAR 6, 42–50
Rowley, T. & Brown, L. (1981) 'Excavations at Beech House Hotel, Dorchester-on-Thames, 1972', *Oxoniensia* 46, 1–55
Salter, H.E. (1907) 'Ecclesiastical history', in W.Page (ed.), *Victoria County History, Oxfordshire* 2, 1–3
Sawyer, P.H. (1962) 'Dorchester Hundred', in M.D. Lobel (ed.), *Victoria County History, Oxfordshire* 7, 1–4
Seaby, W.A. & Woodfield, P. (1980) 'Viking stirrups from England and their background', *Med. Archaeol.* 24, 87–122
Sherwood, J. & Pevsner, N. (1974) *Buildings of England: Oxfordshire*
Stenton, F.M. (1913) *The Early History of the Abbey at Abingdon*
Stenton, F.M. (1936) 'St. Frideswide and her times', *Oxoniensia* 1, 103–112
Stenton, F.M. (1939) 'Domesday Survey', in L.F. Salzman (ed.), *Victoria County History, Oxfordshire* 1, 372–395
Sturdy, D.A.M. (1972) 'Excavations in St. Peter-in-the-East church, Oxford', *Oxoniensia* 37, 245
Taylor, C. (1975) *Fields in the English Landscape*
Taylor, H.M. & Taylor, J. (1968) *Anglo-Saxon Architecture*
Wolffe, B.P. (1957) 'Beckley' in M.D. Lobel (ed.), *Victoria County History, Oxfordshire* 5, 63–64
Woolner, D. (1965) 'The White Horse, Uffington', *Trans. Newbury Dist. Fld. Club* 11, 3, 27–44

ARCHAEOLOGY OF OXFORD CITY

TOM HASSALL

Since the Middle Ages, scholars have sought to understand the origins of the City and the University. The first attempts were of an uncritical nature and where the evidence was lacking antiquaries were perfectly prepared to invent a mythical history ascribing the foundation of the town to Mempric in 1009 BC. Many of these myths were believed as late as the early eighteenth century (Parker 1885, 5–62). However, this period also saw the first attempts to reconstruct the history and topography of the City from the mass of documentary sources which survive. In the seventeenth century Brian Twyne (c. 1579–1644) (Clarke 1889–99, 17–18) and later Anthony Wood (1632–95) laid the foundations for the conventional historical research into the City's past. This research has continued into our own century with the well known detailed topographical studies of H.E. Salter (1863–1951) (1936; 1960–69) and with the publication in 1979 of the Victoria County History of Oxford (VCH).

Archaeology itself has had a surprisingly long tradition in the City. The first recorded excavation was in 1583 when a dispute over land ownership necessitated an excavation to establish the line of the City Wall (Turner 1880, 433). But it was not until the nineteenth century that the potential of archaeology began to be recognized. From that time it was seen that in Oxford, like all medieval cities, there were two aspects to archaeological research: first, the evidence of standing structures; second, the evidence from beneath the ground. The former method was pioneered by J.C. Buckler (1793–1894), who with his father is known for his topographical drawings (1951) but less well known for his detailed surveys of buildings during demolition. Their work has preserved a mass of architectural evidence at a time of great change in the City. The second method owed its original impetus to scholars like Herbert Hurst (1900), J.H. Parker (1885) and other members of the Oxford Architectural and Historical Society who carried out pioneering historical and topographical research into the City's past. The most extensive of the early excavations was conducted on the site of the Angel Inn during the construction of the Examination Schools in 1876 (Bruce-Mitford & Jope 1940, 42–4). However, the full scope of archaeology was not recognized until 1937 during the building of the New Bodleian Library. Pantin recorded in detail the medieval and later buildings on the site, developing the techniques which he was later to describe as 'Above Ground Archaeology' (1937). Pantin was to go on to make the study of urban domestic buildings in Oxford and elsewhere, his particular field of interest (1947; 1962–3; 1964). While Pantin recorded the buildings on the site, Bruce-Mitford (1939) recorded the evidence contained in the medieval rubbish pits and wells which are now such a familiar aspect of urban archaeology. Bruce-Mitford's research enabled him to establish the basic typology of medieval pottery for Oxford, probably the first time that this had been attempted for any town. The work at the New Bodleian can claim to be one of the first English medieval urban 'rescue excavations'.

The excavations at the New Bodleian Library established the importance of archaeological examination during redevelopment and demonstrated the basic techniques which were to be employed. The opportunities to put these ideas into practice came from the late 1950s when the commercial centre of Oxford began to be developed. Oxford was fortunate in that it had escaped bombing during the Second World War. But immediately after the war the City began to discuss various plans to demolish and rebuild the commercial centre (Sharp 1948). Pre-war industrial development had led to a massive population growth. Much of the City's nineteenth-century housing was inadequate and overcrowded, and shopping facilities were considered insufficient.

From the late 1940s until the present day a series of development schemes have been discussed. Although these schemes have varied in detail they have all had certain common factors. These factors have been: the need to preserve the historic buildings of the eastern two-thirds of the medieval town; the opportunities in the remaining western third to replace commercial buildings and housing mostly of recent date; finally, the importance of preserving the famous skyline of Oxford by restricting the height of buildings and therefore encouraging underground servicing of shops.

The actual development which has taken place has so far fallen into three distinct phases. Each development phase has also seen a different form of archaeological response. The first phase began in 1954 with a piecemeal development of the traditional historic commercial centre of Cornmarket Street and Queen Street. In this area comparatively few old buildings survived and virtually all those remaining were destroyed to make way for the development. The archaeological investigation of these sites was coordinated at the Ashmolean Museum and depended largely on the work of Pantin, Jope and Sturdy. The most important of the sites examined was that of the Clarendon Hotel when it was demolished to build Woolworths, now the Clarendon Centre. Pantin (1958) examined the buildings during demolition and was able to reconstruct their history. Jope (1958) with Sturdy (1959) carried out limited excavations during the actual construction. The physical evidence was then combined with the documentary history of the ownership of the site to

115

produce a total history of this part of commercial Oxford. Thanks to excavations such as this and in particular to Jope's synthesis of the evidence (1956) the outlines of the late Saxon and early medieval archaeology of the City were becoming clear.

The first phase of development came to an end in 1964 when the City Council decided to begin the wholesale redevelopment of the western part of the medieval town. Although the development proposals covered a wide area, the centre-piece of this development was in the parish of St. Ebbe's where a shopping centre, the Westgate Centre, with underground servicing and associated car parks was built. The scale of these proposals was such that the existing archaeological arrangements in the City based on the Ashmolean Museum and on an *ad hoc* committee formed to co-ordinate the excavations had insufficient resources to meet the challenge. This challenge was clearly spelt out in a report compiled in 1966 by Benson and Cook of the Oxford City and County Museum (founded in 1965), now the Oxfordshire Department of Museum Services. This report, entitled *City of Oxford, Archaeological Implications*, was a pioneering study which was to be copied subsequently in numerous British towns. The report spelt out in language intelligible to the City Council, to the City's planners and to potential developers, the scale of archaeological destruction and the measures required to record this heritage. The publication of this report led to the formation in 1967 of a full-time team of archaeologists in the City under the auspices of the Oxford Archaeological Excavation Committee. Since 1973, the excavations have been under the control of the Oxfordshire, now Oxford, Archaeological Unit with one field officer, Brian Durham, responsible for excavations in the City. The organization of the Unit follows the model which was first established by Biddle in Winchester and has now also been followed in many major cities such as York and Lincoln. The Unit is an independent organization quite separate from the City's two museums or the University but working closely with these institutions. Funding comes from central and local government and sponsorship of many kinds.

During the second phase of development it was possible for the small permanent team of excavators supplemented by voluntary labour to carry out a mixed programme of area and selective excavations combined with the observation of the actual construction of new foundations. These excavations were concerned with such topics as the origins of the medieval City, the plan and date of the defences and the streets, the layout and nature of domestic buildings, and the examination of more specialized buildings such as the Castle, parish **churches and religious houses (Hassall 1972c; 1974a; 1975b).**

In retrospect, the second phase of development was comparatively shortlived and it had come to an end by 1975 when the Westgate shopping centre was officially opened. Even before 1975 the scale of the development had begun to change. Economic pressures combined with a growing concern for the conservation of buildings meant that very large-scale developments were no longer attractive. Instead old buildings have been refurbished and only smaller new buildings have been built. Ironically, this third phase of development has made the archaeology more difficult. Small sites tend to be developed rapidly and large basements are no longer commercially viable. It follows that the recent excavations have tended to be either very small or confined to watching the foundations of buildings under construction. The choice of sites has been even more selective than in the past and they are aimed at answering very specific problems particularly relevant to the earliest history of the town. Nevertheless, the presence of a full-time team of archaeologists has meant that even small-scale excavations and salvage recording can make a significant contribution to our knowledge (Hassall 1982).

In summarizing the results of this long tradition of archaeological research one must begin with the geographical setting of the City. Oxford has a classic Upper Thames siting. It is situated like so many of the oldest settlements where the main river is joined by a tributary. The Thames and its floodplain define the settlement to the south and west and the Cherwell and its smaller floodplain to the east. The town itself was to develop at the southern end of the Summertown-Radley gravel terrace which lies between the two rivers. Its siting was therefore one of relative inaccessibility but with natural defence potential. Only from the north was access unimpeded by rivers.

A variety of soils was available to the earliest farmers ranging from the well-drained gravel terrace to the low-lying floodplain. The gravel terrace is well suited to arable while the floodplain provided and still provides pasture. However, in prehistoric times the floodplain was considerably drier than at present, allowing occupation at, for instance, Port Meadow which is now regularly flooded (Robinson 1980a; Robinson and Lambrick 1984).

Prehistoric finds are relatively scarce from the site of the town. There have been comparatively few recent finds, certainly nothing to alter the generally accepted pattern of early settlement (Hassall 1972, 139–143; Radcliffe 1961–2). Sturdy (1961–2a, 30 and 33) has pointed out the concentration of Neolithic material from the area around Christ Church. The suggestion that this might have been the site of a major settlement similar to that of the causewayed enclosure at Abingdon is certainly an attractive theory. In the Bronze Age the remains of barrows are known from the floodplain on Port Meadow (Atkinson 1942; Lambrick 1982) while there now appears to have been a linear barrow cemetery at the University Parks (Fig. 12). In the Science Area, immediately adjoining the Parks, a double-ditched barrow has been partially excavated (Durham 1983d). A Beaker burial has been found in the **low-lying suburbs at the Hamel in St. Thomas' Street** and the evidence points to a Beaker period settlement site nearby (Palmer 1980, 128–134).

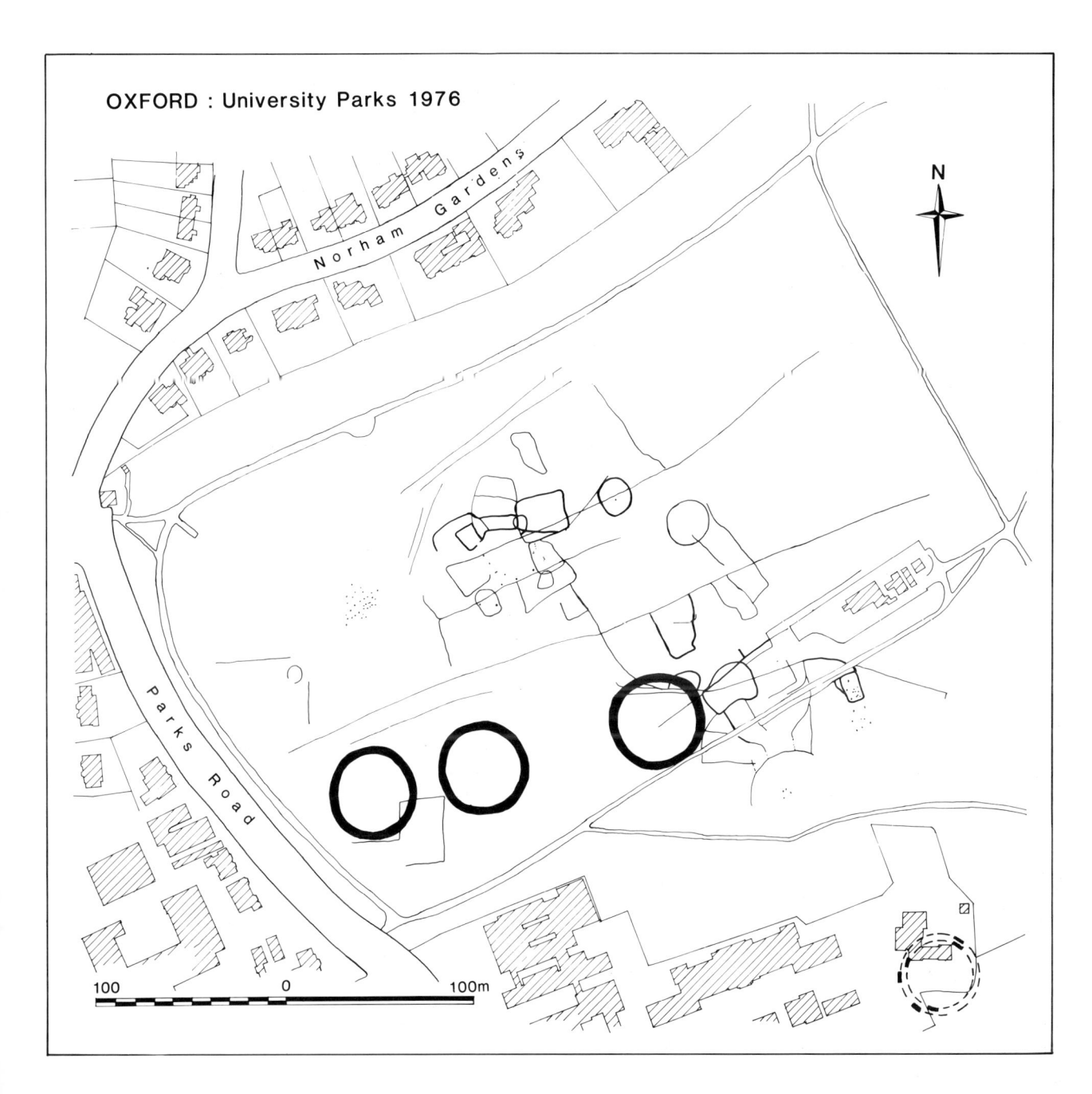

Figure 12. *Cropmarks, University Parks*

Port Meadow has also produced the clearest evidence for Iron Age occupation (Atkinson 1942; Lambrick 1983). Undated sites of possibly similar character are also now known from air photographs of Oxford City football ground and the University Parks (Wilson 1982, 62–3). The enclosures now known to exist at the Parks may well also be of Roman date, since fairly dense Roman settlement has been recognized for North Oxford since the last century (Munby 1972). The most extensive area recently examined has been in Parks Road in front of the University Museum where a ditch and burials were recorded (Hassall 1972a). The north Oxford settlements were probably strung out along a Roman road following approximately the line of the modern Banbury Road. This Roman road ran southwards to cross the floodplain at North Hinksey to head for the unwalled town now known to have existed at Frilford (Hingley 1982).

A branch off this north-south road crossed the floodplain south of Donnington Bridge and presumably joins the main Roman road from Alchester to Dorchester (ibid.). This link road would have served the Roman pottery kilns which are such a feature of the archaeology of modern East Oxford. Young's excavations at the Churchill Hospital in Headington have now become the type site for these Oxford potteries (Young 1972, 1973a and b, 1974).

Evidence for pagan Saxon occupation is sparse and no settlement has yet been identified. However, one can infer that by the eighth century much, if not all, the site of the later town formed part of a royal estate whose centre was to the east at Headington (Cam 1936). At this time the country north of the Thames lay within the kingdom of Mercia with the Thames forming the frontier with Wessex. Stenton (1936) has discussed the legendary history of Oxford and both he and later commentators have supported the view that the history of Saxon Oxford begins *c.* 727. At about that time St. Frideswide, presumably a Mercian noblewoman, is reputed to have founded a monastery on or near the site of the present Cathedral. It is likely that this monastery would have followed contemporary Kentish custom (Rigold 1968). It would, therefore, have been a 'double monastery', in other words a house for both monks and nuns, under the rule of an abbess, presumably St. Frideswide in the first instance. Nothing is known of this early foundation and indeed the first certain reference to it is not until 1004 when it is recorded that it had been burnt down during the 1002 massacre of the Danes in Oxford. However, the likelihood of an early ecclesiastical use of the site has been supported by the discovery of 'charcoal' burials in Tom Quad at Christ Church immediately to the west of the church of the medieval Augustinian Priory of St. Frideswide's (Hassall 1973, 270–4). Radiocarbon dates of these burials indicate a date in the second quarter of the ninth century.

At Abingdon and elsewhere in the Thames Valley the existence of an early monastic site led to the development of first a lay settlement and then a town (Rodwell 1975, 25–34; 109–117). No evidence for such a Mercian settlement has yet been found, but Christ Church would probably occupy the most likely site. The earliest signs of occupation have come from nearby and are associated with the development of the river crossing to the south. Excavations by Durham (1977) at 79–80 St. Aldate's have shown that by the late eighth century it became possible to cross the floodplain of the Thames to the south and that the line of the later St. Aldate's and Abingdon road crossing began to be developed. This southern route formed by natural islands, causeways and fords was to become the main route into Oxford across the river and completely superseded the old crossing at North Hinksey (Davis 1973). In St. Aldate's the evidence points towards the construction of an artificial embankment which can be dated to the reign of Offa of Mercia (757–796). Such a crossing would have played an important part in the economic expansion of Mercia which was a land-locked kingdom with no direct access to the south coast and the important West Saxon port of Southampton (Metcalf 1977). In order that the crossing could be used all the year round the roadway had to be above general flood level and where no firm-bottomed fords existed the bed of the Thames was stabilized. The original clay bank in St. Aldate's was heightened in the first half of the ninth century and silting took place in the upstream side, perhaps encouraged by the building of groins. Under the new Crown Court, formerly the Morris Garages, further south in St. Aldate's, an artificial stone ford has been found which is not later than the ninth or tenth century, but may originally have dated to *c.* 800 (Durham 1982e). This ford became silted up and was probably abandoned in the late eleventh century; by this time at least one of the other branches of the river may also have had a wooden bridge (Durham 1980b). This north-south road through Oxford was to become one of the major arteries of late Saxon and medieval England and replaced the Roman road from Alchester to Dorchester.

The development of Mercian Oxford during the ninth century is not at all clear, but by the early tenth century, if not before, the town had already become the head of a district. As a Mercian frontier town it is conceivable that Oxford was defended like Hereford (Biddle 1976, 23–27; Shoesmith 1982, 74–80). It was certainly defended by 911 by which time Wessex gained control over Mercia and it was brought within the West Saxon scheme of fortified towns or *burhs*. These fortifications were the work of Alfred as one of his measures to combat Scandinavian Viking attacks on his kingdom (Radford 1970). Some of the *burhs*, notably Wareham, Wallingford and Cricklade, display a very rectangular plan in the line of their walls and have a regular grid of streets (Biddle and Hill 1971), while excavations at Winchester have shown that, even where Alfred was reusing Roman defences, internal streets were regularly laid out.

It is possible that Oxford's defences and street pattern were the work of Alfred. Alfred has certainly always been connected with the town in legend. The main archaeological evidence is the 'Orsnaforda' pennies whose originals may have been minted in the town (Cooper 1979, 7). However, the first dated reference to Oxford is in Alfred's son's reign. In 911 Edward the Elder (899–924) took control of the town and it is probably still safest to assume that it was he who was responsible for the town's defences. It is also now virtually certain that he laid out the basic street grid. At the time that these works took place it must be assumed that in addition to St. Frideswide's there must have been a lay settlement so far undiscovered. However, later references to the 'king's eight virgates of land' imply that a very substantial enlargement of the town took place.

The only direct documentary reference to the town's late Saxon defences is contained in the *Burghal Hidage* which provides information on the likely length of the defended perimeter of the town (Hill 1969). It is now agreed that the topographical evidence points towards the original fortifications being smaller than their medieval successors (Hassall 1975a). The Northgate and Southgate were probably in the same position as the medieval north and south gates and marked by the two churches of St. Michael. The original Eastgate may have been near the church of St. Mary the Virgin in the High Street while the western line would have more or less coincided with the eastern defences of the later Norman Castle. In other words, the plan of the town would have been rectangular. A bank and ditch would have been required on its northern, western and eastern sides, but to the south side the line of the Trill Mill stream would have provided a natural defence (CBA 1979; Durham 1983c). The northern line is certain and the early bank, probably later strengthened with a stone facing, and its associated ditch have been investigated at St. Michael's at the Northgate (Durham *et al.* 1983, 14–18; Fig. 13). The sequence can be compared to that at Cricklade (Radford 1972). The north-western corner of the ditch south of George Street has also been identified (ibid. 18–23). In view of this alignment, the Saxon ditch which ran north-south to the west of St. Ebbe's church does not now seem a likely candidate for the western defences (Hassall 1971a, 3–6). The eastern line is more problematic, although the idea of a defensive line running between Catte Street/Magpie Lane and medieval School Street (now the western side of Radcliffe Square)/Oriel Street is supported by a possible southern return in the wall by the old Bodleian Library (Penny 1899) and a ditch in Corpus Christi College (Hassall 1973, 274).

Within the defences the town would have possessed a well-developed street grid. The St. Aldate's/Cornmarket Street line must predate the defences and there must also have been a route to the east, presumably crossing the Cherwell at the ford by the later Magdalen Bridge. Cornmarket Street may originally have been wider than the medieval street (Sturdy

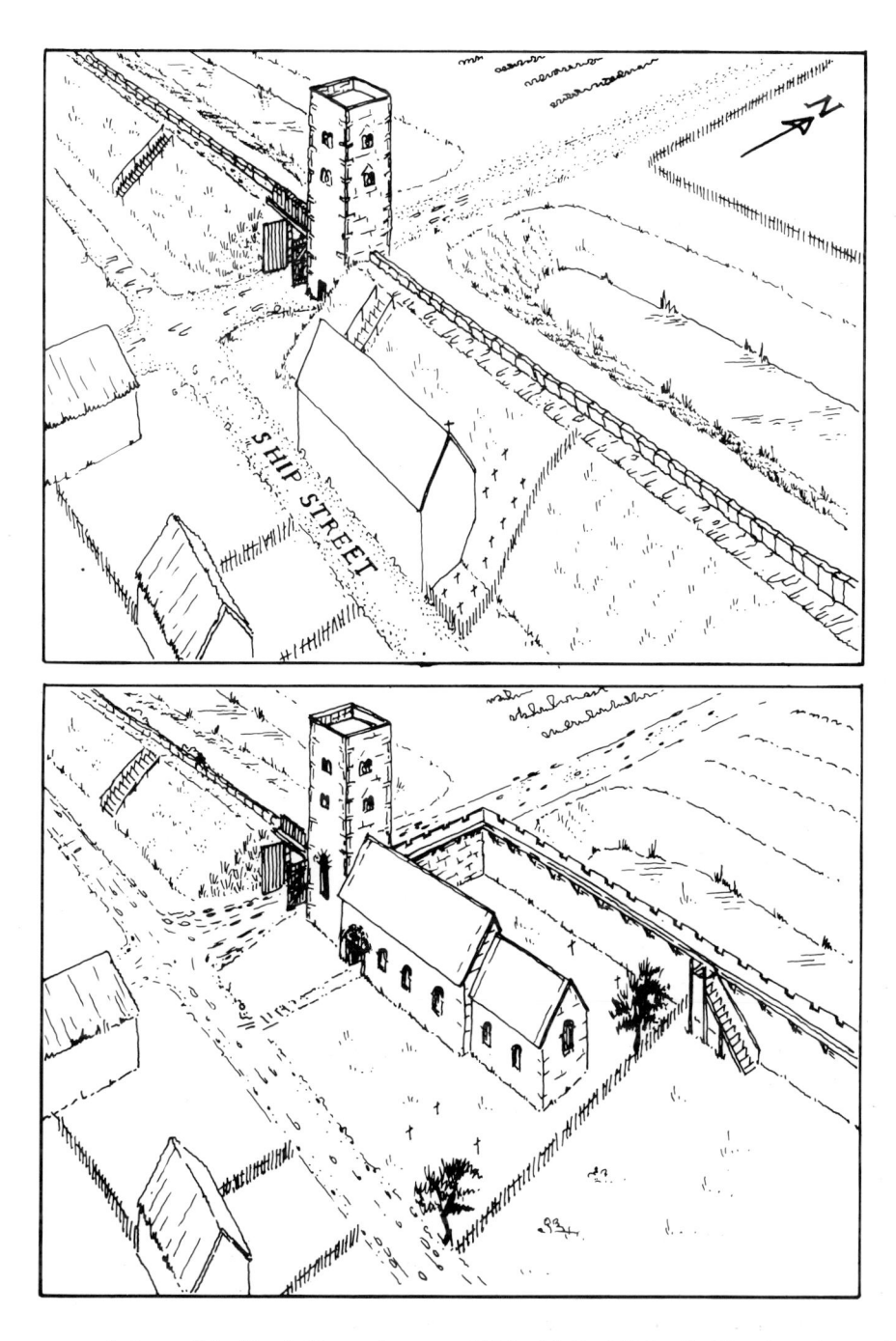

Figure 13. *Reconstructed views of the North Gate: above, c. 1086 with St. Michael's Church conjectured along Ship Street; below, the early 12th-century church built against the gate tower, occupying an enlarged churchyard created by the defensive diversion*

119

1961–2, 6) while St. Aldate's was given a metalled surface which is now recognized as a characteristic of all Oxford's early streets (Durham 1981b). Primary metalling has been recognized in the east-west axis of High Street and Queen Street (Fig. 14). In High Street the original topsoil was stripped off before the metalling was laid and there was a central drain with a timber lining (Durham 1982b); by contrast in Queen Street the topsoil was retained (Hassall 1970, 9). Primary metalling has also been recognized in side streets including the former Church Street and the Turl (Durham 1982f) which was originally straight until All Saints Church blocked off its southern end. Metalling has also been recorded in Catte Street, but since this lies outside the putative original *burh* its existence is rather anomalous (Durham 1981b). The similarity of the metalling throughout the central area and its marked contrast with later poor quality street surfaces points towards deliberate laying-out at one moment in time. The best clue as to the date of this operation is provided by an Edward the Elder penny found resting on the primary surface of New Inn Hall Street (Durham 1980a). This street has been suggested as part of an original intra-mural street system which can be seen in the plan of the northern and eastern sides of the town.

It is only possible to speculate how the ground between the original grid of streets was subdivided. Early documentary evidence relating to properties seems to suggest that individual landowners might possess substantial blocks of properties like that referred to in 1005 when Eynsham Abbey acquired an Oxford estate which included St. Ebbe's church. Later evidence, particularly the Hundred Rolls survey of 1279, points in the same direction. For example, Blair (1978) has suggested that Frewin Hall and its dependent holdings in the thirteenth century seem to represent a large 'urban estate'. However, he warned that such a grouping need not necessarily be of Late Saxon origins. The same caveat is true of the thirteenth-century properties of Abingdon Abbey which Bond (1979) has demonstrated to cluster within the nucleus of the presumed original *burh* and the lower part of St. Aldate's which was developing as a suburb in the second quarter of the tenth century (Durham 1977). Salter (1914) argued that many of the town's thirteenth-century property boundaries did indeed go back to the original laying-out of the town. But recent excavations have suggested that Salter's idea must be treated with caution so far as the property boundaries at right angles to the street are concerned. These properties may have been brought about by the subdivision of original larger blocks (Hassall 1971b). However, the property boundaries at the rear of later medieval tenements and common to all properties fronting on to a particular street are much more likely to be of ancient origin. Similarly, parish boundaries are likely to provide clues as to some, but not necessarily all, of the earliest boundaries (see below). In the original layout of the town some parts of the town may have been left open and undivided in order to provide places of refuge for neighbouring villages, although even open areas may have been designated for the use of particular estates. In Domesday many rural manors possessed properties in the town which were responsible for the maintenance of the wall. This system of 'mural mansions' may reflect part of the original tenth-century arrangements.

It is clear that whatever the property divisions of the tenth-century town, the major street frontages soon became developed. In spite of later cellar digging the most characteristic surviving features of the Late Saxon town are the bottoms of the ubiquitous cellar pits which were first recognized in Cornmarket Street by Jope (1958; cf. Durham 1984a) at the Clarendon Hotel. Further later Saxon cellars have been found on both the west and on the east side of the street by Cherry, Hassall and Sturdy (Oxford Excavations Committee 1963; Hassall 1971b; Sturdy 1960). The evidence for the east side of the street suggests that the street frontage originally lay further east than at present and that the whole street was considerably wider (Sturdy 1960).

On the east-west axis both High Street and Queen Street had built-up frontages. At All Saints church Durham (Hassall 1974a, 54–73; Durham 1981c) found that on the three surviving areas of original topsoil were quantities of very pure carbonized wheat which have produced early tenth-century radiocarbon dates and may be associated with the original laying-out of the site. The first property division on the site dated to the early to mid-tenth century when a sequence of buildings begin. The property boundary remained static until the construction of the first church on the site in the second half of the eleventh century (see below). The site produced one of the most substantial cellars so far discovered in Oxford. It dated to the early eleventh century and must have belonged to a building 3.5m wide by 6.5m long. The cellar's walls were lined with wooden side-posts revetting a wall of horizontal planks. As so often with these Oxford cellar pits this one ended its days as a massive cesspit. Further westwards at 13 High Street more cellar pits have been found (Hassall 1973, 276–80). On the Queen Street frontage the evidence is much the same with cellars on both north and south sides of the street (Davison 1961; Oxford Excavation Committee 1963; Halpin 1983).

Behind the major street frontages the hinterland of the blocks formed by the streets also began to be developed by the eleventh century, although some of the side streets were not opened up until the twelfth century (see below). For instance, evidence from the excavation of the Hinksey Hall site at the centre of the island formed by Queen Street, St. Aldate's, Pembroke Street and St. Ebbe's Street showed that the centre of this island had Late Saxon buildings on it (Halpin 1983). How access to this site was achieved in Late Saxon times is not clear but it may have been from the later Kepeharm's Lane. In the island formed by Cornmarket Street, Queen Street, New Inn Hall Street and St. Michael's Street floors of a probable eleventh-century building have been found fronting Shoe Lane (Durham 1980a).

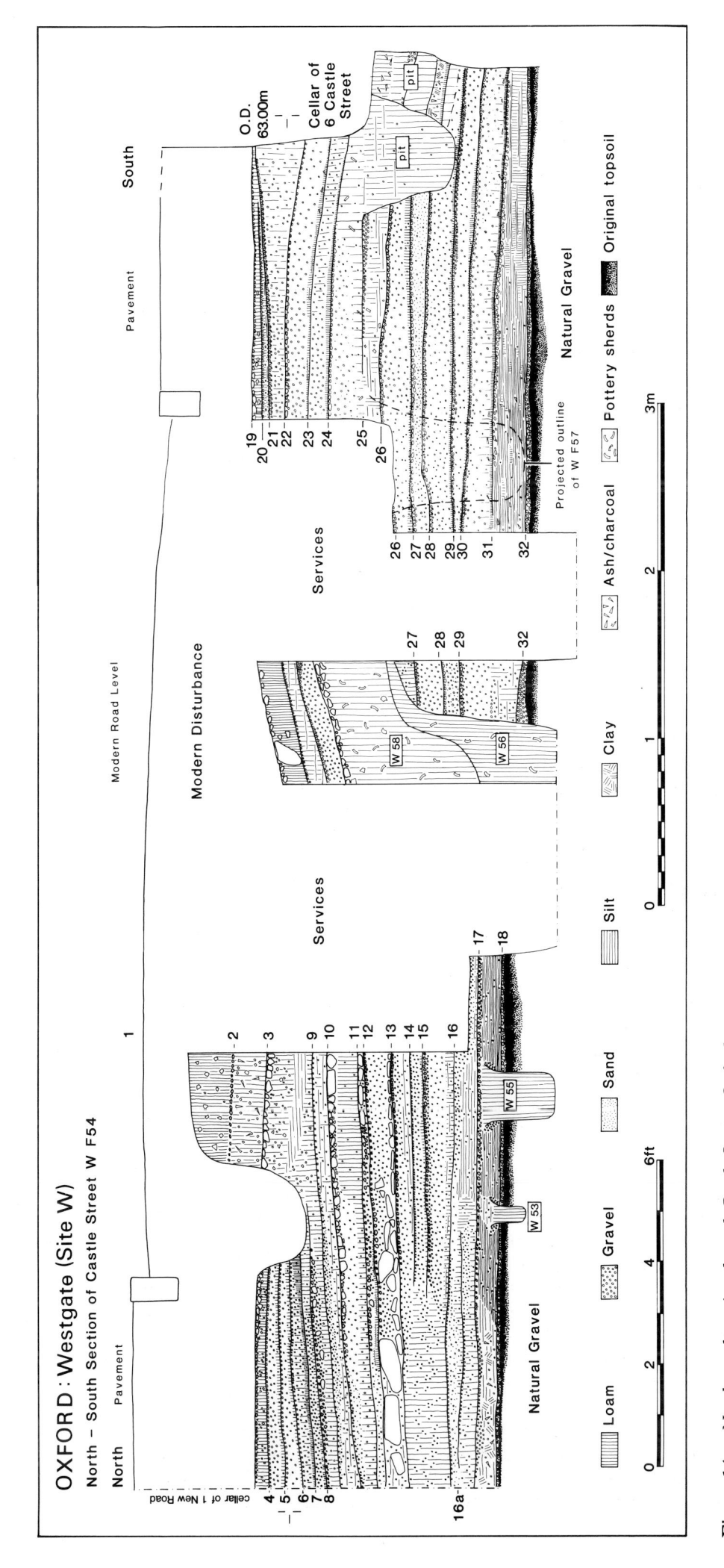

Figure 14. *North-south section through Castle Street, Oxford*

121

Although it is clear that the area within the walls became fully developed during the tenth century, the evidence has come largely from the distribution of cellar pits and rubbish pits rather than from coherent building plans. The excavation sites have, however, produced large quantities of pottery so that it has been possible to amplify the pioneering studies of Bruce-Mitford and Jope (1940). Mellor (1980a) has now been able to take advantage of the well stratified sequence from St. Aldate's (Durham 1977) and further finds from under the Castle (Hassall 1976) to begin to synthesize the evidence for the development of the main types of Late Saxon pottery. The pottery evidence will soon be matched by a synthesis of the animal bone evidence.

In addition to domestic sites a number of the town's churches are known to be pre-Conquest, although the foundation date of many is problematic. There were two and possibly four churches at the original gates: St. Michael's at the Northgate with its eleventh-century tower, St. Michael at the Southgate, St. Mary the Virgin and possibly St. Peter-le-Bailey. These are likely candidates for early foundations. It has been argued, however, that the existing tower of St. Michael at the Northgate may have been separate from the original foundation (Durham *et al.* 1983). Archaeological evidence is lacking for most of the other churches. St. Peter-in-the-East seems to have been preceded by an earlier wooden building (Sturdy 1972a).

While the open spaces within the centre of the town were filling up, suburbs began to develop in the areas outside the defences. In St. Aldate's, the south suburb, Durham (1977) showed that this development began to develop in the second quarter of the tenth century and then continued in an unbroken sequence. Significantly this suburb was the only suburb outside the later medieval wall line which was legally considered to be part of the town (Cam 1963, 117; Keene 1975, 75–6). There is no clear evidence for the north suburb although the church of St. Mary Magdalen is probably pre-Conquest. The history of the development of the original western suburb which probably reached down to the Thames has been confused by the later building of the Castle. However, the discovery of Late Saxon buildings under the Castle first made by Jope (1952–3) and later by Hassall (1976) suggests that Queen Street continued outside the original Saxon Westgate and was lined with buildings. Similar development must have been taking place along High Street between St. Mary's (the presumed site of the original east gate) and the later medieval east gate.

By the Conquest the original eastern suburb had been brought within the defences. This eastern extension is marked by the changes of alignment in the northern and southern wall lines at Smith gate (the northern end of Catte Street) and between Christ Church and Corpus. The date of this extension is unclear but the most likely period would be in the early eleventh century during the period of renewed Danish activity. Following the massacre of the Danes in Oxford the town was itself burnt in 1009. At All Saints Church there is evidence for major burning taking place in the early eleventh century (Durham 1981c). It is inevitably tempting to associate this fire and the finds of Viking-type stirrups from the Cherwell at Magdalen Bridge (Seaby and Woodfield 1980) with the known raid on Oxford. Certainly a disruption took place in the output of the Oxford mint at this time (Lyon 1966), although the fact that royal councils were held in the town shows that it was not completely devastated.

The most obvious effect on Oxford of the Norman Conquest was the building of the Castle by Robert d'Oilly in 1071 (VCH 296–299; Hassall 1971d). The construction of the castle led to the complete disruption of the original western suburb as has been mentioned above. Not only were houses destroyed, but the road to the west had to be diverted south of the new castle site. The castle itself is situated in a classic Norman setting with its eastern side incorporating virtually the entire length of the original Late Saxon western defences while its western side made use of the branch of the Thames which up to that time had defined the western growth of the town. The castle could thus control the town but at the same time its garrison had easy access to open countryside if ever the defences became indefensible. The river whose level was controlled by the castle mill also provided a source of water for the moat which surrounded the castle.

The history of the castle is well known. Only on two occasions in 1142 and in 1216 did the castle actually need to withstand a major siege. It was never as important as, say, its neighbour at Wallingford. So far as archaeology is concerned the greatest interest has been in the pre-castle levels rather than the castle itself. The only examination of the Keep and the chapel of St. George was that by King (1796) which took place in the late eighteenth century before the building of the prison. Otherwise the present buildings of County Hall and the prison, while preserving the administrative and penal functions of the castle, likewise seal its archaeology. The only recent opportunities for excavation have been provided by the County Council's gradual development of the site which has provided opportunities to examine parts of the western and eastern moats, while the building of Westgate Centre allowed the discovery and recording of the eastern barbican (Hassall 1976). This barbican was built in 1216 by Fawkes de Bréauté. The construction involved the demolition of the church of St. Budoc which originally stood opposite the main eastern gateway. The site of this church has also been identified (ibid.). Apart from confirming the position of the barbican these excavations have not added much to our knowledge of the castle itself, but the waterlogged conditions of the moat have produced an interesting collection of finds, notably of late medieval leatherwork.

Robert d'Oilly may also have built Oxford's great southern bridge and causeway system, the Grandpont, which linked the town with Abingdon (Fig. 15). As has been shown, a southern route out of the town had existed since the late eighth century but the various

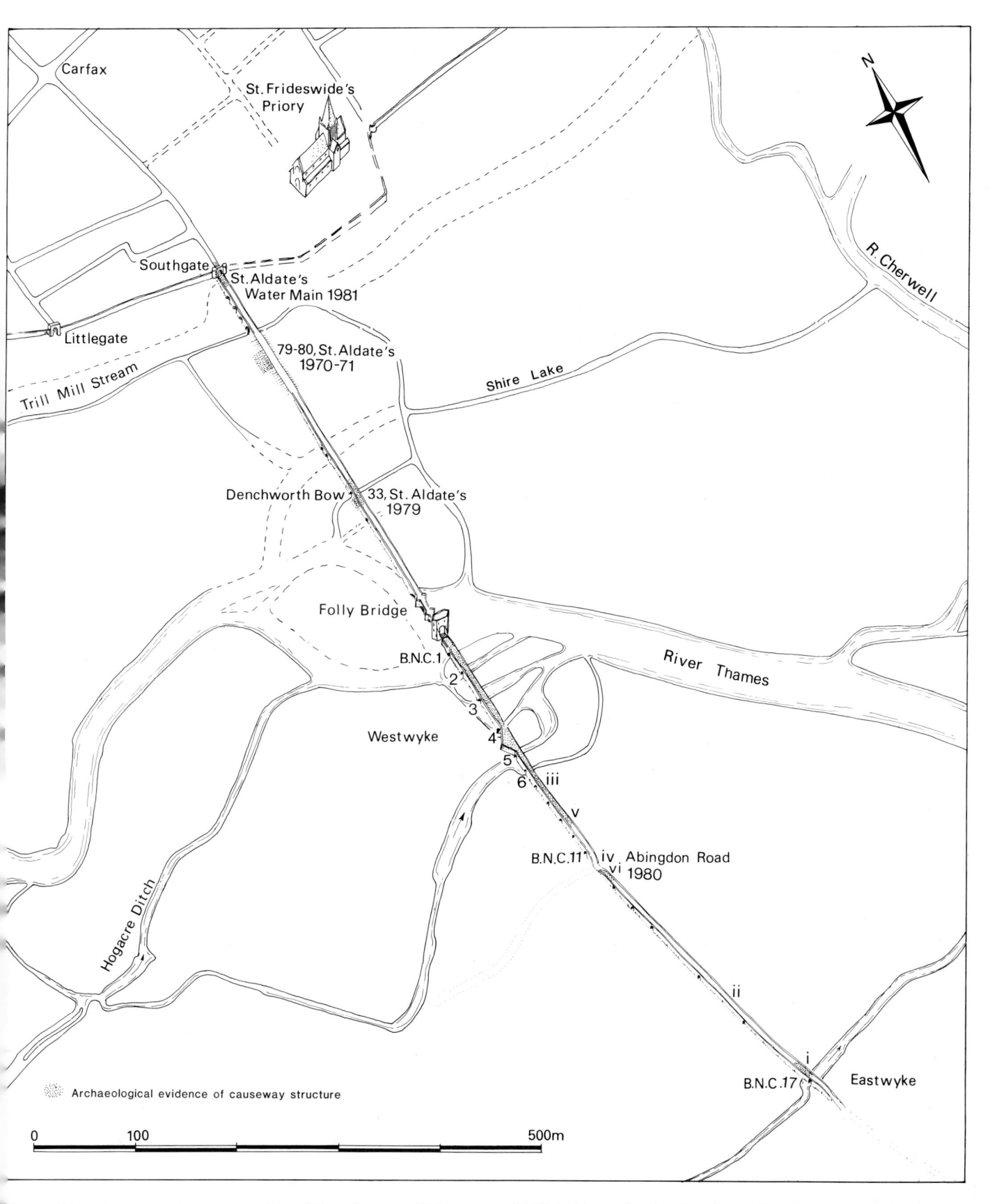

Figure 15. *Axonometric reconstruction of Grandpont c. 13th century: BNC 1–17 are flood-arches depicted on Brasenose College map of the 16th century*

excavations in St. Aldate's have also provided tangible evidence for the Norman bridge system in addition to those arches which are already known to have survived under the Abingdon Road. Observations by Durham show how some of the natural river channels had already began to silt up by the eleventh century (1982e; 1983c) and at least one early artificial ford and a possible early bridge (1980b) were replaced by stone arches

123

linked by a stone causeway which extended underneath both St. Aldate's and the Abingdon Road (1981a).

While Robert d'Oilly was involved in major military and civil engineering the evidence of Domesday suggests that the town itself was at least temporarily in a fairly wasted state. The record suggests that there were many derelict properties within the town. In part this dereliction can be explained by the building of the castle but there must have been additional factors such as either other damage suffered at the Conquest or a more natural disaster like a major fire. It is in this context that Sturdy has suggested that a major replanning of the town may have taken place in the early twelfth century. The chief element of this replanning is a suggested realignment of Cornmarket Street when the western side may have been set back and the east side brought forward (Sturdy 1961–2b; Sturdy 1972b).

However, Oxford's recession can only have been short-lived and the occupied area began to expand both inside and outside the walls. Within the walls the archaeological evidence for this expansion comes from the evidence for the opening up of new streets which provided new frontages for development within the larger Late Saxon property blocks. Thus in the original nucleus of the tenth-century town Brasenose Lane and St. Frideswide's Lane (now part of Christ Church) were opened up in the early to mid twelfth century (Sturdy 1961–2a, 31–2). In the walled suburb to the east Kybald Street (now only surviving in part) and Logic Lane also date from c.1130 (Radcliffe 1961–2). Suburban growth was also marked. Domesday refers to houses both within and without the wall. St. Aldate's was certainly developed by this time. Excavations by Durham (1977) showed that development had already begun there in the tenth century, but by the second half of the eleventh century at 79–80 St. Aldate's at least the frontage had become firmly established. St. Giles' to the north had probably reached its full length by 1150. Its wide form is very suggestive of an external market-place outside the north gate although there is no evidence for its use as a market. Possibly its spacious area was used as a marshalling ground for goods before they entered the town (Keene 1975, 82). There is no archaeological evidence for the growth of the eastern suburb to the ford and bridge at Eastbridge (now Magdalen Bridge) although the hospital of St. John had become established by the end of the twelfth century.

The clearest excavated evidence for suburban growth comes from the western suburb of St. Thomas' (Fig. 16). Here low-lying conditions and an undisturbed street frontage have allowed Palmer (1980) to uncover the building sequence which begins in the late twelfth century. At the time of Domesday this part of west Oxford was divided between the holdings of Robert d'Oilly and Roger d'Ivry. The d'Oilly holding was given to Oseney Abbey at its foundation in 1129. At this time the excavated evidence shows that St. Thomas' was divided by drainage ditches which subdivided meadows. In the late twelfth century Oseney began a development which on the basis of its long property boundary plots and back lane (The Hamel) has all the characteristics of deliberate planning rather than ribbon development. The excavations on the west side of The Hamel showed how two properties – the Hall of St. Helen and Bretel's – developed from this time.

The remaining suburb developed on the northern side of the extra-mural street (now George Street and Broad Street). Bruce-Mitford's pioneering excavation at the site of the New Bodleian extension remains the most graphic demonstration of the way in which this suburb developed in the thirteenth century until its growth was to be checked by the Black Death and subsequent depopulation in the late fourteenth century (Bruce-Mitford 1939).

In spite of Oxford's suburban growth there was no attempt, in the medieval period at least, to defend the houses outside the original walls, with the exception of a gate in the main south bridge and a drawbridge at the Eastgate (Hassall 1979). The line of the walls that had been established pre-Conquest remained the line with only minor alterations. There is little evidence for the wall during the twelfth century, although when King Stephen took the town it was described as strongly defended and the town's twelfth-century seal depicts schematically the town surrounded by a crenellated wall. It is only from 1226 when the town received a series of murage grants that it is assumed that the original earth rampart with stone facing was replaced by a free-standing stone wall with bastions. It was probably at this time that the north-western angle of the walls was realigned to meet the castle in a gentle curve rather than preserving the right-angle of the original Saxon line (Durham et al. 1983, 18–23). The wall was also realigned east of the north gate (ibid., 14–18). As the gate was extended progressively northwards so it was necessary to fill in the original Saxon ditch and create a local diversion in the wall and ditch. The first attempt at building a stone wall in the new position failed, perhaps because of inadequate foundations, and it was necessary to construct a wall on arched foundations. The wall was always stronger on this northern side of the town. The ditch (Daniell 1939) was water-filled and the stone wall itself (Hunter and Jope 1951) was defended by towers. Although some of the towers have disappeared their positions are known and one of the earliest modern excavations was of the tower which stood in the Clarendon Quadrangle (Penny 1899). Other bastions have been drastically altered like the one excavated in 1972 in St. Michael's Street (Hassall 1973, 285–6).

However, far and away the most unusual aspect of Oxford's defences was the double wall line which extended from Smithgate at the northern end of Catte Street to the Eastgate (Fig. 17). This outer wall included bastions in its northern side. The existence of these elaborate defences was proved by Palmer (1976) in excavations in St. Helen's Passage and Hertford College, where the wall and an original postern were found, and at 21 Longwall Street where the outer wall and the outer north-east corner bastion were also located (Durham et al. 1983, 23–26). No other town in

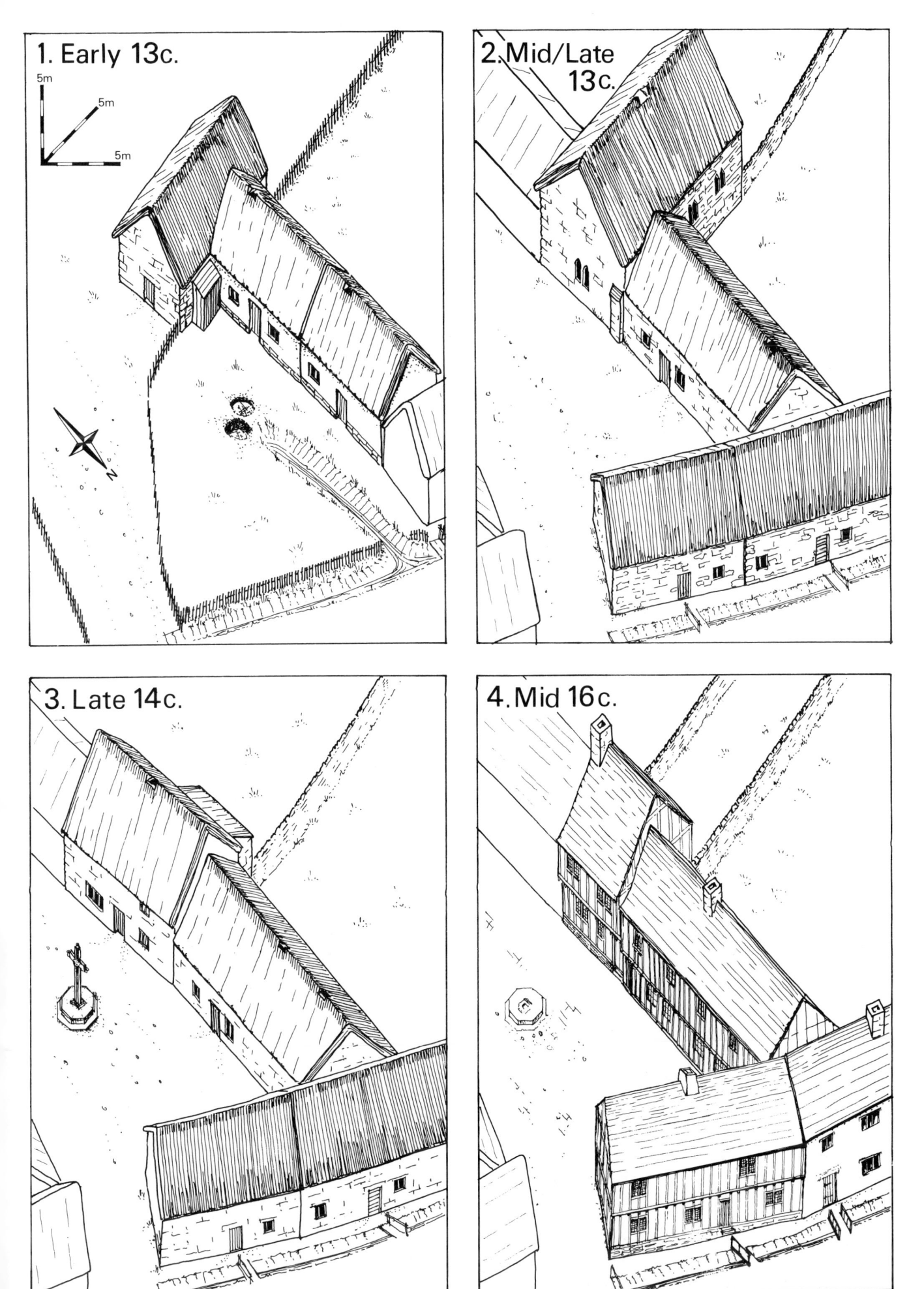

Figure 16. *The Hamel, Oxford: conjectural reconstruction of medieval tenements*

Figure 17. *Oxford's north-western defences: a reconstruction of the double wall line with New College Chapel and the Bell Tower, c. 1400*

England had this form of defence and it is probably best seen as an abortive attempt to apply the principles of concentric castle architecture to Oxford in the late thirteenth century.

In contrast with the north and east walls, the south side of the town was far less securely defended and, as previously, the defence must have relied heavily on the natural defences of the town. The wall survives in both Merton College (Hassall 1971c) and Corpus Christi College. In the latter college the wall now stops at a bastion, but originally turned southwards and then westwards to enclose the precinct of St. Frideswide's Priory. The bastion is, in other words, on an inside angle where under normal circumstances a bastion would not be required. This bastion has been extensively examined (Durham 1982a) and it now seems most likely that it was originally defending an eastern-facing postern and may indeed form the northern side of the postern itself.

The redevelopment of St. Ebbe's has allowed the examination of virtually the entire length of the wall from Littlegate to Westgate. The excavations uncovered the western side of the Littlegate itself and sections through the wall (Hassall 1970, 15–18; Hassall 1972b, 139–143). The wall at this point was complicated by the building of the Greyfriars' church in the 1240s across the line of the wall and no sign of the original defensive wall was seen. The interruption in the wall was supplied by the construction of the north wall of the church in such a way that it provided a continuation of the wall. The foundations of the north wall of the church which fulfilled the double function of church wall and defensive wall have been uncovered (Hassall 1970, 10–15; Hassall 1971, 6–8).

The pattern of property ownership and the layout of tenement boundaries both within and without the wall has been clear since Salter published his map of medieval Oxford (1934) supplemented by the two posthumous volumes of the Survey of Oxford (1960, 1969). Cooper (1972) has also worked out the thirteenth-century layout for St. Thomas'. So far as the structures which occupied these tenement plots are concerned the foundations of their study were laid by Pantin (1937), with his detailed and pioneering examination of the houses in Broad Street demolished to make way for the New Bodleian Library and his studies of Tackley's Inn (1942), the Clarendon Hotel (1958), and the schools and halls of the medieval University (1964). Pantin's synthesis of the medieval English town-house plans in general (1962–3) and his study of Oxford in particular (1947) still remain the standard reference works.

In view of the extent of Pantin's research and the comparative scarcity of surviving medieval domestic buildings it is perhaps surprising how much has been discovered in recent years. At Frewin Hall Blair (1978), following an original idea of Pantin, has recognized and recorded the cellar of a Norman mansion built between 1090 and 1150 which formed part of the principal residence of a large urban estate which later became St. Mary's College. This cellar is now the oldest surviving domestic structure in Oxford, whose only rival in date was the cellar recognized by Jope (1958) and Pantin (1958) beneath the Clarendon Hotel and which re-emerged briefly during the conversion of Woolworth's into the Clarendon Centre. Like the Frewin Hall cellar, this cellar was also only half-sunk into the ground. Durham (1984a) found that this cellar was built in two phases, the earlier perhaps before 1100 with the surviving vault (now reburied) added in the twelfth or thirteenth century. In the intervening period the ground level outside the vault had risen 1.60m with layer upon layer of floors of the adjoining building.

Tackley's Inn has also been reassessed. Munby (1978) has examined the drawings by J.C. Buckler of this building and three adjoining medieval houses similar in date and plan. While the latter buildings have long since been destroyed, Munby's discussion means that they can now be added to the known stock of Oxford's medieval town houses. Munby (1974) also carried out a similar exercise in St. Thomas' where the interpretation of one of Buckler's drawings shows that a house of Wealden type existed there in the fifteenth century when the suburb was enjoying a period of prosperity connected with the cloth industry. Munby (1975) has also recorded a further fifteenth-century building at 126 High Street whose rear has been demolished.

Structures recovered by excavation rather than by above-ground archaeology are naturally ephemeral and difficult to interpret. Within the town walls the survival rate of medieval foundations in well-stratified deposits is very slight. Even in a comparative backwater like the former Church Street, St. Ebbe's, where there were no modern cellars and disturbance was minimal, only one really coherent building plan was found in what to date represents the largest area excavation in the city (Hassall 1969, 7–10; Hassall 1970, 7–10; Hassall 1971a, 3–6). By contrast the best stratified remains of domestic buildings have been found not within the walled area at all but in the low-lying south and west suburbs where ground conditions not only inhibited the digging of cellars, but positively encouraged householders to allow their floor levels to rise and thus become drier. Durham's meticulous excavations of two properties in St. Aldate's coupled with a re-examination of the documentary evidence (1977) has allowed the detailed reconstruction of a sequence of buildings in a very confined site. In the long life of this site which extends from the Late Saxon period through the Middle Ages a variety of building techniques was indicated including cob, a possible cruck construction and stone foundations. In the late twelfth or early thirteenth century, various internal divisions took place followed by a complete rebuilding c. 1400 and again in the mid-sixteenth century when the building was rebuilt in timber to which a central chimney was later added. One of the tantalizing aspects of this site is that a description of 1439 provides a series of dimensions of the building which can be compared, when certain allowances are made, with the excavated structure.

Palmer's excavations of the Hall of St. Helen and Bretel's tenement in St. Thomas' at its junction with The Hamel were on a larger scale (1980). In this suburb newly developed in the late twelfth century the sequence of buildings began in the early to mid-thirteenth century with a row of three buildings with a yard. The entomological evidence shows the change from rural to urban conditions. These first buildings had stone footings, but whether these were dwarf walls to support timber framing or stone walls is not certain. In the mid- to late thirteenth century new buildings were constructed including a new range which protruded into The Hamel. In the late thirteenth century one of the tenements was again rebuilt. In the early sixteenth century further redevelopment took place, the buildings then laid out following the same basic plan as their predecessors, but they lasted until the nineteenth century. This excavation thus produced the most complete sequence of excavated building plans. Its site was carefully chosen because of the well-preserved state of the stratification, but also because it included the actual frontage of The Hamel. The site was also rich in environmental evidence giving an overall impression of filth and decay with beetles eating the timbers of the buildings and living in the thatched roofs and with piles of rotting refuse and dung (Robinson 1980b). For the future it is clear that sites with this combination of accessible frontages, good stratification and preserved environmental remains should receive the highest priority for excavation.

Apart from the survival of well-stratified sequences of structural remains the other striking contrast between the sites in the south and west suburbs and those elsewhere in the town is in the presence or absence of cess-pits and wells. These features are hardly found in St. Aldate's and St. Thomas' but they are the most characteristic element of the majority of sites in the town and were one of the earliest of such features to be recognized. In the case of the excavations in 1877 at the Angel Inn, the excavators mistook such features for the underground houses of a 'British Village'. However, thanks particularly to the excavations first by Bruce Mitford at the New Bodleian (1939) and subsequently by Jope (1950; 1952–3; 1958) and others (Davison 1961; Radcliffe 1961–2), the ubiquity of these humble features is now well known. In some cases the pits were clearly intended as cess-pits as shown by the discovery of human parasite ova (Marples 1977); in other cases the pits may have been dug for gravel and were later used as rubbish but not latrine pits (Robinson 1980).

The largest controlled excavation so far undertaken in the centre of the town at 31–34 Church Street was dominated by pits and wells (Hassall 1969, 7–10; 1970, 7–10; and 1971a, 3–6). Their distribution can give an indication of areas of activity at any one time. By the later Middle Ages the normal layout of a tenement comprised a building on the street frontage, a courtyard with a stone-lined well and cess-pits at the far end of the property. Stone linings to wells and cess-pits began to replace simple shafts dug into the natural gravel from the fourteenth century. By this time the ground within the town must have become very unstable because of earlier digging. The existence of so many pits reflects the problem of night-soil and rubbish disposal in the town, and it is only in the later Middle Ages that there appears to have been a regular system of carting rubbish to tips, some of which are shown in Agas' map of 1578 (1899) in the area around the castle. At an earlier period rubbish could also have had its uses in land reclamation in the south suburb where rubbish-dumping in river channels was found by Durham at 89–91 St. Aldate's in the mid-eleventh century (1983c), at 65 St. Aldate's in the late twelfth to thirteenth centuries (1982e), and at 35–40 St. Aldate's in the fourteenth century (1980b). The island site of the second priory of the Blackfriars was also made habitable in part by the dumping of soil containing domestic rubbish, possibly derived from new pits as they were dug through earlier ones (Lambrick 1984). Apart from controlled tipping exercises such as these it is also clear that then, as now, any hole in the ground was fair game for rubbish disposal, hence the large numbers of medieval and later shoes in the castle moat (Hassall 1976).

Stratified floor levels, wells and pits have all produced profuse quantities of artefacts. Pottery, as one would expect, dominates the record. The Oxford region was one of the first medieval pottery regions to receive serious study. Oxford's medieval pottery typology was established by Bruce-Mitford (1939; 1940), Jope (1942; 1950; 1958) and Sturdy (1959). Building on their earlier studies and using the well-stratified sequences from St. Aldate's (Haldon 1977) and The Hamel, Mellor (1980b) has been able to extend and to refine this study. The majority of the fabrics are of local manufacture and imports usually form only a very small percentage of the total assemblages.

While pottery dominates the artefact record other trades and crafts are also well represented at every excavated site. Butchery provides the most extensive evidence and the contents of both pits and floor levels provide large quantities of animal bone evidence (Marples 1977; Wilson 1980). The standard diet included sheep, ox and pig (the latter presumably often being kept by the individual households). The diet was also supplemented by red and roe deer, later replaced by fallow deer, hare and rabbit. In addition to domestic fowl Oxford's poulterers were also supplying a variety of water and meadow birds including teal, gadwall, shelduck, wigeon, whooper swan, woodcock and golden plover. Fish was available. Recovery of river fish bones has not been great, but marine fish, oysters, mussel, limpets and cockles are found.

Animals were used for more than their meat. Spinning and weaving wool were of crucial importance to the town, although the archaeological evidence is comparatively slight. Spindle whorls are frequently found and fragments of spun thread have been recovered from St. Aldate's (Crowfoot 1977). Where ground conditions are waterlogged actual textiles made up into clothing have been discovered although not necessarily of local manufacture (Crowfoot 1976). The same kind of soil conditions also preserves the products of cordwainers. Leather turnshoes, bags, belts, knife-sheaths and decorated leather have been found in the castle barbican ditch and moat (Henig 1976b; Jones 1976) and The Hamel (Jones 1977). Most sites also produce objects of bone and antler (e.g. Henig 1977). The clearest example of an actual workshop so far excavated is that of Thomas Brikar or Briker in St. Aldate's where bone pegs were being manufactured as part of the process of musical instrument-making (Durham 1977, 163–166).

Apart from the evidence for trades depending on animal products or hide, other artefacts show the range of crafts in the town or at least objects which were available for purchase. All sites have produced iron (I. Goodall 1976, 1977 and 1980). Cutlery includes knives, some with cutler's marks, shears and scissors; amongst the ironmongery are carpenters' tools such as bits, structural ironwork like hinges and door- and window-fittings and horse furniture such as horseshoes, bits and spurs. Copper alloy was reserved for finer objects such as buckles, strap ends, buttons, thimbles, mounts and studs (A.R. Goodall 1977 and 1980). Other trades such as woodworking leave less durable remains. But again, where conditions are wet objects such as wooden pins, combs, bobbins and turned wooden bowls have been found (Henig 1976a).

The synthesis of all this disparate material will help to complement the documentary sources for medieval Oxford's economy. This economy seems to have been particularly sensitive to the ability of Oxford's merchants to navigate the Thames (Davis 1973). Although much evidence has been found relating to early river channels, so far even the low-lying sites have produced little evidence for a formal commercial river front. Wooden waterfronts have been uncovered at 65 St. Aldate's (Durham 1983b) and fourteenth- to fifteenth-century revetments to the Castle Mill stream (OUAS 1978; Durham 1981d). Such waterfronts are more likely to have been connected with fishing and other riverside crafts rather than trade as such.

The spiritual life of Oxford was catered for by numerous parish churches and religious houses. In common with other towns of Late Saxon origin there were many churches in Oxford, eighteen in all including the suburban churches. The early Middle Ages saw an expansion of these churches in response to a growing population. In the case of St. Michael at the Northgate space was so cramped that the northern extension of the church had to be built on the site of the original Saxon defensive ditch. Such unsuitable ground conditions required the new walls to be built on construction arches (Durham et al. 1983, 14–8). The first church to disappear was that of St. Budoc's, demolished in 1215/16, but whose first site in front of the main entrance to the castle has been identified (Hassall 1976). However, Oxford was overprovided with churches, particularly following depopulation after the Black Death, and there has been a constant loss of churches ever since. This process has culminated in the conversion of St. Peter's-in-the-East and All Saints to college libraries. In both cases excavations were possible. Sturdy's (1972a) excavations in St. Peter's-in-the-East were principally concerned with the earliest church, while at All Saints Durham (Hassall 1974a, 54–57) has recovered the plan of the medieval church which was destroyed in 1700 and was replaced by the present eighteenth-century structure. The original church of the second half of the eleventh century was enlarged in the last quarter of the same century by the addition of a chancel, a north chapel and a nave extension (Fig. 18). The north chapel was short-lived because it was built on a back-filled earlier cellar. A bell tower was added probably at the western end of the nave and a north aisle was added c. 1200. After 1326 a new 'chancel' was added to the north aisle and took over the function of the original chancel which became by 1476 the chapel of the Holy Trinity. The chapel of St. Anne was added to the north side of the church in 1333. This sequence of events was discovered by a combination of prior excavation and observation during construction.

Throughout the medieval period Oxford would have been dominated by the buildings and precincts of a series of religious houses (Ashdown and Hassall 1975). The senior house was St. Frideswide's refounded as an

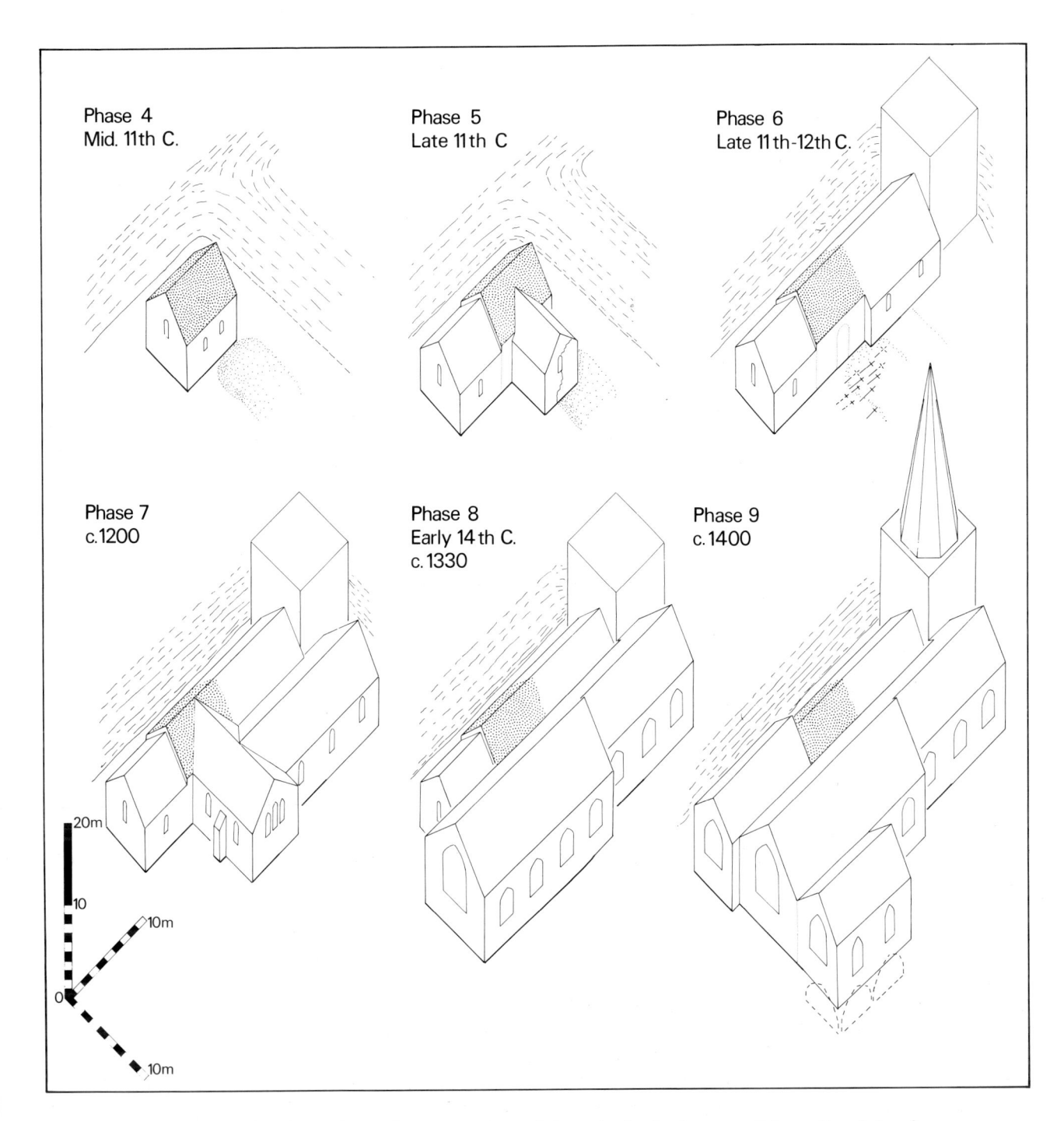

Figure 18. *All Saints Church : conjectural reconstructions of phases in the development of the medieval church*

Augustinian Priory in 1122. The medieval church and east and south range of the cloister survive. Within the cloisters are some enigmatic foundations of apparently late fifteenth- or sixteenth-century date excavated by Sturdy (1957) who has also shown that the arches within the present cathedral once thought to be Saxon are in fact of later date (Taylor and Taylor 1968, 479–8).

The largest monastery in Oxford was Oseney Abbey, a house of Augustinian Canons, founded in 1129. Only a fragment of the buildings survives (Steane and Gosling 1980). However, the foundations of a series of original riverside buildings alongside a river channel filled in in the thirteenth century have been observed (Durham 1983a and 1984b). Three phases of building were recognized beginning in the thirteenth century and including the massive stone foundations of a barn or stable built in the fourteenth and fifteenth centuries.

The most extensive excavations in Oxford have, however, taken place on the site of the second house of the Dominicans and on the site of the Franciscans. The Dominicans arrived in Oxford in 1226 and the general position of their two pre-Reformation sites in the town has been known since Hinnebusch (1938) first collected the evidence. Excavations by Lambrick, Woods and others (1976) have resulted in the recovery of the greater part of the plan of the second priory when it moved from its original site off St. Aldate's to a low-lying island site in the Thames in what is now St. Ebbe's. The buildings were begun in 1236 and precautions were made to raise the ground level. The buildings were of exceptional size and importance although only part of the gateway now survives. The main plan of the church has been recovered together with the great cloister. Unusual features included a long slype south of the choir, a chapter house attached to the back wall of the cloisters and a galilee at the western end of the church. More recent excavations by Lambrick (1980 and 1984) have provided evidence for the great cloister garth, a subsidiary cloister and a reredorter. A northern extension to the church originally thought to have existed now seems unlikely. At the Reformation the buildings were pulled down and the site was laid out as gardens.

The Franciscans came to Oxford in 1224 and also settled in St. Ebbe's. Their site lay between the former Church Street and the Trill Mill stream and was bisected by the Town Wall which was removed to make way for their buildings. The complete plan of the church has now been recovered by excavation (Fig. 19). Like the Dominican church it was very large but unlike that it went through a series of enlargements (Hassall 1969, 11; 70, 10–15; 71a, 6–8). The most notable was the construction of a great northern extension similar to an elongated transept. This feature was called the 'north nave' by William Worcester when he described the church in 1480. The plan of the conventual buildings south of the church is not clearly understood. They were very extensive but in spite of large numbers of trial trenches the plan is difficult to reconstruct (Hassall 1974a, 59–61). At the Reformation the buildings were heavily robbed and the only walls which were left standing were those which served as property boundaries after the site became subdivided.

In addition to these two great mendicant priories there were a number of other friary sites in Oxford. No work has been carried out on these with the exception of that of the Austin Friars who occupied the site of what is now Wadham College from 1268. During new building works Blair (1976) recognized an ancillary building of c. 1500 whose eastern wall survived because it was used as a boundary wall after the Reformation.

One of the latest religious foundations in the town was Rewley Abbey, a Cistercian House. The site now lies beneath the British Rail coalyard. It is somewhat surprising to find a house of that Order so near to a centre of population, but Rewley was originally intended as a house of studies for Cistercian monks, although it was soon elevated to the status of an abbey. Trial work by Durham (1982d) has shown that the foundations of at least the northern range were left in place when the building was demolished to make way for the railway in the 1850s. The site is comparatively unobstructed by modern building although sealed beneath quite a considerable build-up of modern debris.

Rewley, originally founded as a monastic college, and the friars all played an important role within the University. Members of the University were considered to be ecclesiastics and the constituent colleges of the University were also religious foundations. Archaeology, apart from providing the general context of the University, has also provided both direct and indirect evidence for University life. The bulk of the students in the medieval period were accommodated in Academic Halls which were licensed lodging houses. Several have been excavated, including a small hall, White Hall, in St. Ebbe's (Hassall 1969, 7–10; 1970, 7–10; 1971a, 3–6) and the much larger Hinxey Hall (Halpin 1983). This hall began its history as Kepeham Hall, later becoming Hinxey Hall. It existed from the late fourteenth century until the early to mid-sixteenth century. Excavation has confirmed the documentary evidence for this hall and supported Pantin's conjectural ground floor plan (1964, 77–82). This building was almost like a small college in size.

One of the monastic colleges which has been examined is St. Mary's College. This was a college for Austin Canons which existed from 1435 to 1546. Blair (1978) has collated the evidence for the buildings and shown that, although the college incorporated an earlier Norman mansion, its plan was similar to that of Corpus Christi College or Christ Church. The upstanding structure of its New Inn Hall Street range was examined and part of the chapel was excavated. The roof of the chapel still survives having been disassembled in the seventeenth century and re-erected at Brasenose.

Sites not so directly connected with the University have produced objects which are best seen in the context of Oxford academic life. These have included a bone parchment pricker providing evidence for a possible scribe in St. Thomas' (Palmer 1980, 218–9),

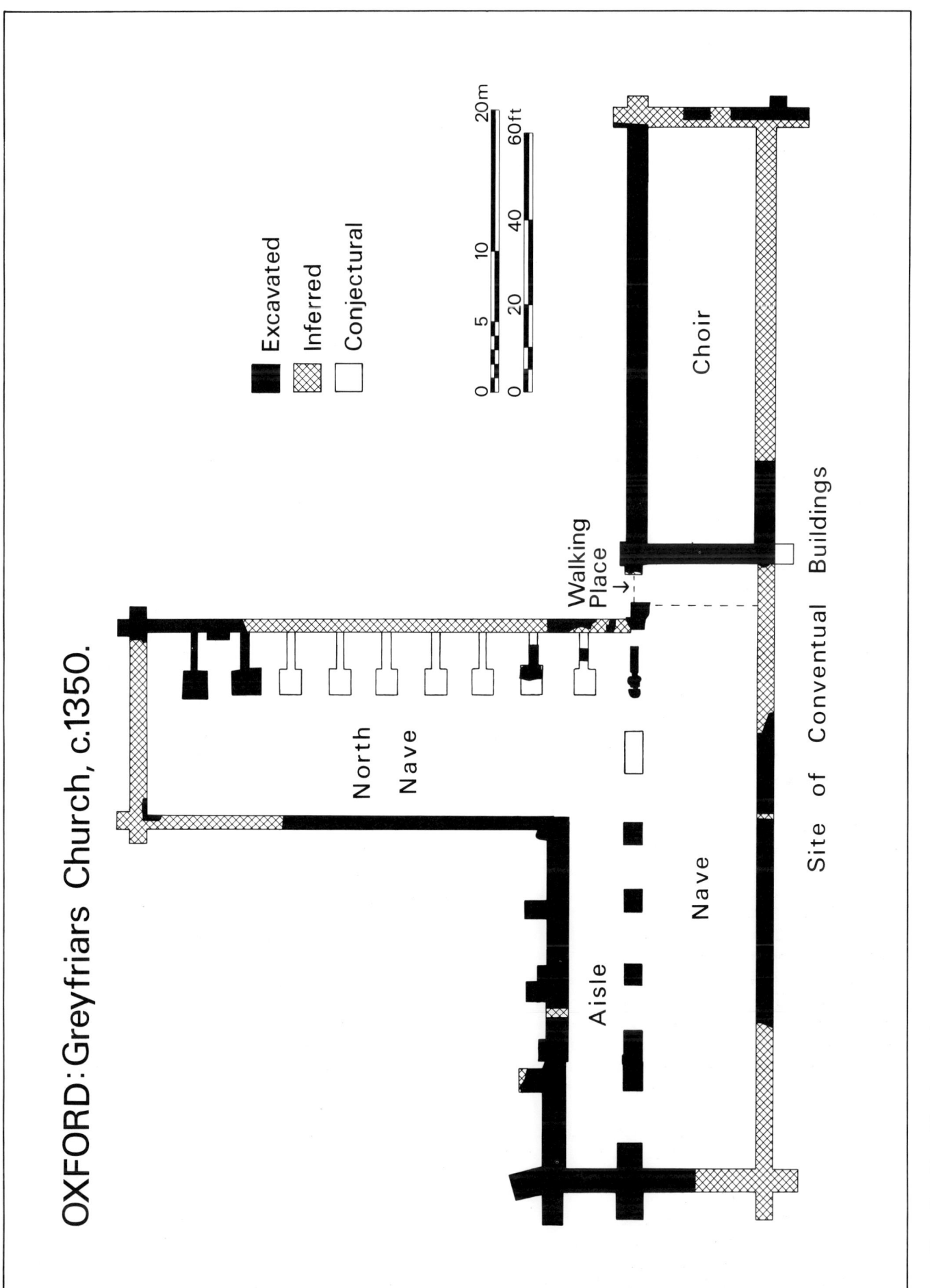

Figure 19. *Greyfriars Church, c. 1350*

and the possible palette of a manuscript illuminator in St. Aldate's (Durham 1977, 169). The harp-making from the same St. Aldate's site (ibid. 163–166) is also a reflection of a craft apparently particularly associated with this university town.

Apart from providing the evidence for physical remains of medieval Oxford, archaeology is also recovering the skeletal remains of its actual inhabitants. The pioneering study of Oxford's medieval anthropology was that of Buxton (1937). He was, however, dependent on a comparatively small sample. The excavations at All Saints and the Dominican and Franciscan sites have provided a much larger sample. At the Dominican site (Lambrick and Woods 1976, 203–5; 226–229), apart from friars, burials included lay people, and juveniles in the chapter house may have been the children of benefactors. Child burials have also been found at two domestic sites: a foetal burial in St. Aldate's (Durham 1977, 166) and a child at The Hamel (Palmer 1980, 219). Presumably these were deliberate concealments of unbaptised infants, but are not necessarily to be taken for evidence of actual infanticide.

For the post-medieval period the main contribution of recent excavations has been in the area of pottery studies and an understanding of the Civil War defences of Oxford. The nature of the Civil War defences has been the subject of much discussion (Lattey et al. 1936; Kemp 1977). It is now clear that probably more refurbishment took place of the medieval defences and particularly the ditch than has previously been thought (Durham et al. 1983). A further bizarre sidelight on Oxford in the Civil War was provided by Durham's examination of a possible strong room beneath the Provost of Oriel's lodging. This construction was later used as a cess-pit whose noisome contents has been the object of a specialist study by Robinson (Durham 1982c).

The scope for further archaeological research into Oxford's past is still considerable. There remain a number of major outstanding questions, above all of which is the nature of Mercian Oxford: where the early settlement was, its size and character and whether it was defended. For later periods the excavations to date have indicated the potential areas of research. What is clear is that by taking whatever opportunities are presented, however small, over a number of years a detailed picture has gradually emerged. For the future the opportunities for excavation will continue to be concentrated in the western part of the city where the redevelopment process appears to be entering a fourth phase with renewed large-scale development. By the end of the 1980s Queen Street will have been virtually rebuilt by a process of piecemeal rebuilding; Gloucester Green is scheduled for large-scale development and so also is the British Rail site at the station. These areas should throw further light on the Saxon town, the early medieval suburban growth and on Rewley Abbey. By the excavation of sites in Oxford and its hinterland archaeology still has a major contribution to play in our understanding of the City's past.

Bibliography

Agas, R. (1899) *Old Plans of Oxford*, Oxford Hist. Soc., 38

Ashdown, J.H. & Hassall, T.G. (1975) 'Oxford', in K. Rodwell 1975, 133–146

Atkinson, R.J.C. (1942) 'Archaeological sites on Port Meadow, Oxford', *Oxoniensia* 7, 24–35

Benson, D. & Cook, J.M. (1966) *City of Oxford Redevelopment: Archaeological Implications*

Biddle, M. & Hill, D.H. (1971) 'Late Saxon planned towns', *Antiq. J.* 51, 70–85

Biddle, M. (1976) 'The Evolution of towns: planned towns before 1066', in M.W. Barley ed., *The plans and topography of medieval towns in England and Wales*, CBA Res. Rept. 14, 19–32

Blair, J. (1976) 'A Monastic fragment at Wadham College', *Oxoniensia* 41, 161–168

Blair, J. (1978) 'Frewin Hall, Oxford: a Norman mansion and a monastic college', *Oxoniensia* 43, 48–99

Bond, C.J. (1979) 'The reconstruction of the medieval landscape: the estates of Abingdon Abbey', *Landscape History* 1, 59–75

Bruce-Mitford, R.L.S. (1939) 'The Archaeology of the site of the Bodleian Extension in Broad Street, Oxford', *Oxoniensia* 4, 89–146

Bruce-Mitford, R.L.S. & Jope, E.M. (1940) 'Eleventh and twelfth century pottery from the Oxford Region', *Oxoniensia* 5, 42–49

Buckler, J.C. (1951) *Drawings of Oxford by J.C. Buckler 1811–1827*, Bodleian Picture Book, 3

Buxton, L.H. Dudley (1937) 'The Anthropology of medieval Oxford', *Oxoniensia* 2, 118–128

Cam, H.M. (1936) 'The Hundred outside the North Gate of Oxford', *Oxoniensia*, 1, 113–128

Cam, H.M. (1963) *Liberties and Communities in Medieval England*

Clark, A. (1889–99) *Survey of the Antiquities of the City of Oxford compiled in 1661–6 by Anthony Wood*, Oxford Hist. Soc. 15, 17, 37

Cooper, J. (1972) 'Hundred Rolls of St. Thomas's parish', *Oxoniensia* 37, 168–73

Cooper, J. & Crossley, A. (1979) 'Medieval Oxford', in A. Crossley ed., *The Victoria History of the County of Oxford* 4, 3–73

CBA (1979) 'Oxford: Late Saxon and early medieval ditches', *CBA 9 Newsletter* 9, 132, fig. 38

Crowfoot, E. (1976) 'The textiles', in Hassall 1976, 271–4

Crowfoot, E. (1977) 'Textiles', in Durham 1977, 154–5

Daniell, J. (1939) 'The City wall and ditch in the Clarendon Quadrangle', *Oxoniensia* 4, 153–161

Davis, R.H.C. (1973) 'The Ford, the river and the City', *Oxoniensia* 38, 258–267

Davison, B.K. (1961) 'Oxfordshire: Oxford, St. Ebbe's corner', in 'Medieval Britain in 1960' in *Med. Archaeol.* 5, 324–5

Durham, B. (1977) 'Archaeological investigations in St. Aldates, Oxford', *Oxoniensia* 43, 83–203

Durham, B. (1980a) 'Oxford, 18–24 New Inn Hall Street', *CBA 9 Newsletter* 10, 157–8

Durham, B. (1980b) 'Oxford, 35–40 and 65 St. Aldates', *CBA 9 Newsletter* 10, 158–60 and fig. 159

Durham, B. (1981a) 'Oxford: Abingdon Road and Folly Bridge', *CBA 9 Newsletter* 11, 129

Durham, B. (1981b) 'Oxford: Catte Street, New Inn Hall Street and St. Aldates', *CBA 9 Newsletter* 11, 131

Durham B, (1981c) 'Oxford: All Saints', *CBA 9 Newsletter* 11, 155–6

Durham, B. (1981d) 'Oxford' in G. Milne & B. Hobley eds., *Waterfront archaeology in Britain and northern Europe*, CBA Res. Report 41, 142–3

Durham, B. (1982a) 'Oxford: Corpus Christi College', *CBA 9 Newsletter* 12, 156–8

Durham, B. (1982b) 'Oxford: High Street', *CBA 9 Newsletter* 12, 158–60

Durham, B. (1982c) 'Oxford: Oriel College, the Provost's Lodging', *CBA 9 Newsletter* 12, 160

Durham, B. (1982d) 'Oxford: Rewley Abbey', *CBA 9 Newsletter* 12, 160

Durham, B. (1982e) 'Oxford: 65 St. Aldates and 92 St. Aldates', *CBA 9 Newsletter* 12, 160–1
Durham, B. (1982f) 'Oxford: Turl Street, new foul sewer', *CBA 9 Newsletter* 12, 161
Durham, B. (1983a) 'Oxford: Oseney Abbey, Mill Street', *South Midlands Archaeology (CBA 9 Newsletter)* 13, 137
Durham, B. (1983b) 'Oxford: 65 St. Aldates', *South Midlands Archaeology (CBA 9 Newsletter)* 13, 138
Durham, B. (1983c) 'Oxford: 89–91 St. Aldates', *South Midlands Archaeology (CBA 9 Newsletter)* 13, 138–140
Durham, B. (1983d) 'Oxford: South Parks Road', *South Midlands Archaeology (CBA 9 Newsletter)* 13, 140–1
Durham, B., Halpin, C. & Palmer, N. (1983) 'Oxford's northern defences: archaeological studies 1971–1982', *Oxoniensia* 48, 13–40
Durham, B. (1984a) 'Oxford: 52 Cornmarket Street, former Woolworths', *South Midlands Archaeology (CBA 9 Newsletter)* 14, 110
Durham, B. (1984b) 'Oxford: Oseney Abbey', *South Midlands Archaeology (CBA 9 Newsletter)* 14, 111
Goodall, A.R. & I.H. (1977) 'Copper alloy objects', in Durham 1977, 143–52
Goodall, A.R. (1980) 'Copper alloy and lead objects', in Palmer 1980, 183–8
Goodall, I.H. (1976) 'Metalwork', in Hassall 1976, 298–303
Goodall, I.H. (1977) 'Iron objects', in Durham 1977, 142–8
Goodall, I.H. (1980) 'Iron objects', in Palmer 1980, 189–191
Haldon, R. (1977) 'Late Saxon and medieval pottery', in Durham 1977, 111–139
Halpin, C. (1983) 'Late Saxon evidence and excavation of Hinxey Hall, Queen Street, Oxford', *Oxoniensia* 48, 41–69
Hassall, T.G. (1969) 'Excavations at Oxford 1968: First Interim Report', *Oxoniensia* 34, 5–20
Hassall, T.G. (1970) 'Excavations at Oxford 1969', *Oxoniensia* 35, 5–18
Hassall, T.G. (1971a) 'Excavations at Oxford 1970', *Oxoniensia* 36, 1–14
Hassall, T.G. (1971b) 'Excavations at 44–46 Cornmarket Street, Oxford, 1970', *Oxoniensia* 36, 15–33
Hassall, T.G. (1971c) 'Excavations in Merton College, Oxford, 1970', *Oxoniensia* 36, 34–48
Hassall, T.G. (1971d) *Oxford Castle*. Oxfordshire Prisoners' Aid Society
Hassall, T.G. (1972a) 'Roman finds from the Radcliffe Science Library extension, Oxford, 1970–1', *Oxoniensia* 37, 38–50
Hassall, T.G. (1972b) 'Excavations at Oxford, 1971: Fourth Interim Report', *Oxoniensia* 37, 137–149
Hassall, T.G. (1972c) *Oxford: the City Beneath your feet*. Oxford Archaeol. Excavation Cttee
Hassall, T.G. (1973) 'Excavations at Oxford, 1972: Fifth Interim Report', *Oxoniensia* 38, 268–298
Hassall, T.G (1974a) 'Excavations at Oxford 1973–4: Sixth and Final Interim Report', *Oxoniensia* 39, 53–61
Hassall, T.G. (1974b) 'Urban surveys: medieval Oxford', in A. Rogers & T. Rowley eds., *Landscapes and Documents*, 49–62
Hassall, T.G. (1975a) 'Topography of pre-University Oxford', in C.G. Smith & D.I. Scargill eds., *Oxford and its Region*, 29–36
Hassall, T.G. (1975b) 'Oxford: an urban case', in *Planning and the Historic Environment I*, OUDES, 61–7
Hassall, T.G. (1976) 'Excavations at Oxford Castle, 1965–73', *Oxoniensia* 41, 232–308
Hassall, T.G. (1979) 'City walls, gates and posterns', in A. Crossley ed. *The Victoria History of the County of Oxford* 4, 300–303
Hassall, T.G. (1982) 'Les Rècherches archéologiques actuelles à Oxford', in *Archéologie Urbaine, Actes du Colloque international Tours*, Association pour les fouilles archéologiques nationales, 67–73
Henig, M. (1976a) 'Wood', in Hassall 1976, 270–1
Henig, M. (1976b) 'Knife-sheaths and decorated leather', in Hassall 1976, 294–6
Henig, M. (1977) 'Objects of bone, antler and shell', in Durham 1977, 160–3

Hill, D. (1969) 'The Burghal Hidage: the establishment of a text', *Med. Archaeol.* 13, 84–92
Hingley, R. (1982) 'Frilford: Noah's Ark', *CBA 9 Newsletter* 12, 150–153
Hinnebusch, W.A. (1938) 'The Pre-Reformation sites of the Oxford Blackfriars', *Oxoniensia* 33, 57–82
Hunter, A.G. & Jope, E.M. (1951) 'Excavations on the City defences in New College, Oxford, 1949', *Oxoniensia* 16, 28–41
Hurst, H. (1900) *Oxford Topography*, Oxford Hist. Soc. 39
Jones, J. (1976) 'The Leather', in Hassall 1976, 275–96
Jones, J. (1980) 'Leatherwork', in Palmer 1980, 193–4
Jope, E.M. (1942) 'Some recent finds of medieval pottery', *Oxoniensia* 7, 71–79
Jope, E.M., Jope, H.M. & Rigold, S.E. (1950) 'Pottery from a late 12th century well-filling, and other medieval finds from St. John's College, Oxford, 1947', *Oxoniensia* 15, 44–62
Jope, E.M. (1952–3) 'Late Saxon pits under Oxford Castle mound: excavations in 1952', *Oxoniensia* 17–18, 77–111
Jope, E.M. (1956) 'Saxon Oxford and its region', in D.B. Harden ed., *Dark-Age Britain*, 234–58
Jope, E.M. (1958) 'The Clarendon Hotel, Oxford. Part 1, The Site', *Oxoniensia* 23, 1–83
Keene, D. (1975) 'Suburban growth', in M.W. Barley ed., *The Plans and Topography of medieval towns in England and Wales*, CBA Res. Rept. 14, 71–82
Kemp, A. (1977) 'The fortification of Oxford during the Civil War', *Oxoniensia* 42, 237–246
King, E. (1976) *Vestiges of Oxford Castle*
Lambrick, G. & Woods, H. (1976) 'Excavations on the second site of the Dominican Priory, Oxford', *Oxoniensia* 41, 168–231
Lambrick, G. (1980) 'Oxford, Blackfriars', *CBA 9 Newsletter* 10, 153–5
Lambrick, G. (1982) 'Thames floodplain survey', *CBA 9 Newsletter* 12, 129–134
Lambrick, G. (1983) 'Thames floodplain survey', *South Midlands Archaeology (CBA 9 Newsletter)* 14, 109–110
Lattey, R.T., Parsons, E.J.S. & Philip, I.G. (1936) 'A Contemporary map of the defences of Oxford in 1644', *Oxoniensia* 1, 161–172
Lyon, C.S.S. (1966) 'Chronology of the coinage of Ethelred II', *Brit. Numis. J.* 35, 34–7
Marples, B.J. (1977) 'Animal bones', in Durham 1977, 166–168
Marples, M.J. (1977) 'Human parasite ova', in Durham 1977, 174
Mellor, M. (1980a) 'Late Saxon pottery from Oxfordshire: evidence and speculation', *Med. Ceramics* 4, 17–27
Mellor, M. (1980b) 'Pottery', in Palmer 1980, 160–182
Metcalf, D.M. (1977) 'Monetary affairs in Mercia in the time of Aethelbald', in A. Dornier ed., *Mercian Studies*, 87–106
Munby, J.T. (1972) 'An inventory of sites and finds from the Science Area, Oxford', in Hassall 1972a
Munby, J. (1974) 'A fifteenth century Wealden house in Oxford', *Oxoniensia* 39, 73–76
Munby, J. (1975) '126 High Street: the archaeology and history of an Oxford house', *Oxoniensia* 40, 254–308
Munby, J. (1978) 'J.C. Buckler, Tackley's Inn and three medieval houses in Oxford', *Oxoniensia* 43, 123–160
Oxford Excavations Committee (1963) *Report to Subscribers for 1962*
OUAS (1978) Oxford University Archaeological Society, 'Oxford, Paradise Street', *CBA 9 Newsletter* 8, 17
Palmer, N. (1976) 'Excavations on the outer City Wall of Oxford in St. Helen's Passage and Hertford College', *Oxoniensia* 41, 148–160
Palmer, N. (1980) 'A Beaker burial and medieval tenements in The Hamel, Oxford', *Oxoniensia* 45, 124–225
Pantin, W.A. (1937) 'The recently demolished houses in Broad Street', *Oxoniensia* 2, 171–200
Pantin, W.A. (1942) 'Tackley's Inn, Oxford', *Oxoniensia* 7, 80–92
Pantin, W.A. (1947) 'Development of domestic architecture in Oxford', *Antiq. J.* 27, 120–150
Pantin, W.A. (1958) 'The Clarendon Hotel, Oxford. Part II. The Buildings', *Oxoniensia* 23, 84–129
Pantin, W.A. (1962–3) 'Medieval English town-house plans', *Med. Archaeol.* 6–7, 202–39

Pantin, W.A. (1964) 'The halls and schools of medieval Oxford: an attempt at reconstruction', in *Studies presented to Daniel Callus*, Oxford Hist. Soc. n.s. 16, 31–100

Parker, J.H. (1885) *The early history of Oxford*. Oxford Hist. Soc. 3

Penny, F.H. (1899) *Buried Oxford Unearthed*

Radcliffe, F. (1961–2) 'Excavations at Logic Lane, Oxford. The prehistoric and early medieval finds', *Oxoniensia* 26–7, 38–69

Radford, C.A.R. (1970) 'The Later Pre-Conquest boroughs and their defences', *Med. Archaeol.* 14, 83–103

Radford, C.A.R. (1972) 'Excavations at Cricklade, 1948–63', *Wilt. Archaeol. Nat. Hist. Mag.* 67, 61–111

Rigold, S.E. (1968) 'Double minsters of Kent', *J. Brit. Archaeol. Ass. Ser. 3* 31, 27–37

Robinson, M. (1980a) 'Flooding and the Bronze Age use of the Thames floodplain in the Oxford district', in N. Palmer 1980, 133–4

Robinson, M. (1980b) 'Waterlogged plant and invertebrate evidence', in Palmer 1980, 199–206

Robinson, M.A. & Lambrick, G.H. (1984) 'Holocene alluviation and hydrology in the upper Thames basin', *Nature* 308, No. 5962, 809–814

Rodwell, K. ed. (1975) *Historic Towns in Oxfordshire*, Oxfordshire Archaeol. Unit Survey No. 3

Salter, H.E. (1914) *A Cartulary of the hospital of St. John the Baptist*, Oxford Hist. Soc. 66, 483–490

Salter, H.E. (1934) *Map of medieval Oxford*

Salter, H.E. (1936) *Medieval Oxford*, Oxford Hist. Soc. 100

Salter, H.E. (1960, 69) *Survey of Oxford*, ed. W.A. Pantin. Oxford Hist. Soc., n.s., 14, 20

Seaby, W.A. & Woodfield, P. (1980) 'Viking stirrups from England and their background', *Med. Archaeol.* 24, 87–122

Sharp, T. (1948) *Oxford replanned*

Shoesmith, R. (1982) *Hereford city excavations, 2. Excavations on and close to the defences*, CBA Res. Rept. 46

Steane, J. & Gosling, P. (1980) 'Oseney Mill. Surviving part of Oseney Abbey', *CBA 9 Newsletter* 10, 96–7

Stenton, F.M. (1936) 'St. Frideswide and her times', *Oxoniensia* 1, 103–112

Sturdy, D. (1959a) 'Oxford, Christ Church', *Oxoniensia* 24, 101

Sturdy, D. (1959b) 'Thirteenth century and later pottery from the Clarendon Hotel and other sites in Oxford', *Oxoniensia* 24, 22–36

Sturdy, D. (1960) 'Oxfordshire: Oxford', in 'Medieval Britain in 1959', *Med. Archaeol.* 4, 148–50

Sturdy, D. (1961–2a) 'Recent excavations in Christ Church and nearby', *Oxoniensia* 26–7, 19–37

Sturdy, D. (1961–2b) 'Oxford, 13–17 Cornmarket Street', *Oxoniensia* 26–7, 338

Sturdy, D.A.M. (1972a) 'Excavations in St. Peter-in-the-East church, Oxford', *Oxoniensia* 38, 245

Sturdy, D. (1972b) 'Correlation of evidence of medieval urban communities', in P.J. Ucko ed., *Man, Settlement and Urbanism*, 864

Taylor, H.M. & J. (1968) *Anglo-Saxon Architecture*

Turner, W.H. (1880) *Selection from the records of the City of Oxford*

VCH (1979) A. Crossley ed., *A history of the County of Oxford. 4. The City of Oxford*

Wilson, B. (1980) 'Animal bone and shell', in Palmer 1980, 198

Wilson, D.R. (1982) *Air photo interpretation for archeologists*

Young, C.J. (1972) 'Excavations at the Churchill Hospital, 1971; interim report', *Oxoniensia* 37, 10–31

Young, C.J. (1973a) 'Excavations at the Churchill Hospital, 1972; interim report', *Oxoniensia* 38, 207–214

Young, C.J. (1973b) 'The Roman Kiln Site at St. Luke's Road, Cowley, Oxford', *Oxoniensia* 38, 215–232

Young, C.J. (1974) 'Excavations at the Churchill Hospital, 1973; interim report', *Oxoniensia* 39, 1–12

THE OXFORD REGION IN THE MIDDLE AGES
JAMES BOND

Introduction

There has been no general synthesis of the medieval archaeology of the Oxford region since the publication of Hoskins & Jope's chapter in the British Association handbook in 1954. During the ensuing thirty years, however, the progress of fieldwork, aerial photography, excavation, documentary research and other techniques of investigation has gained such momentum that it now almost threatens to bury us under an avalanche of undigested detail. Some attempt needs to be made to review the achievement and the shortcomings of the last few decades' work, and to assess the present state of knowledge, even if the unrelenting pace at which new data are being accumulated means that this summary itself will soon have become outdated.

The heritage of settlements, sites, buildings and landscape features now recognized as surviving from the Middle Ages is more impressive in both quantity and quality than that from any previous period. Moreover, the archaeological evidence surviving in the landscape can now be studied alongside other complementary sources of historical information, such as place-names and documentary records, which add a further dimension to our understanding. The sheer volume of available information has made it impractical to present all the medieval sites upon a single map; instead, a thematic approach has been adopted, with a series of maps depicting the known distributions of selected classes of sites. John Steane has discussed elsewhere in this volume the basis for compiling these maps from the County Sites and Monuments Record and other sources, and has indicated some of their limitations. Perhaps the most important caveat is that each map spans a period of nearly five centuries between the Norman Conquest and the Dissolution of the Monasteries; considerable changes were taking place during this period, and some maps, therefore, present a misleadingly static picture; while many of the sites shown were occupied or in use contemporaneously, it is certainly not intended to imply that all of them were. Other anomalies will be indicated in the more detailed commentaries which follow. Finally, it will be evident that there remain many aspects of medieval social and economic history which for various reasons have not been mapped, but some of these will receive brief consideration in the text.

Medieval Towns

It is now generally accepted that the renewal of town life in the late Saxon period was reinforced by a further wave of new urban promotions during the twelfth and thirteenth centuries (Beresford 1967; Rodwell 1975). We are faced, nonetheless, with considerable difficulties when we look for simple criteria which will provide a satisfactory definition of what constituted a town in the Middle Ages; and for this reason a range of factors which contribute towards urban status has been selected for plotting in Map 13.

A distinctive characteristic of many medieval towns is their status as boroughs (Beresford & Finberg 1973). Borough status conveyed upon the community a degree of administrative independence and freedom from manorial control which could not be attained in the rural countryside. There were various types of borough, from the late Saxon royal foundations of Wallingford and Oxford, where the burgesses in effect rented the borough from the king, thereby ensuring for themselves a considerable measure of self-government, right down to the rudimentary boroughs of Eynsham and Deddington where the only distinctive feature was burgage tenure, the right to buy, sell or bequeath tenements freely, so that investment in property there had potential attractions as a source of profit (Emery 1974). Significant though borough status was, however, it will not serve as a watertight test of urban character. Towns like Wantage, Bicester, Charlbury and Watlington served as important local centres of commerce without ever aspiring to burghal rank, while by contrast chartered boroughs such as Middleton Stoney and Chinnor failed to acquire any other lasting urban functions.

The commercial function of towns is best illustrated by their activities as market centres. A developing network of markets went hand-in-hand with other aspects of medieval expansion. Their origin is sometimes difficult to trace: not infrequently they are recorded as being held of ancient right, without any real indication of when they were first established. The map indicates the first reasonably unambiguous mention of each market, but this should be treated with caution. The Domesday survey, for example, records a market at Bampton and a group of ten traders dwelling outside the abbey gate at Abingdon, but it fails to mention any market at Oxford, though it is inconceivable that the county town had not acquired commercial functions by that date. Similarly, although many new market charters were acquired by seigneurial authorities during the twelfth and thirteenth centuries, some of these may represent merely a legal endorsement of long-established practices, while others are probably to be seen as a declaration of intent which was never brought to fruition. Some of the places chartered to hold markets, such as Kingston Lisle, Bignell or Radcot, had

135

no other urban qualifications or pretensions whatsoever. Fairs, usually but not invariably located within market centres, have also been depicted on Map 13 as another important facet of commercial activity.

Perhaps the most effective test of the success of a medieval town was whether it continued to operate as a borough or, perhaps even more importantly, retained its market function, over a long period of time. To separate the 'genuine' towns from the numerous abortive urban promotions, the places which were still boroughs and/or market towns in the nineteenth century have been distinguished by solid symbols on the map. Transport improvements and other factors led to a further weeding-out process during the course of the nineteenth century, which has been discussed elsewhere (Bond 1980).

As far as the surrounding countryside was concerned, the market was the most important of the services provided by the town. An overall pattern seems to have evolved whereby few villages were more than 8–10 km from their nearest market centre, the maximum convenient distance for a man to cover on foot with goods, returning home the same day. As Map 13 shows, however, there was considerable imbalance in the distribution of markets. The large empty gap between Oxford, Wallingford and Thame is particularly striking, especially when the absence of any significant market centre within the adjoining area of Buckinghamshire is considered. It is difficult to explain this void solely by reference to the superior facilities of Oxford, when there is a ring of rival market centres well within the standard 8–12 km radius around the western side of the county town. Nor can it be dismissed as an area of poor soils, low productivity, low population or lack of rural settlements – the Lay Subsidy quotas of 1334 show this area to have been one of the wealthier parts of the county. By contrast, the western end of the Vale of the White Horse appears overendowed. The fact that, out of the nine market centres licensed in this area, only Faringdon and Wantage survived as towns, might suggest that the concentrated competition was too great for most of them to prosper; but the question remains, how did such a cluster arise in the first place? Some sort of circuit arrangement may be implied by the holding of Faringdon market originally on a Monday, East Hendred on Tuesday, Hinton Waldrist on Wednesday, Stanford-in-the-Vale on Thursday, Radcot on Friday and Wantage on Saturday. Only in the extreme south-west of the county was there a group of four contiguous markets all at one time held on a Thursday, and even here the settlement in the middle of the group, Baulking, had altered its market day to Tuesday as early as 1219.

Although several Oxfordshire towns – Abingdon, Bicester, Chipping Norton, Thame, Wantage and Wallingford – partly or wholly overlie the sites of fairly extensive Romano-British settlements, there is little evidence for the survival of any Roman plan elements. The first signs of anything resembling town planning occur in the two late Saxon *burhs* of Oxford and Wallingford, discussed by Tom Hassall in previous chapters. The circumstances of their origin and early development bequeathed certain distinctive features to the plan of both towns: the cruciform street layout within a rectangular defensive circuit, the apparent lack of any original internal market-place, and the multiple provision of parish churches.

Today the internal street-plan of both former *burhs* resembles a grid, but it would be wrong to assume that all elements of this belong to an entirely contemporary late Saxon layout. Major modifications occurred through the later superimposition of castles and religious houses, and more subtle adjustments to the street-plan were taking place a century or more after the Norman Conquest. In Oxford, where more archaeological work has taken place, observations during redevelopment in Cornmarket, the main road north, have shown that the whole street was narrowed and shifted a few metres to the west in the early twelfth century. Some of the smaller internal lanes seem to have been cut through older properties in the early or mid-twelfth century, notably St. Frideswide's Lane (closed again in the fourteenth century) and Brasenose Lane. The present pattern of streets was fully established by the thirteenth century, when many are first documented by name, though there have been a few later diversions and closures. Property boundaries within Saxon Oxford seem to have been remarkably fluid, and evidence from Cornmarket, St. Aldate's and Church Street suggests that many were not fully stabilized before the twelfth century. Subsequently boundaries were more static, although there were continual modifications through amalgamation and subdivision. The history of many Oxford tenements has been documented in remarkable detail (Salter 1960, 1969).

Oxford had already expanded beyond the perimeter of its original ramparts by the end of the tenth century. The defended area was almost doubled by an extension to the east completed before *c.* 1100, which left its mark on the course of the medieval walls in the Smith Gate re-entrant. On the opposite side of the city a smaller extension was linked with the building of the castle in 1071 and the consequent resiting of the West Gate. Further minor modifications resulted from the encroachments of religious precincts over the defences, at St. Michael-at-the-North-Gate church, at the Grey Friars and possibly at St. Frideswide's Priory. The ramparts had locally been reinforced with masonry before the receipt of the first murage grant in 1227, but the building of the town walls in their present form began in the second quarter of the thirteenth century. In 1244 the Grey Friars received permission to demolish part of the south-western defences to extend their precinct within a new crenellated wall, and archaeological evidence from the Littlegate area suggests that this work was begun; but they seem to have been unable to complete the task, and in 1248 were allowed instead to build the north wall of their church across the gap in the defences. Despite this documentation, no evidence of town walls predating the friary was detected archaeologically, the church wall being instead built over a twelfth- and thirteenth-century occupation area (Hassall 1972a). Later in the thirteenth century an outer concentric wall was begun in the north-eastern quarter of the city (Palmer 1976), a feature without any known parallel in medieval town defences in Britain. In their final form, Oxford's medieval walls enclosed an area of *c.* 38 hectares, with five main gates, a detached bridge-gate, about a dozen posterns and at least 21 bastions. In the meantime, expansion outside the defences had continued, with suburbs such as St. Giles' and St. Thomas' growing up in the twelfth century and being served by new extra-mural parish churches.

Oxford's economic fortunes suffered a considerable decline during the fourteenth century, when the documentary evidence records falling rents, deserted tenements and houses being demolished and replaced by gardens. The consequent widespread availability of cheap property allowed a great expansion of University institutions at this time. College precincts spread over the sites of former entire streets of domestic buildings. Oriel College occupied the site of 17 tenements, only three of which were occupied at the time when they were first acquired. Merton College garden occupies the site of a dozen abandoned tenements, and the redundant parish church of St. John was absorbed as the college chapel. New College acquired in 1379 a site formerly occupied by over thirty houses and an intra-mural street.

Wallingford has received less archaeological investigation than Oxford, but here the essential features of the late Saxon *burh* appear to have been less altered by later medieval modifications. The rectangular outline of the Saxon earthen defences is still visible, and there has been no extension of the *enceinte* since it was first enclosed in the late ninth century, although the north gate of the town was rebuilt in stone shortly before its obliteration by an extension to the castle in the later thirteenth century (Brooks 1965–6). The rectilinear street plan appears in its broad outlines to be contemporary with the original defences, though there have been some changes: the market-place looks like a later intrusion, created by widening the main street south of the central crossroads by clearing the properties along its western side; the main road north was shifted some 30m to the west in the thirteenth century when the castle was enlarged; a couple of streets in the north-west quadrant have been lost; and there has been a post-medieval realignment of Thames Street.

Wallingford entered a period of decline in the mid-thirteenth century, which continued disastrously throughout the later Middle Ages. The building of a new bridge over the Thames at Abingdon in 1416, which diverted much of the traffic on the route from London to South Wales, contributed to this, though it was far from being the only factor. By 1439 only four of Wallingford's eleven parish churches were still in use; recent excavation has located the churchyard of St. Rumbold's in Goldsmith's Lane, abandoned in the fourteenth century, following an earlier examination of part of St. Michael's cemetery in the south-east quadrant. Kine Croft was already a large open space within the south-west angle of the defences by the sixteenth century. This decline was not reversed until long after the end of the Middle Ages.

All other places in Oxfordshire possessing any serious claims to urban status emerged in this role between the tenth and thirteenth centuries. The distinction sometimes made between 'organic' and 'new' medieval towns is not a very satisfactory one. It becomes ever more difficult to identify a truly 'organic' town which has evolved spontaneously at some place of superior geographical advantage; indeed, it may be questioned whether an organism as complex as a town could ever develop without some degree of deliberate promotion or support by an individual or corporate estate-owner. Most towns in fact contain more than one element. Often an earlier village nucleus can be detected, with a new, planned urban settlement grafted onto it. Sometimes a more complex pattern occurred, with successive phases of medieval accretions producing a superficially rather formless plan. Nonetheless, such places were in reality no less 'artificial' or 'planned' than the occasional *de novo* foundation with an entirely contemporary layout.

In cases where the urban genesis was brought about primarily by a concerted action at one particular date, this may be reflected topographically by a certain regularity of plan. The exact form this takes may, however, vary considerably. Since commerce was now more important than defence, the key feature was often a new market-place, which would normally be lined with burgage tenements, the rear of which would sometimes terminate in a back lane parallel with the market frontage. In Thame and Henley the new market axis takes a cigar-shaped form, in Witney and Banbury it is wedge-shaped, in Bicester triangular, in Wantage, Deddington and Chipping Norton rectangular, in Burford simply a broad main street.

The best-known of the so-called 'new' towns is probably Thame, but even here the development was not a simple one-stage plantation. The original agricultural village, Old Thame, was centred on the existing parish church, and the curious curving circuit of Bell Street may preserve the alignment of part of its boundary. The liberty of Priestend at the western extremity of the town may have been laid out as a separate small planned unit after the establishment of the prebend in 1146. Exactly when New Thame, the main part of the present town lining the market-place, was founded is still not entirely clear; but it had probably been laid out before 1219, when the bishop of Lincoln acquired a licence to divert the Oxford-Aylesbury road into the town. A survey of the bishop's estates in *c.* 1230 listed 63 burgages in New Thame: these had been set out directly over open-field lands to standard dimensions of one acre each, for which an annual rent of one shilling was charged. Thame's subsequent modest prosperity resulted in the subdivision of many of these properties into half-acre and quarter-acre strips, but their general grain is still clearly visible, some of their boundaries retaining a slight aratral curve which fossilizes the alignment of the underlying open-field ploughstrips. Little archaeological excavation has taken place in Thame, and the couple of burgage frontages which have been examined proved unrewarding in terms of surviving medieval evidence.

A similar development seems to have occurred at Witney, perhaps as a response to the great expansion of cultivated land around the southern fringes of Wychwood through assarting during the twelfth and thirteenth centuries. The details are obscure, but the Winchester pipe roll of 1208–9 includes the first reference to Witney as a borough. Account rolls of 1211 and 1220 were already recording the borough as an entity separate from the manor. The topography of the present town suggests a major replanning, involving the total realignment of the roads through the settlement. The old crossing of the Windrush at Cogges and the east-west route along what is now Crown Lane and Corn Street were much reduced in importance. A new bridge was built some 600m upstream, giving access to the apex of a vast new market-place, orientated from north to south and cutting across the older road system, with the old parish church, substantially rebuilt and extended during the thirteenth century to serve the new urban community, occupying the southern end. An annual payment of 6d is by far the commonest rent recorded in the Hundred Rolls of 1279, a degree of standardization typical of 'new' towns. A clear pattern of burgage tenements is still visible on either side of the market-place, though this is suffering much erosion through modern redevelopment. Recently completed excavation on the site of the demolished Crown Inn fronting the market-place revealed a sequence of medieval hearths and floor levels.

There are other, even less well-documented, examples where the regular layout suggests a simple *de novo* plantation. At Chipping Norton the town centre, with its long rectangular market-place surrounded by burgage tenements, located a short distance above the parish church and castle, was probably developed by the FitzAlans in the twelfth century, but clear documentary evidence is lacking. Excavation on one market-place frontage has yielded hints of thirteenth- and fourteenth-century occupation, but as at Thame any remains of medieval structures were much disrupted by later activity (Chambers 1975a).

The disposition of streets and property boundaries often betrays changes in form, either through the imposition of new planned elements over an earlier pattern, or by the failure of a planned layout to maintain its original integrity. At Abingdon the development of a broad open market-place just outside the abbey gate clearly cut across the course of two older roads, East and West St. Helen's Streets, which focussed upon the minster church of St. Helen (Lambrick 1968a); this change presumably occurred some time between the refoundation of the abbey in the mid-tenth century and the first indications of the presence of a market in the mid-eleventh. Considerable archaeological work has taken place in and around Abingdon, but by and large this has thrown more light upon the pre-urban settlement of the area, or on special areas such as the abbey precinct, than upon the medieval town itself. Excavation in West St. Helen's Street has produced evidence of timber building in the twelfth and thirteenth centuries, superseded in the fourteenth century by a building with stone footings, both phases accompanied by many pits (Miles 1975). At the north end of the town, in Broad Street, another stone building, probably of thirteenth- or fourteenth-century date, with further pits, has been examined (Parrington & Balkwill 1975). More medieval pits and possible wharf structures have been excavated off Bridge Street (Parrington 1975). At the time of writing a site in Lombard Street is under investigation, and this has already produced an exotic import, a fragment of a medieval Islamic enamelled glass beaker.

Evidence of similar fundamental changes in plan can be detected even in the case of classic *de novo* planted towns. New Woodstock was certainly, and Henley-on-Thames probably, a foundation of Henry II. Both display many typical symptoms of plantation, such as anomalies in ecclesiastical status – Woodstock church was a chapelry of Bladon and Henley church a chapelry of Benson. At New Woodstock the rectilinear outline of the borough and the curiously cruciform alignments of some of the minor lanes and property boundaries within it may imply that the original intention there was to lay out the new town on a grid system. However, Woodstock's elevated status as a royal borough was not matched by its economic prosperity, tenements were not taken up as quickly as had apparently been hoped, and if any regular layout was ever intended it soon seems to have broken down into a main axis centred on a triangular market-place, one side of which cuts obliquely across the grain of the putative grid. At Henley the original planned axis appears to have been orientated from east to west, with the new church and bridge at the lower end, opening into a cigar-shaped market-place rising up to Gravel Hill. However, towards the upper end of this axis the pattern of burgages and their parallel back lanes fades out, and it looks as if the higher part was never fully occupied (there is a similar blank area at the south-eastern end of Thame). During the later Middle Ages a secondary north-south route now represented by Duke Street and Bell Street, which intersected the market-place at right-angles, seems to have assumed greater prominence, with increased development also taking place along the original back lanes of Friday Street and New Street; this may reflect the increasing river trade and increasing importance of the valley-side route.

Other changes involve the extension of towns by successive planned accretions. This is demonstrated particularly clearly in the topography of Eynsham (Aston & Bond 1976, 81–3). The central focus here is the small square outside the abbey gate which, as at

Abingdon, may have been superimposed over an older road pattern. The street issuing westwards from it, Acre End Street, from the evidence of its name may well represent a pre-urban agricultural nucleus; the alignment of the tenements and back lane on its northern side demonstrates quite clearly that it was fully occupied before a new row of tenements began to be developed along Mill Street, running north from the market-place. This in turn seems to have been developed before Newland Street was laid out. The Newland development was regarded as a completely separate new borough (Beresford 1967): it was founded by a charter of 1215, which permitted the abbot of Eynsham to divide up his demesne land between the old town and the street leading to Cassington Bridge, together with half a furlong to the north of the street, into 80 equal quarter-acre plots, to be let out at a standard annual rent of 1s. each. The road itself clearly already existed, and the new tenements were laid out over former agricultural land, probably, as at Thame, retaining in outline the grain of the underlying open-field strips.

Extensions of the Newland type, often bearing that same name, are not uncommon in Oxfordshire and neighbouring counties (cf. Bond 1977, 23–6). Following the promotion of Witney to borough status by the bishop of Winchester at the beginning of the thirteenth century, the lord of the manor of Cogges, on the opposite bank of the Windrush, attempted a similar venture in 1212–13, cutting 23 holdings of two acres each out of his demesne alongside the main Oxford road, and offered these for rent at 1s. per acre (Beresford 1967). At Banbury another new suburb called Newland had been laid out over the fields and meadows outside the East Bar of the town before 1285 (Harvey 1969). At Deddington a series of new tenements was laid out along the main Oxford-Banbury road some time in the thirteenth century, as an extension to the older town centred on the market-place.

Part of the development at Deddington still bears the name New Street, and the occurrence of this name elsewhere betokens more modest changes or extensions to the original plan. New Street in Henley was probably originally simply a back lane to the properties fronting the main road to the bridge, but later on it acquired a well-marked pattern of tenements in its own right – the evidence of existing buildings indicates that this had been developed by the fifteenth century. New Street in Chipping Norton, first recorded by name in 1549, appears to be a late medieval diversion leading the Worcester road into the centre of the market-place; the line of the older road which it superseded can still be traced as a hollow-way running up towards West End.

The most widespread manifestation of the breakdown of planning in the later Middle Ages is the reduction of market-places by encroachment. This was a result of pressure from three sources: from frontagers who wished to extend their premises forwards, from market stallholders who left their stalls in position from one market-day to the next and built them up into more and more permanent structures, and from the need to site important new public buildings in a central location. In 1284 the Justices in Eyre ordered the removal of stalls which had so narrowed the thoroughfare in the market-place of Wantage that carts could no longer pass; but in the following year permission was acquired for their re-erection. In 1221 it was reported that the bishop of Lincoln had 'made on the king's highway in the Forum of Thame an encroachment where he raised houses to increase his rent, to the length of 100 feet in all'. Thirty years later one of his successors erected eighteen stalls on the market-place, and encroachments were 'augmented . . . from year to year'. Here and elsewhere in Oxfordshire island blocks of building within the market-place, often including a town hall and market cross, have left a permanent mark upon the townscape.

Town defences were a significant feature only in Oxford and Wallingford. Elsewhere they were of minor importance. There is an antiquarian tradition of a Saxon rampart around Witney; the town had a mint in the eleventh century, and the reputed circuit is topographically attractive, but archaeological observations have so far failed to confirm its existence. Banbury certainly had a town ditch, four stone gates and possibly also a bargate upon the bridge in the early thirteenth century (Harvey 1969). Walls are recorded in Henley's town records from 1397 to 1531, and a 'Town Ditch' is marked on the first edition of the Ordnance Survey 1:2500. A tenement in Abingdon was located *extra barres* in 1478–9 (Kirk 1892, 139). Such gates and ditches probably had little military value, being more concerned with delimiting the borough boundary, controlling people and goods entering the market, and enabling tolls to be collected. Woodstock had a single murage grant for three years in 1322, but it is doubtful whether walls were ever built as a result. At Wantage the market-place lies in the centre of a large ovoid *enceinte* defined by Garston Lane and Ormond Road which would repay further examination.

Finally, special archaeological interest may be attached to areas of medieval occupation which have been vacated through the contraction or reorganization of the town plan, such as the open spaces within the defences of Wallingford. There may be some doubt whether the empty plots fronting one end of the market-place at both Thame and Henley were ever taken up for occupation. At Deddington, however, there are earthworks suggesting a series of abandoned house-plots fronting a former street linking Horse Fair with the Clifton Road. At Bicester a plan of 1753 shows a range of buildings along the north side of the King's End green which were swept away later in the century for an extension to the grounds of Bicester House, and a short distance to the east in Lower Home Close a further area of abandoned medieval settlement has recently been recognized.

Medieval Rural Settlement

It has become increasingly evident in recent years that the large nucleated village, which has remained the most characteristic feature of rural settlement in the greater part of Oxfordshire from the Middle Ages into the present century, was not, as was once thought, an introduction of the first English settlers. This traditional hypothesis has been overturned by new information from archaeological evidence which indicates a much more dispersed pattern of early Saxon settlement, and the tendency towards nucleation must now be viewed as a late Saxon, perhaps in some cases even a post-Conquest phenomenon. The reasons for the change are still far from certain, but the influences at work probably include the rising pressure of population, the need to organize agricultural production more efficiently, the evolution of the classic communal open-field system, the reorganization of the early church into the parochial system, and the imposition of feudal authority. These factors doubtless interacted with one another in a variety of ways over a considerable period of time, and the process is unlikely to have been a simple or uniform one.

Although the tendencies towards nucleation and towards greater stability of site had become pronounced by the time the high-water mark of medieval settlement was reached towards the end of the thirteenth century, significant changes were still taking place. Apart from the widespread desertions of many villages and hamlets in the later Middle Ages, to be examined further below, there is also much evidence for village contraction, migration and replanning (cf. Taylor 1978). Map 14, which attempts to plot all nucleated medieval rural settlements in Oxfordshire, therefore in some ways presents a misleadingly static picture. Nonetheless it has some value both in demonstrating the sheer number of medieval villages and hamlets in existence, and in illustrating their general distribution – the absence of settlement on the highest crests of the Berkshire Downs and Chilterns and the string of villages along the spring-line below the scarp of the Downs are especially striking. Moreover, the deserted settlements, which have on several previous occasions been presented in isolation, can here be seen in their proper context in the overall settlement pattern.

The settlements plotted on Map 14 have been subdivided in two ways:–

(i) The larger symbols indicate *villages* which contained the main focal point of ecclesiastical, and often also of manorial, administration within each medieval parish. During the early Middle Ages they were often, but not invariably, the largest settlement in the parish. The smaller symbols represent *hamlets* or townships of nucleated form which were originally administratively subordinate to the first group, though some of them acquired independent parochial status at a later date. It should be emphasized that the smaller symbols do not necessarily imply that these places were smaller in extent, had smaller populations, or were of later origin than the central settlement in the parish. Isolated medieval homesteads have been omitted from this map altogether, since their distribution is too imperfectly investigated at present.

(ii) The shading of the symbols distinguishes fairly crudely between places which survive to the present day apparently intact within their medieval perimeter, places which have undergone a degree of contraction or shift, and places which have become deserted. There are, obviously, many difficulties in attempting to impose such a rigid classification over a subject as fluid and dynamic as rural settlement. Particular problems surround the definition of 'settlements with evidence of contraction': at one end of the scale, many large and thriving villages include the odd gap where one or two medieval crofts are no longer occupied, while at the other end of the scale few so-called 'deserted' villages are entirely devoid of occupied buildings and a single farm or cottage remains on most sites of this type. Within this range of options any division is, of necessity, an arbitrary and somewhat subjective one. Moreover, even where earthwork evidence or medieval pottery scatters can be traced adjoining an extant settlement, it may be very difficult to determine whether these represent a genuine contraction or simply a local shift of site which did not necessarily involve any loss of population.

The map also includes an attempt to reconstruct the boundaries of the medieval parishes and townships, so far as currently-available information permits, and with the reservation that, in a few areas, further work may necessitate a few modifications to the pattern shown here. The main point to emerge from this exercise is the range of relationships between parishes, villages and hamlets. Some parishes contain a single nucleated settlement, either an extant village such as Wigginton, Towersey or Chilton, or a deserted site such as Eaton Hastings or Godington. By contrast, there are numerous large multi-township parishes such as Cumnor, Enstone, Great Haseley and Great Milton; within such parishes the subsidiary settlements frequently comprised smaller, more compact land units over which they operated field systems independently of those of the main village; but occasionally, as in the Baldons, several townships shared an integrated field system which was worked in common.

Many aspects of medieval rural settlement still require further investigation. The fundamental question of continuity of estates and the relationship between medieval and earlier settlement patterns and forms remains, and there is much more work to be done upon the morphology of villages and the evolution of the characteristic medieval and post-medieval plan types (cf. Bond 1985).

Deserted and Shrunken Villages

The realization that deserted medieval villages are a common and widespread phenomenon has been probably the most important contribution of work on rural settlement since the Second World War. Map 15 is a direct abstraction from the preceding map, all the extant settlements and boundaries having been eliminated in order to give the distribution of deserted and shrunken settlements greater prominence. Much of the information presented here is derived from the two standard works (Allison et al. 1965; Beresford & Hurst 1971), which list just over a hundred deserted sites within the historic county of Oxfordshire. The boundary extension which took in the Vale of the White Horse in 1974 and the continuing progress of discovery of new sites which has been recorded in the Annual Reports of the Medieval Village Research Group since the late 1960s has now increased the number of deserted medieval villages known in Oxfordshire to nearly 150. With about 24 per cent. of all the medieval villages in the county now deserted, it appears as one of the most heavily-affected parts of England. The distribution of 'shrunken' settlements, hitherto unpublished, is also presented on this map, subject to the caveats expressed in the preceding section.

It must be emphasized at the outset that the causes and chronology of village desertion are immensely varied and complex and still not yet fully understood. Map 15 includes sites deserted at many different dates for many different reasons. Beresford & Hurst (1971, 12) suggest that the chronology of desertion in Oxfordshire is as follows:– 1% of sites deserted before c.1100, 8% between c.1100 and c.1350, 30% from c.1350 to c.1450, 45% from c.1450 to c.1700 and 3% after c.1700, with the remaining 13% of desertions being undatable within even the widest limits. Even within the same period many different causes may operate, and it is highly dangerous to attempt to project an overall picture from the example of one or two well-documented or well-researched sites.

The overall distribution of sites is therefore of limited meaning unless the different periods and causes of desertion could be identified and plotted separately, and this could not yet be attempted with any great confidence. Nonetheless, some general comments can be made. Few parts of Oxfordshire are now seen to be devoid of deserted and shrunken sites. The principal exceptions are in the south, along the chalklands of the Berkshire Downs and Chilterns, and to a lesser extent in the central Wychwood area and in the dissected uplands of Bloxham Hundred in the north. Here, it has been suggested, the greater pastoral element in the economy permitted relative immunity. By contrast, some of the greatest densities occur in the vale between the Chilterns and the River Thame where, in the early Middle Ages, open-field farming had spread out to the limits of each parish, reducing the permanent pasture to a minimum, despite the fact that the heavy clay soils probably favoured grass rather than corn. However, the pattern as a whole is too complex to permit any simplistic explanation based primarily on the geological background.

During the general economic expansion of the early Middle Ages few villages became deserted. The exceptional instances which can be documented usually seem to be a result of seigneurial reorganization, with the inhabitants being resettled elsewhere. Early desertions are sometimes associated with the foundation of Cistercian abbeys and granges. The village of Treton, which had been a substantial settlement of 23 holdings in 1086, formed part of the endowment of Bruern Abbey in 1147 and was converted to a grange; Bruern Abbey may also have had a hand in the depopulation of other sites in the area such as Dunthrop and Sewell. Monastic houses of other orders seem to have followed the same practice on occasions. The inhabitants of Ash, a hamlet on the edge of Otmoor which was granted to Studley Priory in about 1176, may have been removed and resettled at Studley itself. The village of Fulwell became a grange of Oseney Abbey in 1205, and by the end of the thirteenth century most of its land had been converted to sheep pasture and its inhabitants removed to Mixbury. Similar migrations may also have occurred on lay estates: the desertion of the village of Cogges appears to coincide with its lord's attempt to found a new borough elsewhere in the parish in the early thirteenth century.

By the beginning of the fourteenth century economic decline was beginning to set in, and a few settlements on marginal land probably proved untenable. Langley, on a bleak and exposed position on the Windrush-Evenlode watershed over 180m above sea level, may be an example – there had been 18 tenants there in 1279, but only four remained by 1327. However, very little land in Oxfordshire can truly be described as poor farmland, and it would be wrong to claim the retreat from the margins of cultivation as a major factor in village desertions. The distribution map confirms that most desertions occurred, not in the areas of new colonization around Wychwood or in the Chilterns, but in the old-settled lands in the clay vales, the Upper Thames Valley and the Cotswold dip-slope. In such regions local variations in soil quality may have been a factor of some significance, and there may be a decline in some of the secondary hamlets established during the land hunger of the eleventh and twelfth centuries; but there was no wholesale abandonment of newly-colonized land.

A substantial reduction of population was brought about by the Black Death of 1349. Generally few villages suffered total destruction by this epidemic. Oxfordshire does, however, contain two classic examples: the site of Tusmore has been recorded (Miles & Rowley 1976), but the exact location of the hamlet of Tilgarsley in Eynsham remains controversial. One or two more Oxfordshire desertions may have been a direct result of the plague. Thrupp in Radley received a massive tax abatement in 1352. At Coat in Charlbury an early fourteenth-century Eynsham Abbey rental lists 12 tenants, but the abbot received no rents in 1350 and, ten years later, was excused payment of tax because he no longer had lands or tenements there. Remarkably clear earthworks including a roadway, boundary bank and about a dozen building platforms survived here until 1981, when parts were levelled and ploughed; pottery from the site confirms the mid-fourteenth century desertion.

Although the population was greatly reduced during

the second half of the fourteenth century, most villages were able to recover to some extent from the immediate impact of the Black Death. The effect was, however, to afford surviving tenants a much greater mobility. Settlements where holdings were less attractive than those of neighbouring villages by reason of poorer yields, more burdensome services or higher rents now found themselves at a distinct disadvantage: their tenants were now much more likely to abandon their holdings to seek a better living elsewhere, and it was increasingly difficult to find new tenants to replace them. At Oseney Abbey's manor of Brookend, a new settlement founded in the twelfth century on the waste of Chastleton, vacant holdings were beginning to appear after 1381, by 1422 the abbey was suffering serious loss of rents, and twenty years later only three tenants remained (Lloyd 1964–5). Similarly at Shifford accounts and court rolls for 1458–1467 yield many references to ruinous messuages which were not repaired.

In general it was the smaller settlements closely hemmed in by neighbouring communities, the settlements with limited land resources entirely devoted to open-field farming with inadequate reserves of pasture, and those on marginally poorer soils which were most likely to disappear. Variations in tenure were probably more important than any other single factor, however, in determining which settlements were to fail and which to survive: places with a high proportion of customary tenants more heavily burdened with rents, with standardized inflexible holdings which could not readily be adapted to suit changing social and economic conditions, were especially vulnerable.

Depopulation caused by the lord of the manor carrying out forced evictions in order to enclose land for sheep pasture was reaching its peak during the period 1450–1485 (Beresford 1954), but this no longer seems quite such a dominant reason for village desertions as was once thought. Far from being invariably the villain of the piece, the manorial lord often had much to lose from depopulation because of declining income from rents. The Brookend evidence shows Oseney Abbey attempting to resist the decay of the village by a deliberate policy of seeking new tenants for abandoned holdings for as long as possible. A final decision to enclose and convert to pasture was often taken only some time after depopulation, as a means of cutting the losses when all else had failed. Even where forced evictions did occur, the process had largely been completed before 1488, the limitation date set upon the Inquiry of 1517, the returns from which are one of the principal sources for this type of depopulation. The extent of land recorded as converted to pasture in the 1517 returns is rarely more than a couple of hundred acres, and the houses destroyed in each village were usually numbered in ones and twos. Only exceptionally, as at Wheatfield, where John Streatley had evicted 54 people and destroyed 7 houses, were more substantial depopulations recorded. At Eaton Hastings sheep-farming is cited as the principal cause of a relatively late depopulation occurring between 1509 and 1523 (Brooks 1969).

Post-medieval village depopulations are relatively uncommon, and are usually connected with changes carried out under seigneurial control, in particular the removal of settlements which were in the way of landscaping schemes in the vicinity of a big house and the resettling of their inhabitants in a new estate village outside the park. Nuneham Courtenay (Batey 1968, 1978) and Middleton Stoney are the classic Oxfordshire examples, but partial destructions by emparkment can also be detected on several other sites, including Bletchingdon and Chesterton.

Many deserted and shrunken villages are still recognizable from surviving earthworks, but their numbers are being relentlessly reduced by ploughing and other destructive agencies, and the need to record them is urgent. About 20 of the best-quality earthwork sites have so far been subjected to measured surveys (e.g. Reeves 1971, and Annual Reports of the Medieval Village Research Group), and over 30 more have been provisionally recorded by sketch surveys. Earthwork surveys have their limitations, since they only reflect the village plan during its later stages of occupation. Nonetheless, some significant recurrent features have been observed, such as the presence of ridge and furrow underlying crofts at Somerford, Tusmore and Water Eaton, which implies the encroachment of settlement over former open-field lands. Minor alterations in plan are illustrated at Coat, where one range of buildings has clearly encroached over a former roadway, causing its diversion. Useful evidence has also come from watching-briefs and fieldwalking operations on ploughed sites. Asterleigh, Ilbury, Rofford, Walcot and Wilcote have all produced pottery predominantly of twelfth- to fourteenth-century date, but at Astrop the sequence seems to begin in the eleventh and terminate in the mid-thirteenth century. Thomley has produced some early medieval pottery, but the bulk of it dates from the thirteenth to fifteenth centuries, as does the material recovered from the site of the new village hall recently built in the shrunken village of Sandford-on-Thames. Another modern disturbance at Attington yielded mainly fifteenth-century pottery.

The number of excavations has been more limited, although the investigation of the site of the church and other medieval buildings at Woodperry in the 1840s (Wilson 1846) must rank as one of the earliest excavations ever carried out on a deserted village in England. Medieval villages, perhaps above all other types of site, require large-scale open-area excavations carried out to meticulously high standards before they can be fully understood, and no research excavation of this nature has yet been possible on any Oxfordshire example. Only at Seacourt has initial trial-trenching (Bruce-Mitford 1940) been followed up by the more extensive examination of several house sites and further salvage recording during bulldozing as the site was bisected by the construction of Oxford's western by-pass (Biddle 1961–2). No structures earlier than the mid-twelfth century were found, suggesting that the area examined was an extension from the original village nucleus. The earliest peasant buildings were of timber, employing both post-hole and sill-beam construction, but between the mid-thirteenth and early fourteenth centuries they were being replaced in stone. The road was also metalled in the thirteenth century. The houses were mostly rectangular, with a single hearth centrally-placed or against the centre of the end wall. Several subsidiary farm buildings were recorded. No examples of the longhouse, with living-accommodation, cross-passage and byre all under the same roof, were encountered, however. The results of the excavation supported the documentary evidence for Seacourt's decline and desertion in the mid-fourteenth century.

More limited excavation at Lea in Swalcliffe in the 1950s revealed a building of greater pretensions, a large stone house occupied from the fourteenth to the seventeenth century which appears to have been the immediate predecessor of the existing farmhouse. Three more sites were examined during the 1960s, none yet fully published. At Dornford a sequence of peasant houses and outbuildings dating apparently from the eleventh to the fifteenth century was recognized. One building was excavated at Pinkhill, producing evidence of occupation from the twelfth to the fifteenth century. Work at Tulwick also indicated occupation continuing into the fifteenth century. Another small excavation at Thomley in 1970 located foundations and clay and stone-pitched floors.

More recent work has concentrated upon shrunken rather than completely deserted sites. Two areas of contraction on the southern side of Tetsworth were examined prior to their destruction by the M40: limited work on one of those sites produced evidence of occupation from the eleventh to the fourteenth century (Hinton 1973), while more extensive excavation of the other revealed a substantial twelfth-century farmhouse within an enclosure, replaced in the early thirteenth century by a more ordinary house and barn, which was finally abandoned at the end of the thirteenth century (Robinson 1973). Rescue excavation prior to a building development at Hanwell revealed several stone buildings apparently resulting from an expansion of the village in about the thirteenth century reversed by desertion by the early eighteenth century (Chambers 1975b). Observations of a pipe trench have suggested that part of Somerton may have ceased to be occupied before the mid-fourteenth century (Chambers 1977).

Although deserted isolated medieval farmsteads have not been considered in the above discussion, brief mention should be made of two sites of this nature recently examined by excavation. A site discovered in 1972 at Sadler's Wood in Lewknor has produced evidence for substantial stone buildings occupied from the early or mid-thirteenth to the later fourteenth century (Chambers 1973), and a second thirteenth-century assart farmstead at Slape Copse in Glympton has also received limited investigation.

Monastic Houses

Well before the Norman Conquest a variety of monastic and ecclesiastical foundations had been established along the Thames in the richer anciently-settled areas. The Roman town of Dorchester, where Birinus had founded the first see of Wessex in 634, was subsequently the centre of a Mercian diocese until this was transferred to Lincoln in 1070, and a community of secular canons survived there up to the time of the Augustinian refoundation in about 1140. Frideswide's eighth-century minster at Oxford, destroyed in 1002, was also re-established as a house of secular canons, which survived at least up to $c.1111$.

The great English monastic revival of the tenth century saw the foundation of two important Benedictine houses. Abingdon, originally a seventh-century foundation, was refounded in 954 and then maintained a continous existence until the Dissolution. Richly-endowed with extensive estates, it was by far the wealthiest monastic house in the Upper Thames region. Upstanding remains include the gatehouse with the adjoining church of St. Nicholas, built to serve the abbey's lay tenants and servants, and important fragments of some of the peripheral administrative and domestic ranges; but the church was completely dismantled after the Dissolution, although some evidence for its plan was recovered by excavation in 1922 (Biddle 1968). Using the documentary evidence (e.g. Kirk 1892) alongside the excavated and upstanding remains, a valuable, if partly tentative, plan of the entire precinct has been reconstructed (Lambrick 1968b).

The second new Benedictine foundation, at Eynsham, was removed after the Norman Conquest to Stow in Lincolnshire, but the community returned to Eynsham in 1094. While it never rivalled Abingdon, it still became the third richest abbey in the county. Relatively little is known about the early layout of its precinct, but there is both documentary and field evidence of a major later extension (cf. Chambers 1936). In 1217 a new grange or barn was built near the old barton, and a road realigned around the new western boundary of the precinct: the new road must be the present Station Road (formerly New Bridge Street), and its predecessor can still be traced as a hollow-way southwards from the cul-de-sac of Abbey Street to the earlier crossing of the Chil Brook. At least one plot containing a house had to be acquired by the abbey in order to carry out this precinct extension, and the documentary description of its location suggests a very plausible identification with a platform still visible alongside the old road south of the Chil Brook. Another survey of $c.1360$ describes the garden, the fishponds then recently made, and the agricultural buildings around the court to the west of the abbey. The ruins of the abbey church survived into the seventeenth century, and the gatehouse later still, but no visible upstanding masonry remains and, apart from slight traces of an unusually complex flight of fishponds, the site is levelled. However, desultory excavation in 1851, observations during grave-digging in the churchyard extension and trial excavations in 1962–3 and 1970 (Gray & Clayton 1978) have shown that important remains survive below ground, and the site has considerable potential for future examination.

No further major Benedictine abbeys were founded after the Conquest, but there were a number of smaller houses. Wallingford Priory was established as a dependency of St. Alban's Abbey in the later eleventh century. It was demolished after the Dissolution, and much of its stone reused in 1530 to repair Wallingford Bridge. Its site lay somewhere in Bull Croft in the north-west quarter of the *burh*. No details of its plan are known, though there have been some chance discoveries: burials were located nearby in 1983. The small priory of Pheleley near Charlbury developed out of a Wychwood hermitage some time early in the twelfth century; it was absorbed by Eynsham Abbey in 1145, there are no known remains, and even its exact location is controversial.

Several small alien Benedictine priories were established during the course of the twelfth century: Cogges Priory was founded as a dependency of Fécamp in 1103, Steventon Priory as a dependency of Bec at about the same time, and Minster Lovell Priory as a dependency of Ivry in about 1183. Some documentary evidence exists for these houses (cf. Salter 1930; Taylor 1937), but their general plan is imperfectly understood. Fragments of a twelfth-century structure incorporated into the farmhouse north of Minster Lovell church may be part of the priory building. More complete remains of a mid-thirteenth-century hall are incorporated into the vicarage north of Cogges church (Blair & Steane 1982). In both cases the present parish church would also seem to have served as the priory church. At Steventon part of a late medieval hall and solar which may belong to the priory also remains.

Three Benedictine nunneries were also founded during the twelfth century. By far the most important of these was Godstow, established in 1133. Substantial ruins and earthworks still remain (R.C.H.M. 1939), and the location and appearance of other buildings now demolished is known from earlier descriptions and prospects (Ganz 1972). Alterations to the course of the Thames at various dates since 1780 have brought to light stone coffins and tiles, and further information has come from small excavations in 1939, 1959 and 1971, but the site has yet to receive detailed archaeological investigation. A smaller nunnery was founded at Littlemore around 1140 and, unusually, the eastern range of its cloister garth, incorporating the dormitory and chapter-house, survive in the present Minchery Farm building (Pantin 1970). The buildings of the nunnery of Studley, founded around 1175, were largely demolished to make way for the Tudor mansion which now occupies the site; but the discovery of medieval foundations was reported in the nineteenth century.

The only other order to achieve any major presence in Oxfordshire was the Augustinian canons, for whom six new houses were founded during the twelfth and early thirteenth centuries. The first was St. Frideswide's Priory in Oxford, refounded in 1122 on or near the site of the Saxon minster. Little is known of the Augustinian phase archaeologically, but some of the monastic buildings were incorporated into Wolsey's Cardinal College (now Christ Church) in 1525. The new college buildings caused the removal of the western three bays of the church, the west cloister range, kitchen and refectory, and subsequently also the prior's lodging. The surviving Augustinian remains include the remainder of the nave, aisles, transepts, crossing-tower, presbytery and chapels of the church, dating mainly from the twelfth century with late medieval alterations (used since 1546 as the cathedral of the diocese of Oxford); the twelfth-century slype below the south transept; the early thirteenth-century chapter-house and dorter range; and the fifteenth-century frater, with three sides of the cloister (R.C.H.M. 1939).

Seven years later a second Augustinian abbey was founded about 1km to the west at Oseney. This flourished, developing into one of the largest Augustinian abbeys in England, and locally exceeded in wealth only by the Benedictine house of Abingdon. After the Dissolution its church served briefly as the cathedral of the new diocese, but after four years this function was removed to St. Frideswide's. Piecemeal robbing and demolition caused the disappearance of almost all the buildings between 1547 and 1725. One small stone building with a fine fifteenth-century roof and an adjoining wall pierced by a four-centred arch of similar date survives, together with a few architectural fragments. A single rectangular fishpond survived into the early part of the present century. There is a long record of chance discoveries of foundations, stone coffins, moulded masonry, tiles and other finds since the eighteenth century, which have made a tentative reconstruction of the plan possible (Squires 1928), but no controlled archaeological excavation took place until 1983, when foundations of a long barn or stable and other medieval structures at the southern end of the precinct were examined.

Dorchester Abbey, refounded as an Augustinian house in 1140, succeeded an earlier community of secular canons, as did St. Frideswide's. Its church passed into parochial use after the Dissolution, and all but the north transept and chapel still remains. The greater part of the building dates from the twelfth century, the south aisle was added in the fourteenth century, and the west tower was largely rebuilt in 1602. Substantial remains of the main claustral buildings, which (unusually for a non-urban site without obvious topographical constraints) lay on the north side of the church, were destroyed in the late seventeenth or early eighteenth century; the extent of the cloister was demonstrated by small-scale excavations in 1960–62 (Cunningham & Banks 1972). Remains of a detached medieval stone building west of the church, probably the guesthouse, were incorporated into the later Grammar School house and still survive. A much-altered fishpond also survives. Unfortunately, however, a substantial timber barn which probably belonged to the abbey's demesne farm was swept away to make room for new housing in the mid-twentieth century.

A smaller Augustinian priory with a hospital attached was established at Cold Norton some time between 1148 and 1158. It was largely demolished soon after the Dissolution, although a Buck prospect of 1729 shows a medieval ruin, which had gone by *c*.1850, surviving among the later farm buildings, and fragments of a gatehouse are reputed to have survived until 1962. Chance discoveries of tiles, window tracery and burials have been recorded, but there has been no controlled archaeological excavation (Hookins 1853–5; Wing 1853–5).

Rather more is known of Bicester Priory, founded *c*.1182–85. Here, too, the church was dismantled immediately after the Dissolution, and though some of the other buildings were converted to domestic use, they also were demolished after 1673. The gatehouse survived up to about 1800. The present Church Meeting House and the seventeenth-century dwelling called the Old Priory both include reused monastic stonework. Excavation in 1819 located massive stone foundations (Dunkin 1823). The site was largely destroyed by housing development in 1964–66, during which observation and limited trial excavation recovered a partial plan of the church and other claustral buildings (Hinton 1968, 1969); part of the south transept was seen during further building works in 1983.

The last Oxfordshire house of Augustinian canons was founded at Wroxton in 1217. Fragments of the priory buildings were incorporated into the existing seventeenth-century mansion; other remains were levelled during the landscaping of its grounds. Unpublished excavations carried out in 1956 and 1964 are said to have revealed conduits and foundations of the priory church and of some of the outbuildings. The only Augustinian nunnery in Oxfordshire was at Goring, founded some time early in the twelfth century: here the nunnery church was built as an eastern extension of the parish church. It was demolished soon after the Dissolution, but foundations excavated in 1892 showed that the nunnery church was cruciform, with cloisters, dormitory and chapter-house wing and refectory attached (Stone 1893).

Compared with the Benedictine monks and Augustinian canons, the reformed orders were able to make only a limited impact on Oxfordshire. The most important were the Cistercians, but while they successfully established three abbeys during the twelfth and thirteenth centuries, none of these was of the first rank. They illustrate several distinctive features of Cistercian colonization. The order preferred remote, isolated areas with reserves of uncultivated land: correspondingly, the first, short-lived Cistercian house in Oxfordshire was established in 1138 in the marshy clayland of Otley near the edge of Otmoor, while Bruern Abbey was founded in 1147 on a heath on the north-west side of Wychwood Forest. The very uncharacteristic suburban location of Rewley Abbey derived from its founder's intention in 1280 to establish a monastic college, but it was reorganized as an orthodox Cistercian abbey the following year. Cistercian houses were also somewhat prone to being uprooted and transferred to different sites, and this occurred twice in Oxfordshire. The monks at Otley found the site too wet even for them, and moved to a new locality within the old deer park of Thame in 1140, retaining their original home as a grange. The Cistercian community established at Faringdon in 1203 found itself in an insufficiently secluded locality, where it was brought too much into collision with neighbouring monastic interests, and in 1204–5 it moved out of the county altogether to Beaulieu (Hants.), with the old site again being retained as a grange.

None of the Oxfordshire Cisterican abbeys appear very impressive today. The principal survival is at Thame, where the *capella ad portam* was retained as a private chapel and part of the abbot's lodging and another medieval range were encased within the Palladian mansion of Thame Park. Some details of the remainder of the monastic plan were recovered in *c*.1840 (Lee 1888), but there has been no subsequent archaeological work. At Rewley some ruins survived into the eighteenth century, but today only part of the precinct wall with a fifteenth-century doorway is visible. The allotments, railway sidings and coal depot which cover the site are ripe for redevelopment, and although trial holes and observations have so far been relatively uninformative, it is likely that more extensive excavation would yield significant results. At Bruern no traces remain and nothing is known of the plan or extent of the monastic buildings.

Of the reformed orders of canons, only the Gilbertines had interests in Oxfordshire. Their priory at Clattercote was developed from an earlier leper hospital in about 1150. Its remains were incorporated into an early seventeenth-century mansion and are depicted in a Buck prospect of 1729, but further rebuilding since that date has left only a few thirteenth- and fourteenth-century details in the east wing of the house.

The two main military orders are both represented locally. The Knights Templars established their first preceptory at Cowley in 1136, subsequently acquiring considerable estates and founding another preceptory at Merton and camerae at Sibford, Warpsgrove and Westcot in Sparsholt. In 1240 a new preceptory was founded at Sandford-on-Thames which then became the main administrative centre for all the Templar estates in Oxfordshire, Berkshire and Hampshire, while Cowley and Merton were reduced to the status of camerae. Part of the thirteenth-century chapel at Sandford is incorporated into a barn at Temple Farm. When the order was suppressed in 1308, its possessions were transferred to the Knights Hospitallers. Their main local preceptory was at Clanfield, the site of which is indicated by the moat at Friars Court, though none of the medieval buildings remain.

Collegiate churches were located within the castles of both Oxford and Wallingford. A college of secular canons attached to the church of St. George in the Castle in Oxford, founded in 1074, was absorbed by Oseney Abbey in 1149, but by about 1480 another college of priests had emerged there, and this survived until the Dissolution. At Wallingford there was a church and college of St. Nicholas in the outer bailey by 1200, and this was refounded with a more generous endowment in 1280. Documentary evidence records its further enlargement with a bell-tower, gallery and kitchen early in the sixteenth century. After the Dissolution its residential buildings were acquired by the canons of Christ Church, Oxford, and a survey of 1548 suggests that the priests' lodgings were arranged around a small cloistered quadrangle immediately south of the church. The buildings were ruined in the Civil War, and only fragmentary remains of walling with a fifteenth-century doorway and windows now remain.

About two dozen medieval hospitals are recorded, but it is difficult to arrive at a definitive total since some were poorly-documented, short-lived, absorbed into other institutions or refounded for different purposes. When hospitals first appeared, in the early twelfth century, their function was simply to provide shelter and hospitality for travellers of all kinds, and only later on did they come to cater more specifically for the sick. This change of function is sometimes reflected in a change of plan, the large common dormitory being replaced by a range of separate rooms. One institution known to have changed its role in this way is the Hospital of St. John the Baptist in Oxford, first recorded in 1180 as a hostel for travellers, but refounded in 1231 as an infirmary for the sick: in 1457 it was absorbed into the new foundation of Magdalen College, and parts of its extensive premises were incorporated into the High Street front and kitchens of the college. Part of its burial ground was uncovered in 1976–77. Hospitals frequently had their own chapel. The Norman church at Crowmarsh probably had its origins as the chapel of the leper hospital of St. Mary Magdalene outside Wallingford, founded before 1142. The chapel of St. Bartholomew's Hospital in Oxford was built soon after 1328, when the foundation was acquired by Oriel College as a rest-house. Fragments of St. John's Hospital in Burford, St. John's Hospital in Abingdon and St. John's Hospital in Wallingford all survive incorporated into later buildings, but otherwise the earlier medieval hospitals have left few visible remains.

Before the fifteenth century most hospitals were located in the towns: the greatest concentration was in Oxford itself, but several of the smaller market towns had two or three examples. Being relative late-comers, they were often situated towards the margins of the built-up area, a position which suited their function both as hospices for travellers and as lazar-houses. The later medieval hospitals were more frequently in rural locations, and this often signifies a further change of function: they were now primarily almshouses for the aged, poor and infirm, and lepers and the incurably sick were often firmly excluded. At Ewelme the original buildings of the almshouses founded by the Earl of Suffolk in 1437 still remain, and these are notable not only for their early use of ornamental brickwork, but also for their innovatory plan: making a complete break with previous tradition, they consist of thirteen separate dwellings around a cloister. This is very reminiscent of the distinctive plan of monasteries of the Carthusian order, and it may be significant that the Earl's grandfather had founded a Charterhouse in Hull some 60 years earlier. This form of plan proved very suitable for its purpose, and was soon being imitated elsewhere. At Fyfield a hospital was founded in conjunction with a chantry in the parish church in 1442, and the original priest's house is now the White Hart Inn. The last pre-Reformation foundation of this type was a small almshouse founded in 1526 at Childrey (Markham 1979).

The various orders of friars which made such an impact on religious and intellectual life during the thirteenth century were concentrated exclusively in Oxford. The first to arrive were the Dominicans or Black Friars, who in 1221 acquired a cramped site in Little Jewry east of St. Aldate's for what was only their second foundation in England. In 1245 they moved to an extra-mural location in St. Ebbe's south of the Trill Mill stream, where there was more room for expansion (Hinnebusch, 1938). Most of the buildings of the second Blackfriars were dismantled in 1544, though a fifteenth-century gatehouse survived, only recently recognized; excavation prior to redevelopment has enabled a considerable part of the plan of the church, claustral and subsidiary buildings to be recovered (Hassall 1973, 1974; Lambrick & Woods 1976).

The Franciscans or Grey Friars arrived in Oxford in 1224, and by about 1235 they had acquired a site between St. Ebbe's church and the city wall, where they began their first buildings. In 1244 they acquired a large adjoining plot outside the city wall, with permission to extend their claustral buildings and precinct across the line of the original defences. Extensive excavations prior to the destruction of the site during the Westgate Centre redevelopment in 1970–71 revealed the peculiar T-shaped plan of the church, confirming the description given by William Worcestre in 1480, and located some of the subsidiary buildings (Hassall 1969, 1970, 1971, 1974).

Of the Oxford friaries only the Blackfriars and Greyfriars have received extensive examination below ground. The Carmelites or White Friars acquired a site in Worcester Street in 1256 where they built their first friary, but in 1318 Edward II granted them the disused royal lodging of Beaumont Palace. The palace buildings were converted by the Carmelites for their own use and their earlier premises were sold to the Benedictines for the use of Gloucester College. The last remains of the second Whitefriars were destroyed by the building of Beaumont Street in 1825. The Austin Friars, who acquired their first premises outside the East Gate in 1267, also moved shortly afterwards to a better site outside the Smith Gate in St. Cross parish; most of their buildings were demolished after the Dissolution, but a few fragments were later incorporated into Wadham College (Blair 1976). Other orders, such as the Friars of the Sack, the Trinitarians and the Crutched Friars, had only a short tenure in Oxford, and virtually nothing is known of their buildings.

A more unusual type of monastic establishment, also entirely restricted to Oxford, is represented by the monastic colleges attached to the University. All but one of these were absorbed by post-Dissolution colleges, and considerable portions of their late medieval buildings remain in use. The first three all belonged to the Benedictines. The earliest, and the chief seat of the Benedictine monks in the University, was Gloucester College, founded in 1283, and now incorporated into Worcester College. Durham College was founded in 1291 as a cell of Durham Priory, and its buildings were later taken into Trinity College. Canterbury College, founded in 1362, was absorbed into Henry VIII's foundation of Christ Church, and none of its buildings survive. The Cistercian College of St. Bernard, founded in 1437, was re-established as St. John's College in 1554, and its original buildings survive in the present front quadrangle. The only monastic college not perpetuated in a post-Dissolution foundation was the Augustinian College of St. Mary in New Inn Hall Street. This was founded in 1435, but its ambitious suite of buildings was not completed till after 1518. The remains of its gatehouse have long been visible, but only recently has the roof of what may have been one of its ancillary buildings been identified concealed within a later building further south, while trial excavations in 1976–77 identified fragments of the chapel (Blair 1978).

Monastic houses were supported by income drawn from a wide variety of sources. For some orders their greatest wealth lay in their landed estates, which were exploited in a variety of ways. The larger Benedictine abbeys in particular were often richly endowed with extensive estates over which they maintained comparative security of tenure for five or six centuries, and they therefore had ample opportunity and incentive to invest their capital in projects which produced major changes in the landscape. The Cistercians too, so often cast in the role of colonizers of under-exploited land, were perhaps even more active within a rather shorter time-span.

The local focus of monastic land management is frequently described as a 'grange', a rather unsatisfactory term projected from contemporary Cistercian usage, which can mean either a largely consolidated and independently-operated estate, or the range of buildings from which any monastic landed property was worked, or simply the great barn which was often the most important element of those buildings. It has become increasingly clear that, after the twelfth century, there was less to distinguish the estate management practices of the different orders than was once supposed (Platt 1969). There is not always any clear distinction between a 'grange' in the original Cistercian sense and an ordinary manorial estate held in demesne by an abbey of a different order, and both may include a very similar range of buildings.

Map 16 incorporates an attempt to plot some of the more important monastic demesne farms which included significant complexes of buildings. The problems of definition and the uneven coverage of research demand that this provisional distribution should be treated with extreme caution; but the apparent concentration in the Vale of the White Horse is probably not entirely illusory, although it may be a little overemphasized by published work on the Abingdon estates (Bond 1979). The buildings present on such sites might include domestic accommodation, chapel, barn, granary, stable, byre and dovecote in varying combinations; and the relative prominence of each element will itself vary according to whether the house was more or less frequently employed as a residence or rest-house, whether the estate was predominantly arable or pastoral, and various other factors. Substantial domestic ranges survive on the Abingdon estates, notably at Charney Bassett, Sutton Courtenay and Culham, while the details of the demolished house of Cumnor Place are well-documented and the site appears archaeologically little disturbed. A further Abingdon grange at Dean Court, not adequately identified in the 1979 survey, may shortly become available for archaeological examination.

The most distinctive medieval buildings surviving on the outlying monastic estates are the great barns, the finest local examples of which were all built by monasteries themselves located outside Oxfordshire. The well-known aisled barn at Great Coxwell (Horn & Born 1965; Siebenlist-Kerner et al. 1978) and the recently-recognized barn at Shilton (Heyworth 1971) both belonged to the Cistercian abbey of Beaulieu (Hants.). The vast barn at Cholsey, pulled down in 1815 and known only from earlier drawings and measurements (Horn 1963), belonged to Reading Abbey. The smaller barn at Church Enstone with its genuine but reset 1382 datestone (Wood-Jones 1956) belonged to Winchcombe Abbey (Gloucs.). Smaller barns also survive on the Abingdon properties of Northcourt, Shippon and Tadmarton (Bond 1979).

The broader economic and historical aspects of monastic estate management have been the subject of numerous important studies (e.g. Morgan 1946; Harvey 1977; Postles 1975a, 1975b, 1977), but the topographical expression of these varied activities would amply repay further examination, while the archaeological investigation of monastic granges and estate farms locally has hardly begun.

Castles and Moated Sites

Map 17 shows the distribution of a miscellaneous group of medieval sites whose principal feature in common is that they contain a defensive or quasi-defensive component. It embraces a wide chronological, tenurial and morphological range of sites, from the great royal castles begun immediately after the Norman Conquest down to the small moated homesteads occupied later in the Middle Ages by families often of sub-seigneurial status. Some of the major sites are very well documented and have received considerable archaeological investigation, but comparatively little is known about most of the lesser sites.

The plotting of this particular range of monuments poses exceptionally difficult problems of classification. Neither in contemporary medieval sources nor in modern usage does the popular nomenclature correspond precisely with recognizable physical categories of site. There are areas of overlap and difficulties of definition even within the different types of site which have been distinguished – the classification applied here is often extremely tentative due to the uneven spread of field investigation or the lack of sufficiently clear remains, and it is not always easy to distinguish where one type of site has evolved into, or been replaced on exactly the same location by another (for example, the conversion of a ringwork to a motte and bailey). Another difficulty arises from concentrating upon a single function of these sites, their 'defensive' role, out of a whole range of functions which they may have fulfilled. In physical terms this is expressed in the particular attention paid to the nature of the perimeter (curtain wall, towers, gatehouse, rampart or moat) in defining the class of site, rather than to the interior buildings and other structures. The result is that very disparate sites may all be classified under the same symbol, while many of those sites may not be significantly different in status or purpose from others which do not happen to be surrounded by any sort of 'defensive' perimeter and are therefore not mapped here. One obvious anomaly is that several monastic sites appear on this map as well as on Map 16 simply because they happen to be surrounded by a moat. Similarly, many of the moated manorial sites and sub-manorial farmsteads indicated on the map by the symbol for 'other moated sites' would have had virtually identical ranges of buildings and identical functions to numerous other manor-houses and farmsteads not marked here because they were never moated.

The more strongly-defended sites are conveniently referred to under the popular generic term 'castles', but this title conceals a wide range of forms of earthworks and buildings. The development of castles in Oxfordshire can be summarized as follows:–

(1) First to be built were the two great royal castles in the Saxon *burhs* of Wallingford and Oxford, both of which had come into being by 1071. Priority was accorded to these sites probably because the *burhs* were viewed as potentially dangerous centres of discontent, and both controlled strategic crossings over the Thames. Athough both were nominally royal strongholds, they were from the outset usually garrisoned and maintained by supporters of the Norman kings – the d'Oillys at Oxford, Miles Crispin and then Brian FitzCount at Wallingford. The building of both castles involved the clearance of previously-occupied parts of the town – at Oxford late Saxon pits and buildings were sealed beneath the defences (Jope 1952–3; Hassall 1976), while at Wallingford the Domesday survey records that eight properties (*hagis*) were destroyed in order to accommodate the castle into the north-eastern quarter of the town. Both strongholds took the form of a motte and bailey, though at Oxford there are grounds for suspicion that the motte may have been added to a pre-existing ringwork which already incorporated the stone tower of St. George's church (Hassall 1976). The subsequent development of both sites is well documented (Brown *et al.* 1963). Both saw military action on several occasions, notably during the Anarchy and during the reign of King John. During the twelfth century their bailey ramparts were superseded or reinforced by stone curtain walls with square interval towers. At Oxford Castle the defences of the south-east gate were strengthened in 1216, when Fawkes de Bréauté diverted a road and demolished the old church of St. Budoc to make way for a great semicircular barbican, recorded during the construction of the Westgate Centre in 1969–70 (Hassall 1976). After the later twelfth century there was a general tendency for square interval towers to be superseded by round ones: a new round tower was built at Oxford in 1235, the base of which may still be that surviving within the prison precincts.

By the mid-thirteenth century Oxford Castle's importance had declined, and despite sporadic efforts to patch it up, the structure fell into decay. Demolition and redevelopment between 1649 and 1971 reduced the site to the point where its only visible remains today are the motte with its internal well-chamber, St. George's Tower, the crypt of St. George's chapel, the base of one round tower on the southern side of the bailey, and the general outline of the bailey in so far as it is fossilized in the street-plan (R.C.H.M. 1939, 156–8).

In contrast to Oxford, Wallingford Castle's importance increased after the end of the Norman period, and it was enlarged in the later thirteenth century by the addition of an outer bailey and the digging of an additional outer moat. The spoil from the ditches was spread over the interior of the outer bailey, burying earlier structures which included a remarkable cob-walled house with its walls surviving to a height of 2m, probably of late twelfth-century date (Selkirk 1972). The construction of the castle's outermost ditch also involved the diversion of one of the town's main streets and the destruction of the original North Gate (Brooks 1965–6). Developments during the middle and later fourteenth century were primarily of a domestic and residential nature (Brown *et al.* 1963, 850–2). By the time of Leland's visit it was partly in ruin, and its defences were ordered to be slighted in 1652. The motte, the successive bailey ditches and substantial fragments of curtain wall survive. Apart from a large house which occupied part of the outer bailey from 1837 to 1972, there has been little post-medieval disturbance within the castle precincts, and it remains a prime archaeological site.

(2) Smaller motte and bailey castles appeared in

some numbers during the late eleventh and twelfth centuries, and some of these have also been investigated archaeologically. The smaller earthwork castles often had a shorter life than Oxford or Wallingford, and their essential characteristics are less blurred by the modifications of later centuries. The most remarkable group is at Ascott-under-Wychwood, where three sites lie within a few hundred metres of each other: the central one at Ascott d'Oilly was examined in 1946–47 as part of a programme of research excavations on castles believed to have had a restricted period of occupation, and it was shown there that the motte actually encased a stone tower standing on the original ground level (Jope & Threlfall 1959). At Hinton Waldrist and Swerford the motte appears to have been simply a mound of spoil, with no evidence for a tower (Gardiner & Jope 1940; Jope, 1938). More recent work at Middleton Stoney, however, has shown that the supposed earthen motte was in reality a mound of tumbled stonework around the ruins of a large tower (Rahtz & Rowley, 1984).

(3) A smaller group of eleventh- and twelfth-century castles followed the ringwork tradition. The best-preserved unmodified ringwork is probably the poorly documented site in Ardley Wood. The small moated mound at Fitzharris just outside Abingdon can be ascribed to one of the military tenants forcibly settled upon Abingdon Abbey's estates after the Conquest (Preston 1934). At Cogges the pattern of the earthworks suggests a small moated ringwork to which a subsidiary enclosure has been attached later. At Chipping Norton the well-preserved earthworks of the FitzAlans' castle appear to include a much larger ringwork containing substantial internal buildings, with two subsidiary outer enclosures. None of these sites have been subject to excavation. At Deddington the earliest phase of the castle, built before 1100, consisted of an embanked enclosure some 3.4 ha in extent, which is probably to be regarded as a large, eccentrically-shaped ringwork rather than the outer bailey of a now-vanished motte. A polygonal inner bailey was inserted during the tenure of the Chesney family, excavations here in 1947–51 and 1976–79 (not yet fully published) revealing a strong stone curtain wall and gatehouse dating from the early twelfth century. Timber buildings within the interior were superseded by a stone hall in c.1160 with a slightly later solar; a kitchen, thirteenth-century chapel and other buildings were also located. The site was apparently abandoned after the fourteenth century, and survives only as an earthwork (Colvin 1963).

(4) By the early twelfth century alternative forms to the ringwork or motte and bailey were already beginning to appear. The castle built at Banbury by Alexander, bishop of Lincoln, some time after 1125, took the form of a large quadrilateral enclosure surrounded by a thick embanked curtain wall, possibly reinforced by rectangular corner and interval towers, and surrounded by a relatively slight ditch (Rodwell 1976). Beaumont Castle at Mixbury consists of a pair of conjoined quadrilateral moated enclosures, though whether these existing earthworks really date back to the time of Roger d'Ivry, the Domesday lord, as is usually claimed, is open to doubt. The quadrilateral moated form became widely used in the thirteenth century, for example at the Audleys' castle at Stratton Audley.

(5) The most concentrated period of military activity in Oxfordshire was the struggle between Stephen and Matilda, which lasted from 1139 to 1153. Oxford and Wallingford were both held for Matilda, and both suffered protracted sieges during which elaborate earthworks were thrown up by the attacking forces. At Oxford it was probably Stephen who was responsible for the construction of Mount Pelham and Jew's Mount (both levelled after the sixteenth century) outside the north bailey wall in 1141, while opposite Wallingford at Crowmarsh a whole sequence of siege-forts was developed during the actions of 1139, 1145–46 and 1152. Virtually nothing of these survives.

Many smaller 'adulterine' castles of varying forms were built during the same period, but many of the suspected examples are poorly documented, while many of the documented examples are difficult to identify on the ground. Some of the latter were probably fairly ephemeral structures. Of Matilda's three 'castles' built in 1141 at Woodstock, Radcot and Bampton, the last was simply a temporary fortification of the church tower, while no certain remains of the other two can be traced. Another castle built for Matilda at Faringdon in 1144 and taken by storm the following year by Stephen remains unlocated, though a distinctive circuit of streets at Bromsgrove in the south-west quarter of the town might conceivably preserve its outline. The remains of a tower surrounded by a rampart and concentric ditches at Faringdon Folly, once thought to represent the site (Leeds 1936, 1937), are now reassigned by the corrected dating of the pottery to the thirteenth century. The castle of *Burtuna* which was attacked by Henry Plantagenet in 1147 is conceivably to be equated with a ploughed-out motte-like mound at Black Bourton, though there is an alternative identification with Purton Castle in Wiltshire. Another castle called *Bretewelle*, whose defenders delayed Henry's advance on Wallingford in 1153, might plausibly be identified with moated sites at either Brightwell-cum-Sotwell or Britwell Salome.

After the middle of the twelfth century many of the castles built or garrisoned during the Anarchy were deliberately slighted. Hinton Waldrist and Swerford produced virtually no pottery of later date. At Ascott d'Oilly the tower seems to have been dismantled around 1180. At Middleton Stoney the archaeological evidence supports the documented destruction date of 1216.

(6) By the thirteenth century the Oxfordshire castles had been greatly reduced in numbers, though the most important sites which remained were still being strengthened and elaborated. Significant new techniques in fortification were introduced probably in the late thirteenth century at Banbury. Bishop Alexander's castle was completely reconstructed according to principles developed during the Edwardian campaigns in Wales, with a symmetrical plan, concentric lines of

defence, and circular drum towers punctuating the curtain wall. It may be significant that Edward I visited Banbury in person several times during the 1270s. Banbury Castle retained this form up to the Civil War, when its defences were again modified. It was totally demolished after its surrender in 1646, but excavation prior to modern redevelopment has yielded much valuable information (Fasham 1973; Rodwell 1976).

(7) After the late thirteenth century the construction of private castles was controlled by the granting of crenellation licences. Such licences must be regarded with some caution as evidence for the dating of defensive works. Sometimes they were acquired as a safeguard merely to legalize an already-existing situation. In other cases they were acquired with the intention of building a fortification at some future date, the achievement of which might be long delayed or, indeed, never realized at all. Not infrequently a major landowner took out licences to crenellate several of his houses at the same time. Most of the buildings to which crenellation licences were applied were never major military works, merely ordinary manor houses elaborated with relatively slight defensive works – often simply a moat with a gatehouse and curtain wall. At Bampton (licensed in 1315) parts of the moat remain and the gatehouse arch is visible in the wall of the present farmhouse. Quadrangular plans with corner towers are common during this period, and probably owe their inspiration to the symmetrical Edwardian design – examples survive at Greys Court (1347) and, more completely, at Shirburn (1377), the latter the first major brick building in Oxfordshire. Perhaps the best-preserved of the later medieval fortified manor houses is at Broughton, where a crenellation licence was acquired in 1406, perhaps to complete the defences of an already moated manor house (Slade 1978).

(8) The final stage of castle-building is exemplified by Hanwell, begun about 1500 and completed in the 1520s. Although nominally a castle, the requirements of comfortable residential accommodation took precedence, and the corner towers, central gatehouse and battlemented parapets were here entirely for show. Much of Hanwell was demolished in the eighteenth century, but one of the corner towers and part of the south range survive.

The sites identified on Map 17 as 'Other moated sites' represent a class of monument which is far more numerous than the castles, but less well-known either archaeologically or historically. Indeed, until comparatively recently there has been little systematic study of moated sites at national level, and the work in Oxfordshire was particularly slight (Aberg 1978). The balance is now slowly being redressed, but it still has to be admitted that the study of moats in Oxfordshire remains in its infancy. There remain major difficulties of definition, identification and dating. There is not always a clear distinction between castle defences, 'true' moated sites, and ditched crofts. The readiness with which moats can become overgrown, infilled or obliterated by building often makes their recognition in the field difficult, and even where the earthworks are perfectly clear it is not always possible to prove a medieval origin from fieldwork alone. The sub-seigneurial sites in particular are generally poorly documented.

These difficulties make it improbable that a definitive total of the medieval moated sites in Oxfordshire can ever be determined. On present evidence the incidence of moats in Oxfordshire appears to lie somewhere in the middle of the range for the country as a whole – the county is neither exceptionally heavily nor exceptionally sparsely endowed. Excluding ten sites which have been classified as moated castles and six more which are moated monastic sites or granges, Map 17 shows a total of 96 other moats. Of these, 75 examples can be identified with a reasonable degree of confidence, the remaining 21 being probable sites awaiting confirmation. Fourteen sites once listed as medieval moats have since been rejected through reinterpretation as post-medieval earthworks or as some other class of site. It is likely, however, that these totals will be modified yet further as survey work proceeds.

The distribution of moats is clearly concentrated in the clay vales, particularly on the Gault and Kimmeridge Clay below the Chiltern scarp, and to a slightly lesser extent on the Oxford Clay in the Upper Thames Valley and in north-east Oxfordshire. A high proportion are sited directly on the spring-line at the interface between the clays and the chalk or greensand, or where a local capping of drift produces a perched water-table. The comparative scarcity of moated sites in the Cotswolds, on the Corallian escarpment and on the Chilterns reflects the greater difficulties involved in excavating a water-holding ditch on the more permeable soils. Most moats are located where water was plentiful and could be retained, and in some cases elaborate leat systems were excavated to divert water into the moat: these facts seem to negate the suggestion sometimes made that they were dug merely to drain the area upon which the interior buildings stood.

The location of moated sites in respect to other settlements is of considerable interest. An estimated 48 per cent of all moats at present known in Oxfordshire lie within the bounds of existing villages and a further 23 per cent are associated with deserted medieval village sites. Only 28 per cent are in locations which might be described as isolated or distant from nucleated settlements. While there can be no simple equation between location and social status, it might appear from this that the greater proportion of Oxfordshire moats belong to sites of manorial rank, and that the number associated with assarting and colonization of waste and forest is relatively low. The motives which led some manorial lords to construct moats around their properties while their neighbours, faced with similar physical conditions and opportunities, made a decision not to do so, are now almost impossible to identify. It was generally a matter of personal choice, though occasionally there may be hints of a wider estate policy: on the Abingdon Abbey estates, for example, it appears that those manor houses which remained part of the monastic demesne also remained unmoated, while moats were frequently made around those which had been in the hands of tenants from an early period (Bond 1979).

The chronology of moated sites in Oxfordshire is insufficiently known from direct evidence, but work so far has not produced any evidence to conflict with the pattern which can be projected from neighbouring areas. The origin of the moat tradition is probably derived from the ringwork castle, and elsewhere circular or oval moats seem to appear early in the sequence, during the twelfth century. Locally the transitional stage from ringwork to moat is probably represented by Cogges Castle, which itself seems to have been superseded by the unmoated Manor Farm nearby in about 1250. From the beginning of the thirteenth century there was generally a rapid increase in the number of moats built, and in the late thirteenth and early fourteenth centuries some of them seem to have been drastically modified by enlargement, realignment or other forms of elaboration. In the late Middle Ages the practice of moat-building seems to have declined, perhaps reflecting the general economic decline of the period, and possibly also related to the onset of wetter climatic conditions in the mid-fourteenth century which may in some cases have encouraged a move to drier sites. After c.1600, however, the practice of digging new moats or modifying pre-existing ones as an element in garden layouts reappears, and it is sometimes difficult to distinguish sites of this type from their medieval predecessors.

The shape and size of Oxfordshire moats awaits systematic study. The most common type would appear to be the single quadrilateral enclosure, but field investigation often shows that these are not quite as simple as they appear on the map, and the proportion with subsidiary enclosures is probably higher than is at present recognized. Apart from the circular ringwork-derived forms, other shapes occasionally occur: the largest of the three moats at Caswell is pentagonal. Moats sometimes have two or more islands, as at Sugarswell. Concentric moats seem relatively rare: at the most elaborate example, the Beckley Park lodge, documentary evidence suggests that the triple ditches there are not all contemporary, for when the lodge was rebuilt in 1376 it was recorded that 15 men were employed for 18 days to dig the outermost ditch. A number of sites appear to have moats which formed an incomplete enclosure from the outset, and do not owe their incompleteness to partial infilling at a later date. This lends support to the suggestion that many of the lesser moats had no defensive value in themselves but were in effect a status symbol conceived in conscious imitation of the defences of buildings occupied by the higher ranks of society. In several places, notably Caswell and Standlake, physically separate moats are grouped in twos or threes: it is not yet clear whether these represent cases of replacement, where one of the moats has superseded its neighbour, or whether some functional differentiation is implied, perhaps with one moat enclosing the main dwelling and subsidiary moats enclosing agricultural buildings, gardens, orchards or serving as fishponds. The size of Oxfordshire moats varies considerably, but here, as elsewhere, the majority fall within the range 0.3–0.8 hectares.

The range of structures to be expected on and around a moat are clearly described in the accounts of the Merton College manor of Cuxham, which refer to a detached kitchen, dairy, bakehouse, barns, byre, stable, carthouse, granary, hayhouse, pigsty, henhouse, dovecote, mills, gardens and orchard in addition to the manor house itself. At Cuxham the moat is fairly restricted in size, and clearly can only have accommodated the main domestic buildings, while the ancillary features and farm buildings were mostly enclosed by cob walls (Harvey 1965). Limited excavations had taken place at Lilley Farm near Mapledurham, at Moat Cottage in Kidlington, and at Manor Farm in Kingham, but only total excavation can explore the complexities which the Cuxham documentation implies. So far only one opportunity has arisen, on a moat at Chalgrove first discovered from the air as recently as 1976, when it was already under threat of levelling for a playing-field. A delay in this operation permitted extensive excavation between 1977 and 1979. Late twelfth- and early thirteenth-century structures predating the moat included a cob building. The moat itself seems to have been dug after the mid-thirteenth century, when an aisled stone hall was built on the larger of the two islands. This also contained a range of subsidiary domestic and agricultural buildings, including a detached kitchen and bakehouse, a large barn and a dovecote, and later a chapel. In the late fourteenth century a new kitchen, agricultural buildings and walled garden were made. The site may have gone out of use when it passed into the hands of Magdalen College in 1484, though a later barn and rectangular dovecote survived until 1520.

Forests and Parks

The Domesday Survey records that the king's Oxfordshire demesne forests of Shotover, Stowood, Woodstock, Cornbury and Wychwood extended for nine leagues in length and nine leagues in breadth. Map 18 shows that these royal forests formed a discontinuous band across the centre of the county, continued eastwards into Buckinghamshire by the Forest of Bernwood. The medieval concept of forest was primarily a legal one, signifying an area subject to Forest Law and retained under royal control as a hunting preserve. It did not imply a continuous swathe of dense woodland: even the Domesday surveys record six villeins and eight bordars operating three and a half ploughteams within the forest, and from later evidence it is clear that it included much open countryside, fields and even entire villages. Nonetheless, woodland and wood-pasture were essential components, and the distribution of place-names containing elements such as *wudu* and *lēah* (Gelling 1953–4) and Domesday vills which included woodland amongst their economic resources (Jope & Terret 1971) leaves little doubt that in the early Middle Ages many parts of this central band of Oxfordshire were comparatively well-wooded – as, indeed, is still to some extent the case.

There is no convenient explanation for this concentration of woodland in purely physical terms. It spans a wide geological range from the Lias to the Lower Greensand, including clays, limestones and sandstones, and it rises from about 60m to 200m above sea level. Little of it can be regarded as truly marginal land. As the sequence of distribution maps relating to previous chapters shows, many parts of it were fully settled in the prehistoric and Roman period, and it clearly cannot therefore be regarded as a virgin remnant of the primeval woodland. One possible explanation of its origin may be that it fossilizes a post-Roman frontier, a sort of buffer of secondary woodland regenerating between the zones of Hwiccan and Middle Anglian settlement prior to the emergence of the heptarchy. Once established, the woodland would have represented a valuable economic resource, which was exploited even by relatively distant settlements in a complex pattern of inter-commoning (cf. Sturdy 1963). Vestiges of these arrangements survived into the Middle Ages – Charlbury, Finstock and Fawler in Wychwood belonged to the bishop of Lincoln's Banbury estate centred 24km away before the late eleventh century, and long afterwards remained a detached part of Banbury Hundred. Similarly, King's Wood in Stonesfield was formerly called Bloxham Wood and belonged to the manor of that name some 17km to the north.

The legal extent of the forest fluctuated at different periods, and this is particularly the case with Wychwood, the largest and most important of the Oxfordshire forests. The documentary evidence for Wychwood has been studied in some detail (Wickham Steed 1961, 1962; Schumer 1984), and it has been possible to define its bounds at three different periods:– (i) the Norman bounds, which remained up to the mid-twelfth century; (ii) the great extension of the area under Forest Law carried out by Henry II to cover most of west Oxfordshire between the Thames, Cherwell and Swere; the bounds of this extension are referred to in King John's Great Charter of 1215 and Henry III's Forest Charter of 1217; (iii) the bounds defined by the perambulation of 1300, by which time the Forest had been divided into three physically separate portions, based on the two royal estates of Woodstock and Cornbury and on the bishop of Winchester's manor of Witney. The bounds of Shotover Forest have been plotted from the perambulation of 1298 (Roberts 1963). The bounds of Bernwood have been plotted in tentatively on Map 18, but this now needs revision in the light of subsequent work (Steane, 1985).

Assarting was actively reducing the physical extent of the woodland during the early Middle Ages. In Wychwood, not only were the old-established settlements around its margins pushing forward their cultivation frontier, new villages such as Leafield, Ramsden, Finstock, Fawler, Hailey and Crawley had been established within its bounds before the thirteenth century. Nonetheless it is clear that some of the woods which survive today have had an unbroken continuity as woodland through from the Middle Ages. Substantial fragments of Stowood escaped the formal disafforestation of Shotover in 1660. Waterperry and Whitecross Green Woods are remnants of Bernwood. Although what was left of Wychwood was disafforested in 1857 and much of it was finally enclosed for agriculture in 1862, some woodland remained on the Cornbury estate, in the western part of Blenheim Park and elsewhere. It is now appreciated that this ancient woodland, where it has not been treated with herbicides or converted to commercial forestry, is of considerable interest to historical ecologists (Bowen 1977, 1980).

The royal forests were not the only parts of the county which were well-wooded during the Middle Ages. Two other areas, not distinguished on Map 18 because they were never legally forest, are the Chilterns and the hills of Wytham and Cumnor to the west of Oxford in the great loop of the Thames. The Domesday survey records a string of vills along the foot of the Chiltern scarp to which woodland areas belonged. The parishes here originally extended, and to some extent still do extend, in long ribbons across the geological grain of the country (cf. Map 14), and there can be no doubt that the woods themselves were almost all on the Chiltern dip-slope. Charcoal remains from the Chalgrove moated site suggest that the firewood being brought there was already predominantly beech. By contrast, the Domesday record for the Wytham-Cumnor area makes no mention of woodland (Campbell 1971), but the evidence of place-names (Gelling 1972–3) and Abingdon charters of the eleventh and twelfth centuries makes it quite clear that the Domesday record is here defective, and that the hills were then well-wooded, as indeed they still are today.

Both within and outside the royal forests some individual medieval woods are very well documented, and in addition to their potential ecological interest some of them are distinctive archaeologically. Where their primary purpose was timber production or coppice growth, they needed protection from livestock, and this often resulted in their enclosure by a bank with an external ditch. Their tendency towards a rounded outline also often distinguishes them from later plantations. Burleigh Wood on the bounds of Bladon and Cassington, Cogges Wood, Stanton Great Wood in Stanton St. John, and Stoke Wood and Stoke Little Wood in Stoke Lyne are a few typical examples. The woodland banks sometimes survive as an earthwork even after the removal of the wood itself – in one case near South Lawn in Swinbrook such a bank bisects what appear to be the earthworks of an earlier settlement.

No attempt has been made on Map 18 to map the extent of medieval woodland, either within or outside the forests. However, it has been possible to show the distribution of medieval parks, a type of wood-pasture enclosure theoretically licensed by royal grants to serve as small private game preserves. While there is a fairly widespread scatter of parks throughout the county, it is possible to discern a certain tendency for greater concentrations in the more wooded areas, especially in Wychwood and the Chilterns. The origin of many parks is difficult to establish. In Oxfordshire only about a quarter of all the known medieval examples are recognized from emparking licences, the majority having been detected only from incidental references once they were already in existence. Even emparking licences must be treated with caution – like market charters or crenellation licences, they may represent an attempt to legitimize an established situation or they may only be a declaration of intent, and in neither case would they provide reliable dating evidence.

The earliest park in Oxfordshire was almost certainly that attached to the royal manor of Woodstock, enclosed at the very beginning of the twelfth century by Henry I. The only other example documented before the middle of the twelfth century is the bishop of Lincoln's park at Thame, which was clearly already in existence before 1131, when Henry I licensed an exchange of lands to allow the bishop to enlarge it. The main period of park creation appears to have been the thirteenth and early fourteenth centuries, reaching a peak in the second half of the thirteenth century when about a third of the Oxfordshire parks are recorded for the first time.

The distribution and chronology of parks in the royal forest are of special interest. In some areas parks only seem to make their appearance after legal disafforestation, but in Wychwood only one example, Minster Wood, was emparked after the area had been taken out of the forest. Five private parks lie within the new extension of Wychwood taken in by Henry II, and all three of those whose origins are dated were licensed when the area concerned was legally within the forest. Of the three or four parks which remained within the reduced area of forest after 1300, all were in royal hands (since Map 18 was drawn, Beryl Schumer has produced evidence to suggest that the ambiguous royal park at 'Combe' recorded in 1362, here tentatively placed at Combe by Woodstock, can more probably be identified with Coombe Park in Whitchurch).

The parks created during the early Middle Ages tended, on the whole, to be on marginal land, waste or woodland, where competition with more demanding types of land use was minimized. Emparking licences often indicated the type of land being enclosed – Crouch Spinney (1215), Standlake Wood (1230), Pinsley Wood (1270), Elsfield Wood (1327), 100 acres of wood and 40 acres of waste at Shirburn (1336). This preference for marginal land and manorial waste, which often lay towards the edge of the parish, means that medieval parks are frequently at some distance from the house or palace to which they belonged; in this respect they are in sharp contrast with the landscaped parks which often formed the setting of post-medieval mansions. Witney Park in the Middle Ages was 2km west of the bishop of Winchester's palace, Shirburn Park 2.5km from the castle and Watlington Park 3km from Watlington Manor.

The principal purpose of the early medieval park was to enclose deer, and this dictated their characteristic shape, size and perimeter form. Deer can leap an obstacle of up to 6m horizontally or 2.7m vertically, so the park needed a formidable boundary. This usually took the form of a high bank topped by a paling fence, with a wide internal ditch which prevented the deer already inside the enclosure from being able to clear the fence. A few traces of these massive earthwork boundaries remain here and there, but generally their survival in Oxfordshire does not appear particularly impressive. Woodstock Park was enclosed not by a paling fence, but by a stone wall, which is always claimed to be the earliest stone park wall in England: there are frequent references to its repair in the thirteenth century. Perhaps inspired by Woodstock, several other local parks were also enclosed with stone walls, including Beckley (1296–7) and Middleton Stoney (1328). Hedges were also apparently sometimes used – there is a reference to 207 perches of hedging made round Watlington Park in 1296.

Unless there were constraints imposed by pre-existing boundaries, the shape of the park was influenced primarily by the labour and expense of paling or walling. The ideal shape was a perfect circle, which gave the maximum internal area for the minimum perimeter length. The characteristic circular or ovoid outline can often be detected in the alignment of field boundaries long after the park itself has ceased to exist – Beckley Park is probably the best example in Oxfordshire. The average size of park enclosures was commonly about 100 hectares, but Woodstock Park appears to have been over 400 hectares, while at the other end of the scale an enclosure as small as twelve hectares could still support some 40 or so fallow deer. There are frequent references in the thirteenth century to the construction of deer-leaps, which allowed the one-way passage of deer from surrounding woods into the park, but although the probable sites of one or two of these have been identified, none have yet been examined archaeologically.

Because the medieval park was often distant from the palace, castle or manor to which it pertained, there was often some sort of hunting-lodge accommodation on the bounds of or within the park itself. King John ordered the building of a timber lodge in Finmere Park in 1207, while Cornbury had a lodge of stone and timber in 1337. The moated sites which survive at Barley Park, Mapledurham and Cokethorpe Home Wood (the last probably the medieval Standlake Park) probably represent the sites of park lodges. In a few cases the lodge itself became elaborated into a residence of considerable pretensions. At Beckley the moated park lodge was comprehensively rebuilt in 1375–6 and maintained in good repair at least up to 1441, and it is clear that this had come to replace the old manor house in the village, which was in ruins before the middle of the thirteenth century. At Woodstock the house in the park which started as a simple hunting lodge was expanded by Henry II into a full-scale palace, with a very elaborate suite of accommodation and all sorts of outbuildings and supplementary structures (Brown et al. 1963).

The fallow deer enclosed within the parks were not only hunted for recreation, but provided an important source of animal protein when other stock had to be killed off before winter. There are frequent references in the Close Rolls to the king granting deer from royal parks such as Woodstock to other individuals and institutions during the thirteenth century, and through the winter months the Liberate Rolls include a succession of orders for deer to be killed at Woodstock, salted down and sent to Westminster or Winchester or wherever the king happened to be. The royal forests and parks were also used as a source of live deer, conveyed as a royal favour for the stocking of private parks. For Oxfordshire three sources of supply recur in the documentation: Windsor Forest supplied the south-east of the county, while Woodstock Park and Wychwood Forest supplied the centre and west. The distances over which quantities of live deer might be moved were sometimes considerable: the grant of eight live does and four bucks granted from Wychwood in 1284 for the stocking of Haseley Park would have involved a journey of well over 30km.

Parks often had a range of supplementary functions in addition to serving as reservoirs of live deer. The exploitation of park timber and underwood for building materials, fuel and other purposes is particularly well documented for Woodstock Park (Bond 1981), Cornbury and Beckley. In many cases the enclosure of a park had not completely extinguished all common rights over the land, and receipts of pannage from tenants who retained the privilege of turning out their pigs to forage on the manorial waste were still being recorded from Woodstock, Beckley and Watlington Parks in the late thirteenth centuries. The presence of other livestock is also sometimes recorded: parts of the royal stud were housed in Woodstock and Cornbury Parks during the fourteenth century, and Woodstock Park contained Henry I's menagerie of exotic beasts. Fishponds and warrens were also common adjuncts to a park. The fishponds in Woodstock Park are especially well documented during the thirteenth and early fourteenth centuries. Artificial rabbit-warrens, often within or adjoining parks, were beginning to appear in Oxfordshire by the early fourteenth century, the earliest examples being at Watlington (1337), Finmere (1339) and Banbury (1348–9).

During the economic decline of the later Middle Ages, fewer new parks were being created, though occasionally population decline and agricultural retreat provided unprecedented opportunities. In 1358 Roger de Cottisford paid the king half a mark to enclose and empark the site of the village of Tusmore, recently entirely depopulated by the Black Death, and to divert the old road from Cottisford to Souldern which ran through the deserted village. The parks which were created or extended during the later Middle Ages tended to suffer much greater constraints from existing field and property boundaries. The enlargement of Watlington Park in 1392 involved the addition of 20 acres which were already enclosed with dykes and hedges, and William Lovell's new park made in 1442 involved the disafforestation of Minster Woods and the enclosure of two adjoining fields. Parks of their period tend to have a much more irregular and rectilinear outline than those created at an earlier date.

Elsewhere in Oxfordshire the widespread decline which began in the later fourteenth century was finalized by formal disparking, woodland clearance and subdivision into separate fields. Many parks, such as Hook Norton, Bucknell and Ewelme, had disappeared off the map by the seventeenth century. The survivors were those which succeeded in changing their entire purpose, from reservoirs of game to ornamental settings for great houses (Woodward 1982).

Other aspects

The series of maps which relate to this discussion illustrates a limited range of themes, selected for plotting in this way both because the number of known sites is felt to represent a reasonably high proportion of the total which once existed, and because their distributions, being not unduly imbalanced by the uneven progress of investigation, are felt to have some intrinsic significance. There clearly remain many other aspects of the medieval landscape which have not received similar treatment, either because of recognized serious imperfections in their known distributions or because their distributions are not independently valid or, in themselves, particularly meaningful. It will not be possible to treat the many unmapped themes in any detail here, but a few comments on the present state of knowledge and the archaeological potential may not be inappropriate in conclusion.

Churches are the subject of a vast literature, and the number of extant and demolished medieval church buildings in Oxfordshire is reasonably completely known, at least for the post-Conquest period. The value in plotting their bald distribution is limited, however, since it would to a large extent mirror the distribution of settlements shown on Map 14. Despite the long tradition of studying ecclesiastical architecture, there has been comparatively little opportunity for archaeological investigations. Large-scale church excavations have been confined to Oxford, where the redundant churches of All Saints and St. Peter-in-the-East have been examined prior to their conversion to other uses. Smaller opportunist excavations and watching-briefs have been carried out during alterations elsewhere, for example at Waterperry (Hassall 1972b), Westcott Barton (Chambers 1979), Great Coxwell and Marcham, and re-examination of the standing fabric has also yielded significant new information at Cottisford (Milnes-Walker 1978), Tackley and Hook Norton.

Domestic buildings have also been the subject of many

studies, though the geographical coverage is much more uneven. Survival is, not unexpectedly, biased towards the higher levels of society. Merchants' houses and shops, sometimes with vaulted cellars, survive in several Oxfordshire towns. Medieval town houses have been most thoroughly investigated in Oxford itself, where the general outlines of development established by Pantin (1947) have been amplified by subsequent detailed studies of individual buildings (e.g. Munby 1975). The more substantial rural manor houses have long been recognized (for a convenient summary see, e.g., Long 1938-40, 1940-41), but more recent work has identified further examples such as the aisled hall at Lewknor, now used as a barn (Turner 1972; Morrey & Smith 1973; Fletcher 1975), and has greatly advanced understanding of special building techniques and forms such as the crown-post roof (Fletcher & Spokes 1964) and the aisled hall (Fletcher & Currie 1979). Considerable work has been carried out on cruck-framed buildings, the building and occupation of which extended below the manorial threshold to the more prosperous free tenants. Crucks have a markedly western distribution in Britain as a whole, and Oxfordshire lies entirely within, but towards the eastern margins of, the sharply-defined zone within which they occur. Over 150 cruck buildings of various types have now been identified in the county (Alcock 1981). The greatest known concentration lies towards the east end of the Vale of the White Horse, where several parishes – Steventon, Long Wittenham, East Hendred, Harwell – contain between half a dozen and a dozen examples each (Fletcher 1965-6, 1968; Portman 1958). There has been much debate about the origins of this form of construction, but the application of scientific archaeological techniques such as radiocarbon dating and dendrochronology has demonstrated that cruck-framing was already being used in this area by the end of the thirteenth century (Fletcher 1970; Currie & Fletcher 1972; Hillam & Fletcher 1983).

Medieval agriculture has been most widely studied from the documentary sources. Statistical details mapped from the Domesday survey (Campbell 1971; Jope & Terrett 1971) seem to imply that there were, by the late eleventh century, some fundamental contrasts in the distribution of arable land, meadow, woodland and pasture. Some of the contrasts shown on the Domesday Geography maps may reflect contemporary reality, but others, such as the apparent absence of woodland from the Chiltern dip-slope and of pasture from Wychwood, are entirely illusory. The practice of the Domesday assessors in describing agricultural resources under the heading of the manor to which they belonged rather than under the locality in which they actually occurred gives rise to many anomalies, and is a major obstacle to the interpretation of the document in geographical terms. Later medieval sources such as manorial accounts and extents indicate that many parts of the county were under the midland type of open-field cultivation, with two-field systems tending to predominate on the Cotswolds and Berkshire Downs and three-field systems more prevalent in the clay vales and Chiltern fringes. In the Chilterns there was more emphasis on mixed farming, with open-field land concentrated around the main settlements, but detached communally-worked furlongs also often scattered amongst the common grazing and private woodlands (Roden 1973). The medieval conversion of woodland by assarting to hedged enclosures under individual occuption is well documented in the Wychwood area.

The archaeological investigation of medieval agriculture has been much more limited. There is now little doubt that much ridge and furrow surviving today is a product of former open-field practices, and in some parishes it is possible to demonstrate a direct connection between the ridges and the strips shown on pre-enclosure maps. The countywide distribution of ridge and furrow has been the subject of a preliminary study from aerial photographs (Sutton 1964-5), and is seen to be concentrated on the lias and in the Oxford, Kimmeridge and Gault clay vales and largely absent from the oolite, corallian and chalk uplands. This distribution is a very imperfect reflection of the known extent of open-field systems, and clearly the drainage properties of the soil were a major consideration in determining whether the selions were ploughed ridged or unridged. The pattern of ridge and furrow has been plotted in more detail from fieldwork in a few parishes – Water Eaton, Ducklington, Shenington and Alkerton – but there is scope for much more recording of this sort, in particular to examine the relationship between furlongs and earlier fields, which may shed light upon the origins of open-field agriculture, and to investigate the changes which have sometimes occurred in the length, breadth and orientation of the ridges, reflecting adaptations taking place while the open-field system was in operation.

Medieval industry in Oxfordshire is to a large extent dominated by the extractive industries (stone quarries, tile- and pottery-kilns) and the processing of agricultural produce (corn-milling, malting, cloth-making). Water-mills for grinding corn are occasionally documented in pre-Conquest sources, and the Domesday survey records over 250 mills within the present bounds of Oxfordshire; many more are known from later sources. Archaeologically, however, little is known of them; their sites have often continued in use, with consequent drastic alterations, well into the post-medieval period. However, a number of abandoned medieval watermills have been recognized from earthwork evidence, and where these can be linked with a documentary *terminus post quem* – for example, a site discovered in 1976 within the bounds of Blenheim Park which may be identical with a mill which Edward III had dismantled in 1334 – they are of obvious archaeological importance.

Windmills first appeared in England in the last quarter of the twelfth century. The Knights Templars may have been instrumental in their introduction, and it is possible that one of the two mills listed on the

Templars' lands at Merton in 1185 may have been a windmill. The first unambiguous references are the records for South Stoke (1220) and Thame (1237), and by the end of the fourteenth century at least 25 examples are known. Windmill mounds are common features of the landscape, and some of them may be medieval – it is tempting to link one at Launton with the site of a windmill recorded there in 1279.

The application of power from the more rapid streams to the fulling of woollen cloth is documented from the end of the twelfth century. Monastic houses seem to have been the pioneers: amongst the earliest known Oxfordshire examples are Winchcombe Abbey's fulling-mill at Cleveley, recorded c.1190, and the Cistercians' fulling-mill at Thame, recorded in 1197. At least twenty more examples are documented before c.1550, but again archaeologically little work has been done. The decline of the urban cloth industry in Oxford is possibly related to the advent of the fulling-mill.

Oxfordshire is well endowed with good building stone, and the quarrying industry was highly organized by the Middle Ages. The hills west of Oxford were being quarried for coral rag at Chilswell in the eleventh century, and by the fifteenth century further quarries had opened nearby at Cumnor, Bayworth, Dry Sandford and Besselsleigh. South-east of Oxford the place-name Standhill (OE *stāngedelf*) indicates that the local Portland beds were being exploited by the eleventh century. Corallian and Portland stone was being quarried at Wheatley on a large scale from the late thirteenth century, and was used not only for major buildings in Oxford but also sent downriver to Abingdon, Wallingford and Windsor and overland as far south as Highclere in 1370. The Headington quarries opened up after 1400, supplying much stone to Oxford buildings. Further west the oolite of the Cotswolds provided some of the finest of all building stones. The Taynton quarries figure in the Domesday survey and over the next four centuries Taynton stone was carried throughout Oxfordshire and used for prestigious buildings as far afield as Windsor, Eton, Sheen and Westminster. One of the Taynton quarries also produced roofing slates, used at Pershore Abbey in 1381–2. Upton-by-Burford was another important source of freestone for Oxford buildings after the thirteenth century, and there were smaller quarries at Hanborough, Bladon and Bicester. In the north of the county the Middle Liassic marlstone was quarried at Bloxham and Hornton. Some work has been done on the distribution of the more important medieval building stones, primarily from documentary sources (e.g. Jope 1948, 1956), but since Arkell (1947) there has been little systematic enquiry into the geological origin of stone used in local buildings.

The widespread use of roof and floor tiles is indicated by both documentary and archaeological evidence after the thirteenth century, and from the mid-fourteenth century tiles made at Nettlebed were being used at Wallingford Castle, Abingdon Abbey and elsewhere. Tilers are also recorded at Oxford, Banbury, South Stoke and Henley. Brick first makes its appearance as a major constituent of a building in Shirburn Castle (1377), and in 1416–17 there is documentary evidence of a large consignment of bricks being made at Crocker End near Nettlebed and taken to Stonor, where they were probably used for the still-extant chapel tower. Another major group of brick buildings dating from the 1430s is at Ewelme. By the later fifteenth century brick was becoming more widely used, even in the stone districts of Oxfordshire at Hanwell Castle (Bond *et al.* 1980).

Bladon is one of only three places in England where a pottery industry is recorded in the Domesday survey, and there may be a link between it and the potters and kilns recorded in the Hundred Rolls at nearby Woodstock in 1279. There are also documentary indications of potters at Leafield (1272), on Benson Manor (1296–7) (perhaps actually located at Henley, where potters are independently recorded), at Nettlebed (1442) and at Marsh Baldon (1514). The local potteries were overshadowed, however, by the important production centre of Brill, just over the Buckinghamshire border, which was sending fine wares into Oxfordshire in quantity from the thirteenth century. Long sequences of well-stratified pottery deposits from recent excavations in the city of Oxford have been the subject of detailed analyses (e.g. Haldon 1977; Mellor 1980), and the continuing examination of material from other sites is throwing important new light upon marketing areas and the changing balances between local and imported wares. It is, however, ironic that no kilns have yet been located or excavated in any of the documented production centres in Oxfordshire itself. Wasters from Ascott-under-Wychwood probably indicate a thirteenth-century production centre nearby (Jope & Threlfall 1959; Mellor 1982), but it was as recently as 1982 that the first medieval kiln and workshop were pinpointed by magnetometer survey following the discovery of later fourteenth- and fifteenth-century pottery in Swyncombe parish north of Soundess during fieldwalking in advance of gas pipeline construction.

Acknowledgements

It is impossible to acknowledge fully the almost innumerable debts which have been incurred in the preparation of this discussion. I would, however, like to thank my past and present colleagues in Oxfordshire County Council Department of Museum Services, the staffs of the Oxford Archaeological Unit, University of Oxford Department for External Studies, and the Ashmolean Museum, members of local archaeological and historical societies, and numerous other individuals who have advanced the study of medieval archaeology in Oxfordshire. Some of their works are listed in the bibliography below. Interim reports on other sites mentioned in the text but not referenced to published sources will normally be found in the annual *CBA Group 9 Newsletter (South Midlands Archaeology* since 1983) or the Oxford Archaeological Unit's newsletter.

Other previously unpublished material is drawn from the County Sites and Monuments Record housed in the Oxfordshire County Museum at Woodstock.

Note

This text was submitted in April 1984 and, apart from the completion of bibliographical information for references whose publication was known to be pending at that time, it has not been possible to incorporate the results of work undertaken, completed or published since that date.

References

Aberg, F.A., ed. (1978) *Medieval Moated Sites*. CBA Research Report 17

Alcock, N.W., ed. (1981) *Cruck Construction: an Introduction and Catalogue*. CBA Research Report 42

Allison, K.J., Beresford, M.W. & Hurst, J.G. (1965) *The Deserted Villages of Oxfordshire*. Leic. Univ. Dept. of Local History, Occasional Paper 17

Arkell, W.J. (1947) *Oxford Stone*

Aston, M. & Bond, C.J. (1976) *The Landscape of Towns*

Batey, M. (1968) 'Nuneham Courtenay: an Oxfordshire eighteenth century deserted village', *Oxoniensia* 33, 108–124

Batey, M. (1978) 'Nuneham Courtenay: Goldsmith's Deserted Village', *Oxoniensia* 43, 258–259

Beresford, M.W. (1954) *The Lost Villages of England*

Beresford, M.W. (1967) *New Towns of the Middle Ages: Town Plantation in England, Wales and Gascony*

Beresford, M.W. & Finberg, H.P.R. (1973) *English Medieval Boroughs: a Hand-List*

Beresford, M.W. & Hurst, J.G. (1971) *Deserted Medieval Villages*

Biddle, M. (1961–2) 'The Deserted Medieval Village of Seacourt, Berkshire', *Oxoniensia* 26/27, 70–201

Biddle, M. (1968) 'The Excavations at Abingdon Abbey, 1922', *Medieval Archaeol.* 12, 60–69

Blair, J. (1976) 'A Monastic fragment at Wadham College, Oxford', *Oxoniensia* 41, 161–167

Blair, J. (1978) 'Frewin Hall, Oxford: a Norman mansion and a monastic college', *Oxoniensia* 43, 48–99

Blair, J. & Steane, J.M. (1982) 'Investigations at Cogges, Oxfordshire, 1978–81: the priory and parish church', *Oxoniensia* 47, 37–125

Bond, C.J. (1977) 'The Topography of Pershore', *Vale of Evesham Hist. Soc. Research Papers* 6, 2–38 (pp. 23–6 discuss 'Newland' suburbs in Oxfordshire and elsewhere)

Bond, C.J. (1979) 'The Reconstruction of the medieval landscape: the estates of Abingdon Abbey', *Landscape History* 1, 59–75

Bond, C.J. (1980) 'The Small Towns of Oxfordshire in the Nineteenth Century', in R.T. Rowley (ed.), *The Oxford Region* 55–79

Bond, C.J. (1981) 'Woodstock Park under the Plantagenet kings: the exploitation and use of wood and timber in a medieval deer park', *Arboricultural J.* 5, 201–213

Bond, C.J. (forthcoming) 'Medieval Oxfordshire villages and their topography: a preliminary discussion', in D. Hooke (ed.), *Medieval Villages: a Review of Current Work*. Univ. of Oxford Inst. of Archaeol.

Bond, C.J., Gosling, S. & Rhodes, J.G. (1980) *Oxfordshire Brickmakers*. Oxfordshire Museums Services Publication 14

Bowen, H.J.M. (1977) 'Indicators of old forest', *Reading Naturalist* 29, 2–8

Bowen, H.J.M. (1980) 'A Lichen flora of Berkshire, Buckinghamshire and Oxfordshire', *Lichenologist* 12, 199–237

Brooks, J. (1969) 'Eaton Hastings: a deserted medieval village', *Berks. Archaeol. J.* 64, 1–8

Brooks, N.P. (1965–6) 'Excavations at Wallingford Castle, 1965: an interim report', *Berks. Archaeol. J.* 62, 17–21

Brown, R.A., Colvin, H.M. & Taylor, A.J. (1963) *The History of the King's Works*. Vol. 2, *The Middle Ages*

Bruce-Mitford, R.L.S. (1940) 'The Excavations at Seacourt, Berks., 1939: an interim report', *Oxonienisa* 5, 31–41

Campbell, E.M.J. (1971) 'Berkshire', in H.C. Darby & E.M.J. Campbell (eds.), *The Domesday Geography of South-East England*, 239–286

Chambers, E. (1936) *Eynsham under the Monks*. Oxfordshire Rec. Soc. 18

Chambers, R.A. (1973) 'A Deserted medieval farmstead at Sadler's Wood, Lewknor (M40 Site 13)', *Oxoniensia* 38, 146–167

Chambers, R.A. (1975a) 'Excavations at No. 12 Market Place, Chipping Norton, Oxon., 1974', *Oxoniensia* 40, 211–217

Chambers, R.A. (1975b) 'Excavations at Hanwell near Banbury, Oxon., 1974', *Oxoniensia* 40, 218–237

Chambers, R.A. (1977) 'Observations at Somerton, Oxon., 1973', *Oxoniensia* 42, 216–225

Chambers, R.A. (1979) 'Excavations in Westcote Barton parish church, Oxon., 1977', *Oxoniensia* 44, 99–101

Colvin, H.M. (1963) *A History of Deddington, Oxfordshire*

Cunningham, C.J.K. & Banks, J.W. (1972) 'Excavations at Dorchester Abbey', *Oxoniensia* 37, 158–164

Currie, C.R.J. & Fletcher, J.M. (1972) 'Two early cruck houses in North Berkshire identified by radiocarbon', *Medieval Archaeol.* 16, 136–142

Dunkin, J. (1823) *History and Antiquities of the Hundreds of Bullingdon and Ploughley*

Emery, F. (1974) *The Oxfordshire Landscape*

Fasham, P.J. (1973) 'Excavations in Banbury, 1972: first report', *Oxoniensia* 38, 312–338

Fletcher, J.M. (1965–6) 'Three medieval farmhouses in Harwell', *Berks. Archaeol. J.* 62, 45–69

Fletcher, J.M. (1968) 'Crucks in the West Berkshire and Oxford region', *Oxoniensia* 33, 71–88

Fletcher, J.M. (1970) 'Radiocarbon dating of medieval timber-framed cottages, in R. Berger (ed.), *Scientific Methods in Medieval Archaeology*

Fletcher, J.M. (1975) 'The Medieval hall at Lewknor', *Oxoniensia* 40, 247–253

Fletcher, J.M. & Currie, C.R.J. (1979) 'The Bishop of Winchester's medieval manor house at Harwell, Berkshire, and its relevance in the evolution of timber-framed aisled halls', *Archaeol. J.* 136, 151–172

Fletcher, J.M. & Spokes, P.S. (1964) 'The Origin and development of crown-post roofs', *Medieval Archaeol.* 8, 152–183

Ganz, D. (1972) 'The Buildings of Godstow Nunnery', *Oxoniensia* 37, 150–157

Gardiner, H. & Jope, M. (1940) 'The Earthwork at Hinton Waldrist', *Berks. Archaeol. J.* 44, 49–60

Gelling, M. (1953–4) *The Place-Names of Oxfordshire*. English Place-Name Soc. vols. 23 & 24

Gelling, M. (1972–3) *The Place-Names of Berkshire*. English Place-Name Soc. vols. 49 & 50

Gray, M. & Clayton, N. (1978) 'Excavations on the Site of Eynsham Abbey, 1971', *Oxoniensia* 43, 100–122

Haldon, R. (1977) 'Late Saxon and medieval pottery', in B. Durham, 'Archaeological investigations in St. Aldate's, Oxford', *Oxoniensia* 42, 111–139

Harvey, B. (1977) *Westminster Abbey and its Estates in the Middle Ages*

Harvey, P.D.A. (1965) *A Medieval Oxfordshire Village: Cuxham, 1240–1400*. Oxford Hist. Ser., 2nd ser.

Harvey, P.D.A. (1969) 'Banbury', in *Historic Towns Atlas* vol. 1

Hassall, T.G. (1969) 'Excavations at Oxford, 1968: first interim report', *Oxoniensia* 34, 5–20

Hassall, T.G. (1970) 'Excavations at Oxford, 1969: second interim report', *Oxoniensia* 35, 5–18

Hassall, T.G. (1971) 'Excavations at Oxford, 1970: third interim report', *Oxoniensia* 36, 1–14

Hassall, T.G. (1972a) 'Excavations at Oxford, 1971: fourth interim report', *Oxoniensia* 37, 137–149

Hassall, T.G. (1972b) 'Excavation at the Saxon church at Waterperry, Oxon.', *Oxoniensia* 37, 245

Hassall, T.G. (1973) 'Excavations at Oxford, 1972: fifth interim report', *Oxoniensia* 38, 268–298

Hassall, T.G. (1974) 'Excavations at Oxford, 1973–4: sixth and final interim report', *Oxoniensia* 39, 53–61

Hassall, T.G. (1976) 'Excavations at Oxford Castle, 1965–1973', *Oxoniensia* 41, 232–308

Heyworth, P.L. (1971) 'A Lost Cistercian barn at Shilton, Oxon.', *Oxoniensia* 36, 52–54

Hillam, J. & Fletcher, J. (1983) 'Tree-ring dates for buildings with oak timber', *Vernacular Architecture* 14, 61–62

Hinnebusch, W.A. (1938) 'The Pre-Reformation sites of the Oxford Blackfriars', *Oxoniensia* 3, 57–82

Hinton, D.A. (1968) 'Bicester Priory', *Oxoniensia* 33, 22–52

Hinton, D.A. (1969) 'Excavations at Bicester Priory, 1968', *Oxoniensia* 34, 21–28

Hinton, D.A. (1973) 'Excavations at Church Piece, Tetsworth (M40 Site 5)', *Oxoniensia* 38, 116–118

Hookins, P. (1853–5) 'Notes on Cold Norton Priory', *Trans. North Oxfordshire Archaeol. Soc.* 79–88

Hoskins, W.G. & Jope, E.M. (1954) 'The Medieval period', in A.F. Martin & R.W. Steel (eds.), *The Oxford Region: A Scientific and Historical Survey*, 103–120

Horn, W. (1963) 'The Great Tithe Barn of Cholsey, Berkshire', *J. Soc. of Architectural Historians* 22, 13–23

Horn, W.E. & Born, E. (1965) *The Barns of the Abbey of Beaulieu at its Granges of Great Coxwell and Beaulieu St. Leonards*

Jope, E.M. (1938) 'Castle Hill, Swerford', *Oxfordshire Archaeol. Soc. Report* no. 84, 85–93

Jope, E.M. (1948) 'Abingdon Abbey craftsmen and building stone supplies', *Berks. Archaeol. J.* 51, 53–64

Jope, E.M. (1952–3) 'Late Saxon pits under Oxford Castle mound: excavations in 1952', *Oxoniensia* 17/18, 77–111

Jope, E.M. (1956) 'The Archaeology of Wheatley stone', in W.O. Hassall (ed.), *Wheatley Records, 956–1956*. Oxfordshire Record Soc. 37, 17–26

Jope, E.M. & Terrett, I.B. (1971) 'Oxfordshire', in H.C. Darby & E.M.J. Campbell (eds.), *The Domesday Geography of South-East England*, 186–238

Jope, E.M. & Threlfall, R.I. (1959) 'The Twelfth-century castle at Ascott d'Oilly, Oxfordshire', *Antiq. J.* 39, 219–273

Kirk, R.E.G., ed. (1892) *Accounts of the Obedientiars of Abingdon Abbey*. Camden Soc. n. s. 51

Lambrick, G. (1968a) 'The Foundation-traditions of the Abbey (Abingdon)', *Medieval Archaeol.* 12, 26–34

Lambrick, G. (1968b) 'Buildings of the monasteries at Abingdon from the late seventh century to 1538', *Medieval Archaeol.* 12, 42–59

Lambrick, G., & Woods, H. (1976) 'Excavations on the second site of the Dominican Priory, Oxford', *Oxoniensia* 41, 168–231

Lee, F.G. (1888) 'The Abbey and mansion house of Thame Park', *Building News*, 455–457

Leeds, E.T. (1936) 'An Adulterine castle on Faringdon Clump, Berkshire', *Antiq. J.* 16, 165–178

Leeds, E.T. (1937) 'An Adulterine castle on Faringdon Clump, Berkshire: second report', *Antiq. J.* 17, 294–298

Lloyd, T.H. (1964–5) 'Some documentary sidelights on the deserted Oxfordshire village of Brookend', *Oxoniensia* 29/30, 116–128

Long, E.T. (1938–40) 'Medieval domestic architecture in Oxfordshire', *Oxfordshire Archaeol. Soc. Reports* 84, 45–56; 85, 97–105; 86, 3–17

Long, E.T. (1940–41) 'Medieval domestic architecture in Berkshire', *Berks. Archaeol. J.* 44, 39–48, 101–113; 45, 28–36

Markham, M. (1979) *Medieval Hospitals in Oxfordshire*. Oxfordshire Museums Services Information Sheet 12

Mellor, M. (1980) 'Pottery', in N. Palmer, 'A Beaker burial and medieval tenements in The Hamel, Oxford', *Oxoniensia* 45, 160–182

Mellor, M. (1982) 'Medieval pottery from the Wychwood', *Oxoniensia* 47, 133–136

Miles, D. (1975) 'Excavations at West St. Helen Street, Abingdon', *Oxoniensia* 40, 79–101

Miles, D. & Rowley, T. (1976) 'Tusmore deserted village', *Oxoniensia* 41, 309–315

Milnes-Walker, H. (1978) 'A Saxon church at Cottisford?', *Oxoniensia* 43, 255–256

Morgan, M. (1946) *The English Lands of the Abbey of Bec*. Oxford Hist. Ser.

Morrey, M.C.J. & Smith, J.T. (1973) '"The Great Barn", Lewknor: the architectural evidence', *Oxoniensia* 38, 339–345

Munby, J. (1975) '126 High Street: the archaeology and history of an Oxford house', *Oxoniensia* 40, 254–308

Palmer, N. (1976) 'Excavations on the outer city wall of Oxford in St. Helen's Passage and Hertford College', *Oxoniensia* 41, 148–160

Pantin, W.A. (1947) 'The Development of domestic architecture in Oxford', *Antiq. J.* 27, 120–150

Pantin, W.A. (1970) 'Minchery Farm, Littlemore', *Oxoniensia* 35, 19–26

Parrington, M. (1975) 'Excavations at the Old Gaol, Abingdon', *Oxoniensia* 40, 59–78

Parrington, M. & Balkwill, C. (1975) 'Excavations at Broad Street, Abingdon', *Oxoniensia* 40, 5–58

Platt, C. (1969) *The Monastic Grange in Medieval England*

Portman, D. (1958) 'Cruck houses in Long Wittenham', *Berks. Archaeol. J.* 56, 35–45

Postles, D. (1975a) *Oseney Abbey, 1129–1348*. Univ. of Leicester PhD thesis

Postles, D. (1975b) 'The Estate stewards of Oseney Abbey, c.1245–1340', *Oxoniensia* 40, 326–328

Postles, D. (1977) 'Problems in the administration of small manors: three Oxfordshire glebe-demesnes, 1278–1345', *Midland History* 4, 1–14

Preston, A.E. (1934) 'A Moated mound at Abingdon, Berks.', *Antiq. J.* 14, 417–421 and *Berks. Archaeol. J.* 38, 167–170

Rahtz, S. & Rowley, R.T. (1984) *Middleton Stoney: Excavation and Survey in a North Oxfordshire Parish, 1970–1982*

Reeves, C.J. (1971) 'A Medieval village (Broadstone nr. Enstone)', *Oxoniensia* 36, 49–57

Roberts, E. (1963) 'The Boundary and woodlands of Shotover Forest, circa 1298', *Oxoniensia* 28, 68–73

Robinson, M. (1973) 'Excavations at Copt Hay, Tetsworth (M40 Site 4)', *Oxoniensia* 38, 41–115

Roden, D. (1973) 'Field systems of the Chiltern Hills and their environs', in A.R.H. Baker & R.A. Butlin (eds.), *Studies of Field Systems in the British Isles*, 325–376

Rodwell, K., ed. (1975) *Historic Towns in Oxfordshire: a Survey of the New County*. Oxfordshire Archaeol. Unit, survey no. 3

Rodwell, K. (1976) 'Excavations on the site of Banbury Castle, 1973–4', *Oxoniensia* 41, 90–147

Rowley, R.T. (1972) 'First report on the excavations at Middleton Stoney Castle, 1970–71', *Oxoniensia* 37, 109–136

RCHM (1939) *An Inventory of the Historical Monuments in the City of Oxford*. R. Commission on Hist. Monuments (England)

Salter, H.E. (1930) 'Cogges Priory', *Oxfordshire Archaeol. Soc. Reports* 75, 321–325

Salter, H.E. (1960, 1969) *Survey of Oxford*, ed. W.A. Pantin. Oxford Hist. Soc. n. s. 14 & 20

Selkirk, A. (1972) 'A Medieval "Cob" Building (at Wallingford)', *Current Archaeol.* 35, 318

Schumer, B. (1984) *The Evolution of Wychwood to 1400: Pioneers, Frontiers and Forests*. Leic. Univ. Dept. of Local History Occasional Papers, 3rd ser. no. 6

Siebenlist-Kerner, V., Schove, D.J. & Fletcher, J.M. (1978) 'The Barn at Great Coxwell, Berkshire', in J.M. Fletcher (ed.), *Dendrochronology in Europe*, BAR Internat. Ser. 51, 295–302

Slade, H.G. (1978) 'Broughton Castle, Oxfordshire', *Archaeol. J.* 135, 138–194

Squires, T.W. (1928) *In West Oxford*

Steane, J.M. (1985) 'Bernwood Forest, past, present and future', *Arboricultural J.* 9, 39–55

Stone, P.G. (1893) *An Exact Account of the Church and Priory at Goring*

Sturdy, D. (1963) 'Traces of Saxon nomadic life near Oxford',

Oxoniensia 28, 95–98
Sutton, J.E.G. (1964–5) 'Ridge and furrow in Berkshire and Oxfordshire', *Oxoniensia* 29/30, 99–115
Taylor, A.J. (1937) 'The Alien Priory of Minster Lovell', *Oxoniensia* 2, 103–117
Taylor, C.C. (1978) 'Aspects of village mobility in medieval and later times', in S.Limbrey & J.G. Evans (eds.), *The Effect of Man on the Landscape: the Lowland Zone*, CBA Research Report 21, 126–134
Turner, H.L. (1972) '"The Great Barn", Lewknor: the documentary evidence', *Oxoniensia* 37, 187–191

Wickham Steed, V. (1961, 1962) 'The Bounds of Wychwood Forest', *Top. Oxon.* 7 & 8
Wilson, J. (1846) 'Antiquities found at Woodperry, Oxon.', *Archaeol. J.* 3, 116–128
Wing, W. (1853–5) 'Cold Norton Priory', *Tr. North Oxfordshire Archaeol. Soc.* 75–78
Wood-Jones, R.B.(1956) 'The Rectorial barn at Church Enstone', *Oxoniensia* 21, 43–47
Woodward, F. (1982) *Oxfordshire Parks*. Oxfordshire Museums Services Publication 16

COMMENTARY TO ACCOMPANY DISTRIBUTION MAPS OF THE ARCHAEOLOGY OF OXFORDSHIRE

JOHN STEANE

The preparation of archaeological distribution maps is now a well established practice in the English topographical tradition. We look back particularly to the work of O.G.S. Crawford and Sir Cyril Fox. Crawford's work in the mapping of Neolithic Wessex (Crawford 1932) led the way in the series of national period maps produced by the Ordnance Survey. Fox had already produced valuable distribution maps of archaeological periods in the Cambridge region (Fox 1923). His work was extended to a national scale twenty years later (Fox 1943). In the meantime the *Victoria County History for Oxfordshire* had prepared maps for its chapters on prehistoric, Roman and Anglo-Saxon periods (V.C.H. 1939). *Oxoniensia*, the Journal of the Oxford Architectural and Historical Society, founded in 1936, has published distribution maps of certain types of sites and artefacts in the Oxford region. A series of maps summarizing the interim state of archaeological knowledge in the area was published in 1954 (Martin and Steel, 1954).

The present series has been prepared from information held in the Oxfordshire Sites and Monuments Record. This was established by Don Benson, the first keeper of the Field Section of the Oxfordshire County Council Department of Museum Services. Its operation has already been described in some detail (Benson 1972, Bond and Campbell 1980). It has now (1981) accumulated records of over 12,800 archaeological and historic sites in the county and about 600 sites are being added each year. The sources for this information are worth describing briefly before we can judge the value of the present series of distribution maps. A major source at the beginning of the record was the record cards of the Ordnance Survey. These have been supplemented by information from aerial photographs, in particular by the pioneer work of Major Allen who flew over the Upper Thames Valley in the 1930s and whose valuable collection of air photographs of archaeological sites is outstanding. More recently the exceptional quality of the work of J. K. St. Joseph and the Cambridge Committee for Aerial Photography has added much to our understanding of Oxfordshire landscapes. The National Monuments Record has provided a further fruitful source of photographs taken for archaeological purposes. Non-specialist vertical photography includes the RAF cover taken in 1947, the Fairey Surveys collection of the whole of Oxfordshire (2,200 prints carried out in 1962 for the County Planning Department and various surveys carried out for particular projects e.g. A34, M40, Ridgeway Path. Study of these not only facilitates the plotting of ancient sites showing up in shadow, soil- or crop-marks, it also enables the great changes in the last twenty years to be monitored. The stages in the collation and documentation from aerial photographs in the Oxford region were discussed some years ago (Benson 1975). More recently attention has been focussed on recording broader aspects of the historic environment, such as ancient hedges, woods, parks, commons and greens (Bond and Campbell 1980). Other categories of data such as field names, ancient parish, estate and farm boundaries, hedge species counts and the distribution of ridge and furrow are plotted onto transparent overlays. The source for much of this information about the environment has been local groups and individuals working in the field. Their accumulation of material is gradually being built up into a series of parish surveys.

The value of distribution maps on a county scale, derived from such sources, must be judged against the background of a variety of constraining factors. These have been discussed by Fowler (1977) and more recently in the particular context of a neighbouring county by the Royal Commission on Historical Monuments (*Northamptonshire, An Archaeological Atlas*, 1980). Another commentary on a more generous scale has recently been made for a county in the highland zone (West Yorkshire 1981).

Two general points, one concerning time and the other concerning space, need to be made. A group of material, sites or finds, dating from a certain period, is abstracted from the general archaeological record and is plotted on the same map. The results appear to indicate human activity at a single point of time whereas they are actually showing the accumulated evidence of archaeological observations of human occupation over long periods of time. During these periods considerable changes were taking place. Clearly if it was possible to date finds more accurately instead of applying blanket terms like "Roman" or "Iron Age" we could construct a series of overlays each representing a chronological sub-division which would demonstrate more accurately the evolution of human occupation within an area. It might well be argued that a map designated "Roman" and including the location of evidence dating from a period of 400 years is of a limited value in showing relationships between man and his environment.

The second problem concerns the actual area of study. The county of Oxfordshire is an artificial creation of the early Middle Ages for administrative purposes. Its boundaries were adjusted recently by the 1972 Local Government Act effective from 1 April 1974, when a large portion of north-west Berkshire was added. The new Oxfordshire has little relevance as a land unit to the pattern of human occupation of the earlier periods. When one considers its considerable variations of relief and physical topography, it is clear that it is not a geographical region, but cuts across a whole series of such regions. It includes the broad winding river valley of the Upper Thames and the narrower valleys of the Cherwell and the Ock, the high limestone Cotswold hills and two great ridges of chalk downland, the Chilterns and the Berkshire Downs, as well as intervening clay vales. If we look at the more debatable matter of cultural boundaties (Jope 1963) it is again clear that it straddles a number of regions.

Let us turn now to the variety of factors both physical and human which have restricted the recovery of archaeological material located on these maps.

1. *The vagaries of the human observer*. This has been humorously referred to as "the fifteen bicycling miles from Oxford factor" and it is obvious that the activities of archaeologically minded members of the University have been a major factor in the accumulation of the records of the past in the area. Oxford gardens have yielded an unusual number of antiquities and this has arisen partly because there is a higher chance of their being recognized. The University Archaeological Society has made a major contribution to the collection of data over the years but the fluctuating membership which results from the brevity of undergraduate life has resulted in a somewhat uneven processing of the results of fieldwork. Again there has been a considerable input from the work of the University's Department for External Studies which has put on a series of courses and has trained a large number of fieldworkers.

There are in addition nearly 50 local societies all recording history and archaeology as well as some redoubtable individuals working in the field. All this makes for a fortuitous pattern of sites and finds. One fieldworker has been responsible for recovering flint artefacts in the Eynsham and Minster Lovell areas. Another anomalous grouping of finds results from the fieldwalking of members of the Weed Research Organisation at Begbroke in their lunch hours! Such local densities remind us that archaeological maps inevitably tend to show the distribution of modern workers in archaeology rather than complete pictures of human occupation in the county during different periods.

Another problem arises from the differing quality of records. "All observations, all perceived facts depend on the observer, his state of mind, his frame of reference and personal idiosyncrasies ... the observer, consciously or unconsciously, selects the 'facts' to be perceived and no two observers need record the same perceptions about even a single artefact" (Clarke 1968).

2. The factors affecting the recording of artefacts is related to the *nature of the finds themselves*. Some types of finds are readily discovered by non-archaeologists. Sir John Evans was able to build up a vast and compendious collection of prehistoric stone and metal tools because they were so easily recognizable by the Victorian navvy or farm-worker. Other types of flint tools, not so easily recognizable, such as scrapers, have not so frequently figured. Hence axes tend to dominate the find spots of Neolithic distribution maps. Again certain types of material have attracted the attention of archaeologists because of their high survival rate and because they are easy to recognize in consequence. Scatters of Romano-British pottery are easily detectable on a field surface: being well made and thoroughly fired it has a better chance of surviving the abrasion of the plough and the erosion of weathering. Prehistoric and Saxon pottery disintegrates more easily and often is hardly discernible in colour from the soil. Some finds are so anomalous that they must be put in the category of non-archaeological finds. The recovery of an ancient lamp from the Eastern Mediterranean in a North Oxford garden, a North American Indian arrowhead from a field near Banbury, a Nigerian snuff tray, 20 feet down in undisturbed chalk on the Chilterns, and an Indian tulwar (sabre) found in a gravel pit in the Vale of the White Horse pose puzzles in detection rather than archaeological problems (*ex inf*. J.G. Rhodes).

3. *Factors concerning the recognition of sites.*
(a) Parts of Oxfordshire are under permanent pasture and woodland; other areas are built over or have been destroyed by gravel or ironstone extraction. This means that a considerable area is unlikely to yield information on archaeological sites. Woodland inhibits fieldwork; dense undergrowth and thick layers of leaf mould make ground examination difficult and yet it is clear that such areas often contain settlement sites (Taylor 1975). Policies followed by certain landowners in restricting access to their land may lead to blanks in the archaeological record. The pessimist might conclude that archaeological maps recording the evidence collected by fieldwalkers are merely pinpointing the areas owned by amenable farmers whose land happened to be under arable cultivation in the 1970s and 80s!

(b) The type of soil exercises a constraint on aerial photography. The large areas of gravel in the Upper Thames Valley have produced optimum conditions for the growth of cropmarks readily discernible by aerial photography. The generally blank stretches of the ironstone areas in the northern part of the county are an indication of soils largely composed of sandstones and liassic clays which do not in general produce cropmarks. The presence of a number of defended sites shows that man was there in the Iron Age in considerable strength. The fact that there is no supporting evidence for settlement or field systems must mean that we have not found them. Again there is a series of blank areas on the map in the Upper Thames region. To what extent is this attributable to a lack of human settlement? Or alternatively have the gravels which produce cropmarks been overlain in these areas by silt, which does not? Former forest areas such as Wychwood, Shotover and the Chilterns are also zones understandably devoid of cropmarks but by no means devoid of other evidence of early human habitation. Paradoxically, as modern farming obliterates more and more archaeological field monuments we shall find that a residue will be likely to survive only in secondary woodland. It has already been noticed that Ashdown Park has considerable relics of early field systems under its protecting trees whereas all around they have been ploughed flat (Steane and Dix 1978).

A further difficulty with regard to aerial photography is that it is difficult and dangerous to interpret sites or to assign them to any archaeological period without further fieldwork and perhaps even excavation. Consequently some of the numerous cropmarked sites which are shown on the Iron Age map may well, with further study, be attributed to other periods.

(c) The uneven progress of archaeological studies exercises a constraint on the collection of cartographical data. Fifty years ago the tide of Romano-British studies was running high. Chapters in the *Victoria County History* were devoted to the Roman period. Each site was gazetteered. The medieval antiquities, apart from fortified earthwork sites, were ignored. From the early 1950s this position has been reversed. Through the influence of Beresford and Hurst deserted medieval villages began to be located as grassy banks, and hollows were recognized for what they were. Since that time other aspects of the medieval landscape, fishponds, mill dams, parks, have been receiving attention. As the tide of destruction caused by the ever-increasing scale of mechanization in modern farming has gathered speed, it has been recognized that many field boundaries, hedgerows and woodlands are relics of ancient landscapes and need to be recorded before being swept away. The modern trend is towards total archaeology, and it is now becoming important to study the botanical and zoological components of ancient landscapes. It is realized that much of our study of past societies has been unduly artefactually orientated. Distribution maps which rely so heavily on artefact locations are seen as ignoring the fashionable cult of environmental archaeology. This disparate level of progress in archaeological studies is mirrored in the policies followed by the field section of the Museum itself. Some categories of sites and finds have been recorded more systematically than others. A second general problem arises out of a fact of administrative geography. The Vale of the White Horse District was attached to Oxfordshire in 1974. The old county of Berkshire at that time had not yet started a sites and monuments record. Seven years later the maps demonstrate that our knowledge of this area is still rather thin. The relative blanks on the map do not so much reflect a lack of human occupation in the past as a lack of systematic study in the present.

(d) A fourth factor is the uneven rate of decomposition or destruction of ancient sites. Some societies built entirely of wood and only in exceptional cases will their constructions be observable by the field archaeologist. Again some communities built massive communal tombs which still survive as long barrows, others like the Anglo-Saxons were content with slipping their dead into inconspicuous pits. Clearly the field record only contains that which is recordable and this will vary in different societies at different times. Political crisis may bring a tremendous stimulus to fortify on a grand scale. The Iron Age hillforts are the most spectacular prehistoric structures in the Oxfordshire landscape. The undoubtedly far-reaching influence of the Romans on the economy of the area has not left nearly such impressive marks. Equally important in influencing the survival rate of ancient sites is the pattern of subsequent land use. It used to be assumed that prehistoric man favoured the chalk downlands because most of the earthwork evidences of his occupation were there. If we glance at the Iron Age map we might conclude (wrongly) that the only area to be cultivated during the Iron Age was the western end of the Berkshire Downs. In fact we now increasingly realize that on the downland until recently the survival rate of ancient field systems and occupation sites was greater. Elsewhere in the valleys the obliterating effects of later agriculture have been more complete. Where large areas have been excavated by scientific archaeology as at Ashville near Abingdon, it is realized that the valleys could have been densely settled in the Bronze and Iron Ages. Again at Farmoor and Mingie's Ditch, Hardwick near Witney, extensive evidence for pastoral farming in the river valleys has been found.

4. *Sites and Finds*. The later maps representing the sites dating from the Medieval period probably portray a reasonably complete picture of the county at this time. Sites are of more significance than finds, as one would expect when surveying the tolerably well-preserved evidence of human occupation between 500 and 1,000 years ago. As one goes further back into the past, one is forced to rely more and more heavily on finds. Finds often divorced from their original contexts begin to outnumber sites. We can still recognize occupation sites in some numbers in the Iron Age. They become less numerous in the Bronze, very rare in the Neolithic, and vanish altogether beyond this time. This means that our maps get generally less reliable the further back we go. For the Mesolithic and Palaeolithic we have nothing but a few scattered and mostly unrelated artefacts.

The initial work on the maps was carried out by members of the Field Section staff at the Oxfordshire County Museum and by trainees from the Department of Archaeological Sciences at the University of Bradford. Brendan Grimley (Bradford) prepared the first draft of the Palaeolithic map. Mike Heaton (Bradford) drew the Bronze Age map, with advice from Richard Bradley (University of Reading), and the Romano-British map, with advice from Christopher Young (Department of Environment, Ancient Monuments Division). James Bond drew the six medieval maps. John Steane drew the final version of the Palaeolithic map with advice from Derek Roe of the Donald Baden-Powell Quaternary Research Centre, University of Oxford, the Mesolithic and Neolithic maps with advice from Humphrey Case of the Ashmolean Museum, the Early Iron Age map with advice from David Miles of the Oxford Archaeological Unit and the Early Saxon map with advice from Sonia Hawkes of the Institute of Archaeology, University of Oxford. Work on the late Saxon map was carried out by Paul Gilman, with advice from Tom Hassall and John Blair. The maps were prepared for publication by Mélanie Steiner.

Palaeolithic

The small amount of material displayed on this map reflects our very restricted understanding of this period in Oxfordshire. Commercial gravel digging by hand in the late 19th and early 20th centuries accounts for the preponderance of the finds. Unfortunately large-scale methods of mechanical extraction have now cut the flood of artefacts discovered to a mere trickle. Occasionally workers spot a broken axe when it drops from the cleaning screens onto the conveyor belt. Otherwise the archaeologists have to rely on the chance visit of a specialist to the quarry face. The net effect of recording such finds is to build up a map of gravel pits rather than a true distribution of Palaeolithic material.

The basic data for the earlier finds is largely derived from Ordnance Survey records. These have been supplemented more recently by the work of Roe (1968) and Wymer (1968)). More recently still the fieldwork of R. Macrae of Eynsham has been noteworthy. Occasionally finds come to light during controlled excavation but in almost every case in Oxfordshire the context of the Palaeolithic finds seems to be secondary. It is not possible to claim a single habitation site.

The distribution of the finds suggests that at some periods during the Palaeolithic, hunters were present in some numbers on the Chilterns. Their artefacts mingled with the solifluxional material and ultimately were deposited in the fan gravels at the foot of the Chilterns. Other artefacts are found on the ground terraces on both sides of the Thames. No artefacts have been found as yet in the Cotswolds and it may well be that this represents a significant lack of human activity at this early stage.

Mesolithic

If anything this map is likely to be even less representative of the true distribution. In the first place very little material has been recorded in Oxfordshire. There have been few fieldworkers with an ability to recognize Mesolithic material. An attempt to map the sparse distribution was made in 1952 (Case in Martin and Steel). Since then a few further find-spots have been recorded (Wymer 1977).

When one compares the dense complex of sites along the river Kennet and the sparseness along the comparable environments provided by the Thames, Ock and Cherwell, the explanation is the presence of an outstanding fieldworker in Berkshire (Froom 1972a and 1972b). The generally scattered distribution of Mesolithic-type flint artefacts, especially in the northwest part of the county, suggests that the activities of these hunters were widespread and that they had penetrated well beyond the river valleys. Far more information needs to be collected, however, before any valid generalizations can be made.

Neolithic

The considerable amount of material dating from this period makes it tempting to begin to make some generalizations from the evidence. Unfortunately non-archaeological factors are again reflected to a large extent in the distributions. Axes in particular are readily discovered by non-archaeologists. Other types of tools, such as scrapers, which were not so easily recognizable have not so frequently been collected. Hence axes tend to dominate the finds located on Neolithic distribution maps. It is not surprising that many have been found round Oxford. As at Northampton (Royal Commission 1980), the number found may simply reflect the concentration of modern populations rather than any prehistoric cultural presence. On the Cotswolds the nature of the soil is a prime determinant in the pattern of find-spots (Tyler 1976). The heavy clay soil of the valleys is used for permanent grassland which precludes flint-collecting. On the hills where soil is lighter axes and flint arrowheads are found with ease.

Axes have often been regarded in the past as isolated losses. Grimes (1951) saw them as evidence for lines of communication. Taylor (1979) has recently exploded the myth of the Jurassic way and it is difficult to see very much evidence for Neolithic communications in the Oxfordshire evidence. In particular there is no linear spread of lost Neolithic axes along the Ridgeway. If there was a crossing place at Goring–Streatley one would expect a concentration of lost finds here. In fact most of the axes dropped either accidentally or for ritual purposes into the river Thames occur some miles north at Wallingford (Adkins and Jackson 1978). There is just a possibility of a route from the Corallian ridge towards the chalk downland marked by finds (Case et al. 1964/65).

More recently it has been claimed that Neolithic axes may be evidence of contemporary occupation and that therefore they indicate areas of settlement. As against this there is an almost total lack of correlation between the find-spots of stone axes and the distribution of field monuments in large parts of Oxfordshire. A similar lack of correlation has been noted by Bradley in the Lake

District (Bradley 1972–3). He suggests that axes were linked with the thinning of tree cover and the lopping of leaf fodder well beyond the limits of domestic settlement. It is perhaps significant that a score of Neolithic axes have been picked up in the Chilterns. There is a similar widespread scatter in the Cotswolds (Tyler 1976). He suggests that the distribution there is predominantly lowland occurring below 400 feet. "These may have been thickly forested areas in Neolithic times, the axes being used and lost in the forest."

Preliminary study suggested, as in Northamptonshire, that there was no marked difference in the distribution of various petrological groups represented. Accordingly it was decided not to plot them in the interests of not overloading an already complex map with detail.

The other flint material such as scrapers, arrowheads, waste flakes and cores is not so easily found as axes. In Oxfordshire the majority of such material has been retrieved by archaeologists rather than by casual finders. Doubtless if detailed and standardized fieldwork was attempted in many other places it would change the distribution map out of all recognition. For instance, in 1978 a survey was organized of the interior of the ploughed-out Iron Age hillfort of Madmarston. Over a hundred worked flints including several arrowheads were found (Steane and Dix 1979). Again the presence of a lone fieldworker at Charney Bassett has resulted in the finding of a large number of arrowheads (Bradley and Ellison 1975). Doubtless other sites would be located in the areas of the Thames gravels where ring-ditches lie thickly clustered if such fieldwork were carried out.

Arrowheads are relatively easy to recognize as human artefacts, particularly on fields of limestone soil, and there is a wide distribution over the Cotswolds; indeed much denser concentrations have been found in neighbouring counties. It is noteworthy that in the North Cotswolds there is a correlation between the area in which the long barrows are sited and the arrowheads are located. A recent interpretation sees flint arrowheads as primarily weapons of warfare. Concentrations are claimed as representing favoured and wealthy areas for which competition was severe (Green 1980). On the other hand the concentration of leaf-shaped arrowheads in the vale has been equated with a hunting territory (Bradley and Ellison 1975).

The Bronze Age

This map emphasizes the very partial evidence which we have for the study of the Bronze Age in Oxfordshire. Burials abound, and a certain number of metal artefacts have been recovered from the river Thames but there is an almost total lack of settlement evidence. Consequently we are forced to rely for socio-economic, environmental, and chronological information on the burials themselves. Rams Hill (Bradley and Ellison 1975), the only substantial excavated Bronze Age settlement, stands alone.

The barrows on the chalk downland have attracted interest since Sir Richard Colt Hoare's ride along the Ridgeway in 1815. They were the subject of destructive investigation by a number of Victorian barrow diggers such as Martin-Atkins, Wilson and Canon Greenwell. Grinsell listed them before the war (Grinsell 1935) and Case has studied the famous barrow group at Lambourn (Case 1956) which is just over the county boundary with Berkshire and has been included on the map. They have recently been re-surveyed (Bradley and Ellison 1975 and Richards 1978) and many more examples have been added to the great congregation at Lambourn. Here the immediate area of the Seven Barrows now is seen to include 46 mounds and ring-ditches while a scattered group of a dozen is known from Nutwood Down. Clearly the great density of Bronze Age barrows in the south-west corner of the map is partly to be explained by these concentrated bursts of fieldwork.

The map shows a sinuous band of ring-ditches, running across the centre of the county, following the course of the Thames Valley. The gravels of the Upper Thames Valley have been constantly flown over since Major Allen's sorties of the 1930s and the high rate of discovery is clearly linked with the great interest roused by these early air photographs.

Ploughing has been intense and has reduced most of these burial mounds to ring-ditches which show up as cropmarks. A good deal of excavation has arisen out of gravel extraction and the building of airfields which has resulted in field survey (Grimes 1960 and Case et al. 1964/5). Grimes suggested that the 57 ring-ditches which he found near Stanton Harcourt were due to the presence of the henge monument known as the Devil's Quoits which may have attracted barrows towards it as did Stonehenge. Similar groupings are to be found in the Abingdon/Radley, Dorchester and Wallingford areas. In each case when the Neolithic map is compared there is seen to be a continuity of sacred function in these areas.

Recent fieldwork shows that the Vale of the White Horse is not nearly so blank as was formerly thought. Because of later land-use no field systems remain but a series of 14 probable barrows can be traced; the majority of these sites are in the north of the vale but not all are on Corallian limestone and seven are in fact on clay. They all lie in an area which has produced many surface flints.

On the Cotswolds there is a scatter of barrows with no marked concentrations. The condition of the monuments is much better, as one would expect, with less intensive ploughing. One curious anomaly is the lack of a density around the henge monument, the Rollright Stones on the Warwickshire border, but future fieldwork may well remedy this. In general county boundaries seem to act with an inhibiting effect on archaeological research.

One important factor which may have a bearing on the location of archaeological sites in the Thames Valley has been noticed recently (Robinson 1980). The flood-plain appears to have been drier and better drained in the Bronze Age and may well have been as suited for arable as the First and Second Gravel Terraces. Since then forest clearance, expansion of arable agriculture, the introduction of winter cereals and an increase of rainfall of the sub-Atlantic phase have all combined to increase surface water run-off and river sediment load. This has caused an aggradation of alluvium which has covered many sites and caused a rise in the water-table and an increase in flooding. This silt undoubtedly masks much of the gravel in particular in the western half of the county and may well account for the less intensive cropmarks distinguishable by aerial photography there.

Turning to artefacts, there is a pronounced linear distribution of find-spots in and along the banks of the River Thames which shows a radical lack of correlation with the distribution of burial mounds and ring-ditches. Fox (1943) noticed "that the great river, practically from end to end from Oxford to Shoeburyness, is marked by a string of finds, the most extended and continuous in the country", and he considered that the well-drained gravel terraces were attractive to human occupation in the Bronze Age. Recent discussion (Ehrenberg 1977) has pointed out that non-archaeological factors also have an important bearing on this distribution. The Thames has been dredged almost continously since the mid-19th century to allow vessels of increasingly large burden to travel up-river and hundreds of artefacts have been found by the dredger crews. Ehrenberg points out that 105 finds of Bronze Age metalwork are known to have come from the Berkshire stretch of the river before 1932 and since then 27 have been recorded. Very few of the provenances are exact since dredger crews tended to cite the find-spots only in terms of the nearest town or bridge, so it is impossible to be sure whether finds are parts of hoards, or whether supposed concentrations truly mark the position of fords or settlement sites.

The vast majority of Bronze Age metal finds from Berks., Bucks. and Oxon. are weapons; tools in general are smaller and may have been missed by dredger crews. Consequently dredging which may be seen as a regular search for finds has badly distorted the distribution of finds. Ehrenberg has considered the mechanisms whereby finds were lost and in addition to the obvious ones such as accidental losses, capsizing from boats, battles, also suggests that they were meant to propitiate the watergods, following the increased rainfall and waterlogging of the late Bronze Age. Her most interesting suggestion, however, is the possibility that weapons which had formerly been buried in barrows were now cast into rivers because of a fundamental change in burial rite. The erosion of settlements which has only produced one example, at Wallingford, is largely discounted.

Iron Age

The first thing that strikes one when looking at this map, which attempts to display the total number of sites and finds broadly attributable to the Iron Age, is the close correspondence between the known sites and the superficial geological deposits of the gravel terraces. The gravels are of course especially suitable for revealing cropmarks from the air and they have also acted as a magnet to commercial gravel digging. This in turn has elicited the most powerful archaeological response. Despite these reservations, expressed by Harding (Harding 1972), the distribution pattern has not been supplemented by surface finds to such an extent as to invalidate the first impression in favour of the gravel terraces. Only the wide dispersal of coin finds suggests some kind of economic penetration into most parts of the country. There are in fact considerable geographical blanks in the archaeological record which may show that these areas were devoid of settlement in Iron Age times. Sites and finds are conspicuously few in the areas east of Oxford, the Otmoor region and the eastern corner of the county.

The second noticeable fact is the large number of defended sites, twenty-four, with three possibles. They are categorized here as hillforts but do in fact include the valley forts of Cherbury, Cassington and the Belgic promontory fortress of Dyke Hills. This contrasts with neighbouring Northamptonshire (Royal Commission 1980) which produces a plethora of Iron Age sites but can only muster four hillforts. Clearly Oxfordshire was in the hillfort-dominated zone which stretched from North Wales to Kent (Cunliffe 1976). There has been a disappointingly small amount of controlled excavation limited to sections across entrances and defences. Almost nothing is known of the interiors of Oxfordshire hillforts. The lower-status sites on the gravel-bearing soils on the other hand have been the subject of a number of large-scale and informative excavations.

The field systems which form such an important element on the south-western edge of the map and which spread down the dip-slope of the chalk into Berkshire have been shown at their fullest extent. They were not marked on the Bronze Age map for reasons of lack of space caused by the concentrations of burial mounds, but they have been assigned with almost equal force to the Bronze Age. It would seem reasonable to suppose that they were growing as clearance along the chalk was progressing, but "their chronology is for the most part vague and almost totally relative" (Richards 1978). The extent of prehistoric field systems has been mapped from aerial photography. Rhodes produced a pioneer survey (Rhodes 1950) which has been supplemented by a more intensive search round Rams Hill (Bradley and Ellison 1975) and a more general survey (Richards 1978). Little progress has been made with dating but it has been noticed that blocks of fields appear to occupy complementary areas of the landscape to the grass-grown Lambourn valley already occupied with barrows. The fields would in many cases appear to be aligned on barrows and in some cases avoid covering them. In general there seems to be a major division in land-use between the more arable west and the more pastoral east. The map shows also a long linear ditch known as Grim's Ditch which stretches from Lattin Hill eastwards for about 12 miles. What the map does not show clearly, because they are mostly in Berkshire, is the presence of six major linear ditches, amounting to a length of 20 kms in all which run between the scarp slope and the Lambourn river which divide the downland into distinct blocks. The majority of these ditches run through areas of fields and suggest an element of extensive and cohesive planning dividing the landscape into economic units which remind us of the medieval strip parishes. Apart from scraps of indecisive date the field networks described are the only ones remaining in the county. The question immediately is posed : where are the Iron Age fields of the Thames Valley? (Miles 1978). A possibility is that "in the river gravels where drainage was not needed, and where the flat ground would not create lynchets, there is therefore no need to expect traces of 'Celtic fields'" (Royal Commission 1980). The map marks only three pit alignments, which seem rarer in the Upper Thames than in the Welland valley. The almost ubiquitous presence of pits, which on excavation have proved the presence of grain and arable weeds, and the finding of corn-drying ovens show the importance of grain-growing in the Iron Age and Romano-British period. It would appear that the main arable areas were simply located between the settlement sites, though some areas as at Farmoor and Mingie's Ditch, Hardwick, seem to have been pastoral farms perhaps occupied during the summers only.

One final feature, the Berkshire Ridgeway, has not been inserted on the map, partly because its course is so well known and partly because it would have confused the picture which was already covered with field systems and linear ditch systems. This may well have originated in the Bronze Age as a processional route weaving its way through a linear spread of barrows. It is slightly disturbing to note that the present course cuts decisively through a block of prehistoric fields south of Ham Wood. Similarly it cuts off the stub ends of the network south of East Hendred. Comparisons of the course noticed in the Rocque map and the tithe maps of the 1840s and the Ordnance Survey maps of 1883 show that the Ridgeway has changed course considerably since the 18th century. It may be suggested that it began as a broad zone of communication and has steadily been restricted in width under the more intense farming pressures. There is a general distinction between the narrow curving constrained course of the western half and the broad braided multiplicity of lines of the eastern half (Steane 1983).

They coincide with the division in land-use noticed when the field systems were discussed. This suggests that the route had already become contained within a network of fields in the prehistoric. There is little or no evidence of prehistoric trade along it, no linear spreads of finds, and a complete blank apart from one axe at the supposed Goring-Streatley crossing.

Roman

This map seeks to locate all known Roman sites and finds in the county. This, of course has been attempted before, by the *Victoria County History* (1939), Martin and Steel (1954) and Young (1978). Each map has traced the steady growth of local interest in the period. Fieldwork has not, however, been as intense as in the neighbouring county of Northamptonshire. Here a recent map of the distribution of Roman finds has plotted 900 symbols (Royal Commission 1980). It is likely that the present map represents what is probably the most accurate overall distribution of sites and finds in the series before the medieval period. This is partly owing to the great interest in the Roman period shown by a University whose contribution to classical studies is distinguished. It is also partly because of the relative ease with which Romano-British building material and pottery may be identified. However it is still very doubtful whether the present picture represents anything like the true density of sites. There are a number of blanks on the map, particularly to the east and north-east. Further, the county boundary to the west seems to have acted as a distorting factor. Recent work at the western end of the Vale of the White Horse (Miles and Hingley 1980 unpub.) which has located a number of sites serves to show what may be possible in other areas. Another considerable problem is the static nature of the information shown on the map which represents material from four hundred years. Only recently has there been detailed study undertaken on the dating of the products of local pottery kilns (Young 1977) and as yet these findings have not been applied to elucidate the chronology of settlement within the county.

The most obvious innovation of the Roman Conquest here as elsewhere was the development of towns and roads. It is clear from the map that the most important east-west through route was Akeman Street linking the towns of Cirencester and Verulamium across the northern part of the county. There was also a north-south route which crosses Akeman Street near Alchester and connects Alchester through Dorchester to Silchester.

Both these roads are marked in on the *Ordnance Survey Map of Roman Britain* (4th edn). Parts of a third major route which ran north-east from Wantage are known for certain as far north as the temple site at Frilford. Thereafter the course is uncertain (Young 1977). A network of minor roads and trackways also doubtless existed (Hargreaves and Parker 1972, Hargreaves, Parker and Boarder 1973) and some of the more likely (e.g. Aves ditch) have been drawn on the map. Recently a bridge has been found in the centre of Otmoor carrying the Roman road over the river Ray (Chambers 1981).

The effect of these roads was doubtless to penetrate the area to the east of the Thames and Cherwell and this was aided by the establishment first of forts and then of defended towns at Dorchester and Alchester. It is particularly noticeable when we compare the Iron Age and Romano-British distributions in the hinterland of Alchester that the town has obviously had the effect of opening up an area previously little settled. A similar effect is seen in the area to the east and north-east of Dorchester. Clearly the Romano-British farmers were not afraid of the intractable clay soils of the vales.

There are two good examples of continuity of a political/economic focus from the Iron Age into the Roman period. The best known is the sequence in the Dorchester area; here the Iron Age hillfort on Wittenham Clumps was followed by a slight shift to the north when the Belgic promontory fortress of Dyke Hills was occupied. The Romans also recognized the importance of the region by founding their walled town of Dorchester within half a mile of Dyke Hills. In the north of the county below the Iron Age hillfort of Madmarston, an extensive urban site at Swalclifffe Lea was founded which ultimately spread over 40 acres. Despite a search at Graven Hill, a likely hillfort site south of Bicester, no Iron Age precursor has been found for the Romano-British town of Alchester. One other town at least as large as Dorchester existed at Abingdon at the confluence of the Ock and Thames (Young 1977). Another settlement which had some of the characteristics of a small town existed at Asthall. The map makes it clear that in general the urban settlements acted as a stimulus on rural growth. Abingdon must have provided the market for the Barton Court villa for instance, Mount Farm no doubt sold produce at Dorchester. The villas occur on the valley gravels only close to Abingdon and Dorchester.

The location of the kiln sites has already been discussed in detail by Young (1977). The key conditions seem to have been availability of clay, water, fuel and ease of communications. Undoubtedly his group 3 sites east of Thames and Cherwell had the edge on the others and the map shows that this was provided by three factors, proximity to two major market centres, situation on the north-south road and east-west river route, and the facility of a self-regenerating fuel source in the Shotover-Bernwood region (see Medieval map).

When we turn to the west central part of the county two aspects are particuarly noticeable. The first is the great concentration of villas, eleven in number, within the area enclosed by stretches of the Iron Age linear ditch and bank, the Oxfordshire Grim's Ditch. The limestone region extending across the centre of Oxfordshire and dissected by the rivers Glyme, Evenlode and Windrush had already attracted the attention of Belgic farmers. The siting of the Roman villas suggests that their owners preferred to settle within the vicinity of two or more different soils. The effect would have been to provide villa farms such as Shakenoak and North Leigh with an area of arable in close conjunction with wooded clay country, furnishing fuel, pannage and grazing for cattle and goats. Studies of the siting of Romano-British farms in relation to soils in the Vale of the White Horse show a similar predilection for mixed soils. Of 42 sites, 14 are on pebbly or fine sandy loams, 10 are on medium loam, loam-sandy soils. The Gault and Kemmeridge clays are virtually empty of occupation (Applebaum 1972).

The second surprising fact arises out of the almost total blank of Romano-British sites in the western margin of the Upper Thames Valley. When we look at the Iron Age map we see that there is an exceptionally dense cluster in this area – west of Bampton. Two suggestions may be made. The first is that these sites (Miles and Hingley 1980 unpub.) are almost entirely identified from aerial photography. Such crop-marked sites are not of course easy to date unless the identification is backed up by fieldwalking. It may well be that more fieldwork will assign a number of them to the Romano-British period. A second possibility is that this area was already intensively farmed and Romano-British farmers simply kept out but it is strange that there are not more casual find-spots of Roman material.

Three temple sites are plotted. Woodeaton and Frilford were sites where there was a continuity of sacred function. Lowbury has a more questionable status (Atkinson 1916): its hill-top site is certainly suggestive of a temple and it was also the centre of converging routes all over this part of the Downs. The chalk downland has not produced evidence for a very intensive Roman settlement. In Berkshire Richards points out the lack of any formal road system and the sparseness of substantial settlements. Only Maddle Farm, where the settlement area extends to the Oxfordshire boundary, shows occupation spreading over 75 acres and evidence of one major building with tesselated pavements (Richards 1978).

Early Saxon

This map attempts to delineate archaeological data of the pagan Saxon period principally derived from individual burials and cemeteries, superimposed on certain aspects of the late Roman settlement pattern of Oxfordshire. It does not provide sufficient evidence for making generalized statements concerning early Saxon settlement patterns or territorial arrangements. Certain categories of information have in fact been deliberately left out. These include the Old English place-names (which were mapped for Oxfordshire by Gelling 1953 and for Berkshire by Gelling 1971–4. The Old English charter bounds are not mapped here (the Berkshire charters are covered by Gelling 1976). Nor are the structures of Saxon churches located on the present map.

The burials themselves provide a somewhat uneven category of information. The great majority have been discovered accidentally by gravel and stone quarrying, the construction of railways and canals and building works. Consequently their location tells us more about the main areas of industrial activity in the county in the 19th and 20th centuries than about the Saxon landscape. They have been haphazardly and inadequately recorded. There are only seven sites with more than forty recorded graves and for only eight cemeteries is there any sort of grave plan (Dickinson 1976). Since

1840 each decade has seen the discovery of between five and ten new cemeteries, but, despite the spread of urban sprawl, from 1970 to 1976 only four new cemeteries were found. They are only rarely detectable on aerial photographs. The circumstances of their discovery nearly always mean that a certain part has been destroyed in the process. The cemeteries frequently provide us with the graves of the richer folk so we are apt to get a biased view of Saxon society from studying the remains.

The information derived from Saxon cemeteries is therefore unsatisfactory in several ways, but it is far more bulky than the knowledge we have of settlement sites. Aerial photography is not very successful at revealing the presence of Saxon settlements. Sometimes silt has masked them; sometimes undistinguished blobs may or may not be the remains of Grubenhäuser. At New Wintles only the Bronze Age ring-ditches showed up but a Saxon settlement appeared on excavation. Again extensive gravel quarrying has been a major factor in the discovery of sites. It has been claimed by Berisford (1973) that 27 sites are known and by Dickinson (1976) that 40 have been found. Whatever the truth of the matter the settlements are outstripped by the numbers of cemeteries, nearly 60 in the Thames gravels between Lechlade and Goring. Clearly many more remain to be discovered along the tributaries of the Thames and the higher ground. Moreover most of the settlements so far found failed to survive into the Mid-Saxon period; this seems connected with a valley-ward shift or can be attributed to their small size or poverty. Because Cassington has been virtually surrounded by gravel pits we can trace this process in some detail. It is possible to pair off cemeteries and settlements (Berisford 1973). Similarly at Eynsham there are abandoned Saxon settlements and cemeteries to the north and south of the present centre. This phenomenon of settlement-shift has been noticed in other areas, notably Maxey (Cambridgeshire) and Chalton (Hampshire). The fact that many settlements were sited some distance from Roman villas implies that the newcomers lived side-by-side with the Romano-British farmers, perhaps even being content to take the less desirable land.

The map does not contribute a great deal to the much-debated question of continuity between the Roman and Saxon periods. It would have been better served if it had been possible to map the areas where 4th- and 5th-century Roman material has been found. The evidence for the hypothesis that the first German settlers were invited over by the sub-Roman administration to defend such towns as Silchester and Dorchester is rather sparse. Recently it has been stated (Richards 1978 quoting Young) that the burials from Dorchester-on-Thames (Kirk and Leeds 1952–3) often quoted as Germanic are in fact merely those of soldiers in the late Roman army. Certainly the distribution of the complex of early Saxon finds and burials in the Dorchester and Abingdon areas implies continuity. There is no such evidence around Alchester. In one rural area again the presence of German mercenaries has been detected at Shakenoak, perhaps placed there on the edge of the great North Leigh estate to which Shakenoak seems to have been subordinate in the late Roman-British period. Berisford (1973) is not convinced of the evidence for continuity and thinks that the site was abandoned during the 5th century and partially re-occupied later.

When we turn briefly to finds we notice that there is a distinct linear distribution along the river Thames as on the Bronze Age map. Myres (in Martin and Steel 1954) considered "more significant perhaps is the considerable number of pagan Saxon weapons that has been recovered from the bed of the Thames at many points in its course through the Oxford region". He thought that loss of valuable arms in the river itself was more likely to occur in the course of battle than by mere accident. It seems however that the mechanics of discovery are also relevant. The decisive factor is the dredging practices of the Thames Conservancy. Dredging is in fact a comparatively thorough method of search: it has produced an artificially linear distribution of finds of the pagan Saxon period which in its way is as unhelpful as the location of cemeteries by gravel extraction.

Late Saxon

This map illustrates the archaeology of Oxfordshire in the three centuries which preceded the Norman Conquest. During the Late Saxon period historical sources increase in value and number through narrative accounts such as the Anglo-Saxon Chronicle, various laws and acts of government, land charters, and monastic records. Consequently it is possible to locate and name more places than in the maps illustrating previous periods. In compiling it a start was made by referring to the Ordnance Survey's *Britain before the Norman Conquest*. The sites of the major monasteries are marked on this and some of the minster churches. These have been supplemented by information from Dr. W.J. Blair (The Queen's College, Oxford). Churches containing building work of this period have been taken from Pevsner's *Buildings in England, Oxfordshire* (Sherwood & Pevsner 1979).

A few finds of late Saxon date are culled from the Ordnance Survey's map; these have been added to from the much fuller archive in the Sites and Monuments Record, Oxfordshire County Museum. In two places, Wallingford and Oxford, the amount of Late Saxon material derived from recent archaeological work is so prolific that no attempt has been made to include it on the county map. The location of the *villae regales* has been taken from the map in Steel and Martin 1954. The Old Norse and Scandinavian names are those mentioned in Gelling (1953).

Medieval

The period to be covered by the maps was defined as that between two major events, the Norman Conquest,

1066, and the Reformation of c.1530. Both saw revolutions in land ownership which reverberated over the whole country. When approaching the problem of mapping the archaeological material for this period a number of difficulties arise. There is a greater quantity of information available for the Middle Ages compared with other earlier periods. This has arisen for two main reasons. More sites, finds, and monuments have survived than from earlier times. In some categories of monuments, such as rural parish churches, a very large proportion of the total number which ever existed have come down to us in fact. In some areas (Cogges is a good example) much of the medieval landscape, and structural elements associated with it, have lasted to the present day. Not only is the archaeological record rich, it is supplemented and complemented by documentary evidence which not only aids interpretation of known sites, but also can point to the existence of undiscovered or long-since destroyed sites. For these reasons it is possible to map a far more complete picture for the Middle Ages than for earlier periods. Such a plethora of material is so extensive, however, that it cannot be realistically plotted on a single map. A different approach has been adopted with maps being produced on a thematic rather than a chronological basis.

(1) Medieval rural settlement and parishes:
   from which is abstracted:–
(1a) Deserted and shrunken villages.
(2) Medieval boroughs and market centres.
(3) Medieval forests and parks.
(4) Medieval castles and moated sites.
(5) Medieval monastic sites.

Despite the wealth of information displayed on these maps it remains only a very partial selection of the total available. Among the many aspects of the medieval archaeological record which have not been plotted are parish churches and chapels, domestic buildings, the remains of field systems, and the extent of woodland, fishponds, and industrial features like mills, kilns and quarries. The distribution of churches and chapels would largely duplicate rural settlements. The mapping of church buildings dating from different periods might give a useful index of economic prosperity or contraction in different areas. Domestic buildings are very inadequately recorded and continually fresh discoveries are being made. Any distribution map of survivals is likely to be strongly biased by the work of Wood-Jones in the Banbury Region and by Currie and Fletcher in the south of the county. Some other aspects of the medieval landscape have already been the subject of distribution maps published elsewhere. Domesday woodland and mills, for instance, have been published in Darby and Campbell 1962. Other aspects, such as field systems, although widespread, are as yet imperfectly mapped. The location of medieval industry in Oxfordshire is inadequately known. Despite the intensive work done by Mellor and others on the medieval pottery, hardly anything is known about the location of kilns in the county.

Finally a few comments will be made on each map pointing out the more obvious anomalies. The question of sources is dealt with more thoroughly in the text of the accompanying chapter.

(1) *Rural settlement and (1a) Deserted and Shrunken villages*. Medieval archaeology is a comparatively recent field of study. It began promisingly enough in Oxfordshire in the early Victorian period when the Rev. Dr. J. Wilson carried out one of the first excavations of a deserted medieval village in the county at Woodperrry (Wilson 1846). Thereafter archaeological energies were directed into the narrow, if profitable, channels of college, church and manor house. An excavation at Seacourt (Bruce-Mitford 1940) revived interest, but it was really the work of the Medieval Village Research Group during the last 30 years which has led to the remarkable accumulation of evidence on which these maps are based. Systematic scanning of aerial photographs, earthwork surveys, fieldwalking, selective excavation, and research among documents have produced a distribution of rural settlement which in totality cannot be far from a complete picture. There are very few sites whose names are not known and equally few names without locations. The main anomaly is that the map represents an unduly static picture. As has recently been emphasized (Taylor 1983), settlements in the mid- to late Saxon period were constantly coming and going, sometimes shifting with the same name following a site which might move several times over 500 years. Certainly settlement in the landscape was becoming considerably more stable after 1066 but it is still true to say that at any one time it is unlikely that Oxfordshire would have been so completely filled up with settlements as the map suggests.

(2) *Medieval boroughs and market centres*. This map *par excellence* brings out the problems of definition when dealing with a phenomenon such as the medieval borough. The county has already had its historic towns covered by an archaeological implications survey (Rodwell 1974), but this was limited to the major market centres of whatever period and many of the 'minute failed market towns of the medieval period' were excluded. This map attempts to fill the gaps and the result emphasizes the density of market centres. It is clear that no-one in Oxfordshire lived more than a day's journey from a market centre. Recent work on the temporal spacing of such centres in other areas of the Midlands (such as Nottinghamshire) shows that overlapping was more apparent than real.

(3) *Medieval forest and parks*. Woodland played an important part in the medieval economy despite the fact that modern studies (e.g. Rackham 1980) indicate that only a small proportion of the county was still tree-covered. Unfortunately it is not possible yet to map medieval woodland at all fully because the detailed

topographical research has not yet been done in Oxfordshire, although the Nature Conservancy is aware of the importance of distinguishing between the surviving scraps of ancient woodland and the more extensive secondary areas. Woodland is of course difficult country for archaeologists. It is less susceptible to exploration by aerial photography, while tree roots and undergrowth inhibit excavation and field survey. It is possible that in the long run earthworks will stand a better chance of preservation if they are in woodland and already it has been noticed that some early field systems have only survived when protected by woodland cover (Steane & Dix 1978). The map of Forests and Parks is based largely on surviving legal records and to a lesser extent on topographical or archaeological input. Much of the data for the Wychwood Forest area was derived from the researches of Mrs. Wickham-Steed, lodged in the Sites and Monuments Record. It does bring out the constant fluctuations in the boundaries of the forest which the Angevin kings attempted to expand up till about 1200, and which thereafter contracted, and by 1300 were reduced to three main areas. Work recently done on Bernwood Forest (Steane 1985) shows that its origins are likely to be in an Early Iron Age 'multiple estate' and that its boundaries, originally extending from Aylesbury to Bicester, had shrunk very considerably by 1300. Some revision of the plotted boundaries shown on the map is now thought necessary. The distribution map of parks is likely to be reasonably complete since the subject has been intensively studied (Woodward 1983). The correlation between the dense concentration of parks in the south-east part of the county and the thickly-wooded Chiltern Hills is striking. There is another group clearly related to the royal forest of Wychwood. The others are scattered over the landscape and prompt no particular explanation except to stress that the privilege of possessing a park was widely sought after by the gentry, ecclesiastics and nobles of medieval Oxfordshire.

(4) *Medieval castles/moated sites.* Large strides have been taken in the study of ancient earthwork defensive sites since the last county-wide survey (Victoria County History 1907). At that time earthworks from all periods were lumped together and little was known of the dating of such sites. It was wrongly believed that "excavation affords the only method of ascertaining the age of most earthworks". An attempt was made then to classify them on typological grounds. Since then most medieval castles have been firmly located and dated by means of documents. Several have been subjected to scientific excavation (Banbury, Deddington and Oxford in particular). An alternative and more detailed classification is now proposed. It is now recognized that the basic defensive enclosures of the Saxon-Norman period were the ring-works and these were added to and adapted. The result was in some cases the motte-and-bailey castle and in other cases the developed ring-work castle. In others earthwork banks do not appear to have been very important but moats figure prominently in the defences of crenellated manor houses, castles and some monastic sites. Strategic considerations do not seem to have played a large part in the siting of Oxfordshire castles. Only at Oxford and Wallingford were castles built to dominate towns and river-crossings. The locations chosen for the rest depended on local tenurial considerations. Defences in fact were required for buildings which otherwise had mainly residential or administrative functions connected with estate management. "Other moated sites" are the most numerous defensive category but also the most enigmatic. Only one has been extensively excavated, at Chalgrove. Often it is not possible to date them accurately because their defences are not mentioned in the documents, but it is a reasonable supposition that, in common with other areas of the Midlands, most of the Oxfordshire moats date from the 13th–14th centuries. There is the same broad correlation between their location and the clay vales as elsewhere. The greater density of such sites in the main areas of medieval woodland may link some of them with the assarting movement which was gathering momentum as the population expanded in the 13th century. However many of the areas of active assarting in Oxfordshire are on chalk and limestone which are not particularly suitable for moating. It is likely that a much higher proportion of the Oxfordshire moats was manorial than was the case in Warwickshire or Worcestershire.

5 *Medieval Monasteries.* Monastic sites are well known and monastic histories have been the subject of thorough research in the Oxford region, hardly surprising in view of the number of scholars working in a University famed for its medieval studies. The map is based on the information available in the Sites and Monuments Record, and as such is more complete than the Ordnance Survey *Monastic Map of Southern Britain*. One shortcoming is that the distribution of granges is probably incomplete and the density may be a little biased to the Vale of the White Horse where the estates of the Abbey of Abingdon have been the subject of a recent study (Bond 1979). One interesting observation is the magnetic attraction of the river Thames particularly for the siting of the older Benedictine houses. If we include twenty in Oxford, twenty-nine out of fifty Oxfordshire religious foundations were on or near the river and these include the oldest and wealthiest. The neighbouring county of Berkshire shows the same phenomenon: altogether eighteen out of thirty-five religious houses were situated on or very near the Thames. The ease with which cumbersome building materials such as stone (Jope 1948/9) and timber (Steane 1981) could be moved along the river may have been one attraction. The proximity to rich farmlands which formed the congeries of estates supporting these houses was a more likely reason. This map more than most in the series is a record of sites because it can hardly be claimed that monastic ruins figure in, much less dominate, any part of the landscape of the Upper Thames Valley. There is no Fountains or Rievaulx to

fire the imagination. The combined effects of deliberate destruction at the time of the Dissolution, the sale of building materials in an area where there was little fine building stone, and the pressure of redevelopment especially on urban sites, have reduced most monasteries, priories, and hospitals in the Oxford Region simply to memories.

Bibliography

Adkins, R. and Jackson, R. (1978) *Neolithic Stone and Flint Axes from the River Thames.* British Museum Occas. Paper No. 1
Applebaum, S. (1972) 'Agriculture in Roman Britain', in Finberg, H.P.R., *Agrarian History of England and Wales* I. ii
Atkinson, D. (1916) *The Romano-British Site on Lowbury Hill in Berkshire*
Benson, D. (1975) 'The application of aerial photography in the Oxford Region', in Wilson, D.R. (ed.), *Aerial Reconnaissance for Archaeology.* CBA
Berisford, F. (1973) *The Early Anglo-Saxon Settlement Sites in the Upper Thames Basin with special reference to the area around Cassington and Eynsham.* Oxford B. Litt. Thesis
Bond, C.J. (1979) 'The reconstruction of the medieval landscape. The estates of Abingdon Abbey', *Journal of Landscape History* 1, 59–75
Bond, C.J. and Campbell, J.M. (1980) 'Environmental record centres as a source for local historians. The case of Oxfordshire', in Brandon, P. and Millman, R. (eds.), *Recording Historic Landscapes.* Polytechnic of North London, Dept. of Geography Occasional Papers No. 2
Bradley, R. (1972–3) 'Prehistorians and pastoralists in Neolithic and Bronze Age England', *World Archaeol.* 4, 192–204
Bradley, R. and Ellison, A. (1975) *Rams Hill.* BAR 19
Bruce-Mitford, R.L.S. (1940) 'Excavations at Seacourt', *Oxoniensia* 5, 31–40
Case, H. (1956) 'The Lambourn Seven Barrows', *Berks. Archaeol. J.* 55, 15–31
Case, H. *et al.* (1964–5) 'Excavations at City Farm, Hanborough, Oxon.', *Oxoniensia* 29–30, 1–99
Chambers, R. (1981) 'Fencott and Murcott', *CBA Group 9 Newsletter* 11, 122–3
Clarke, D.L. (1968) *Analytical Archaeology*
Crawford, O.G.S. (1932) *Ordnance Survey Map of Neolithic Wessex*
Cunliffe, B. and Rowley, T., eds. (1976) *Oppida : The Beginnings of Urbanisation in Barbarian Europe.* BAR S11
Dickinson, T. (1976) *The Anglo-Saxon burial sites of the Upper Thames Region and their bearing on the history of Wessex c. 400–700 AD.* Oxford Ph.D thesis
Ehrenberg, M.R. (1977) *Bronze Age Spearheads from Berks, Bucks and Oxon.* BAR 34
Fowler, P.J. (1977) *Approaches to Archaeology*
Fox, C. (1923) *The Archaeology of the Cambridge Region*
Fox, C. (1943) *The Personality of Britain*
Froom, F.R. (1972a) 'Some Mesolithic sites in South West Berkshire', *Berks. Archaeol. J.* 66, 11–22
Froom, F.R. (1972b) 'A Mesolithic site at Wawcott, Kintbury, Berkshire', *Berks. Archaeol. J.* 66, 23–44
Gelling, M. (1953) *Place-names of Oxfordshire*
Gelling, M. (1973–6) *Place-names of Berkshire*
Green, H.S. (1980) *The Flint Arrowheads of the British Isles.* BAR 75
Grimes, W.F. (1951) 'The Jurassic Way' in Grimes, W.F. (ed.), *Aspects of Archaeology*
Grimes, W.F. (1960) *Excavations on Defence Sites 1939–45* Vol. 1

Grinsell, L.V. (1935–6) 'An analysis and list of Berkshire barrows. Parts 1 and 2', *Berks. Archaeol. J.* 39, 171–191 and 40, 21–58
Harding, D.W. (1972) *The Iron Age of the Thames Valley*
Hargreaves, G.H. and Parker, R.P.F. (1972) 'Kirtlington Port Way Roman Road', *CBA Group 9 Newsletter* 2, 15
Hargreaves, G.H., Parker, R.P.F. and Boarder, A.W.F. (1974) 'Aves Ditch', *CBA Group 9 Newsletter* 4, 10–11
Hingley, R. (1982) 'Noah's Ark, Frilford', *CBA Group 9 Newsletter* 12, 150
Jope, E.M. (1948/9) 'Abingdon Abbey, craftsmen and building-stone supplies'. *Berks. Archaeol. J.* 51, 53–64
Jope, E.M. (1963) 'The Regional cultures of medieval Britain', in Foster, I.Ll. and Alcock, L. *Culture and Environment, essays in honour of Sir Cyril Fox*, 327–351
Kirk, J.R. and Leeds, E.T. (1952–3) 'Three early Saxon graves from Dorchester, Oxfordshire', *Oxoniensia* 17/18, 63–76
Lambrick, G. (1983) *The Rollright Stones.* Oxf. Archaeol. Unit
Martin, A.F. and Steel, R.W. (1954) *The Oxford Region*
Miles, D. (1978) 'The Upper Thames Valley', in Bowen, H.C. and Fowler, P.J. *Early Land Allotment in the British Isles.* BAR 48
Miles, D. and Hingley, R. (1980) Map of Iron Age settlement sites in Oxfordshire. Unpublished, deposited in Oxon. County Museum
Ordnance Survey, *Map of Monastic Britain.* 2nd edn. South Sheet, 1954
Ordnance Survey, *Map of Britain before the Norman Conquest.* 1974
Ordnance Survey, *Map of Roman Britain.* 4th edn. 1978
Rackham, O. (1980) *Ancient Woodland*
Rhodes, P.P. (1950) 'The Celtic Field Systems on the Berkshire Downs', *Oxoniensia* 15, 1–28
Richards, J. (1978) *The Archaeology of the Berkshire Downs*
Robinson, M. (1980) 'Flooding and the Bronze Age use of the Thames floodplain in the Oxford District' in Palmer, N., 'A Beaker burial and medieval tenements in the Hamel, Oxford', *Oxoniensia* 45, 133–4
Rodwell, K. (1974) *Historic Towns in Oxfordshire.* Oxford Archaeological Unit
Roe D.A. (1968) *Gazetteer of Lower and Mid Palaeolithic Sites.* CBA Research Report 8
Royal Commission on Historical Monuments, England (1980) *Northamptonshire, an Archaeological Atlas*
Sherwood, J. and Pevsner, N. (1979) *Buildings of England. Oxfordshire*
Steane, J.M. and Dix, B.F. (1978) *Peopling Past Landscapes.* CBA
Steane, J.M. (1981) 'The Medieval forests, woods and parks of Berkshire', *Arboricultural J.* 5, 189–200
Steane, J.M. (1983) 'How old is the Berkshire Ridgeway?', *Antiquity* 57, 103–8
Steane, J.M. (1985) 'Bernwood Forest, past, present, future', *Arboricultural J.* 9, 39–55
Taylor, C.C. (1975) 'Roman settlement in the Nene Valley', in Fowler, P.J. (ed.), *Recent Work in Rural Archaeology*, 107–20
Taylor, C.C. (1979) *Roads and Trackways in Britain*
Tyler, A. (1976) *Neolithic Flint Axes from the Cotswold Hills.* BAR 25
Victoria County History of Oxfordshire. Vol. I (1939)
West Yorkshire. An Archaeological Survey to AD 1500. West Yorks. Metropolitan C.C., 1981
Wilson, J. (1846) 'Antiquities found at Woodperry, Oxfordshire', *Archaeol. J.*, 111, 116–28
Wood-Jones, R.B. (1963) *Traditional Domestic Architecture of the Banbury Region*
Woodward, F. (1982) *Oxfordshire Parks*
Wymer, J.J. (1968) *Lower Palaeolithic Archaeology in Britain*
Wymer, J.J. and Bonsall, W. eds. (1977) *Gazetteer of Mesolithic sites in England and Wales.* CBA
Young, C.J. (1977) *Oxfordshire Roman Pottery.* BAR 43

OXFORDSHIRE
PALAEOLITHIC FINDS

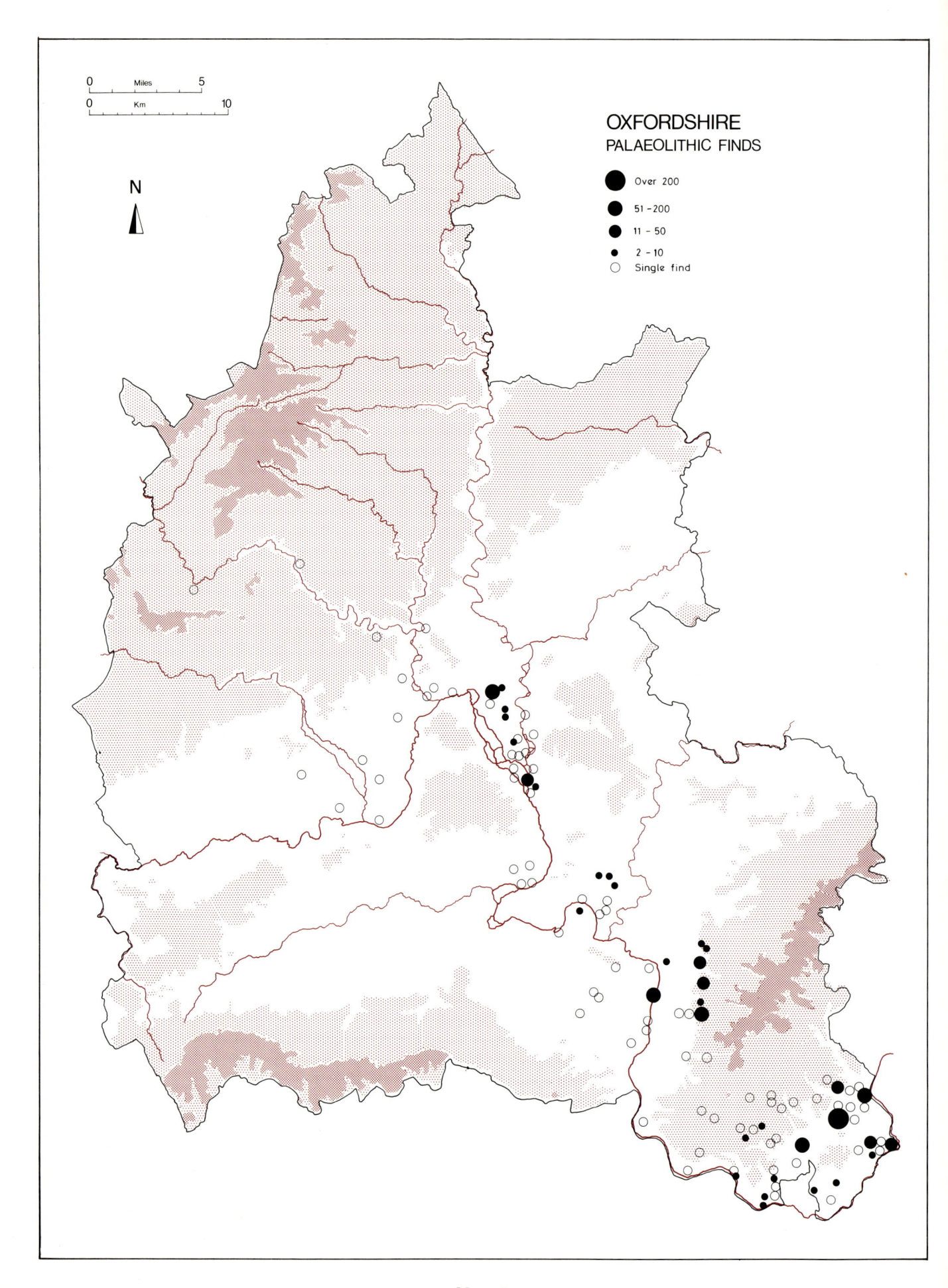

- Over 200
- 51 – 200
- 11 – 50
- 2 – 10
- Single find

Map. 1

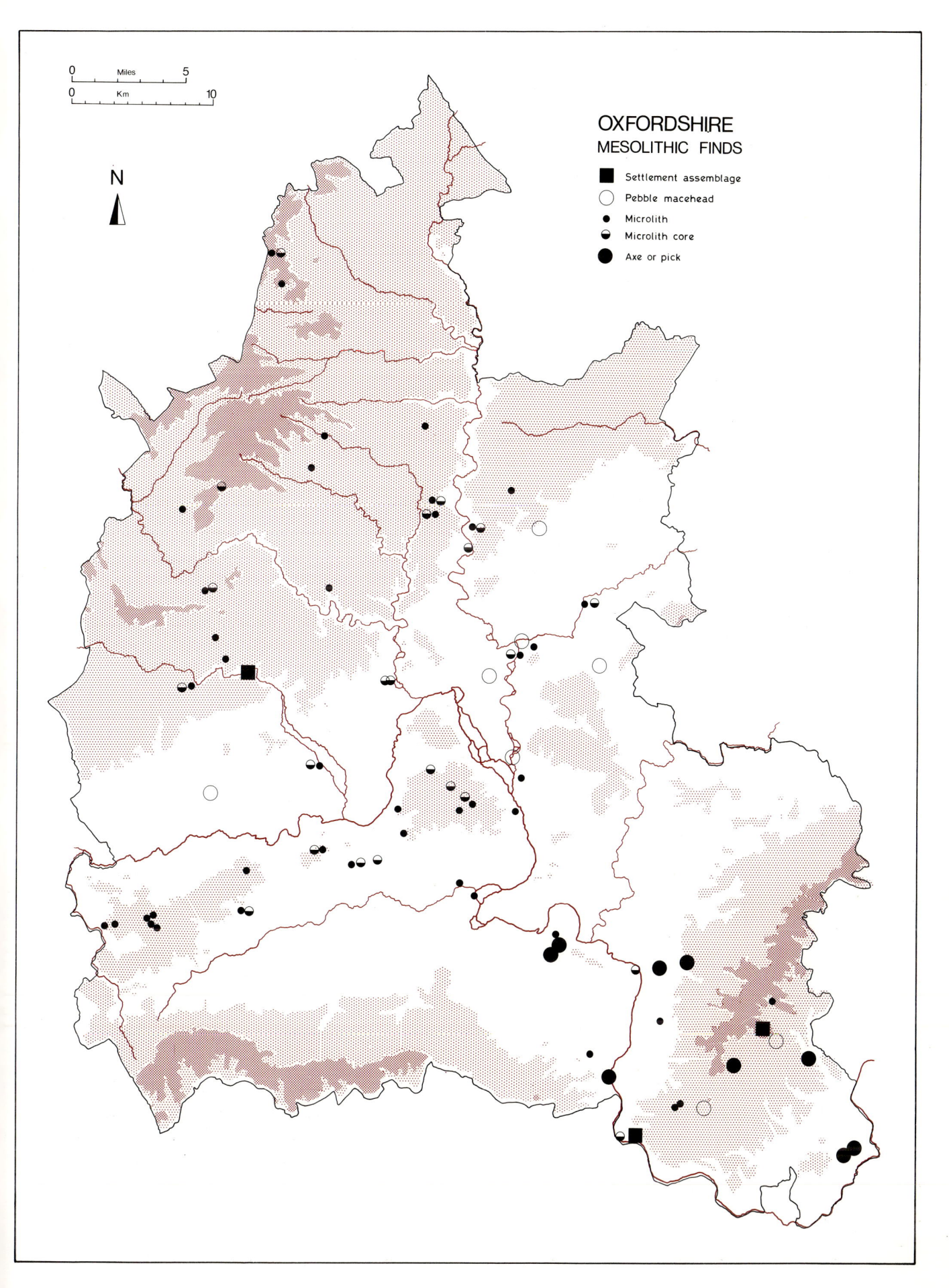

Map. 2

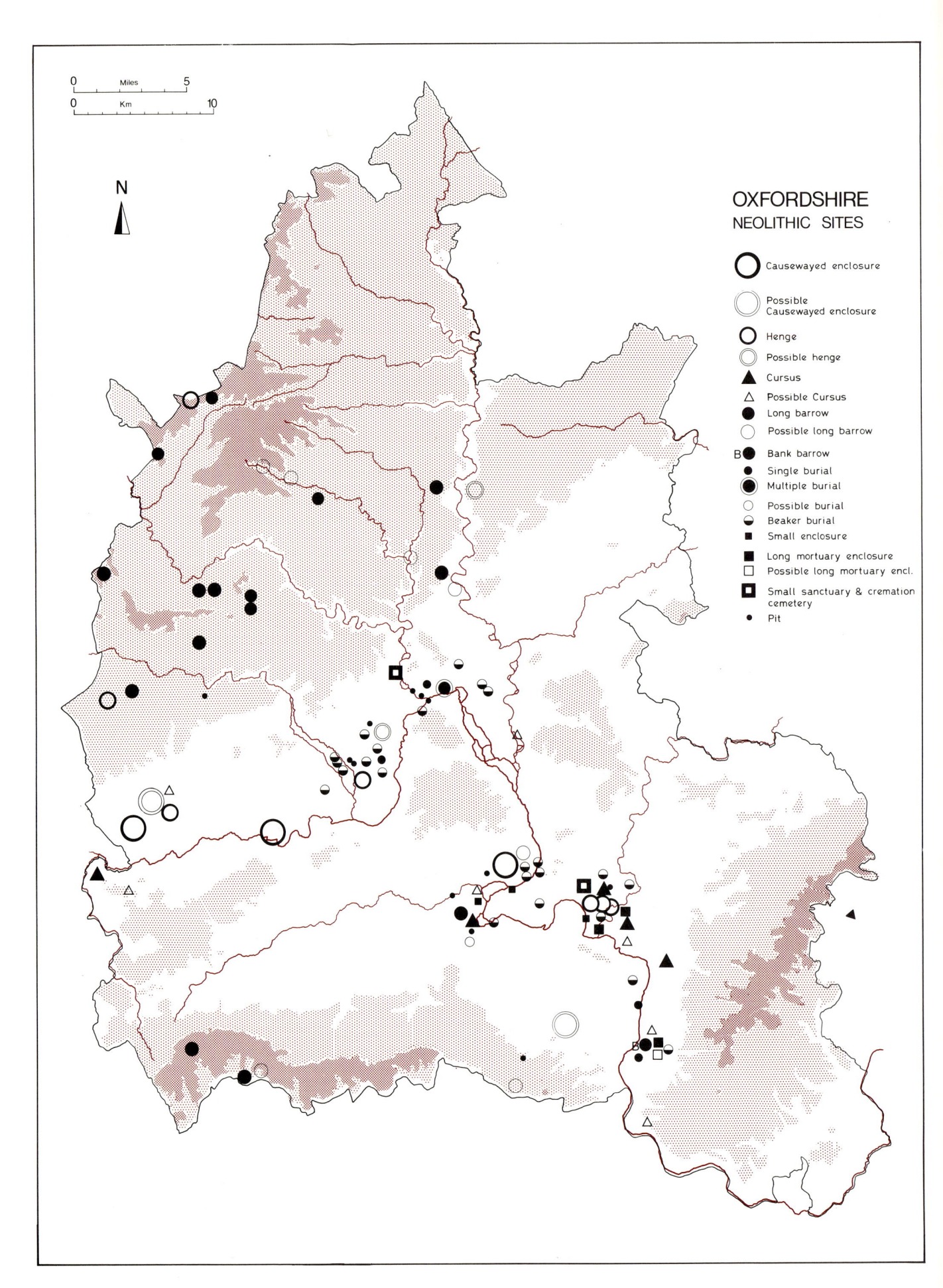

Map. 3

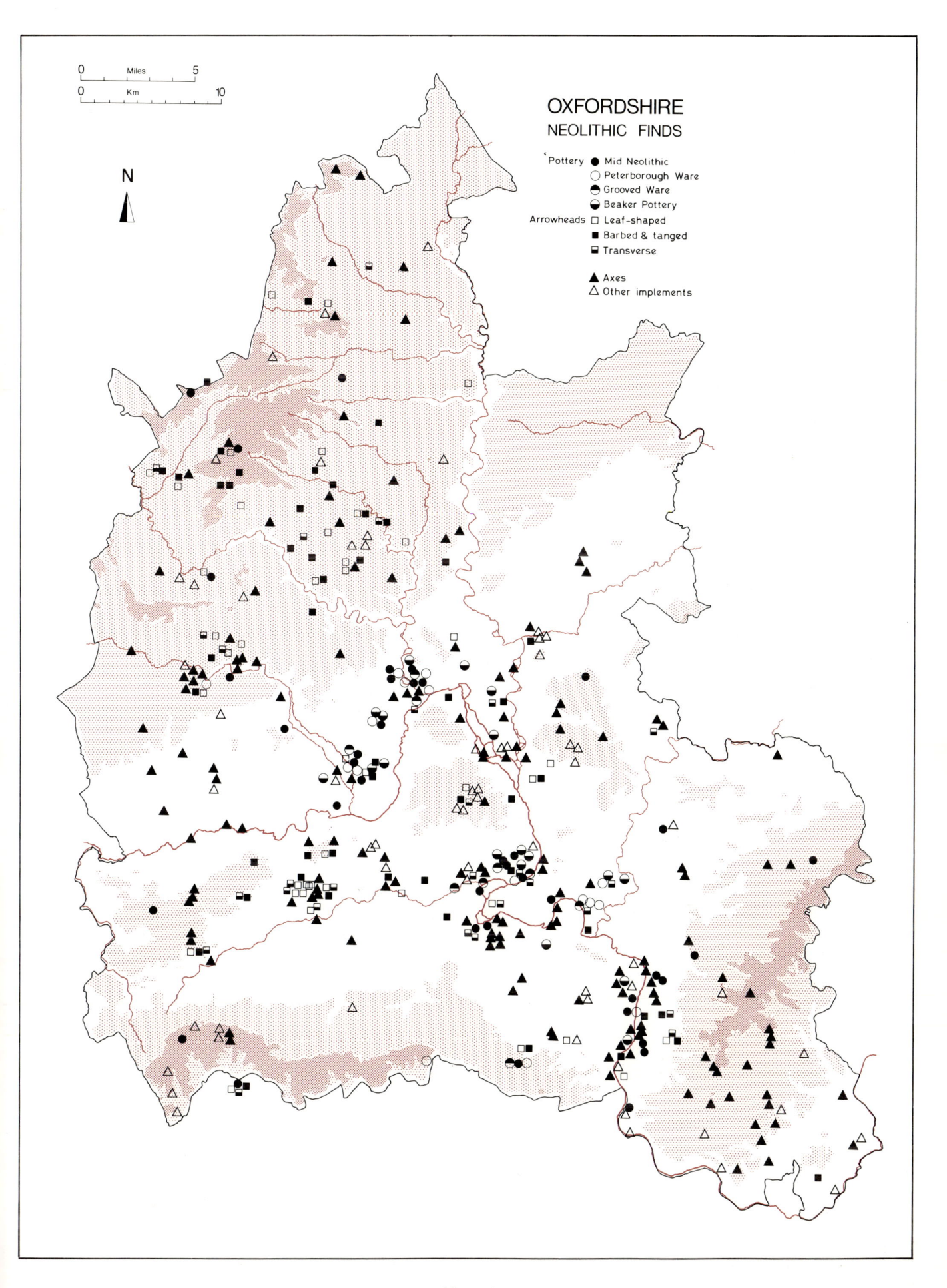

Map. 4

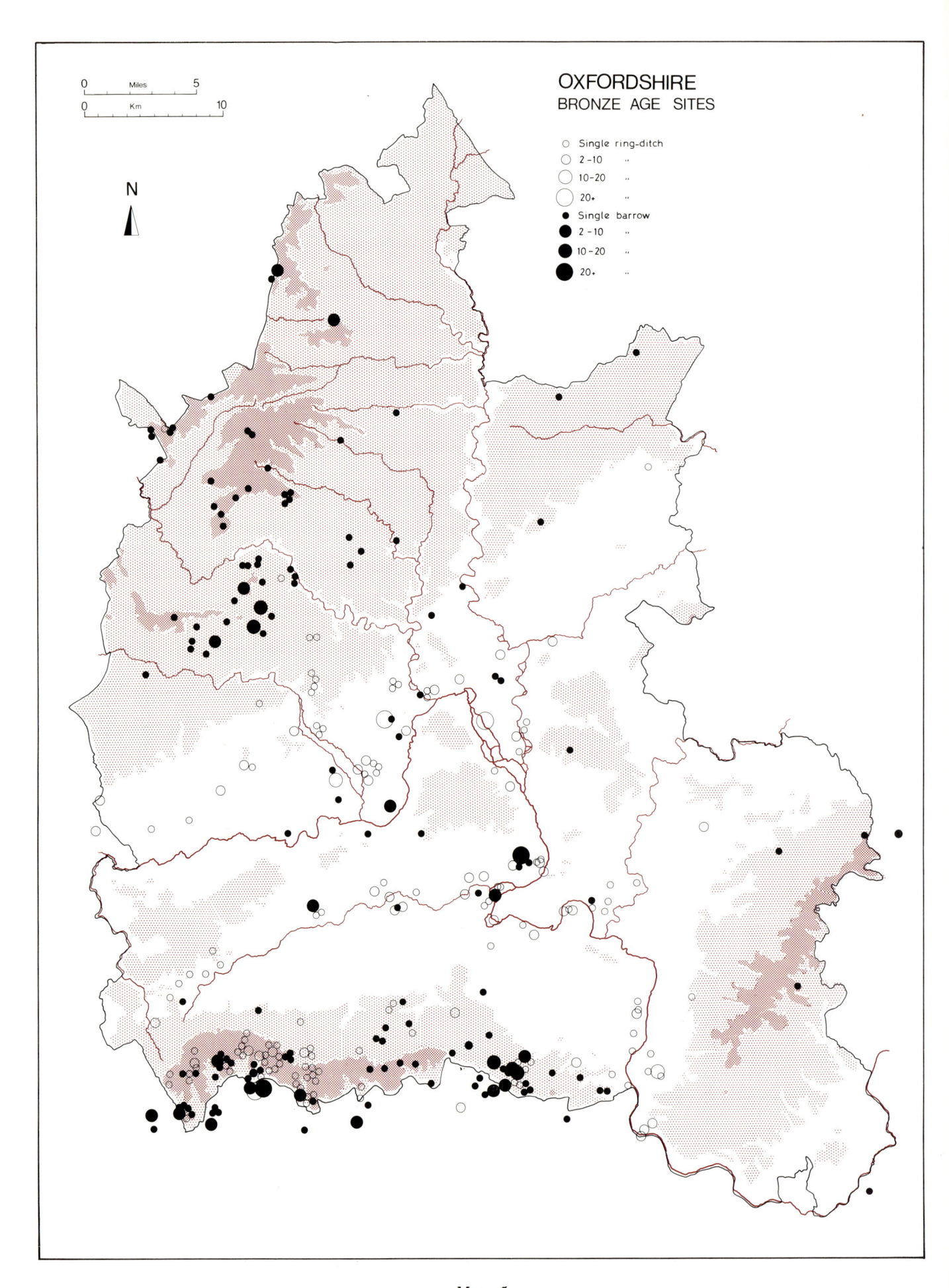

Map. 5

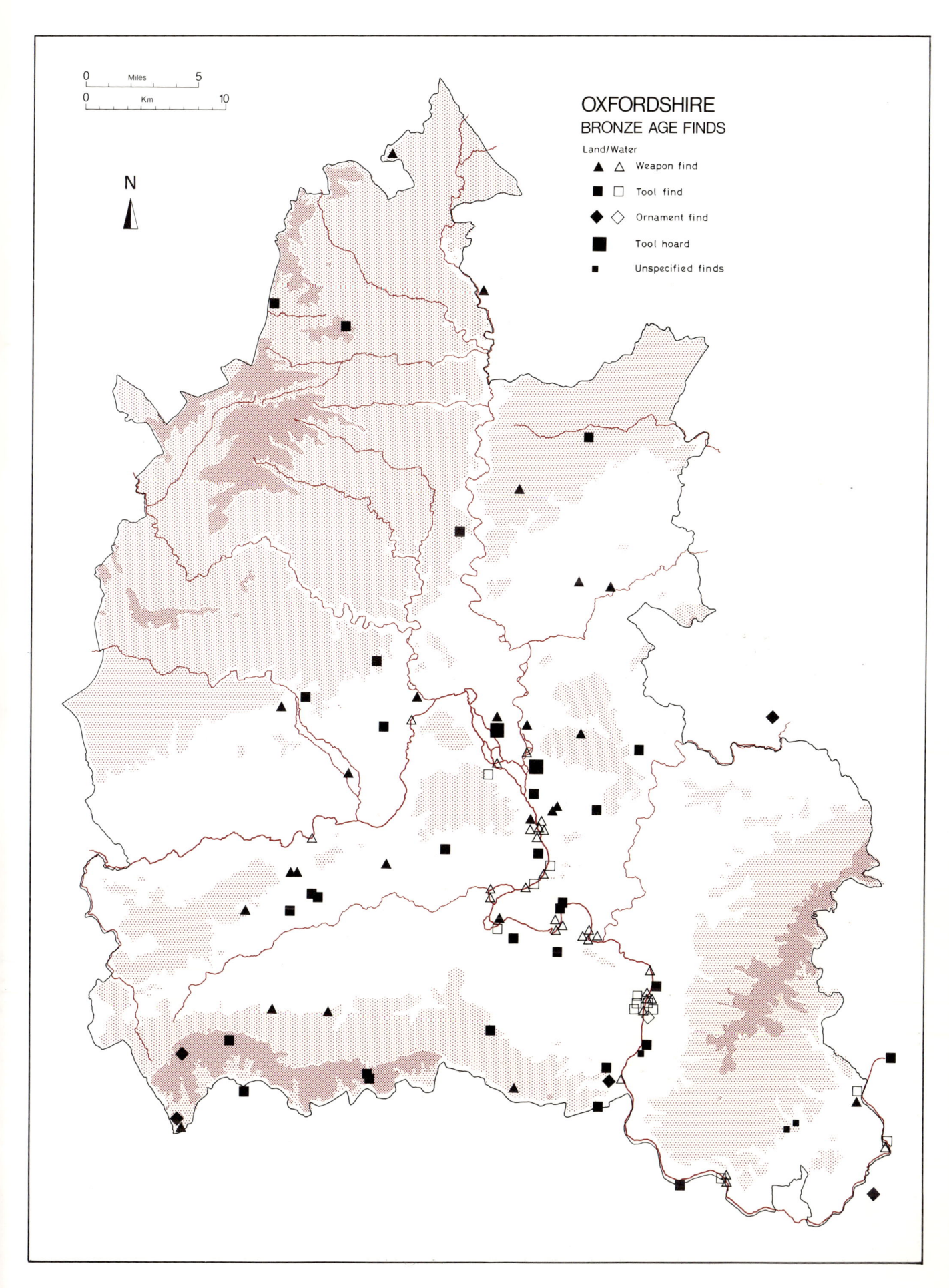

Map. 6

OXFORDSHIRE
IRON AGE SITES

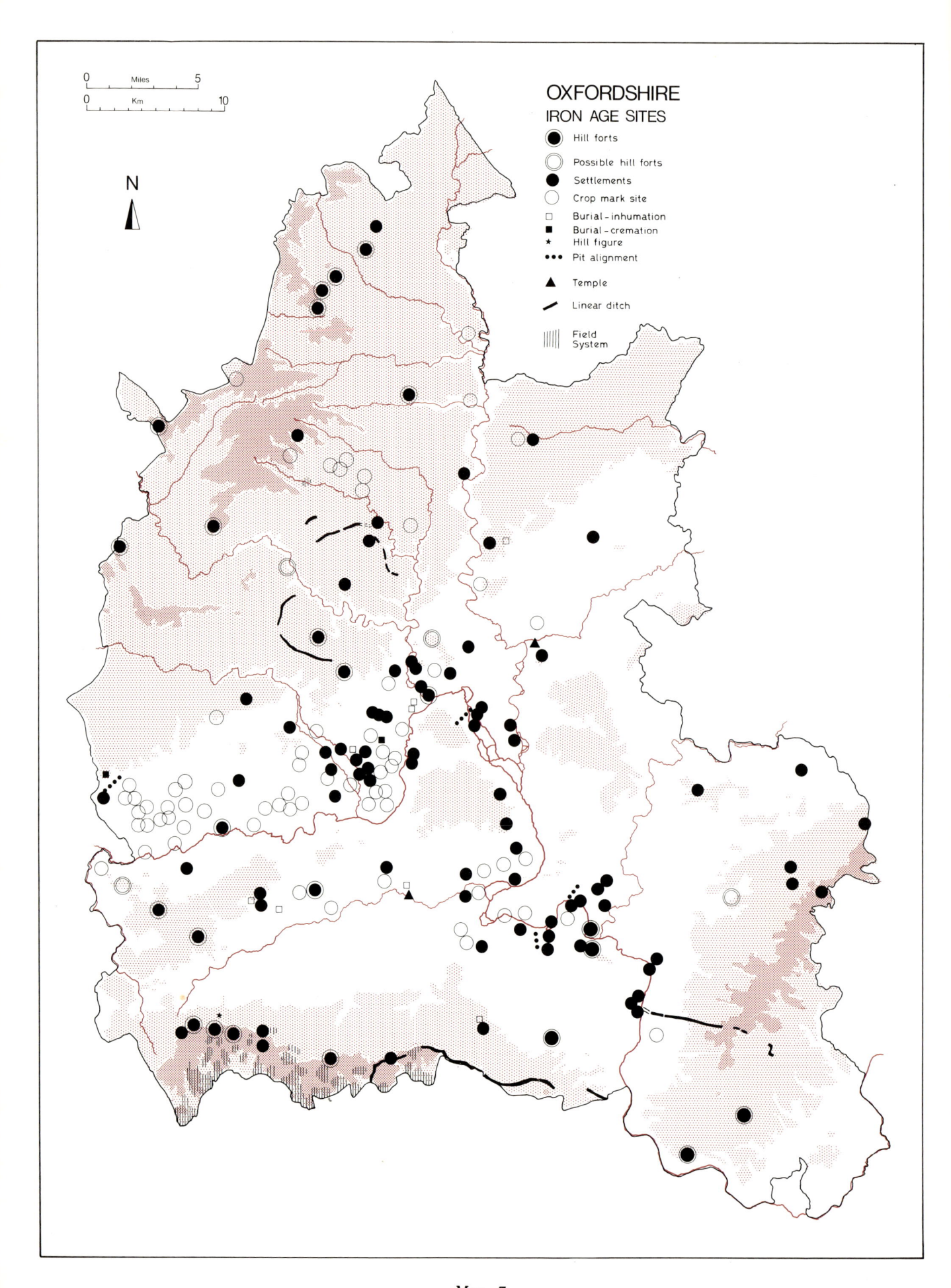

- ● Hill forts
- ○ Possible hill forts
- ● Settlements
- ○ Crop mark site
- □ Burial - inhumation
- ■ Burial - cremation
- ★ Hill figure
- ••• Pit alignment
- ▲ Temple
- / Linear ditch
- ||||| Field System

Map. 7

OXFORDSHIRE
IRON AGE FINDS
● Coins
○ Other finds

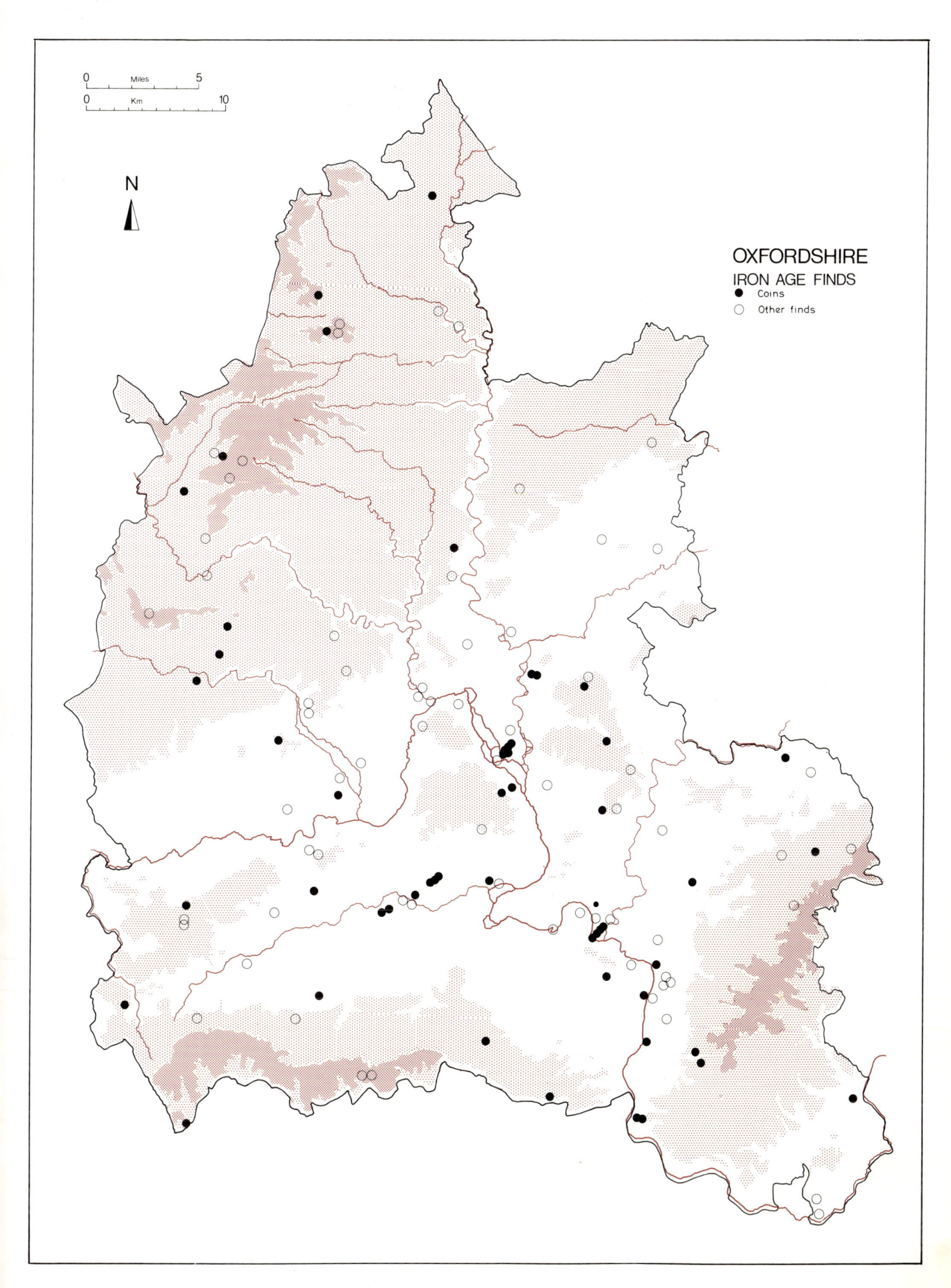

Map. 8

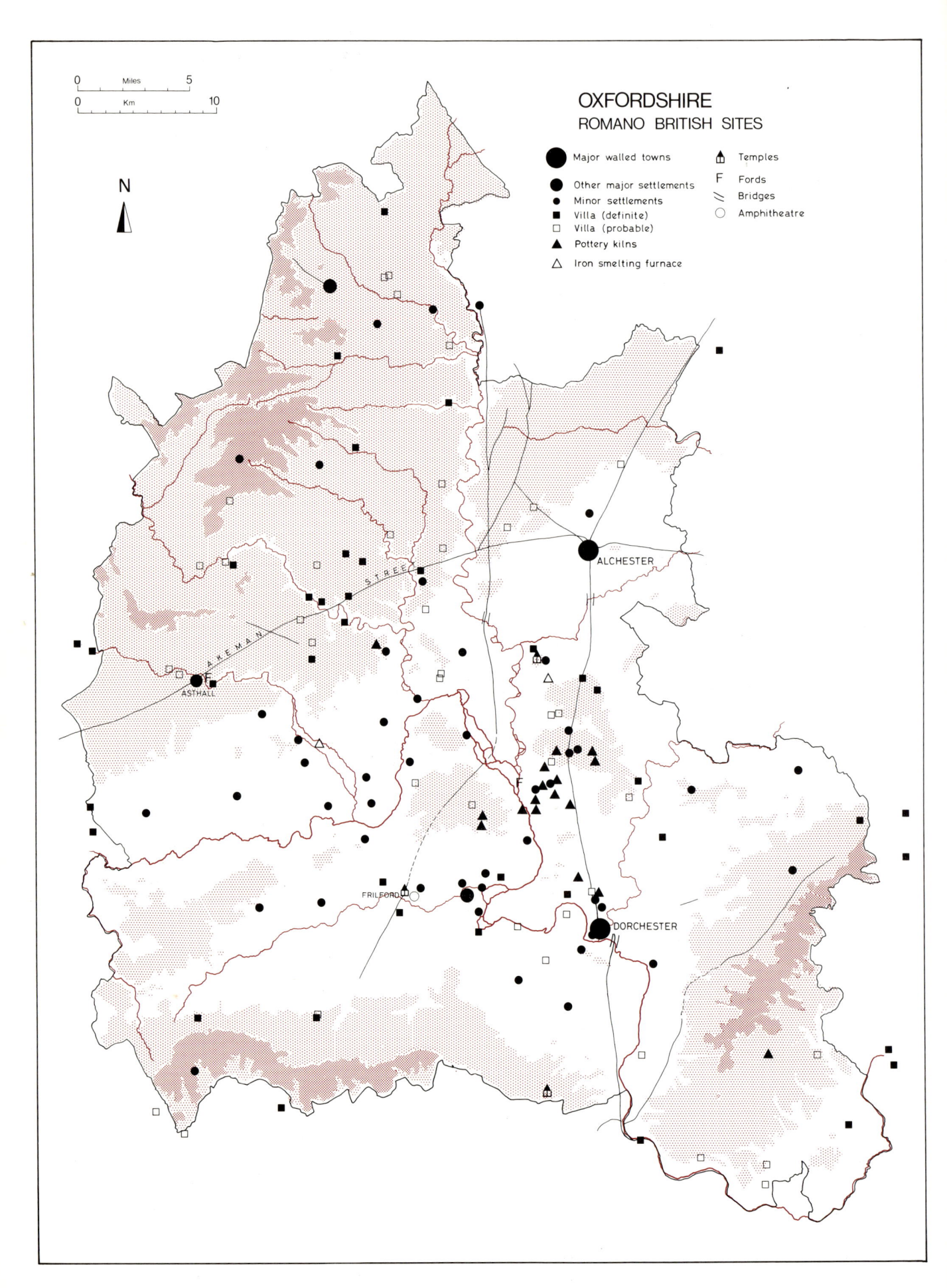

Map. 9

OXFORDSHIRE
ROMAN FINDS

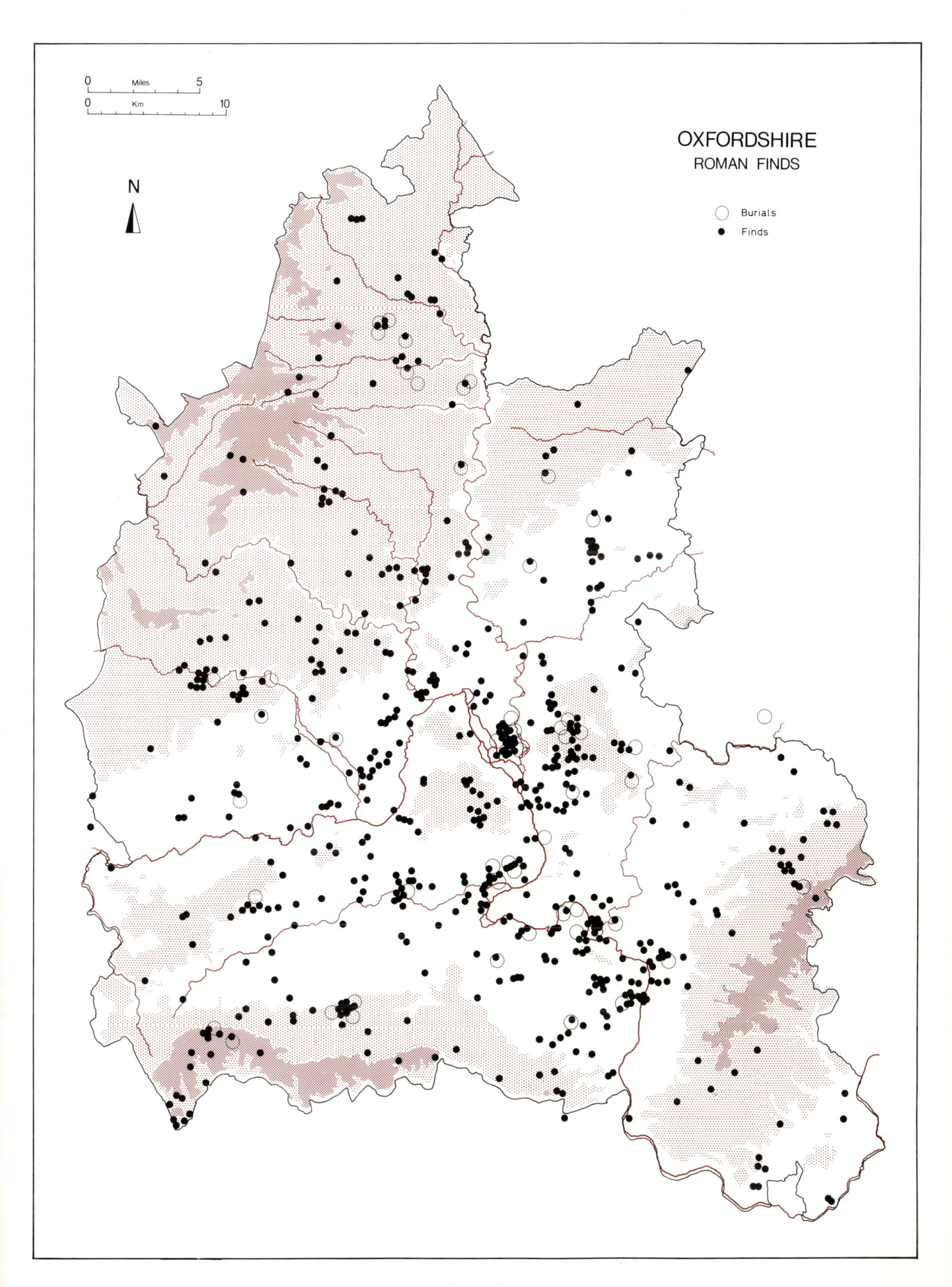

○ Burials
● Finds

Map. 10

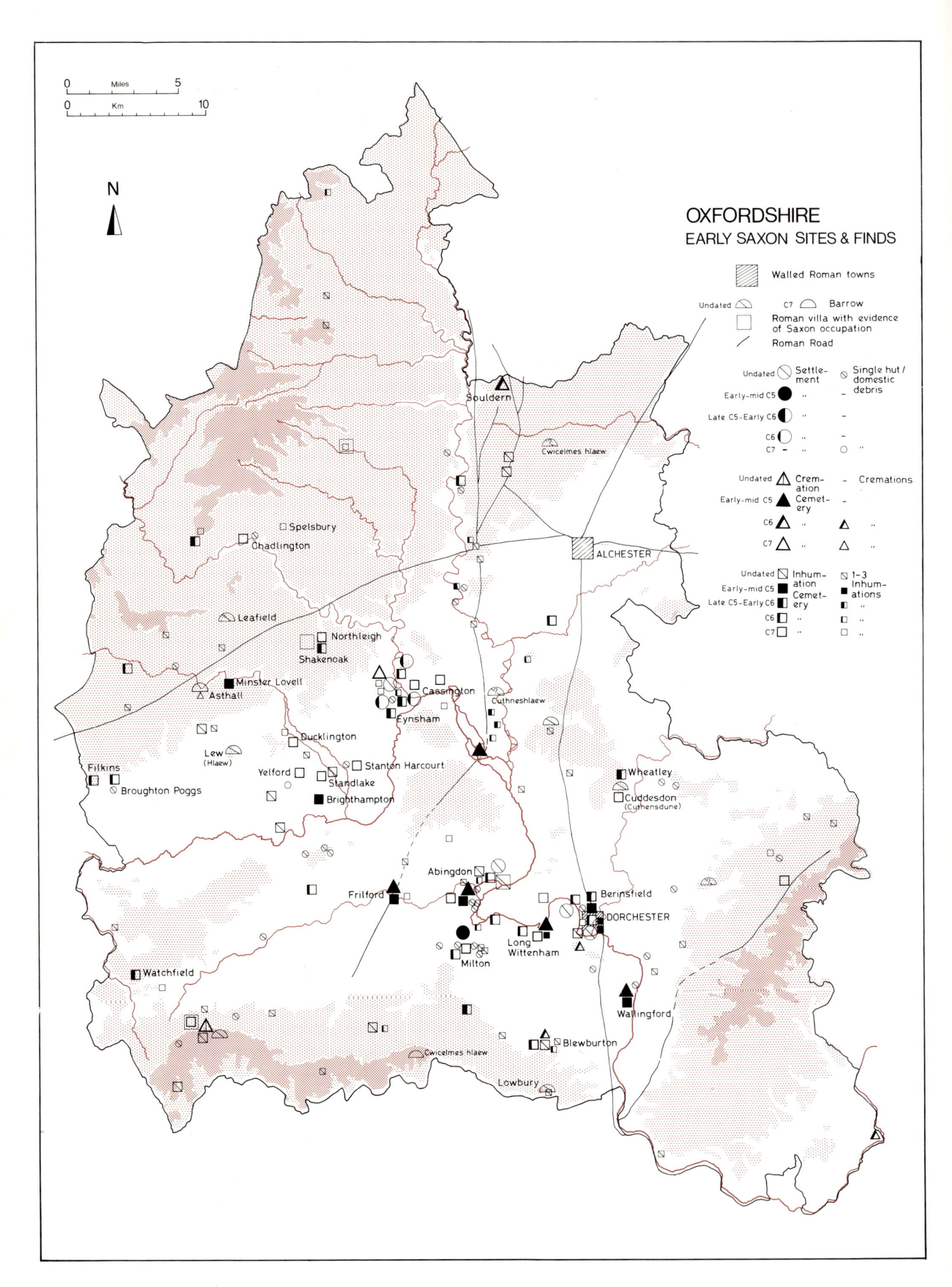

Map. 11

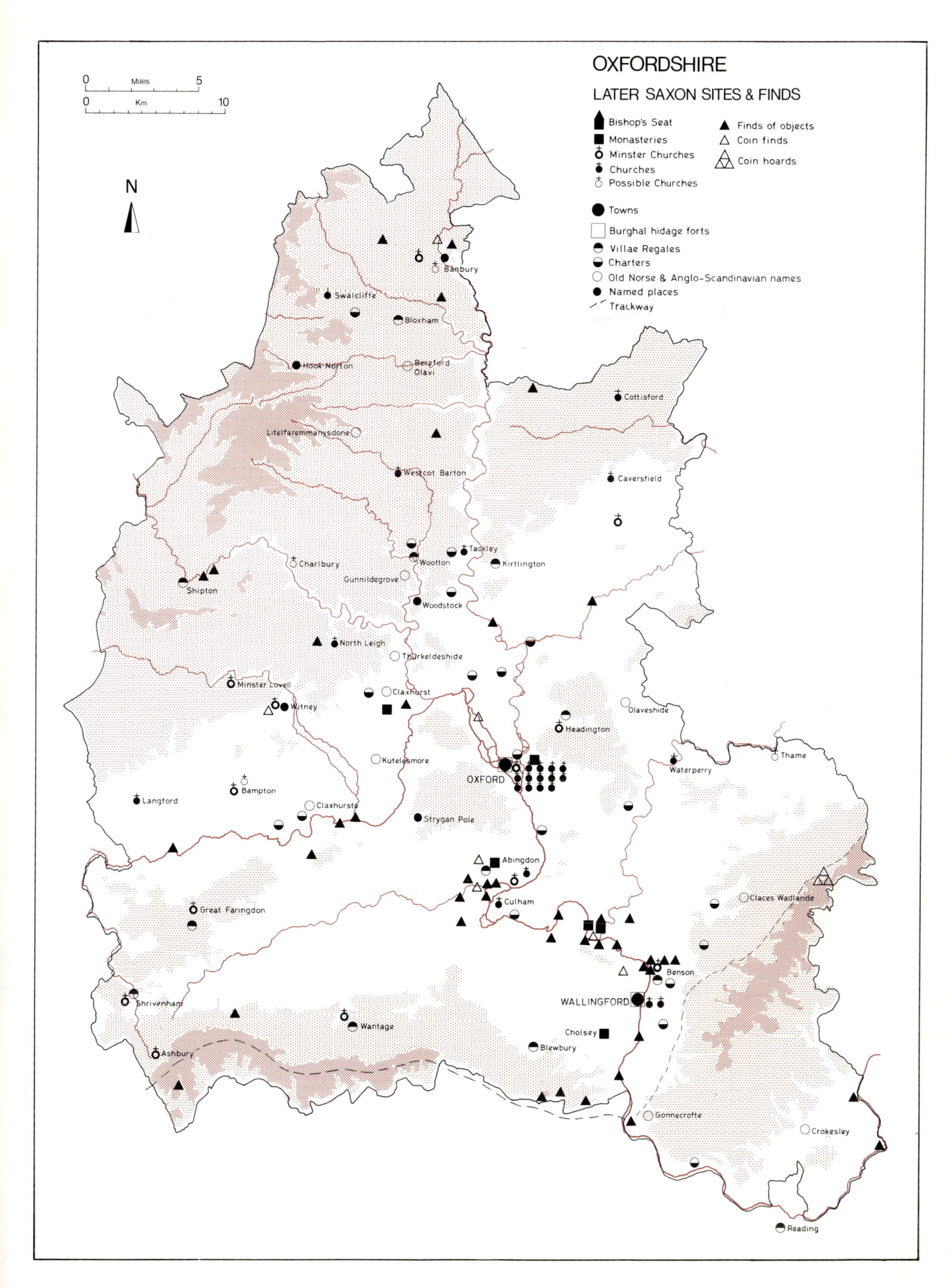

Map. 12

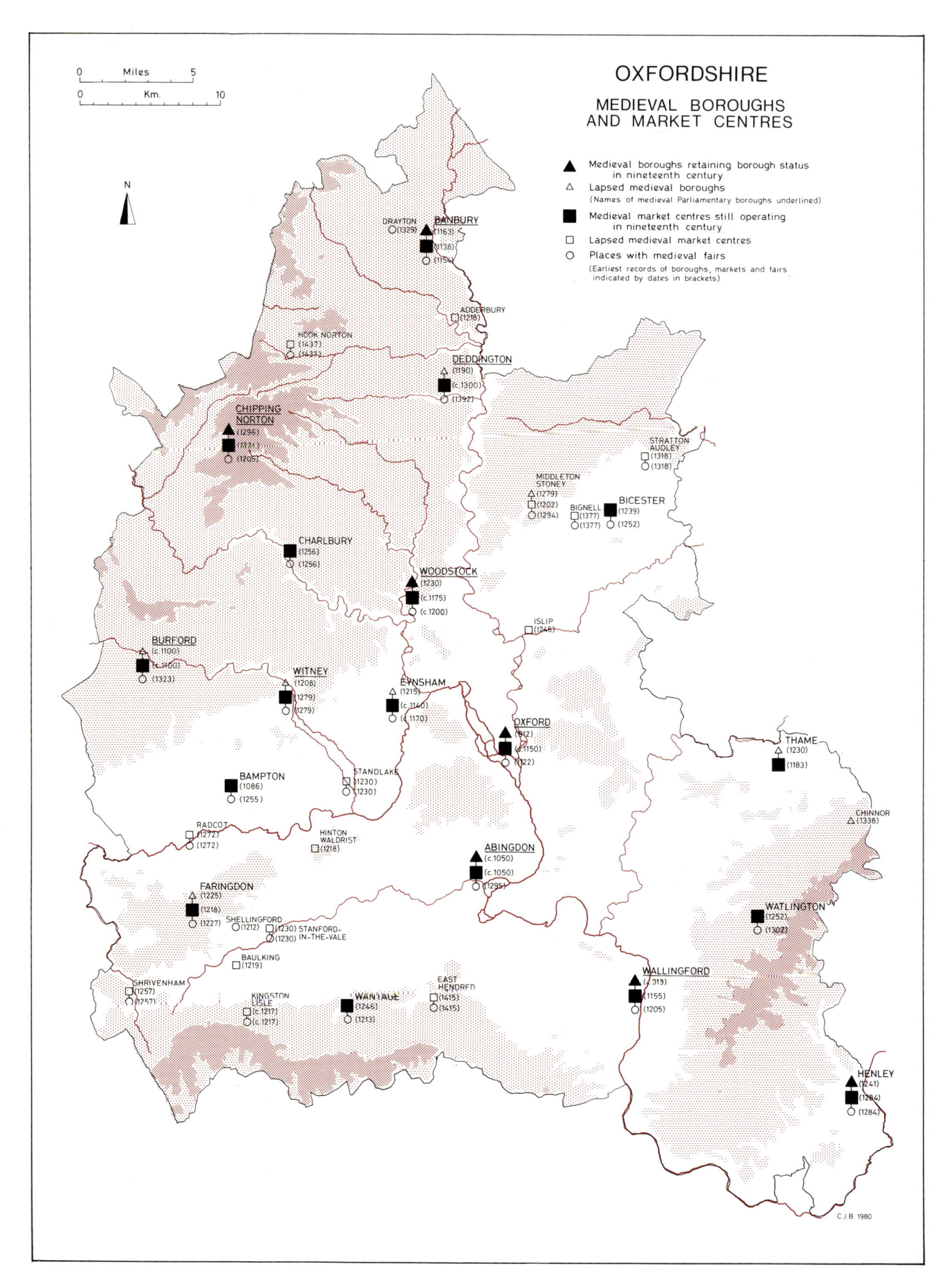

OXFORDSHIRE
MEDIEVAL BOROUGHS AND MARKET CENTRES

▲ Medieval boroughs retaining borough status in nineteenth century
△ Lapsed medieval boroughs
(Names of medieval Parliamentary boroughs underlined)
■ Medieval market centres still operating in nineteenth century
□ Lapsed medieval market centres
○ Places with medieval fairs
(Earliest records of boroughs, markets and fairs indicated by dates in brackets)

Map. 13

OXFORDSHIRE
MEDIEVAL RURAL SETTLEMENT

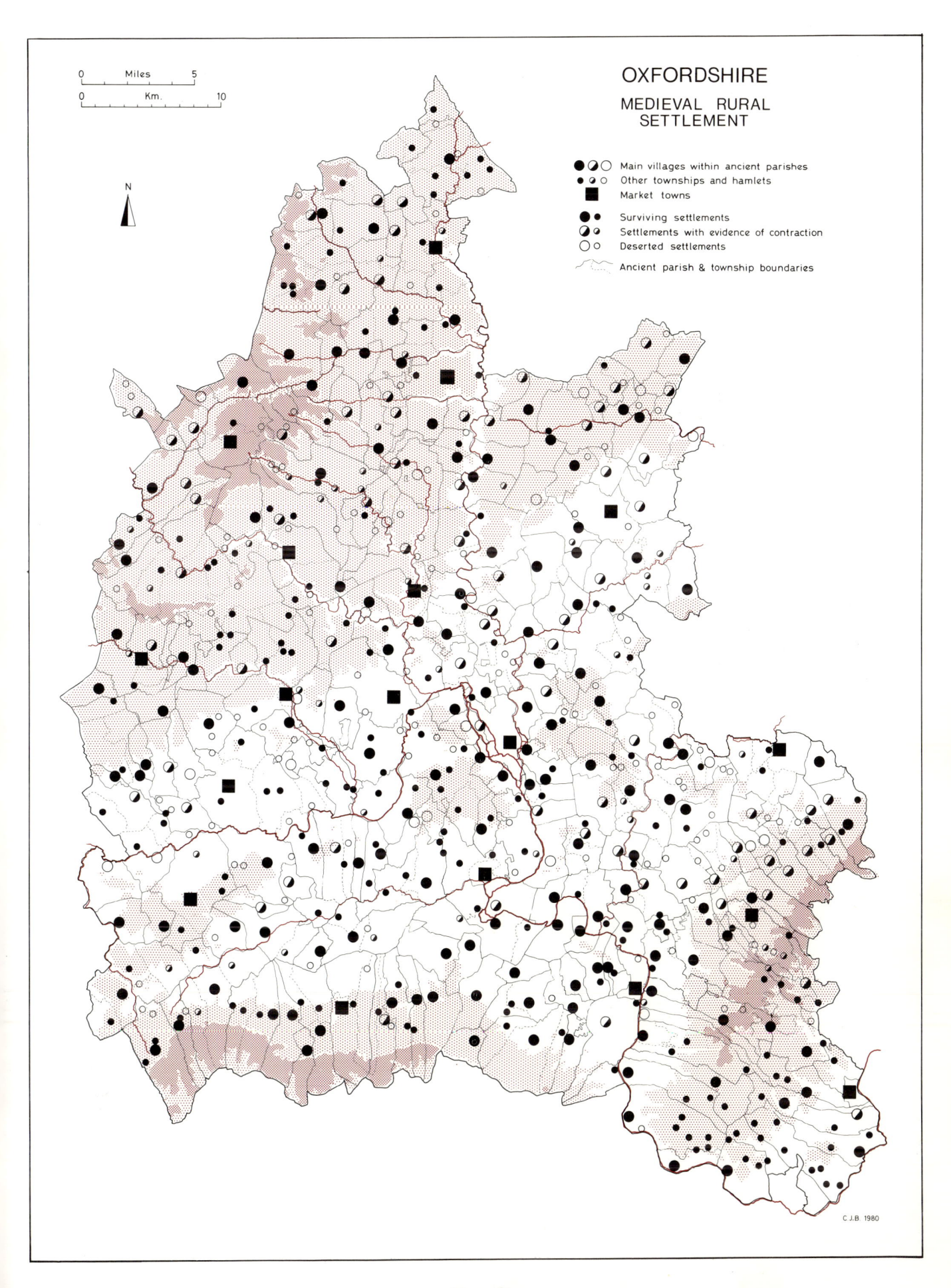

- ● ◐ ○ Main villages within ancient parishes
- • ◐ ○ Other townships and hamlets
- ■ Market towns
- ● • Surviving settlements
- ◐ ◐ Settlements with evidence of contraction
- ○ ○ Deserted settlements
- Ancient parish & township boundaries

Map. 14

185

OXFORDSHIRE
DESERTED & SHRUNKEN VILLAGES

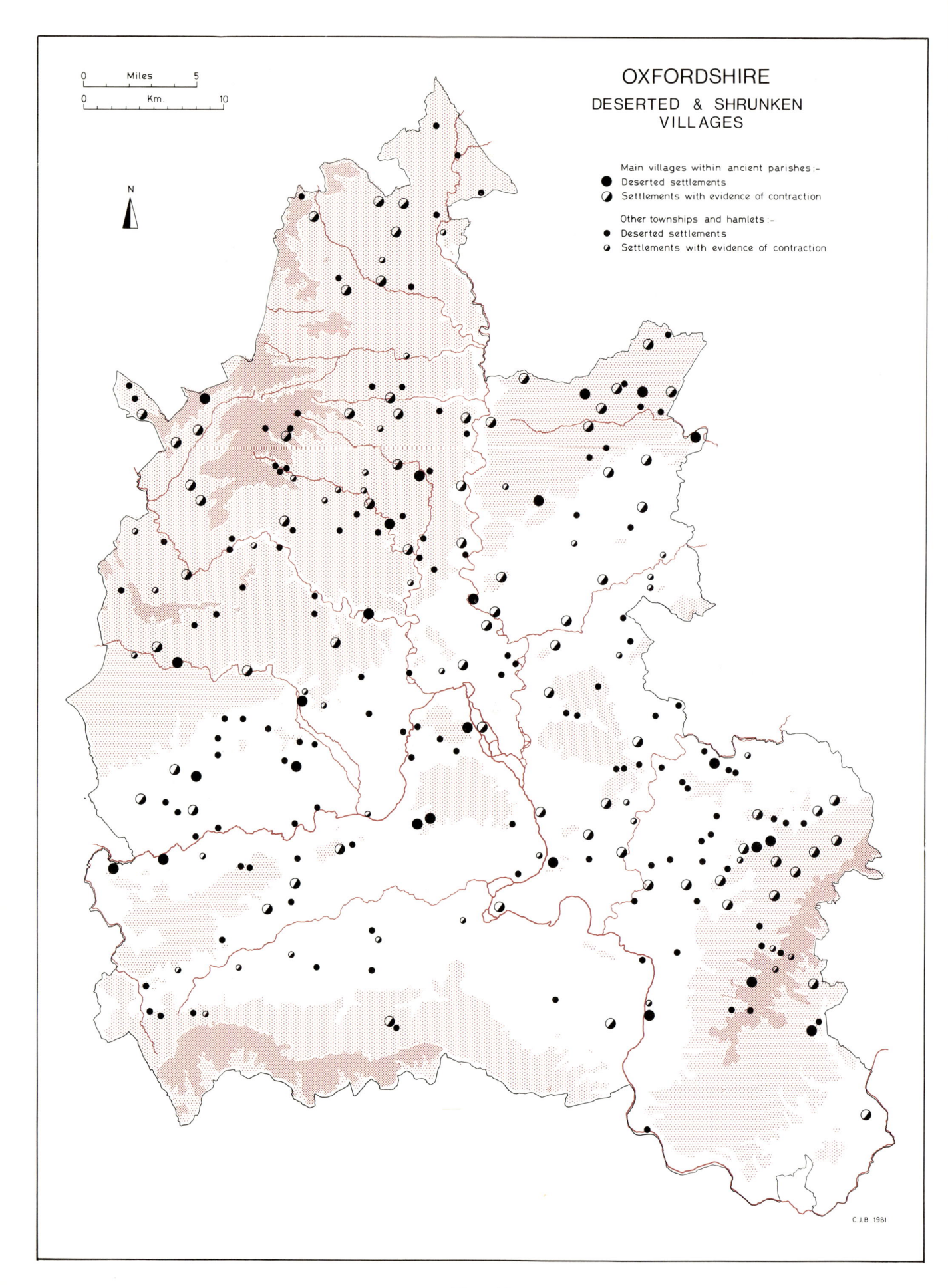

Main villages within ancient parishes:-
- ● Deserted settlements
- ◐ Settlements with evidence of contraction

Other townships and hamlets:-
- • Deserted settlements
- ◌ Settlements with evidence of contraction

Map. 15

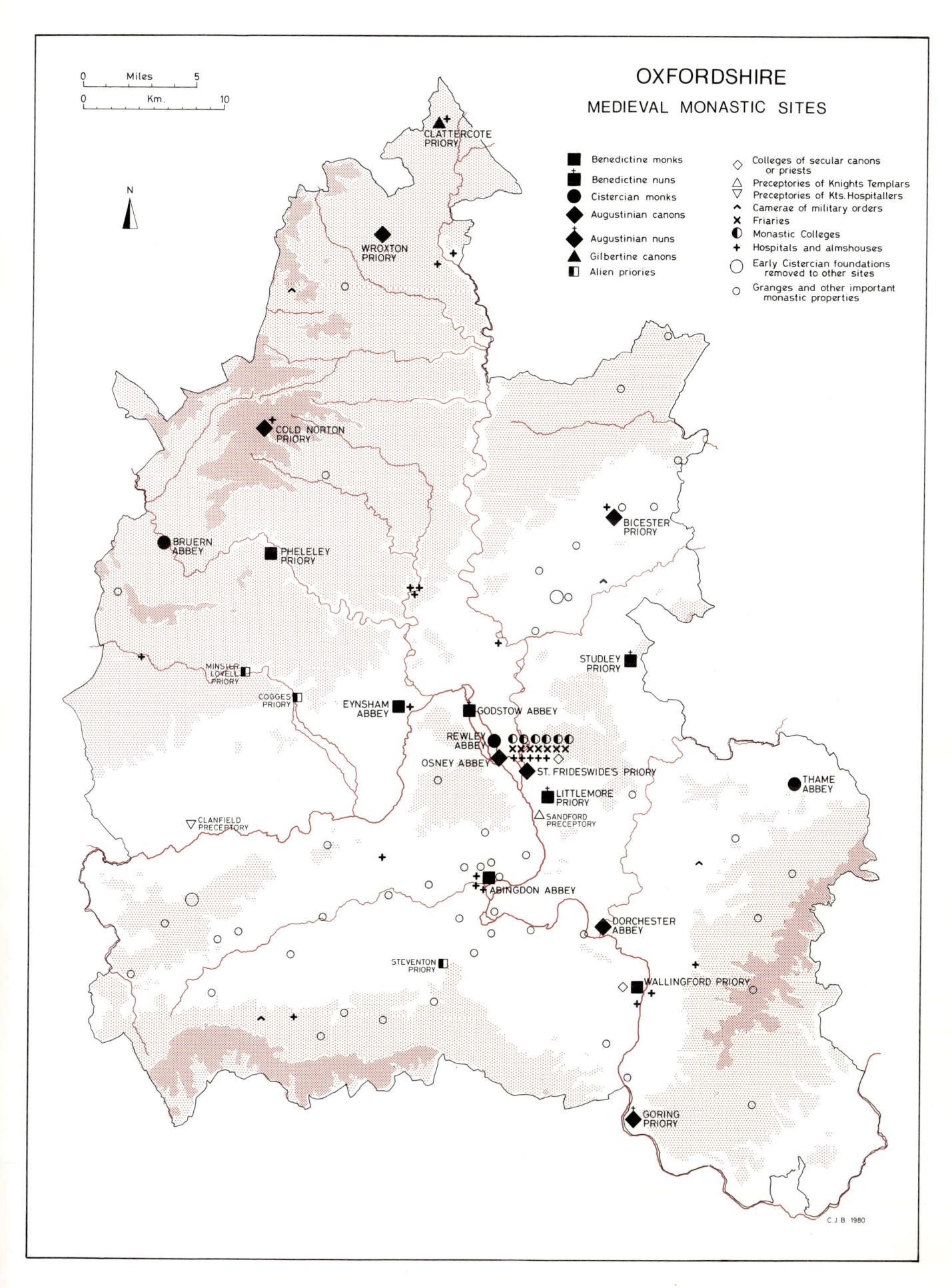

Map. 16

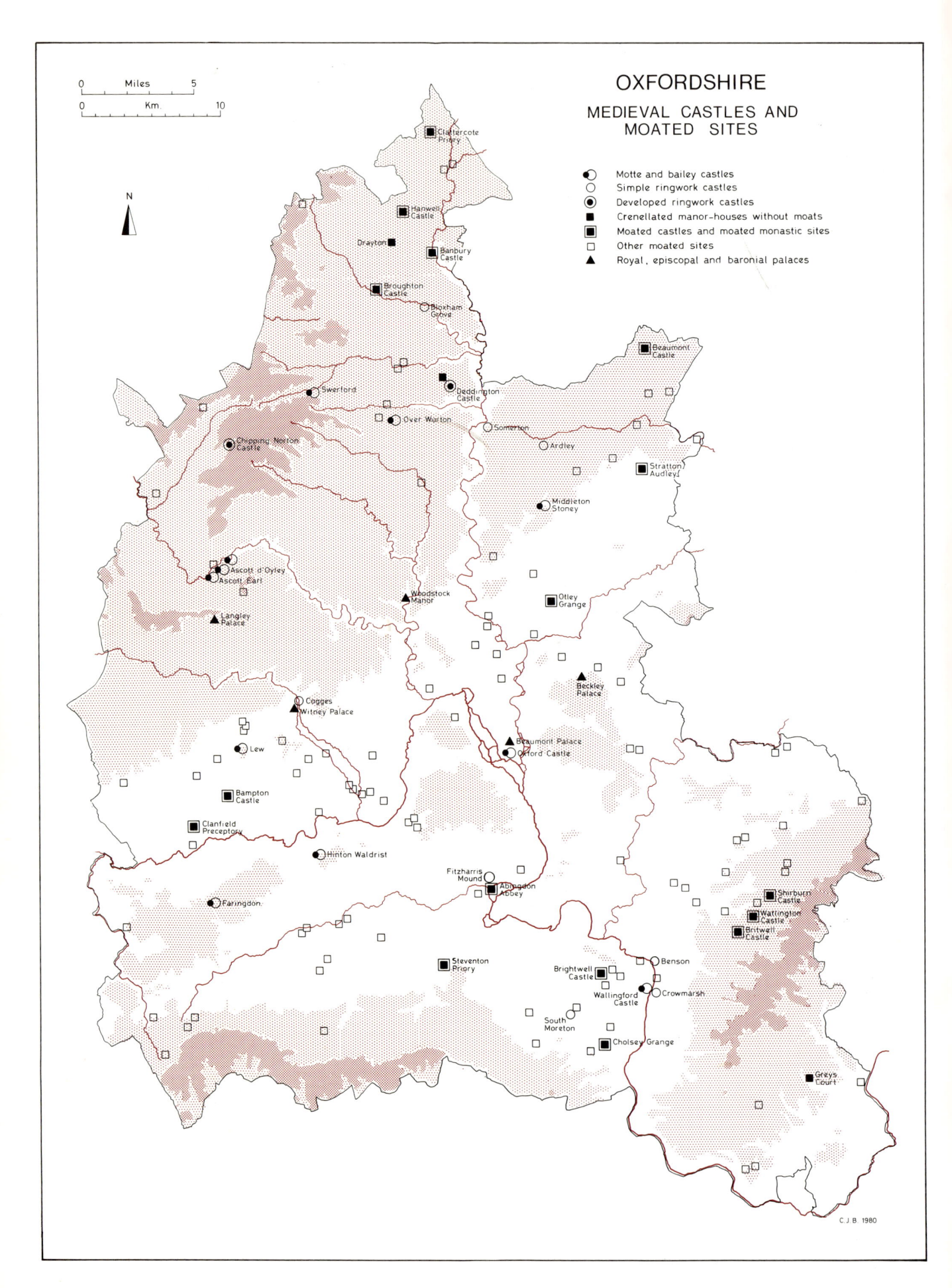

OXFORDSHIRE
MEDIEVAL CASTLES AND MOATED SITES

- ◐ Motte and bailey castles
- ○ Simple ringwork castles
- ⊙ Developed ringwork castles
- ■ Crenellated manor-houses without moats
- ▣ Moated castles and moated monastic sites
- ▢ Other moated sites
- ▲ Royal, episcopal and baronial palaces

Map. 17

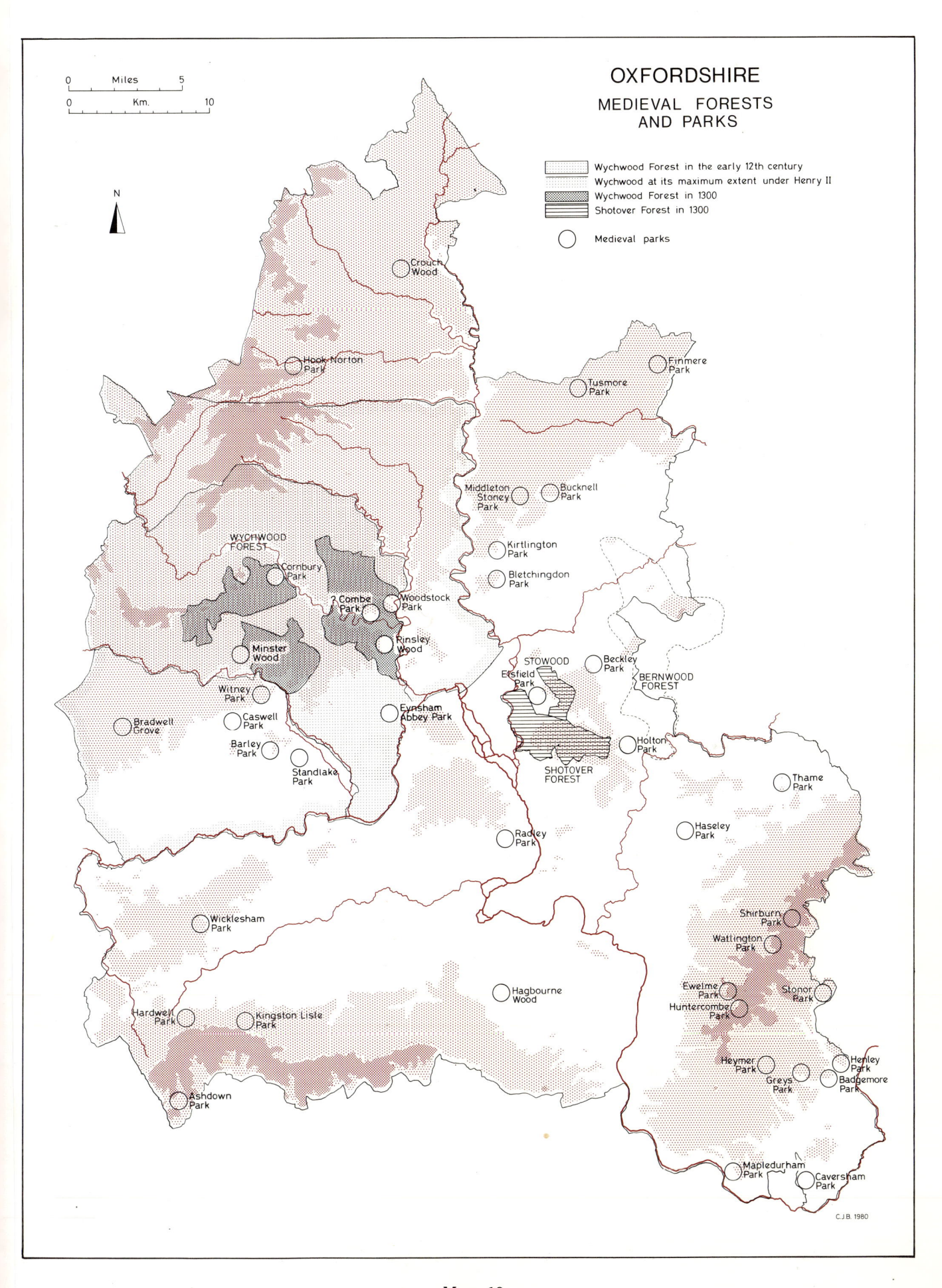

Map. 18.